Control Language Programming

for the AS/400

second edition

BY BRYAN MEYERS AND DAN RIEHL

A Division of
Penton Technology Media

221 E. 29th Street • Loveland, CO 80538 USA
(800) 650-1804 • (970) 663-4700 • www.29thStreetPress.com

Library of Congress Cataloging-in-Publication Data

Meyers, Bryan, 1948–
    Control language programming for the AS/400 / by Bryan Meyers and
Dan Riehl. — 2nd ed.
        p. cm.
    Includes bibliographical references and index.
    ISBN 1-882419-76-6 (pbk.)
        1. IBM AS/400 (Computer)—Programming. 2. Job Control Language
(Computer program language)   I. Riehl, Dan, 1953–   . II. Title.
QA76.8.I25919M49 1997
005.4'34—dc21   97-33820
                                                          CIP

29th Street Press® is a division of
Penton Technology Media
Loveland, Colorado USA

This book was printed and bound in Canada.

ISBN 1-882419-76-6

2004 2003 2002 WL 3 2 1 10 9 8 7 6 5 4

To our families:
Kris, Heather, Donn, and Simone Riehl;
Sandy, Jason, and Lindsey Meyers.
Thank you for your love and patience.

Acknowledgments

Our deep gratitude goes to all who participated in making this second edition a reality: 29th Street Press (formerly Duke Press) publisher Dave Bernard and managing editor Trish Faubion performed the editing work. Trish also shepherded the chapters through production, proofreading, and indexing. Martha Nichols and Lynn Riggs performed the actual production work, while art director John Morris-Reihl revised the cover.

Special thanks go to Dr. Judy Yaeger, Susan Guthrie of Lakeland Community College, and Bernie Cinkoske of Ivy Tech State College, all three of whom have provided invaluable technical reviews and suggestions.

Table of Contents

INPUT/OUTPUT IN A CL PROGRAM

Preface

This book can be logically divided into five sections:

1. Introduction to Control Language (Chapters 1–4)
2. Basic CL Programming (Chapters 5–12)
3. Input/Output in a CL Program (Chapters 13–15)
4. Advanced CL Programming (Chapters 16–22)
5. Creating Your Own Commands (Chapters 23–25)

In most cases, an instructor will be able to use the text sequentially to build a complete CL instructional track.

The first section deals generally with CL as the primary interface to AS/400 functions. If students have previous experience with the AS/400, this section will serve as review and reinforcement; an instructor most likely will be able to cover this section of the book in a very short time.

The next section, Basic CL Programming (Chapters 5–12), begins to introduce the concept of a CL program and its components. This section also covers many of the capabilities of CL programs, along with discussions about program logic, expressions, program calls, and basic error trapping. After finishing this section, students should be able to read a CL program, identify its function, and write a simple CL program.

During the study of Chapters 5–12 and throughout the rest of the book, students often will find it useful to refer to the appendices. Appendix A is a "quick reference" to nearly 100 CL commands used most often in CL programs. If students have no experience with Programming Development Manager (PDM) or Source Entry Utility (SEU), Appendices B and C provide introductions to these facilities.

To further build the students' knowledge of CL, the third section (Chapters 13–15) covers CL's various input and output capabilities; for example, parameters, files, data areas, and system values. After finishing this section of the text, a student should be able to write a CL program to perform a relatively complex function.

While the next section (Chapters 16–22) is presented as "advanced," several topics in this section should be part of even a minimal CL course of study. Chapters 16, 17, and 19, in particular, which cover messages, error handling, file overrides, and APIs, should always be included. Chapter 22 discusses fundamental changes that the Integrated Language Environment (ILE) introduces to the AS/400's execution model; this information is relevant not only to CL and should be covered thoroughly so that the student understands how ILE changes some of the traditional AS/400 concepts.

Chapters 23–25 discuss the construction of user-defined commands; a knowledge of this facility will give students an advantage in the AS/400 job market, and its coverage is well worth the time spent studying it. If the length of a course does not permit inclusion of user-defined commands, the instructor should encourage self-study in this area.

A suggested course of study for a 13-session course follows, assuming that exercise labs are held separately from classroom sessions:

1. Chapters 1–4
2. Chapters 5–6
3. Chapters 7–8
4. Chapters 9–10
5. Chapters 11–12
6. Chapters 13–14
7. Chapter 15
8. Chapter 16
9. Chapters 17–18
10. Chapters 19–20
11. Chapters 21–22
12. Chapters 23–24
13. Chapter 25, Review

The end of each chapter includes a list of terms defined in the chapter and in the glossary. These terms are for class discussion to ensure that students grasp the concepts presented in the chapter. Some of the review questions also lend themselves more to classroom discussion than to individual testing.

Some of the exercises at the end of each chapter build upon previous exercises — an important consideration if all the exercises in a chapter cannot be completed in the computer lab. With this constraint in mind, choose those exercises that you feel will be most beneficial to the student.

Chapter 1

What Is CL?

Chapter Overview

This chapter examines the unique role of the AS/400 Control Language (CL) in relation to other computer languages and describes CL's strengths and weaknesses. Emphasis is placed on the use of CL to control workflow and to define job streams to the AS/400 computer. You will become familiar with the contrast between CL and typical high-level languages (HLLs) — for example, Cobol and RPG. This chapter also contains a brief discussion of compiled and interpreted CL, along with an explanation of the execution environment restrictions in effect when using CL commands.

What CL Is

AS/400 Control Language (CL) is a set of commands that you use to control operations and to request system-related functions on the IBM AS/400 computer. IBM provides CL as an integrated part of the OS/400 operating system, not as a separate product.

As a means of controlling workflow, CL serves purposes comparable to Job Control Language (JCL) on mainframe computers. CL, however, provides much more functionality than JCL. In some respects, CL is similar to the PC-DOS commands you may use on a PC. DOS operations like copying files, redirecting output, and making directories have direct CL counterparts.

CL originated on the IBM System/38 computer in the late 1970s and continued as the principal system control language when the AS/400 was introduced in 1988. The AS/400 version of CL provided many enhancements over the S/38 version, including new commands and other added functionality. However, because of similarities between the S/38 and AS/400 versions of CL, many S/38 CL commands and programs can be used on the AS/400, and vice versa.

A single CL statement is called a **command**. A CL command is the primary means of interacting with the AS/400. Nearly everything the AS/400 does is requested by a command. There are commands to create and delete objects, commands to start programs, a command to power down the system, and even a command to create a command.

You can think of a command as an instruction to the computer to perform a function. For example, the DLTF (Delete File) command instructs the AS/400 to delete a file from the system; this command would be comparable to the DEL command, which is a part of DOS on personal computers.

Most CL commands are supplied by IBM as part of the operating system, but you also can create your own commands, customized to your own installation's particular needs.

CL, as shipped by IBM, consists of more than 1,000 commands but still maintains a useful consistency that makes the language easy to learn and to understand. Most CL commands can be used at least two ways: (1) by typing them individually onto an AS/400 command line, or (2) by grouping them together into a **CL program**. CL programs typically consist of multiple CL commands that define procedures or operations on the AS/400. By combining multiple commands within a CL program, you can automate most AS/400 operations.

You should write CL programs to perform repetitive processing because CL programs will reduce errors and operator/user intervention. CL also is a natural choice for many utility programs that control or monitor system-related activities on the AS/400. Listed below are a few of the many functions that CL can perform:

- Start jobs by calling programs or by submitting jobs for batch processing.
- Control the sequence of processing within a program and among different programs.
- Check for the existence of objects in the system and check for security authorizations to objects.
- Create and manage system objects (e.g., files, programs, or commands).
- Handle error conditions caused by commands or programs.
- Control the operation of an application by establishing the value of variables used in the application, such as date, time, and other external information.
- Control communications.
- Send messages between programs and users or between programs and other programs.
- Manage work on the system.
- Create the environment in which a job will execute, controlling such attributes as which objects it will use, what its execution priority will be, and how it will respond to unexpected errors.
- Manipulate variable information, byte strings, and date formats.
- Change the configuration of your AS/400 and define the devices attached to it.

What CL Is Not

Although CL is very rich in function, it is *not* — in the classical sense of the term — considered to be a high-level language (HLL). You would not, for example, write a payroll application using CL exclusively. For such application programming on the AS/400, you would use a combination of CL and a HLL such as RPG or Cobol. You would use CL to implement the system-related procedures and functions of the application and you would use the HLL to perform such operations as screen handling, file updates, and complex business logic. CL is used to manipulate and control the application's execution environment, generally as a "front end" to the HLL application programs.

Why wouldn't you use CL exclusively to create a typical business application? Because many functions perform better or are easier to write using a HLL, and CL just cannot do some computer operations. For example, CL programs cannot add or update records in a database file and CL has very limited printing capabilities. CL programs do not support the use of AS/400 subfiles within application displays, nor do they support individual fields in AS/400 program-described files. Database manipulations are limited to reading files and only a single file can be opened for I/O operations in a CL program. These missing pieces in CL make it unsuitable for developing a complete business application.

Controlling Workflow with CL

CL programs control the workflow of an application by allowing you to create job-streams, which consist of CL commands to be executed in order. Within a CL program you can alter the order of execution by testing various conditions that may exist during the execution of a job. You can monitor for errors that might occur while running a job and perform corrective actions or abort the job. You can pass values, or parameters, to and from CL programs to make them more flexible and to permit or restrict the execution of blocks of program code. A CL program can incorporate conditional logic and special functions that are not available when you enter individual commands on a command line. You can also test and debug a CL program, just like any HLL program.

CL programs, unlike JCL, are implemented as **compiled program objects**, rather than **interpreted job streams**. A CL program is a permanent object on the AS/400, created by compiling a group of CL commands.

CL Execution Environment and Restrictions

As mentioned, individual CL commands may be entered into the system interactively on an AS/400 command line or included in a CL program. Individual CL commands and compiled CL programs can be submitted for batch processing using the SBMJOB (Submit Job) command. Commands can also be included within an AS/400 REXX language procedure.

If you group CL commands together, they may be compiled into a program object or submitted for interpretation during a batch process using the SBMDBJOB (Submit Database Job) command.

Some CL commands (e.g., STRSEU, to start the Source Entry Utility) are valid only when used interactively. Others (e.g., CRTCLPGM, to compile a CL program) should be used only within a batch process.

Several CL commands (e.g., GOTO and ENDPGM) are valid only when they appear within a CL program. You will become familiar with any such restrictions as we discuss the individual commands in detail later.

An Introductory Program

So what does a CL program look like? The example shown in Figure 1.1 is a simple CL program that sends a message to the user who runs the program.

Figure 1.1
A Simple CL Program

```
GREET:  PGM

        DCL &user    *CHAR 10
        DCL &date    *CHAR  6
        DCL &time    *CHAR  6

        RTVJOBA    USER(&user)
        RTVSYSVAL SYSVAL(QDATE)     RTNVAR(&date)
        RTVSYSVAL SYSVAL(QTIME)     RTNVAR(&time)

        SNDPGMSG   MSG('Hello,' *BCAT &user            +
                            *TCAT '. Login date-'       +
                            *CAT &date                  +
                            *BCAT 'time-'               +
                            *CAT &time)                 +
                   MSGTYPE(*COMP)

        ENDPGM
```

We discuss the fine details of CL programming later. For now, here's an overview of what is happening in the program in Figure 1.1:

1. The program defines three variables that will be used later in the CL program: the user of the program (&user), the current system date (&date), and the current system time (&time).
2. The name of the current user (i.e., the person who is signed on to the AS/400) is retrieved, along with the current date and time.
3. The system "glues together" a message, then sends the message to the user. For example:

```
"Hello, JSMITH. Login date-010198 time-152307"
```

As you progress through this text, you will become familiar with these and other CL commands, and with the flavor of a CL program.

Chapter Summary

The AS/400 Control Language (CL) is a set of commands included with the OS/400 operating system. CL is used to control operations and request system-related functions on the AS/400.

Even with more than 1,000 IBM-supplied commands, CL maintains a consistency that makes it easy to use and to learn. You can type individual CL commands on an AS/400 command line or you can group commands together and compile them into a CL program.

CL programs can be used to perform repetitive processing, thus reducing errors and the need for operator intervention.

CL is not a high-level language (HLL), in the classical sense of the term, like Cobol or RPG.

CL programs are compiled objects, not interpreted job streams.

CL commands can be entered interactively on a command line. A CL command or program can be submitted for batch processing using the SMBJOB (Submit Job) command. A group of CL commands can be compiled to form a program object, or they can be interpreted in a batch process using the SBMDBJOB (Submit Database Job) command.

Some CL commands are valid only when run interactively. Other CL commands are valid only when they appear within a CL program.

Terms

CL program

command

compiled program objects

interpreted job streams

Review Questions

1. Which of the following programming objectives might be satisfied with CL programming?

   a. Provide unattended overnight backup of AS/400 objects that have changed since the last weekly backup.

   b. Control a sequence of programs to write vendor checks and post them to a general ledger.

   c. Enforce a policy of changing a user's password every 50 times (s)he signs on to the AS/400.

   d. Provide unattended change of the system clock to or from Daylight Savings Time.

   e. Store comprehensive information about a firm's customers in an AS/400 database.

   f. Monitor the status of all communications lines attached to an AS/400.

   g. Calculate the amortization of a loan.

   h. Calculate payroll amounts for standard deductions and federal income withholding.

   i. Print a vendor listing including vendor name, address, and amount owed.

2. CL can be used on which of the following computers?

   a. DEC VAX

   b. IBM PC or PS/2

   c. IBM AS/400

   d. Apple Macintosh

   e. IBM 3090 mainframe

   f. IBM System/38

   g. IBM RS/6000

3. Which of the following file operations can you perform with CL?

   a. Read records from a database file.

   b. Update records in a database file.

   c. Read the records from several database files.

   d. Make a copy of a file.

   e. Delete a file.

Chapter 2

Control Language Command Names

Chapter Overview

This chapter addresses the way CL command names are structured. You will become familiar with the abbreviations used to denote common actions, subjects, adjectives, and subject phrases used to determine CL command names.

Verbs and Subjects

You learned in Chapter 1 that AS/400 CL is made up of more than 1,000 IBM-supplied commands. How will you ever learn them all? Although CL command names may seem foreign to you initially, learning them will not be as daunting a task as it first seems. IBM developed the language in a logical, consistent manner that makes it relatively easy to determine the name of a command required to accomplish a given task. Once you learn the simple logic behind the IBM naming conventions, you will find it easy to understand and use most of the commands.

CL command names are a shorthand form of the standard grammar for an English language imperative statement. Each command is an instruction to the computer to perform an action. The commands consist of a verb, or action, followed by the subject that will be acted upon (in English grammar we refer to the subject as the object, but because *object* has a specialized meaning on the AS/400, for clarity we use the word *subject*). For example, the CL command to display the contents of a magnetic tape is DSPTAP, the imperative statement being "display a tape." The command consists of two parts: the verb *DSP*, an abbreviated form of the English verb *display*; and the subject *TAP*, a shorthand form of the word *tape*.

If you were to guess what the CL command would be to "delete a program," you might guess correctly that the verb would be *delete* and the subject would be *program*. Shortening the verb *delete* would produce the CL verb *DLT*, and shortening the word *program* would produce the CL subject *PGM*. When you combine the CL verb and subject, the result is the CL command DLTPGM.

Command names are limited to a maximum length of 10 characters. The verbs are usually represented by three characters (e.g., *DLT* for delete), and the subjects are usually represented by one to three characters (e.g., *F* for file, *E* for entry, *PGM* for program).

A challenge exists when you know the imperative statement that describes the function you want the computer to perform, but you do not know the CL abbreviation for the verb or subject. For example, suppose you want to "send a message" to someone on the system, telling him or her that you are free for a meeting today at two o'clock. You know that the verb is *send* and the subject is *message*. But how do you correctly guess the CL shorthand version of the verb and subject? There are a number of choices for an abbreviated version of the verb *send*: You could guess SEN, SND, SED, or even the entire verb SEND. The abbreviated version of the subject *message* could be MES, MSG, M, or many other combinations of the letters contained in the word *message*. The correct CL command for "send a message" is SNDMSG. *SND* is the CL shorthand for the verb *send* and *MSG* is the abbreviated version of the subject *message*. However, as you can see, determining the correct shorthand version could require some guesswork on your part.

A general rule of thumb is that CL abbreviates words to their three most significant consonants. When a CL abbreviation includes a vowel, it is usually the first vowel or the only vowel in a word. Fortunately, once you know CL's shorthand version of a word, that shorthand version usually will be consistent, regardless of where in the command name it is used. For example, you read earlier that the command to display a tape is DSPTAP. If you change the subject from *tape* to *diskette*, you still use the same verb shorthand, *DSP*, but you use the shorthand *DKT*, for diskette, the new subject. When you combine the two abbreviations, you get the command DSPDKT, to "display a diskette." Figure 2.1 lists some common English verbs and their CL abbreviations.

Figure 2.1
Examples of
Common Verb
Abbreviations in CL

English Verb	CL Abbreviation	English Verb	CL Abbreviation
Add	ADD	Hold	HLD
Allocate	ALC	Initialize	INZ
Call	CALL	Move	MOV
Change	CHG	Override	OVR
Clear	CLR	Reorganize	RGZ
Copy	CPY	Release	RLS
Create	CRT	Remove	RMV
Declare	DCL	Restore	RST
Delete	DLT	Retrieve	RTV
Do	DO	Save	SAV
Display	DSP	Send	SND
End	END	Start	STR
Go to	GOTO	Work with	WRK

While many English verbs have their consistent shorthand version in CL, so also do subjects. For example, you know the command to display a tape is DSPTAP. *DSP* is the verb and *TAP* is the subject. CL also allows you to *initialize* a tape. In this case, the subject *TAP* does not change, but the action you want to perform, the verb, changes from *display* to *initialize*. The standard CL verb for *initialize, INZ*, replaces the verb *DSP* to form the command INZTAP (Initialize Tape). Figure 2.2 lists some commonly used subjects and their CL abbreviations.

Figure 2.2
Examples of
Common Subject
Abbreviations in CL

Subject	CL Abbreviation	Subject	CL Abbreviation
Attribute	A	Job	JOB
Authority	AUT	Library	LIB
Configuration	CFG	List	L
Command	CMD	Member	M
Communication	CMN	Message	MSG
Description	D	Object	OBJ
Diskette	DKT	Program	PGM
Document	DOC	Queue	Q
Entry	E	Subsystem	SBS
File	F	System	SYS
Folder	FLR	Tape	TAP

By using the verb and subject charts, you can easily determine the verb and subject to combine to produce a completed CL command. For example, if you want to "create a command," you can see by referring to the charts that the verb for *create* is *CRT* and the subject for *command* is *CMD*. Therefore the complete CL command would be CRTCMD. Similarly, if you want to "display a job," the command is DSPJOB.

Not all verbs are applicable to each subject. For example, if you combine the verb *CRT* and the subject *TAP*, you end up with the command CRTTAP (Create Tape). Although we all would like to help our companies save money on computer supplies, it is beyond the ability of CL to create magnetic tapes. CRTTAP is *not* a valid CL command.

A few CL commands do not require that a subject be specified. The CL command GOTO stands alone as a verb with no need for an added subject. Similarly, the CL commands CALL, DO, and ENDDO require no subject.

Adjectives and Subject Phrases

As you have learned, CL commands are formed by combining abbreviated versions of English verbs and subjects. This allows us to specify a command like WRKJOB (Work with Job). Sometimes, however, using a simple subject is not sufficient. In these cases, CL also allows you to specify an adjective to be associated with the subject. For example, if you want to look only at jobs that are currently *active* on the system, you could specify the command WRKACTJOB (Work with Active Jobs). Specifying the adjective *ACT*, CL shorthand for the adjective *active*, effectively limits the scope of the command to working with active jobs only. Together, the verb

(WRK), adjective (ACT), and subject (JOB) comprise the CL command to be executed. If you want to work only with jobs for one specific *user* on the system, you would use the CL command WRKUSRJOB (Work with a User's Jobs). In this instance, *USR* is the CL shorthand for the adjective *user*. Many CL commands use the verb, adjective, subject format. For example, to create an RPG/400 program, the CL command is CRTRPGPGM (Create RPG Program); to create a COBOL/400 program, the CL command is CRTCBLPGM (Create Cobol Program); and to create a standard CL program, the command is CRTCLPGM (Create CL Program). In these cases, the adjective qualifies the subject by specifying the kind of program to be created.

Let's look at a few more examples of CL's verb, adjective, subject command name format. The CL command to create a physical file is not simply CRTF (Create File). The AS/400 must know the type of file to create so you must specify the file type. For example, the CL command to create a physical file is CRTPF (Create Physical File); to create a logical file, the command is CRTLF (Create Logical File); to create a printer file, the command is CRTPRTF (Create Printer File); and to create a display file, the command is CRTDSPF (Create Display File). In each of these examples, the adjective becomes an integral part of the command.

In some rare cases, the name of a command does not fit into the verb/adjective/subject structure. In these cases, an even more detailed syntax is necessary. For example, consider the DSPPFM (Display Physical File Member) command. This command combines the verb *DSP* (display) with a subject phrase containing an adjective, *P* (Physical), and two subjects, *F* (File) and *M* (Member). Other commands, like ADDPFM (Add Physical File Member), CHGPFM (Change Physical File Member), and RGZPFM (Reorganize Physical File Member) use the same subject phrase (PFM). This verb/subject phrase structure complicates selecting the correct name of a CL command, but the structure is not used heavily in CL. In general, if you can learn the approximately 40 CL verbs and the approximately 100 subject abbreviations, you will have no trouble learning the names of the more than 1,000 CL commands.

Chapter Summary

AS/400 CL consists of more than 1,000 IBM-supplied commands. Each command is a shorthand version of an imperative statement, or instruction, to the computer to perform an action.

A command consists of a verb (or action) followed by a subject, which may be a simple subject, an adjective/subject combination, or a subject phrase.

Each verb and subject uses a standardized abbreviation scheme, usually consisting of the three most significant consonants in the verb, subject, and adjective. If there is a vowel in the abbreviation, it is usually the first or only vowel in the original word.

Review Questions

1. Using what you know about abbreviated verbs and subjects, identify the function of the following AS/400 CL commands:

    a. ADDLIBLE

    b. CHGPGM

    c. CLRPFM

    d. RMVMSGD

    e. DSPOBJAUT

    f. HLDJOB

    g. INZDKT

    h. MOVOBJ

    i. RSTLIB

    j. RTVJOBA

    k. SNDMSG

    l. STRSBS

    m. WRKFLR

2. Using the verb and subject charts, and other information found in this chapter, determine the names of the CL commands that perform the following functions:

    a. Remove a member

    b. Allocate an object

    c. Restore an object

    d. Change a library

    e. Create a library

    f. Create a message queue

    g. Create a job queue

    h. Remove a library list entry

    i. Create an RPG program

    j. Create a CL program

Chapter 3

Command Parameters

Chapter Overview

In this chapter we discuss using parameters to add flexibility and utility to CL commands. You learn about using keyword and positional notation to specify command parameters. We discuss the different types of command parameters and introduce you to default values, predefined values, special values, qualified values, generic values, and list values.

Command Parameters

Most CL commands allow you to specify one or more **command parameters** to define what a CL command will do. A parameter is simply a value, specified along with the command, that tells the command explicitly what to do or how to do it. In Chapter 2 we discussed the DSPTAP (Display Tape) command. If you enter only the CL command DSPTAP, the AS/400 will not have enough information to process the command. The AS/400 can have several different magnetic tape devices attached to it, and each tape device will have its own name. To display the contents of a tape, the computer needs to know specifically the name of the tape device you want to use. To direct the AS/400 to use a certain tape device, you must specify, along with the DSPTAP command, the name of that device. You would need to enter the command as

```
DSPTAP    DEV(TAP01)
```

where DSPTAP is the command to execute, DEV is the **parameter keyword**, and TAP01 is the **parameter value** — in this case the name of the tape device that will be used. You must separate the command and each of its parameters with one or more spaces. When you use parameter keywords like DEV, the actual parameter value must be enclosed in parentheses.

Required and Optional Parameters

Most CL commands have multiple parameters that may be specified to further define what the command should do. These parameters fall into two categories: **required** and **optional**. A required parameter is one that must be specified for the AS/400 to execute a CL command. An optional parameter may be specified, but is not required for successful execution of the CL command. A few commands, such as DO and ENDDO, have no parameters.

In our example above, you learned that the value for the DEV parameter keyword on the DSPTAP command must be explicitly supplied. Specifying a value for DEV indicates to the AS/400 which tape device to use for the command. The DEV parameter is an example of a required parameter.

The DSPTAP command has four other parameters for which a value may be supplied, but CL does not require that you do so. Parameters such as these are called **optional parameters**. CL assigns *default values* for optional parameters. The defaults are set to values that IBM assumes will be used most often. The default value will be used during the execution of the command unless you specifically enter a value for the optional parameter. The following example shows the DSPTAP command with the required DEV parameter and its four optional parameters. In this example, the IBM-supplied default values are shown for the optional parameters. (Think of all the lines in this example as a single command, entered on one line. The plus sign (+) is used for continuing a CL command onto more than one line, which we discuss in Chapter 6.)

```
DSPTAP      DEV(TAP01)       +
            LABEL(*ALL)      +
            SEQNBR(1)        +
            DATA(*LABELS)    +
            OUTPUT(*)
```

As you can see, the last command parameter that you may specify for the DSPTAP command uses the parameter keyword OUTPUT. The default value for the parameter is *. When the parameter default of * is not changed, it tells the DSPTAP command to display the contents of the tape interactively on your workstation screen. However, if you want to send the output of the DSPTAP operation to a printed report instead of to your workstation screen, you may enter the display tape command as follows:

```
DSPTAP      DEV(TAP01)       +
            OUTPUT(*PRINT)
```

This command syntax overrides the IBM-supplied default value for the OUTPUT parameter and causes a printed listing to be generated that reports on the contents of the magnetic tape.

Because specifying *OUTPUT(*PRINT)* is not required to execute the DSPTAP command, *OUTPUT* is considered an optional parameter. It is optional because the CL command can be successfully executed by the AS/400 using the IBM-supplied default value * for the parameter. You need to specify only the required parameters, and any optional parameters for which you do not want to use the IBM-supplied default values. Therefore, using either of the following two command syntax forms will produce the same result:

Command syntax including the default values:

```
DSPTAP      DEV(TAP01)       +
            LABEL(*ALL)      +
            SEQNBR(1)        +
            DATA(*LABELS)    +
            OUTPUT(*PRINT)
```

Command syntax omitting the default values:

```
DSPTAP     DEV(TAP01)        +
           OUTPUT(*PRINT)
```

If you use the second syntax shown, the AS/400 assumes you want to use the default values shown in the first syntax structure for the LABEL, SEQNBR, and DATA parameters.

Entering Parameters with Keyword Notation

In the previous examples we have presented CL commands in what is called **keyword notation**. Keyword notation presents all of the command parameters preceded by their corresponding keyword. For instance, in our example using the DSPTAP command,

```
DSPTAP     DEV(TAP01)        +
           OUTPUT(*PRINT)
```

keywords *DEV* and *OUTPUT* are used to identify the associated parameter values, *TAP01* and **PRINT*. When keywords are used, the order in which the parameters are specified is not significant. The keyword itself identifies the parameter to the command. For example, the following two CL command syntax forms shown in keyword notation are equivalent:

```
DSPTAP     DEV(TAP01)        +
           OUTPUT(*PRINT)
```

```
DSPTAP     OUTPUT(*PRINT)    +
           DEV(TAP01)
```

Entering Parameters with Positional Notation

Every CL command that has parameters allows those parameters to be entered in keyword notation. You also have the option to specify many, but not all, parameters in what is called **positional notation**. In positional notation, keywords are not used. Instead, parameters are specified in a predetermined positional order. When you use positional notation, you must specify the parameter values in the correct order. The DSPTAP command is first shown here with keyword notation, then with positional notation.

Keyword notation:

```
DSPTAP     DEV(TAP01)
```

Positional notation:

```
DSPTAP     TAP01
```

Because the DEV parameter is the first command parameter, it must be specified first in positional notation. Usually, commands with only one or two parameters specified are easy to read and understand when presented in positional notation. For example, even without knowing what they do, you can easily read and understand the following CL commands:

```
DSPTAP      TAP01
DSPLIB      MYLIBRARY
GOTO        ENDOFPGM
CALL        PROGRAM1
```

When you specify multiple parameters in positional notation, however, readability suffers. In the following example, the CPYF (Copy File) command is presented. This is the CL command to copy data from one file to another. First the keyword notation is shown for specifying multiple parameters, then the positional notation.

Keyword notation:

```
CPYF        FROMFILE(AFILE)     +
            TOFILE(BFILE)       +
            FROMMBR(MEMBER1)    +
            TOMBR(MEMBER2)      +
            MBROPT(*ADD)
```

Positional notation:

```
CPYF        AFILE               +
            BFILE               +
            MEMBER1             +
            MEMBER2             +
            *ADD
```

You can see from this example of positional notation that, unless you are familiar with the CPYF command, it is difficult to understand the meaning of the command parameters. What makes it difficult is that you cannot see which keywords are being used for which parameters. The keywords provide a frame of reference to the parameters, and in most cases, make the command easier to read.

The Order of Parameters

As we mentioned earlier, when you use positional notation to specify command parameters, you must carefully consider the order in which you specify the parameters. IBM has created the AS/400 CL command set with a predefined order in which you must specify parameters when using positional notation. The IBM publication *Control Language Reference* provides the documentation regarding allowable parameter values and the order in which the parameters must be specified. If you don't have access to that reference, you can find in Appendix A of this text the same information for most of the commands you will normally use.

As an example of the predefined order of parameters, consider again the CPYF command. The CPYF command requires that when using positional notation, the parameters be specified in the order shown below:

```
CPYF        from-file-name          +
            to-file-name            +
            from-member-name        +
            to-member-name          +
            add-replace-option      +
            create-tofile-option
```

1. The file to copy from (FROMFILE keyword). This is a required parameter.
2. The file to copy to (TOFILE keyword). This is a required parameter.
3. The file member to copy from (FROMMBR keyword). This parameter is optional; the default value is *FIRST.
4. The file member to copy to (TOMBR keyword). This parameter is optional; the default value is *FIRST.
5. Option to add or replace records (MBROPT keyword). This parameter is optional; the default value is *NONE.
6. Option to create the to-file (CRTFILE keyword). This parameter is optional; the default value is *NO.

Positional Keyword Limits

Every CL command limits the number of positional parameters that may be specified for the command. For example, the DSPTAP command allows you to use only one positional parameter. Therefore, if you want to specify more than one parameter value, you cannot enter the DSPTAP command in purely positional notation. You *cannot* enter the DSPTAP command as follows:

```
DSPTAP      TAP01                   +
            *ALL                    +
            1                       +
            *LABELS                 +
            *PRINT
```

Even if you could use the above format for the DSPTAP command, the resulting command would be difficult to understand. For the DSPTAP command, you can use positional notation only for the first parameter

```
DSPTAP      TAP01
```

The CPYF command is one command that allows several positional parameters. This command allows up to six positional parameters. So you could enter the CPYF command as follows:

```
CPYF        AFILE       +
            BFILE       +
            MEMBER1     +
            MEMBER2     +
            *ADD        +
            *YES
```

The CPYF command has many more parameters than are shown here, but six is the maximum number of parameters that may be specified using positional notation. This maximum is set individually for each command. You can determine the maximum number of positional parameters that can be used for a CL command by using the DSPCMD (Display Command) command to display a description of the command.

Note that even though some of the parameters for the CPYF command are optional, you may need to include an entry for them if you use positional notation. For example, if you want to specify a value for the fourth parameter (TOMBR), you will have to include a value for the third parameter (FROMMBR), even if that value is the default *FIRST*. Otherwise, the fourth parameter will not be in the fourth position of the parameter list.

Using *N

What if you want to use positional notation for a command, and you want to use default values for some of the parameters? You could explicitly type the default values, but there is an alternative notation you can use to specify default values when using positional notation. The value *N* may be used as a place holder within a positional notation list of parameters. For example, instead of specifying the CPYF command as

```
CPYF        AFILE       +
            BFILE       +
            *FIRST      +
            *FIRST      +
            *REPLACE
```

you could use the place holder *N and specify

```
CPYF        AFILE       +
            BFILE       +
            *N          +
            *N          +
            *REPLACE
```

This command syntax would cause the IBM-supplied default values to be used for parameters 3 and 4 (the FROMMBR and TOMBR keywords), corresponding to the positions of the value *N. The value *N is called a **predefined value**. IBM-supplied predefined parameter values in CL are always preceded by an asterisk (*), helping you to easily identify them.

Mixing Keyword and Positional Notation

The predefined value *N is seldom used because it is not very easy to read or write. When you want to specify only certain parameters, keyword notation is often easier to read and write, and it has the added advantage of being somewhat self-documenting. An alternative to using the value of *N is available. It is possible to combine keyword notation and positional notation on the same command. Consider the following example:

```
CPYF        AFILE           +
            BFILE           +
            MBROPT(*REPLACE)
```

The positional entries of *AFILE* and *BFILE* are followed by the keyword entry of *MBROPT(*REPLACE)*. When positional entries are mixed with keyword entries, the positional entries must be specified first, in the correct order. Keyword entries may then follow in any order. Once you begin using keyword notation in a command, you must use keyword notation for all subsequent parameters for that command. Combining positional notation with keyword notation usually produces the best compromise between readability and ease-of-entry. The use of *N should be discouraged.

At this point you might be asking yourself, "How am I supposed to remember all of the command parameters, let alone remember the exact order in which they must be specified for positional notation?" As you progress through this text, you will become familiar with several CL commands and their associated parameters. However, you do not need to remember every parameter of every command. Because there are more than 1,000 IBM-supplied CL commands on the AS/400, memorizing the AS/400 command set could be a lifelong task. Instead of forcing you to memorize, the AS/400 provides an easy-to-use prompting facility for every CL command. The prompting facility allows you to easily determine the parameters that may be specified for any CL command and will even help you find out which command to use to perform a task. We discuss the prompting facility in detail in Chapter 4. For now, don't try to memorize the commands and parameters. Instead, become familiar with their structures.

Types of Command Parameters

CL commands allow several different types of parameters to be used. Certain parameters require that a character string be specified as the parameter value; others require decimal values. The parameter type will depend upon the context of the parameter; that is, what parameter information the command needs to function. For example, in the DSPTAP command the first parameter, DEV, requires that a device name be specified, as in *DSPTAP DEV(TAP01)*. The third parameter, SEQNBR, requires that a numeric integer value of the tape sequence number be specified, as in *DSPTAP DEV(TAP01) SEQNBR(1)*.

Names and integer values are only two of the parameter types that may be used by a CL command. A list of some of the basic parameter types and their allowable values is shown in Figure 3.1.

Figure 3.1
Common Types of
Parameter Values

Parameter Type	Allowable Value
Character	Any character string
Command String	Any CL command
Date	A character string denoting the date, as in *123197*
Decimal	A decimal number, as in *5* or *3.14*
Generic Name	A partial name followed by an (*) asterisk, as in P* or PAY*. Identifies a group of objects
Hexadecimal	A hexadecimal number using digits 0–F
Integer	A numeric integer value as in 1 or 500
Logical	A logical value of 1 or 0
Name	A character string whose first character is alphabetic (A–Z), $, #, or @, and remaining characters are alpha-numeric (A–Z), (0–9), $, #, @, _ (underscore) or . (period)
Time	A character string specifying a time of day, as in *123000*

Parameter Special Values

When you use the DSPTAP command, you will notice that some of the parameter values begin with an asterisk (*).

```
DSPTAP    DEV(TAP01)        +
          LABEL(*ALL)       +
          SEQNBR(1)         +
          DATA(*LABELS)     +
          OUTPUT(*PRINT)
```

In the command above, you can see that we specified the LABEL parameter as *ALL*, the DATA parameter as *LABELS*, and the OUTPUT parameter as *PRINT*. Parameter values such as these that begin with an asterisk (*) are called **special values**. A special value allows a parameter value to be outside the normal checking rules for parameters. For example, the DSPTAP command expects to see a file label name as the value for the LABEL parameter. But the command allows you to specify the value *ALL, instead of a valid file label name, to indicate that all files on the tape are to be processed. In this case, CL reserves the meaning of the value *ALL* for a specific purpose. Many command parameters allow you to choose from one or more special values that are predefined for the parameter. Note that, although the predefined value *N begins with an *, it is not considered to be a special value; it is simply a place holder when positional notation is used.

Qualified Values

Occasionally, a command parameter allows you to specify a two- or three-part parameter value, known as a **qualified value** or **qualified name**. This form of parameter value is usually used when dealing with system objects such as file names or job names. For example, if you wanted to refer to the file named *CUSTOMER* in library *ARLIB*, you could specify a single entry, *ARLIB/CUSTOMER*. The slash (/) is the qualifier character, separating the two parts of the value. In the following example, the DSPPFM (Display Physical File Member) command uses a qualified parameter value to specify the file name:

```
DSPPFM       FILE(ARLIB/CUSTOMER)
```

Parameter Value Lists

Some command parameters allow you to list more than one value. For example, the RSTOBJ (Restore Object) command allows you to specify the names of one or more (up to 300) objects that you want to restore from backup media. This command uses a simple list to identify these objects

```
RSTOBJ       OBJ(CUSTOMER INVOICES PAYMENTS)    +
             SAVLIB(ARLIB)                       +
             DEV(TAP01)                          +
             OBJTYPE(*FILE)
```

In this example, we want to restore three files: CUSTOMER, INVOICES, and PAYMENTS. The elements of the list in the OBJ parameter must be separated by at least one blank.

When you use a parameter value list, you must enclose the list in parentheses, even if you use positional notation for the parameters. The following example, while it might seem correct at first glance, will *not* work:

```
RSTOBJ       CUSTOMER INVOICES PAYMENTS         +
             ARLIB                               +
             TAP01                               +
             *FILE
```

Because we are using positional notation, the AS/400 reads the first three values as individual parameters, not as elements of the OBJ parameter list. Consequently, the AS/400 will try to restore CUSTOMER to a library named INVOICES, using the tape on the non-existent device named PAYMENTS. In addition, the computer will not know how to handle what it sees as three additional positional parameter values: ARLIB, TAP01, and *FILE. The following example corrects the situation by enclosing the list parameter in parentheses:

```
RSTOBJ       (CUSTOMER INVOICES PAYMENTS)       +
             ARLIB                               +
             TAP01                               +
             *FILE
```

Complex Lists

In rare situations, you will have parameter values that include a list within another list, also called a **complex list**, as in the following example:

```
RSTOBJ      OBJ(*ALL)                                              +
            SAVLIB(ARLIB)                                          +
            DEV(TAP01)                                             +
            OBJTYPE(*ALL)                                          +
            FILEMBR((CUSTOMER (COMP01 COMP02))      +
                    (INVOICES (COMP01 COMP02))      +
                    (PAYMENTS (COMP01 COMP02)))     +
            MBROPT(*ALL)
```

In this example, we are restoring only the file members COMP01 and COMP02 from each of the files CUSTOMER, INVOICES, and PAYMENTS. The major list and the sublist are each enclosed in their own sets of parentheses, so it's not a trivial task to read the command as it is written. Fortunately, this type of parameter construction does not occur often, and you may use the command prompting facility, which is discussed in Chapter 4, to help match parentheses and to organize the list.

Chapter Summary

Most CL commands allow the specification of one or more command parameters; that is, values that will add to the flexibility and utility of commands. CL requires that you enter some parameter values (required parameters), but provides default values for other optional parameters.

You can enter *any* parameter using keyword notation. In keyword notation, you enter the parameter keyword, followed by the parameter value enclosed in parentheses. In addition, most commands allow you to enter some parameter values positionally, in a predetermined order, without entering the keyword name. When using keyword notation, you can specify parameters in any order. Positional notation requires that parameters be designated in a specific order.

You can combine positional and keyword notations for the same command, but you must specify the positional parameters first. When using positional notation, you can use the predefined value *N as a place holder to indicate the use of the parameter default value. But the use of *N is discouraged because it is difficult to read and write.

CL reserves certain predefined *special values* for some command parameter values. Each of these special values is preceded by an asterisk (*).

Some parameters allow the use of a *qualifier character* (/) to more specifically identify a parameter value. Qualified names are typically used to identify system objects within libraries.

Some command parameters allow you to specify lists of values. The list itself is enclosed within parentheses and each value in the list must be separated by at least one blank. In rare cases, it will be necessary to specify a parameter list within other lists.

Terms

command parameters
complex list
keyword notation
optional parameter

parameter keyword
parameter value
positional notation
predefined value

qualified values
required parameter
special values

Review Questions

1. How do parameters add flexibility to CL commands?
2. Explain the difference between required and optional parameters.

3. Explain the difference between keyword and positional notation. Which is generally easier to write and to read?
4. What does IBM call parameter values that begin with an asterisk (*)? What purpose do they serve?

Exercises

1. For each of the following CL command entries, decide whether the entry uses correct CL syntax. If an entry is not correct, correct it.
    a. DSPTAP
    b. CRTRPGPGMPGM1
    c. GOTO LUNCH
    d. CPYF
    e. CPYF NEWCUST ALLCUST
    f. CPYF FROMFILE(NEWCUST)   +
            TOFILE(ALLCUST) *N *N *ADD
    g. CPYF NEWCUST ALLCUST   +
            MBROPT(*ADD)
    h. DSPTAP TAP01 *ALL 1 *LABELS *PRINT
    i. DSPTAP *N

2. Which of the following entries are valid for specifying an Integer type parameter value?
    a. 1.75
    b. 565
    c. 400
    d. −356.56

3. Which of the following entries are valid for specifying a Name type parameter value?
    a. BOB
    b. #1SON
    c. $$BILL.1
    d. @$$$
    e. A&&B.6
    f. 00009
    g. NAME_1
    h. 1TAP01

4. Using Appendix A as a reference, list all of the parameter keywords for the following CL commands:
    a. SIGNOFF
    b. PGM
    c. RTVCLSRC
    d. CALL
    e. RCVF
    f. SNDPGMMSG
    g. CHGMSGQ
    h. RETURN

Exercises continued

Exercises continued

5. Which of the following are CL special values?

   a. NO
   b. *N
   c. *NO
   d. *LABELS
   e. *YES
   f. *CURRENT
   g. *LIBL
   h. BIG/LARGE
   i. (SIX SEVEN EIGHT)

6. The following list contains a mixture of simple values, special values, qualified values, generic values, and list values that may be used as parameters. Identify the type of parameter listed.

   a. MYLIBRARY/MYPROGRAM
   b. (JOB SIX FIVE)
   c. PROGRAM1
   d. *YES
   e. RET*
   f. (FILE1 FILE2)
   g. (LIB1/PGM1)
   h. (*LIBL/MYPGM)
   i. (KING*)
   j. (*JOB (*FIRST 1 2))

Chapter **4**

The AS/400 User Interface

Chapter Overview

This chapter introduces you to practical operational matters on the AS/400, including how to navigate the AS/400 menu system, how to use the command line, how to use function keys, and how to use the command prompting facility.

The AS/400 Menu System

When you first sign on to the AS/400, you are presented with the system's Main Menu display (Figure 4.1 — page 26). This display is usually the first screen presented to an AS/400 user. If your particular user profile has been customized, you might see a different display. If you do not see the system Main Menu, but some other display, type the command *GO MAIN* on any AS/400 command line and press the Enter key. This action takes you to the Main Menu.

The Main Menu you see might not include all the options shown in Figure 4.1. The options you are shown are determined by the security setup on your particular AS/400. The AS/400 provides hundreds of different **menus**. The Main Menu is just one of them. These AS/400 menus provide access to system functions in a way that is both easy to learn and easy to use.

All menus provide a command line (A in Figure 4.1) on which you can enter any of the valid option numbers (B) from the menu, or a CL command. The menus also provide a standard set of function keys (C) that provide additional functionality from within the menu.

All menus have a name. The name of the Main Menu is *MAIN*. The name of each menu is shown in the upper left corner of the menu (D in Figure 4.1). The title of the menu and the current AS/400 system name also are displayed.

When you know the name of a menu, you can go directly to it by using the CL command GO, followed by the name of the menu. Suppose you wanted to perform some kind of magnetic tape operation on the AS/400. You could go to any command line, type the command *GO TAPE*, and press the Enter key. The AS/400 would display the menu named *TAPE* (Figure 4.2). If you wanted to perform an operation on a data file, you could enter the command *GO FILE*. The menu named *FILE* would then be displayed.

Figure 4.1
AS/400 Main Menu

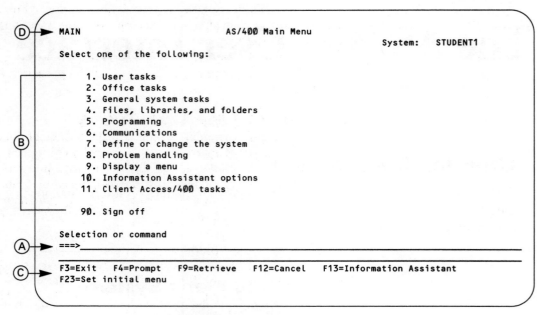

```
 D →   MAIN                          AS/400 Main Menu
                                                          System:    STUDENT1
       Select one of the following:

              1. User tasks
              2. Office tasks
              3. General system tasks
              4. Files, libraries, and folders
              5. Programming
 B            6. Communications
              7. Define or change the system
              8. Problem handling
              9. Display a menu
             10. Information Assistant options
             11. Client Access/400 tasks

             90. Sign off

       Selection or command
 A →   ===>_____

 C →   F3=Exit    F4=Prompt    F9=Retrieve    F12=Cancel    F13=Information Assistant
       F23=Set initial menu
```

Figure 4.2
AS/400 Tape Menu

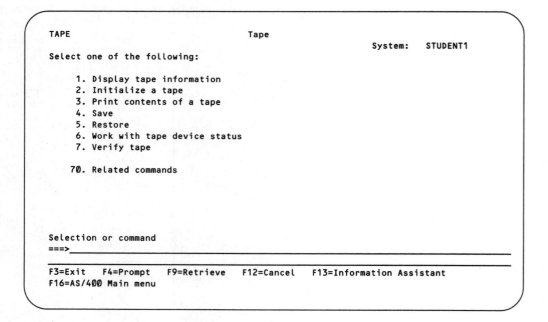

```
       TAPE                              Tape
                                                          System:    STUDENT1
       Select one of the following:

              1. Display tape information
              2. Initialize a tape
              3. Print contents of a tape
              4. Save
              5. Restore
              6. Work with tape device status
              7. Verify tape

             70. Related commands




       Selection or command
       ===>_____

       F3=Exit    F4=Prompt    F9=Retrieve    F12=Cancel    F13=Information Assistant
       F16=AS/400 Main menu
```

Using the GO command, you also can specify a menu name as a *generic* parameter. Generic parameters are used to broaden the scope of a command from a single entry to all entries that fit a character pattern. For example, if you wanted to see all menus that start with the letter T, you could enter the command *GO T**. Or if you wanted to choose from all menus that start with the letters TAP, you could enter the command *GO TAP**.

Using the GO command, you also can specify the special value **ALL*, as in *GO *ALL*. When you enter this command, you will be presented with a listing of all AS/400 menus.

Command Line Operations

Every menu includes a command line near the bottom of the display. Some screens, like the programmer's Source Entry Utility (SEU) edit screen, provide a special function key that can be used to access a command line. An extended command line display is also available by calling a special IBM-supplied program named QCMD. You can access this function by typing *CALL QCMD* on a command line.

You have already learned that you can enter the GO and CALL command on a command line. In fact, you can enter any CL command on a command line. For example, if you wanted to display the contents of a magnetic tape on your workstation screen you could simply type *DSPTAP TAP01* on a command line and press the Enter key. (We assume, in this case, that the tape device is named TAP01.) Or if you wanted to display the contents of a library named MYLIBRARY, you could enter the command *DSPLIB MYLIBRARY*.

Command Line Function Keys

Any time you have a command line on your screen, there are at least four active **function keys** that can be used. Function keys are special keys on the keyboard, normally labeled F1 through F12 or F1 through F24, depending on your keyboard. If the keys are labeled F1 through F12, you must use the Shift key to access F13 through F24: Shift F1 would be treated as F13, Shift F2 would be treated as F14, and so on.

The four function keys that are always valid when a command line is displayed are F3, F4, F9, and F12. F3 is the exit function on the AS/400. When you want to exit from the screen that is currently displayed , you would use the F3=Exit key. F12 is the cancel function on the AS/400. F12=Cancel will return you to the previous screen. Many times the action performed by F3 is identical to F12.

The F9 function key is used to retrieve commands previously entered on the command line. Instead of repeatedly typing similar or identical commands on the command line, you can use the F9=Retrieve key to scroll back through commands previously entered. The commands then may be re-executed, or modified and then executed. Each time you sign-on to the AS/400 you start a new command retrieval list.

The F4 function key is the prompt key. Whenever you press the F4=Prompt key, you invoke the AS/400 prompting facilities. When used from a screen containing a command line, the F4=Prompt key helps you enter commands correctly, and even helps you find the command you should use to accomplish a given task.

The AS/400 Prompt Facility

When you type the name of a CL command on a command line, you can press F4=Prompt, instead of Enter, to invoke the **command prompt display**. For example, when you type *DSPTAP* on a command line and press F4=Prompt, the AS/400 displays a formatted prompt for the parameters of the DSPTAP (Display Tape) command (Figure 4.3).

Figure 4.3
Prompted DSPTAP
(Display Tape)
Command

```
                                 Display Tape (DSPTAP)

 Type choices, press Enter.

 Device . . . . . . . . . . . . .   _____    Name
 Volume identifier . . . . . . .    *MOUNTED       Character value, *MOUNTED
 File label . . . . . . . . . . .   *ALL
 Sequence number . . . . . . . .    1              1-9999
 Data type . . . . . . . . . . .    *LABELS        *LABELS, *SAVRST
 Output . . . . . . . . . . . . .   *              *, *PRINT, *OUTFILE
 End of tape option . . . . . . .   *REWIND        *REWIND, *UNLOAD




                                                                        Bottom
 F3=Exit   F4=Prompt   F5=Refresh   F12=Cancel   F13=How to use this display
 F24=More keys
```

The prompt asks for the parameter values needed by the DSPTAP command. You simply fill in the parameter values. When you press the Enter key, the system executes the command using the parameters you specified.

Or you also can type the name of a CL command and its parameters from a command line and then press the F4=Prompt key. For example, if you type the command *DSPTAP TAP01 OUTPUT(*PRINT)* on a command line and then press F4=Prompt, the parameters will be presented already filled in on the prompt (Figure 4.4). You then can modify those parameters, change other parameters, or simply press the Enter key to execute the command.

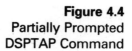

Figure 4.4
Partially Prompted
DSPTAP Command

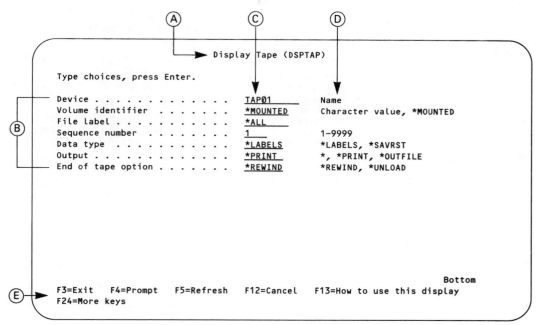

The Command Prompt Display

Regardless of the CL command you are prompting, consistency among prompt displays makes them easy to work with. As with the command prompt display for the DSPTAP command (Figure 4.4), a description of the command and the command name always appear at the top of the screen (A in Figure 4.4). Below the command name, you will find a list of the command parameters. In the case of the DSPTAP command, you are shown seven parameters that can be specified. From left to right on the display you see a description of each parameter (B in Figure 4.4), an input-capable field for each parameter value (C), and a list of allowable values that can be specified for the parameter (D). At the bottom of the screen is a list of the allowable function keys (E).

In our sample DSPTAP command display, the first parameter, labeled "Device," is a required parameter. Required parameters are easily identifiable on any prompt screen because the underline for their input-capable field is always highlighted. Because the other six parameters for the DSPTAP command are optional, the system fills in their default values for you.

Determining Allowable Values

If you are unsure what to enter in any parameter input field, you can determine the correct entry in one of three ways. If, for instance, you do not know what value to enter for the third parameter (*File Label*) of the DSPTAP command, you could enter a question mark (?) in the File Label input field (Figure 4.5) and press Enter.

Figure 4.5
Prompting for
Individual Parameter
Values with a
Question Mark (?)

```
                              Display Tape (DSPTAP)

 Type choices, press Enter.

 Device . . . . . . . . . . . . .    TAP01         Name
 Volume identifier  . . . . . . .    *MOUNTED      Character value, *MOUNTED
 File label . . . . . . . . . .      ?
 Sequence number  . . . . . . . .    1             1-9999
 Data type  . . . . . . . . . .      *LABELS       *LABELS, *SAVRST
 Output . . . . . . . . . . . .      *             *, *PRINT, *OUTFILE
 End of tape option . . . . . . .    *REWIND       *REWIND, *UNLOAD




                                                                       Bottom
 F3=Exit    F4=Prompt    F5=Refresh    F12=Cancel   F13=How to use this display
 F24=More keys
```

The resulting screen (Figure 4.6) prompts you to specify a value for the *LABEL* parameter. Information on the screen tells you to specify a character type parameter. However, you also can enter a special value of *ALL* (A in Figure 4.6). Any allowable special values are listed on the display (B). In the case of the DSPTAP command's LABEL parameter, only one special value (*ALL) is permitted.

Figure 4.6
Example of
CL Parameter
Prompting

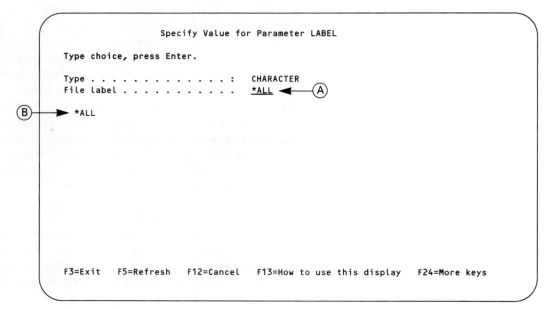

```
                        Specify Value for Parameter LABEL

 Type choice, press Enter.

 Type . . . . . . . . . . . . . :   CHARACTER
 File label . . . . . . . . . .     *ALL  ◄────(A)

(B)──►  *ALL









 F3=Exit    F5=Refresh    F12=Cancel    F13=How to use this display    F24=More keys
```

Another way to determine the value of the LABEL parameter is to place the cursor in the input field for the parameter and then press the F4=Prompt key. Using the F4=Prompt key produces the same result as placing a question mark in the parameter input field. You will see a display identical to the one shown in Figure 4.6. In either case, you can type the desired parameter value directly onto this display, and the value will "carry back" to the previous display.

The third, and perhaps best, way to determine a parameter's allowable values is to use the Help key. Place the cursor in the input field of the parameter in question, then press the Help key. If you have trouble locating the Help key on your keyboard, you can use the F1=Help function key instead. For all IBM-supplied screens(e.g., Menus, Command Prompts), pressing the F1 key is the same as pressing the Help key.

When you press the Help key, you are presented with a help text window. Figure 4.7 shows the help text window for the LABEL parameter. In the window you can see a description of the parameter (A) and a list of possible values with a description of each (B). You can access additional online documentation from the help text window by keying F11=InfoSeeker (InfoSeeker is the name the AS/400 gives to its facility for accessing books online). If you press F2=Extended help from this window, you will see the extended help listing for the DSPTAP command. Or you can print the help text from this window by pressing F14=Print help. Unlike the display presented when you press the F4=Prompt key, however, you cannot type the value you want to use directly onto the help text window.

Figure 4.7
Example of
Help Window

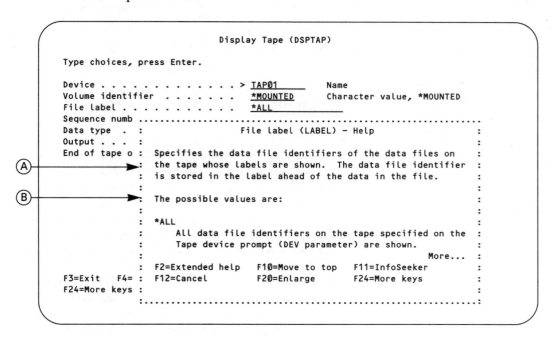

If the lower right corner of the help window contains the notation "More...", you need to use the Page Down (or Roll Up) key to view all the help text. To enlarge the help text to a full-screen window (Figure 4.8), press F20=Enlarge. To automatically have full-screen help text windows, ask your AS/400 system administrator to modify your user profile.

Figure 4.8
Example of Full-Screen
Help Window

```
                          Display Tape (DSPTAP)
 ...........................................................................
 :                      File label (LABEL) - Help                          :
 :                                                                         :
 : Specifies the data file identifiers of the data files on the tape whose :
 : labels are shown.  The data file identifier is stored in the label ahead:
 : of the data in the file.                                                :
 :                                                                         :
 : The possible values are:                                               :
 :                                                                         :
 : *ALL                                                                    :
 :     All data file identifiers on the tape specified on the Tape device  :
 :     prompt (DEV parameter) are shown.                                   :
 :                                                                         :
 : data-file-identifier                                                    :
 :     Specify the data file identifier (17 alphanumeric characters        :
 :     maximum) of the data file for which label information is shown.      :
 :                                                                         :
 :                                                                         :
 :                                                               Bottom    :
 : F2=Extended help    F3=Exit help   F10=Move to top   F11=InfoSeeker     :
 : F12=Cancel          F13=Information Assistant         F14=Print help     :
 :                                                                         :
 :........................................................................:
```

Command Prompt Function Keys

Now that you are familiar with the action of the F4=Prompt key and the Help key when used from the command prompt display, let's look at several other function keys that are active when a command prompt is shown on the screen.

Look again at Figure 4.5 on page 30. You will notice that besides the F3=Exit and F12=Cancel function keys, other valid function keys are F4=Prompt, F5=Refresh, F13=How to use this display, and F24=More keys.

The F5=Refresh key refreshes the display, ignoring anything you have typed into the parameter input fields and redisplaying an initial command prompt. This function key is useful if you decide you have entered several parameters in error, and you want to start fresh.

The F13=How to use this display function key takes you to a series of screens that describe how command prompt screens work. Review these screens at least once to become more familiar with command prompts.

Because space can be limited on a CL prompt screen, all valid function keys are not listed initially. To see other valid function keys, press the F24=More keys function key. For example, when you press F24 from the screen shown in Figure 4.4, the resulting screen (Figure 4.9) shows you can use additional function keys F9, F11, F14, and (again) F24. Whenever you press F24, the screen rotates through different groups of available function keys. You can use any function key listed for these screens, even when it is not shown at the bottom of the screen.

Figure 4.9
Prompted Command
Screen with
Additional Function
Keys Displayed

```
                          Display Tape (DSPTAP)

  Type choices, press Enter.

  Device . . . . . . . . . . . . .   TAP01        Name
  Volume identifier . . . . . . .    *MOUNTED     Character value, *MOUNTED
  File label . . . . . . . . . . .   *ALL
  Sequence number . . . . . . . .    1            1-9999
  Data type . . . . . . . . . . .    *LABELS      *LABELS, *SAVRST
  Output . . . . . . . . . . . . .   *PRINT       *, *PRINT, *OUTFILE
  End of tape option . . . . . . .   *REWIND      *REWIND, *UNLOAD




                                                                     Bottom
  F9=All parameters    F11=Keywords    F14=Command string   F24=More keys
```

Pressing the F9=All parameters function key causes the computer to display all valid parameters for a command. Depending on the command, all the valid parameters may not fit on one display screen; you may need to use the Page Down (or Roll Up) key to see them all. Because the DSPTAP command has no more parameters than are shown on the screen in Figure 4.9, pressing the F9=All parameters function key would have no effect. But some commands, like the CPYF command presented earlier, have many parameters. Some of the parameters are seldom used, however, so they are not displayed on the initial command prompt. To access all command parameters, use the F9=All parameters function key.

F11=Keywords acts like a toggle switch: It displays either the keywords for each displayed parameter or a list of possible choices. When F11=Keywords is pressed, the F11=Keywords function key becomes the F11=Choices function key. Press F11=Choices and the display once again shows parameter choices instead of parameter keywords.

Figure 4.10 shows the keyword prompt. You can have your user profile changed to initially display the keywords, instead of parameter value choices; however, most programmers find it more useful to see the choices.

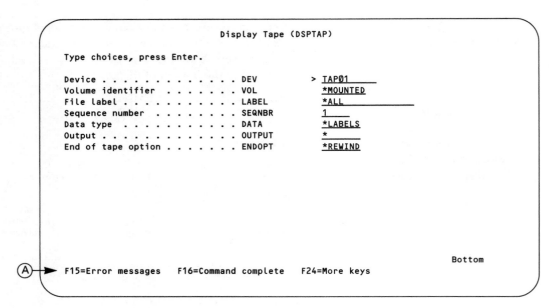

Figure 4.10
Prompted CL
Command in
Keyword Format

```
                                Display Tape (DSPTAP)

 Type choices, press Enter.

 Device . . . . . . . . . . . . . DEV        >  TAP01
 Volume identifier . . . . . . . VOL           *MOUNTED
 File label . . . . . . . . . . LABEL          *ALL
 Sequence number  . . . . . . . . SEQNBR       1
 Data type  . . . . . . . . . . DATA           *LABELS
 Output . . . . . . . . . . . . OUTPUT         *
 End of tape option . . . . . . ENDOPT         *REWIND




                                                                    Bottom
 F15=Error messages    F16=Command complete    F24=More keys
```

(A)

Pressing the F14=Command string key displays a screen containing the current command prompt as a CL command string — the actual CL command that will be executed when you press the Enter key from the command prompt.

And as you learned earlier, pressing F24=More keys presents more valid function keys at the bottom of the display. In this case, the additional function keys you can use are F15=Error messages and F16=Command complete (A in Figure 4.10).

For whichever command you might be using the prompt facility, the F15=Error messages key allows you to display any errors detected by the prompter. This is a particularly useful function for finding an error on a command prompt that spans several screens.

Pressing the F16=Command complete key tells the command prompter that you have finished entering parameter values and are ready to execute the command. You use this function key only on a multiscreen prompt, when you do not want to fill in any more parameter values on successive screens of the prompt.

Additional Parameters

Some CL command prompt screens allow you to use an F10=Additional parameters function key. Most commands have more parameters than you would need to use regularly. In these cases, the command prompt initially shows you only the required parameters and those others that you would be most likely to change. As an example, Figure 4.11 shows a command prompt to create a CL program. When you create a CL program, you usually need to supply a value for only the parameters shown on the initial screen (those shown in Figure 4.11). However, there may be situations when you need to specify values for additional parameters. When this occurs, you

Figure 4.11
Prompted CRTCLPGM

```
                          Create CL Program (CRTCLPGM)

 Type choices, press Enter.

 Program . . . . . . . . . . . . .    _____      Name
   Library . . . . . . . . . . . .    *CURLIB       Name, *CURLIB
 Source file . . . . . . . . . . .    QCLSRC        Name
   Library . . . . . . . . . . . .    *LIBL         Name, *LIBL, *CURLIB
 Source member . . . . . . . . . .    *PGM          Name, *PGM
 Text 'description'  . . . . . . .    *SRCMBRTXT    _____
 _____




                                                                   Bottom
 F3=Exit    F4=Prompt    F5=Refresh    F10=Additional parameters    F12=Cancel
 F13=How to use this display          F24=More keys
```

can press the F10=Additional parameters key to see and modify any other parameters for the command.

There is a subtle difference between the F9=All parameters and the F10=Additional parameters keys. While pressing F9 shows all the parameters for a command, pressing F10 takes advantage of the AS/400's "smart prompting" feature, showing only those parameters that are applicable to a given situation. Usually, you will use F10. Rarely would there be a need to use F9.

Figure 4.12 shows the screen that appears after you press F10=Additional parameters from the command prompt shown in Figure 4.11. The additional parameters are listed and the value "More…" is shown at the bottom of the display, indicating that the Page Down (or Roll Up) key can be used to see even more parameters.

Figure 4.12
Prompted CRTCLPGM
Command Showing
Additional Parameters

```
                        Create CL Program (CRTCLPGM)

 Type choices, press Enter.

 Program . . . . . . . . . . . . .   _____      Name
   Library . . . . . . . . . . . .   *CURLIB      Name, *CURLIB
 Source file . . . . . . . . . . .   QCLSRC       Name
   Library . . . . . . . . . . . .   *LIBL        Name, *LIBL, *CURLIB
 Source member . . . . . . . . . .   *PGM         Name, *PGM
 Text 'description'  . . . . . . .   *SRCMBRTXT


                        Additional Parameters

 Source listing options  . . . . . .   _____    *SOURCE, *NOSOURCE, *SRC
              + for more values  .     _____
 Generation options  . . . . . . . .   _____    *NOLIST, *LIST, *NOXREF
              + for more values  .     _____
 User profile  . . . . . . . . . .     *USER      *USER, *OWNER
 Log commands  . . . . . . . . . .     *JOB       *JOB, *YES, *NO
                                                             More...
 F3=Exit   F4=Prompt   F5=Refresh   F12=Cancel   F13=How to use this display
 F24=More keys
```

Prompt Special Characters

To use the command prompt, you need to be familiar with five special characters. These characters are *question mark* (?), *ampersand* (&), *plus* (+), *greater than* (>), and *less than* (<). You are already familiar with the operation of the question mark (?), which performs the same function as the F4=Prompt key when entered in a parameter input field.

The & is entered into a blank prompt input field to increase the size of the parameter value typing area on the prompt. Figure 4.13 shows the result of placing an & in the *Device* input field of the DSPTAP command prompt. As you can see, the typing area becomes larger, allowing the parameter value to be longer. Because CL programs allow you to use long expressions as parameter values, you usually need the & only when writing CL programs. In this example, using & expands the 10-character input field for parameter *Device*.

The rest of the special prompting characters — plus (+), greater than (>), and less than (<) — can be used when a parameter allows you to enter a list containing more than one value.

The + lets you add entries at the end of a parameter list. For example, the DSPLIB (Display Library) command allows you to specify a list of libraries that you want to display. You can see in Figure 4.14 that the initial DSPLIB command prompt provides room to enter the names of only two libraries.

Figure 4.13
Prompted DSPTAP
Command Showing
Extended Tape Device
Input Field

```
                              Display Tape (DSPTAP)

 Type choices, press Enter.

 Device . . . . . . . . . . . . .   ('TAP' *CAT &DEVICE *TCAT  '1')

 Volume identifier  . . . . . .     *MOUNTED     Character value, *MOUNTED
 File label . . . . . . . . . .     *ALL
 Sequence number  . . . . . . .     1            1-9999
 Data type  . . . . . . . . . .     *LABELS      *LABELS, *SAVRST
 Output . . . . . . . . . . . .     *            *, *PRINT, *OUTFILE
 End of tape option . . . . . .     *REWIND      *REWIND, *UNLOAD




                                                                    Bottom
 F3=Exit   F4=Prompt   F5=Refresh   F12=Cancel   F13=How to use this display
 F24=More keys
```

Figure 4.14
Using Plus Sign (+)
to Expand a
Parameter List

```
                             Display Library (DSPLIB)

 Type choices, press Enter.

 Library . . . . . . . . . . . . . . .   library1       Name, *LIBL, *USRLIBL
                 + for more values  . . .   +
 Output  . . . . . . . . . . . . . . .   *              *, *PRINT








                                                              Bottom
 F3=Exit   F4=Prompt     F5=Refresh   F12=Cancel   F13=How to use this display
 F24=More keys
```

If you want to look at several libraries at one time, you need to extend the list. To do this, enter the name of the first library you want to display. Then enter the + in the second entry field, where the prompt states "+ for more values". When you press the

Enter key, you are shown the screen in Figure 4.15. This screen allows you to type in the names of several libraries, which will be added to the original entry.

Figure 4.15
Expanded
Parameter List

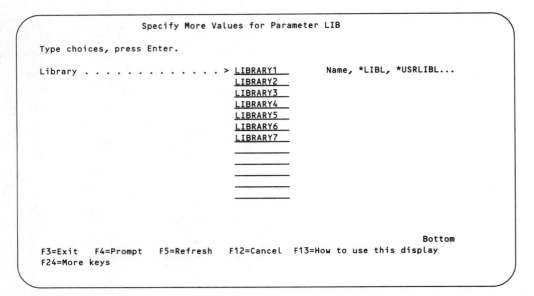

```
                        Specify More Values for Parameter LIB

    Type choices, press Enter.

    Library . . . . . . . . . . . . . >  LIBRARY1          Name, *LIBL, *USRLIBL...
                                         LIBRARY2
                                         LIBRARY3
                                         LIBRARY4
                                         LIBRARY5
                                         LIBRARY6
                                         LIBRARY7

                                         _____
                                         _____
                                         _____
                                         _____


                                                                        Bottom
    F3=Exit    F4=Prompt    F5=Refresh    F12=Cancel  F13=How to use this display
    F24=More keys
```

When you press the Enter key from the display shown in Figure 4.15, you return to the original prompt, only now the additional values are shown on the display (Figure 4.16). Notice that to the left of the list entry for **LIBRARY7** the value "+ for more values" is again shown. This indicates that you may enter a + on the **LIBRARY7** line to add more entries. The **LIBRARY7** entry is not removed when you do this.

There are occasions when you might want to insert an entry in the middle of a list of values. For instance, if you want to place the library name **LIBRARYA** between **LIBRARY3** and **LIBRARY4**, you could either retype the list of libraries to put them in the right order, or you could insert the entry for **LIBRARYA** using greater than (>). Figure 4.17 illustrates this technique. As you can see, entry **LIBRARY3** has been replaced with >. When you press the Enter key, the system prompts you for the names of the libraries to insert at that place in the list.

When you want to delete entries from the list parameter, you may do so by using less than (<). Figure 4.18 (page 40) illustrates the use of < to remove an entry — in this example, **LIBRARY4** — from the list. When you press the Enter key, the **LIBRARY4** entry is removed.

You also can remove entries from a list by overtyping the value displayed with blanks, or by using the Field Exit key. Simply place the cursor on the first character of the entry to be removed and press the Field Exit key. If you are unsure which key on your particular keyboard is the Field Exit key, ask your AS/400 system administrator.

Figure 4.16
Prompted DSPTAP
Command with
Expanded
Parameter List

```
                              Display Library (DSPLIB)

Type choices, press Enter.

Library   . . . . . . . . . . .     LIBRARY1        Name, *LIBL, *USRLIBL...
                                    LIBRARY2
                                    LIBRARY3
                                    LIBRARY4
                                    LIBRARY5
                                    LIBRARY6
                + for more values   LIBRARY7
Output  . . . . . . . . . . . .     *               *, *PRINT




                                                                    Bottom
F3=Exit    F4=Prompt   F5=Refresh   F12=Cancel  F13=How to use this display
F24=More keys
```

Figure 4.17
Inserting a Value into
a Parameter List

```
                              Display Library (DSPLIB)

Type choices, press Enter.

Library   . . . . . . . . . . .     LIBRARY1        Name, *LIBL, *USRLIBL...
                                    LIBRARY2
                                    >
                                    LIBRARY4
                                    LIBRARY5
                                    LIBRARY6
                + for more values   LIBRARY7
Output  . . . . . . . . . . . .     *               *, *PRINT




                                                                    Bottom
F3=Exit    F4=Prompt   F5=Refresh   F12=Cancel  F13=How to use this display
F24=More keys
```

Figure 4.18
Deleting a Value
from a Parameter List
Using Less Than (<)

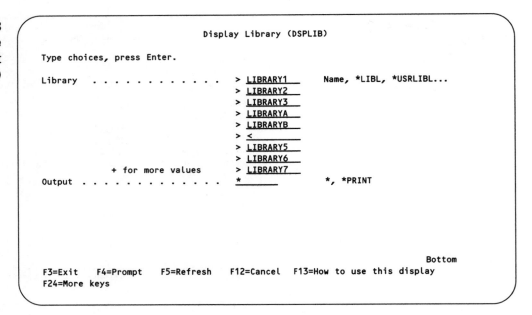

```
                              Display Library (DSPLIB)

Type choices, press Enter.

Library  . . . . . . . . . . .  > LIBRARY1      Name, *LIBL, *USRLIBL...
                                 > LIBRARY2
                                 > LIBRARY3
                                 > LIBRARYA
                                 > LIBRARYB
                                 > <
                                 > LIBRARY5
                                 > LIBRARY6
               + for more values > LIBRARY7
Output . . . . . . . . . . . .  *             *, *PRINT




                                                                    Bottom
F3=Exit   F4=Prompt   F5=Refresh   F12=Cancel   F13=How to use this display
F24=More keys
```

Finding the Right CL Command

Sometimes you will not know the name of the CL command that will do what you want to do. In these instances, you can use the prompting facility to help you find the command you are looking for.

To search for the name of a command, go to a menu or other screen that contains a command line, and without making any entry on the command line, press the F4=Prompt key. This results in a display of the menu named MAJOR (Figure 4.19).

The MAJOR menu provides a listing of the major command groups available on the AS/400. Because the MAJOR menu contains the phrase "More..." at the end of the list of options (A in Figure 4.19), you can press the Page Down (or Roll Up) key on your keyboard to see more options. The additional options from the MAJOR menu are shown in Figure 4.20.

The MAJOR menu allows you to find the command you are looking for by means of several different command grouping methods. Depending upon the command you are looking for, and how much you know about formulating command names, you usually will find that one grouping method makes more sense than another.

MAJOR menu option 1 allows you to "Select Command by Name." When you take this option you are presented with the menu named SLTCMD, which contains a listing of every CL command on the system in alphabetical order. This choice might be okay if you are looking for a command that starts with the letter A — for example, ADDPFM (Add Physical File Member). But if the command you need happens to start with the letter T — for example, TFRCTL (Transfer Control) — you would have to scroll through about 900 commands before you find the command you want.

Figure 4.19
Major Command
Groups Menu

```
MAJOR                        Major Command Groups
                                                          System:   STUDENT1
Select one of the following:

        1. Select Command by Name                         SLTCMD
        2. Verb Commands                                  VERB
        3. Subject Commands                               SUBJECT
        4. Object Management Commands                      CMDOBJMGT
        5. File Commands                                   CMDFILE
        6. Save and Restore Commands                       CMDSAVRST
        7. Work Management Commands                         CMDWRKMGT
        8. Data Management Commands                         CMDDTAMGT
        9. Security Commands                               CMDSEC
       10. Print Commands                                 CMDPRT
       11. Spooling Commands                              CMDSPL
       12. System Control Commands                         CMDSYSCTL
       13. Program Commands                               CMDPGM
                                                              More...

Selection or command
===> _____


F3=Exit    F4=Prompt    F9=Retrieve    F12=Cancel    F13=Information Assistant
F16=AS/400 Main menu
```

Ⓐ

Figure 4.20
Additional Commands
from Major Command
Groups Menu

```
MAJOR                        Major Command Groups
                                                          System:   STUDENT1
Select one of the following:

       14. Office Commands                                CMDOFC
       15. Database Commands                              CMDDB
       16. Communications Management Commands             CMDCMNMGT
       17. Distribution Services Commands                 CMDDSTSRV
       18. Configuration Commands                         CMDCFG
       19. Problem Management Commands                    CMDPRBMGT
       20. Message Handling Commands                      CMDMSGHDL
       21. Performance Commands                           CMDPFR
       22. System/36 Commands                             CMDS36
       23. System/38 Commands                             CMDS38




                                                              Bottom
Selection or command
===> _____


F3=Exit    F4=Prompt    F9=Retrieve    F12=Cancel    F13=Information Assistant
F16=AS/400 Main menu
```

If you know the CL verb of the command you are looking for, you might use option 2 from the MAJOR menu, to select "Verb Commands." The resulting VERB menu contains many CL verbs, again in alphabetical order. If you were looking for a command containing the CL verb DSP, you might page through many, many "Display" commands before finding the command you want — for example, DSPPFM (Display Physical File Member).

You also could look for the command name by using option 3 from the MAJOR menu, which takes you to the SUBJECT menu (Figure 4.21), where you can locate a command based on subject. For instance, if you know you want to do some operation on a file, you can look for the subject "file." There are fewer items listed in the SUBJECT menu than in other menus, which means you can find commands faster. So when you know the subject of the command you want, the SUBJECT menu can be a better choice than options 1 or 2.

Figure 4.21
Subject Commands
Menu

```
 SUBJECT                          Subject Commands

 Select one of the following:

      1. Abnormal Commands                                  CMDABN

      3. Access Code Commands                               CMDACC
      4. Access Group Commands                              CMDACCGRP
      5. Accounting Commands                                CMDACG

      7. Action Entry Commands                              CMDACNE
      8. Active Commands                                    CMDACT

     11. Adopt Commands                                     CMDADP
     12. Adapter Commands                                   CMDADPT
     13. Address Commands                                   CMDADR

     19. Autostart Job Entry Commands                       CMDAJE
                                                              More...
 Selection or command
 ===> _____

 _____
 F3=Exit    F4=Prompt    F9=Retrieve    F12=Cancel    F16=Major menu
```

If you know more detail about the command you are looking for, other options available on the MAJOR menu would be more appropriate than options 1, 2, or 3. Look again at Figures 4.19 and 4.20, and you will see that menu options offering narrower command selections are available (e.g., option 5, File Commands; option 7, Work Management Commands; option 10, Print Commands).

If you know, for example, that you want a command to "Delete a file," the best option from the MAJOR menu would be option 5, File Commands. Selecting this option will display the CMDFILE menu (Figure 4.22).

You would select option 7 from the CMDFILE Menu to access the Delete File command. Notice that directly across from option 7, on the right side of the display, is the CL command you are looking for, *DLTF*.

As you can see, you can find a command in several different ways using the MAJOR menu as a starting point (by command name, by verb, by subject, etc.). You normally can find the CL command using any of these options. But you can reduce your search time considerably by becoming familiar with and working with the different options.

Using the CMD Menus

As you become more familiar with CL commands, you could bypass the MAJOR menu altogether. Because CMDFILE (Figure 4.22) is a menu, you could enter *GO CMDFILE* on any command line and that menu would be displayed. The result is the same as if you selected the MAJOR menu first, but it's easier to use the GO CMDFILE command. There are many, many menus on the system that begin with the letters CMD. Each of these menus is designed to help you find commands that deal with a certain subject. For instance, the CMDADD menu displays all of the ADD commands on the system (e.g., ADDPFM, ADDWSE, and ADDTRC). To see a listing of all CMD type menus on the system, type the command GO CMD* on any command line.

Figure 4.22
File Commands Menu

```
CMDFILE                        File Commands

Select one of the following:

  Commands
        1. Close File                              CLOF
        2. Copy File                               CPYF
        3. Copy From Stream File                   CPYFRMSTMF
        4. Copy To Stream File                     CPYTOSTMF

        6. Declare File                            DCLF
        7. Delete File                             DLTF
        8. Delete Override                         DLTOVR
        9. Display File Description                DSPFD
       10. Display File Field Description          DSPFFD
       11. Display Override                        DSPOVR
       12. Start TCP/IP File Transfer              FTP
       13. Receive File                           RCVF
                                                       More...
  Selection or command
  ===> _____

  _____
  F3=Exit    F4=Prompt    F9=Retrieve    F12=Cancel    F16=Major menu
```

Chapter Summary

The AS/400 menu system consists of hundreds of different menus, each with a unique name. The name of the main system menu is MAIN.

AS/400 menus can be accessed by using the CL command GO and supplying the name of the menu as a parameter. The menu parameter of the GO command allows you to name an individual menu, a generic entry (e.g., T*, to see all names beginning with that letter), and to specify the value *ALL, which gives a listing of all AS/400 menus.

Every menu and several other AS/400 screens contain a command line on which CL commands may be entered. Several standard function keys are available when the command line is displayed.

The CL command prompt facility allows you to easily enter the parameters for a command. Help facilities and standard function keys can assist you in filling in the prompt. Special prompt characters are available within the prompt. You use the special character ? to determine allowable values for a parameter input field. You can use the special character & to increase the length of an input field. You use the special characters +, >, and < to manipulate entries in a list of parameter values.

You can search for the name of a command using the prompt facilities. Pressing the F4 function key from an empty command line displays the MAJOR menu. The MAJOR menu presents a listing of the major command groupings available on the AS/400. These groupings include commands listed alphabetically by command name, by verb name, by subject, and by command categories (e.g., File Commands, Work Management Commands, and Print Commands).

The CMD menus, such as CMDFILE, are useful in listing all of the commands for a specific subject.

Terms

command prompt display   function keys   menus

Review Questions

1. How does the AS/400 menu system make it easier for you to navigate the system?

2. How can you use a command line on the AS/400?

3. What are function keys on the AS/400? How would you use them?

Exercises

1. Perform the following functions:
   a. Sign on to the AS/400 and go to the menu named MAIN.
   b. Press the F4=Prompt key to display the menu named MAJOR.
   c. Using the MAJOR menu as a starting point,
      1) Find the names of the CL commands to perform the following functions:
         - Work with submitted jobs
         - Work with your spooled files
         - Start a print writer
         - Work with configuration status
         - Create a display file
         - Monitor for a message
         - Create a save file
         - Receive a message
         - Start a Source Entry Utility (SEU) session
      2) Then determine which command parameters are required and which are optional, and determine the allowable values for any required parameters.

2. Using the Help key from a command prompt screen, display a help text window. Press F2=Extended help and examine the resulting display. What, in your opinion, does the F2=Extended Help screen provide?

3. Prompt for the command DSPTAP. Once the prompt is displayed, press the F13 function key. Browse though the information presented. Is the information useful? Why or why not?

4. Match the functions in the left column with the menu names in the right column, to identify those menus you might use to perform the functions.

Function	Menu
a. Display the contents of a file	1. CMDOFC
b. Edit an OfficeVision/400 document	2. SAVE
c. Edit the source for a CL program	3. STATUS
d. Perform a daily backup to tape	4. CFGLCL
e. Add a new local printer to the configuration	5. SECURITY
f. Display current status of communications lines	6. CMDFILE
g. Add a new user to the list of authorized users	7. PROGRAM

Chapter 5

Creating CL Programs

Chapter Overview

This chapter helps you understand the usefulness of CL programs and explains the steps needed to create a CL program. We also discuss the CL compiler, emphasizing CL compiler options and how to analyze the reports that the compiler generates.

The Capabilities of CL Programs

In many instances, only one CL command is required to perform a function. For instance, if you wanted to back up an accounts payable library on the system to a magnetic tape, you could type the CL command

```
SAVLIB LIB(APLIB) DEV(TAP01)
```

on any command line and press Enter. But what if you also wanted to send messages to users in the accounts payable department, first informing them that you will be backing up their library, and then letting them know when the backup is completed? You could do this from a command line by typing in a series of CL commands similar to those shown in Figure 5.1.

Figure 5.1
Sample CL Commands
Required to
Perform Backup

```
SNDBRKMSG MSG('The backup of accounts payable is starting') TOMSGQ(APDSP1)
SNDBRKMSG MSG('The backup of accounts payable is starting') TOMSGQ(APDSP2)
SNDBRKMSG MSG('The backup of accounts payable is starting') TOMSGQ(APDSP3)
SNDBRKMSG MSG('The backup of accounts payable is starting') TOMSGQ(APDSP4)
SAVLIB LIB(APLIB) DEV(TAP01)
SNDBRKMSG MSG('The backup of accounts payable is completed') TOMSGQ(APDSP1)
SNDBRKMSG MSG('The backup of accounts payable is completed') TOMSGQ(APDSP2)
SNDBRKMSG MSG('The backup of accounts payable is completed') TOMSGQ(APDSP3)
SNDBRKMSG MSG('The backup of accounts payable is completed') TOMSGQ(APDSP4)
```

But if this were a backup routine performed regularly, typing the required series of CL commands each time the backup was to run would be tedious and error-prone. A better solution would be to write a CL program that incorporates all the commands. Then, instead of typing the CL command sequence like that shown in Figure 5.1, you would type one command to call your program. For example, if your program containing the series of CL commands were called APBACKUP, to execute the program, you would type the command

```
CALL APBACKUP
```

CL programs also allow you to specify simple and complex logic to perform different operations based upon information external to the program itself. External data can come from many sources, including program input parameters, data files, data areas, AS/400 system values, and job attributes. For example, using system values you could cause your program to perform some commands if the time of day is before noon and perform different commands if it is after noon.

CL programs also can be written to manipulate AS/400 system information and the job's work environment. Languages like RPG and Cobol are very good for processing data files, providing display screen functions, printing reports, and processing complex business logic. But, unlike CL, these languages do not allow you to directly access system-level operations.

How to Create a CL Program

At Version 3 of the OS/400 operating system, IBM introduced CL's participation in the Integrated Language Environment (ILE), a new program execution model for the AS/400. ILE changes the program creation process somewhat; we discuss those changes in Chapter 22. For now, we concentrate on creating programs that run in the AS/400's Original Program Model (OPM). For nearly all CL programming, OPM principles and methods still apply, and at this writing are more prevalent than ILE principles and methods.

Here are the four steps typically involved with creating a CL program:

1. Create a source physical file in your library to hold the source code for your CL programs.
2. For each specific program, add a member to the source physical file.
3. Type all the needed CL commands into the source member.
4. Compile the CL program, creating a program object.

Let's look at each of these steps in detail.

Creating a Source Physical File

A **source physical file** is a special kind of AS/400 file intended to hold, among other things, CL source statements. Each source physical file is broken into partitions, called members. Each distinct member contains the actual source statements (i.e., CL commands) needed to construct a CL program object. For example, if you create a CL program called APBACKUP, a member within the source physical file also will be named APBACKUP. There will be one CL source member for each CL program object.

Figure 5.2 shows a source physical file that contains six members. Like source member APBACKUP in Figure 5.2, each of the other members contains source statements.

Figure 5.2
Illustration of
Members within a
Source Physical File

Member APBACKUP	Member MYPROGRAM	Member PROGRAM2	Member PROGRAM3	Member PROGRAM4	Member PROGRAM5

```
PGM
SNDBRKMSG MSG('The backup of accounts payable is starting') TOMSGQ(APDSP1)
SNDBRKMSG MSG('The backup of accounts payable is starting') TOMSGQ(APDSP2)
SNDBRKMSG MSG('The backup of accounts payable is starting') TOMSGQ(APDSP3)
SNDBRKMSG MSG('The backup of accounts payable is starting') TOMSGQ(APDSP4)
SAVLIB LIB(APLIB) DEV(TAP01)
SNDBRKMSG MSG('The backup of accounts payable is completed') TOMSGQ(APDSP1)
SNDBRKMSG MSG('The backup of accounts payable is completed') TOMSGQ(APDSP2)
SNDBRKMSG MSG('The backup of accounts payable is completed') TOMSGQ(APDSP3)
SNDBRKMSG MSG('The backup of accounts payable is completed') TOMSGQ(APDSP4)
ENDPGM
```

Following IBM naming standards, we name the file QCLSRC, the default of the source physical file for CL source members. The defaults for other source physical files are QRPGSRC for RPG source members, QLBLSRC for Cobol source members, and QDDSSRC for Data Description Specification (DDS) source members. Although you don't have to use the IBM naming standards for source physical files, the standards are widely accepted and they are used in this text.

Because a source physical file can contain many members, you don't need to create a source physical file for each new member. Normally, you would create the QCLSRC source file in your library only once and then use that file to hold all your CL members.

The following command would create source physical file QCLSRC in library PGMTEST:

```
CRTSRCPF  PGMTEST/QCLSRC                      +
          TEXT('Control Language source')
```

Adding a Member to File QCLSRC

The CL command to add a member to a file is ADDPFM (Add Physical File Member). Typically, however, a programmer will use the Programming Development Manager (PDM) to add members to a source file. PDM, a programming environment that lets you work easily with source members and other objects, provides one function key (F6=Create) to add a member to a source file; using the ADDPFM command requires many keystrokes. (For a detailed discussion of PDM, see Appendix B.)

To access the Work with Members using PDM display shown in Figure 5.3, you would type the command

WRKMBRPDM

Figure 5.3
Example of
WRKMBRPDM
Display

```
                        Work with Members Using PDM              STUDENT1

 File . . . . . .    QCLSRC
   Library . . . .   PGMTEST             Position to . . . . .  _____

 Type options, press Enter.
   2=Edit          3=Copy  4=Delete 5=Display      6=Print    7=Rename
   8=Display description 9=Save  13=Change text  14=Compile  15=Create module...

 Opt  Member     Type     Text
 __   CALCPMT    CLP      Calculate monthly payment
 __   GETDOW     CLP      Get day of week subprocedure
 __   MYPROGRAM  CLP      Program to create a library and source file
 __   NULLDATE   CLP
 __   NULLDATEST CLP
 __   NULLDATES2 CLP
 __   NULLDATES3 CLP
 __   PRTAUTUSR  CLP      Print authorized users
                                                                  More...
 Parameters or command
 ===> _____
 F3=Exit          F4=Prompt           F5=Refresh          F6=Create
 F9=Retrieve      F10=Command entry   F23=More options    F24=More keys
```

If you press function key F6=Create from the display shown in Figure 5.3, the system presents a display similar to the one shown in Figure 5.4. This display is the command prompt for command STRSEU (Start Source Entry Utility). Source Entry Utility (SEU) is IBM's primary source editor for the AS/400; it is installed on most AS/400s used for software development and maintenance.

Figure 5.4
STRSEU Prompt
Display

```
                    Start Source Entry Utility (STRSEU)

 Type choices, press Enter.

 Source file . . . . . . . . .    QCLSRC      Name, *PRV
   Library . . . . . . . . . .    PGMTEST     Name, *LIBL, *CURLIB, *PRV
 Source member . . . . . . . .    APBACKUP    Name, *PRV, *SELECT
 Source type . . . . . . . . .    CLP         Name, *SAME, BAS, BASP, C...
 Text 'description' . . . . . .   Accounts Payable Backup Program


                                                                  Bottom
 F3=Exit   F4=Prompt   F5=Refresh   F12=Cancel   F13=How to use this display
 F24=More keys
```

The STRSEU command display prompts you for the answers to five questions.

1. What is the name of the source file you are working with? For this example the answer is *QCLSRC*.

2. What is the name of the library in which the source file resides? For this example the library is named *PGMTEST*.

3. What is the name of the source member you want to edit? Usually, you should give the same name to a CL program and its corresponding source member. For instance, if you name the program APBACKUP, the source file member also should be named *APBACKUP*, as in this example.

4. What type of source member will you be editing? For this example the answer is a source type of *CLP*, meaning this is the source member for a CL program. The correct response is RPG if you are editing an RPG source member, or CBL for a Cobol source member. The value you enter for this parameter defines the type of syntax checking you want SEU to perform and identifies this member as CL program source for other PDM functions.

5. What text description do you want to associate with this member? For this example the text is *Accounts Payable Backup Program*.

After you have typed answers to the questions, press Enter and the system presents the SEU work display. You are now ready to enter CL commands into the source member.

Entering CL Commands into a Source Member

You use SEU, or some other source editor, to enter and edit CL commands in a source member. We discuss the rules for entering CL source statements in Chapter 6. For now, the display shown in Figure 5.5 illustrates a sample SEU editing session. You can find more detailed information about using SEU in Appendix C.

Figure 5.5
Sample SEU
Editing Session

```
Columns . . . :   1  71              Edit                    PGMTEST/QCLSRC
SEU==> _____ APBACKUP
 FMT **  ...+... 1 ...+... 2 ...+... 3 ...+... 4 ...+... 5 ...+... 6 ...+... 7
 *************** Beginning of data **************************************
0001.00 PGM
0002.00 SNDBRKMSG MSG('The backup of accounts payable starting') TOMSGQ(APDSP1)
0003.00 SNDBRKMSG MSG('The backup of accounts payable starting') TOMSGQ(APDSP2)
0004.00 SNDBRKMSG MSG('The backup of accounts payable starting') TOMSGQ(APDSP3)
0005.00 SNDBRKMSG MSG('The backup of accounts payable starting') TOMSGQ(APDSP4)
0006.00 SAVLIB LIB(APLIB) DEV(TAP01)
0007.00 SNDBRKMSG MSG('The backup of accounts payable complete') TOMSGQ(APDSP1)
0008.00 SNDBRKMSG MSG('The backup of accounts payable complete') TOMSGQ(APDSP2)
0009.00 SNDBRKMSG MSG('The backup of accounts payable complete') TOMSGQ(APDSP3)
0010.00 SNDBRKMSG MSG('The backup of accounts payable complete') TOMSGQ(APDSP4)
0011.00 ENDPGM
 ***************** End of data ******************************************


 F3=Exit   F4=Prompt   F5=Refresh   F9=Retrieve   F10=Cursor   F11=Toggle
 F16=Repeat find       F17=Repeat change          F24=More keys
```

Compiling the CL Program

After you enter the source statements that will comprise the CL program, you need to create the CL program. The CL source statements stored in the source member must go through a process that translates source statements into a CL program object. This translation process is called compiling a program and is performed by the **CL compiler**.

The CL compiler is a special IBM-supplied program that reads the source statements you supply and determines whether the CL program will compile correctly. The compiler then generates a report that shows any errors the compiler may have found. When no severe errors are found in the source statements, the compiler creates a CL program object that can be executed by using the CALL command; for example,

```
CALL APBACKUP
```

Using the CL Compiler

You start the CL compiler by executing the CRTCLPGM (Create CL Program) command. The CRTCLPGM command can be issued from any command line, but PDM offers a user-friendly alternative.

The WRKMBRPDM display shown in Figure 5.6 shows our example source member (APBACKUP) with source type CLP. When you type option 14 (for compile) next to this member, PDM executes the CRTCLPGM command for that source member. (Option 14 also works with other source member types — e.g., RPG or Cobol; the source type tells PDM which compiler to use.) The CRTCLPGM command will run either interactively or in batch mode, depending on your PDM session defaults. But always set your PDM defaults to submit compile operations for batch processing, which frees your workstation for other jobs and improves overall system throughput because batch jobs run at a lower priority than interactive jobs.

CL Compiler Options

Once you type option 14 next to a CLP source member and press Enter, the system executes the CRTCLPGM command automatically, without any additional input from you. However, if you want to view or change the options the compiler will use to create your program, you can press function key F4=Prompt instead of pressing Enter. The system would present the CRTCLPGM command prompt display shown in Figure 5.7.

The display prompts you for the program name (i.e., the name by which the program will be known to the system) and for the name of the library in which the program will be created. In this example, PDM has already filled in these fields for you, using the source file member name (APBACKUP) and library name (PGMTEST) from the previous display.

PDM also has filled in the name of the source physical file (QCLSRC) that contains the source member and the name of the library (PGMTEST) in which the source physical file exists.

Figure 5.6
Compiling a Program
Using PDM

```
                        Work with Members Using PDM                    STUDENT1
    File . . . . . .    QCLSRC
      Library . . . .    PGMTEST           Position to . . . . .  _____

    Type options, press Enter.
     2=Edit        3=Copy  4=Delete 5=Display      6=Print    7=Rename
     8=Display description  9=Save  13=Change text  14=Compile  15=Create module...

    Opt  Member     Type    Text
    14   APBACKUP   CLP     Accounts Payable Backup Program
    __   CALCPMT    CLP     Calculate monthly payment
    __   GETDOW     CLP     Get day of week subprocedure
    __   MYPROGRAM  CLP     Program to create a library and source file
    __   NULLDATE   CLP
    __   NULLDATEST CLP
    __   NULLDATES2 CLP
    __   NULLDATES3 CLP

                                                                      More...
    Parameters or command
    ===> _____
    F3=Exit          F4=Prompt          F5=Refresh          F6=Create
    F9=Retrieve      F10=Command entry  F23=More options    F24=More keys
```

Figure 5.7
Prompted CRTCLPGM
Command

```
                        Create CL Program (CRTCLPGM)

    Type choices, press Enter.

    Program . . . . . . . . . . . . > APBACKUP    Name
      Library . . . . . . . . . . . > PGMTEST     Name, *CURLIB
    Source file . . . . . . . . . . > QCLSRC      Name
      Library . . . . . . . . . . . > PGMTEST     Name, *LIBL, *CURLIB
    Source member . . . . . . . . . > APBACKUP    Name, *PGM
    Text 'description' . . . . . . .  *SRCMBRTXT
    _____

                        Additional Parameters

    Source listing options . . . . .  _____   *SOURCE, *NOSOURCE, *SRC...
             + for more values        _____
    Generation options . . . . . . .  _____   *NOLIST, *LIST, *NOXREF...
             + for more values        _____
    User profile . . . . . . . . . .  *USER        *USER, *OWNER
    Log commands . . . . . . . . . .  *JOB         *JOB, *YES, *NO
                                                                      More...
    F3=Exit   F4=Prompt   F5=Refresh   F12=Cancel   F13=How to use this display
    F24=More keys
```

In addition, PDM has assumed the source member name (APBACKUP) will be the same as the one you typed a 14 next to on the display in Figure 5.6. This is the name of the source physical file member that contains the source statements that make up the program.

The text description describes the purpose of the program. The PDM default is to use the same text description written for the source file member ("Accounts Payable Backup Program"). In PDM, this text is assigned using the special value *SRCMBRTXT.

Whenever anyone displays information about this program, they will see this text. You should, therefore, make the text as descriptive as possible.

Under "Additional Parameters," the display prompts you for "Source listing options." This prompt is actually quite misleading. In reality, you are being asked for four pieces of information: the source listing option, the cross-reference option, the second-level text option, and the program creation option.

Normally, when you compile a CL program, the following options are in effect:

1. Print a listing of the CL source member.

2. Within the compiler reports that are generated, include a cross-reference listing of variables and data items used within the program.

3. When printing error messages, *do not* include more detailed (second-level) message text that may help in diagnosing problems.

4. Create a CL program from the CL source member.

You can change any of these compile options by specifying certain values in the "Source listing options" parameter. You can tell the compiler that you do not want to include a listing of the CL source member by specifying the option *NOSRC* or *NOSOURCE*. There is no difference in the way these options work; they are just two ways to spell the same option. To suppress the cross-reference listing, specify the option *NOXREF*. If, by chance, you *do* want second-level text included in the listing, be sure to specify *SECLVL*.

You can tell the compiler *not* to create a program object from a source member by specifying option *NOGEN*. The *NOGEN option is useful if you want to generate the compiler reports but do not want to actually create the program.

The "Generation options" shown in Figure 5.7 generally are not used and are beyond the scope of this text. Suffice it to say, they let you print the compiler's "intermediate representation" of the program (*LIST and *XREF), as well as generate a "program patch area" (*PATCH). You can safely ignore these prompts at this point in your CL programming career.

The "User profile" parameter is used by the AS/400 to determine how authority checking should be performed when a program is executed. AS/400 security determines which CL commands and objects a person is authorized to use. For the user profile parameter you would normally choose the default value, *USER*, which means that the person using the program must be authorized to do everything the program does. If a person is not authorized, the program terminates abnormally. In situations where you want a person to temporarily use a command or object specified in a program, you can specify *OWNER* for the user profile parameter. In this case, the person who uses the program (the *USER) would have the same authority within this program as the person who created the program (the *OWNER).

The "Log commands" parameter determines whether the CL commands executed in a program will be written to the job log. The default value for this parameter is *JOB*, which means that if the job that runs the program is already sending the executed CL commands to the job log it will continue to do so. You can also specify *YES or *NO to explicitly control whether the commands are written to the job log.

Pressing the Page Down key from the display in Figure 5.7 gives you the display shown in Figure 5.8, which shows the remaining parameters that are used when compiling a CL program.

Figure 5.8
Additional CRTCLPGM
Command Parameters

```
                            Create CL Program (CRTCLPGM)

  Type choices, press Enter.

  Allow RTVCLSRC . . . . . . . . .   *YES        *YES, *NO
  Replace program  . . . . . . . .   *YES        *YES, *NO
  Target release . . . . . . . . .   *CURRENT    *CURRENT, *PRV, V2R1M0...
  Authority  . . . . . . . . . . .   *LIBCRTAUT  Name, *LIBCRTAUT, *CHANGE...




                                                                          Bottom
  F3=Exit    F4=Prompt    F5=Refresh    F12=Cancel   F13=How to use this display
  F24=More keys
```

Specifying the default (*YES) for the Allow RTVCLSRC (Retrieve CL Source) parameter can be a lifesaver. You actually can "decompile" a CL program if you create it using the *ALWRTVSRC(*YES)* option. Taking this option causes a CL program to be stored on the AS/400 in such a way that the original source statements used to create the program can be retrieved from the program object. Then if you lose the source member used to compile the program, the source statements can be re-created by retrieving them from the compiled program object. You would use the RTVCLSRC command to retrieve the source statements. If you specify *NO, you lose the ability to retrieve source statements from the program object. You might use RTVCLSRC(*NO) if you are selling or distributing a program, or if the program you are creating has security implications; in these cases you would not want to allow the option to decompile the program.

When compiling a new version of a program object that already exists on your system, you will want to specify *YES for the "Replace program" parameter. This directive determines what will happen if the program you are compiling already exists. If you specify *YES, the existing program will be renamed and moved to a library named QRPLOBJ, and the new program will be created in the library you originally specified. The "User profile" and "Authority" parameter values will be copied from the program being replaced to the new program, regardless of the values you specify for the new program. If *NO* is specified, the program is not replaced, and the new program object is not created if an older version already exists.

The "Target release" parameter specifies the OS/400 operating system release level for the program. This parameter is useful if you need to move the program to another AS/400, which might be at a previous release level of the OS/400 operating system. The parameter default value is *CURRENT*, which means the program object will be created for the release level currently installed on the AS/400 used for the compilation.

The "Authority" parameter determines what ability the public users on the system will have regarding this program. The term "public *users*" refers to users who do not have special authorities, or who do not have specific authority to the program being created. If you specify *ALL*, any public user on the system can run the program, change the program, or delete the program. If you specify *USE*, the public user will be able to run the program, but not change or delete it. If you specify *CHANGE*, the public user can run the program, and change certain characteristics of the program, but cannot delete the program. If you specify *EXCLUDE*, the public user cannot run, change, or delete the program.

The default value for the authority parameter is *LIBCRTAUT*, which means the authorization to a program is determined by the creation authorization assigned to the library in which the program is created.

Although a detailed discussion of AS/400 security, including authorization lists, is beyond the scope of this text, note that an authorization list name also can be specified for the authority parameter. In this case, authorization to a program will be determined by the corresponding authorization list entries.

CL Compiler Reports
During its execution, the CL compiler generates various reports, depending upon the compiler options you have specified. If the compiler detects no severe errors in the source member it is processing, it creates a CL program object. Figure 5.9 shows a sample CL source member named MYPROGRAM. MYPROGRAM is a member of file QCLSRC in library PGMTEST. The purpose of the program is to create a library named MYPGMTEST and then create source physical file QCLSRC within the library. Error-trapping commands also are included in the program in case unexpected errors occur during its execution.

If this source member were compiled using option 14 from PDM, and using the PDM defaults, the compiler would generate the report shown in Figure 5.10 (pages 58–59).

Figure 5.9
CL Program
MYPROGRAM

```
/*  Program name..... MYPROGRAM                                    */
/*  Author........... Joe Programmer                              */
/*  Date Completed... June 12, 1997                               */
/*  Program Purpose.. To create a test library and a source       */
/*                    physical file for CL source                 */
/*  Service Request#. NONE                                        */

        PGM

        DCL       VAR(&MSGID)    TYPE(*CHAR) LEN(7)
        DCL       VAR(&MSGDTA)   TYPE(*CHAR) LEN(100)
        DCL       VAR(&MSGF)     TYPE(*CHAR) LEN(10)
        DCL       VAR(&MSGFLIB)  TYPE(*CHAR) LEN(10)
        DCL       VAR(&ERRORSW)  TYPE(*LGL)

        MONMSG    MSGID(CPF0000) EXEC(GOTO CMDLBL(TAG))

        CRTLIB    LIB(MYPGMTEST) TYPE(*TEST) TEXT('Programmer    +
                    test library')

        CRTSRCPF  FILE(MYPGMTEST/QCLSRC) TEXT('Control          +
                    Language Source Physical File')

        RETURN    /* Normal end of program */

TAG:    RCVMSG    MSGTYPE(*LAST) MSGDTA(&MSGDTA) MSGID(&MSGID)   +
                    MSGF(&MSGF) SNDMSGFLIB(&MSGFLIB)
        MONMSG    CPF0000

        SNDPGMMSG MSGID(&MSGID) MSGF(&MSGFLIB/&MSGF)            +
                    MSGDTA(&MSGDTA) MSGTYPE(*ESCAPE)
        MONMSG    CPF0000

        ENDPGM
```

Analyzing Compiler Reports

Let's take a closer look at the compiler report in Figure 5.10. At the top of the report is descriptive information about the compilation, including the current release level of the OS/400 operating system (A), the time and date of the compile operation (B), and the compile options that were in effect for this compilation (C).

The source member listing (D in Figure 5.10) includes the source member sequence number, the source statements, and the date that the line of the source member was last changed.

Following the source listing is a cross-reference listing for the variables used in the program (E). For each variable defined in a program, the cross-reference shows the variable name, the line on which the variable is defined, the variable type, the variable length, and the line number of all references to the variable in the source member listing. The cross-reference also lists any labels used in the source member (F). The label name is listed, followed by the line number on which the label is defined and the line number of all references to that label name.

Following the list of labels is the summary of warnings or errors detected by the compiler during the compilation process (G). The total number of errors and warnings is listed first, followed by a breakdown of errors and warnings by severity level.

Figure 5.10
continued

```
5716SS1 V3R7M0  961108              Control Language              PGMTEST/MYPROGRAM      06/12/97 18:49:14      Page    2
                                    Cross Reference
(E) Declared Variables
    Name              Defined    Type        Length      References
    &MSGDTA           1100       *CHAR       100         2600    3100
    &MSGF             1200       *CHAR       10          2700    3000
    &MSGFLIB          1300       *CHAR       10          3700    3000
    &MSGID            1000       *CHAR       7           2600    3000
(F) Defined Labels
    Label             Defined    References
    TAG               2700       1500
                      * * * * *  E N D   O F   C R O S S   R E F E R E N C E   * * * * *


5716SS1 V3R7M0  961108              Control Language              PGMTEST/MYPROGRAM      06/12/97 18:49:14      Page    3
                                    Message Summary
                  Severity
(G) Total         0-9   10-19  20-29  30-39  40-49  50-59  60-69  70-79  80-89  90-99
        0         0     0      0      0      0      0      0      0      0      0
(H) Program MYPROGRAM created in library PGMTEST on 06/12/97 at 18:49:30.
    Program MYPROGRAM created in library PGMTEST. Maximum error severity 00.
                  * * * * *  E N D   O F   M E S S A G E   S U M M A R Y   * * * * *
                  * * * * *  E N D   O F   C O M P I L A T I O N   * * * * *
```

In this example, no errors were detected. Because no errors were detected, a message at the end of the report (H) states that the program was created (i.e., it compiled normally) and placed in library PGMTEST. Following successful compilation, the program can be executed by typing the command

    CALL MYPROGRAM

on any command line.

Diagnosing Compile-Time Errors

Many times your program will not compile correctly the first time. This can happen for any number of reasons. For instance, you could spell something wrong, or you could forget to declare a variable or a label. When an error occurs during the compilation of a program, the compiler listings are very helpful in diagnosing the problem.

Figure 5.11 shows a CL source member named MYPROGRAM2, which is supposed to do everything that MYPROGRAM did in the previous example, as well as create a source physical file named QRPGSRC if the user running MYPROGRAM2 is BOB.

Figure 5.11
CL Program
MYPROGRAM2

```
/*  Program name..... MYPROGRAM2                                   */
/*  Author........... Joe Programmer                              */
/*  Date Completed... June 12, 1997                               */
/*  Program Purpose.. To create a test library and a source       */
/*                    physical file for CL source                 */
/*                    If BOB is the user of the program, then      */
/*                    create an RPG source file also.             */
/*  Service Request#. NONE                                        */

            PGM

            DCL         VAR(&MSGID)    TYPE(*CHAR) LEN(7)
            DCL         VAR(&MSGDTA)   TYPE(*CHAR) LEN(100)
            DCL         VAR(&MSGF)     TYPE(*CHAR) LEN(10)
            DCL         VAR(&MSGFLIB) TYPE(*CHAR) LEN(10)

            MONMSG      MSGID(CPF0000) EXEC(GOTO CMDLBL(TAG))

            CRTLIB      LIB(MYPGMTEST) TYPE(*TEST) TEXT('Programmer   +
                          test library')

            CRTSRCPF    FILE(MYPGMTEST/QCLSRC) TEXT('Control         +
                          Language Source Physical File')
            IF          COND(&USER = 'BOB') THEN(DO)
               CRTSRCPF    FILE(MYPGMTEST/QRPGSRC) TEXT('RPG Source   +
                             Physical File')
            RETURN      /* Normal end of program */

TAG:        RCVMSG      MSGTYPE(*LAST) MSGDTA(&MSGDTA) MSGID(&MSGID)  +
                          MSGF(&MSGF) SNDMSGFLIB(&MSGFLIB)
            MONMSG      CPF0000

            SNDPGMMSG   MSGID(&MSGID) MSGF(&MSGFLIB/&MSGF)           +
                          MSGDTA(&MSGDTA) MSGTYPE(*ESCAPE)
            MONMSG      CPF0000

            ENDPGM
```

When you attempt to compile program MYPROGRAM2, the report in Figure 5.12 is generated.

The message at the end of the report tells you clearly that this program did not compile successfully. A quick review of the report gives you the reasons. First, you see error message CPD0727 (A): *Variable &USER is referred to, but not declared.* The error message refers to the line immediately before it — the CL command *IF COND(&USER = 'BOB') THEN(DO)*. This source statement references the variable &USER but because it is not defined in the program, the compiler does not know what the variable looks like. This condition is not allowed: All variables used in a program must be defined in the program.

Second, error message CPD0714 (B) states (with questionable grammar) that there is *"No matching ENDDO command for DO command for 1 do groups."* This means that somewhere in the source member the DO command is used but the matching ENDDO command is not in the member. Every time you use the DO command, you must always specify the ENDDO command at the end of the DO group. Because the

Figure 5.12
Compiler Listing for CL
Program MYPROGRAM2

```
5716SS1 V3R7M0  961108                    Control Language              PGMTEST/MYPROGRAM2    06/12/97 19:30:43        Page    1
Program . . . . . . . . . . . . . . . . . . . . :   MYPROGRAM2
  Library . . . . . . . . . . . . . . . . . . :   PGMTEST
Source file . . . . . . . . . . . . . . . . . :   QCLSRC
  Library . . . . . . . . . . . . . . . . . . :   PGMTEST
Source member name . . . . . . . . . . . . . . :   MYPROGRAM2  06/12/97 19:30:39
Source printing options . . . . . . . . . . . :   *SOURCE  *XREF  *GEN  *NOSECLVL  *NOSRCDBG
Program generation options  . . . . . . . . . :   *NOLIST  *NOXREF  *NOPATCH
User profile  . . . . . . . . . . . . . . . . :   *USER
Program logging . . . . . . . . . . . . . . . :   *JOB
Allow RTVCLSRC command  . . . . . . . . . . . :   *YES
Replace program . . . . . . . . . . . . . . . :   *YES
Target release  . . . . . . . . . . . . . . . :   V3R7M0
Authority . . . . . . . . . . . . . . . . . . :   *LIBCRTAUT
Sort sequence . . . . . . . . . . . . . . . . :   *HEX
Language identifier . . . . . . . . . . . . . :   *JOBRUN
Text  . . . . . . . . . . . . . . . . . . . . :   Program to create a library and source file
Compiler  . . . . . . . . . . . . . . . . . . :   IBM AS/400 Control Language Compiler
                                           Control Language Source
SEQNBR  *...+... 1 ...+... 2 ...+... 3 ...+... 4 ...+... 5 ...+... 6 ...+... 7 ...+... 8 ...+... 9 ...+.   DATE
   100- /*  Program name..... MYPROGRAM2                                      */            06/12/97
   200- /*  Author........... Joe Programmer                                  */            06/12/97
   300- /*  Date Completed... June 12, 1997                                   */            06/12/97
   400- /*  Program Purpose.. To create a test library and a source          */            06/12/97
   500- /*                    physical file for CL source.                    */            06/12/97
   600- /*                    If BOB is the user of the program, then         */            06/12/97
   700- /*                    create an RPG source file also.                 */            06/12/97
   800- /*  Service Request#. NONE                                           */            06/12/97
   900-                                                                                     06/12/97
  1000-           PGM                                                                       06/12/97
  1100-                                                                                     06/12/97
  1200-           DCL       VAR(&MSGID)   TYPE(*CHAR) LEN(7)                                06/12/97
  1300-           DCL       VAR(&MSGDTA)  TYPE(*CHAR) LEN(100)                              06/12/97
  1400-           DCL       VAR(&MSGF)    TYPE(*CHAR) LEN(10)                               06/12/97
  1500-           DCL       VAR(&MSGFLIB) TYPE(*CHAR) LEN(10)                               06/12/97
  1600-                                                                                     06/12/97
  1700-           MONMSG    MSGID(CPF0000) EXEC(GOTO CMDLBL(TAG))                           06/12/97
  1800-                                                                                     06/12/97
  1900-           CRTLIB    LIB(MYPGMTEST) TYPE(*TEST) TEXT('Programmer  +                  06/12/97
  2000                        test library')                                               06/12/97
  2100-                                                                                     06/12/97
  2200-           CRTSRCPF  FILE(MYPGMTEST/QCLSRC) TEXT('Control  +                         06/12/97
  2300                        Language Source Physical File')                              06/12/97
  2400-                                                                                     06/12/97
  2500-           IF        COND(&USER = 'BOB') THEN(DO)                                    06/12/97
```

Ⓐ * CPD0727 40 Variable '&USER   ' is referred to but not declared.

```
  2600-           CRTSRCPF  FILE(MYPGMTEST/QRPGSRC) TEXT('RPG Source  +                    06/12/97
  2700                        Physical File')                                              06/12/97
  2800-           RETURN    /* Normal end of program */                                     06/12/97
  2900-                                                                                     06/12/97
  3000-                                                                                     06/12/97
  3100- TAG:      RCVMSG    MSGTYPE(*LAST) MSGDTA(&MSGDTA) MSGID(&MSGID) +
  3200-                     MSGF(&MSGF) SNDMSGFLIB(&MSGFLIB)
  3300-           MONMSG    CPF0000
  3400-
  3500-           SNDPGMMSG MSGID(&MSGID) MSGF(&MSGFLIB/&MSGF)           +
  3600-                     MSGDTA(&MSGDTA) MSGTYPE(*ESCAPE)
  3700-           MONMSG    CPF0000
  3800-
  3900-                     ENDPGM                                                          06/12/97
```

Ⓑ * CPD0714 30 No matching ENDDO command for DO command for 1 do groups.

```
                    * * * * *  E N D   O F   S O U R C E  * * * * *
```

continued

Figure 5.12
continued

```
5716SS1 V3R7M0  961108            Control Language        PGMTEST/MYPROGRAM2   06/12/97 19:30:43      Page    2
                                  Cross Reference
Declared Variables
Name             Defined      Type          Length       References
&MSGDTA          1300         *CHAR         100          3100   3600
&MSGF            1400         *CHAR         10           3200   3500
&MSGFLIB         1500         *CHAR         10           3200   3500
&MSGID           1200         *CHAR         7            3100   3500
Defined Labels
Label            Defined      References
TAG              3100         1700
                    * * * * *  E N D   O F   C R O S S   R E F E R E N C E   * * * * *


5716SS1 V3R7M0  961108            Control Language        PGMTEST/MYPROGRAM2   06/12/97 19:30:43      Page    3
                                  Message Summary
                 Severity
Total            0-9  10-19  20-29  30-39  40-49  50-59  60-69  70-79  80-89  90-99
    2             0     0      0      1      1      0      0      0      0      0
Program MYPROGRAM2 not created in library PGMTEST. Maximum error severity 40.
                    * * * * *  E N D   O F   M E S S A G E   S U M M A R Y  * * * * *
                    * * * * *  E N D   O F   C O M P I L A T I O N  * * * * *
```

compiler cannot detect the omission of an ENDDO command until it reaches the end of the source member, this message does not appear on the line immediately following the DO command.

The CL compiler cannot create a program object when it detects an error with a severity of 30 or higher. The compiler detected two errors in this program and summarized them at the end of the report (C). One error has a severity of between 30 and 39; the other has a severity of between 40 and 49. Because the maximum error severity in this program is 40, the compiler will not create a program object from the source member. When you find and correct the errors in the source member, you can compile the program successfully.

The CL Program Object

Most AS/400 HLL compilers generate program objects that are directly executable by the computer. The compiler translates the HLL instructions into low-level instructions the AS/400 can understand. When the CL compiler creates a program object, however, the resulting CL program is not actually a stand-alone executable program. Most CL commands from the source member are actually tokenized within the program object. (A **command token** is a compressed representation of the CL command that appears in the source member.) This tokenized format is not directly executable.

The low-level instructions needed to execute most individual CL commands are generated when the program is run, not when it is compiled. When a CL program is run, the AS/400 must examine each tokenized command, find the definition of the command, and generate the low-level instructions required to process the command.

If, at the time the program is run, the needed CL command cannot be found within a library on the job's library list, the program terminates abnormally.

Chapter Summary

A CL program consists of a series of CL commands that you compile and run as a group. With CL programs, you can use information external to the program itself (e.g., program input parameters, data files, data areas, AS/400 system values, job attributes) to control program operations. You also can write CL programs that directly access system-level operations, which you cannot do with RPG or Cobol programs.

The commands that comprise a CL program are stored within a member of a source physical file. Source physical files can contain many members that, in turn, contain source for many CL programs. The default source file name for CL program source is QCLSRC. To create a source physical file, use the CRTSRCPF (Create Source Physical File) command.

The Source Entry Utility (SEU) is the primary means of editing source members on the AS/400. The Programming Development Manager (PDM) is an IBM programming environment that provides easy access to SEU.

After the necessary commands are entered into a source member, they must be compiled into an executable program object. The command to start the CL compiler is CRTCLPGM (Create CL Program). The CL compiler produces a listing that documents CL compilations; when a source member does not compile, the listing is helpful in diagnosing problems.

If you compile a program with the ALWRTVSRC(*YES) attribute, you can use the RTVCLSRC (Retrieve CL Source) command to "decompile" the CL program object.

CL programs, unlike most HLL programs, contain "tokenized" commands, without all the necessary low-level code to be directly executable. At run time, the AS/400 generates the low-level instructions required to run the command.

Terms

CL compiler   command token   source physical file

Review Questions

1. What is a source physical file and what does it contain?

2. What steps would you follow to create a CL program?

3. Which CL compiler option allows you to "decompile" a CL program after it has been compiled?

4. When will the CL compiler not produce a CL program object?

Exercises

1. Create a source physical file in your library that will contain CL source members. (If you already have a source physical file for CL source members, skip this step.)

   (To accomplish the following exercises, refer to Appendix B about PDM and Appendix C about SEU.)

2. Add a member named SA0501*XXX* to the source physical file. (Replace *XXX* with your initials or other unique identifier assigned by your instructor.) SA0501 stands for chapter 05, member 01.

3. Edit the source member to contain the following CL source statements at the line numbers indicated. (Replace *XXX* with your initials and insert your name and the current date.)

```
0001.00 /*  PROGRAM NAME..... SA0501XXX                              */
0002.00 /*  AUTHOR........... (Your Name)                            */
0003.00 /*  DATE COMPLETED... (enter the current date)              */
0004.00 /*  PROGRAM PURPOSE.. SEND A MESSAGE INDICATING THE TIME OF DAY  */
0005.00 /*  CHAPTER 5, MEMBER 1                                      */
0006.00
0007.00           PGM
0008.00
0009.00           DCL        VAR(&TIME) TYPE(*CHAR) LEN(6)
0010.00
0011.00 START:    RTVSYSVAL  SYSVAL(QTIME) RTNVAR(&TIME)
0012.00
0013.00
0014.00           SNDPGMMSG  MSG('THE CURRENT TIME IS ' *CAT &TIME)
0015.00
0016.00           RETURN     /* NORMAL END OF PROGRAM */
0017.00 END:      ENDPGM
```

Exercises continued

Exercises continued

4. Compile the CL program. The name of the program will be SA0105*XXX*, where *XXX* is your initials. If the program does not compile successfully, fix any errors until it does compile successfully.

5. Print the compile listing.

6. Identify on the compile listing where the following information is located:
   a. The error message summary
   b. The variable cross-reference
   c. The source listing
   d. The label cross-reference
   e. The compile options
   f. The maximum error severity found

7. From the compile listing, answer the following questions:
   a. On which line is the variable &TIME defined?
   b. Can the RTVCLSRC command be used to decompile this program?
   c. What is the target release for this program?
   d. Can a "public user" run this program?
   e. Which lines within the member refer to the &TIME variable?
   f. In which library was the program object created?

8. Execute the program, using the CALL command. What does the program do? Refer to Appendix A to learn the meanings of the commands in the example.

Chapter 6

The Structure of a CL Source Member

Chapter Overview

This chapter introduces you to the basic CL program structure and its free-format entry. You will become familiar with the four sections of a CL program and learn the methods used to enter comments and declare labels for procedures.

Entering CL Source Statements

Recall from Chapter 5 that a CL source member contains source statements. These source statements consist of CL commands and any optional comments that you choose to include. The source member is used as input to the CL compiler; the output is a CL program object. For the compiler to successfully create the CL program, the source statements must be entered into the member according to the general rules of CL programming. A discussion of these rules follows.

Free-Format Statement Entry

Many computer languages have rigid rules regarding the physical placement of source statements within a source member. The source statements entered into the member must adhere to these rules or the language's compiler considers them invalid. Even if the statements are valid for a particular language, they must be entered into the proper column. The columnar format with its rigid rules comes from the early history of computers, when many programming languages were entered on punch cards.

RPG is an example of a programming language that has strict rules regarding the columnar positioning of statements within a source member. (The traditional RPG columnar format is based on an 80-column punch card. The new RPG IV syntax relaxes the rules for some specifications.) Cobol also has restrictions on columnar positioning of statements within a source member, but Cobol is not as restrictive as RPG.

Figure 6.1 shows a sample RPG source member. With RPG, the statements must be aligned in the columns as shown or the source member will not compile.

Figure 6.1
Sample RPG
Source Member

```
......*..1 ...+... 2 ...+... 3 ...+... 4 ...+... 5 ...+... 6 ...+... 7
      FQADSPOBJIF E                     DISK
      FBDF810  CF E                     WORKSTN
      F                                        RRN   KSFILE SFLREC
       *
      I          DS
      I                                          1   6 ODSDAT
      I                                          1  60SAVDAT
      I          DS
      I                                          1   6 PRMDAT
      I                                          1  60SAVSYS
      C          *ENTRY    PLIST
      C                    PARM             SYSDAT  6      LAST SAVSYS
```

CL has no restrictions regarding columnar placement of source member statements. Consider the sample CL source member shown in Figure 6.2.

Figure 6.2
Sample CL
Source Illustrating
Free-Format Entry

```
... + ...1 ...+... 2 ...+... 3 ...+... 4 ...+... 5 ...+... 6 ...+... 7
         PGM       PARM(&user &reply &text)
         DCL       &user   *CHAR 10
         DCL       &reply  *CHAR 1
         DCL       &text   *CHAR 255
         DCL       &sender *CHAR 10

         MONMSG    MSGID(CPF0000) EXEC(GOTO ERROR)

      /* Is a reply to this message requested? */
         IF        (&reply = 'Y')  DO
           RTVUSRPRF  MSGQ(&sender)
           SNDMSG     MSG(&text) TOUSR(&user) MSGTYPE(*INQ)   +
                      RPYMSGQ(&sender)
           ENDDO
         ELSE      DO
           SNDMSG     MSG(&text) TOUSR(&user) MSGTYPE(*INFO)
           ENDDO

         SNDPGMMSG MSGID(CPF9898) MSGF(QCPFMSG)              +
                   MSGDTA('The message has been sent')       +
                   MSGTYPE(*COMP)
ERROR:   RETURN                         ↑
         ENDPGM                                      (A)
```

Notice in Figure 6.2 that most CL commands start in column 14. This is an arbitrary choice. You can start CL commands in any column you choose. Notice also the even indentation of many of the command parameters following their respective commands and of the commands within the CL "DO" groups. CL does not require indentation, but indentation improves the source member's readability.

Uppercase and Lowercase

Commands, their parameters, and comments can be entered in uppercase or lowercase. The only restriction on case occurs when dealing with quoted character strings (A in Figure 6.2). Characters inside a quoted character string are interpreted the same way in which they are entered; that is, either as uppercase or lowercase.

Many CL programmers have adopted the standard that program variable names should always be entered in lowercase, which makes the CL source statements easier to read. If you use the SEU command prompter, you enter only uppercase characters, except within quoted strings. If you prefer lowercase characters, you can switch to the SEU edit display, which allows lowercase characters. For information about SEU, see Appendix C.

Using Blank Lines

The CL program shown in Figure 6.2 also demonstrates the use of blank lines, inserted between source member statements to improve the source member's readability. You may use one or more blank lines anywhere within the source member.

Keyword and Positional Notation

Source statements can be entered in either keyword or positional notation, or a combination of the two (see Chapter 3). Typically, commands like DCL, IF, ELSE, CHGVAR, and GOTO are written in positional notation because it is easier to read than the corresponding keyword notation. If you use the SEU command prompter to enter these commands, they always appear in keyword notation. If you like the readability provided by positional notation, however, you can switch to the SEU edit display, which allows you to remove keywords.

Entering Program Comments

You can enter explanatory comments within a CL source member on any line. These comments allow the programmer to document the CL program's functions within the source member itself. Information such as the CL program name, the author of the program, the date written, and the purpose of the program should be included in every CL source member.

You begin and end a comment line in a CL source member with the characters /* and */, respectively. Figure 6.3 shows several sample comment lines. As you can see, CL offers a great deal of latitude regarding the entry of comments.

Figure 6.3
Entering Comments

```
/*   Program Name..... PROGRAM1                              */
/*   Author........... Joe Programmer                        */
/*   Date Completed... June 12, 1997                         */
/*   Program Purpose.. To illustrate the use of comments     */
/*   Service Request#. NONE                                  */

GOTO LOOP  /* Comment AFTER command */

/*  Comment BEFORE command */ GOTO LOOP

/*  Comment BEFORE command */ GOTO LOOP /* and AFTER command */

    IF   (&var1 = &var2)  GOTO LABEL1
         /* comment within IF/ELSE group */
    ELSE  GOTO LABEL2
```

Command Continuation (+ and −)

Often, when you enter a CL command into a source member, the command requires more than the 80 columns provided in the source member line. When this occurs, special **command continuation characters** must be used. Within a CL source member, the command continuation characters are the plus sign (+) and the negative sign (−), or hyphen. Both of these command continuation characters allow you to continue a CL command on more than one line, but there are differences in the way they work.

The + continuation character indicates that the command continues from the line on which the + is placed to the first non-blank character on the next line. The continuation character must always be the last non-blank character on a line that is to be continued. Figure 6.4 shows examples of valid and invalid uses of the + command continuation and, in each case, the way in which the command would be interpreted.

In the first two examples (A and B in Figure 6.4), two versions of the SNDPGMMSG (Send Program Message) command are continued onto two additional lines so that all the necessary parameters can be specified. Both versions adhere to the CL rule that at least one blank character must separate command parameters and they will be interpreted identically. When you continue a command onto more than one line, any blanks preceding the + are considered as one occurrence of the blank character. Continuing commands in this way allows you to align the continuation characters by inserting blank characters before the +. The result is a more readable program.

In example C, the + on each line is not preceded by a blank character. Because the + continuation character continues the command with the first non-blank character of the next line, there is no blank inserted between the command parameters. Because the blank character is omitted, the result is an invalid CL command.

Example D uses + to continue command parameters and (in the second line) to continue a parameter value. In the second case, the parameter value is a quoted string of characters. Because no blank characters are desired within the quoted string of alphabet characters, the + is placed directly after the last character on the line, with no intervening blank characters.

Figure 6.4
Command Continuation

```
         **    ...+... 1 ...+... 2 ...+... 3 ...+... 4 ...+... 5 ...+... 6 ...+... 7
       0001.00       SNDPGMMSG  MSGID(CPF9898) MSGF(QCPFMSG)               +
  (A)  0002.00                           MSGDTA('The message has been sent')     +
       0003.00                           MSGTYPE(*COMP)

       0001.00       SNDPGMMSG  MSGID(CPF9898) MSGF(QCPFMSG) +
  (B)  0002.00                           MSGDTA('The message has been sent') +
       0003.00                           MSGTYPE(*COMP)

Valid continuation; both examples interpreted the same:
SNDPGMMSG MSGID(CPF9898) MSGF(QCPFMSG) MSGDTA('The message has been sent') MSGTYPE(*COMP)


       0001.00       SNDPGMMSG  MSGID(CPF9898) MSGF(QCPFMSG)+
  (C)  0002.00                           MSGDTA('The message has been sent')+
       0003.00                           MSGTYPE(*COMP)

Invalid continuation; interpreted as:
SNDPGMMSG MSGID(CPF9898) MSGF(QCPFMSG)MSGDTA('The message has been sent')MSGTYPE(*COMP)


       0004.00       CHGVAR     &alphabet                                  +
  (D)  0005.00                  ('ABCDEFGHIJKLMNOPQRSTUVWXYZabcdefghij+
       0006.00                  klmnopqrstuvwxyz')

Valid continuation; interpreted as:
CHGVAR VAR(&ALPHABET) VALUE('ABCDEFGHIJKLMNOPQRSTUVWXYZabcdefghijklmnopqrstuvwxyz')


       0007.00
       0008.00       CHGVAR     &alphabet                                  +
  (E)  0009.00                  ('ABCDEFGHIJKLMNOPQRSTUVWXYZabcdefghij  +
       0010.00                  klmnopqrstuvwxyz')

Valid continuation, but interpreted as:
CHGVAR VAR(&ALPHABET) VALUE('ABCDEFGHIJKLMNOPQRSTUVWXYZabcdefghij  klmnopqrstuvwxyz')


       0011.00 CHGVAR       &newvalue        ((&LENGTH * &WIDTH) + +
  (F)  0012.00                           (3.14 * &RADIUS) + (255 / &HEIGHT) + 623)

Valid continuation; interpreted as:
CHGVAR VAR(&NEWVALUE) VALUE((&LENGTH * &WIDTH) + (3.14 * &RADIUS) + (255 / &HEIGHT) + 623)


       0014.00       /* This is a comment that requires more than one line. It may be continued on  +
  (G)  0015.00          the next lines with command continuation characters. The comment must still +
       0016.00          end with the end comment characters */

Interpreted as a program comment
```

Example E shows what would happen within the string of alphabet characters if blanks preceded the +. Any blanks before the + are interpreted as being part of the string of alphabet characters.

Example F presents an easy solution to a special problem. The programmer needs to continue an arithmetic expression that contains a +. Because the + is entered twice, the compiler interprets the first + as part of the expression and the second + as a continuation character.

The last example (G in Figure 6.4) illustrates how to continue program comments onto more than one line.

The –, or hyphen, continuation character works differently than the + continuation character. The – indicates that the command is to be continued from the line on which the – is placed to the first position (column 1) of the next line. In Figure 6.5, an example from Figure 6.4 is rewritten using the – as a continuation character.

Figure 6.5
Command Continuation
with the Minus Sign (–)

```
CHGVAR      VAR(&alphabet) -
            VALUE('ABCDEFGHIJKLMNOPQRSTUVWXYZabcdefghij-
            klmnopqrstuvwxyz')


Interpreted as:
CHGVAR VAR(&ALPHABET) VALUE('ABCDEFGHIJKLMNOPQRSTUVWXYZabcdefghij          klmnopqrstuvwxyz')
```

In this example, all the blank characters on the last line are included in the interpreted value of the command. While the – continuation character is allowed within a CL source member, it is not generally used. Most CL programmers prefer to use the + continuation character.

When you use IBM's SEU CL command prompter, the prompter automatically places the + command continuation characters on the continued lines for you. But if you are not using the command prompter to enter commands, or if you are editing lines within an existing CL source member, you must ensure that the + or – command continuation characters are entered correctly.

Using Labels

Labels, while not required in a CL source member, can be used for two purposes: (1) a label can provide extra documentation for a command or block of commands, and (2) a label can be the target of the CL GOTO command. The GOTO command requires a label name within the source member to "go to," as in GOTO LOOP1.

A label name can be from one to 10 characters in length and must be immediately followed by a colon (:). The one to 10 characters that make up a label name must be specified according to the rules for entering an **AS/400 name**. A name is a character string whose first character is alphabetic (A–Z), $, #, or @, and whose additional characters are alphanumeric (A–Z and 0–9), $, #, @, underscore (_), or period (.). If a label will be the target of a GOTO command, you cannot use a period in the label name.

Labels can appear either on the same line as a CL command, or as the only entry on a line. Figure 6.6 illustrates the use of labels.

Figure 6.6
Using Labels

```
          PGM        PARM(&user &reply &text)
          DCL        &user   *CHAR  10
          DCL        &reply  *CHAR  1
          DCL        &text   *CHAR  255
          DCL        &sender *CHAR  10
          DCL        &number *DEC   (3 0)

          MONMSG     MSGID(CPF0000) EXEC(GOTO ERROR)
STARTIT:
          RTVJOBA    USER(&sender)
                                        /* Send a message 3 times  */
LOOP1:    IF         (&number < 3)  DO
          SNDMSG     MSG(&text) TOUSR(&user) MSGTYPE(*INQ)       +
                     RPYMSGQ(&sender)
          CHGVAR     &number (&number + 1)
          GOTO       LOOP1
          ENDDO
ENDIT:
          SNDPGMMSG  MSGID(CPF9898) MSGF(QCPFMSG)                +
                     MSGDTA('The message has been sent')         +
                     MSGTYPE(*COMP)
ERROR:    RETURN
          ENDPGM
```

The Sections of a CL Source Member

There are few hard and fast rules for structuring entries within a CL source member. A valid CL source member can consist of several thousand lines of CL commands and comments, or it can consist of none. (The CL compiler will compile a source member that contains no statements; of course, the resulting program will not do anything.) Depending on the processing that the CL program must perform, and also depending on the programmer who writes it, the source member will contain a wide variety of functions and programming styles. To write CL programs that ensure proper functionality, however, and to remain consistent with the rules of good programming style, you need to include certain sections within the source member.

CL source members, when properly structured, contain the following four sections, which appear within a source member in the order shown here:

1. The program information section
2. The program linkage section
3. The declarations section
4. The procedure section

The Program Information Section

The **program information section** appears first in a CL source member. Although this section is not required, good programming style dictates that it should be present in every CL source member. You use this section, which consists entirely of comments, to provide information and documentation about the source member and the program that will be created from the source member.

Figure 6.7 shows a sample program information section for a CL source member. This section should identify the program name, the author of the program, the date the program was first completed, and the purpose of the program. Many shop standards dictate that you also include a log of any changes made to the program. This log would be in the program information section.

Figure 6.7
The Program
Information Section

```
/*   Program Name..... APPGM1                                        */
/*   Author........... Joe Programmer                                */
/*   Date Completed... July 15, 1997                                 */
/*   Program Purpose.. This program sends a message to a user,       */
/*                     optionally requesting a reply;                */
/*                     the message text, user, and whether or not    */
/*                     a reply is desired are received as parameters */
/*                     from another program.                         */
/*   ============================================================    */
```

The Program Linkage Section

The **program linkage section** marks the beginning of the CL program. It is required and always contains only one CL command: the PGM (Program) command. The PGM command serves as the beginning boundary of the executable program. No other CL command can precede the PGM command within a CL source member. You can use this section of the program to establish a link between a program and the program that called it. CL uses this link to share information between the two programs. The CL program receives this shared information in the form of program parameters. The optional PARM keyword entry of the PGM command identifies the received parameters, which can be accessed, manipulated, and changed within the CL program. Figure 6.8 shows an example of the program linkage section. In this example, the CL program receives three parameters — *&user*, *&reply*, and *&text* — when it is executed.

Figure 6.8
The Program
Linkage Section

```
PGM           PARM(&user &reply &text)
```

The Declarations Section

The **declarations section**, which declares (defines) any variables or files that will be used in a CL program, follows the program linkage section. All received parameters, as well as any other variables used in the CL program, must be declared in the declarations section. In those rare instances where a CL program needs no variables or files, you can omit the declarations section.

The DCL (Declare Variable) command defines the variable name, type, length, and any initial value to be stored in the variable. The declarations section also allows you to identify a file that will be processed by input/output statements within the program. To declare a file for use in a program, use the DCLF (Declare File) command. CL allows only one DCLF command in a CL program.

Chapter 7 presents a thorough discussion of variables and their use within a CL program, and of the DCL and DCLF commands. For now, Figure 6.9 shows the CL syntax to declare variables for the *&user, &reply,* and *&text* parameters from Figure 6.8, as well as an additional entry to declare a variable for a user ID (*&sender*).

Figure 6.9
The Declarations
Section

```
DCL       &user      *CHAR   10
DCL       &reply     *CHAR   1
DCL       &text      *CHAR   255
DCL       &sender    *CHAR   10
```

The Procedure Section

The **procedure section** specifies which procedures and processes the program will perform. This section immediately follows the declarations section and contains CL commands that specify what the program will do at execution time. For instance, if the CL program will back up a library onto a magnetic tape, the SAVLIB (Save Library) command will appear somewhere within the procedure section.

The procedure section starts with the first CL command following the declarations section and ends with the ENDPGM (End Program) command, a compiler-directing statement that causes the CL compiler to ignore any source member lines that appear after it. Every CL source member should include one ENDPGM command as the last line of the member.

In all but the simplest CL programs, the procedure section starts with one or more MONMSG (Monitor Message) commands. These **global MONMSG commands** identify the major error-handling facilities used within the CL program. If, while the CL program is being executed, an unexpected error occurs, the MONMSG command intercepts the error message and tells the program how to proceed. Most of the time, the program will GOTO another section of the program, identified by a label. We discuss the MONMSG command in detail in Chapter 12.

Following the global MONMSG command(s), the procedure section can be divided into two segments: the *standard procedure segment* and the *error procedure segment.* The standard procedure segment includes all normal processing performed

by the program and is usually ended by the *RETURN* command, which identifies an
exit from the CL program and causes the program to end. Although CL allows more
than one RETURN in a program, good programming practice dictates that only one
RETURN statement appear in a single program. It is the standard ending point of
the program when the program executes without unexpected errors.

The error procedure segment appears in all but the simplest CL programs and
includes the major error-handling procedures used by the program. The beginning
of the error procedure segment is identified by a label, the same label specified in a
global MONMSG command, and can be ended in a variety of ways. The most common
way to end this segment is to execute a CL command that sends a special type of
message, called an **escape message**, which immediately ends the CL program. The
contents of the message indicate the error that caused the program to fail. We discuss how the error-handling segment of the procedure section works in Chapter 16.
For now, you need only realize that it is part of the procedure section of the CL program. Figure 6.10 shows a typical CL procedure section.

Figure 6.10
The Procedure Section

```
             MONMSG     (CPF0000) EXEC(GOTO ERROR)
/* Send message, requesting reply if required                          */
             IF         (&reply = 'Y')    DO
             RTVUSRPRF  MSGQ(&sender)
             SNDMSG     MSG(&text) TOUSR(&user) MSGTYPE(*INQ)           +
                        RPYMSGQ(&sender)
             ENDDO
             ELSE       DO
             SNDMSG     MSG(&text) TOUSR(&user) MSGTYPE(*INFO)
             ENDDO

             SNDPGMMSG  MSGID(CPF9898) MSGF(QCPFMSG)                    +
                        MSGDTA('The message has been sent')            +
                        MSGTYPE(*COMP)
             RETURN /* Normal end of program */

ERROR:              /* Standard Error Procedure */
             IF         &errorsw                                       +
                        (SNDPGMMSG MSGID(CPF9999)  MSGF(QCPFMSG)       +
                                   MSGTYPE(*ESCAPE)) /* Function check */
             CHGVAR     &errorsw   '1'
ERROR2:      RCVMSG     MSGTYPE(*DIAG)   MSGDTA(&msgdta) MSGID(&msgid) +
                        MSGF(&msgf)      MSGFLIB(&msgflib)
             IF         (&msgid = '       ')  (GOTO  ERROR3)
             SNDPGMMSG  MSGID(&msgid)    MSGF(&msgflib/&msgf)          +
                        MSGDTA(&msgdta) MSGTYPE(*DIAG)
             GOTO       ERROR2
ERROR3:      RCVMSG     MSGTYPE(*EXCP)   MSGDTA(&msgdta) MSGID(&msgid) +
                        MSGF(&msgf)      MSGFLIB(&msgflib)
             SNDPGMMSG  MSGID(&msgid)    MSGF(&msgflib/&msgf)          +
                        MSGDTA(&msgdta) MSGTYPE(*ESCAPE)

             ENDPGM
```

When all four CL program sections are placed together, in order, you have the basis for a well-structured and highly documented CL source member. Figure 6.11 shows a CL source member that includes all four sections. You can use this sample CL program as a starting point for the CL programs you develop in this text.

Figure 6.11
A CL Source Member

Program Information Section ─┐

Program Linkage Section ─────

Declarations Section ─

Procedure Section ─

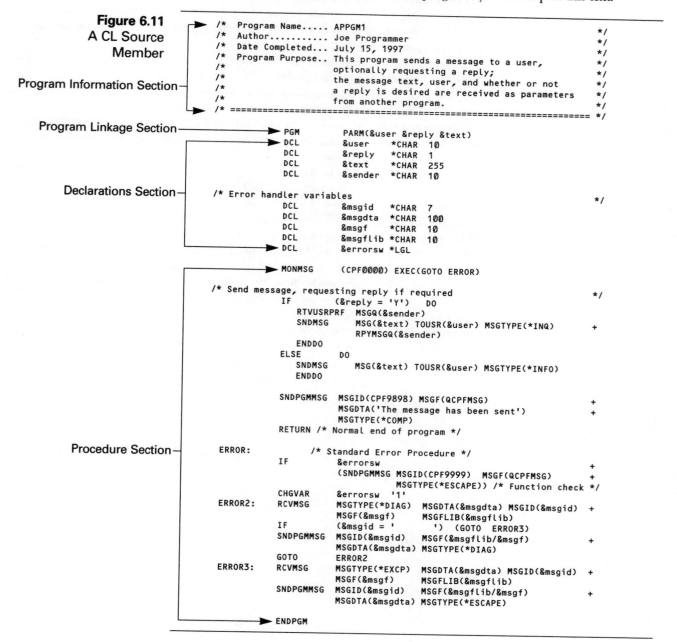

```
/*  Program Name..... APPGM1                                              */
/*  Author.......... Joe Programmer                                       */
/*  Date Completed... July 15, 1997                                       */
/*  Program Purpose.. This program sends a message to a user,             */
/*                    optionally requesting a reply;                      */
/*                    the message text, user, and whether or not          */
/*                    a reply is desired are received as parameters       */
/*                    from another program.                               */
/*  ===================================================================== */

PGM           PARM(&user &reply &text)
DCL           &user     *CHAR   10
DCL           &reply    *CHAR   1
DCL           &text     *CHAR   255
DCL           &sender   *CHAR   10

/* Error handler variables                                                */
DCL           &msgid    *CHAR   7
DCL           &msgdta   *CHAR   100
DCL           &msgf     *CHAR   10
DCL           &msgflib  *CHAR   10
DCL           &errorsw  *LGL

MONMSG        (CPF0000) EXEC(GOTO ERROR)

/* Send message, requesting reply if required                            */
IF            (&reply = 'Y')  DO
  RTVUSRPRF   MSGQ(&sender)
  SNDMSG      MSG(&text) TOUSR(&user) MSGTYPE(*INQ)             +
              RPYMSGQ(&sender)

ENDDO
ELSE          DO
  SNDMSG      MSG(&text) TOUSR(&user) MSGTYPE(*INFO)
ENDDO

SNDPGMMSG     MSGID(CPF9898) MSGF(QCPFMSG)                      +
              MSGDTA('The message has been sent')              +
              MSGTYPE(*COMP)
RETURN /* Normal end of program */

ERROR:            /* Standard Error Procedure */
IF            &errorsw                                          +
              (SNDPGMMSG MSGID(CPF9999)  MSGF(QCPFMSG)          +
                         MSGTYPE(*ESCAPE)) /* Function check */
CHGVAR        &errorsw  '1'
ERROR2:  RCVMSG  MSGTYPE(*DIAG)  MSGDTA(&msgdta) MSGID(&msgid)  +
              MSGF(&msgf)        MSGFLIB(&msgflib)
IF            (&msgid = '       ')  (GOTO  ERROR3)
SNDPGMMSG     MSGID(&msgid)      MSGF(&msgflib/&msgf)           +
              MSGDTA(&msgdta) MSGTYPE(*DIAG)
GOTO          ERROR2
ERROR3:  RCVMSG  MSGTYPE(*EXCP)  MSGDTA(&msgdta) MSGID(&msgid)  +
              MSGF(&msgf)        MSGFLIB(&msgflib)
SNDPGMMSG     MSGID(&msgid)      MSGF(&msgflib/&msgf)           +
              MSGDTA(&msgdta) MSGTYPE(*ESCAPE)

ENDPGM
```

Chapter Summary

A CL source member consists of CL commands and comments. Because CL is a free-format programming language, source statements can begin in any column of the source member. This is in contrast to languages such as RPG or Cobol, which have rules regarding the physical placement of source statements within a source member.

To improve readability of your source member, you can insert blank lines anywhere in a source member.

Commands and comments can be entered in uppercase or lowercase and you can enter commands in either positional or keyword notation.

Comments, which allow a programmer to document a CL program's functions, start and end with the characters /* and */, respectively.

When a command does not fit onto one line of a source member statement, use the command continuation characters + or −. CL programmers usually prefer + because it is less error-prone.

Use labels, which can be from one to 10 characters in length, to add documentation to a program or as the target of a GOTO command.

There are four sections of a CL source member: (1) the program information section, which includes program documentation; (2) the program linkage section, which marks the beginning of a CL program; (3) the declarations section, which defines variables and files used in a CL program; and (4) the procedure section, which specifies what a CL program will do when executed.

Normally, the procedure section comprises two segments: the standard procedure segment and the error procedure segment. The standard procedure segment includes all normal processing performed by a program and is usually ended by a RETURN command. The error procedure segment includes the major error-handling procedures used by a program.

Terms

AS/400 name

command continuation
characters

declarations section

escape message

global MONMSG command(s)

procedure section

program information section

program linkage section

Review Questions

1. Why is CL called a free-format programming language?
2. How might you use a label in a CL source member?

3. What are the four sections of a CL source member? What would be included in each section?

Exercises

Figure 6A
Source Member for Exercises 1–7

```
                PGM
        DCL     VAR(&date) TYPE(*CHAR) LEN(6)
         DCL        VAR(&msgid) TYPE(*CHAR)     LEN(7)
       DCL      VAR(&msgdta) TYPE(*CHAR) LEN(100)
         DCL      VAR(&msgf) TYPE(*CHAR) LEN(10)
      DCL      VAR(&msgflib)      TYPE(*CHAR) LEN(10)
         DCL      VAR(&errorsw)     TYPE(*LGL)
           MONMSG          MSGID(CPF0000) EXEC(GOTO ERROR)
        RTVSYSVAL  SYSVAL(QDATE) RTNVAR(&date)
         SNDPGMMSG     MSG('The current date is ' *CAT &date)
           RETURN
  ERROR:     IF        COND(&errorsw) THEN(SNDPGMMSG MSGID(CPF9999)    +
                         MSGF(QCPFMSG) MSGTYPE(*ESCAPE))
       CHGVAR      &errorsw   '1'
  ERROR2:    RCVMSG     MSGTYPE(*DIAG) MSGDTA(&msgdta) MSGID(&msgid)   +
                      MSGF(&msgf)     SNDMSGFLIB(&msgflib)
      IF        (&msgid *EQ '       ') GOTO      ERROR3
        SNDPGMMSG  MSGID(&msgid) MSGF(&msgflib/&msgf)                  +
                       MSGDTA(&msgdta)      MSGTYPE(*DIAG)
        GOTO           ERROR2
       ERROR3:    RCVMSG     MSGTYPE(*EXCP) MSGDTA(&msgdta) MSGID(&msgid) +
                         MSGF(&msgf) SNDMSGFLIB(&msgflib)
        SNDPGMMSG  MSGID(&msgid) MSGF(&msgflib/&msgf)                  +
                        MSGDTA(&msgdta) MSGTYPE(*ESCAPE)

       ENDPGM
```

1. Add a member named SA0601*XXX* to source physical file QCLSRC. Replace *XXX* with your initials. The purpose of this program (Figure 6A) will be to display the current date within a message sent to you.

Exercises continued

Exercises continued

2. Edit the source member to contain the statements shown in Figure 6A.

   a. Make sure the characters are typed in uppercase or lowercase, as shown.
   b. As you enter the commands, line up the command and the command parameters to make the program easier to read.

3. Insert within the member the missing program information section.

4. Insert blank lines to improve readability.

5. Insert comments to identify the different sections of the program.

6. Compile the program.

7. Run the program. What is the result?

Chapter 7

Declaring Program Variables

Chapter Overview

This chapter discusses the use of program variables in a CL program. You learn the rules about naming variables, the types of variables that CL supports, and how these variables are declared in a CL program.

What Is a Program Variable?

A **program variable** is a named field used to store a value. For example, a variable named *&filename* might contain the value *CUSTFILE*, or a variable named *&custnbr* might be used to store the value *53124*. Unlike a constant, which has a value that never changes, the value stored in a variable can change every time a CL program is run. You also can change a variable's value many times during the execution of a CL program. A typical use of a CL program variable might be to act as a counter within a program to control how many times a loop is processed.

Variables also can be used within CL commands as substitutes for almost all command parameters. For example, instead of specifying the command

```
DSPTAP DEV(TAP01)
```

in a CL program, you could replace the fixed value (TAP01) in the DEV parameter with a variable named *&tapedevice*

```
DSPTAP DEV(&tapedevice)
```

The value of variable *&tapedevice* would be determined when the program is executed. In effect, the DEV parameter of command DSPTAP could contain a different value each time the program is run, adding flexibility to the command's use in your program.

Program variables exist only within the program in which they are used; when the program ends, the values stored within the variables are no longer accessible. You can use variables to add flexibility to your CL programs and to pass information between programs.

How to Declare a Variable

For a variable to be used in a CL program, the variable must be defined. You define the variable name and its characteristics, such as data type and length, with the DCL

(Declare) or DCLF (Declare File) command. All DCL and DCLF commands must appear in the declarations section of a CL source member, immediately following the PGM (Program) command.

The DCL Command

The DCL command explicitly defines an individual variable in your program. For example, the command

```
DCL     VAR(&dayofweek)     +
        TYPE(*CHAR)         +
        LEN(9)
```

defines a variable named *&dayofweek*, which a program could use to store the day of the week. The variable is defined to hold character data (*CHAR), and is nine characters long. This declaration allows you to store a value such as "Wednesday" in the &dayofweek variable.

Naming Variables

The first parameter on the DCL command, *VAR*, is required. The VAR parameter assigns a name to the variable. Every variable name begins with an ampersand (&), followed by one to 10 characters that uniquely identify the variable. The characters following the & must be one of the characters A–Z, a–z, @, #, or $. The remaining characters can also include the numbers 0–9 and the underscore (_) character. Variable names cannot contain embedded blanks or other special characters, such as !, %, or *.

Specifying the Data Type

The *TYPE* parameter on the DCL command also is required. This parameter specifies the type of data the variable can contain. CL supports only three data types when declaring variables:

- *CHAR for variables containing character data
- *DEC for variables containing decimal data
- *LGL for variables containing logical data

Character type (*CHAR) variables can be used to hold any character or string of characters. The characters are stored as consecutive bytes, one byte per character.

Decimal type (*DEC) variables are used to hold numeric data. The numeric data is stored in packed-decimal format within the program's storage. CL *does not* support binary or zoned-decimal variables.

Logical type (*LGL) variables, sometimes called flags, switches, or indicators, are used to store a Boolean data value. Boolean data values are not used by many programming languages and may be new to you. These Boolean logical variables are stored as single-byte fields that can contain only a '1' (on) or a '0' (off) to indicate either a *true* or *false* condition.

Specifying the Variable Size

The DCL command's optional *LEN* (length) parameter specifies the variable's length. The maximum length allowed for a variable depends on its data type. Although the length parameter is not required, it is nearly always used for character and decimal variables. If the length parameter is not specified, a default length is assigned to the variable (Figure 7.1).

Figure 7.1
Length Guidelines
for CL Variables

Variable Type	Minimum/Maximum Length	Default Length
*CHAR	1–9999	32
*DEC	1–15 (0–9 decimal places)	15 (5 decimal places)
*LGL	1	1

To specify the length for a *CHAR or *DEC variable, enter the maximum number of characters you want the variable to hold. For example,

```
DCL     VAR(&your_name)   +
        TYPE(*CHAR)       +
        LEN(40)

DCL     VAR(&my_number)   +
        TYPE(*DEC)        +
        LEN(5)
```

Because *LGL type variables are always one character long, you usually do not specify their length. For example, instead of

```
DCL     AR(&flag_1)       +
        TYPE(*LGL)        +
        LEN(1)
```

you would omit the LEN parameter from the specification

```
DCL     VAR(&flag_1)      +
        TYPE(*LGL)
```

For *DEC variables, you can specify an assumed decimal point. To indicate where the decimal point should be placed, you use a different form of entry for the LEN parameter. The length would be specified by using a pair of integers separated by a blank. The first integer defines the length of the variable; the second integer indicates how many digits within the variable fall to the right of the decimal point. For example, the following command defines a number 15 digits long, with five digits to the right of the decimal point:

```
DCL     VAR(&my_number)              +
        TYPE(*DEC)                   +
        LEN(15 5)
```

The variable defined above could hold a number up to 9,999,999,999.99999. Up to nine digits may appear to the right of the decimal point.

Because the LEN parameter, in this case, is a list type parameter (i.e., the parameter includes more than one value), you must enclose the two integers in parentheses regardless whether you use keyword or positional notation.

Initializing the Value of a Variable

You can assign an initial value to a variable by using the optional *VALUE* parameter on the DCL command. For example, if you specify the following command, you would be declaring the *&dayofweek* variable and assigning it an initial value of *Wednesday*:

```
DCL     VAR(&dayofweek)              +
        TYPE(*CHAR)                  +
        LEN(9)                       +
        VALUE('Wednesday')
```

If the VALUE parameter is not specified, variables are automatically initialized to their default values. For *CHAR variables, the default initial value is blanks. For *DEC variables, the default initial value is zero. For *LGL variables, the default initial value is '0'.

When you supply an initial value for a variable, you must specify a value of the same type as the TYPE parameter. For example, to initialize a *CHAR variable, you must specify a *character string* as the VALUE. A *DEC variable, however, requires a *numeric* VALUE.

Assigning Values to *CHAR Variables

Assigning an initial value to a *CHAR variable is fairly straightforward. The value can consist of a string of any combination of characters, with few restrictions. The following are valid declarations:

```
DCL     VAR(&my_name)                +
        TYPE(*CHAR)                  +
        LEN(15)                      +
        VALUE('This is my name')

DCL     VAR(&my_name)                +
        TYPE(*CHAR)                  +
        LEN(15)                      +
        VALUE('THIS/IS=MY%NAME')

DCL     VAR(&my_number)              +
        TYPE(*CHAR)                  +
        LEN(5)                       +
        VALUE('12345')
```

You may have noticed in the above examples that the string of characters defining a variable's value is enclosed in apostrophes. (Many programmers refer to the apostrophe as a single quote, and some call it a tick mark.) This format is called a **quoted string**. The character value you specify within apostrophes can consist of any alphabetic, alphanumeric, or special characters. When an apostrophe is to appear within a quoted string, you must enter two apostrophes.

```
DCL     VAR(&END)                           +
        TYPE(*CHAR)                         +
        LEN(16)                             +
        VALUE('That''s all folks')
```

Although not required, you may find that always enclosing a character value in apostrophes makes good sense. If you do not use a quoted string, you will need to remember the following restrictions, which affect the value's validity. Character values in unquoted strings

- cannot consist solely of numbers
- cannot contain a blank
- cannot include CL special characters (e.g., *, &, /, (,), ., +, or –)

For example, the following command is invalid because the value in the unquoted string is considered to be a list of values, not a single value:

```
DCL     VAR(&my_name)                       +
        TYPE(*CHAR)                         +
        LEN(15)                             +
        VALUE(This is my name)
```

You must be especially careful to include numeric values in quoted strings if they are to be the initial values for *CHAR variables. In the following examples, the unquoted numeric values are considered to be numeric data, not character data, so these examples are invalid:

```
DCL     VAR(&my_number)                     +
        TYPE(*CHAR)                         +
        LEN(5)                              +
        VALUE(12345)

DCL     VAR(&my_number)                     +
        TYPE(*CHAR)                         +
        LEN(5)                              +
        VALUE(-12345)

DCL     VAR(&my_number)                     +
        TYPE(*CHAR)                         +
        LEN(5)                              +
        VALUE(+12345)
```

You also cannot specify another CL variable when assigning the initial value of a variable. And because CL reserves the ampersand (&) to identify variables, you cannot use the ampersand unless you include it in a quoted string. For example, the following command is invalid:

```
DCL     VAR(&my_number)      +
        TYPE(*CHAR)          +
        LEN(7)               +
        VALUE(&MYNAME)
```

If you want to include the ampersand in the value for a variable, you must specify the value as a quoted string. For example,

```
DCL     VAR(&my_number)      +
        TYPE(*CHAR)          +
        LEN(7)               +
        VALUE('&MYNAME')
```

However, be aware that this does not assign the value of the variable &MYNAME to the variable &my_number; it assigns the character string '&MYNAME'.

Occasionally, you may need to initialize a *CHAR variable to a value that cannot be represented by a character from your computer keyboard. In these cases, you can set the value of the variable to a **hexadecimal number**. The following command assigns a hexadecimal value to a character variable.

```
DCL     VAR(&hex_number)     +
        TYPE(*CHAR)          +
        LEN(1)               +
        VALUE(X'FC')
```

The set of hexadecimal numbers contains the values 0–9 and A–F. Hexadecimal numbers, although not often used in CL, can be used for such things as manipulating screen attributes, processing lists of values, and assisting in data comparison operations. To specify hex notation, CL uses an *X*, followed by a quoted character string consisting of pairs of hexadecimal numbers. For example, if you want to initialize a *CHAR variable to the hexadecimal value of *FFFF*, you would enter the following DCL statement:

```
DCL     VAR(&hexff)          +
        TYPE(*CHAR)          +
        LEN(2)               +
        VALUE(X'FFFF')
```

Assigning Values to *DEC Variables

When you want to assign an initial value to a *DEC variable, you must use a numeric value: characters 0–9, period (.), and the positive (+) and negative (−) signs. You cannot use a comma (,) to separate millions or thousands. However, to conform with international conventions, a comma can be used in place of a period to represent a decimal point. Only one period (or comma) may appear in a numeric value to specify

Coding in Style

- CL doesn't care whether or not you name variables with uppercase or lowercase characters. It will treat *&DAYOFWEEK* and *&dayofweek* as the same variable. But to make your source code more readable, type variable names in lowercase.
- The DCL command is more readable if you omit the following common keywords:

  VAR
  TYPE
  LEN

  For example, instead of using keyword notation,

```
DCL   VAR(&custnbr)   +
      TYPE(*DEC)      +
      LEN(5 0)
```

use the following positional notation:

```
DCL   &custnbr   *DEC   (5 0)
```

the position of the decimal point. If a sign (+ or −) is included in the numeric value, it must appear as the first character of the value. The following examples are valid declarations of initial values for *DEC variables (note how much more readable these commands are when we combine keyword and positional notation):

```
DCL   &my_number    *DEC (5 0)   VALUE(523)
DCL   &my_number    *DEC (5 2)   VALUE(3.14)
DCL   &my_number    *DEC (5 2)   VALUE(-256.78)
DCL   &my_number    *DEC (5 2)   VALUE(+256)
```

You cannot use a quoted string as the initial value for a *DEC variable, nor can you assign alphabetic characters. The following commands are invalid:

```
DCL   &my_number    *DEC (5 0)   VALUE('523')
DCL   &my_number    *DEC (5 0)   VALUE(ABC)
```

If you include a sign in the initial value, it must precede the numeric value. The following command is invalid:

```
DCL   &my_number    *DEC (5 0)   VALUE(25677-)
```

You also must ensure that the decimal places in the initial value will fit into the declared length. The following examples are invalid because the values indicate decimal alignment different from the decimal positions specified in the LEN parameter:

```
DCL   &my_number    *DEC (5 0)   VALUE(256.13)
DCL   &my_number    *DEC (3 3)   VALUE(1.23)
```

Assigning Values to *LGL Variables

The rule for specifying an initial value for a *LGL variable is easy. An important point here is that logical variables can hold only '0' (False) or '1' (True). These are character values, not numeric, so they must be enclosed in apostrophes. The initial value *must* be character value '1' or '0', as the following examples illustrate:

```
DCL  &flag_1    *LGL VALUE('0')
DCL  &flag_1    *LGL VALUE('1')
```

The following examples break the true/false rule, so they are *not* valid:

```
DCL  &flag_1    *LGL VALUE('2')
DCL  &flag_1    *LGL VALUE(0)
DCL  &flag_1    *LGL VALUE(1)
```

Miscellaneous Rules for Initial Values

When you specify an initial value for a variable, you must not only ensure that you use the correct data type, you also must take into account the length of the initial value. If you specify a value on the LEN parameter that is too small to hold the assigned value, the command is invalid. If the length (LEN) specified is larger than that of the value, the CL compiler appends blanks or zeros to the value to match the specified length. For *CHAR variables the initial value will be left-adjusted within the variable and will be padded to the right with blanks. In the following example, the variable *&name* will be initialized to the value *MARYɃɃɃɃɃɃɃɃɃɃɃɃɃɃɃɃɃɃɃɃɃɃ* (where Ƀ indicates a blank):

```
DCL  VAR(&name)     +
     TYPE(*CHAR)    +
     LEN(30)        +
     VALUE('MARY')
```

For *DEC variables, the value will be placed in the variable according to the decimal alignment specified and, if necessary, padded to the right and left with zeros. For example, the following command will initialize the variable *&number* to the value *00016.10*:

```
DCL  VAR(&number)   +
     TYPE(*DEC)     +
     LEN(7 2)       +
     VALUE(16.1)
```

You should note that if you specify the VALUE parameter of the DCL command *without* specifying the LEN parameter, CL sets the length of the variable according to the length of its VALUE, ignoring the guidelines shown in Figure 7.1. For example, the following command would assign a length of seven bytes to the variable *&mylibrary*, even though Figure 7.1 indicates that a *CHAR variable with an unassigned length defaults to 32 bytes:

```
DCL   VAR(&myLibrary)      +
      TYPE(*CHAR)          +
      VALUE('PGMTEST')
```

The following command would assign a length of three bytes, with two decimal places, to the variable *&pi*, just as if you were to specify LEN(3 2):

```
DCL   VAR(&pi)             +
      TYPE(*DEC)           +
      VALUE(3.14)
```

To improve the readability and maintainability of your CL programs, you should never assign an initial value to a character or decimal variable when the length (LEN) is not specified.

You cannot assign an initial value to a variable if the variable name being declared also appears in the PARM parameter of the PGM command. In this case, the value of the variable is determined at runtime by a value passed to the program from another program. The following is an *invalid* combination of code because the program must receive the initial value of the *&library* parameter when the program is called.

```
PGM   PARM(&library)
DCL   VAR(&library)        +
      TYPE(*CHAR)          +
      LEN(10)              +
      VALUE('MYLIBRARY')
```

More DCL Examples

It might be useful to examine additional examples of DCL command usage, applying the rules you have learned. Following each set of DCL commands below is an explanation of each example.

```
DCL   VAR(&state) TYPE(*CHAR) LEN(2) VALUE('  ')
DCL   VAR(&state) TYPE(*CHAR) LEN(2)
DCL   &state *CHAR 2 VALUE('  ')
DCL   &state *CHAR 2 VALUE(X'4040')
DCL   &state *CHAR 2
```

All of these examples define a variable named *&state*, two characters long, initialized to blanks. The hexadecimal representation of the blank character is '40'.

```
DCL   &state *CHAR 2 VALUE('CA')
DCL   &state *CHAR 2 VALUE(CA)
DCL   &state *CHAR 2 VALUE(ca)
DCL   &state *CHAR 2 VALUE(X'C3C1')
```

All of these examples define the variable *&state* and initialize its value to *CA*. In the third example, CL converts the lowercase *ca* to uppercase characters because they are not enclosed in single quotes.

```
DCL &state *CHAR 2 VALUE('Ca')
```

This example defines the variable *&state* with an initial value of *Ca.* CL does not convert the case of the value because the value is a quoted string.

```
DCL &name *CHAR
```

In this example, the *&name* variable defaults to 32 characters long, initialized to blanks.

```
DCL &name *CHAR VALUE('Mr. Jones')
```

In this example, the *&name* variable is nine characters long, initialized to 'Mr. Jones'.

```
DCL VAR(&profit) TYPE(*DEC) LEN(7 2) VALUE(00000.00)
DCL &profit *DEC (7 2) (0)
DCL &profit *DEC (7 2)
```

These examples define *&profit* as a decimal variable, with a total length of seven digits, two of them following the decimal point. The initial value in all these examples is zero. The LEN parameter is enclosed in parentheses in all the examples to group the two integers that define the length and number of decimal positions.

```
DCL &phone *DEC 10
```

This example declares *&phone* as a decimal variable 10 digits long, no decimal places, initialized to zeroes.

```
DCL &weight *DEC
```

In this example, the variable *&weight* defaults to 15 digits long, with five digits to the right of the decimal point. The initial value is zero.

```
DCL &pi *DEC VALUE(3.14)
```

In this example, the variable *&pi* is three digits long, with two digits to the right of the decimal point. The initial value is 3.14.

```
DCL VAR(&FLAG) TYPE(*LGL) LEN(1) VALUE('0')
DCL &flag *LGL 1
DCL &flag *LGL
```

In these examples, the variable *&flag* is defined as a logical variable, initially off (or false).

```
DCL &flag *LGL VALUE('1')
```

In this example, the logical variable *&flag* is initially on (or true).

The DCLF Command

A CL program can process a display file or a database file. You can use a display file to send a screen to a workstation and to receive from the workstation information that you will use in the program. The display file would contain the screen layout, including the fields that you can display or key into. You also can use your CL program to read records from a database file. If your CL program uses either a display file or a database file, you must declare the name of the file to the program using the DCLF (Declare File) command. For example, the command

```
DCLF FILE(PAYROLL/EMPMAST)
```

makes the database file *EMPMAST* (an employee master file) in library *PAYROLL* available for processing in a CL program. When you declare a display or database file in a CL program, the file must exist on your system before you can compile the program successfully.

In the example above, if the file EMPMAST contains fields named *EMPNBR*, *NAME*, and *RATE*, the CL compiler automatically declares the variables *&EMPNBR*, *&NAME*, and *&RATE* for use in your program. These variables would have the same attributes as the fields in the file (i.e., the same length and data type.)

A CL program can use only one file; that is, only one DCLF command is allowed per CL program. For database files, only input operations are allowed. You cannot use a CL program to write or update a record in a database file.

Be careful to make the distinction between processing a file in your program and using your program to perform an action using a file object. For example, you can use the CPYF (Copy File) command to copy a file without declaring the file in your program. If, however, your CL program performs read operations from the file (using the CL command RCVF), you must declare the file. Chapter 15 covers file processing in detail.

DCLF Examples

The following examples will help you better understand how the DCLF command functions.

```
DCLF FILE(INVENTORY/STOCK)
DCLF INVENTORY/STOCK
DCLF *LIBL/STOCK
DCLF STOCK
```

These examples make the fields in file *STOCK* available to your program as variables. The first two examples explicitly state that the file is found in library *INVENTORY*; the last two examples assume that file *STOCK* will be found in a library in your job's library list. When you compile the program, any fields in file *STOCK* will be declared as variables in your CL program automatically.

The example below makes available to your CL program all the fields defined in display file *CUSTDSP*. Because no library is specified for file *CUSTDSP*, the compiler will search for the file in your job's library list. When the compiler finds the file, all fields in the file will be declared for use in the CL program automatically.

```
DCLF FILE(CUSTDSP)
```

Chapter Summary

Program variables are fields within a CL program used to store values. Program variables exist only within the program in which they are used; when the program ends the values stored in the variables are no longer accessible.

You must declare (define) all variables to the CL program before the program can use them (i.e., the program must define the variable name and its characteristics, such as data type and length). You use the DCL (Declare) command or the DCLF (Declare File) command to declare CL variables.

The DCL command defines an individual variable; the DCLF command defines all variables in a display file or a database file. The DCL and DCLF commands must precede all other commands (except the PGM command) in a CL program.

Variable names always begin with an ampersand (&), followed by one to 10 characters that uniquely identify the variable (e.g., &dayofweek, &name, &number).

CL supports three data types for variables: *CHAR (character), *DEC (decimal) and *LGL (logical).

You can assign an initial value to a variable. If you don't, CL initializes the variable to blanks for *CHAR variables, zeros for *DEC variables, and '0' (off) for *LGL variables.

Terms

hexadecimal number   program variables   quoted string

Review Questions

1. What is a CL program variable?

2. How and where do you declare variables in a CL program?

3. CL provides two commands to declare variables. Name the commands and explain their function.

4. What three data types does CL support when declaring variables?

Exercises

1. Determine which of the following variable names are valid and which are invalid. If the variable name is invalid explain why.

   a. `&MEMBER`
   b. `&12345`
   c. `*NUMBER`
   d. `&1FIRST`
   e. `&NUMBER1`
   f. `&MYFIRSTNUMBER`
   g. `&@@@@A`
   h. `@&&MASTER`
   i. `&#@$_16`
   j. `&my_number`
   k. `&dues`
   l. `&john doe`
   m. `&$dollars`

2. Determine the initial value and length of the following variables.

   a. `DCL &number *DEC VALUE(16)`
   b. `DCL &name *CHAR 10`
   c. `DCL &size *DEC (2 0)`
   d. `DCL &width *DEC VALUE(154.6789)`
   e. `DCL &height *DEC VALUE(1)`
   f. `DCL &city *CHAR VALUE('Memphis')`
   g. `DCL &state *CHAR`

   h. `DCL &phone *CHAR 15      +`
      `    VALUE('555-1212')`
   i. `DCL &tax_rate *DEC (4 3)  +`
      `    VALUE(3.625)`

3. Consider the following variable declarations. Which are valid declarations? Which are invalid? If they are invalid, explain why.

   a. `DCL &name`
   b. `DCL &first_name 3 *CHAR   +`
      `    VALUE('Bob')`
   c. `DCL VAR(&lastname) LEN(5) +`
      `    TYPE(*CHAR) VALUE('Jones')`
   d. `DCL &city *CHAR (10 0)`
   e. `DCL &State *CHAR          +`
      `    VALUE('Mississippi')`
   f. `DCL &countryname *CHAR VALUE('USA')`
   g. `DCL &number *DEC VALUE(6.123456)`
   h. `DCL &NEXT *DEC           +`
      `    VALUE(234.9645375676)`
   i. `DCL &NAME2 *CHAR VALUE(1623)`
   j. `DCL &NAME3 *CHAR          +`
      `    VALUE(Robert Frost)`
   k. `DCL &switch16 *LGL LEN(1) +`
      `    VALUE('0')`

   Exercises continued

Exercises continued

```
l. DCL &switch65 *LGL VALUE(1)
m. DCL &Address_1 *CHAR 10000
n. DCL &zip_code *DEC (17 9)
```

4. Which of the following are invalid character (*CHAR) type values? Why? How would you correct them?

   a. `VALUE(12345)`
   b. `VALUE(-12345)`
   c. `VALUE(X'ABCD')`
   d. `VALUE('Today is Sunday')`
   e. `VALUE(Today is Monday)`
   f. `VALUE(today)`
   g. `VALUE('*$%@)(@#PRT123')`
   h. `VALUE(SIXTY)`
   i. `VALUE(*hjert)`

5. Which of the following are invalid decimal(*DEC) type values? Why? How would you correct them?

   a. `VALUE(0)`
   b. `VALUE(123A)`
   c. `VALUE(-476.8)`
   d. `VALUE(1776)`
   e. `VALUE(John Doe)`
   f. `VALUE('123.99')`
   g. `VALUE($2.99)`
   h. `VALUE(3.14+)`
   i. `VALUE('0')`

6. In this exercise, you practice declaring variables for use in a CL program. The program sends you a message when it is done.

   a. Add a member named SA0701*XXX* to source physical file QCLSRC. Substitute your initials for *XXX*.

   b. Add the program information section and the program linkage section to the member.

   c. Declare the following variables for use in the program:

      1) A character variable named *Time*, six positions long, with an initial value of blanks.

      2) A character variable named *User*, 10 positions long, with an initial value of blanks.

      3) A decimal variable named *Customer*, seven positions long, with an initial value of 55345.

      4) A decimal variable named *Taxrate*, five positions long, four of which are to the right of the decimal point. Give the variable an initial value of 7.1625.

      5) A logical variable named *Errorflag*, initially false.

   d. Include the following statements in the procedure section:

      ```
      SNDPGMMSG ('I''m done now')
      RETURN
      ENDPGM
      ```

   e. Compile the program.

   f. Examine the variable cross-reference in the compile listing to see whether your variable declarations are correct.

      You should notice several errors in the compile listing. These errors are mostly CPD0726, telling you that you have declared variables within the program, but have not referred to them. Notice that these errors have a severity level of 10. Because the errors have a severity level less than 30, they do not stop the program from compiling successfully. They are simply there to warn you that you might have a problem, because normally you would not declare variables that you don't use.

      The other warning is CPD0791. This message, which has a severity level of 00, appears if you do not use labels within your program. It is not necessarily an error, but the compiler wants you to know there could be a problem.

   g. Run the program. What is the result?

Chapter 8

Manipulating Variables with the CHGVAR Command

Chapter Overview

In this chapter we introduce the CHGVAR (Change Variable) command, which can be used to change the value of a program variable during execution of a CL program. You learn how to use the CHGVAR command to move data into a variable and to convert data from one data type to another. We also discuss CL's "built-in" functions, %SUBSTRING and %BINARY.

The CHGVAR (Change Variable) Command

In Chapter 7 we explained how to use the DCL (Declare) command within the declarations section of a CL program to assign an initial value to a variable. Once you have declared a variable with the DCL command or the DCLF command, you can use the CHGVAR command to assign a new value to the variable. The CHGVAR command may appear anywhere within the procedure section of the program. When a program executes a CHGVAR command, the named variable is assigned a new value. For example, in standard algebra we can use the statement (A = 5) to assign the value 5 to the variable A. In CL you would write that same statement as

```
CHGVAR    &A        5
```

In another example of CL's syntax (here we use the keyword format of the CHGVAR command), the following command changes the contents of the variable *&dayofweek* to the value *Thursday*:

```
CHGVAR    VAR(&dayofweek)    +
          VALUE('Thursday')
```

The two parameters supported by CHGVAR, *VAR* and *VALUE*, are required. The VAR parameter names the variable to which you are assigning a value (i.e., the **receiver variable**); the VALUE parameter contains the value that will be assigned to the variable. The CHGVAR command *replaces* the current value of a variable with the value from the VALUE parameter of the command, padding with blanks or zeros if necessary.

Unlike many HLLs, CL uses the same command (CHGVAR) to assign values to any variables, regardless of their data type. You can use the CHGVAR command in any of these cases with equal ease:

- To assign a character value to a character type variable
- To assign a decimal value to a decimal type variable
- To assign a logical value to a logical type variable

In addition, you can use the CHGVAR command for data conversion. The CHGVAR command can

- convert a numeric value to a character value and store the result in a character variable
- convert a character value to a decimal value and store the result in a decimal variable

Certain rules apply when performing simple assignment operations and when performing data conversion operations. We discuss each of these cases individually. Most of the rules are the same ones you learned in Chapter 7 when we discussed assigning an initial value to a variable. When there are differences, we will note them.

Using CHGVAR with Character Variables

Perhaps the simplest use of the CHGVAR command is to assign a character value to a character (*CHAR) variable. With one exception, you apply the same rules when using the CHGVAR command as you would when using the DCL command to assign an initial value to a variable. In Chapter 7 you learned that when using the DCL command and assigning an initial value, you must ensure that the variable is long enough to hold the entire initial value. When you use the CHGVAR command, however, if the receiving variable is too short to contain the value specified, extra characters in the value are truncated. Consider the following example:

```
DCL      &name *CHAR 10                +
         VALUE('Billy Golf')
CHGVAR   VAR(&name)                    +
         VALUE('John D. Smithson')
```

In this case, the length of the variable *&name* is declared to be 10 characters. But the value specified by the CHGVAR command is 16 characters long. When the CHGVAR command is executed, CL truncates the extra characters specified in the VALUE parameter and the variable *&name* will contain the truncated value *John D. Sm.*

Remember that the CHGVAR command replaces the current value of the entire receiver variable with the value from the VALUE parameter of the command. For example, if variable *&dayofweek* is a character variable nine characters long with a

value of *WEDNESDAY*, the following command changes the value of *&dayofweek* to
MONDAYᵇᵇᵇ (ᵇᵇᵇ represents three blanks):

```
CHGVAR    VAR(&dayofweek)   +
          VALUE(Monday)
```

Because the character string *Monday* is not enclosed in apostrophes, the CHGVAR
command also converts the lowercase characters in *Monday* to uppercase.

If you wanted to retain the original case, you would specify the value as a
quoted string:

```
CHGVAR    VAR(&dayofweek)   +
          VALUE('Monday')
```

Using CHGVAR with Decimal Variables
If the receiver variable of the CHGVAR command is a decimal (*DEC) data type, you
must keep the following guidelines in mind:

- The VALUE specified can contain only digits, the decimal point (or comma),
  and a leading sign (+ or −).
- The value moved into the receiver variable will be properly aligned at the
  decimal point, as declared in the DCL command for the receiver variable. If a
  decimal point is not included in the VALUE, the VALUE is assumed to be an
  integer, with no decimal positions.
- If the VALUE contains more digits to the right of the decimal point than the
  receiver variable, the extra digits will be truncated without causing an error.
- Specifying a VALUE with more digits to the left of the decimal point than the
  variable can hold will result in an error at the time the program is executed.

To illustrate the use of the CHGVAR command with *DEC variables, consider a
program that declares a decimal variable named *&number*, five digits long, with no
decimal places. The following commands would declare this variable, then change its
value to *00123*:

```
DCL    &number          +
       *DEC (5 0)

CHGVAR    VAR(&number)      +
          VALUE(123)
```

Because the receiver variable *&number* is too small to hold the value 999999, the following command would be *in error*:

```
CHGVAR    VAR(&number)      +
          VALUE(999999)
```

You can see that the VALUE parameter contains six digits, but the variable is declared as being only five digits long. The CL compiler will not catch this error, but when you attempt to run the program, the system will issue an error message.

The following command, on the other hand, may not produce the desired result, but it will not cause an error

```
CHGVAR    VAR(&number)    +
          VALUE(499.99)
```

Even though the VALUE parameter includes two decimal positions, and the receiver variable is declared with none, CL does not consider this an error. CL simply ignores the digits to the right of the decimal point. The value of *&number* after executing this command would be *499* (CL will not round the number up to 500).

Using CHGVAR with Logical Variables

Only one consideration applies if you want to use CHGVAR to assign a value to a logical (*LGL) variable:

- The value must be true ('1') or false ('0').

CL will accept only these two values (true or false) for logical variables, which act as flags, or toggle switches, in a CL program. For example, the following assignment will change the logical variable named *&expired* to true:

```
CHGVAR    VAR(&expired)    +
          VALUE('1')
```

The following assignment, on the other hand, might look correct to you, but CL will reject it because *Y* is not a valid value to assign to a logical variable.

```
CHGVAR    VAR(&expired)    +
          VALUE('Y')
```

Performing Data Conversion with CHGVAR

The CHGVAR command allows you to convert decimal data to character data and character data to decimal data. This conversion will occur whenever the CHGVAR command is executed, if the receiver variable (VAR) is not of the same type as the VALUE specified. The conversion will happen automatically, with no special action required on your part. There are, however, several rules you must follow when you want to use this data conversion facility.

Converting Decimal Data to Character Data

You can assign a numeric value to a character variable. CL will implicitly convert decimal values to character values, but you must be aware of the following rules:

- The numeric value cannot be a quoted string.

- The value, when placed into the receiver variable, will be *right*-justified and padded to the left with zeroes.
- If the numeric value is negative, the leftmost position of the receiver variable will contain the sign.
- The receiver variable will contain the decimal point, if any.
- You must ensure that the receiver variable is long enough to accommodate all the numbers, the sign, and the decimal point.

It is common practice to use the CHGVAR command to convert numeric values to character values. If variable *&datea* is declared as a character variable eight characters long, the following command would assign the value *00123199* to *&datea*:

```
CHGVAR    VAR(&datea)      +
          VALUE(123199)
```

If you were to enclose the value *123199* within apostrophes, you would have an entirely different result because CL would treat the value as character data, not numeric. CL would not, therefore, perform the data conversion.

```
CHGVAR    VAR(&datea)      +
          VALUE('123199')
```

The above command would result in *&datea* having a value of *123199øø*, left-justified with two trailing blanks.

When you assign a numeric value to a character variable, the decimal point (if present) will be included in the receiver variable. For example, the command

```
CHGVAR    VAR(&amtduea)    +
          VALUE(976.43)
```

would assign variable *&amtduea* a value of *00000976.43* (assuming *&amtduea* is declared with a length of 11). If the value is negative, the sign is placed in the leftmost position of the receiver variable. For example, the command

```
CHGVAR    VAR(&amtduea)    +
          VALUE(-976.43)
```

assigns variable *&amtduea* a value of *-0000976.43*.

Converting Character Data to Decimal Data

You can assign a character value to a decimal variable, given the following restrictions:

- The character value can consist only of numbers, a decimal point, and a sign (+ or −). If a sign is included, it must be the leftmost character in the value.
- If the character value contains a decimal point, the data will be aligned according to the declaration of the receiver variable.

- Within the value specified, excess characters to the right of the decimal point are truncated without error. Excess characters to the left of the decimal point will cause an error at the time the program is executed.

The following command will assign the value *098.6* to the decimal variable *&normaltemp*, declared with LEN(4 1):

```
CHGVAR    VAR(&normaltemp)    +
          VALUE('+98.6')
```

Because the quoted character string in the VALUE parameter follows the rules for converting character values to a decimal variable, CL will convert the value correctly. The following assignment, however, would be invalid because only numeric characters can be specified as a VALUE for this variable:

```
CHGVAR    VAR(&normaltemp)    +
          VALUE('Fever')
```

Using a Variable to Specify VALUE

Thus far, we have demonstrated only how to use the CHGVAR command to assign a literal value to a variable. But you also can assign a value stored in a variable to another variable.

To change the value of a receiver variable to the value stored within another variable, you would specify the other variable as the VALUE in the CHGVAR command:

```
CHGVAR    VAR(&dayofweek)    +
          VALUE(&today)
```

The example above assigns variable *&dayofweek* the same value as variable *&today*. The value in *&today* must conform to the same rules you would follow if you were specifying a literal for the VALUE parameter. The value stored in the variable *&today* will be copied, or converted if necessary, according to the same rules that apply when you specify the VALUE as a literal value. For example, if the current value of the variable *&today* is *Monday*, the following CL commands are equivalent:

```
CHGVAR    VAR(&dayofweek)    +
          VALUE('Monday')

CHGVAR    VAR(&dayofweek)    +
          VALUE(&today)
```

Using an Arithmetic Expression to Specify VALUE

Perhaps the most flexible uses of the CHGVAR command capitalize on its ability to evaluate expressions. For example, to increment the value of a decimal variable by 1, you would use the following command:

```
CHGVAR    VAR(&count)        +
          VALUE(&count + 1)
```

This command will add 1 to the value of the variable *&count*. CL supports the common arithmetic operators (+, −, /, *), parenthetical expressions, and normal rules of precedence. The expression can be as simple or as complex as necessary, and can include other variables.

```
CHGVAR    VAR(&area)                                    +
          VALUE(3.14159 * &radius * &radius)
```

For instance, in the example above, *&radius* and *&area* both must be declared as *DEC type variables. If variable *&area* was declared as a *CHAR type variable, you might think that decimal-to-character conversion would take place. However, the CHGVAR command does not support data conversion when an arithmetic expression is used as the VALUE. Chapter 10 covers the use of arithmetic expressions in depth.

Using a Character String Expression to Specify VALUE

In addition to arithmetic expressions, you can use the CL **concatenate operator** (*CAT*) to specify character string expressions for the VALUE parameter. *CAT joins two character values together, allowing you to connect multiple values and store the result in a character variable. Each value specified in a character string expression must be either a character literal (e.g., 'Tuesday') or a character variable. For example, after executing the command

```
CHGVAR    VAR(&message)                                 +
          VALUE('Today is ' *CAT &today)
```

variable *&message* will contain the value *Today is Tuesday* (assuming that variable *&today* is defined as a *CHAR variable containing the value *Tuesday*).

Two variations of the *CAT operation make it even more useful. These variations are *TCAT* (Concatenate with truncation) and *BCAT* (Concatenate with a blank).

*TCAT will connect two values and remove all intervening blanks. Consequently, if variable *&today1* is a *CHAR variable six positions long and has a value of *Tuesϕϕ*, and variable *&today2* is a *CHAR variable with a value of *day*, the following command will assign variable *&today* a value of *Tuesday*:

```
CHGVAR    VAR(&today)                                   +
          VALUE(&today1 *TCAT &today2)
```

If you were to use the *CAT operation instead of *TCAT, *&today* would have a value of *Tuesϕϕday*, because the trailing blanks in *&today1* would be included in the variable *&today*.

*BCAT works almost like *TCAT: *BCAT joins two values and removes intervening blanks; but *BCAT always leaves, or inserts, a single blank between the values. For example, the following command assigns variable *&message* a value of *Today is Tuesday*:

```
CHGVAR    VAR(&message)                                 +
          VALUE('Today is' *BCAT 'Tuesday.')
```

Whether or not a variable contains trailing blanks, if you use *BCAT to attach it to another variable, the resulting value will always have one blank between the two connected values. Figure 8.1 provides examples of character string expressions.

Figure 8.1
Character String
Expressions

Length and beginning values of *CHAR type variables:

LEN(23)	&a = ƀƀƀƀƀƀƀƀƀƀƀƀƀƀƀƀƀƀƀƀƀƀƀ
LEN(10)	&b = Johnƀƀƀƀƀƀ
LEN(1)	&c = I
LEN(10)	&d = Smithƀƀƀƀƀ

CHGVAR command	**Resulting value of &a**
CHGVAR &a (&b *CAT &c *CAT &d)	JohnƀƀƀƀƀƀISmithƀƀƀƀƀ
CHGVAR &a (&b *TCAT &c *TCAT &d)	JohnISmithƀƀƀƀƀƀƀƀƀƀ
CHGVAR &a (&b *BCAT &c *BCAT &d)	JohnƀIƀSmithƀƀƀƀƀƀƀƀ
CHGVAR &a ('Dear' *BCAT &b *BCAT &d)	DearƀJohnƀSmithƀƀƀƀƀ

Using Built-In Functions

When using the CHGVAR command, you can take advantage of CL's three **built-in functions**: the %SUBSTRING function, the %BINARY function, and the %SWITCH function. The most widely used is the %SUBSTRING function. The %BINARY function is used only when you need to manipulate binary numbers. The %SWITCH function, a throwback to punch-card-based operating systems that allows you to test certain settings and control program flow, is rarely used in CL programs and is not covered in this text.

CL's %SUBSTRING function allows you to use the CHGVAR command to assign only a portion of another variable to a receiver variable. The %SUBSTRING function extracts specified characters from a variable and moves them to the receiver variable. The %SUBSTRING function takes the following form:

```
CHGVAR    VAR(&dayofweek)                    +
          VALUE(%SUBSTRING(&today 1 3))
```

The above command extracts only the first three letters in variable *&today* and places them into the receiver variable *&dayofweek*. In this example, if *&today* has a value of *Tuesday*, variable *&dayofweek* will have a value of *Tue* after the CHGVAR command is executed. The %SUBSTRING function has three arguments: (1) the variable name from which to extract the characters, (2) the first position in the variable to extract, and (3) the total number of consecutive characters to extract. Because the %SUBSTRING function can operate only on character data, it can only be used with character (*CHAR) variables. Chapter 10 covers the %SUBSTRING function in detail.

The %BINARY function provides rudimentary CL support for binary data. CL by itself does not handle signed binary integers, but many other AS/400 facilities, including some application program interfaces (APIs), require the use of binary numbers. The %BINARY function can be used to extract a binary integer from a character (*CHAR) variable. The syntax of the %BINARY function takes the following form:

```
CHGVAR    VAR(&decnbr)                    +
          VAL(%BINARY(&binnbr 1 2))
```

In this example, if the character variable *&binnbr* contains the hexadecimal character value *002F*, the CHGVAR statement would treat *&binnbr* as a binary integer instead of a character variable and would assign the decimal value *47* (hex 002F) to the *DEC variable *&decnbr*. Even though you can treat *&binnbr* as a binary integer, you must still declare it with a *CHAR data type. Using the %BINARY function in the VALUE parameter of the CHGVAR command causes a binary-to-decimal data conversion. In Chapter 10, we cover the %BINARY function in more detail.

Using Built-In Functions in the Receiver Variable

You have seen how to use the built-in %SUBSTRING and %BINARY functions within the VALUE parameter of the CHGVAR command. It is also possible to use these functions within the VAR parameter to modify only certain character positions within the receiver variable.

In the following example, variable *&text* is defined as a *CHAR variable 15 positions long. The initial value of the variable is *Bob is the boss*. The following command will replace only the first three characters in *&text*, resulting in a value of *Joe is the boss*:

```
CHGVAR    VAR(%SUBSTRING(&text 1 3))    +
          VALUE('Joe')
```

If we perform another CHGVAR command, we can change the value of *&text* even further. The command

```
CHGVAR    VAR(%SUBSTRING(&text 8 3))    +
          VALUE('NOT')
```

will replace the portion of the variable beginning at the eighth character for a length of three characters with the value *NOT*. Variable *&text* would then contain the value *Joe is NOT boss*.

When you use the %SUBSTRING function in the receiver variable, the VALUE specified will be truncated to accommodate the length specified in the %SUBSTRING function. In the following example, two characters are to be moved into variable *&state*, starting at the first position:

```
CHGVAR    VAR(%SUBSTRING(&state 1 2))    +
          VALUE('CALIFORNIA')
```

Because the value *CALIFORNIA* contains more than two characters, the substring function will start at the leftmost position of the value *CALIFORNIA* and move only the two characters *CA* to the first and second characters of the variable *&state.*

Within the same CHGVAR command, both the receiver variable and the value may contain a %SUBSTRING function. The following CHGVAR commands would be valid:

```
CHGVAR    VAR(%SUBSTRING(&string 1 4)         +
          VALUE(%SUBSTRING(&other 4 4))
CHGVAR    VAR(%SUBSTRING(&name 1 10)          +
          VALUE(%SUBSTRING(&data 50 10))
```

In addition to using a variable for the first argument of the %SUBSTRING function, you also can specify *DEC variable names for the other arguments, as the following command illustrates:

```
CHGVAR    VAR(%SUBSTRING(&string &pos &len))  +
          VALUE('ABCDEFG')
```

The %BINARY function also can be used within the receiver variable. When used in the receiver variable, the %BINARY function performs decimal-to-binary conversion. For example, in the following command

```
CHGVAR    VAR(%BINARY(&binnbr 1 2))           +
          VALUE(&decnbr)
```

if the *DEC variable *&decnbr* contains the decimal value *47*, the CHGVAR command would convert the value *47* into a binary value, moving it to the first two positions of receiver variable *&binnbr*, which would then contain the character hexadecimal value *002F*. Even though you can treat *&binnbr* as a binary integer, you must still declare it with a data type of *CHAR.

As with the %SUBSTRING function, the %BINARY function supports using *DEC variables for other arguments, as illustrated by the following command:

```
CHGVAR    VAR(%BINARY(&binnbr &pos &len))     +
          VALUE(55)
```

Chapter Summary

In a CL program, the CHGVAR (Change Variable) command lets you assign a value to a variable. With the CHGVAR command, you can assign a literal value, the value of another variable, or the result of an expression to the receiver variable. The CHGVAR command can assign values to any variables, regardless of their data type. Specific rules apply for each type of assignment. Specific rules also apply to data conversion, which the CHGVAR command performs automatically if the receiver variable is not of the same type as the value specified.

To connect multiple character values and store the result in a *CHAR variable, you can use a character string expression. The concatenation operators (*CAT, *BCAT, and *TCAT) are used to connect values in character string expressions.

Special capabilities built into CL provide access to additional functions, called built-in functions. The %SUBSTRING special function allows CHGVAR to extract or manipulate only a part of a character string. The %BINARY special function treats a character value as a binary integer.

Coding in Style

- The CHGVAR command is more readable if you omit the keywords VAR and VALUE. For example, instead of using keyword notation,

```
CHGVAR    VAR(&custnbr)                              +
          VALUE(12345)
```

use the following positional notation:

```
CHGVAR    &custnbr 12345
```

When using positional notation, you need to enclose expressions in matching parentheses:

```
CHGVAR    &custnbr  (&custnbr + 1)
```

- The concatenation operations support a shorthand notation. Instead of *CAT, *TCAT and *BCAT, you can use ||, |< and |>, respectively. Consequently, both of the following commands accomplish the same end:

```
CHGVAR    &message                                  +
          ('Today is' *BCAT &today *TCAT '.')
```

```
CHGVAR    &message ('Today is' |> &today |< '.')
```

- The substring and binary functions have abbreviated versions. You can specify either %SUBSTRING or %SST to indicate a portion of a character string. For the binary function, code either %BINARY or %BIN. Most programmers prefer the abbreviated versions. CL treats the following commands identically, but the short version is normally used:

```
CHGVAR    &library %SUBSTRING(&fullname 11 10)
CHGVAR    &library %SST(&fullname 11 10)
```

The DMPCLPGM Command

In the lab exercises for this chapter, you will be writing CL programs that change the values stored within CL variables. One of the best ways to determine whether you have changed the variables correctly is to simply write the contents of the variables into a report that can then be printed. You can accomplish this end with the DMPCLPGM (Dump CL Program) command. To determine whether the programs you write for this chapter's exercises are changing the variables correctly, you will include the DMPCLPGM command in each of the source members where each exercise indicates. When a CL program executes the DMPCLPGM command, it creates a report with the spooled file name QPPGMDMP. You can then view the spooled file, or print it. DMPCLPGM does not stop the program execution. It simply dumps the program and continues with the next command. Figure 8A is a QPPGMDMP spooled file created by including the DMPCLPGM command within the CL source member for the first exercise in this section.

Figure 8A
The Output of the
DMPCLPGM Command

```
5738SS1 V2R2M0 920925                        CL Program Dump                    7/15/97  17:29:35         Page  1
    Job name . . . . . . . . :   DSP13      User name . . . . . . . . :   STUDENT1 Job number  . . . . . :   121281
(A) Program name  . . . . . . :   SA0801XXX  Library . . . . . . . . . :   CLTEXT   Statement  . . . . . :   2200
                                                        Messages
             Message                         Message              From                    To
    Time     ID              Sev    Type    Text                  Program      Inst       Program          Inst
(B) 172935                   00     CMD     2200 - DMPCLPGM       QCADRV       0000       SA0801XXX        0000
                                                        Variables
    Variable      Type        Length          Value                      Value in Hexadecimal
                                          *...+....1....+....2....+    * . . .+ . . .1 . . .+ . . . .2 . . . .+
(C) &CHAR10       *CHAR         10        'My Library'               D4A840D38982998199A8
    &CHAR24       *CHAR         24        'This variable is 24 long'  E38889A240A5819989981829385408 9A240F2F44093969587
    &DEC50        *DEC          5 0       12345
    &DEC72        *DEC          7 2       12345.67
    &LGL1         *CHAR         1         '1'                        F1
                                  * * * * *  E N D   O F   D U M P  * * * * *
```

You need to be familiar with three distinct sections of a program dump. The heading information (A in Figure 8A) lists the names of the job and the program that were running when the dump occurred. Other information about the program is also displayed in the heading. Following the heading information is a list of all the messages generated by the program (B).

Next (C) is the listing of the program variables. The report lists the variable's name, followed by its type and its length. Then the report lists the value of the variable at the time the program was dumped, followed by the hexadecimal representation of the variable value. In the report, *LGL variables declared in the program are listed as *CHAR. This is a little confusing, but as long as you remember that that's how they are dumped, you won't have a problem understanding the report. Also notice that no hexadecimal representation is shown for *DEC type variables. You can see the actual *DEC variable values under the VALUE column on the report.

Terms

built-in functions   concatenate operator   receiver variable

Review Questions

1. What is the primary function of the CHGVAR command?

2. What two parameters are supported by the CHGVAR command and what is their purpose?

3. With which variable types can you use the CHGVAR command?

4. What is the purpose of the concatenate operator, and what are its three forms?

5. What are the two commonly used built-in CL functions, and how are they used?

Exercises

1. What will be the value of the declared variables after executing each of the following code examples?

    a. ```
       DCL &dayofweek *CHAR 9 VALUE('Wednesday')
       CHGVAR VAR(&dayofweek) VALUE('Thursday')
       ```
    b. ```
       DCL &dayofweek *CHAR 9 VALUE(Wednesday)
       CHGVAR VAR(&dayofweek) VALUE(Thursday)
       ```
    c. ```
       DCL &dayofweek *CHAR 9 VALUE(' ')
       CHGVAR VAR(&dayofweek) VALUE(Thursday)
       ```
    d. ```
       DCL &dayofweek *CHAR 9 VALUE('Wednesday')
       CHGVAR VAR(&dayofweek) VALUE(23)
       ```
    e. ```
       DCL &dayofweek *CHAR 3
       CHGVAR VAR(&dayofweek) VALUE('Thursday')
       ```
    f. ```
       DCL &dayofmonth *DEC (2 0)
       CHGVAR VAR(&dayofmonth) VALUE(23)
       ```
    g. ```
       DCL &dayofmonth *DEC (2 0)
       CHGVAR VAR(&dayofmonth) VALUE('27')
       ```
    h. ```
       DCL &dayofmonth *DEC (2 0)
       CHGVAR VAR(&dayofmonth) VALUE(27.3)
       ```
    i. ```
       DCL &top_score *DEC (2 0) VALUE(93)
       DCL &low_score *DEC (2 0) VALUE(67)
       DCL &difference *DEC (2 0)
       CHGVAR VAR(&low_score) VALUE(73.7)
       CHGVAR VAR(&difference) VALUE(&top_score - &low_score)
       ```
    j. ```
       DCL &qual_name *CHAR 21
       DCL &object    *CHAR 10 VALUE('QPRINT')
       DCL &library   *CHAR 10 VALUE('QGPL')
       CHGVAR &qual_name VALUE(&library *CAT '/' *CAT  &object)
       ```

Exercises continued

Exercises continued

```
k. DCL &qual_name *CHAR 21
   DCL &object    *CHAR 10 VALUE('QPRINT')
   DCL &library   *CHAR 10 VALUE('QGPL')
   CHGVAR &qual_name VALUE(&library *TCAT '/' *CAT &object)
l. DCL &qual_name *CHAR 20 VALUE('QPRINTbbbbQGPLbbbbbb')
   DCL &object    *CHAR 10
   DCL &library   *CHAR 10
   CHGVAR (%SUBSTRING(&qual_name 7 1) VALUE('S')
   CHGVAR &object  (%SUBSTRING(&qual_name 1 10))
   CHGVAR &library (%SUBSTRING(&qual_name 11 10))
```

2. In this exercise, you will practice changing variables within a CL program. The program will produce a report so you can determine whether the variables have been changed successfully.

   a. Add a member named SA0801*XXX* to source physical file QCLSRC. Substitute your initials for *XXX.*

   b. Add the program information section and the program linkage section to the member.

   c. Declare the following five variables for use in the program. Do not specify initial values for these variables.

   - A character variable named *&CHAR10*, 10 positions long.
   - A character variable named *&CHAR24*, 24 positions long.
   - A decimal variable named *&DEC50*, five positions long.
   - A decimal variable named *&DEC72*, seven positions long, two of which are to the right of the decimal point.
   - A logical variable named *&LGL1*.

   d. Using the CHGVAR command, change the values of the five variables as indicated:

Variable name	Change the value to
&CHAR10	My Library
&CHAR24	This variable is 24 long
&DEC50	12345
&DEC72	12345.67
&LGL1	True

   e. Include the following three statements in the procedure section after the CHGVAR commands:

DMPCLPGM	RETURN	ENDPGM

   f. Compile and run the program. The program will create the report (spooled file) named QPPGMDMP. Examine the spooled file to determine whether the CHGVAR commands worked correctly.

3. In this exercise, you will practice changing variables within a CL program when those variables have been assigned an initial value. The program will produce two reports: one report will show you the initial value of the variables; the second report will show you the value of the variables after the CHGVAR commands have been executed.

   a. Copy member SA0801*XXX* to a member named SA0802*XXX* in the source physical file QCLSRC. Substitute your initials for *XXX.*

   b. Modify the program information section to reflect the current exercise number, program name, and date.

Exercises continued

Exercises continued

c. Add a VALUE parameter to the DCL command for each of the five variables according to the following table:

Variable name	Initial value	Variable name	Initial value
&CHAR10	History	&DEC72	3.14
&CHAR24	Mississippi	&LGL1	'0'
&DEC50	198		

d. Following the last DCL command, insert a line with the DMPCLPGM command. Leave all the other lines in the program as is.

e. Compile and run the program. The program will create two reports named QPPGMDMP. The first report will show the value of the program variables before the CHGVAR commands are executed; the second report will show the value of the variables after the CHGVAR commands are executed. Examine the spooled files to determine whether the DCL and CHGVAR commands worked correctly.

4. In this exercise, you will practice using the data conversion facilities of the CHGVAR command. The program will produce two reports: One report will show you the value of the variables after execution of the first set of CHGVAR commands; the second report will show you the value of the variables after execution of the second set of CHGVAR commands, which perform data conversion.

a. Copy member SA0802*XXX* to a member named SA0803*XXX* in the source physical file QCLSRC. Substitute your initials for *XXX*.

b. Modify the program information section to reflect the current exercise number, program name, and date.

c. Modify the declarations section of the program to declare the following four variables, without specifying any initial values:

Variable name	Variable type	Length	Variable name	Variable type	Length
&CHAR05	character	5	&DEC50	decimal	(5 0)
&CHAR10	character	10	&DEC72	decimal	(7 2)

d. Immediately after the declarations section, insert CHGVAR commands to store the following values within the variables specified. The last two CHGVAR commands will perform character-to-decimal data conversion.

Variable name	Value	Variable name	Value
&CHAR05	'12345'	&DEC50	&char05
&CHAR10	'12345.67'	&DEC72	&char10

e. Modify the second block of CHGVAR commands (after the first DMPCLPGM command) to change the variables specified to the values indicated. The last two CHGVAR commands will perform decimal-to-character data conversion.

Variable name	Value	Variable name	Value
&DEC50	54321	&CHAR05	&dec50
&DEC72	76543.21	&CHAR10	&dec72

f. Compile and run the program. The program will create two reports named QPPGMDMP. The first report will show the value of the program variables after execution of the first block of CHGVAR commands. The second report will show the value of the variables after execution of the second block of CHGVAR commands. Examine the reports. If the results are not what you expected, determine why.

Exercises continued

Exercises continued

5. In this exercise, you will practice using expressions within the CHGVAR command. The program will produce two reports to show you the values of the variables at two different points in the program.

    a. Copy member SA0803*XXX* to a member named SA0804*XXX* in the source physical file QCLSRC. Substitute your initials for *XXX*.

    b. Modify the program information section to reflect the current exercise number, program name, and date.

    c. Modify the declarations section to declare the following twelve variables, with no initial values:

Variable name	Type	Length	Variable name	Type	Length
&CHAR10	character	10	&DEC50	decimal	(5 0)
&CHAR25	character	25	&DEC72	decimal	(7 2)
&TEXT	character	80	&NUM1	decimal	(15 5)
&TEXT2	character	80	&NUM2	decimal	(15 5)
&TEXT3	character	80	&NUM3	decimal	(15 5)
&TEXT4	character	80	&NUM4	decimal	(15 5)

    d. Modify the first block of CHGVAR commands to assign the following four variables the specified values:

Variable name	Value
&CHAR10	'My name is'
&CHAR25	[*Your name*]
&DEC50	1
&DEC72	20

    e. Modify the second block of CHGVAR commands (after the DMPCLPGM command) to assign new values to the following eight variables, using expressions.

Variable name	Expression value
NUM1	&num1 + 1
NUM2	&dec72 + &dec50
NUM3	&num2 + &num1
NUM4	&dec72 − 8
TEXT	&char10 *CAT &char25
TEXT2	'My friend is' + *BCAT &char25
TEXT3	%SST(&text2 1 12) + *BCAT 'Bill Jones'
(%SST(&TEXT4 10 35))	&text

    f. Compile and run the program. The program will create two reports named QPPGMDMP. The first report will show the value of the program variables after executing the first block of CHGVAR commands; the second report will show the results after executing the second block of CHGVAR commands. Examine the reports. Can you explain why the variables have the values shown in the reports?

Chapter 9

CL Control Structures

Chapter Overview

In this chapter we review the control structures and rules of structured programming, and how they are carried out in the AS/400 Control Language. We discuss the GOTO command, IF/THEN/ELSE structures, and DO/ENDDO groups.

CL and Structured Programming

One of CL's weakest points is its lack of support for structured programming control structures. Modern programming languages typically allow the control structures illustrated in Figure 9.1.

The only control structures that CL supports directly are SEQUENCE and IF/THEN/ELSE. There is no DOWHILE, DOUNTIL, or CASE command within CL. The CL programmer is at a further disadvantage in that CL also does not support internal subroutines. Because of this lack of support for structured programming control structures, use of the CL GOTO command is extensive. These limitations make it difficult, if not almost impossible, to write a well-structured CL program.

Normally, commands in a CL program are processed consecutively (SEQUENCE). That is, the program executes the first command in the program, then the next one, and so on to the end of the program. This type of "top down" execution is typical among most languages. But CL, like most other languages, gives you some control over the execution order of the program's commands by allowing you to alter this order of execution. By using the GOTO command, you can skip entire portions of the program, if that is appropriate to your application.

The GOTO Command

One way you can alter the execution flow is by using the GOTO command to cause **unconditional branching**. Unconditional branching occurs when a CL program executes the GOTO command, causing the program to jump to another section. The jump, or branch, is performed no matter what conditions exist at the time the program encounters the GOTO instruction. The GOTO command always instructs the program to "go to" a label name within the program. The label name is specified in the CMDLBL parameter of the GOTO command:

```
GOTO CMDLBL(label-name)
```

Figure 9.1
Structured Programming
Control Structures

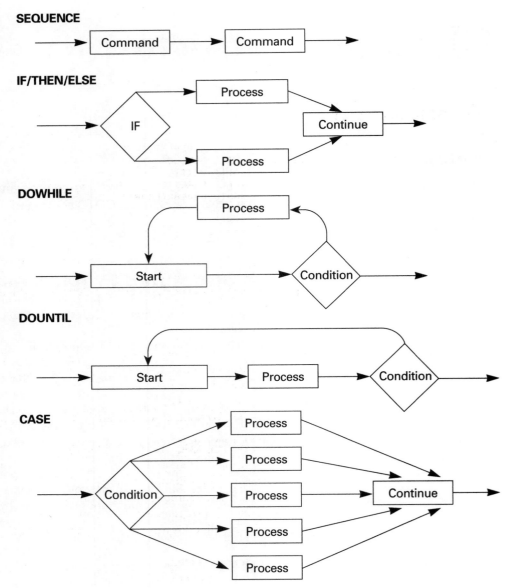

Figure 9.1
Structured Programming
Control Structures

With GOTO, you can branch forward or backward within a program. After the program has branched, or gone to the label, sequential processing resumes.

The GOTO label specified must, of course, exist in your program. If the label does not exist, compilation of the program fails. Recall from Chapter 6 that any CL command in a program can have a label. You can specify the label to the left of the command if it is on the same line as the command, or you can specify the label on a separate line all by itself. Label names cannot exceed 10 characters in length, and they must be followed by a colon. When you specify the label name in the GOTO command, however, you do not include the colon. Figure 9.2 illustrates the use of the GOTO command.

Figure 9.2
Using GOTO with a Label

```
          .
          .
          .

          GOTO CMDLBL(RESUME)
LOOP1:    CALL PGMPROC
          DLTF WRKFILE
          CALL RESET
          GOTO CMDLBL(LOOP1)
RESUME:   RETURN
          ENDPGM
```

Many languages have a GOTO operation, but most structured programming theory discourages its use. Unrestricted use of the GOTO operation often leads to haphazard "spaghetti code" program logic that is difficult to understand and prone to error. So even though CL offers no real alternative in many situations, exercise care and discretion when you use the GOTO command in your programs. Try to organize your program so that the top-down execution order will handle most situations you encounter. And a good rule to follow is that the GOTO command should always refer to a label that follows its occurrence in the program. The one exception to this rule is when your program needs to process a section of code repeatedly in a loop, in which case the GOTO command would usually occur in your program after the target label. We look at some examples of looping later.

IF/THEN/ELSE Structure

You can use the GOTO command by itself to cause an unconditional branch at any time, but usually you will want to branch to another section of code only under specific conditions. For example, you might process one section of code if one particular user is running the program, but skip that section of code if another user is running the program. CL handles this type of **conditional branching** through the IF/THEN/ELSE control structure.

Conditional branching is handled by the IF command. The IF command defines a condition and another CL command:

```
IF        COND(condition)    THEN(CL-command)
```

The CL program evaluates the condition in the COND parameter. That condition is typically a relational expression that compares two values:

```
(&a = 5)
```

If this expression occurs in the COND parameter of an IF statement, and the condition is true, the command specified in the THEN parameter is executed. Otherwise, the program skips to the next statement. The IF command, by itself, does not support the idea of processing an "if group" of statements. Instead, the IF command always identifies in the THEN parameter a single CL command to execute. The condition can be as simple or as complex as necessary. Chapter 10 deals extensively with the use and formation of expressions that you can use on the IF command. Figure 9.3 illustrates the use of a single CL command in the THEN parameter.

Figure 9.3
IF/THEN Logic

```
IF        COND(&user = 'STUDENT1')              +
          THEN(DSPTAP TAP01 OUTPUT(*PRINT))

IF        COND(&user = 'JOAN')                  +
          THEN(GOTO CMDLBL(SKIP1))

IF        COND(&number = 15)                    +
          THEN(CHGVAR &number (&number - 1))
```

Nested IF Structures

The THEN parameter identifies a single CL command that will be executed if the condition is true. To create a **nested IF control structure**, another IF command can be specified for the THEN parameter. Figure 9.4 illustrates nested IF structures.

Figure 9.4
Nested IF Structure

```
Example 1
IF  COND(&user = 'STUDENT1')                    +
    THEN(IF   COND(&number = 5)                 +
              THEN(DSPTAP TAP01 OUTPUT(*PRINT)))

Example 2
IF  (&user = 'STUDENT1')                        +
    IF   (&number = 5)                          +
         DSPTAP TAP01 OUTPUT(*PRINT)

Example 3
IF  (&user = 'STUDENT1')                        +
    IF   (&number = 5)                          +
         IF   (&day = 'Tuesday')                +
              DSPTAP TAP01 OUTPUT(*PRINT)
```

The first example in Figure 9.4 shows the IF command in keyword notation. If the first condition (&user = 'STUDENT1') is true, then the second condition (&number = 5) is evaluated. If that condition is also true, then the DSPTAP command is executed and the program's execution continues with the next command in sequence.

The second example in Figure 9.4 shows the same nested IF command structure presented in positional notation. Notice how much easier it is to read the structure when positional notation is used. For this reason, the IF command is usually entered in positional notation with each nesting level indented. (The term **nesting level** is a means of describing how many IF statements are nested.) When you enter the IF command so that it spans several source lines, you must remember to include the + command continuation character on each line.

The third example shows three nesting levels. CL supports up to 10 nesting levels. For the DSPTAP command to be executed, all three IF conditions must be true.

Using the ELSE Command

A CL program often will use an IF command with an ELSE command. The ELSE command specifies a single CL command to execute if the condition associated with the IF command is *not* true (i.e., if the condition fails). The syntax of the ELSE command is

```
ELSE CMD(CL-command)
```

The ELSE command must follow the IF command and cannot exist without an associated IF command. Figure 9.5 is an example of combining IF/THEN/ELSE commands used to control branching in a CL program.

Figure 9.5
IF/THEN/ELSE Logic

```
      PGM

      ...

LOOP:
      SNDRCVF

      IF        COND(&option = 1)        +
                THEN(GOTO CMDLBL(OPT1))

      IF        COND(&option = 2)        +
                THEN(GOTO CMDLBL(OPT2))

      CHGVAR    VAR(&option) VALUE(0)
      CALL      PGM(PGM0)

      IF        COND(&continue = 'Yes')  +
                THEN(GOTO CMDLBL(LOOP))

      ELSE      CMD(GOTO CMDLBL(END))

OPT1:
      CALL      PGM(PGM1)
      GOTO      CMDLBL(LOOP)

OPT2:
      CALL      PGM(PGM2)
      GOTO      CMDLBL(LOOP)

END:  RETURN
      ENDPGM
```

In this example, the CL program uses the SNDRCVF (Send/Receive File) command to send a display screen to a workstation and wait for a response. It then tests the value of the response, (i.e., the *&option* parameter). If the value of *&option* is equal to *1* or *2*, processing skips down to the appropriate labels, OPT1 or OPT2, where it calls PGM1 or PGM2, respectively, and then branches back to the LOOP label. If the option is neither 1 nor 2, the program changes the value of *&option* to *0*, then calls another program, PGM0. If *&continue* is *Yes*, processing loops back up to the LOOP label. If *&continue* is anything other than *Yes*, the program branches to the END label, where the program ends.

Nested IF/THEN/ELSE Structures

In the case of nested IF commands, you can specify the ELSE command for each nesting level, but you must be careful to match the ELSE command to the correct IF command. When an ELSE command appears within a nested IF structure, the IF and ELSE commands are paired together. This means that when an ELSE command is found, it is paired with the last IF command that is not already paired to an ELSE command. If an outer nesting level of the IF command requires an ELSE command, all inner levels also must specify the ELSE command. Otherwise, the ELSE command is paired with the last IF command that has an unpaired ELSE. See the example in Figure 9.6.

Figure 9.6
Nested IF/THEN/ELSE
Structures

```
Example 1
IF    (&user = 'STUDENT1')                        +
      IF    (&number = 5)                         +
            DSPTAP TAP01 OUTPUT(*PRINT)
      ELSE IF    (&day = 'Tuesday')               +
            GOTO NEXT1
            ELSE GOTO LOOP1
ELSE GOTO ENDIT

Example 2
IF    (&user = 'STUDENT1')                        +
      IF    (&number = 5)                         +
            IF    (&day = 'Tuesday')              +
                  DSPTAP TAP01 OUTPUT(*PRINT)
            ELSE GOTO NEXT1
      ELSE GOTO LOOP1
ELSE SNDPGMMSG 'This is an error'
```

The code in Figure 9.6 is indented to show three nesting levels. In the first example, you see that the IF command at nesting level 3, *IF (&day = 'Tuesday')*, is the single command specified for the ELSE command at nesting level 2. This is permitted within CL.

In the second example, if the ELSE command at nesting level 3 (*ELSE GOTO NEXT1*) is omitted, the next ELSE command found (*GOTO LOOP1*) would be paired incorrectly with the command *IF (&day = 'Tuesday')*. Consequently, the next ELSE command (*SNDPGMMSG...*) would be paired incorrectly with the command *IF (&number = 5)*. So you can see that avoiding the use of many nesting levels within CL when specifying the ELSE command helps keep your program clear.

DO Groups

Recall that the IF and ELSE commands allow you to specify only a single CL command for the THEN and CMD parameters. However, a single command often will not suffice. Other options are to condition *each* command using an IF command, or to condition a GOTO command to direct processing to another block of the program; but these two approaches are difficult to read and error-prone.

For such situations, CL uses the DO and ENDDO (End Do) commands to extend the usefulness of IF and ELSE commands. The DO command lets you define a processing block, called a DO *group,* to process a group of commands together. A DO group would include all the commands between the DO command and the ENDDO command. The DO command is commonly associated with the THEN parameter of an IF command or the CMD parameter of an ELSE command, which enables you to execute several commands. After the commands within a DO group are performed and the ENDDO command executes, processing continues.

Figure 9.7 illustrates the use of DO groups to define processing blocks. The CL code in this figure follows the same logic as the code in Figure 9.5. By using DO groups, we have made this program more readable, more logical, and thus more maintainable. Because the program follows a more logical path in Figure 9.7, we also have eliminated the need for the ELSE test after the call to PGM0.

Figure 9.7
DO Groups

```
        PGM

        ...

LOOP:
        SNDRCVF

        IF        COND(&option *EQ 1) THEN(DO)
                  CALL PGM(PGM1)
                  GOTO CMDLBL(LOOP)
        ENDDO

        IF        COND(&option *EQ 2) THEN(DO)
                  CALL PGM(PGM2)
                  GOTO CMDLBL(LOOP)
        ENDDO

        CHGVAR    VAR(&option) VALUE(0)
        CALL      PGM(PGM0)
        IF        COND(&continue = 'Yes')          +
                    GOTO CMDLBL(LOOP)
END:    RETURN
        ENDPGM
```

The CL compiler listing does not indicate the beginning or ending of DO groups. You must ensure that for every DO command, there is a balancing ENDDO command, and that for every ENDDO command, there is a balancing DO command. If there are unmatched DO or ENDDO commands, the compilation will fail. Indenting your source statements enables you to "desk check" your program to identify DO/ENDDO pairs.

DO groups can be used within nested IF/THEN/ELSE structures, up to the maximum of 10 levels. Figure 9.8 illustrates the use of nested IF/THEN/ELSE structures containing DO groups.

Figure 9.8
Nested DO Groups

```
PGM

...

IF   (&option *EQ 1) DO
                          IF (&answer *EQ 'Y') DO
                              CALL PGMYES
                              DLTF TRANSFILE
                              ENDDO

                          ELSE DO
                              CALL PGMNO
                              CALL RESET
                              ENDDO
                      ENDDO
ELSE                  DO
                          DLTF WORKFILE
                          SIGNOFF
                      ENDDO

RETURN
ENDPGM
```

As you can see, the program's logic can become very complex if you nest conditional processing groups. Again, indenting the code shows the logic visually. This example specifies different processing for three different conditions:

1. The value of *&option* is 1 and the value of *&answer* is Y,
2. The value of *&option* is 1 but the value of *&answer* is not Y,
3. The value of *&option* is not *1*.

Program Looping

Because there is no DOWHILE or DOUNTIL structure in CL, loops are frequently used to simulate their structures. You can use GOTO within a loop to create your own DOWHILE or DOUNTIL structure, as shown in Figure 9.9. As you can see in Figure 9.9, even with its limitations, the GOTO command can be used to add a lot of flexibility to your CL program, especially when used with the IF/THEN/ELSE structure.

Figure 9.9
Using GOTO to Create a
DOWHILE Structure

```
          CHGVAR    &count      0

LOOP:     IF   (&count = 3)   GOTO ENDLOOP
          SNDPGMMSG ('This is one of three messages')
          CHGVAR    &count      (&count + 1)
          GOTO LOOP

ENDLOOP:
```

Chapter Summary

CL is hampered by its lack of support for standard control structures such as DOWHILE, DOUNTIL, and CASE. To help compensate for this lack of control structures, the GOTO command is frequently used. While CL programs normally execute statements in a top-down sequence, the GOTO command causes the program to branch to a statement identified by a label. This is called unconditional branching.

For conditional branching, when you want a program to branch to another section of code only under specific conditions, the IF/THEN/ELSE control structure is CL's primary means. The IF command defines a condition and specifies a command to execute if the condition is true. The ELSE command specifies a command to execute if the condition in the associated IF command is not true. IF/THEN/ELSE structures can be nested up to 10 levels.

The DO and ENDDO commands form the boundaries of a DO group, a block of commands that are processed together. DO groups allow you to process more than one command as the result of an IF or ELSE command.

Finally, you can use the GOTO command within a loop to simulate the DOWHILE or DOUNTIL structures not available in CL.

Coding in Style

- Labels should clearly identify entry points into specific areas of the CL program. To find labels easily, always begin them in column 1 of the program source. Lend readability to a program by placing a label alone on a line, with no other code.

- To help identify the code in a DO group, you should always indent the code. Instead of the following style, for example,

```
IF COND(&option *EQ 1) THEN(DO)
CALL PGM(PGMA)
CALL PGM(PGMB)
ENDDO
ELSE CMD(DO)
CALL PGM(PGMC)
CALL PGM(PGMD)
ENDDO
```

  indent the DO groups to make them easier to read:

```
IF    COND(&option *EQ 1) THEN(DO)
      CALL PGM(PGMA)
      CALL PGM(PGMB)
      ENDDO
ELSE CMD(DO)
      CALL PGM(PGMC)
      CALL PGM(PGMD)
      ENDDO
```

- Use positional notation, instead of keyword notation, when using the IF, ELSE, and GOTO commands.

  For example, instead of

```
IF COND(&answer *EQ 'Y') THEN(GOTO CMDLBL(YES))
ELSE CMD(GOTO CMDLBL(NO))
```

  use the following notation, to make the code easier to read:

```
IF    (&answer = 'Y') GOTO YES
ELSE GOTO NO
```

- Good programming practice requires that you *always* use DO groups in connection with the IF and ELSE commands, even if only a single command will be executed because of the condition. This technique makes a program easier to maintain because it lets you easily insert commands into a DO group. And because this approach generally limits the IF command to one line, the program is easier to read.

Terms

conditional branching
nested IF control structures

nesting level
unconditional branching

Review Questions

1. Examine the following code, which is part of the procedure section of a CL program. Assume that the first time it executes, the variable *&option* has a value of 2. Check the lines that will execute only on the first iteration of the loop and not thereafter.

```
a. LOOP:
b.        SNDRCVF
c.        IF        (&option *EQ 1) DO
d.                  CALL PGM(PGM1)
e.                  GOTO LOOP
f.                  ENDDO
g.        IF        (&option *EQ 2)        +
h.                  CALL PGM(PGM2)
i.                  GOTO END
j.        CHGVAR    &option 0
k.                  CALL PGM(PGM0)
l.        IF        (&continue = 'Yes')    +
m.                     GOTO CMDLBL(LOOP)
n. END: RETURN
o.        ENDPGM
```

2. Examine the following code, which is part of the procedure section of a CL program. Which lines will never execute, regardless of variable values?

```
a. LOOP:
b.        SNDRCVF
c.        IF        (&option *EQ 1) DO
d.                  CALL PGM(PGM1)
e.                  GOTO LOOP
f.                  ENDDO
g.        IF        (&option *EQ 2) DO
h.                  CALL PGM(PGM2)
i.                  GOTO LOOP
j.                  ENDDO
k.        ELSE      GOTO END
l.        CHGVAR    &option       0
m.        CALL      PGM(PGM0)
n.        IF        (&continue = 'Yes')       +
o.                     GOTO CMDLBL(LOOP)
p. END: RETURN
q.        ENDPGM
```

3. The following code segments illustrate the use of common structured programming constructions. Match the construction with the code fragment.   a. DOWHILE   b. DOUNTIL   c. CASE

```
1) LOOP:    SNDPGMMSG MSG('This is one of three messages')
            CHGVAR    &count  (&count + 1)
            IF  (&count < 3)  GOTO LOOP

2)          CHGVAR    &count  1
   LOOP:    IF  (&count > 3)    GOTO ENDLOOP
            SNDPGMMSG MSG('This is one of three messages')
            CHGVAR    &count  (&count + 1)
            GOTO LOOP
   ENDLOOP:

3) IF       (&month = '04') SNDPGMMSG MSG('This month has 30 days.')
   ELSE IF  (&month = '06') SNDPGMMSG MSG('This month has 30 days.')
   ELSE IF  (&month = '09') SNDPGMMSG MSG('This month has 30 days.')
   ELSE IF  (&month = '11') SNDPGMMSG MSG('This month has 30 days.')
   ELSE IF  (&month = '02') SNDPGMMSG MSG('This month has 28 or 29 days.')
   ELSE     SNDPGMMSG MSG('This month has 31 days.')
```

Exercises

1. In this exercise, you will practice using the IF command and the GOTO command with labels. The program will send a message to the bottom of your display. The content of the message will be determined in the program and will be sent to your display using the SNDPGMMSG (Send Program Message) command. To send a message with the SNDPGMMSG command, enter the command SNDPGMMSG followed by the message that you want to send. The message should be enclosed in apostrophes. For example, the following command will send the specified message to the bottom of your display:

```
SNDPGMMSG MSG('Today is Tuesday')
```

The SNDPGMMSG command is valid only when used in a CL program. It cannot be used from a command line.

   a. Copy an existing CLP type source member to a member named SA0901*XXX* in the source physical file QCLSRC. Substitute your initials for *XXX*. As always, update the program information section.

   b. Modify the source member to accomplish the following tasks.
      Your program should:
      - Declare a character type variable named *&company* that is four characters long. Assign this variable an initial value of 'ACME'.
      - Using the IF command, perform the following (*Do not* use DO groups, nested IFs, or ELSE commands for this exercise):
         1) If the company name is 'ABCO', go to a label named ABCO. At the ABCO label, you will send the message 'Company is ABCO'. After sending the message, go to a label named ENDOFPGM. At the END-OFPGM label only two commands should appear, RETURN and ENDPGM. These must be the last statements appearing in the source member.
         2) If the company name is 'ACME', go to a label named ACME. At the ACME label, you will send the message 'Company is ACME'. After sending the message, go to the ENDOFPGM label.
         3) If the company name is neither of the above, send a message that states 'Unknown company.' Then go to the ENDOFPGM label.

   c. Compile and run the program. Do you get the message 'Company is ACME'? Change the initial value of variable *&company* to 'ABCO'. Compile and run the program. Do you get the message 'Company is ABCO'? Change the initial value of variable *&company* to a value of 'AAAA'. Compile and run the program. What is the result?

2. In this exercise, you will practice using the IF command with DO groups. The program will send a message to the bottom of your display. The content of the message will be determined in the program, and will be sent to your display using the SNDPGMMSG command.

   a. Copy source member SA0901*XXX* to a member named SA0902*XXX* in the source physical file QCLSRC. Substitute your initials for *XXX*. As always, update the program information section.

   b. Modify the source member to accomplish the same tasks as the program in Exercise 1, except this time use DO groups to simplify the structure of the CL program. *Do not* use nested IF commands or ELSE commands.

   c. Compile and run the program. Do you get the message 'Company is ACME'? Change the initial value of variable *&company* to 'ABCO'. Compile and run the program. Do you get the message 'Company is ABCO'? Change the initial value of variable *&company* to a value of 'AAAA'. Compile and run the program. What is the result?

Exercises continued

Exercises continued

3. In this exercise, you will practice using nested IF and ELSE commands. DO groups will also be used. The program will send two messages to the bottom of your display. The contents of the messages will be determined in the program, and will be sent to your display using the SNDPGMMSG command.

    a. Copy source member SA0902*XXX* to a member named SA0903*XXX* in the source physical file QCLSRC. Substitute your initials for *XXX*. As always, update the program information section.

    b. Modify the source member to accomplish the following tasks.

    Your program should:

    - Declare a character type variable named *&company*, four characters in length. Assign this variable an initial value of 'ACME'.
    - Declare a character type variable named *&goodone*, one character long. An initial value need not be assigned.
    - Using DO groups, IF/THEN/ELSE structures, and nested IF/THEN/ELSE structures where indicated, perform the following tasks:

    ```
    IF the company name is 'ABCO',
          DO the following:
                Change the variable &goodone to a value of 'Y'.
                Send the message 'Company is 'ABCO'.
    ELSE
          IF the company name is 'ACME'
          DO the following:
                Change &goodone to 'Y'.
                Send the message 'Company is ACME'.
     ELSE DO the following:
                Change &goodone to 'N'.
                Send the message 'Unknown company'.
    ```

    At the end of the program, enter the commands to find out whether the company is a good one. If it is a good one (&goodone = 'Y'), send the message 'This is a good one'. Otherwise, send the message 'This is a bad one'.

    c. Compile and run the program. You should get two messages. The first one should say 'Company is ACME'. Far to the right on the message line you should see a + sign. This means that there are more messages you can see. If you place your cursor on the message line and press the Page Up key, the next message will appear. It should say 'This is a good one'. Change the initial value of the variable *&company* to 'ABCO'. Compile and run the program. DO you get the correct messages? Change the initial value of the variable *&company* to a value of 'AAAA'. Compile and run the program. What is the result?

Chapter 10

Expressions

Chapter Overview

In this chapter you learn how to use expressions within CL commands. The chapter begins with a general overview of expressions and their use, followed by a discussion of the four different types of expressions allowed within a CL command.

What Is an Expression?

An **expression** is a group of symbols used to represent a single value. The group of symbols in the expression *5 +1*, for example, can be used to represent the value 6, as can the expression *12/2*.

Expressions can be used within most CL command parameters. Recall from Chapter 8 that we used expressions with the CHGVAR (Change Variable) command. In the following example,

```
CHGVAR      &var1      (&var2 + 1)
```

the expression *&var2 + 1* will be evaluated when the CHGVAR command is executed and the single derived value of the expression will be placed within the variable *&var1*. In this case, the derived value will be the current value of *&var2* added to the decimal number *1*.

An expression can contain constants and variables. Expressions usually contain more than one value (or **operand**) separated by an **operator**, such as + or − . In the expression *&var2+1* from the previous example, the two operands are *&var2* and *1*, and they are separated by the addition operator (+).

Four types of expressions can be used to represent CL command parameter values:

- Arithmetic expressions
- Character string expressions
- Logical expressions
- Relational expressions

The derived value of an arithmetic expression will always be a single numeric value. The derived value of a character string expression will always be a single character string value. The derived value of a relational or logical expression will always be a single logical value of *true* ('1') or *false* ('0').

The type of command parameter (e.g., character, decimal, or integer) will determine which expression type can be used to represent its value. That is, you could not specify an arithmetic expression as the value of a *CHAR data type command parameter. For example, the expression in the following command would *not* work:

```
DSPTAP    DEV(6 + 1)
```

Because the DEV parameter of the DSPTAP command requires a character type value, this usage would be an obvious error. Instead, you could use a character string expression:

```
DSPTAP    DEV('TAP' *CAT &DEV)
```

Some command parameters (e.g., the COND parameter of the IF command) *require* that you use an expression. For example, in the following command,

```
IF    (&a > &b) GOTO LOOP
```

the relational expression *&a* > *&b* represents a single evaluated result of either *true* or *false*, depending on the values of variables *&a* and *&b*.

If two or more expressions are combined, they form a **complex expression**. The following command contains a complex expression:

```
IF    ((&a > &b) *AND (&number = 5))    +
      GOTO LOOP
```

In this case, even though the command contains more than one expression, the evaluated result will still be a single value: either *true* or *false*.

Using Arithmetic Expressions

In CL, you can use an arithmetic expression in only three situations:

- within the VALUE parameter of the CHGVAR command
- within the COND parameter of the IF command
- within the MAPFLD parameter of the OPNQRYF command (discussed in Chapter 17)

Because you cannot use an arithmetic expression to specify the value on any other command parameter, the following uses of arithmetic expressions would be *invalid*:

```
DCL       &VAR1                         +
          VALUE(16 + 32)
DCL       &VAR2                         +
          VALUE(&VAR1 + 1)
DSPTAP    DEV(TAP01)                    +
          SEQNBR(&COUNT + 1)
```

An arithmetic expression will always contain at least two operands separated by arithmetic operators. The operands can be decimal constants or decimal variables. The following arithmetic operators can be used within an arithmetic expression:

- addition (+)
- subtraction (−)
- multiplication (*)
- division (/)

The derived value of an arithmetic expression is always a single numeric value. For example, the derived value of the expression (6 * 3) is the number 18. Arithmetic expressions are always enclosed within parentheses:

```
(&number + 16 / 3)
```

Within an arithmetic expression, blanks can be used to separate operands from operators, but, with one exception, they are not required. The exception involves using a variable name with a division operator (/). If a variable name is followed by the division operator, the operator must be preceded by a blank (the blank allows CL to recognize use of the / as an operator rather than as a qualifier character). For example, you could specify

```
(&DEC /5)
```

but not

```
(&DEC/5)
```

Each operand in the expression can contain an optional sign to indicate that the operand has a positive or negative value. The sign, if used, must immediately precede the value, with no intervening blanks (e.g., −5). If the operand does not contain a sign, it is considered to be positive.

The following are valid arithmetic expressions:

```
(&number+1)
(1 + &number)
(16/30)
(16 / 30)
(&number + 16 / 3 + &number2)
(&number+16/3+&number2)
```

The following valid expressions use signed numbers. In the first two examples, −1 is a signed number; in the third example, the sign of the value in variable &number is reversed.

```
(&number* -1)
(&number*-1)
(&number / 5 + 2 / -&number2)
```

Arithmetic Order of Operations

When more than one operator appears within an arithmetic expression, you must be aware of the order in which the operators are evaluated. CL follows the algebraic standard order of operations:

Order	Operator
1	Signed decimal values (such as −3 or +&num1)
2	Multiplication (*) and division (/)
3	Addition (+) and subtraction (−)

When operators of the same order appear within an expression, the operations are performed from left to right. Consider the following expression:

```
(5 + 3 / 3 - 2)
```

CL will first divide 3 by 3 to produce an intermediate result of 1. Next, 5 and 1 will be added, resulting in a value of 6. Then CL will subtract 2 from 6 to produce the final value of 4.

You can change the order in which an expression will be evaluated by using parentheses. For example, the following modification to the above example changes the way CL evaluates the expression:

```
((5+3) / (3-2))
```

In this case, CL will first add 5 and 3 to produce an intermediate result of 8. Next, 2 will be subtracted from 3, resulting in a value of 1. Then 8 will be divided by 1, resulting in a final value of 8.

Using the %BIN Function

CL does not directly support a binary number data type. The only numeric data type CL supports is *DEC (decimal). But CL does provide a way to extract a number stored in binary format and convert it to a decimal variable: by using the %BIN (binary) built-in function as an operand in an arithmetic expression.

The %BIN function operates on a *CHAR variable, extracting a binary numeric value that can be used in an arithmetic expression. %BIN can extract either 2 or 4 bytes from the character variable. (On the AS/400, binary numbers always occupy either 2 or 4 bytes.) The following example uses the %BIN function in an arithmetic expression:

```
(%BIN(&number 1 2) + 16)
```

CL would evaluate the above expression as follows: (1) extract the binary number from the character variable *&number* starting at position 1 for a length of 2, then (2) add the extracted value to the number 16 to produce the derived value of the expression.

If you want to extract the binary equivalent of an entire variable, you don't need to specify a starting position or length for the %BIN function. For instance, the previous example could be written as

```
(%BIN(&number) + 16)
```

In this case, CL assumes that you want to extract a binary number from an entire variable.

Using Character String Expressions

You can use a character string expression to combine character data into one derived value. The following character string expression is evaluated as the single character string value *My name is Barb*:

```
('My name is ' *CAT 'Barb')
```

In Chapter 8, which discussed using character string expressions with the CHGVAR command, you learned how to specify character string expressions using the *CAT, *BCAT, and *TCAT operators. The rules that you learned in Chapter 8 regarding the formation of character string expressions apply regardless of the command that you are entering.

You can use a character string expression to supply a value for almost all CL command parameters. The exceptions to this rule are rare, but one worth noting is that character string expressions cannot be used to initialize the value of a variable in the DCL (Declare) command. You *cannot* specify the value of a variable in the following way:

```
DCL    &VAR1      *CHAR LEN(20)               +
       VALUE('My value' *CAT ' is 10')
```

Character string expressions are always enclosed within parentheses and always contain at least two operands separated by character string operators. The operands can be quoted or unquoted character strings or *CHAR variables. The %SST (substring) built-in function also can be used to specify an operand. You can use the following character string operators within a character string expression:

- *CAT (concatenation)
- *BCAT (concatenation with a blank)
- *TCAT (concatenation with truncation)

or you can use the respective symbols in place of the predefined values:

- || (*CAT)
- |> (*BCAT)
- |< (*TCAT)

Within a character string expression, you can use blanks to separate operands from operators, but blanks are required only when an operator is one of the predefined values (i.e., *CAT, *BCAT, or *TCAT). If the symbols ||, |>, or |< are used, blanks are optional.

Let's look at an example of a character string expression. Assume that, at the end of your CL program, you want to send a message indicating the current time of day and the current date. Figure 10.1 shows two approaches you might use.

Figure 10.1
Using a Character
String Expression to
Send a Message

```
Example 1
PGM

DCL   &time    *CHAR 6
DCL   &date    *CHAR 6
DCL   &message *CHAR 50

RTVSYSVAL QTIME &time   /* This command gets the time */
RTVSYSVAL QDATE &date   /* This command gets the date */

CHGVAR &message                                             +
       ('The time is ' *CAT &time *TCAT ' on'              +
        *BCAT &date)
SNDPGMMSG MSG(&message)

RETURN
ENDPGM

Example 2
PGM

DCL   &time    *CHAR 6
DCL   &date    *CHAR 6

RTVSYSVAL QTIME &time   /* This command gets the time */
RTVSYSVAL QDATE &date   /* This command gets the date */

SNDPGMMSG MSG('The time is ' *CAT &time *TCAT ' on'        +
          *BCAT &date)

RETURN
ENDPGM
```

In Example 1, variable *&message* is declared to hold the message text that will be built using the CHGVAR command. Example 2 shows you how to build the message without declaring variable *&message* and without using the CHGVAR command. In this example, the character string expression is used with the SNDPGMMSG (Send Program Message) command. Although the processing steps are different, both examples serve the same purpose: to build and send a message.

Using the %SST Built-In Function

As mentioned earlier, a character string expression can contain the %SST (substring) built-in function as an operand. In Chapter 8, we discussed the basic method of using the %SST function with the CHGVAR command. You can, however, use the %SST function in any command that allows parameters with string expressions. Figure 10.2 shows how you might use the %SST function with the SNDPGMMSG command.

The program in Figure 10.2 retrieves the time of day in HHMMSS (hours, minutes, seconds) format. Then the program builds a message using a character string expression. If the time of day is exactly noon, the message will say, *The time is 12:00:00.*

Figure 10.2
Using %SST with the
SNDPGMMSG
Command

```
PGM

DCL        &time      *CHAR 6

RTVSYSVAL QTIME &time
SNDPGMMSG MSG('The current time is' *BCAT      +
              (%SST(&time 1 2)) *CAT ':' *CAT  +
              (%SST(&time 3 2)) *CAT ':' *CAT  +
              (%SST(&time 5 2)))

RETURN
ENDPGM
```

The program substrings the variable *&time* into three pieces: (1) the hour of the day (the first two characters of *&time*), (2) the minutes (the third and fourth characters of *&time*), and (3) the seconds (the last two characters of *&time*). The program also inserts colons (:) between each time segment to produce a nicely formatted message. The %SST built-in function provides this extra bit of editing functionality within a character string expression.

Using Relational Expressions

A relational expression contains two operands that are compared. The comparison performed depends on the relational operator that appears between the operands. Examples of relational expressions are *(&A > &B)* and *(&state = 'MAINE')*. The derived value of the expression will be either true ('1') or false ('0'), depending on the result of the comparison.

Relational expressions can be used within only a few CL commands. The main use of relational expressions is to specify the COND parameter of the IF command, as we discussed in Chapter 9. Another use of relational expressions is in the VALUE parameter for the CHGVAR command. We examine both usages in this chapter.

The operands in a relational expression can be any of the following:

- Decimal constants
- Decimal variables
- Arithmetic expressions
- Character constants
- Character variables
- Character string expressions
- Logical constants
- Logical variables
- Logical expressions

Although you can use any of these operands in a relational expression, the two operands must be of the same data type. Because the relational expression performs a comparison, it would make no sense to compare two operands with different data types.

For example, it would make no sense to compare the decimal number *5* to the character string *Apples*. Therefore, you could *not* use the following relational expressions:

```
('Apples' = 5)
((&A + 5) = 'Apples')
```

Relational Operators

Figure 10.3 lists the operators that can be used in a relational expression. You can use either the predefined values or the representative symbols.

Figure 10.3
Relational Operators

Relationship	Predefined Value	Symbol
Equal to	*EQ	=
Greater than	*GT	>
Less than	*LT	<
Greater than or equal to	*GE	>=
Less than or equal to	*LE	<=
Not equal	*NE	¬=
Not greater than	*NG	¬>
Not less than	*NL	¬<

Relational expressions must always be enclosed within parentheses. If the operator is a predefined value, you must include blanks to separate the operands from the operator. If the operator is specified as a symbol, blanks are optional. Figure 10.4 provides examples of how relational expressions would be evaluated.

Figure 10.4
Examples of
Relational Expressions

(&number *EQ &pi)	This expression is true if *&number* and *&pi* have equal values.
(&number = 3.14159)	This expression is true if the value of *&number* is 3.14159.
(&salary *GE 57900)	This expression is true if the value of *&salary* is 57,900 or greater.
(%SST(&answer 1 1) = 'Y')	This expression is true if the first character in *&answer* is Y.
(&newpay / &oldpay > 1.05)	This expression is true if dividing the value of *&newpay* by the value of *&oldpay* results in a value greater than 1.05.

Character Operands of Different Lengths

When the operands in a relational expression contain character data and the operands are not the same length, before the comparison is performed, the shorter operand is extended with blanks to match the length of the longer operand. Let's look at a few examples of relational expressions using the following declarations:

```
DCL   &var1     *CHAR 3    VALUE('ABC')
DCL   &var2     *CHAR 10   VALUE('ABCDEFGHIJ')
DCL   &var3     *CHAR 10   VALUE('ABC        ')
DCL   &var4     *CHAR 10   VALUE('           ')
```

Expression 1: (&var1 = &var2)

In this case, before the comparison occurs, *&var1* would be extended with blanks to match the length of *&var2*, giving *&var1* a value of *ABCƀƀƀƀƀƀƀ*. This value does not equal *ABCDEFGHIJ*, the value of *&var2*, so the expression is false.

Expression 2: (&var1 = &var3)

In this example, the expression is *true*. After *&var1* is extended with blanks to match the length of *&var3*, the two operands are equal.

Expression 3: (&var4 = ' ')

In this example, the expression is *true*. After CL pads the character literal ' ' with blanks to match the length of *&var4*, the two operands are equal.

Using Relational Expressions with the CHGVAR Command

You can use relational expressions to specify the VALUE parameter of the CHGVAR command. In this case, the variable you are changing must be a logical variable. Consider the following:

```
DCL       &var1     *DEC (5 0)        VALUE(500)
DCL       &flag     *LGL             VALUE('0')
CHGVAR    &flag     (&var1 = 500)
```

In this case, the relational expression *(&VAR1 = 500)* is true. Therefore, when the CHGVAR command is executed, the value of the logical variable *&flag* will be set to '1', or true. Using the CHGVAR command in this manner allows you to perform two operations with the same command: (1) to make a comparison, and (2) to set the value of a variable (in this case, *&flag*). You could employ a variation on this technique with the IF and ELSE commands, as in the following example, but the preferred method would be to use the CHGVAR command, as in the previous example:

```
DCL   &var1     *DEC (5 0)       VALUE(500)
DCL   &flag     *LGL
IF    (&var1 = 500)                              +
      CHGVAR &flag '1'
      ELSE CHGVAR &flag '0'
```

Using Logical Expressions

Logical expressions, which evaluate the logical relationship between two operands, are very similar to relational expressions. As with relational expressions, the value of a logical expression is evaluated as either being true ('1') or false ('0'). And both relational and logical expressions are used primarily with the IF and CHGVAR commands.

A logical expression may contain only one operand, but it usually contains two or more. If you specify more than one operand, the operands must be separated by a logical operator (i.e., *AND, *OR, or *NOT). The logical operators that can be used within a logical expression are shown in Figure 10.5. You can use either the predefined values or the symbols.

**Figure 10.5
Logical Operators**

Predefined Value	Symbol	Meaning
*AND	&	The expression is true if both operand 1 and operand 2 are true
*OR	|	The expression is true if either operand 1 or operand 2 is true
*NOT	¬	The value of the expression would be reversed

Logical operators are used to specify the logical relationship between operands. Remember that, as in the case of a relational expression, the derived value of the logical expression will be either true ('1') or false ('0').

The operands used in a logical expression are usually relational expressions. You can, however, also use logical variables and logical constants. Consider the following example:

```
(&flag1 *OR &flag2)
```

In this case, both variables, *&flag1* and *&flag2*, must be defined as logical (*LGL) type variables.

Logical expressions with more than one operand must always be enclosed within parentheses. If the operator is a predefined value, one or more blanks must be used to separate the operands from the operator. If the operator is specified as a symbol, blanks are optional. Consider the following example of a logical expression used with the IF command:

```
DCL    &a      *DEC (3 0)      VALUE(5)
DCL    &b      *DEC (3 0)      VALUE(2)
IF     ((&a = 5) *AND (&b = 2)) GOTO LOOP
```

Here's how CL will evaluate this expression. The first operand of the logical expression, *(&a = 5)*, is a relational expression. It is evaluated as true ('1'). The second operand, *(&b = 2)*, another relational expression, also is true ('1'). The two true operands are combined (using *AND) to produce the final evaluated result of the expression, which is true ('1').

Evaluating Logical Relationships

Logical relationships are evaluated according to the operator used. For an *AND relationship to be evaluated as true, *both* of the operands must be true. For an *OR relationship to be true, *either or both* of the operands must be true. Figure 10.6 illustrates various combinations of true and false operands and shows how a particular expression would be evaluated.

Figure 10.6
Logical Evaluation

Operand 1 Evaluation	Logical Operator	Operand 2 Evaluation	Expression Evaluation
True	*AND	True	True
True	*AND	False	False
False	*AND	True	False
False	*AND	False	False
True	*OR	True	True
True	*OR	False	True
False	*OR	True	True
False	*OR	False	False

The *NOT operator is used to reverse the value of a logical value from true to false, or from false to true. The following example evaluates to a value of true:

```
((10 > 1) *AND *NOT (6 > 8))
```

Because the evaluation of the above expression might not be immediately apparent, let's break it down. The first operand is the relational expression *(10 > 1)*, which is true. The second operand is the relational expression *(6 > 8)*, which is false. But the *NOT operator, when applied to the second operand, reverses the value of the second operand from false to true. Because both operands are now true, when they are combined by the *AND operator, the entire expression becomes true. Figure 10.7 illustrates how the *NOT operator, when used with the second operand, can affect the evaluation of certain expressions. Within a logical expression, you can use the *NOT operator with either operand.

Figure 10.7
Logical Evaluation
with *NOT

Operand 1 Evaluation	Logical Operator	Operand 2 Evaluation	Expression Evaluation
True	*AND *NOT	True	False
True	*AND *NOT	False	True
False	*AND *NOT	True	False
False	*AND *NOT	False	False
True	*OR *NOT	True	True
True	*OR *NOT	False	True
False	*OR *NOT	True	False
False	*OR *NOT	False	True

Using Logical Variables and Logical Constants

Up to this point, we have discussed logical expressions whose operands are relational expressions. But logical variables and logical constants also can be used as operands within a logical expression. A logical variable or constant can be used as the only operand within a logical expression, or it can be one of the operands specified. You also can specify both operands as logical variables or constants. The following examples demonstrate each of these uses:

1. Using only one operand, a logical variable named *&errorflag*

   ```
   IF      &errorflag      GOTO ERROR
   ```

   Because *&errorflag* is defined as a logical variable, it can be used as the only operand within a logical expression. If the value of *&errorflag* is true, the expression will be evaluated as true. If *&errorflag* is false, the expression is false.

2. Using a logical variable (*&errorflag*) as one of two operands

   ```
   (&errorflag *AND (&A > &B))
   ```

   In this case, the second operand contains a relational expression.

3. Using logical variables for both operands

   ```
   (&errorflag *OR &endofpgm)
   ```

Using More Than Two Operands

Normally, logical expressions will contain only one or two operands. You can, however, use more than two operands, which allows you to include complex logic within your CL program. In the following example, all three operands must be true for the expression to be true:

```
(&A *AND &B *AND &C)
```

In the next example, you can see that a logical expression can be quite complex:

```
(((&A > &B) *AND (&C = &D)               +
*OR                                      +
((&hour > '05') *AND *NOT &errorflag)))
```

As with arithmetic expressions, you can use parentheses to change the order of evaluation of a logical expression. Figure 10.8 shows how some logical expressions would be evaluated.

Figure 10.8 Evaluation of Logical Expressions		
`(&in03 *OR &in12)`	The condition will be true if either *&in03* or *&in12* is true ('1').
`(&flag *AND &in03)`	Both *&flag* and *&in03* must be true for this condition to be true.
`(*NOT (%SST(&answer 1 1) *EQ 'Y'))`	This condition is true if the first character in *&answer* is any character other than Y.
`(&active *AND (&salary > 50000))`	This condition will be true for instances when *&active* is true and *&salary* is greater than 50,000.
`(*NOT &flag *AND &in03)`	The *NOT in this condition only applies to *&flag*. So this expression will be true if *&flag* is false ('0') and *&in03* is true.
`(*NOT (&flag *AND &in03))`	The *NOT in this condition applies to both *&flag* and *&in03*, because they are enclosed in parentheses. The condition will be true if *&flag* and *&in03* are not both true (i.e., if either or both are false).
`(*NOT &flag *OR *NOT &in03)`	This condition is equivalent to the previous example. The condition is true if either *&flag* or *&in03* is false.

Expression Order of Evaluation

You have learned, with arithmetic expressions, for example, that it is important to understand the order in which an expression will be evaluated in CL. It is equally important, when combining expressions to form compound logical expressions, to know the order in which operators will be evaluated. Figure 10.9 shows the order in which CL evaluates operators in CL expressions. When an expression contains operators of the same order, those operations are performed from left to right. But parentheses can be used to alter the order.

Figure 10.9
Order of Evaluation

1	+, − (when used as signs with decimal values), *NOT, ¬
2	*, /
3	+, − (when used as operators in expressions)
4	*CAT, ‖, *BCAT, |>, *TCAT, |<
5	*EQ, =, *GT, >, *LT, <, *GE, >=, *LE, <=, *NE, ¬ =, *NG, ¬ >, *NL, ¬ <
6	*AND
7	*OR

Chapter Summary

An expression is a group of symbols used to represent a single value. Expressions can be used within most CL command parameters and can contain constants and variables.

Four types of expressions can be used to represent CL command parameters: (1) arithmetic expressions, (2) character string expressions, (3) logical expressions, and (4) relational expressions. Arithmetic expressions always evaluate to a single numeric value. Character expressions always result in a character string. Logical and relational expressions are always either true ('1') or false ('0').

An arithmetic expression always consists of at least two operands separated by arithmetic operators. Arithmetic expressions are always enclosed in parentheses.

The %BIN (binary) built-in function can be used as an operand in an arithmetic expression to extract a binary numeric value from a *CHAR variable.

String expressions combine character data into one character string, using the string operators *CAT, *TCAT, and *BCAT, or their respective symbols: ‖, |>, and |<. String expressions always consist of at least two operands separated by string operators and are enclosed in parentheses.

The %SST (substring) built-in function can be used as an operand in a string expression to extract a portion of a character string.

Relational expressions contain two operands that are compared with each other. If the comparison is true, the expression is true ('1'); otherwise, the expression is false ('0'). Relational expressions are always enclosed in parentheses.

A relational expression will evaluate only operands of identical data types. When the operands in a relational expression contain character data and the operands are not the same length, before the comparison is performed, the shorter operand is extended with blanks to match the length of the longer operand.

Logical expressions evaluate the logical relationship between two operands. The operands used in logical expressions are often themselves relational expressions. The value of a logical expression is evaluated as either being true ('1') or false ('0').

Logical expressions use the logical operators *AND, *OR, and *NOT to make the logical evaluation. A logical expression may contain only one operand, but usually it contains two or more.

Terms

complex expressions
expressions

operand
operator

Review Questions

1. What are expressions and how are they used in CL?
2. Describe the difference between logical, relational, character string, and arithmetic expressions.
3. Examine the following expressions and determine which types of expressions are used.

   a. `(&a + &b)`
   b. `(%SST(&name 1 10) *CAT ' is the name.')`
   c. `(&c *OR &d)`
   d. `(&a > 5)`
   e. `((&a > 5) *AND (%SST(&name 1 10) = 'BOB'))`
   f. `(&c *AND (&b > 16))`
   g. `((&a + 16 / 2) * 3.14)`

4. Using the following declarations, evaluate the expressions in Question 3.

   ```
   DCL    &a      *DEC (5 0)   VALUE(14)
   DCL    &b      *DEC (7 0)   VALUE(6)
   DCL    &c      *LGL         VALUE('1')
   DCL    &d      *LGL
   DCL    &name   *CHAR 15     VALUE('ROBERTA')
   ```

Exercises

1. In this exercise, you will practice using arithmetic expressions. The program will dump the variables so that you can see whether your expressions are constructed correctly.

   a. Copy an existing CLP type source member to a member named SA1001*XXX* in the source physical file QCLSRC. Substitute your initials for *XXX*.
   b. Modify the program information section to reflect the current exercise number, program name, and date.
   c. Modify the declarations section to declare the following variables, with the initial values stated:

Variable Name	Data Type	Length	Initial Value
&num1	Decimal	(3 0)	1
&num2	Decimal	(3 0)	2
&num3	Decimal	(3 0)	3
&num4	Decimal	(3 0)	4
&rslt1	Decimal	(15 5)	0
&rslt2	Decimal	(15 5)	0
&rslt3	Decimal	(15 5)	0
&rslt4	Decimal	(15 5)	0

Exercises continued

Exercises continued

d. Add the commands to perform the following
(the first four commands will use literal numbers
in arithmetic expressions):

- Add 2 to 1 and place the result in &rslt1.
- Subtract 2 from 1 and place the result in
  &rslt2.
- Multiply 1 by 2 and place the result in &rslt3.
- Divide 1 by 2 and place the result in &rslt4.
- Dump the CL program.

(The next four commands will use variables in
arithmetic expressions.)

- Add &num2 to &num1 and place the result
  in &rslt1.
- Subtract &num2 from &num1 and place the
  result in &rslt2.
- Multiply &num1 by &num2 and place the
  result in &rslt3.
- Divide &num1 by &num2 and place the
  result in &rslt4.
- Dump the CL program.

(The next four commands will use signed variables in arithmetic expressions.)

- Multiply &num1 by the negative value of
  &num2 and place the result in &rslt1.
- Divide &num1 by the negative value of
  &num2 and place the result in &rslt2.
- Multiply the negative value of &num1 by
  &num2 and place the result in &rslt3.
- Divide the negative value of &num1 by
  &num2 and place the result in &rslt4.
- Dump the CL program.

(The last four operations will use more than two
operands and parentheses to group the order of
operations.)

- Multiply &num2 by &num3 to produce an
  intermediate result; add &num1 to the
  intermediate result and place the final result
  in &rslt1.

- Multiply &num2 by 2 to produce an intermediate result; divide &num4 by the intermediate
  result and place the final result in &rslt2.
- Add &num1 to &num2 to produce an intermediate result; multiply the intermediate result
  by &num4 and place the final result in &rslt3.
- Divide &num2 by 2 to produce an intermediate
  result; subtract the intermediate result from
  &num4 and place the final result in &rslt4.
- Dump the CL program.

e. Compile and run the program. The program
will create four reports named QPPGMDMP.
Examine the reports. Are the results what you
expected? Did your expressions work correctly?

2. In this exercise, you will practice using numeric
expressions to increment a counter. You will also
practice using the data conversion facility of the
CHGVAR (Change Variable) command. The
program will send a message to your user message queue three times. The message will be
built using character string expressions and will
be sent to your user message queue via the
SNDMSG (Send Message) command.

a. Copy an existing CLP type source member to a
member named SA1002XXX in the source physical file QCLSRC. Substitute your initials for
XXX. As always, update the program information section.

b. Modify the source member to accomplish the
following tasks. (You must determine which variables you need to declare and which commands
should be used to accomplish the tasks. Some
hints are provided.)

Exercises continued

Exercises continued

Your program should do the following:

- Use a loop structure to send a message three times. The first message should say, 'This is message 1'; the second message should say, 'This is message 2'; and the third message should say, 'This is message 3'. Use a variable within the character string expression used to build the message.

Hints:

```
            RTVJOBA   USER(&user)
LOOP:       IF        (&counter = 3)   +
                      GOTO ENDLOOP
            CHGVAR    &counter         +
                      (&counter + 1)

            . . .

            SNDMSG    MSG(&message)    +
                      TOUSR(&user)
            GOTO      LOOP
ENDLOOP:    RETURN
```

c. Compile and run the program. Did your expressions work correctly?

3. In this exercise, you will practice using character string expressions. The program will send a message to the bottom of your display. The message will be built using character string expressions and will be sent to your display via the SNDPGMMSG (Send Program Message) command.

a. Copy an existing CLP type source member to a member named SA1003*XXX* in the source physical file QCLSRC. Substitute your initials for *XXX*. As always, update the program information section.

b. Modify the source member to accomplish the following tasks. (*You* must determine which variables you need to declare, and which commands should be used to accomplish the tasks. Some hints are provided.)

Your program should do the following:

- Retrieve the job attribute that identifies the current user of the program.

Hint: `RTVJOBA USER(&user)`

- Retrieve the system value that identifies the current time of day.

Hint: `RTVSYSVAL QTIME &time`

- Send a program message that says, "Hi *XXXXXXX*, the time is HH:MM:SS." Replace *XXXXXXXX* with the current user and replace HH:MM:SS with the current time. (Colons (:) should be inserted between the hour, minute, and second.)

    The message might look like this:

    Hi STUDENT1, the time is 11:30:45.

    Hint: `SNDPGMMSG`

c. Compile and run the program. Did your expressions work correctly?

4. In this exercise, you will practice using character string expressions, relational expressions, and (perhaps) complex logical expressions. The program will send a message to the bottom of your display. The message will be built using character string expressions and will be sent to your display via the SNDPGMMSG command.

a. Copy an existing CLP type source member to a member named SA1004*XXX* in the source physical file QCLSRC. Substitute your initials for *XXX*. As always, update the program information section.

b. Modify the source member to accomplish the following tasks. (*You* must determine which variables you need to declare, and which commands should be used to accomplish the tasks.)

Exercises continued

Exercises continued

Your program should do the following:

- Retrieve the job attribute that identifies the current user of the program.
- Retrieve the system value that identifies the current time of day.
- Use SNDPGMMSG to send a program message. If the time of day is before 12 noon the message should say, "Good morning XXXXXXX, the time is HH:MM:SS." If the time of day is between 12 noon and 5 P.M., the message should say, "Good afternoon XXXXXXX, the time is HH:MM:SS." Otherwise, the message should say, "Good evening XXXXXXX, the time is HH:MM:SS."

In each of these cases, replace *XXXXXXXX* with the &USER who is running the program and replace HH:MM:SS with the current time, including colon separators (:).

The message might look like this:

Good evening STUDENT1, the time is 23:30:45.

c. Compile and run the program. Do your expressions and IF conditions work correctly? How can you test to determine whether this program will work correctly regardless of the time of day?

Chapter 11

Controlling Workflow

Chapter Overview

In this chapter we define jobs on the AS/400 and introduce the CL commands that control a job's workflow (i.e., that allow you to pass control back and forth between programs, along with information that those programs will use). In addition, we emphasize understanding program invocation levels and the use of the SBMJOB (Submit Job) command.

AS/400 Work Management Overview

How the AS/400 organizes, manages, and processes work is called **work management**. Work management is a complex topic, linking together many facets of the OS/400 operating system. To understand how you can use CL to control workflow, you must first understand a few key work management concepts:

- Interactive jobs
- Batch jobs
- Job descriptions
- Job queues
- Library lists

What Is a Job?

The term **job**, on the AS/400, generally refers to a unit of work, including all the programs and instructions necessary to perform that work. A job can be a simple task, such as producing a report, or it can involve a very complex series of tasks, such as the entire payroll operation. There are two basic types of jobs: *interactive jobs* and *batch jobs*.

When you sign on to the AS/400, you start an interactive job. When you sign off, you end the job. Everything you do between signing on and signing off is part of the same job. Interactive jobs, true to their name, require constant interaction between the user and the computer. The user can perform a number of tasks one at a time, such as selecting a menu option or typing a command. Interactive jobs usually involve typing information into a display screen and waiting for the computer to respond.

A batch job, on the other hand, requires little or no interaction with a workstation user. Usually, you submit a batch job from your interactive job. Some operating systems, such as Microsoft Windows, refer to batch jobs as background jobs. Once you submit a job to batch, it runs without any further input from you. In fact, while the batch job runs, you can continue to do work in your interactive job. Batch jobs usually involve printing reports or processing long-running transactions.

The AS/400 assigns a unique identifier to every AS/400 job. The job identifier consists of three parts: a system assigned job number; the user profile of the user associated with the job; and a general job name identifying either the purpose of the job for batch jobs, or the workstation name for interactive jobs. The job name is a **qualified value**, with the three parts separated by a slash (/). The following are valid job names:

```
024681/DJONES/DSP01
135792/JSMITH/MONTHEND
```

What Is a Job Description?

Every active job on the AS/400 is associated with a job description. Usually, your system administrator assigns a job description to you when (s)he creates your user profile. When you sign on to the system or submit jobs, this job description is used.

A **job description** is an AS/400 object (type *JOBD) containing a set of attributes that define how a job is to be processed. It contains such attributes as the job's execution priority, the name of the printer upon which reports will be printed, the name of the job queue upon which batch jobs will be placed, and the library list that will be associated with the job.

What Is a Job Queue?

When you submit a job for processing, it is not processed immediately. Instead, it is placed into a job queue to wait for available processor resources. A **job queue** is an AS/400 object (type *JOBQ) that acts as a "waiting room" where batch jobs wait in line (queue) for their turn at batch processing. Using a job queue, the AS/400 can run its job load evenly and avoid becoming bogged down by processing too many batch jobs at once. Usually, batch jobs execute in the order they were placed on the job queue; you can, however, hold and release jobs on a job queue or you can assign higher priorities to important jobs that must run before others.

What Is a Library List?

A job's **library list** defines the path of libraries that the job follows when trying to locate programs, files, or other AS/400 objects.

If you are familiar with DOS commands on a personal computer, setting the library list would be analogous to the SET PATH= statement. On the AS/400, if you don't specifically tell the computer in which library an object resides, the job searches its library list for the first occurrence of the object. When a job tries to refer to an object that is not found within the libraries on the library list, an error occurs. You can access an object in a library that is not in the library list if you specifically qualify the name of an object with its library:

```
CALL LIBRARY1/PROGRAM1
```

In the above example, LIBRARY1 need not be within the library list. If, however, you simply specify the following command, the library list is searched for the program named PROGRAM1:

```
CALL PROGRAM1
```

If PROGRAM1 is not found within a library on the library list, an error occurs. The libraries within the library list are searched in a sequential order starting at the top and continuing down until either the program is found or the end of the list is reached. A library list consists of four parts (Figure 11.1).

Figure 11.1
The Library List

Portion of Library List	Abbreviation	Examples of Contents
System library list	SYSLIBL	QSYS QHLPSYS QUSRSYS
Product library	PRDLIB	QPDA
Current library	CURLIB	STUDENT1
User library list	USRLIBL	QTEMP TESTFILES TESTPGMS

The *system library list* contains up to 15 libraries needed by the system to operate. The *product library* is an optional entry, automatically managed by the system when using certain commands, such as STRPDM (Start Program Development Manager). The *current library* is the default library into which newly created objects are placed. The *user library list* contains the names of those libraries containing your programs and applications; the user library list can contain up to 25 library names.

A library list is *not* an AS/400 object. It is, instead, an attribute of a job. The library list is determined primarily by the job description. You can use the following CL commands to display and/or alter the contents of a library list:

- ADDLIBLE (Add library list entry)
- CHGCURLIB (Change current library)
- CHGLIBL (Change library list)
- CHGSYSLIBL (Change system library list)

- DSPLIBL (Display library list)
- EDTLIBL (Edit library list)
- RMVLIBLE (Remove library list entry)

Executing Programs with the CALL Command

On the AS/400, the CALL command is used to run a program. When a program is run, it is in control of the job that issued the CALL command. When the called program ends, control returns to the job, for the next processing step. The CALL command takes the form

```
CALL PGM(library-name/program-name)   +
     PARM(parameter-values)
```

The PGM parameter, which is required, identifies the program you want to CALL. The parameter value is a **qualified name** containing the name of the library in which the program resides and the name of the program itself. For example, if you wanted to run program UPDCUST, which exists in library ARLIB, you enter the command

```
CALL PGM(ARLIB/UPDCUST)
```

The library-name portion of the PGM parameter has a default value of *LIBL. If you use the default value (i.e., you don't specify a library), the AS/400 searches your job's library list to find the program. Thus, the following two commands are equivalent:

```
CALL PGM(*LIBL/PGMA)
CALL PGM(PGMA)
```

In addition to *LIBL, you can specify *CURLIB for the library-name portion of the qualified program name, to indicate that the program resides in the job's current library.

The program and/or the library name can be a CL variable. For example, if a program has declared two variables, &lib and &pgm, to contain a library name and a program name, you could call a program with the command

```
CALL PGM(&lib/&pgm)
```

This command would call the program identified by the value in variable &pgm, which exists in the library identified by the value of variable &lib.

If you include the CALL command in a CL program, the called program need not exist on your system at the time you compile your program. The AS/400 does not try to find the program until you execute your program. However, the called program must be on your system at the time you run your program; otherwise, an error occurs.

When you CALL a program, you can pass values to it. These values are called **parameters**. The called program can access these parameters, and even modify them.

The parameter values are listed in the PARM parameter of the CALL command. Three steps are necessary to pass parameters between two programs:

1. You must list the parameter values in the PARM parameter of the CALL command in the calling program.
2. The PARM parameter of the PGM statement of the called program must list the CL variables that correspond to the parameter values being passed to it.
3. The CL variables for the passed parameters must be declared in the called program.

Figure 11.2 illustrates the mechanism behind passing parameters between programs.

Figure 11.2
Passing Parameters
Between Programs

```
PGMA:     PGM
          CALL PGM(PGMB)                              +
                    PARM('UPDATE' 1357.92)
          RETURN
          ENDPGM
```

```
PGMB:     PGM   PARM(&mode &key)
          DCL   &mode      *CHAR 6
          DCL   &key       *DEC (15 5)
          IF    (&mode *EQ 'ADD   ') DO
                CALL PGM(PGMC) PARM(&key)
                GOTO END
                ENDDO
          IF    (&mode *EQ 'UPDATE') DO
                CALL PGM(PGMD) PARM(&key)
                GOTO END
                ENDDO
          IF    (&mode *EQ 'DELETE') DO
                CALL PGM(PGME) PARM(&key)
                GOTO END
                ENDDO

          IF    (&mode *EQ 'VIEW  ') DO
                CALL PGM(PGMF) PARM(&key)
                ENDDO
END:      RETURN
          ENDPGM
```

In Figure 11.2, PGMA calls PGMB, passing the values *UPDATE* and *1357.92* as parameter values. When PGMB starts running, it automatically receives the passed values, moving them into variables *&mode* and *&key*. PGMB can treat these parameters just like any other CL variable (e.g., testing their values, passing them on to other programs, changing their values). In this case, PGMB tests the value of variable *&mode* to determine which program to call in turn. It then calls either PGMC, PGMD, PGME, or PGMF, passing along the value of variable *&key* (1357.92). In Chapter 13, we discuss the use of parameters in more detail.

ILE Considerations

The Integrated Language Environment (ILE) offers an alternative way to call procedures. The CALLPRC (Call Bound Procedure) command calls an ILE procedure and passes control to it, along with optional parameters. The CALLPRC command can be used in only compiled ILE CL programs; you cannot execute it from a command line or from an Original Program Model (OPM) CL program. We discuss ILE and the CALLPRC command in Chapter 22. The discussion in this chapter relates only to the use of the CALL command.

The Call Stack

When you CALL a program on the AS/400, the calling program remains active, waiting for the called program to end before it resumes execution. The active programs within a job are referred to collectively as the **call stack** (or program stack, or sometimes program invocation stack). The call stack is a list of the active programs in a job, in the order in which they were called. In Figure 11.2, when PGMA calls PGMB, PGMA remains active, waiting at the CALL command until PGMB finishes execution. When PGMB ends by executing a RETURN command, PGMA resumes at the statement following the CALL command — in this case, another RETURN command. While PGMB is active, both PGMA and PGMB are in the call stack. When PGMB ends, it is no longer in the stack. When PGMA ends, neither PGMA nor PGMB is in the call stack.

When a program calls another program, the called program executes at a lower **invocation level** in the call stack. You can think of invocation levels as nesting levels within a job. Invocation levels identify the relationship between active programs in the stack. Figure 11.3 illustrates the invocation levels in a call stack. (All of the programs are assumed to be CL programs.)

Notice in Figure 11.3 that every time a program calls another program, the called program exists at a new invocation level. After MAIN (at level 1) calls PGMA, two programs are in the stack:

1. MAIN
2. PGMA

PGMA subsequently calls PGMB, creating another invocation level, so now there would be three programs in the stack:

1. MAIN
2. PGMA
3. PGMB

PGMB creates yet another invocation level by calling PGMC, resulting in a call stack with four levels:

1. MAIN
2. PGMA

Figure 11.3
Invocation Levels
in a Program Stack

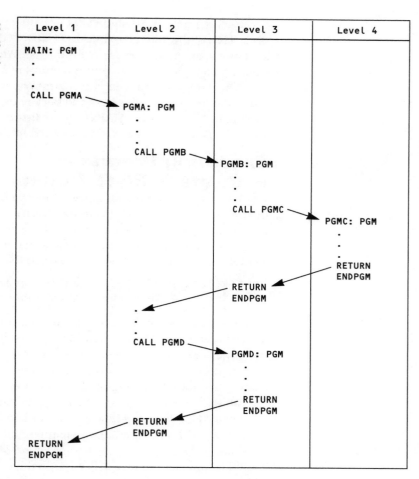

3. PGMB
4. PGMC

When PGMC ends, control returns to PGMB, which also ends, passing control up the stack to PGMA. At this point, we again have two programs in the stack:

1. MAIN
2. PGMA

Instead of ending, however, PGMA later calls PGMD, thus re-creating a third invocation level:

1. MAIN
2. PGMA
3. PGMD

Because programs PGMB and PGMC are no longer active, they no longer exist on the stack. That is why, when PGMA calls PGMD, PGMD executes at the third invocation level, not at an entirely new level for the job. When PGMD ends, it returns control to PGMA, which also ends and returns control to MAIN at the first invocation level.

Whenever a program ends, it returns control to the next program up the stack. When the program at the top of the stack ends, the OS/400 operating system ends the job. In Figure 11.3, if MAIN is at the first invocation level when it ends, the entire job ends. That is, the workstation is signed off.

Executing Programs with the TFRCTL Command

Unlike the CALL command, which allows the calling program to remain active in the call stack, the TFRCTL (Transfer Control) command calls a program, passes control to that program, *then removes the calling program from the call stack*. The TFRCTL command, while beneficial to job management in some cases, is rarely used.The TFRCTL command takes the same form as the CALL command:

```
TFRCTL    PGM(library-name/program-name)   +
          PARM(parameter-variables)
```

When you use the TFRCTL command, even if there appear to be further statements to process in the calling program, they will be ignored and the program that transfers control will end. Reducing the number of programs in the call stack can have a performance benefit. You must keep in mind, however, that the called program cannot return to the calling program. Because the calling program is no longer in the call stack, control will be returned to the next higher program in the stack.

Figure 11.4 illustrates how the call stack in Figure 11.3 would change if TFRCTL instead of CALL were used to invoke programs.

Initially, Figure 11.4 shows one program, MAIN, in the call stack. MAIN uses the TFRCTL command to invoke PGMA, then is dropped from the stack. So when PGMA begins, there is still only one program in the stack, PGMA. PGMA executes PGMB using the CALL command, thus creating another invocation level. There are now two programs in the stack:

1. PGMA
2. PGMB

PGMB uses TFRCTL to execute PGMC. Because TFRCTL drops the calling program from the stack, there are still two programs in the stack:

1. PGMA
2. PGMC

When PGMC ends (at the RETURN command), control is passed back up the stack — not to PGMB, even though it called PGMC, but to PGMA, which then resumes

Figure 11.4
Invocation Levels
in a Program Stack
when Using the
TFRCTL Command

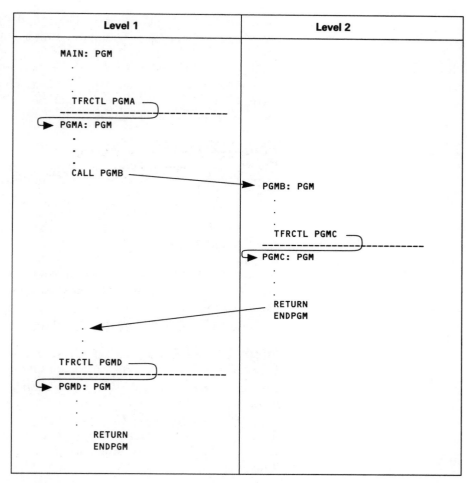

processing. PGMC is dropped from the stack and we again have one program (PGMA) in the call stack at the first invocation level. Later, PGMA uses TFRCTL to pass control to PGMD, then drops out of the stack. During this last step in the process, only PGMD exists in the call stack. When PGMD ends, the job ends.

By using TFRCTL instead of CALL to invoke programs, you can save AS/400 main storage (memory), as well as the machine overhead involved with keeping track of information specific to the invocation levels. Because of these factors, TFRCTL offers a performance advantage over CALL.

When the purpose of a program is to call another program, then end, TFRCTL may be a better choice than CALL. If, however, the calling program needs to complete further processing after starting another program, you must use the CALL command to ensure that the calling program stays active in the stack and receives control again when the called program ends.

There are a few restrictions on the use of the TFRCTL command. The command is valid only within a CL program; you cannot enter it on an interactive command line. If you use TFRCTL to pass parameters, those parameters must be CL variables, not literals. In addition, the parameters passed by the TFRCTL command must have been received by the transferring program as input parameters (i.e., they must have been specified on the PGM statement of the transferring program). Chapter 13 discusses in greater detail parameters as they relate to the TFRCTL command.

The RETURN Command

The RETURN command ends a CL program and removes it from the call stack. Control is returned to the next program up the call stack, where processing resumes at the line following the CALL command. Once a program encounters a RETURN command, processing ends, even if there appear to be subsequent statements in the program that could be processed. If a program running at the first execution level executes a RETURN command, the job ends.

Any time a CL program ends, even if the CL RETURN command is not executed, an implicit RETURN operation occurs. While it is standard practice, it is not required that a CL program contain a RETURN command. When a program reaches the ENDPGM command, or if it sends an escape message (discussed in Chapter 16), the program ends just as surely as if you had specified a RETURN command.

High-Level Language Considerations

Most AS/400 HLLs (e.g., RPG/400 and COBOL/400) allow you to end a called program but have it stay available in the invocation level. For example, a CL program could CALL an RPG/400 program. When the RPG/400 program completes its processing, it can return control to the CL program and remain suspended in the call stack until the CL program CALLs it again, or until the CL program ends. CL programs offer no such capability. When a CL program ends, its invocation is dropped and the program is no longer in the stack.

Executing Commands in Batch Using SBMJOB

The SBMJOB (Submit Job) command allows you to submit a batch job to a job queue. The SBMJOB command has many parameters, but in its simplest form it is expressed as follows:

```
SBMJOB    CMD(CL-command)
```

Once you have submitted a batch job, you are allowed little or no interaction with the job. For example, a batch job normally does not display a screen on your workstation and wait for your input. You can, however, monitor the progress of your batch job using the CL command WRKSBMJOB (Work with Submitted Jobs). Batch processing typically is used for long-running jobs that require no workstation input, such as those that produce printed reports or process a large number of transactions.

A batch job is entirely separate from the job that submitted it, with its own call stack and its own main storage requirements.

Usually you submit a batch job from an interactive workstation. The main advantage of batch processing is that you can continue to do other work on your workstation without waiting for the batch job to finish. Unlike an interactive job, when a batch job is executing, it does not prevent you from using your workstation. Batch processing typically occurs at a lower priority than interactive processing, taking advantage of "lulls in the action" when the AS/400 is not servicing higher priority work, such as interactive workstation jobs. By running long processes in batch, you can improve overall system throughput and maintain faster interactive response times. Running long processes interactively at a high priority, on the other hand, drags down the interactive performance of the AS/400 and can affect every user on the system.

The CMD Parameter of the SBMJOB Command

Let's look at an example of the SBMJOB command.

```
SBMJOB CMD(DSPTAP DEV(TAP01) OUTPUT(*PRINT))
```

In this example, we use the DSPTAP (Display Tape) command to print a report of a tape's contents. Notice that the entire DSPTAP command, including all its parameters, is enclosed within the parentheses of the CMD parameter keyword. You may also have noticed that this command appears to break some of the rules we discussed for command parameters in Chapter 3. At first glance, the value of the CMD parameter would appear to be a character string, but it is not presented as a quoted string. Also, because the value is not a quoted string, you might think that CL would interpret the values within the parentheses as a list of values instead of a single command.

The CMD parameter of the SBMJOB command is a special type of parameter, called a **command string** (*CMDSTR) **parameter**. The correct value for a *CMDSTR parameter is any valid CL command, but *it cannot be enclosed in apostrophes*. Because the system expects a CL command as the value for this parameter, it does not require, and will not allow, a quoted string. Instead, the system checks the command within the CMD parameter separately from the SBMJOB command to be sure the command specified is valid. When you key the SBMJOB command into a CL source member, you must be careful to match beginning and ending parentheses, both for command parameters within the CMD parameter value, and to enclose the entire command string itself. This can be particularly complex if you use keyword notation for the command within the CMD parameter, as we did in the above example. The SEU syntax checker and the CL compiler both reject unmatched parentheses.

A *CMDSTR type parameter also offers you "prompting within prompting" so that you can key the command string using the CL command prompter. When you type *SBMJOB*, then press F4=Prompt to invoke the CL prompter, you can position the cursor on the input line for the CMD parameter value and type a valid command. Then, if you press F4=Prompt again, the CL prompter is invoked a second time, this time for the CL command you typed on the input line. When you fill in the correct parameters for the prompted command, the correct command string is returned within the CMD parameter of the SBMJOB command.

What if you want to run a program rather than execute a CL command when you submit a batch job? That's easy to accomplish. On the SBMJOB command, simply specify the CALL command for the value of the CMD parameter:

```
SBMJOB    CMD(CALL PGM(UPDCUST)    +
          PARM('UPDATE' 1357.92))
```

You might be wondering what a batch job's call stack looks like. Normally, when you use SBMJOB to submit a job for batch processing, the AS/400 puts its own command request processing program, QCMD, at the top of the stack. After that, whatever programs are needed are included in the stack, following the logic that we discussed earlier in this chapter.

Other SBMJOB Parameters

The SBMJOB command offers many parameters to help you specify the environment in which you want a batch job to execute, as well as the job's attributes. Under most circumstances, you will not need to specify these additional parameters, although you may find that using them can make your batch job easier to identify or help you customize the processing of a specific job. We look at only a few of these in this text:

- JOB
- JOBQ
- JOBD
- SYSLIBL
- CURLIB
- INLLIBL
- PRTDEV
- OUTQ
- HOLD
- SCDDATE
- SCDTIME

Job Definition Parameters for SBMJOB

The JOB, JOBQ, and JOBD parameters of the SBMJOB command help define the attributes of the submitted job, and through which job queue it will be submitted. The JOB parameter specifies the name of the job to be submitted; this parameter can help you to identify a batch job by name. You can type a job name in this parameter or use the default special value *JOBD to indicate that the name will come from the entry in the JOBD parameter.

SBMJOB uses the value of the JOBQ parameter to specify the name of the job queue to which this batch job will be submitted. You can type the qualified name of an existing job queue, or you can leave the default special value of *JOBD*, indicating that you want the system to use the JOBQ associated with the job description in the JOBD parameter.

The JOBD parameter identifies the job description that will be used for the batch job. The JOBD parameter has a default value of *USRPRF* (to use the job description specified in your user profile), but you can specify the qualified name of another job description, if necessary.

Library List Parameters for SBMJOB

The SYSLIBL, CURLIB, and INLLIBL parameters of the SBMJOB command define the library list a batch job will use to find programs, files, or other AS/400 objects.

The SYSLIBL parameter of the SBMJOB command determines which libraries will appear in the system portion of the library list for the batch job. For this parameter you cannot specify individual library names. You must use either the default special value *CURRENT* or the other allowable special value *SYSVAL*. *CURRENT tells the system to use the submitting job's current system library list. *SYSVAL indicates that the batch job is to take its system library list from entries in the system value *QSYSLIBL*. (We talk more about system values in Chapter 14.)

The CURLIB parameter allows you to specify the *current library* for the batch job. You can specify the name of an existing library, or you can leave the default value of *CURRENT* (use the submitting job's current library), or you can specify either of the additional special values: *USRPRF* (use the current library indicated in your user profile) or *CRTDFT* (use the system's default current library, QGPL).

The INLLIBL parameter lets you specify a list of libraries that will initially be in the user portion of the library list. This is the library list option that gives you the most flexibility in determining the library list. You can list up to 25 library names in this parameter, but you cannot duplicate a name that already appears in any other portion of the library list. You also can use any of the special values: the default *CURRENT* (use the submitting job's user library list), *SYSVAL* (use the library list entries specified in the system value QUSRLIBL), or *NONE* (the submitted job's user library list will be empty).

SBMJOB Output Parameters

You would use the PRTDEV and OUTQ parameters of the SBMJOB command to determine which printer will be used for reports generated by the batch job. Usually, reports are not printed directly on the printer. Instead, they are stored on an **output queue**. An output queue is an AS/400 object used to hold reports until a printer has time to print them. Usually, the name of the output queue matches the name of the actual printer device.

The PRTDEV parameter specifies the name of the default printer device for the batch job. You can specify the name of a printer device for this parameter, or you can use any of the allowed special values: *CURRENT* (the default) tells the batch job to use the same printer that the submitting job (usually your interactive job) is using; *USRPRF* indicates that the batch job is to use the device named in the your user profile; *SYSVAL* uses the device named in the system value QPRTDEV; and *JOBD* specifies that the batch job is to use the printer device named in the job description.

The OUTQ parameter specifies the qualified name of the output queue into which the batch job will place its reports. You can specify the qualified name of an actual output queue, or you can use one of the following special values: *CURRENT* (the default) uses the output queue associated with the submitting job; *USRPRF* specifies that the batch job will use the output queue specified in your user profile; *DEV* tells the batch job to use the output queue that is associated with the printer device named in the PRTDEV parameter; and *JOBD* uses the output queue named in the job description.

Scheduling Parameters for SBMJOB

If you specify HOLD(*YES) on the SBMJOB command, the batch job will be held on the job queue and will not be processed until someone (usually the system operator) releases it with the RLSJOB (Release Job) command.

If you specify HOLD(*NO), the job will not be held on the job queue and will be processed when its turn comes up. You also can use the default HOLD(*JOBD) to indicate that the hold attribute of a job is to be taken from its job description.

The SCDDATE and SCDTIME parameters let you schedule a batch job to run on a specific date at a specific time. If you use the default values SCDDATE(*CURRENT) and SCDTIME(*CURRENT), the job will be processed as soon as resources are available. In addition to *CURRENT*, you can specify a specific date and time for the job to run. For example, you could use the following command to submit a job to run on January 15, 1998, at 2:00 P.M..:

```
SBMJOB    CMD(CALL PROGRAM1)    +
          SCDDATE(011598)       +
          SCDTIME(140000)
```

Notice that the time is specified in 24-hour (military) format. It's also worth noting that the date must be in the same format as your job's date format. In the United States, this usually will be month/day/year format, but in other countries it may be different.

The SCDDATE parameter also allows some extra flexibility in scheduling. You can indicate special values to run a job on a particular day (e.g., *SUN* for Sunday, *MON* for Monday, and *TUE, *WED, *THU, *FRI,* or *SAT*). In addition, the special values *MONTHSTR* and *MONTHEND* allow you to specify that a job should run on the first or last day of the month, respectively. The system also considers the SCDTIME in determining the date to run the job. If, for example, it is Monday morning and you specify the following command, the job will run the same day:

```
SBMJOB    CMD(CALL PROGRAM1)    +
          SCDDATE(*MON)         +
          SCDTIME(120100)
```

If, on the other hand, it is Monday evening and you enter the above command, the job will run *the following* Monday because the scheduled time has passed.

The Self-Submitting Program

Submitting long-running jobs to batch will enhance your AS/400's overall performance and should be encouraged wherever it is practical to do so. One way that you can enforce the batch processing of a specific program is to have the program submit itself for batch processing. You can do this by taking advantage of one of the job's attributes, the *job type*, which indicates the environment in which a job is running: interactive or batch. It is possible to retrieve this information within a CL program using the RTVJOBA (Retrieve Job Attributes) command. We talk more about the RTVJOBA command in Chapter 14, but a brief discussion of the self-submitting technique is appropriate here. The program in Figure 11.5 illustrates a method of enforcing batch processing of a program.

The program in Figure 11.5 receives two parameters and declares a one-character variable called *&jobtype*, which will be used to store the job's environment (batch or interactive). The RTVJOBA command that follows the declaration of variables retrieves the job attribute TYPE. If the job is interactive, the TYPE attribute placed in the *&jobtype* variable will be a *1*; if the job is running in batch, a *0* is placed in variable *&jobtype*.

Figure 11.5
Self-Submitting
Program

```
UPDCUST:  PGM        PARM(&mode &custnbr)

          DCL        &mode      *CHAR 6
          DCL        &custnbr   *DEC (15 5)
          DCL        &jobtype   *CHAR 1

          RTVJOBA    TYPE(&jobtype)

          IF         (&jobtype = '1')    DO
          SBMJOB     CMD(CALL  PGM(UPDCUST) +
                     PARM(&mode &custnbr))
          RETURN
          ENDDO

          ...
          (Continue processing)
          ...

          ENDPGM
```

Next, the program tests the value of variable *&jobtype*. If the variable has a value of *1*, indicating that it is running interactively, the program executes a SBMJOB command. This command submits a job for batch processing that will CALL the same program and pass the same parameters; it then ends with a RETURN command. If, on the other hand, variable *&jobtype* has a value of *0*, indicating the job already is running in batch, the program skips over the DO/ENDDO group and continues with its processing. If you use this technique, the program will always do the bulk of its processing in batch, even if the user runs the program interactively with the CALL command:

```
CALL PGM(UPDCUST)                       +
      PARM('UPDATE'   1357.92)
```

Notice that even after the program executes the SBMJOB command, it continues to execute. You could follow the SBMJOB command with a message to the user informing him or her that the job was submitted. Remember to follow the SBMJOB command with a RETURN command; otherwise, the program will continue to execute subsequent commands. The submitted job executes independently of the submitting (interactive) job.

Chapter Summary

Work management on the AS/400 describes how the machine organizes, manages, and processes work. A unit of work on the AS/400 is a job. A job includes all programs, and instructions necessary to perform work. There are two basic types of jobs: interactive and batch.

A job description is an AS/400 object containing a set of attributes that define how a job will execute. A job queue is an AS/400 object that holds batch jobs and releases them for processing as system resources are available. A job's library list defines the path of libraries that will be used when trying to find programs, files, or other AS/400 objects.

The CALL command runs a program and passes control to that program. When the called program ends, control is returned to the next command in the calling program.

When you call a program, you can pass parameters to that program. The called program can use and/or modify the parameters. When a program is called, it is placed in the call stack, a list of the active programs in a job, in the order in which they were called. When you use CALL to run a program, the called program runs at a lower invocation level than the calling program.

The TFRCTL (Transfer Control) command calls a program, passes control to it, then removes the calling program from the call stack. The TFRCTL command is valid only in a CL program. When you use TFRCTL to run a program, the called program runs at the same invocation level as the calling program, which is no longer in the call stack. Though seldom used, the TFRCTL command may improve performance by decreasing the size of the call stack and by decreasing the overhead required to keep track of programs in the stack.

The RETURN command ends a program and removes it from the call stack. When a CL program ends, a RETURN command is always executed, even if it is not specifically coded in the program.

The SBMJOB (Submit Job) command allows a job to submit a batch job to a job queue. Processing long-running programs and commands in a batch environment offers an overall system performance advantage. Batch jobs usually run at a lower priority than interactive jobs. The CMD parameter of the SBMJOB command is a special type of parameter, called a command string (*CMDSTR). *CMDSTR parameters can contain any valid CL command not enclosed in apostrophes. *CMDSTR parameters offer an additional level of CL prompting. The SBMJOB command offers many parameters that you can use to further define or customize a batch job. These parameters allow you to specify such things as job name, library list, printer device, and scheduling information for a batch job.

Terms

call stack	job description	qualified name
command string parameter	job queue	qualified value
invocation level	library list	work management
job	parameters	

Review Questions

1. How would you define work management on the AS/400?

2. What are the two basic types of AS/400 jobs?

3. What is a library list, and what are its four components?

4. Name two CL commands that allow you to execute a program. In what ways is each of them unique?

5. What mechanism can you use to communicate values between programs? What are the three basic requirements necessary to accomplish this end?

6. Examine the following segment of code from a CL program. List, in order, the contents of the program invocation stack as this program executes the statement at label A, then again at labels B and C. (Assume no programs other than the ones shown here are active. Assume all the programs are CL programs.)

```
PGMA:       PGM
A:          CALL      CHGCUST
B:          IF        (&IN03)     GOTO END
C:          TFRCTL    APPCUST
END:        ENDPGM
```

7. In the segment of code shown for Question 6, what will happen to the program stack and to the job when program APPCUST ends?

Exercises

1. In this exercise, you practice using the CALL command with parameters. A knowledge of character string expressions is required. The program accepts a parameter and includes the parameter in a message that will be sent to the bottom of your screen via the SNDPGMMSG command.

   a. Copy an existing CLP-type source member to a member named SA1101XXX in the source physical file QCLSRC. Substitute your initials for XXX. As always, update the program information section.

   b. Modify the source member to accomplish the following tasks:
      - Accept a character parameter that is three characters long. The name of the parameter should be &char3. Hint: You accept a parameter on the PGM command, but you also need to use the DCL (Declare) command.
      - Declare a variable named &text that contains the character string *The PARM is*.

Exercises continued

Exercises continued

- Send a message with the command SNDPGMMSG. If the value of *&char3* is *Bob*, the message should say *The PARM is Bob*.

c. Compile the program. Go to an AS/400 command line and call the program several times, supplying a different three-character PARM value each time. For example:

```
CALL SA1101XXX PARM('Bob')
```

2. From a command line, use the SBMJOB command to submit the program from the job in Exercise 1 for batch processing. (Don't forget to supply the PARM keyword value.) On the SBMJOB command, specify the LOG parameter as 4 0 *SECLVL*. For example:

```
SBMJOB   CMD(CALL SA1101XXX PARM('Dot'))  +
         LOG(4 0 *SECLVL)
```

This specification for the LOG parameter of the SBMJOB command ensures that a job log is produced. The job log contains all messages generated by your program. You can see the job log by finding the spooled output file named QPJOBLOG and either viewing or printing it. You can monitor the progress of your batch job and view any spooled files created by the job by using the WRKSBMJOB (Work with Submitted Jobs) command. Examine the QPJOBLOG spooled file. Do you see the message that you sent from your program?

3. In this exercise, you again practice using the CALL command with parameters. The program displays the contents of an AS/400 library on your workstation screen. When the program is submitted for batch processing, a printed listing of the contents of a library is generated.

    a. Copy an existing CLP-type source member to a member named SA1103*XXX* in the source physical file QCLSRC. Substitute your initials for *XXX*. As always, update the program information section.

b. Modify the source member to accomplish the following tasks:

- Accept a character parameter that is 10 characters long. The name of the parameter should be *&library*.
- Use the DSPLIB (Display Library) command to display the contents of the library specified as the PARM. The command that you will use is:

```
DSPLIB LIB(&library)
```

c. Compile the program. Go to an AS/400 command line and call the program, supplying the name of your library as the parameter. For example:

```
CALL SA1103XXX PARM('MYLIBRARY')
```

d. Call the program again. This time, use a different library name. (Note: If you specify the name of a library that does not exist on your system, you will get an error message: *CPF2110 Library not found*. Press the Enter key and the message will disappear. You learn in Chapter 12 how to deal with these error messages correctly.)

4. From a command line, use the SBMJOB command to submit the job for batch processing. (Don't forget to supply the name of your library for the PARM keyword value.) When you submit the job, give the job a name you can remember. For example:

```
SBMJOB                                      +
    CMD(CALL SA1103XXX PARM(MYLIB))  +
    JOB(MY_DISPLAY)
```

Caution: When running this program in batch mode with the SBMJOB command, be sure to enter the name of a valid AS/400 library. If you supply the name of an AS/400 library that does not exist, an error message will be sent to the AS/400 system operator.

Exercises continued

Exercises continued

When this program is submitted for batch processing, a printed listing of the library will be generated even though you did not specify OUTPUT(*PRINT) on the DSPLIB command. This occurs because a batch job cannot normally send screens to a workstation. Using the WRKSBMJOB command, find the spooled file that is created by the batch job. Does it contain any information that is not shown when it is displayed on your workstation screen? If so, what?

5. In this exercise you write a "self-submitting" program. The program prints the contents of an AS/400 library. When the job is submitted, a message will be sent to the workstation screen.

   a. Copy the CLP source member from Exercise 3 to a member named SA1105*XXX* in the source physical file QCLSRC. Substitute your initials for *XXX*. As always, update the program information section.

   b. Modify the source member, if necessary, to accomplish the following tasks:

      • Accept a character parameter that is 10 characters long. The name of the parameter should be *&library*.

      • Determine whether the job is running interactively or in batch mode.

      • If the job is running interactively, submit the job to batch. Give the batch job a descriptive name that you can remember. If you need help, refer to Figure 11.5.

      • After the job is submitted, use the SNDPGMMSG command to send the work-station user a message indicating that the batch job has been submitted.

      • If the job is running as a batch job, use the DSPLIB command to print the contents of the library specified as the PARM.

   c. Compile the program. From an AS/400 command line, call the program, supplying the name of your library as the parameter.
      Use the WRKSBMJOB command to monitor the progress of your submitted job and to view the spooled files.

   d. Call the program again, this time using a different library name.

      Caution: When running this program, be sure to enter the name of a valid AS/400 library. If you supply the name of an AS/400 library that does not exist, the error message will be sent to the AS/400 system operator.

   e. As in the previous exercise, when this program is submitted for batch processing, a printed listing of the library will be generated even though you did not specify OUTPUT(*PRINT) on the DSPLIB command. Using the WRKSBMJOB command, view or print the spooled file created by the job. Was a spooled file named QPJOBLOG also printed for this job?

6. When signed on to the AS/400, press the System Request (SysRq) key. Press the Enter key to access the System Request menu. Select menu option 3 to display the current job. Then select option 11 to view your program invocation stack. What programs are currently in your job's invocation stack? What can you conclude from this?

7. From an AS/400 command line, enter the command DSPLIBL (Display Library List). Identify which libraries are in which portion of your library list. What can you conclude from this?

Chapter 12

Basic Error Handling

Chapter Overview

This chapter introduces ways to handle expected and unexpected errors that may occur when a CL program is executed. We discuss the CL MONMSG (Monitor Message) command and the concept of command-level and program-level message monitors.

Types of Errors

There may be occasions when a CL program cannot successfully execute some or all of the commands contained within the program. The result is a program error.

Some program errors can be anticipated. For instance, if a CL program contains a command to check for the existence of a file, you could reasonably expect that the file might not exist. When the command is executed and the file you are checking for does not exist, an error condition occurs.

At times, you cannot anticipate program errors. For example, suppose a CL program calls another program named PROGRAM2. If someone has deleted PROGRAM2 without your knowledge, a CALL to PROGRAM2 causes an error condition.

Yet another type of error, caused by an abnormal cancellation, can occur during a system power failure, or if someone terminates the job in which your program is running. In these situations, your program ends immediately, with no chance to recover from the error. Aside from including specific restart logic within a program, there is no way to handle abnormal cancellation errors.

It is your responsibility as a programmer to ensure that a program will handle errors correctly. The remainder of this chapter demonstrates how to handle expected and unexpected errors.

Error Messages

If an error condition occurs during execution of a CL program, a special kind of message, called an **escape message** (*ESCAPE), is automatically sent to the program. The escape message identifies the specific error that occurred. Consider the following example: You would use the CHKOBJ (Check Object) command in a CL program if you wanted to determine whether a particular object existed on the system:

```
CHKOBJ STUDENT1/ZZZZZ    *FILE
```

In this example, if the file ZZZZZ exists in library STUDENT1, your program simply continues on to the next command. However, if the file cannot be found in the library, an escape message is sent to your program indicating the specific error that occurred. In this case, the escape message would state, *Object ZZZZZ in library STUDENT1 not found.*

If the system detects an escape message, the system sends an inquiry (*INQ) message to the end user (for an interactive job) or to the system operator (for a batch job), and does not continue until the end user or the system operator responds. Figure 12.1 shows the Program Messages display received by the interactive user of a program containing an error. Notice that the user of the program is presented with the error message followed by four possible actions (s)he can perform. A line is provided at the bottom of the display to enter the user's reply. If the user enters *C* (cancel), the program will be cancelled. If the user enters *D* (dump), a program dump will be printed and the program will be cancelled. If an *I* (ignore) is entered, the error will be ignored and the program will continue as if no error had occurred. Finally, if *R* (retry) is entered, the command in error will be tried again. (See "The CHKOBJ Command," at right.)

Figure 12.1
Program
Messages
Display

```
                          Display Program Messages
 Job 122723/STUDENT1/DSP13 started on 07/15/93 at 08:47:22 in subsystem QINTER in
 CPF9801 received by PROGRAM1 at 2000. (C D I R)














 Type reply, press Enter.
   Reply . . .  _____


 F3=Exit    F12=Cancel
```

Many AS/400 programmers refer to the screen in Figure 12.1 as the "ugly screen" because when this unfriendly screen is displayed to a user, it can produce an ugly situation. The end user, not the programmer, is in control of what happens next (i.e., whether the program is canceled or the command in error dumped, ignored, or retried) — a situation that should not occur. In "The MONMSG Command," you see how you can minimize the chances that the user of a program sees this screen.

The CHKOBJ Command

The CHKOBJ (Check Object) command is used primarily to determine whether a particular object exists, and optionally to check a user's authority to the object. The syntax of the command is as follows:

```
CHKOBJ    OBJ(library-name/object-name)   +
          OBJTYPE(object-type)            +
          MBR(member-name)                +
          AUT(authority-to-check)
```

Using the CHKOBJ command, you can request that one or more tests be performed on an object. If the object being tested does not successfully meet the test criteria, an escape message is generated. The escape message identifies the test that the object failed to pass.

The Object Existence Test

To determine whether an object exists, you can perform an object existence test by using the following CHKOBJ command format:

```
CHKOBJ    OBJ(MYLIBRARY/MYFILE)           +
          OBJTYPE(*FILE)
```

You would specify the object name and the object type. In this example, the object name is *MYFILE* in library *MYLIBRARY*. The object type is a *FILE*. Because the default value for the object library is *LIBL*, you could use the command

```
CHKOBJ    OBJ(MYFILE)                     +
          OBJTYPE(*FILE)
```

to check for the existence of a file named *MYFILE* that exists within a library on the library list.

The OBJTYPE parameter can be any AS/400 object type — for example, *FILE* (file), *PGM* (program), *CMD* (command), or *MSGF* (message file). If the object or library you specify is *not found,* an escape message is generated. If the object is found, *no message* is generated and the program continues with the next command.

The File Member Existence Test

You can use the CHKOBJ command to determine whether a member exists within a file. Using this type of test, you actually are performing two tests in one: one to determine whether the file exists and one to determine whether the member within the file exists. To perform this type of test, the object type must be *FILE* :

```
CHKOBJ    OBJ(MYFILE)                     +
          OBJTYPE(*FILE)                  +
          MBR(MEMBER1)
```

Continued

The CHKOBJ Command continued

In this example, you are testing to see whether the file exists within a library on your library list and to see whether there is a member in the file with the name *MEMBER1*. If either of these tests fails, an escape message is generated.

The default value of the MBR parameter is *NONE*, which would mean that a file would not be checked for members. As we did in the above example, you must specify a value for the MBR parameter to check for the existence of a member.

The Object Authority Test

The object authority test allows you to determine what authority a user has to a specified object. This type of test also executes the object existence test, and if specified, the file member existence test. Any object type can be used for this test:

```
CHKOBJ      OBJ(LIB1/MYPROGRAM)      +
            OBJTYPE(*PGM)            +
            AUT(*ALL)
```

In this example, the object existence test is used to determine whether program *MYPROGRAM* exists in library *LIB1*. If the program does not exist, an escape message is generated and checking stops. If the program does exist, the authority of the object is checked to determine whether the user running the program has *ALL authority to the program. If the user does not have *ALL authority, an escape message is sent. If the user does have *ALL authority, no message is generated and the program continues with the next command.

The default value for the AUT parameter, *NONE*, means no authority checks would be performed. The following values are allowed for the AUT parameter:

```
*NONE            *OBJMGMT
*CHANGE          *OBJOPR
*ALL             *ADD
*USE             *DLT
*EXCLUDE         *READ
*AUTLMGT         *UPD
*OBJEXIST
```

Up to seven of the above values can be specified as a list value for the AUT parameter, as shown in the following example:

```
CHKOBJ      OBJ(LIB1/MYFILE)         +
            OBJTYPE(*FILE)           +
            AUT(*READ *DLT *UPD)
```

Message Files

The descriptions of all IBM-supplied messages are stored in a special type of file, called a **message file**. Message files (AS/400 object type *MSGF) are similar to database files (object type *FILE), but they are used specifically to store the descriptions of messages. Most messages that can be generated within a CL program are stored in an IBM-supplied message file named QCPFMSG in library QSYS. You can display the contents of a message file by using the DSPMSGD (Display Message Description) or WRKMSGD (Work with Message Description) commands. Figure 12.2 shows a partial display of message file QCPFMSG.

Figure 12.2
QCPFMSG
Message File
Partial List

```
                        Work with Message Descriptions
                                                      System:    STUDENT1
    Message file:   QCPFMSG        Library:   QSYS

    Position to . . . . . . .  _____     Message ID

    Type options, press Enter.
      2=Change   4=Delete   5=Display details   6=Print

    Opt   Message ID   Severity   Message Text
     _     CPF9509        40       Space access error.
     _     CPF98A1        40       Cannot find object to match specified name.
     _     CPF9801        40       Object &2 in library &3 not found.
     _     CPF9802        40       Not authorized to object &2 in &3.
     _     CPF9803        40       Cannot allocate object &2 in library &3.
     _     CPF9804        40       Object &2 in library &3 damaged.
     _     CPF9805        40       Object &2 in library &3 destroyed.
     _     CPF9806        40       Cannot perform function for object &2 in library &3
                                                                      More...
    Parameters or command
    ===> _____
    F3=Exit   F5=Refresh   F6=Add   F12=Cancel   F24=More keys
```

In Figure 12.2, you can see that each message has a unique **message identifier** and descriptive text. When an error occurs in your program, the system sends the corresponding message to your program. For example, when an object is not found by the CHKOBJ command, the message identifier used is CPF9801. The descriptive text for the message CPF9801 in the message file is *Object &2 in library &3 not found.* Before the message is sent to your program, the system replaces any substitution variables (e.g., &2 and &3) with the appropriate data, and sends the message to the program as an escape message.

Note: Most messages in the QCPFMSG message file are not intended to signal error conditions. In fact, many messages are used to signal the successful completion of an operation. The description of a message in a message file does not contain information as to how the message will be used. The same message could, for example, be used by one program as an escape message and by another as a completion message, to signal the successful completion of a process.

The message prefix (e.g., *CPF* in CPF9801) indicates which functional portion of the AS/400 sent the message. The prefix CPF indicates that the message was sent by the base OS/400 operating system. If the message prefix is *RPG* or *CBL*, the message was sent from the runtime support modules of RPG or Cobol, respectively. The AS/400 has dozens of IBM-supplied message files and message prefixes.

Following the prefix is a four-position message ID (e.g., *9801* in message identifier CPF9801). The message ID is a numeric value that can contain the numbers 0–9 and the hex numbers A–F. So a message ID of CPFABC9 would be considered valid. The prefix is CPF and the message ID is ABC9.

The MONMSG Command

To detect when an escape message has been sent to a program, you must use the CL MONMSG (Monitor Message) command, designed specifically for that purpose. The MONMSG command monitors for the arrival of an escape message within a program and allows you to take the appropriate action within the program to fix the problem that caused the message to be generated. Appropriate use of the MONMSG command properly ensures that an end user won't see the "ugly screen."

There are many types of messages that can be sent to your program. These include escape messages, diagnostic messages, completion messages, and notify messages. The different types are covered in detail in Chapter 16. For now, it's important for you to know that The MONMSG command can detect only escape messages, and under very rare circumstances, status and notify messages; it cannot detect diagnostic or completion messages.

As a rule, you should always use the MONMSG command within your CL programs to detect escape messages. If an error occurs and you do not monitor for the escape message, the Program Messages display appears; or in the case of a batch job, the system operator receives an inquiry message and must supply the correct reply.

The syntax of the MONMSG command is as follows:

```
MONMSG      MSGID(message-identifier)   +
            CMPDTA(comparison-data)      +
            EXEC(CL-command)
```

The required MSGID parameter specifies the message identifier of the message you want to monitor for. You can specify a list of up to 50 messages within the MSGID parameter. You cannot specify a variable as a message identifier. Within CL, you deal mostly with OS/400 operating system messages; therefore, the message identifiers almost always start with the prefix CPF.

The optional, and rarely used, CMPDTA parameter specifies any comparison data. The default value, which is almost always used, is *NONE*. You cannot specify a variable for the CMPDTA value.

The optional EXEC parameter specifies a single CL command to be executed if the escape message specified on the MSGID parameter is received. A variable cannot be specified.

Here are three examples of how the MONMSG command would be used:

```
MONMSG      MSGID(CPF9801)                               +
            EXEC(GOTO NOT_FOUND)
MONMSG      CPF9801                                      +
            EXEC(SNDPGMMSG 'File not found')
MONMSG      MSGID(CPF9801 CPF9803 CPF9805)     +
            EXEC(GOTO ERROR)
```

Command-Level MONMSG

Two levels of message monitors are available within a CL program: a **command-level message monitor** (discussed in this section) and a **program-level message monitor** (discussed in the following section). A command-level message monitor checks only for escape messages generated by a single command; a program-level message monitor checks for escape messages issued by all commands within the program.

To monitor for messages generated by a single command (i.e., at the command level), the MONMSG command must immediately follow the command. The sample program in Figure 12.3 shows how you might use a command-level message monitor. The program uses the CHKOBJ (Check Object) command to check for the existence of a file; if the file is not found, the program creates the file using the CRTPF (Create Physical File) command.

Figure 12.3
Sample
Command-Level
MONMSG

```
PGM
CHKOBJ      APFILES/WORKFILE      *FILE
MONMSG      MSGID(CPF9801)                               +
            EXEC(CRTPF APFILES/WORKFILE RCDLEN(80))
CALL        APDAYEND
RETURN
ENDPGM
```

After the command specified on the EXEC parameter is executed, the program continues with the next command in sequence. If the EXEC parameter contains a GOTO command, control is passed to the command specified at that label. If the command specified on the EXEC parameter is the RETURN command, the program ends normally.

In Figure 12.3, if the MONMSG command did not immediately follow the CHKOBJ command, the program would receive an unmonitored escape message. This would cause an inquiry message to be sent and the program would wait until a reply was entered. In such a case, you would not have the option to create the file; instead, you would probably have to cancel the program.

When you use a command-level message monitor, it is in effect only for the *single* command that *immediately precedes it.* Consider the example in Figure 12.4. In this example, assume that the first CHKOBJ command generates the escape message CPF9801 (Object not found). Because a MONMSG command does not immediately follow the first CHKOBJ command, no message monitor would be in effect when the command is executed and an inquiry message would be sent. In this program, a message monitor is in effect only for the second CHKOBJ command.

Figure 12.4
Command-Level
MONMSG Used Once

```
PGM
CHKOBJ     APFILES/WORKFILE      *FILE      /* this is unmonitored */
CHKOBJ     APFILES/WORKFILE2     *FILE
MONMSG     MSGID(CPF9801)                                   +
           EXEC(CRTPF APFILES/WORKFILE2 RCDLEN(80))
CALL       APDAYEND
RETURN
ENDPGM
```

Program-Level MONMSG

A program-level MONMSG allows you to use just one MONMSG command to monitor for error messages generated by all commands within a CL program. Instead of placing a MONMSG command after each command in your CL program, you can specify just one MONMSG command *before* the first executable command within your program.

The program-level MONMSG is often referred to as a **global message monitor** because it affects every command within the program. A program-level MONMSG is specified as the first statement in the procedure section of a CL program and must appear immediately after the declarations section, if that section exists. The command would follow this format:

```
MONMSG     MSGID(CPF0000)            +
           EXEC(GOTO ERROR_RTN)
```

In this example the message monitor checks for the message CPF0000, which is a special message identifier that is used to monitor for *all* messages that begin with the prefix CPF. The characters 0000 are used as a mask, indicating that any message that starts with CPF will be intercepted by the message monitor. We look at this message more closely in "Monitoring for Generic Messages" (page 174).

In the above example, ERROR_RTN is a label that starts an error-handling procedure. When using a program-level — or global — MONMSG, you should always branch to an error-handling routine whenever a monitored message occurs, regardless of where it occurs within the program. When used in this way, the error-handling procedure must be generic enough to properly deal with the error that has occurred.

The example in Figure 12.5 demonstrates the use of a program-level MONMSG and an error-handling routine. Using a MONMSG command as shown would have the same effect as placing the MONMSG command immediately after each command in the program.

In Figure 12.5, if either of the two CHKOBJ commands fails and error message CPF9801 is sent, control passes to label ERROR_RTN. Although the MONMSG command would also be in effect for the rest of the commands in the program, it would be ignored because none of the other commands can generate message CPF9801.

When you enter the MONMSG command at the program level rather than the command level, there is one restriction: The EXEC parameter of a program-level

Figure 12.5
Program-Level
MONMSG

```
PGM
DCL  &var      *CHAR 10
DCL  &var2     *CHAR  2
DCLF MYFILE

MONMSG     MSGID(CPF9801) EXEC(GOTO ERROR_RTN)

...

CHKOBJ     *LIBL/MYFILE   +
           *FILE          +
           MBR(MEMBER1)   +
           AUT(*ALL)      +
CHKOBJ     *LIBL/MYFILE2
           *FILE          +
           MBR(MEMBER2)   +
           AUT(*ALL)

...

CALL MYPGM
GOTO ENDIT

ERROR_RTN:
    DMPCLPGM                          /* Dump the CL program  */
    MONMSG     MSGID(CPF0000) /* Just in case          */
    SNDPGMMSG MSG('Error occurred in program.')

ENDIT:
    RETURN
    ENDPGM
```

MONMSG command, if it is used, *must* specify a GOTO command. No other command can be used with the EXEC parameter at the program level. If the EXEC parameter is omitted, all errors within the program are ignored. (Note: It is seldom reasonable to ignore all error messages within a program because unpredictable results often occur.)

You may have noticed that the DMPCLPGM (Dump CL Program) command that appears in the error routine is followed by a command-level MONMSG. Use of the command-level MONMSG without the EXEC parameter ensures that if an error occurs on the DMPCLPGM command, it will be ignored. If the command-level MONMSG was not included, the program could go into a never-ending loop: If the program encountered an error, it would branch to ERR_RTN. If, in the error-handling routine, the DMPCLPGM command generated an error, the program would again branch to ERR_RTN, which in turn would try to execute DMPCLPGM, which would likely generate another error, causing another branch to ERR_RTN, and so on. This loop would continue until the job was canceled. You should always use a command-level MONMSG for each command within an error-handling routine that can generate an error.

Coding in Style

- The MONMSG command is more readable if you omit the following common keywords:

  ```
  MSGID
  CMPDTA
  ```

  For example, instead of using keyword notation,

  ```
  MONMSG     MSGID(CPF9801)   +
             EXEC(RETURN)
  ```

  use the following positional notation:

  ```
  MONMSG     CPF9801    EXEC(RETURN)
  ```

  Unfortunately, the seldom-used CMPDTA parameter is the second positional parameter in the MONMSG command, while the often-used EXEC parameter is third. You cannot, therefore, use positional notation for the EXEC parameter unless you include the CMPDTA parameter. The following command will not work:

  ```
  MONMSG     CPF9801    RETURN
  ```

  You can, however, include the *N null value for the CMPDTA parameter if you want to specify the EXEC parameter in positional notation:

  ```
  MONMSG     CPF9801    *N RETURN
  ```

  Usually, though, you'll find that the EXEC parameter is specified in keyword notation:

  ```
  MONMSG     CPF9801    EXEC(RETURN)
  ```

- It's good programming practice to always use DO groups in connection with command-level MONMSG commands, even if you will only execute a single command because of the error. This technique lends to the program's ease of maintenance by allowing you the freedom to easily insert commands into a DO group. It also makes the MONMSG specification easier to read, by generally limiting it to one line. Program-level (global) MONMSG commands, however, do not allow a DO group.

Mixing Command- and Program-Level MONMSGs

In the example in Figure 12.5, you saw how a command-level message monitor can be used within a program that contains a program-level message monitor. Using the command-level message monitor allowed the program to ignore a message the program-level message monitor was looking for. Whenever an error message is generated, the program-level message monitor will be used only if there is no command-level message monitor. That is, command-level MONMSG commands are always evaluated first; if a command-level MONMSG is in effect for an error that occurs on a command, the program-level MONMSG is not used. If no message monitor exists at either the program level or the command level, the system's default error-handling routine takes control and sends the "ugly screen." Figure 12.6 illustrates how you might mix program- and command-level message monitors.

Figure 12.6
Mixing Program- and Command-Level MONMSGs

```
        PGM
        DCL     &var    *CHAR 10
        DCL     &var2   *CHAR  2
        DCLF MYFILE

        MONMSG     MSGID(CPF0000)                              +
                   EXEC(GOTO ERROR_RTN)

        ...

        ADDLIBLE   APFILES
        MONMSG     MSGID(CPF2103) /* already in list */
        CHKOBJ     *LIBL/MYFILE                                +
                   *FILE                                       +
                   MBR(MEMBER1)                                +
                   AUT(*ALL)
        MONMSG     MSGID(CPF9801)                              +
                   EXEC(CRTPF APFILES/MYFILE RCDLEN(80))

        CALL       MYPGM                                       +
                   PARM(&var)
        GOTO       ENDIT

ERROR_RTN:
        DMPCLPGM                            /* Dump the CL program  */
        MONMSG     MSGID(CPF0000) /* Just in case          */
        SNDPGMMSG MSG('Error occurred in program.')

ENDIT:
        RETURN
        ENDPGM
```

In this example, a global MONMSG command has been specified to trap any CPF messages by using CPF0000 as the monitored message identifier. The program also contains three command-level MONMSG commands that will be in effect for the three commands they follow: the ADDLIBLE command, the CHKOBJ command, and the DMPCLPGM command. If an error is generated by the ADDLIBLE command and the message ID is CPF2103, the message will be ignored. If the ADDLIBLE command generates any other error message, the program-level MONMSG will cause control to pass to the error-handling routine. If the CHKOBJ command generates an error and that error is CPF9801, the CRTPF command will be executed. If any other error is generated by the CHKOBJ command, the program-level MONMSG will cause control to pass to the error-handling routine. If any error occurs on the CRTPF command, the program-level MONMSG will cause control to pass to the error-handling routine. If the DMPCLPGM command generates an error, it will be ignored. Any other errors generated by commands within this program will be caught by the program-level message monitor, and control will be passed to the error-handling routine.

Monitoring for Generic Messages

While monitoring messages that might be generated when you use the CHKOBJ command, remember that more than one message can be generated, depending on the error that occurs. Figure 12.7 lists possible messages that might be generated when the CHKOBJ command is processed. (Appendix A lists messages that can be generated for the most commonly used CL commands.)

Figure 12.7
Possible Error
Messages for the
CHKOBJ Command

```
CPF0001   Error found on command.
CPF9801   Object not found.
CPF9802   Not authorized to object.
CPF9803   Cannot allocate object.
CPF9805   Object destroyed.
CPF9807   One or more libraries in library list deleted.
CPF9808   Cannot allocate one or more libraries on library list.
CPF9810   Library not found.
CPF9815   Member not found.
CPF9820   Not authorized to use library.
CPF9830   Cannot assign library.
CPF9871   Error occurred while processing.
CPF9899   Error occurred during processing of command.
CPF9901   Request check. Unmonitored message.
CPF9999   Function check. Unmonitored message.
```

Previous examples have monitored for the error message CPF9801 (Object not found). But what if you also wanted to monitor for additional error messages? Remember that the MONMSG command can specify up to 50 message IDs. The following example monitors for error messages CPF9801 and CPF9802 (Not authorized to object) on the CHKOBJ command. If either message is generated, program control passes to a label named SEND_ERR.

```
CHKOBJ     *LIBL/MYFILE              +
           *FILE                     +
           MBR(MEMBER1)              +
           AUT(*ALL)
MONMSG     MSGID(CPF9801 CPF9802)   +
           EXEC(GOTO SEND_ERR)
```

Although you can monitor for multiple error messages, such usage has its limitations. In the above example, for instance, if messages other than the two you are monitoring for occur, the AS/400 will revert to its default error handler, the Program Messages display. Monitoring for messages generically is a better option, because generic message monitoring is easier to code and more inclusive.

Remember that error messages contain a three-character prefix, along with a four-position message ID. For example, in message CPF9801 the prefix is *CPF*, while the message ID is *9801*. You can use the MONMSG command so it will check for messages within a range of message ID values. The numbers *00* and *0000* are used for this purpose. If the value *00* is used in place of the last two digits of the message ID, a MONMSG command will monitor for all messages within a range. For example, you can use the following command to monitor for all messages that begin with CPF98 (i.e., messages CPF9800 through CPF98FF):

```
CHKOBJ     *LIBL/MYFILE              +
           *FILE                     +
           MBR(MEMBER1)              +
           AUT(*ALL)
MONMSG     MSGID(CPF9800)           +
           EXEC(GOTO SEND_ERR)
```

By using the message monitor generically to check for all messages beginning with *CPF98*, you can trap nearly all the messages that might be generated by the CHKOBJ command.

You may have noticed that some messages listed in Figure 12.7 do not begin with *CPF98*. Specifically, CPF0001, CPF9901, and CPF9999 do not fit the pattern. Because you need to make sure that your program handles any error condition properly, you must monitor for these messages also. To do this, your generic message monitor would use the value *0000* to monitor for any escape message with a prefix of *CPF*, as in this example:

```
CHKOBJ     *LIBL/MYFILE              +
           *FILE                     +
           MBR(MEMBER1)              +
           AUT(*ALL)
MONMSG     MSGID(CPF0000)           +
           EXEC(GOTO SEND_ERR)
```

Using this form of the MONMSG command, any error message that can be generated by the CHKOBJ command would be monitored because every error message that can be generated by the CHKOBJ command has a prefix of *CPF*. Incidentally, you could also use a combination of generic and specific message IDs in a single MONMSG command:

```
CHKOBJ     *LIBL/MYFILE                                    +
           *FILE                                           +
           MBR(MEMBER1)                                    +
           AUT(*ALL)
MONMSG     MSGID(CPF0001 CPF9800 CPF9901 CPF9999)  +
           EXEC(GOTO SEND_ERR)
```

Specifying Multiple MONMSG Commands

To control the processing performed by your program based upon the error that occurs, you can specify several MONMSG commands following any one command. The following example again uses the CHKOBJ command and monitors for error messages CPF9801 and CPF9802:

```
CHKOBJ     *LIBL/MYFILE                                    +
           *FILE                                           +
           MBR(MEMBER1)                                    +
           AUT(*ALL)
MONMSG     MSGID(CPF9801)                                  +
           EXEC(CRTPF APFILES/MYFILE RCDLEN(80))
MONMSG     MSGID(CPF9802)                                  +
           EXEC(GOTO ERROR_RTN)
```

In this example, if message CPF9801 is generated, the command to create the missing file is executed. If message CPF9802 is generated, program control passes to a label named *ERROR_RTN*. Both of the MONMSG commands are in effect when the CHKOBJ command is executed.

Errors within a MONMSG

You also need to monitor for errors generated by commands specified on the EXEC parameter that might generate an error. In the previous code, for example, if the CRTPF command generated an error, that error would be unmonitored. A program-level MONMSG can be used to handle problems that could occur within a MONMSG EXEC parameter. You also can monitor for messages generated by commands within the EXEC parameter by specifying a DO group for the EXEC parameter:

```
CHKOBJ     *LIBL/MYFILE                                    +
           *FILE                                           +
           MBR(MEMBER1)                                    +
           AUT(*ALL)
```

```
MONMSG      MSGID(CPF9801) EXEC(DO)
                CRTPF       APFILES/MYFILE              +
                            RCDLEN(80)
                MONMSG      MSGID(CPF0000)              +
                            EXEC(GOTO ERROR_RTN)
                ENDDO
MONMSG      MSGID(CPF9802) EXEC(GOTO ERROR_RTN)
```

In the above example, the two MONMSG commands are still in effect for the CHKOBJ command. However, a DO group is specified as the EXEC parameter value of the first MONMSG command. If the CRTPF command generates an error message, the MONMSG after the CRTPF command will be in effect, and it passes control to the label named ERROR_RTN.

Ignoring Error Messages

If the EXEC parameter of the MONMSG command is not specified, the error messages you are monitoring for are ignored. Normally, when an error occurs, you will want to take some type of action; otherwise, unpredictable results can occur within the program. You specify this action in the EXEC parameter.

Occasionally, however, the occurrence of an error can be ignored. An example would be adding a library to your job's library list:

```
ADDLIBLE    MYLIBRARY
MONMSG      CPF2103        /* Already exists in library list */
```

In this case, message CPF2103 would be issued if library MYLIBRARY already existed within the job's library list. If you try to add this library to the list and it's already there, the error can be safely ignored and you don't need an EXEC parameter on the MONMSG command.

Receiving Escape Message Text

In previous examples, when an error was detected within a program, a generic message was sent (e.g., *Error occurred in program*). This message is ambiguous and gives no indication about what error caused the program to fail. You know only that something didn't work. To send a more informative error message, you can receive the actual error message text into your program and resend it to the calling program. If you are running an interactive job from an AS/400 command line, the message appears at the bottom of your display.

When the MONMSG command detects an escape message, the error message text can be received into a program variable using the RCVMSG (Receive Message) command in the following format:

```
RCVMSG      MSGTYPE(*LAST) MSG(&msg)
```

The RCVMSG command above receives the last (*LAST) message your program generated (i.e., the escape message) and places the message text into variable *&msg*.

You then can include the *&msg* variable in a message you can send to the bottom of your display. To accomplish this, you would include the RCVMSG command in your error-handling procedure. Figure 12.8 illustrates this technique.

Figure 12.8
Receiving Escape
Message Text

```
      PGM
      DCL        &msg *CHAR 80

      MONMSG     MSGID(CPF0000) EXEC(GOTO ERROR)

      ADDLIBLE   MYLIBRARY

      CHKOBJ     MYLIB/MYFILE +
                 *FILE         +
                 AUT(*ALL)
      CALL       PROGRAM1
      GOTO       ENDIT

ERROR:
      RCVMSG     MSGTYPE(*LAST) MSG(&msg)
      MONMSG     CPF0000                     /* Just in case */
      SNDPGMMSG  MSG(&msg)
      MONMSG     CPF0000                     /* Just in case */

ENDIT:
      RETURN
      ENDPGM
```

In this example, the program-level MONMSG passes control to label ERROR if an escape message is generated within the program. If control passes to label ERROR, the last message generated (i.e., the escape message) is received via the RCVMSG command. The escape message text is loaded into variable &msg. The error message text is then sent to the bottom of your display using the SNDPGMMSG command. The message text indicates the exact error that caused the program to fail. In this case, if the CHKOBJ command cannot find file MYFILE in library MYLIB, the following message will be sent: *Object MYFILE in library MYLIB not found.* We examine the RCVMSG command in greater detail in Chapter 16.

Chapter Summary
Several types of errors can occur when a CL program is executed. With the exception of abnormal cancellation errors, CL allows a programmer to handle all errors that can occur.

Errors within a CL program are detected as messages being sent to the program. These error messages are *ESCAPE type messages that result in the display of the Program Messages screen if not handled correctly.

Error messages are stored within a message file. The main IBM-supplied message file is QCPFMSG in library QSYS.

Errors that result in escape messages can be monitored for within the program by using the CL MONMSG (Monitor Message) command. You can include the MONMSG command in a CL program as a command-level message monitor and as a program-level message monitor.

Message identifiers (e.g., CPF9801) have a three-character prefix (CPF), followed by a four-position message ID (9801).

You can use the MONMSG command to monitor for a specific message (e.g., MONMSG MSGID(CPF9801)). Or you can monitor for a generic range of messages (e.g., MONMSG MSGID(CPF9800) or MONMSG MSGID(CPF0000)).

If the EXEC parameter of the MONMSG command is not specified, the message you are monitoring for is ignored. When using a program-level MONMSG, the EXEC parameter, if specified, can contain only the GOTO command.

The RCVMSG (Receive Message) command can be used to receive escape message text into a CL program variable. The message then can be resent using the SNDPGMMSG (Send Program Message) command.

The Interactive Job Log

The interactive job log allows you to display on your screen details about the processing of an interactive program. To view the job log, type the command DSPJOBLOG (Display Job Log) on any command line and a Job Log display similar to that shown in Figure 12A would appear. To see more detail pertaining to a certain command, or a group of commands, press the F10=Display detailed messages key and a display similar to that shown in Figure 12B will appear.

Figure 12A
DSPJOBLOG
Display

```
                              Display Job Log
                                                    System:   STUDENT1
Job . . :   DSP13          User . . :   STUDENT    Number . . . :   124660

2 > call sa1201xxx parm('Myfile')
2 > dspjoblog
2 > call sa1201xxx parm('qclsrc')
2 > call sa1201xxx 'qclsrc'
    Program completed normally
2 > call sa1201xxx 'xxxxxx'
2>> dspjoblog




                                                                    Bottom
Press Enter to continue.

F3=Exit    F5=Refresh    F10=Display detailed messages    F12=Cancel
F17=Top    F18=Bottom
```

Continued

The Interactive Job Log continued

Figure 12B
Detailed Message
Display

```
                              Display All Messages
                                                  System:   STUDENT1
Job . . :   DSP13           User . . :   STUDENT   Number . . . :   124660
2 > call sa1201xxx 'xxxxxx'
      1200 - CHKOBJ OBJ(xxxxxx) OBJTYPE(*FILE)
    Object XXXXXX in library *LIBL not found.
    CPF9801 received by SA1201XXX at 1200. (C D I R)
  ? C
2>> dspjoblog




                                                         Bottom
Press Enter to continue.

F3=Exit    F5=Refresh    F12=Cancel    F17=Top    F18=Bottom
```

You can see in Figure 12B information about messages generated during your job. For example, the message *CPF9801 received by SA1201XXX at 1200. (C D I R)* tells you that escape message CPF9801 was generated by your CL program at CL source statement number 12.00. This source statement relates directly to your CL source member line number. You also can see from the job log that the job received a *C* reply to the message, cancelling the job. The AS/400 job log is covered in more detail in Chapter 21.

Terms

command-level message monitor   message file
escape message   message identifier
global message monitor   program-level message monitor

Review Questions

1. Referring to Appendix A, identify the error messages that the following commands can generate (you may omit those errors that may be generated by all commands):

    a. `ADDLFM`
    b. `SBMJOB`
    c. `SNDPGMMSG`
    d. `ADDLIBLE`
    e. `DO`
    f. `RMVLIBLE`

2. What would be the effect of placing this command

    `MONMSG      CPF0000`

    a. as the first command following the declarations section?
    b. following an individual command?

Exercises

1. In this exercise, you write a CL program that executes a CHKOBJ command to determine whether a file exists. The object checked will vary depending on an input parameter that you will supply with the CALL command. If the program finishes normally, it will send a message via the SNDPGMMSG command. This exercise also introduces you to the AS/400 interactive job log. (See "The Interactive Job Log," pages 182–183, for more information.)

    a. Copy an existing CLP type source member to a member named SA1201XXX in the source physical file QCLSRC. Substitute your initials for XXX. As always, update the program information section.

    b. Modify the source member to accomplish the following tasks:

        • Accept a character parameter that is 10 characters long. The name of the parameter should be &file. Remember: You accept a parameter

        on the PGM command, but you also need to use the DCL (Declare) command.

        • Using the CHKOBJ command, test to see whether there is a file within a library on your library list whose name matches the input parameter.

        Hint: `CHKOBJ &file *FILE`

        • Do not use the MONMSG command anywhere within the program.

        • Before the program ends, send a message that indicates that the program completed normally.

    c. Compile the program. Go to an AS/400 command line and call the program several times, supplying a different 10-character PARM value each time. For example:

        `CALL SA1201XXX PARM('QCLSRC')`

        Exercises continued

Exercises continued

d. When the parameter you supply is not the name of a file object within your library list, the Program Messages display will be shown. Execute the program with a bad file name several times. Each time the Program Messages display appears, select a different option as the reply (i.e., C, D, I, or R). What happens after each response? When the Program Messages display is shown, press the Help key. What happens?

e. When a job is cancelled (option C), you receive a message that the job ended abnormally. The message also tells you to look at your job log for more information. Display the job log of your current interactive job. You can do this by entering the command DSPJOBLOG on any command line. The job log is a view of what has happened within your job. From the job log display, press the F10=Detail messages key. Now you can see the actual messages that were generated by your program. Place the cursor on an error message and press the Help key. What is the result?

2. In this exercise, you again write a CL program that executes a CHKOBJ command to determine whether a file exists, but this time you will include a message monitor. The object checked will vary depending on an input parameter that you will supply with the CALL command. If the program finishes normally (i.e., the object does exist), a message indicating the successful completion will be sent via the SNDPGMMSG command. If the object is not found, the SNDPGMMSG command will send an error message to the bottom of your display.

a. Copy the CLP source member from Exercise 1 to a member named SA1202*XXX* in source physical file QCLSRC. Substitute your initials for *XXX*. As always, update the program information section.

b. Add the following enhancements to this source member:
   - Use a command-level message monitor to check for an error if the file does not exist.

   Hint: `MONMSG MSGID(???????) EXEC(DO)`

   If this error is generated, send a message: *Cannot find file MYFILE.* Substitute MYFILE with the name of the file that was not found (i.e., the one requested in the input parameter). (You will need to use a character string expression.) After sending the message, go to label ENDIT. At the ENDIT label, issue the RETURN command followed by the ENDPGM command.
   - If the object is found, send a message: *Program completed normally.*

c. Compile the program. Go to an AS/400 command line and call the program several times, supplying a different 10-character PARM value each time. For example:

   `CALL SA1202XXX PARM('QCLSRC').`

d. Does your program send the correct message each time it is called?

3. In this exercise, you write a CL program that executes several commands that may generate errors. The program will use a program-level message monitor and will forward any error messages to the bottom of your display using the RCVMSG and SNDPGMMSG commands.

a. Copy the CLP source member from Exercise 2 to a member named SA1203*XXX* in source physical file QCLSRC. Substitute your initials for *XXX*. As always, update the program information section.

Exercises continued

Exercises continued

b. Modify the source member to accomplish the following tasks:

- Accept two character parameters, each of which are 10 characters long. The name of the first parameter should be *&file*; the name of the second should be *&library*.

- Include a program-level MONMSG command to check for any messages within the prefix CPF. The EXEC parameter of the MONMSG command should pass control to label *ERROR*.

- Using the input parameters *&file* and *&library*, check to see whether the file exists within the library.

- Execute the DSPFD (Display File Description) command for the file identified by input parameters *&file* and *&library*.

- Execute the DSPLIB (Display Library) command to see the contents of the library identified by input parameter *&library*.

- After processing these commands, go to label *ENDIT*.

- At label ENDIT, include a RETURN command and an ENDPGM command.

- If any errors occur during processing, control will pass to label *ERROR*. At the ERROR label, include the following processing:

  1) Receive (RCVMSG) the error message generated, placing the error message text into variable *&msg*.

  2) Using the SNDPGMMSG command, send the received error message to the bottom of the display.

c. Compile the program. Go to an AS/400 command line and call the program several times, supplying different parameter values each time. Remember: This time the program must receive two parameters. For example:

```
CALL SA1203XXX PARM('QCLSRC'  'MYLIB')
```

d. Do you get the correct results each time you call the program?

Chapter 13

Passing Program Parameters

Chapter Overview

This chapter defines program parameters and discusses how they are used to pass information between programs. You learn how CL uses program parameters with the PGM, CALL, TFRCTL (Transfer Control), and SBMJOB (Submit Job) commands (presented in Chapter 11).

What Are Program Parameters?

Recall that CL allows you to use the DCL (Declare) command to define program variables for use within a CL program. When a variable is defined within a CL program, all commands within that program can reference the variable.

Although program variables can be used and manipulated easily within the CL program in which they are defined, they normally are not accessible by other programs. But there is one exception: A program can share data with a program that it calls. When you specify values for the PARM keyword of the CALL or TFRCTL (Transfer Control) command, the calling program passes the values to the called program, which then can use and/or manipulate the values.

A value that a calling program passes to a called program is commonly called a **program parameter**. A program parameter controls the actions of a program by providing an input value to a program. You can use program parameters to share information between two programs. You would specify program parameters by indicating the value within the PARM keyword in the CALL, TFRCTL, and PGM commands. A program parameter can be a program variable or a constant. Figure 13.1 shows how a program variable can be used as a program parameter.

In this example, PGMA declares the variable *&name* and then issues a CALL to PGMB, specifying variable *&name* as a parameter (PARM) that will be passed to PGMB. PGMB must be able to accept the value contained in variable *&name* or the CALL will fail.

To allow PGMB to accept the passed value, the PGM command within PGMB must specify a variable name into which the passed value will be placed. In our example, the PGM command in PGMB is followed by the PARM keyword, which specifies variable *&name* as the receiver variable for the passed value.

Figure 13.1
Passing Values
Using a Program
Variable

```
PGMA:
        PGM
        DCL      &name   *CHAR 10  VALUE('BOB')
        CALL     PGMB    PARM(&name)
        RETURN
        ENDPGM


PGMB:
        PGM         PARM(&name)
        DCL         &name        *CHAR 10
        SNDPGMMSG   ('My name is' *CAT &name)
        RETURN
        ENDPGM
```

Defining Parameters in a Called Program

As mentioned earlier, to receive parameters from another program, the PGM command of the called program must include the PARM parameter. The command can be written either in keyword notation

```
PGM      PARM(&CL-variable-name)
```

or positional notation

```
PGM      &CL-variable-name
```

In the above PGM commands, the program would receive a single parameter value from another program. This value would be placed within the variable specified on the PARM parameter. The called program must use the DCL command to define the variable, which can be used as any other program variable within the called program.

The PARM parameter also can contain a list of variables. The program would receive as many values as are indicated on the PGM command, placing those values into the corresponding parameters. For example, the following PGM command lists two incoming parameter variables, *&cusnbr* and *&cusname*:

```
PGM      PARM(&cusnbr &cusname)
```

Receiving the value of a variable from the calling program has the same effect within the called program as assigning an initial value to the variable. Because the calling program is already sending an initial value, you cannot assign an initial value to an incoming parameter variable. For example, the following is *not* allowed:

```
PGM      PARM(&name)
DCL      &name *CHAR 10  +
         VALUE('Mary')
```

As mentioned earlier, program parameters must be received into variables. Because CL supports only three types of variables, it follows that all incoming parameters must be defined as one of those types: character (*CHAR), decimal (*DEC), or logical (*LGL). The names of the variables can be any valid variable name; they need not necessarily be the same names that the calling program uses for any corresponding variables. In the following example, three parameters (one of each variable type supported by CL) are received by the program:

```
PGM        PARM(&name &number &flag)
DCL        &name      *CHAR9
DCL        &number    *DEC (15 5)
DCL        &flag      *LGL
```

The parameters must appear within the PGM command in the same order in which they will be sent to the program with the CALL command. The data types in the called program must match those in the calling program. The DCL commands within the calling and called programs can be in any order. For the previous example, the CALL command within the calling program could be written as follows:

```
CALL MYPROGRAM                                        +
     PARM('Christine' 22.5 '1')
```

Because the parameters must be specified in the correct order on the CALL command, you could not use the command

```
CALL MYPROGRAM                                        +
     PARM(22.5 '1' 'Christine')
```

If you were to use this CALL command, the data types of the parameters would not be consistent between the CALL command and the PGM command, and the CALL to the program would fail.

Passing Constants to a Called Program

To pass constants (character, decimal, or logical) as parameters to a called program, you would place the constants within the PARM parameter of the CALL command. You can specify one parameter,

```
CALL MYPROGRAM   PARM('Monday')
```

or up to 50 parameters

```
CALL MYPROGRAM                                        +
     PARM('Monday' 'Tuesday' 'Wednesday')
```

If you specify more than one parameter, the parameter list must be enclosed within parentheses — as is the case with all list type values. If parameters are to be passed to a program from an AS/400 command line, those parameters must always be constants. You cannot use variable names, because variables can exist only within a program.

Passing Character Constants

You can use a character constant as a parameter both interactively from an AS/400 command line and within a CL program. As you have seen, the constant is passed using the CALL command and specifying a character constant as the PARM value:

```
CALL MYPROGRAM                                      +
     PARM('Monday' 'Tuesday' 'Wednesday')
```

When character constants are passed to a program, the called program must declare the parameters as character (*CHAR) type variables. To receive the parameters from the CALL command above, the called program must contain the following commands:

```
PGM     PARM(&day1 &day2 &day3)
DCL     &day1   *CHAR 9
DCL     &day2   *CHAR 9
DCL     &day3   *CHAR 9
```

Notice that the variables are declared in the called program as *CHAR variables with a length of nine characters each — even though two of the character constants (Monday and Tuesday) are shorter than nine characters. When declaring the length of variables used as parameters, you should declare them large enough to hold the largest value that might be passed to them. Because no day of the week has more than nine characters in its name, any parameter used to hold the name of the day of the week should have a length of nine.

When the length of a character variable is longer than the constant being passed to that variable, the constant will be left-adjusted in the receiving variable and padded to the right with blanks. In our example, the values of variables *&day1*, *&day2*, and *&day3* in the called program would be *Monday♭♭♭*, *Tuesday♭♭*, and *Wednesday*, respectively.

If the length of the passed character constant exceeds the length of the receiver variable, the extra positions in the passed constant would be truncated. Consider the following example:

```
CALL MYPROGRAM                                      +
     PARM('Today is Monday'                         +
          'Today is Tuesday'                        +
          'Today is Wednesday')
```

If the variable declarations within the called program are the same as shown earlier, each variable would contain the first nine characters of the corresponding passed parameter value. This value would be *Today is♭* for all three variables. The remaining characters in the three parameter values would be truncated. CL does not issue an error message when it truncates a passed parameter value, so you must make sure your receiver variables are long enough to hold the longest value that will be sent.

You also must be aware of how CL passes character constants of various lengths. All character constants shorter than 33 characters are sent to a called program with a length of 32. Positions beyond the number specified are padded with blanks before the parameter value is sent to the called program. If you specify a character constant longer than 32 characters, it is passed to the called program in its exact length. To help illustrate this point, consider the examples in Figure 13.2.

Figure 13.2
How Character
Constants Are
Passed and Received

Passing parameters

```
CALL    PROGRAM1                                                        +
        PARM('Mary' 'Joe' 'Billie' 'Rumpelstiltskin'                    +
        'This is a long character constant, more than 32')
```

The actual parameters passed are (b̸ represents a trailing blank)

```
                1          2          3       4       4
1........0.........0...........2.......0.....7

Maryb̸b̸b̸b̸b̸b̸b̸b̸b̸b̸b̸b̸b̸b̸b̸b̸b̸b̸b̸b̸b̸b̸b̸b̸b̸b̸b̸b̸
Joeb̸b̸b̸b̸b̸b̸b̸b̸b̸b̸b̸b̸b̸b̸b̸b̸b̸b̸b̸b̸b̸b̸b̸b̸b̸b̸b̸b̸b̸
Billieb̸b̸b̸b̸b̸b̸b̸b̸b̸b̸b̸
Rumpelstiltskinb̸b̸b̸b̸b̸b̸b̸b̸b̸b̸b̸b̸b̸b̸b̸b̸
This is a long character constant, more than 32
```

Receiving parameters

```
PGM PARM(&parm1 &parm2 &parm3 &parm4 &parm5)
DCL     &parm1    *CHAR 10
DCL     &parm2    *CHAR 5
DCL     &parm3    *CHAR 30
DCL     &parm4    *CHAR 32
DCL     &parm5    *CHAR 47
```

The actual parameters received are

```
                1          2          3       4       4
1........0.........0.........0.........0.....7

&parm1  Maryb̸b̸b̸b̸b̸b̸
&parm2  Joeb̸b̸
&parm3  Billieb̸b̸b̸b̸b̸b̸b̸b̸b̸b̸b̸b̸b̸b̸b̸b̸b̸b̸b̸b̸b̸b̸b̸b̸
&parm4  Rumpelstiltskinb̸b̸b̸b̸b̸b̸b̸b̸b̸b̸b̸b̸b̸b̸b̸b̸
&parm5  This is a long character constant, more than 32
```

The examples demonstrate that all character constants passed as parameters are sent as 32 characters long. In the case of *&parm5*, which is longer than 32 positions, the full length of the constant is sent.

The called program receives the parameters with the same data type and in the same order in which they were sent. In the cases where we specified the length of the receiving variables smaller than the length of the parameters that were sent, the extra character positions were truncated when the parameter values were received. In this example, all the truncated characters are blanks.

Because we specified *&parm5* with a length of 47 characters, all 47 characters of the passed parameter will fit into the variable. If the parameter sent was longer than 47, the entire character constant would be sent but only the first 47 characters would be placed into variable *&parm5*; the remaining characters would be truncated.

Sending character constants as parameters can cause problems, if you are not careful. Figure 13.3 illustrates some situations you need to be aware of.

Figure 13.3
Problems That Can
Occur When Passing
Character Constants

Passing parameters

```
CALL    PROGRAM1                                                      +
        PARM('Heather' 'Stephen'                                      +
             'Here is a potential problem'                            +
             'This is a long character constant, more than 32')
```

The actual parameters passed are

```
             1         2           3       4     4
1........0........0...........2.......0.....7

Heatherbbbbbbbbbbbbbbbbbbbbbbbbbb
Stephenbbbbbbbbbbbbbbbbbbbbbbbbbb
Here is a potential problembbbbb
This is a long character constant, more than 32
```

Receiving the passed parameters in the called program

```
PGM     PARM(&parm1 &parm2 &parm3 &parm4)
DCL     &parm1    *CHAR 6
DCL     &parm2    *CHAR 5
DCL     &parm3    *CHAR 40
DCL     &parm4    *CHAR 47
```

The actual parameters received are

```
             1        2        3        4     4
1........0........0........0........0.....7
&parm1  Heathe
&parm2  Steph
&parm3  Here is a potential problembbbbbbThis isb
&parm4  This is a long character constant, more than 32
```

Let's examine how each parameter is handled. Parameter *&parm1* is sent with a value of *Heather*. Because the parameter is a character constant less than 33 positions long, it is passed with a length of 32 characters. The called program declares *&parm1* as only six characters long. In this case, the parameter value *Heather* is truncated to fit into variable *&parm1*, resulting in a value of *Heathe*. The second parameter, *&parm2*, has a similar problem (i.e., the characters *en* are truncated from parameter value *Stephen*). These two examples illustrate an important point: *To avoid truncation, always declare receiving variables large enough to hold the largest value that will be passed to them.*

Parameter *&parm3* illustrates another problem. In the receiving program, part of *&parm4* shows up at the end of *&parm3*! Let's see how this can happen. The calling program sends *&parm3* with a value of *Here is a potential problem*. Because this character constant is less than 33 characters long, it is sent as 32 characters. The called program declares *&parm3* to have a length of 40. Specifying a longer length for *&parm3* in the called program causes the problem. When CL places the parameter value into *&parm3*, it positions all 32 characters of the third parameter into the variable. But because the receiving variable (*&parm3*) is declared as 40 positions long, eight character positions remain unfilled. After variable *&parm3* is filled with the value of the corresponding parameter, the remaining eight positions are filled with the first eight characters of the next parameter. This situation can obviously cause problems in the called program, and there is no guarantee what the contents of the extra character positions will be.

This problem can only occur if, in the called program, you declare a parameter variable with a length greater than 32 characters but you pass a character constant with a length smaller than the receiving variable. A good rule to follow is: *When passing character constants, never declare the parameter variable longer than 32 characters, unless you are certain that you will always pass the correct number of characters.*

In this example, even though *&parm3* will contain extra data from parameter *&parm4*, the fourth parameter will be received correctly within variable *&parm4*; it does not start where *&parm3* left off. Only variable *&parm3* will be incorrect.

Passing Decimal Constants

Like a character constant, a decimal constant also can be used as a parameter both interactively from an AS/400 command line and within a CL program. For example, the following command passes decimal constants as parameters:

```
CALL MYPROGRAM                          +
     PARM(5   3.1416   129.95)
```

When you pass decimal constants to a program, the receiving program must declare the parameters as *DEC variables with a length of 15 digits, including five to the right of the decimal point. There is no allowance for any other length. As in the case of character constants, the parameters received by the called program must be declared as variables with the DCL command, and these variable names must appear on the PGM command. For example:

```
PGM     PARM(&number1 &number2 &number3)
DCL     &number1      *DEC (15 5)
DCL     &number2      *DEC (15 5)
DCL     &number3      *DEC (15 5)
```

CL passes decimal constants as packed-decimal data, with the decimal point properly aligned within the receiver variable. Figure 13.4 shows how CL would handle the parameters from the previous examples. The passed parameters are in packed-decimal format (i.e., two digits per byte). An *F* in the last position indicates a positive number; a *D* indicates a negative number.

Figure 13.4
Passing Decimal
Constants

Passing parameters

```
CALL    MYPROGRAM                    +
        PARM(5  3.1416  129.95)
```

The actual parameters passed are

```
        Constant
                           1 2 3 4 5 6 7 8

        5                  000000000500000F (8 bytes)
        3.1416             000000000314160F (8 bytes)
        129.95             000000012995000F (8 bytes)
```

Receiving parameters

```
PGM     PARM(&parm1 &parm2 &parm3)
DCL     &parm1   *DEC (15 5)
DCL     &parm2   *DEC (15 5)
DCL     &parm3   *DEC (15 5)
```

The actual parameters received are

```
        Decimal            Internal packed
        Value              Representation
                           1 2 3 4 5 6 7 8

&parm1  0000000005.00000   000000000500000F (8 bytes)
&parm2  0000000003.14160   000000000314160F (8 bytes)
&parm3  0000000129.95000   000000012995000F (8 bytes)
```

Passing Logical Constants

Logical constants are passed according to the same rules for passing character constants. When you use the logical constants '0' and '1' as parameters, the system treats them as the character constants '0' and '1'. Logical constants are passed with a length of 32, left-adjusted in the receiving variable, and padded to the right with blanks. Consider the example in Figure 13.5. You can see that the logical constants ('1' and '0') are passed like any character constant (e.g., 'Mary').

Passing Variables to a Called Program

We have been using constants to specify the value of parameters that are to be sent to another program. But you also can use variables within a CL program to store the values that will be passed as parameters. Because variables can exist only within programs, you cannot use variables when entering the CALL command on a command line.

Figure 13.5
How Logical
Constants Are Passed
and Received

Passing parameters

```
CALL      MYPROGRAM PARM('1' '0' 'Mary')
```

The actual parameters passed are

```
            1         2         3    4    4
1.......0.........0...........2.......0.....7

10000000000000000000000000000000000
00000000000000000000000000000000000
Mary0000000000000000000000000000000
```

Receiving parameters

```
PGM       PARM(&parm1 &parm2 &parm3)
DCL       &parm1 *LGL
DCL       &parm2 *LGL
DCL       &parm3 *CHAR 10
```

The actual parameters received are

```
          1         2
1.......0.........0

&parm1    1
&parm2    0
&parm3    Mary00000
```

Here are some examples of how to use the CALL command to pass variables as parameters:

```
CALL PROGRAM1 PARM(&name)
CALL PROGRAM2 PARM(&name &address &phone)
CALL PROGRAM3 PARM(&radius 3.1416 &area)
```

When PROGRAM1 is called in the first example, one parameter (&name) is passed to the program. The second example shows three program variables being passed as parameters to PROGRAM2. The third example, a CALL to PROGRAM3, shows a combination of program variables and constants in the PARM parameter. Three parameters are passed to PROGRAM3. Two of the parameters (&radius and &area) are variables; one is a constant (3.1416).

When you use variables as program parameters, you must, of course, declare the variable names in the calling program. In the following example, PROGRAM1 will call PROGRAM2, passing two parameters (&name and &department) to PROGRAM2:

```
PROGRAM1:
    PGM
    DCL       &name       *CHAR 10
    DCL       &department *DEC (5 0)
    CHGVAR    &name       'Mary'
```

```
CALL        PROGRAM2      PARM(&name &department)
RETURN
ENDPGM
```

The variables *&name* and *&department* are declared within the program, then sent as parameters to PROGRAM2. The passing of the parameters, as you have seen in other examples, is accomplished by using the CALL command and specifying the variables as the parameters that will be sent.

Remember that within PROGRAM2 (the called program) you must declare variables to receive the parameters. The order in which the parameters are listed on the PGM command must be the same as in the CALL command within the calling program. The variable names within the called program need not match the names used in the calling program, but the data type and length should be consistent. The DCL commands used to declare the variables in the calling and called program can be in any order. Here is an example of what PROGRAM2 might look like for the CALL command issued by PROGRAM1:

```
PROGRAM2:
    PGM       PARM(&alpha &dept)
    DCL       &dept  *DEC (5 0)
    DCL       &alpha *CHAR 10
    IF        (&alpha = 'Mary') DO
              CHGVAR   &dept  VALUE(12600)
              ENDDO
    RETURN
    ENDPGM
```

PROGRAM2 accepts two parameters, *&alpha* and *&dept*. As required, the parameters appear in the same order on the PGM command as they did in the CALL command issued by PROGRAM1.

The Mechanics of Passing Variables

When you use the DCL or DCLF command to declare a variable within a program, an area is set up within the program to hold the value you wish to assign to the variable. You saw an example of this when you dumped the storage of CL programs using the DMPCLPGM command. Each variable has an assigned storage area. The declared length of the variable determines the length of the storage area. The storage area for program variables is located within the *Program Automatic Storage Area* (PASA) associated with the program. Each user that runs the program has a unique PASA, so another user cannot access the program storage you use.

When passing variables to a called program, CL does not actually pass the value stored within a variable. Instead, CL passes to the called program a pointer to the first position of the variable within the calling program's storage area. The called program uses this pointer to reference the storage location of the variables that are received as parameters. Within the called program, the incoming parameters are not assigned a new storage space, but instead point to the space that was set aside in the calling program.

Both the calling and the called programs share the same storage space for the parameter variables. Therefore, if the called program makes any changes to the contents of the variables that were passed to it, those changes affect the contents of the storage space that resides in the calling program. When the called program ends, control is returned to the calling program. Because both programs use the same storage area for the variable, a change made to the variable by either program would change the storage area that is shared by both.

The rule to remember about variables is this: *If a variable is passed as a parameter, any change made to the variable in the called program will be reflected in the variable value in the calling program.* But this is not true when constants are passed as parameters. Their value remains constant in the calling program, regardless of any change made to the variable in the called program.

If you want to manipulate a value stored in a variable but you do not want the change reflected in the calling program, you must localize the variable. A **localized variable** exists only in a single CL program. To localize a variable, you would declare an additional variable with the same data type and length as the incoming parameter variable. Then within your called program, you would use the CHGVAR command to assign the value of the parameter to the localized variable. The following example illustrates the technique:

```
PGM       PARM(&name &address)
DCL       &name      *CHAR 20
DCL       &address   *CHAR 35
DCL       &namex     *CHAR 20
DCL       &addressx  *CHAR 35

CHGVAR    &namex     &name
CHGVAR    &addressx  &address
CALL      PROGRAM2   PARM(&name &address)
```

The storage area for *&namex* and *&addressx* is local (i.e., it exists only in this program). The storage area for variables *&name* and *&address* is in the program that called this program. Any change PROGRAM2 makes to *&name* and *&address* will be noticed by the calling program; however, changes made to *&namex* and *&addressx* will not affect the calling program's storage area.

When a program that receives parameters calls another program, the parameters that were originally received can be passed as parameters to the other program. Then that program can send those parameters to another program, and so on. When multiple programs are involved, the variable storage area is still located in the program that issued the first CALL command specifying those parameters. All programs that use these parameters are able to modify the contents of the storage location in the first program by changing the value of the variable used to define the parameter.

Now that you are familiar with the concept of how CL passes parameters, you should easily understand the cardinal rule for passing variables to a called program:

The definition (type and length) of a variable used as a parameter should be identical in both the calling and the called program. This rule applies regardless of the variable's data type. If you follow this rule, you can avoid many long hours debugging your programs.

Considerations When Using the TFRCTL Command

All the considerations for passing parameters we have discussed in connection with the CALL command also pertain to the TFRCTL (Transfer Control) command. However, when using TFRCTL, you need to be aware of two additional considerations:

- If any parameters are passed, they must be variables; constants are not allowed.
- Any CL variables used as parameters must have been received initially as parameters by the program executing the TFRCTL command.

The following uses of the TFRCTL command are *not* valid:

```
PGM
DCL        &custnbr        *DEC (5 0)
TFRCTL     PGMB            PARM(&custnbr)

PGM        PARM(&custnbr)
DCL        &custnbr        *DEC (5 0)
TFRCTL     PGMB            PARM('UPDATE' &custnbr)
```

In the first example, the TFRCTL command is attempting to pass a parameter variable that does not appear in the PGM command. Any parameters in the TFRCTL command must be variables that also appear in the PGM command. In the second example, the TFRCTL command correctly passes *&custnbr*, which appears in the PGM command, but it incorrectly tries to pass the constant *UPDATE*. TFRCTL cannot pass constants as parameters.

These rules may seem restrictive, but when you think about it, they really are quite logical. Recall from Chapter 11 that when a CL program executes the TFRCTL command, the program ends. When the program ends, its variable storage area (the PASA) is no longer accessible. Because variables are passed as pointers to the program's storage area, if that storage area is no longer accessible, the pointers to the variables would not be available to the program receiving control. By requiring that program parameters be passed initially to the program that executes the TFRCTL command, you ensure that the storage area for those parameters still exists when the program containing the TFRCTL command ends.

If you need to send parameters to a program, you may find it easier to use the CALL command. If you need to use the TFRCTL command and you need to send parameters, make sure the program that transfers control receives the same parameters that it sends. This ensures that the pointers will be valid because they will point to the storage area of an active program.

Considerations When Using the SBMJOB Command

The SBMJOB (Submit Job) command allows you to specify a command to execute in a batch environment. You can specify the CALL command as the command to execute, and you can optionally pass parameters on the CALL command. The following code illustrates how to pass parameters via the SBMJOB command within a CL program:

```
PGM
DCL         &name       *CHAR 10
DCL         &number     *DEC (5 2)
. . .       /* manipulate variables */
SBMJOB      CMD(CALL PROGRAMA PARM(&name &number))
RETURN
ENDPGM
```

In this example, we are submitting a job for batch processing that will CALL program PROGRAMA and pass it two parameters: *&name* and *&number.*

Remember that a submitted batch job waits in line until there are machine resources available to process the job. There are occasions when a submitted job waits for several minutes, hours, or even days before it is executed. Recall that when variables are used as parameters on the CALL command, a pointer to the calling program's storage area is passed rather than the actual value of the variable. If this were true in the case of a submitted batch job, that would mean the batch program would try to reference the interactive job that submitted it. If the batch job does not execute until hours later, it is possible that those pointers would no longer be valid (i.e., if the interactive user signs off or starts a different program).

But the CALL command works differently with the SBMJOB command than it does within a CL program or from the AS/400 command line.

When you use the SBMJOB command to CALL a program and pass it variables as parameters, CL automatically translates the variables into constants when the program is submitted. This makes the CALL command quite flexible when used within the SBMJOB command, but you must be aware that variables are translated to *constants*, and you must follow the parameter rules that we discussed earlier for passing constants as parameters. Consider the following example:

```
PROGRAM A:
    PGM
    DCL         &name       *CHAR 10
    DCL         &number     *DEC (5 2)
    CHGVAR      &name       'Bobolink'
    CHGVAR      &number     129.95
    SBMJOB      CMD(CALL PROGRAMB PARM(&name &number))
    RETURN
    ENDPGM
```

In this example, when the batch job is submitted, the parameters within the CALL command are automatically translated into constants. The actual command submitted for batch processing is:

```
CALL PROGRAMB PARM('Bobolink' 0000000129.95000)
```

Let's assume for a moment that PROGRAMB declares its incoming parameters the same as they are declared in PROGRAMA. But remember that the SBMJOB command has translated the variables to constants. Also remember that when you send a decimal constant as a parameter, the incoming parameter *must* be declared as *DEC (15 5). From the perspective of the submitted job, the SBMJOB command effectively changes the definition of variable *&number* from *DEC (5 2) to *DEC (15 5). For PROGRAMB to correctly receive the decimal parameter, which is now a constant, it must be defined in PROGRAMB as *DEC (15 5).

Using Hexadecimal Notation

There will be times, when testing or debugging a program that receives parameters, that you will want to call the program from a command line, even though under normal circumstances the program would be called from another program. Recall that when you CALL a program from the command line, you can pass only constants for parameter values. If the program you want to CALL requires that you pass it a decimal type parameter, you must have defined that decimal variable within the CL program as *DEC (15 5). Herein lies a problem: Many times, this declaration may not fit your particular application.

But there is a way to avoid this problem. It is possible to use *hexadecimal notation* to specify the value of a decimal constant when using the CALL command. Remember that CL passes decimals in packed format. By using hex notation to specify decimals, you can emulate the packed format. Consider the following example:

```
CALL MYPROGRAM PARM(X'0000000000500000F')
```

In this example, the decimal constant 5 is passed to a program that accepts the parameter into a variable defined as *DEC (15 5). This would be the same as specifying the following command:

```
CALL MYPROGRAM PARM(5)
```

You can also use this notation to pass decimal parameters that are not defined as *DEC (15 5). Consider the following examples:

```
CALL MYPROGRAM PARM(X'31416F')
CALL MYPROGRAM PARM(X'0012995F')
CALL MYPROGRAM PARM(X'12995D')
```

Continued

Using Hexadecimal Notation continued

In the first example, the decimal constant *3.1416* is passed to a program that accepts the parameter into a decimal variable defined as *DEC (5 4). If the receiving variable is defined as *DEC (5 0), it would be received as *31416,* without a decimal point. In the second example, the decimal constant *129.95* is passed to a program that accepts the parameter as *DEC (7 2). The third example shows how to pass a negative number. In this case, the decimal constant *129.95–* is passed to a program that accepts the parameter as *DEC (5 2).

There are a few rules to keep in mind when using hexadecimal notation to emulate packed decimals:

- The constant must be preceded by an *X* and must be enclosed in a quoted string.
- The quoted string can contain only the numbers 0–9 and a trailing sign (F or D).
- The quoted string must contain an even number of hexadecimal numbers. Each pair of numbers will be packed into a single byte.
- The quoted string must end in an *F* for a positive number, or a *D* for a negative number.

Normally you would use hex notation to emulate packed decimals only when testing or debugging. For this purpose, hex notation gives you the added flexibility of not having to declare your decimal variables as *DEC (15 5). Within a program, however, the need for hex notation is eliminated by the capability to pass decimal variables other than those defined as *DEC (15 5).

Chapter Summary

A value that a calling program passes to a called program is commonly called a program parameter. A program parameter controls the actions of a program by providing an input value to a program. Program parameters are used primarily to share information between two programs. A program parameter can be a program variable or a constant.

Variables are accessible only to the program in which they are defined, unless they are passed as parameters to another program. Parameters to be passed to another program must be defined in the PARM parameter of the CALL or TFRCTL (Transfer Control) command.

Within a called program, incoming parameters must be declared with the DCL (Declare) command and must appear in the PGM command. The order of the parameters passed must be the same in the CALL command used in the calling program and the PGM command used in the called program.

The parameters passed may be either constants or variables. If you are using the CALL command from a command line, you can use only constants. Up to 50 parameters may be specified on the CALL and PGM commands. Parameters can consist of character, decimal, or logical data.

Character constants less than 33 positions long are passed to the called program with a length of 32. Decimal constants are passed as packed decimal data and must be received in the called program by a variable defined as *DEC (15 5).

When variables are used as parameters on the CALL command, the actual value of the variable is not sent to the called program, but rather a pointer is sent. The pointer allows the called program to reference the same storage area for this variable that the calling program uses for the variable. If a variable is passed as a parameter, any change made to the variable in the called program is reflected in the variable value in the calling program.

When passing parameters with the TFRCTL command, the parameters must be variables that were received as parameters by the program that transfers control.

The SBMJOB (Submit Job) command allows the specification of the CALL command for its CMD parameter. When passing parameters using the CALL command within the SBMJOB command, any variables included are automatically translated into constants.

Terms

localized variable   program parameter

Review Questions

1. Describe the mechanism CL uses to pass information from one program to another.
2. In the following example, PGMA calls PGMB, passing it several parameters. What are the values of the parameters before PGMA calls PGMB? When PGMB begins execution? When PGMA receives control back from PGMB? Use the table to fill in the values.

Variable	Before call	At start of PGMB	After return to PGMA
&name			
&address			
&comment			
&city			
&credlimit			
&highbal			
&active			

```
PGMA:
      PGM
      DCL     &name   *CHAR 20                    +
              VALUE('John J. Smith')
      DCL     &address *CHAR 35                    +
              VALUE('123 Main Street Apartment 45')
      DCL     &comment  *CHAR 55                   +
              VALUE('Long time customer')
      DCL     &credlimit  *DEC (11 2)              +
              VALUE(5000)
      DCL     &active  *LGL                        +
              VALUE('1')

      CALL    PGMB    PARM(&name                   +
                          &address                 +
                          &comment                 +
                          'Philadelphia'           +
                          &credlimit               +
                          55400.10                 +
                          &active)
      SNDPGMMSG MSG('Processing complete.')        +
              MSGTYPE(*COMP)
      RETURN
      ENDPGM
```

Review Questions continued

Review Questions continued

```
PGMB:
        PGM     PARM(&name                                              +
                      &address                                          +
                      &comment                                          +
                      &city                                             +
                      &credlimit                                        +
                      &highbal                                          +
                      &active)
        DCL     &name       *CHAR 20
        DCL     &address    *CHAR 35
        DCL     &city       *CHAR 21
        DCL     &comment    *CHAR 55
        DCL     &credlimit  *DEC (11 2)
        DCL     &highbal    *DEC (15 5)
        DCL     &active     *LGL
        CHGVAR  &name                                                   +
                VALUE('Jerry James')
        CHGVAR  &address                                                +
                VALUE('124 Alderson')
        CHGVAR  &city                                                   +
                VALUE('New York')
        CHGVAR  &comment                                                +
                VALUE(blank)
        CHGVAR  &credlimit                                              +
                VALUE(10000.50)
        CHGVAR  &highbal                                                +
                VALUE(67100)
        CHGVAR  &active                                                 +
                VALUE('0')
        RETURN
        ENDPGM
```

3. The following CL program contains a number of syntax errors. Find the errors.

```
PGMA:
        PGM     ('UPDATE' &custnbr &userid &date)
        DCL     &mode     *CHAR 6
        DCL     &custnbr  *DEC 5
        DCL     &userid   *CHAR 10                                      +
                VALUE('JSMITH')

        IF      (&mode = 'UPDATE')
                SNDPGMMSG MSG('Customer' *BCAT                          +
                              &custnbr *BCAT                            +
                              'has been updated by' *BCAT              +
                              &userid *BCAT on *BCAT &date)
        RETURN:
        ENDPGM
```

Exercises

1. In this exercise, you practice passing parameters to a CL program. The program dumps its storage area so you can determine how the parameters are stored.

   a. Add a member named SA1301*XXX* to source physical file QCLSRC. Substitute your initials for *XXX*.
   b. Add the program information section and the program linkage section to the member.
   c. Accept the following five parameters into your program.
      - A character parameter named TEXT1, 10 positions long.
      - A character parameter named TEXT2, 20 positions long.
      - A character parameter named TEXT3, 50 positions long.
      - A decimal parameter named NUMBER1, whose length is (15 5).
      - A decimal parameter named NUMBER2, whose length is (15 5).
   d. After receiving the parameters, dump the CL program (DMPCLPGM) and return to the calling program (RETURN).
   e. Compile the program.
   f. Run the program several times from an AS/400 command line. Supply different values for the parameters each time. Examine the program dumps.
      - What can you conclude about the contents of the variable storage areas?
      - What do you notice specifically about variable TEXT3?
      - What happens if you do not supply all the parameters within the CALL command?
      - What happens if you use a decimal parameter value for TEXT1, TEXT2, or TEXT3?
      - What happens if you supply a character value for NUMBER1 or NUMBER2?
   g. Using the SBMJOB command, run the program in batch mode. Is there any difference in the variable values than what you saw when running the program from the command line? Why?

2. In this exercise, you write two CL programs. Both programs accept parameters. The purpose of the programs will be to interact with each other to translate a date from the format MMDDYY (month, day, year) into a more readable format (e.g., January 25, 1998). The more readable date format will be sent to the user who called the program.

   The first program should accept a date as a parameter. This date will be in MMDDYY format. The first program will then CALL the second program. In the CALL command to the second program, two parameters will be specified: the date in MMDDYY format and a character parameter that will contain the translated date when the second program ends. After the second program ends, the characters received from the second program will be sent to the user who called the program.

   As an example, a CALL command to the first program would be written as follows:

   ```
   CALL SA1302XXX PARM('123197')
   ```

   When the program finishes, it will send a message to the user with the date translated as 'December 31, 1997'.

   a. Add a member named SA1302*XXX* to source physical file QCLSRC. Substitute your initials for *XXX*. This will be the first (i.e., the calling) program.
   b. Add the program information section and the program linkage section to the member.

Exercises continued

Exercises continued

c. The program will do the following tasks:
- Accept one parameter into the program. This parameter will be a six-character parameter, which will be used to contain a date supplied by the user. The format of the date will be MMDDYY, as in '123197'.
- CALL a program named SA1303*XXX* with two parameters:

    1) the same parameter received by the program. This is the six-character date.
    2) a character variable named &message, 100 positions long. The value of this parameter will be "filled-in" in the called program.

- Send a program message (SNDPGMMSG). The message text will be the "filled-in" parameter value received from the called program, as in 'December 31, 1997'.
- RETURN

d. Add a member named SA1303*XXX* to source physical file QCLSRC. Substitute your initials for *XXX*. This will be the called program.

e. Add the program information section and the program linkage section to the member.

f. The program will do the following tasks:
- Accept two parameters into the program:

    1) The six-character date in MMDDYY format, as in '123197'.
    2) The 100-character message that will be sent back to the calling program. When this program finishes, the six-character date will be translated into a character string that states 'December 31, 1997'.

- Make sure a valid month number has been passed in the first parameter.

    Hint: %SST(&mmddyy 1 2)

- If a valid month number (1–12) has not been entered, change the value of the second parameter to the value 'Invalid date entered. Date must be in MMDDYY format'. If the month number is valid, proceed with the date translation.
- You do not need to include validity checking for the day (DD) and year (YY). So the date February 54, 1900, would be a valid date in this exercise. Also, the century should be assumed to be 19, as in the year 1984.
- Include the CL commands required to translate the date from MMDDYY format into a message that states the date in the readable format:

    'December 07, 1941'

- Include error-message handling where needed.

g. Compile both programs.

h. CALL program SA1302*XXX*, supplying the value '090753' as the parameter:

```
CALL SA1302XXX PARM('090753')
```

If your programs are working correctly, you should receive a message that states 'September 07, 1953'.

i. Call program SA1302*XXX*, supplying different dates. Does the program always work correctly?

Chapter 14

Retrieving and Changing External Attributes

Chapter Overview

This chapter introduces return variables and the RTV (Retrieve) group of commands. Included in this discussion are some of the external attributes such as job attributes, system values, and object descriptions that you can use and modify in your CL programs. We also introduce ways to perform date conversions.

Return Variables

In Chapter 13 you learned that if a calling program passes a variable as a parameter, any change made to the variable in the called program is reflected in the variable value in the calling program. Because the variable is already declared in the calling program, you do not need special coding in the calling program to change the variable's value. The change is performed in the called program.

In some cases, a variable's value in the calling program may not be important until a called program places a value into the variable. For example, a program might need to call another program or execute a command to retrieve an external value, such as a date, then continue processing. That example describes the concept of a **return variable**, that is, a variable that has a significant value only upon the return from another program or command.

In addition to programs you write, a number of CL commands use return variables to return a value to a CL program. In particular, the RTV (Retrieve) group of commands uses return variables extensively to retrieve into a program attributes or information external to the program. Figure 14.1 lists some of the commonly used RTV commands. We look at a few of these in detail, specifically the RTVJOBA (Retrieve Job Attribute), RTVSYSVAL (Retrieve System Value), RTVUSRPRF (Retrieve User Profile), RTVMBRD (Retrieve Member Description), RTVNETA (Retrieve Network Attributes), and RTVOBJD (Retrieve Object Description) commands.

RTVCFGSTS	Retrieve Configuration Status
RTVDTAARA	Retrieve Data Area
RTVJOBA	Retrieve Job Attributes
RTVMBRD	Retrieve Member Description
RTVMSG	Retrieve Message
RTVNETA	Retrieve Network Attributes
RTVOBJD	Retrieve Object Description
RTVSYSVAL	Retrieve System Value
RTVUSRPRF	Retrieve User Profile

The RTVJOBA Command

When a job is active, your CL program can retrieve information about the attributes of the job and place that information into CL variables. Accessing these job attributes allows your program to determine dynamically which functions to perform, or how to perform them. Using the RTVJOBA (Retrieve Job Attributes) command, you can retrieve several different attributes of the current job at once. Some of the job attributes you can retrieve into CL variables are:

- Name of the job (JOB): For an interactive job this is the workstation ID; for a batch job, this is the job name
- Name of the user running the job (USER)
- Job number (NBR)
- The job's output queue (OUTQ)
- The accounting code for the job (ACGCDE)
- The job's execution environment (TYPE); whether the job is batch or interactive
- The execution priority of the job (RUNPTY)
- The job's user library list (USRLIBL)
- The name of the job's current library (CURLIB)
- The name of the job's current printer device (PRTDEV)

When you use the RTVJOBA command, CL places into one or more CL return variables the attributes of the job you are currently running. The command takes the form

```
RTVJOBA    JOB(&CL-variable-name)          +
           USER(&CL-variable-name)         +
           NBR(&CL-variable-name)          +
           OUTQ(&CL-variable-name)         +
           OUTQLIB(&CL-variable-name)      +
           DATE(&CL-variable-name)         +
           TYPE(&CL-variable-name)         +
           RUNPTY(&CL-variable-name)       +
```

```
              USRLIBL(&CL-variable-name)   +
              CURLIB(&CL-variable-name)    +
              PRTDEV(&CL-variable-name)
```

The RTVJOBA command has many other parameters, but these are the ones used most often. To use the RTVJOBA command in a program, you must declare the return variables into which you want the RTVJOBA command to place the values of the job attributes. For example, the following commands in a CL program let you determine whether a job is running interactively or in batch:

```
DCL        &jobtype  *char 1
RTVJOBA    TYPE(&jobtype)
```

These commands declare variable *&jobtype*, into which the RTVJOBA command is to place a code indicating the environment in which the job is running. If the job is running in batch, the command will change the value of *&jobtype* to '0'; otherwise, it will change the value of *&jobtype* to '1'. IBM dictates the format of return variables for the RTVJOBA command. For example, the return variable for the TYPE parameter must be declared as *CHAR LEN(1). Refer to Appendix A to determine the format for many of the return variables of the RTVJOBA command. Figure 14.2 illustrates the use of the RTVJOBA command in a CL program.

Figure 14.2
Using the RTVJOBA
Command

```
UPDCUST:  PGM        PARM(&mode &custnbr)

          DCL        &mode      *CHAR 6
          DCL        &custnbr   *DEC (15 5)
          DCL        &jobtype   *CHAR 1

          RTVJOBA    TYPE(&jobtype)

          IF         (&jobtype = '1')    DO
                     SBMJOB    CMD(CALL  PGM(UPDCUST)           +
                                         PARM(&mode &custnbr))

                     RETURN
          ENDDO

          ...
          (Continue processing)
          ...

          ENDPGM
```

The program in Figure 14.2 declares a one-character variable called *&jobtype*, in which it will store the job's environment type. The RTVJOBA command that follows the declaration determines whether the job is running interactively or in batch.

Next, the program tests the value of variable *&jobtype*. If the variable has a value of '1', indicating that it is running interactively, the program executes a SBMJOB command. This command submits a job for batch processing that will CALL the same program and pass the same parameters; it then ends with a RETURN command.

If, on the other hand, variable *&jobtype* indicates the job is already running in batch (i.e., its value is '0'), the program will skip over the DO group defined by the IF command and continue its batch processing.

Keep in mind that the RTVJOBA command retrieves only the attributes of the job within which the command is executed. You cannot use RTVJOBA to retrieve attributes of other jobs on the system. Also, RTVJOBA is valid only within a CL program and cannot be issued from the AS/400 command line. This restriction makes sense, because the RTVJOBA command requires the use of variables and you cannot declare variables at the command line.

The CHGJOB Command

Often, you will use the RTVJOBA command in conjunction with another CL command, CHGJOB (Change Job). The CHGJOB command lets you change certain attributes of any job on the system. The CHGJOB command follows this form:

```
CHGJOB     JOB(job-number/user-name/job-name)       +
           JOBQ(library-name/job-queue-name)        +
           JOBPTY(job queue-priority)               +
           OUTPTY(output-priority)                  +
           PRTTXT('print-text')                     +
           PRTDEV(printer-device-name)              +
           OUTQ(library-name/output-queue-name)     +
           SCDDATE(date)                            +
           SCDTIME(time)                            +
           DATE(date)                               +
           RUNPTY(machine-running-priority)
```

Like the RTVJOBA command, the CHGJOB command has many other parameters, but these are the most-often used. Many of the command parameters are the same as those used by the SBMJOB command; once again, CL's consistency makes it easy to learn. Some of the parameters also have parallels in the RTVJOBA command. Because the CHGJOB command allows you to change jobs other than your own, the first parameter, JOB, identifies the job to be changed. The default value, *, indicates that you want to change the current job; otherwise, you need to specify the qualified name of the job you want to change.

Some job attributes you can change include the job queue (JOBQ) and the job's priority (JOBPTY) on the job queue. You also can change the output queue (OUTQ), the printer device (PRTDEV), common printed text (PRTTXT) that will print at the bottom of every page, and the priority of reports on the output queue (OUTPTY). Finally, you can adjust the execution attributes of the job, including the time and date it is scheduled to run (SCDDATE and SCDTIME) and its execution priority (RUNPTY). You can even "fool" the job into thinking it is a date other than the actual date (DATE).

The CHGJOB command can run from a command line, as well as within a CL program. When you use the CHGJOB command in a CL program in connection with the RTVJOBA command, you can retrieve the job attribute you plan to change, change the attribute, and then restore the attribute to its original condition. This technique is handy for those times when you want to temporarily change an attribute, such as a job's execution priority, do some processing, and then return the attribute to its original value. Figure 14.3 illustrates a program that lowers its priority on the system to perform a long-running task. Then it returns to its original priority. Using this procedure improves overall system performance by ensuring that long-running interactive processing, which might otherwise be performed in batch, does not drag down performance of other interactive jobs on the system.

Figure 14.3
Using RTVJOBA and CHGJOB in the Same Program

```
PGM
DCL          &runpty    *DEC (2 0)
RTVJOBA      RUNPTY(&runpty)
IF           (&runpty  *LT 50) DO
             CHGJOB     RUNPTY(50)
             ENDDO
  .
  . (Long running processing)
  .
CHGJOB       RUNPTY(&runpty)
RETURN
ENDPGM
```

The program in Figure 14.3 declares a *DEC (2 0) variable *&runpty*, into which the RTVJOBA command places the current execution priority of the job. If the priority is less than 50, indicating that it is running at a high priority, the program uses the CHGJOB command to lower the job's priority to 50. It then performs a long-running task, perhaps displaying or updating a large number of objects in one or more libraries. After the long-running task is complete, the program again uses the CHGJOB command to return the job to its original priority, regardless of what that priority was at the start of the program.

Note that you must use the CHGJOB command if you want to manipulate the attributes of a job. You cannot retrieve a job attribute into a variable, then use the CHGVAR command to change the actual job attribute. You can, however, use CHGVAR to manipulate the variable, then use CHGJOB to change the job attribute. For example, the following code would lower the execution priority of a job by 10 priority "points." For instance, if the current priority is 20, it will be 30 after running the code (the higher the number, the lower the execution priority).

```
RTVJOBA   RUNPTY(&runpty)
IF        (&runpty *LT 90) DO
          CHGVAR   &runpty (runpty + 10)
          CHGJOB   RUNPTY(&runpty)
          ENDDO
```

System Values

The AS/400 has a set of attributes common to the entire system. These attributes, called **system values,** allow you to control and customize certain operating system functions. A system value contains systemwide control information used in day-to-day system operation. Examples of system values would be the system date or the system time of day. System values are not objects that can be created or deleted. IBM supplies them with the AS/400 and assigns default values to each one. The values stored within the system values can be displayed and many of them can be changed. More significant in light of this chapter's topic is the fact that the values stored within system values may be retrieved into CL variables and used within a CL program.

Each system value has a name and a predefined data type and format. For example, the system value named QHOUR contains the current hour of the day. It is stored on the system as a character field, two positions long. At 8 o'clock in the morning the value of QHOUR is '08'.

The RTVSYSVAL Command

You can bring system values into your program and manipulate them as variables using the RTVSYSVAL (Retrieve System Value) command. Unlike the RTVJOBA command, which can retrieve many attributes at once, the RTVSYSVAL command retrieves only one system value at a time. The command places the value into the return variable you specify. The command takes the following form:

```
RTVSYSVAL    SYSVAL(system-value-name)   +
             RTNVAR(&CL-variable-name)
```

The SYSVAL parameter identifies the system value to retrieve. The RTNVAR parameter lets you indicate the return variable that is to contain the system value. For example, the following code would retrieve the value of QHOUR and return it to variable *&thishour.*

```
DCL          &thishour *CHAR 2
RTVSYSVAL    SYSVAL(QHOUR)                  +
             RTNVAR(&thishour)
```

The type and length of the return variable must match the system value attributes. In the case of decimal values, the CL variable can be longer than the system value.

After you have retrieved the system value, you can manipulate the variable within your program without changing the stored system value. In the example above, for instance, using the CHGVAR command to change the value of *&thishour* would *not* change the system value of QHOUR. RTVSYSVAL, like most other RTV commands, cannot be executed from the command line; because it requires a return variable, it is valid only within a CL program.

Figure 14.4 demonstrates the use of the RTVSYSVAL command in a CL program. This program displays the system model and serial number. This information is stored in the system values named QMODEL and QSRLNBR.

Figure 14.4
Using RTVSYSVAL
in a Program

```
PGM
DCL         &model    *CHAR 4
DCL         &srlnbr   *CHAR 8
RTVSYSVAL SYSVAL(QMODEL)                                      +
            RTNVAR(&model)
RTVSYSVAL SYSVAL(QSRLNBR)                                     +
            RTNVAR(&srlnbr)
SNDPGMMSG    MSG('Your AS/400 is a model' *BCAT  +
                  &model *BCAT '                 +
                  'serial number' *BCAT          +
                  &srlnbr)                       +
              MSGTYPE(*COMP)
RETURN
ENDPGMPGM
```

The CHGSYSVAL Command

It is possible to change a system value within a CL program. The CHGSYSVAL (Change System Value) command allows you to make changes to system values. You can execute the CHGSYSVAL command from a command line or from a CL program. Keep in mind, however, that system values are by nature systemwide and that any change you make to a system value has an effect systemwide, not just in your job. The following syntax illustrates the use of the CHGSYSVAL command:

```
CHGSYSVAL    SYSVAL(system-value-name)                 +
             VALUE(new-value)
```

The SYSVAL parameter identifies the system value to be changed, and the VALUE parameter specifies the new value of the system value. Like the RTVSYSVAL command, CHGSYSVAL demands that the value you specify for the VALUE parameter match the predefined attributes of the system value. The program in Figure 14.5 illustrates the use of the CHGSYSVAL command in a program to handle the change to and from Daylight Savings Time.

Figure 14.5
Using CHGSYSVAL
to Handle Daylight
Savings Time

```
PGM       PARM(&springfall)
DCL       &springfall  *CHAR 6

DLYJOB    RSMTIME('020000')

IF        (&springfall = 'SPRING') DO
          CHGSYSVAL   SYSVAL(QHOUR)                +
                      VALUE('03')
          RETURN
          ENDDO

IF        (&springfall = 'FALL') DO
          CHGSYSVAL   SYSVAL(QHOUR)                +
                      VALUE('01')
          RETURN
          ENDDO

ENDPGM
```

The program in Figure 14.5 uses the DLYJOB (Delay Job) command to "fall asleep" until 2 A.M. At that time, it either changes the hour to 3 A.M. or 1 A.M., depending upon the value you specified on the CALL command for parameter *&springfall*. You would probably use the SBMJOB command to submit this job to batch on the Saturday before the time change was to take place on Sunday morning.

Often, you will use the CHGSYSVAL command in connection with the RTVSYSVAL command, first retrieving the value of the parameter, then manipulating the return variable that contains the value of the system value, and finally, specifying the variable as the new VALUE parameter for the CHGSYSVAL command.

Categories of System Values

In addition to the system date and time, model, and serial number, there are system values for such things as default library lists, security attributes, and default job environment specifications. System values are grouped into the following broad categories:

- Date/time
- System control
- Library list
- Editing
- Allocation/storage
- Message/logging
- Security

Let's look specifically at date/time, system control, and library list system values.

Date/Time System Values

The date/time system values let you access and control the date and time on your system. The computer's internal clock automatically updates these system values to reflect the correct date and time. Except to make minor time corrections, you shouldn't have to change them. If you do make changes, they take effect immediately. The major date/time system values are named:

- QDATE
- QCENTURY
- QTIME
- QDATFMT

The QDATE system value holds the system date. QDATE is usually accessed as *CHAR 6. It is made up of three other system values, QMONTH, QDAY, and QYEAR, each *CHAR 2. You can refer to each of these values individually, or you can refer to QDATE as a whole.

The AS/400 stores the year as a two-digit value, even with the advent of the year 2000. To eliminate possible date ambiguities between dates in the twentieth and twenty-first centuries, the QCENTURY system value holds the value of the century for the system date. The system value is a *CHAR 1 value, with a '0' indicating dates between 1928 and 1999 inclusive, or a '1' for dates between 2000 and 2053. System dates with years 1900–1927 or 2054–2099 are not supported by the AS/400.

QTIME is used to store the system time of day in hours/minutes/seconds (HHMMSS) format. It is usually defined as *CHAR 6, but you can gain more precision beyond seconds by using lengths of 7, 8, or 9 (to represent millisecond precision). QTIME is subdivided into values QHOUR, QMINUTE, and QSECOND, each defined as *CHAR 2. QTIME represents the time in a 24-hour-clock format (e.g., '140000' to represent 2 P.M., '000000' for midnight, and '120000' for noon).

You may have noticed that the date/time system values are defined as *CHAR data types, even though these values are generally considered numbers. These values must always be character data rather than numeric data. You must take this fact into account if you ever need to perform arithmetic operations on these system values.

The fourth date/time system value listed above, QDATFMT, really belongs in the editing system values category, but it makes sense to discuss it along with the date system values. QDATFMT contains the systemwide default format for representing dates. QDATFMT can contain any of the following values:

- MDY (month/day/year)
- YMD (year/month/day)
- DMY (day/month/year)
- JUL (Julian format)

In the United States, the date format used normally is MDY. However, users in some countries prefer to see the date in YMD format, and still others (mostly in Europe) prefer DMY. The QDATFMT system value allows flexibility in formatting dates according to the preferred method.

Julian dates are represented using only the year and day of the year. For example, February 28, 1994 (the 59th day of 1994) would be represented as 94059. If your system uses Julian date format, the definitions of QDATE and QDAY change slightly; in this case, QDATE is accessed as *CHAR 5 and QDAY is accessed as *CHAR 3.

System Control System Values

The system control system values provide information specific to your system's operation and configuration. These values can be retrieved or displayed, but many of them cannot be changed. The system control system values that you might normally access in a CL program are:

- QABNORMSW
- QIPLDATTIM

- QIPLSTS
- QMODEL
- QPRTDEV
- QSRLNBR

The system values QABNORMSW and QIPLSTS keep a summary of the circumstances that last caused your system to power down and restart. You cannot change either of these system values. QABNORMSW (*CHAR 1) indicates whether the previous system end was normal or abnormal. It contains a '0' if the previous system shutdown occurred as a result of a PWRDWNSYS (Power Down System) command, without an accompanying ENDJOBABN (End Job Abnormally) command; this is considered a normal shutdown. Otherwise, you will find a '1' in QABNORMSW.

QIPLSTS indicates what type of **IPL** (Initial Program Load) last occurred (an IPL is the AS/400's version of a "boot" process, which loads the operating system when the power is turned on). QIPLSTS (*CHAR 1) can contain several values:

- '0' means the IPL was requested from the operator panel on the computer.
- '1' means the system automatically restarted following a power failure.
- '2' means the system automatically restarted following a PWRDWNSYS command.
- '3' means that the IPL occurred automatically at the date and time set in the QIPLDATTIM system value.
- '4' means that the system has the capability of being remotely started via telephone, and that a remote IPL occurred.

The QIPLDATTIM system value lets you specify a date and time that you want the system to automatically IPL. If the system is powered off when the specified date and time occur, it restarts without intervention. The system provides a power scheduling facility that uses this system value, but you can bypass the scheduling facility and change the system value. The default value for QIPLDATTIM is *NONE. The value is defined as *CHAR 20 and is divided into two parts: the date and the time of day to IPL the system. The two parts must be in a quoted string and must be separated by a space.

The QMODEL and QSRLNBR system values, defined as *CHAR 4 and *CHAR 8, respectively, hold the model number and serial number of the system you are working on. No one can change these system values, but they can be retrieved or displayed.

The QPRTDEV system value (*CHAR 10) holds the name of the system's default printer device. You will not routinely change the value of QPRTDEV, but you might often retrieve it. If you do change the value, the change takes effect for any new jobs that start after it is changed.

Library List System Values

To set up default library lists, you use the library list system values. There are two library list system values: QSYSLIBL and QUSRLIBL.

QSYSLIBL specifies the system portion of the library list that is used for all jobs running on the system. The list can contain the names of up to 15 libraries, each one separated by a blank. Remember that the system searches the system portion of the library list before it searches anywhere else for an object. IBM ships the system value with the value 'QSYS QSYS2 QHLPSYS QUSRSYS', but you can add other libraries to the system library list. You must be careful to include library QSYS, which contains the basic OS/400 operating system, and QHLPSYS, which contains the system help text, in this system value. The QSYSLIBL system value is defined as *CHAR 150.

QUSRLIBL specifies the user portion of the library list used by jobs running on the system. The list can contain up to 25 libraries, each one separated by a blank. Remember that the system searches the user portion of the library list last, after first checking the system library list, the product library, and the current library. IBM ships the system value with the default value 'QTEMP QGPL' but you can add other libraries to the list. You should ensure that libraries QTEMP and QGPL remain in the user library list because these are the generally accepted libraries for temporary objects and for general utility objects. The QUSRLIBL system value is defined as *CHAR 250.

There are no system values for the product library or the current library. The product library is determined automatically when certain commands or functions are used; the current library is set in the user profile, the job description, or by the CHGCURLIB (Change Current Library) command.

Other System Values

There are several groups of system values that you probably will not need to access in a CL program. These values are usually set when your computer is first installed, then rarely changed. A brief overview of these groups is provided here.

The editing system values control the format for displaying dates, currency, and decimals. The allocation/storage system values help you control the number of jobs and the size of memory pools on the system. The message/logging values control how the system logs messages. The security system values set the level of security on your system and also enforce a number of password validation policies. If you need further information about these system values, refer to IBM's *Work Management Guide.*

The RTVUSRPRF Command

The RTVUSRPRF (Retrieve User Profile) command captures information about a user from his/her user profile. A *USRPRF (User Profile) object is created for each user who will perform work on the system. The system security officer or security administrator determines how the profile of each user will be defined. A great deal of information in the user profile deals with a user's authority and environment. You can use this information within a CL program to control processing. RTVUSRPRF is similar to the RTVJOBA command, discussed earlier, in that you can retrieve many attributes with a single command. The RTVUSRPRF command has many parameters, but the following form includes the most-often used:

```
RTVUSRPRF    USRPRF(user-name)                    +
             RTNUSRPRF(&CL-variable-name)         +
             SPCAUT(&CL-variable-name)            +
             INLPGM(&CL-variable-name)            +
             INLPGMLIB(&CL-variable-name)         +
             JOBD(&CL-variable-name)              +
             JOBDLIB(&CL-variable-name)           +
             GRPPRF(&CL-variable-name)            +
             OWNER(&CL-variable-name)             +
             GRPAUT(&CL-variable-name)            +
             ACGCDE(&CL-variable-name)            +
             MSGQ(&CL-variable-name)              +
             MSGQLIB(&CL-variable-name)           +
             OUTQ(&CL-variable-name)              +
             OUTQLIB(&CL-variable-name)           +
             TEXT(&CL-variable-name)              +
             PWDCHGDAT(&CL-variable-name)         +
             USRCLS(&CL-variable-name)            +
             CURLIB(&CL-variable-name)            +
             INLMNU(&CL-variable-name)            +
             INLMNULIB(&CL-variable-name)         +
             LMTCPB(&CL-variable-name)            +
             PRTDEV(&CL-variable-name)            +
             PWDEXP(&CL-variable-name)            +
             STATUS(&CL-variable-name)            +
             PRVSIGN(&CL-variable-name)           +
             NOTVLDSIGN(&CL-variable-name)
```

As you can see, a wealth of information is available in the user profile. Appendix A contains a brief description of each parameter for the RTVUSRPRF command. As with the RTVJOBA command, you must specify a CL variable name to receive each profile attribute that you want to retrieve. Also, as with RTVJOBA, changing the value stored in the variable after the value is retrieved from the user profile does not change the attribute in the user profile.

When you use the RTVUSRPRF command, you specify the user profile you want information about; you also specify which information you are requesting, as the following example illustrates:

```
RTVUSRPRF    USRPRF(BOB)    MSGQ(&msgq)
```

The above example retrieves the name of the message queue assigned to user BOB. In addition to a specific user, you can specify USRPRF(*CURRENT) to retrieve information about the current user, as the following example illustrates:

```
RTVUSRPRF    USRPRF(*CURRENT)    MSGQ(&msgq)
```

Using the USRPRF (User Profile) and RTNUSRPRF (Returned User Profile) parameters together might seem to be redundant. They both refer to the user identification and they both are defined as *CHAR 10. But you use USRPRF to specify to CL which user profile you want to retrieve, and you use RTNUSRPRF to return the name of the user profile that was retrieved. The difference still isn't fully apparent until you realize that the default value for USRPRF is *CURRENT*. If you specify USRPRF(*CURRENT), the RTVUSRPRF command returns to your CL program the user identifier for the user running the program (Figure 14.6). Unless you use USRPRF(*CURRENT), the RTNUSRPRF parameter is redundant.

Figure 14.6
Using RTVUSRPRF
in a Program

```
PGM

DCL       &user      *CHAR 10

RTVUSRPRF USRPRF(*CURRENT)                    +
          RTNUSRPRF(&user)

SNDPGMMSG MSG('User' *BCAT &user *BCAT        +
              'logged in.')                   +
          MSGTYPE(*COMP)
RETURN
ENDPGM
```

The CHGUSRPRF Command

Because there's a CHGJOB command to match the RTVJOBA command, and because there's a CHGSYSVAL command to match the RTVSYSVAL command, you might think there's a CHGUSRPRF command to match the RTVUSRPRF command. You would be right. With the proper authority, you can make changes to a user's profile, changing his or her ability to perform certain operations, or changing the work environment. Because this command deals primarily with system security, however, we won't deal with it in this text.

Other RTV Commands

Several other RTV commands are worthy of mention. A brief discussion of these commands is presented here. For more information, see Appendix A.

The RTVMBRD (Retrive Member Description) command retrieves information about an individual database file member, including the current number of active records in the member, the number of deleted records, the date the member was last saved to a backup medium (such as tape), and the date the member was last used.

The RTVNETA (Retrieve Network Attributes) command retrieves the **network attributes** of your system into CL variables. Network attributes are such things as the name of the system and the name assigned to your communications network. These attributes are usually assigned when your system is set up.

RTVOBJD (Retrive Object Description) provides a way to retrieve descriptive information about a single object on the system into CL variables. This information includes such things as the library in which the object resides, who owns the object, when it was last saved, and when it was last used.

Date Conversion Using the CVTDAT Command

Many of your CL programs will probably use the system date to perform their processing. To perform some tasks, you may need to convert the format of the date to some format other than your system's native format. For example, as we discussed earlier, dates in the United States are usually formatted in month/day/year (MDY) format. But MDY format is inconvenient to use in making date comparisons. You know from experience that the date represented by the character string '01-01-94' is greater than the date represented by '12-31-93'; but CL doesn't support a date data type. So as far as CL is concerned, those character strings are treated strictly as character strings, not dates, and '12-31-93' is greater than '01-01-94'. To make convenient date comparisons, dates could be represented in year/month/day (YMD) format. Then '94-01-01' is greater than '93-12-31', and an accurate comparison can be made. To perform date arithmetic, the easiest data format is Julian format.

CL provides a command to perform just such a conversion. The CVTDAT (Convert Date) command converts a date from one format to another, without changing its value. The format for the CVTDAT command is:

```
CVTDAT   DATE(date-to-be-converted)   +
         TOVAR(&CL-variable-name)      +
         FROMFMT(from-date-format)     +
         TOFMT(to-date-format)         +
         TOSEP(separator-character)
```

The DATE parameter should hold the date you want to convert; it can contain either a constant or a character variable. The value in DATE must be a valid date. The TOVAR parameter allows you to specify a CL character variable into which you want to place the converted value of the date; because the command involves a return variable, it is valid only within a CL program.

The FROMFMT parameter is used to tell CVTDAT in what format the DATE parameter is presented. A number of valid values exist for FROMFMT. The default value is *JOB, indicating that the DATE parameter value is using the same format as the job in which it is running; this format is found in the DATFMT attribute of the job and can be retrieved using RTVJOBA, if necessary. You can also specify FROMFMT(*SYSVAL), to tell the command that the date is in the same format as the system value QDATFMT. Some other commonly used values for the FROMFMT parameter are

- *MDY (month/day/year)
- *YMD (year/month/day)
- *DMY (day/month/year)
- *JUL (Julian format)

To support years from 2000 and beyond, CVTDAT allows these additional formats that use four-digit years:

- *MDYY (month/day/year)
- *YYMD (year/month/day)
- *DMYY (day/month/year)
- *LONGJUL (Julian format)

The TOFMT parameter specifies the format to which you want the date converted. The value can be any of the same values as the FROMFMT parameter, including *JOB* (the default) and *SYSVAL*.

The TOSEP parameter lets you specify that the converted date in the TOVAR variable should include separator characters, and which separator character should be used. The valid characters are the slash (/), hyphen (–), period (.), and comma (,). If you specify TOSEP(*NONE), the variable will not contain separators between the month, day, and year. Specifying TOSEP(*BLANK) separates the portions of the date with blanks. The default TOSEP value, *JOB*, indicates that the converted date should have the separator characters specified in the DATSEP attribute of the job. TOSEP(*SYSVAL) uses the character in the system value QDATSEP.

When you use the CVTDAT command, the length of the value in the DATE parameter and the length of the variable in the TOVAR parameter must correctly match the requirements of the date format. For non-Julian dates, the TOVAR variable must be at least six characters long; for Julian dates, it must be at least five characters long. If you use separator characters, the length must be at least eight characters (six for Julian dates). The four-digit year formats require an additional two characters beyond the two-digit year formats. If you use longer lengths, the variable will be padded on the right with blanks. As with the date/time system values, the CVTDAT command deals with dates as character strings, so the variables must be declared as *CHAR data types.

One common use for the CVTDAT command is to create objects or add file members that are named according to the date they are created. If, for example, you want to separate each day's cash receipts into a separate member in a file named RECEIPTS, you could use the following code to create that file member:

```
DCL          &today     *CHAR 6
DCL          &mbrdate   *CHAR 5
RTVSYSVAL    SYSVAL(QDATE)                  +
             RTNVAR(&today)
CVTDAT       DATE(&today)                   +
             TOVAR(&mbrdate)                +
             FROMFMT(*SYSVAL)               +
             TOFMT(*JUL)                    +
             TOSEP(*NONE)
ADDPFM       FILE(RECEIPTS)                 +
             MBR('CASH' *CAT &mbrdate)
```

In this example, the RTVSYSVAL command determines the current date and copies it into variable &today. Then the CVTDAT command converts the date to Julian format and places the converted date into variable &mbrdate. Finally, the ADDPFM (Add Physical File Member) command adds the member to the RECEIPTS file, creating a name based upon the date. For example, if the current date is February 28, 1997, this code would produce a member named CASH97059.

Chapter Summary

A return variable is a program variable that has a significant value only upon return from a command or from another program. Many CL commands use CL variables to return an external value to a program. The RTV (Retrieve) group of commands uses return variables to provide a program with information external to the program.

The RTVJOBA (Retrieve Job Attributes) command retrieves attributes of the current job and copies them into CL variables. These attributes include such things as the name of the job, who is running it, and whether it is running interactively or in batch. You can also use RTVJOBA in conjunction with the CHGJOB (Change Job) command, if you want to change some attributes of a job and have the ability to change it back to its original state.

System values are customizing specifications that are specific to a single AS/400. System values include such things as the current date and time, default library lists, security attributes, and default job environment specifications. You can retrieve system values using the RTVSYSVAL (Retrieve System Values) command, then use the system values in a CL program. While many system values are set at the time a system is installed, you can change some system values using the CHGSYSVAL (Change System Values) command.

The RTVUSRPRF (Retrieve User Profile) command captures information about a user from that user's user profile object and copies that information into one or more CL variables. With proper authority, you can also change certain attributes of a user profile with the CHGUSRPRF (Change User Profile) command.

To convert the format of a date from one format to another, without changing its value, you can use the CVTDAT (Convert Date) command. CL treats all dates as character strings because it doesn't support a date data type.

Terms

IPL
network attributes

return variables
system values

Review Questions

1. Refer to Appendix A to decide which of the following commands use return variables.
    a. ADDPFM
    b. CALL
    c. CHGJOB
    d. CHGSYSVAL
    e. CHGVAR
    f. CVTDAT
    g. RCVMSG
    h. RTVCLSRC
    i. RTVDTAARA
    j. RTVMSG
    k. RTVOBJD

2. Specify the commands and the parameters that you would use to retrieve the following information into a CL program. Some of the information may be available from more than one command, and some of the information may require more than a single command.

    a. The name of the user who is running the program
    b. The current library and the user portion of a job's library list
    c. The current date
    d. The date on which a job is running
    e. The system name, model, and serial number of your AS/400
    f. The current time, to millisecond accuracy
    g. A user's authority to enter AS/400 commands on a command line
    h. The last date that a program was executed

3. Assume a CL program must calculate the number of days between two dates in the same year. The dates are presented as input parameters to the program in month/day/year format. Which CL commands would you use to perform the calculation? Which date formats would you use?

Exercises

1. Write the program discussed in Review Question 3. The program name will be SA1401*XXX*, where *XXX* is replaced with your initials.

2. Write a program (SA1402*XXX*) that sends a program message to the bottom of your display that states:

    ```
    'You are BOB, signed on at DSP25 on system STUDENT.'
    ```

    BOB is the name of the user of the program. DSP25 is the name of the workstation device (i.e., the JOB name). STUDENT is the system name.

    Exercises continued

Exercises continued

3. Write a program (SA1403 *XXX*) that accepts two parameters:

    a. a database file name
    b. a library name

    Send a message to the bottom of the display that states the following:

    ```
    'File FILE1 in library LIB1 has 00025 active records.'
    ```

    FILE1 is the file name, LIB1 is the library name, and 00025 is the number of active records in the first or only member in the file.

Chapter 15

Files and Data Areas

Chapter Overview

In this chapter you learn how files and data areas are used within a CL program. We discuss database files and display files, along with the data description specifications necessary to define them. In addition, we talk about how and when to use data areas to store and retrieve information.

Working with Files

CL provides input and output commands that allow you to process database and display files within a CL program. You can read information from a database file or, using a display file, you can send a display to a workstation and subsequently receive user input from that display for use in the program. CL supports both types of files with similar commands, but there are differences in the depth of support for each file type. We discuss those differences as we cover each file type in detail.

Database Files

There are two major types of database files on the AS/400: **physical files**, and **logical files**. Physical files contain data that is defined according to a specific layout, called a *record format*. The records in a physical file are physically stored in *arrival sequence* (i.e., the order in which they were added to the file). You can specify an optional *keyed sequence* for a physical file by defining one or more fields in a file as keys. Your program then can process the file's records in the order of the key field, instead of in arrival sequence. Specifying a keyed sequence affects only the order in which a program processes records in a file, not the position of the records in the file.

Logical files are indexes that provide sorting and record selection criteria for physical files. Logical files contain no data records; but programs, including CL programs, can access and manipulate logical files as if they did. A logical file provides an alternate *access path* to records stored in a physical file, perhaps by sorting the records differently or by including only selected data records. The contents of a logical file are dependent upon the contents of one or more related physical files. The logical file acts as a filter, determining which records your program will process and in what order it will process them.

For example, you might have a customer file (a physical file) on your system named CUSTMAS, which contains basic information about each of your customers, past and present, in no particular order. You could define one or more logical files for this physical file to order the data or to filter it. You might want to define one logical file in customer number order and another in customer name (alphabetic) order. Or you might want a logical file in customer number order that contains only currently active customers. One popular method used by AS/400 programmers would have you name the logical files CUSTMAS1, CUSTMAS2, and CUSTMAS3, respectively. Your program could use any of these four files (CUSTMAS, CUSTMAS1, CUSTMAS2, or CUSTMAS3) to access the data in CUSTMAS, but the actual data records would exist only in the physical file CUSTMAS. The logical files would contain only pointers to the records in CUSTMAS, but your program would treat them as if they contained data records. You can have many logical files defined over a physical file. Figure 15.1 illustrates the relationship between a physical file and three logical files.

Display Files

A **display file** is an AS/400 *FILE type object that is not designed to hold data. On the AS/400, a display file belongs in a special category of files called **device files** (a printer file is also a device file). A device file describes the way the AS/400 interacts with a hardware device such as a printer or workstation. Display files contain the descriptions of display screen formats that will appear on a workstation screen. To send a display to a workstation screen, a program writes a display file record.. A user then can type information into the screen. To receive the user's response, the program must read a display file record. A few similarities exist between database files and display files. But as you will see, there are more differences than likenesses.

File Existence Requirements for CL

Most objects referred to in a CL program are not accessed until you run the program. For example, if a CL program calls another program, the called program need not exist when you compile the calling program. Only when you run the calling program do you need to be sure the called program exists on your system.

Files are one of the exceptions to this situation. Database files and display files that are declared in your program must exist on your system at the time you compile the program. When you use the DCLF (Declare File) command to declare a file within a CL program, the CL compiler accesses the file's description to declare the fields in that file as program variables. Remember from Chapter 7 that the CL variable for a field in a declared file is named the same as the field, but preceded by an ampersand (&).

Usually, when you begin writing a CL program, the files you need will already exist on your system. This is especially true of database (physical and logical) files. Even some of the display files you will use for your CL programs may already exist on the system before you begin writing the CL program.

If the file you need doesn't exist, you must create it. To create a file, you first need to define the attributes and layout of the file by entering specifications, called

Figure 15.1
The Relationship Between
Physical and Logical Files

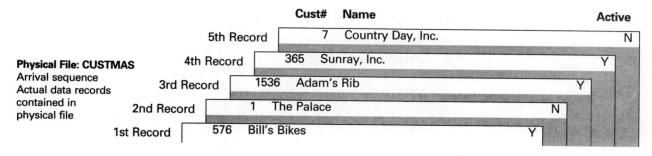

Physical File: CUSTMAS
Arrival sequence
Actual data records
contained in
physical file

	Cust#	Name	Active
5th Record	7	Country Day, Inc.	N
4th Record	365	Sunray, Inc.	Y
3rd Record	1536	Adam's Rib	Y
2nd Record	1	The Palace	N
1st Record	576	Bill's Bikes	Y

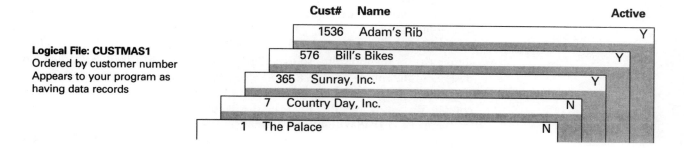

Logical File: CUSTMAS1
Ordered by customer number
Appears to your program as
having data records

Cust#	Name	Active
1536	Adam's Rib	Y
576	Bill's Bikes	Y
365	Sunray, Inc.	Y
7	Country Day, Inc.	N
1	The Palace	N

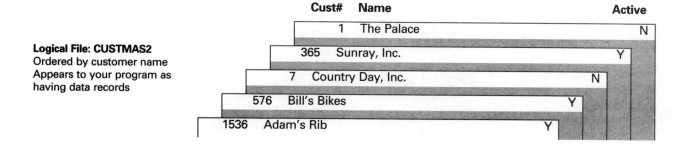

Logical File: CUSTMAS2
Ordered by customer name
Appears to your program as
having data records

Cust#	Name	Active
1	The Palace	N
365	Sunray, Inc.	Y
7	Country Day, Inc.	N
576	Bill's Bikes	Y
1536	Adam's Rib	Y

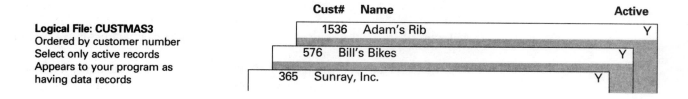

Logical File: CUSTMAS3
Ordered by customer number
Select only active records
Appears to your program as
having data records

Cust#	Name	Active
1536	Adam's Rib	Y
576	Bill's Bikes	Y
365	Sunray, Inc.	Y

data description specifications (DDS), into a source file member. Using DDS, you can describe physical, logical, and display files. Once you have described the file, you then use the appropriate command to create the file object:

- CRTPF   Create Physical File
- CRTLF   Create Logical File
- CRTDSPF   Create Display File

This discussion includes an overview of DDS, so you can create simple files for use with your CL programs, but it is not a DDS tutorial. For more information about using DDS to create files, refer to IBM's *Data Description Specifications Reference.*

Data Description Specifications

Like program objects, display files and database files are created from a source member. However, instead of entering CL source code, as you would when writing a CL program, you enter **data description specifications** (DDS) source code. The standard source file used when entering DDS source is named QDDSSRC. DDS describes the format of the records within the file, as well as the fields within the records. The source type of the individual source member identifies which type of file the member describes. The source type for a display file is *DSPF*, the type for a physical file is *PF*, and the type for a logical file is *LF*. Once you have entered the DDS source, you then compile the source member to create the file object.

Unlike CL, DDS requires that specific entries be entered into specific columnar positions in the source. For example, all DDS include an *A* in column 6. An asterisk (*) in column 7 indicates a comment line. Although, we cannot conduct an exhaustive examination of DDS in this text, Figure 15.2 identifies the major DDS requirements for physical, logical, and display files.

While there are many commonalities in DDS, the specifications vary slightly, depending upon whether they define a physical file, a logical file, or a display file. Let's look briefly at the specifications for each of these file types.

DDS for Physical Files

The specifications that define physical files can include the following:

- Optional file keywords, which describe common characteristics of the file
- A record format specification, which names the record layout and describes some of its characteristics
- Field definition specifications, which describe individual fields within a record format
- Optional key field specifications, which can designate certain fields as key fields

The DDS source member in Figure 15.3 illustrates DDS for a keyed physical file.

Columnar Position	Contents
6	Specification type (always *A*)
7	Comment (* for comments)
17	Type of specification:
	R = Record format
	K = Key field[1]
	S = Select field[2]
	O = Omit field[2]
19–28	Name of record format or field
30–34	Field length
36–37	Decimal positions
38	Usage[3]
	I = Input only
	O = Output only
	B = Input/output
39–41	Display row location[3]
42–44	Display column location[3]
45–80	Keyword entries

Figure 15.2
DDS Overview

[1]Used only for physical and logical files
[2]Used only for logical files
[3]Used only for display files. Position 38 can be used for logical files in rare instances.

Figure 15.3 begins with a comment line (A) containing the file's name (CUSTMAS). The actual AS/400 name of the file is determined by the name you assign when you execute the CRTPF command, not by anything specified within the DDS. Next are file-level keywords (B), which are specified before the record format specification. In this example, the only file-level keyword is *UNIQUE*, which indicates that this file contains unique keys (i.e., it cannot have two records with the same key

Figure 15.3
Physical
File DDS

```
*...+... 1 ...+... 2 ...+... 3 ...+... 4 ...+... 5 ...+... 6 ...+ ... 7
A* File name - CUSTMAS - Customer master file
A                                            UNIQUE
A          R CUSTREC                         TEXT('Customer record')
A            CUCOMP         3  0             TEXT('Company number')
A            CUCUST         7  0             TEXT('Customer number')
A            CUNAME        35                TEXT('Name')
A            CUADDR        35                TEXT('Address')
A            CUCITY        21                TEXT('City')
A            CUSTAT         2                TEXT('State')
A            CUZIPC        10                TEXT('ZIP code')
A            CUCTRY        35                TEXT('Foreign country')
A            CULIM$        11  2             TEXT('Credit limit')
A          K CUCOMP
A          K CUCUST
```

fields). In this case, there cannot be more than one record with the same company number and customer number.

The record-format specification (C) names the record format in the file. The record-format statement is identified by an *R* in column 17 of the specification. Following the record-format specification are several field-level specifications (D) that describe the structure of the data fields within each record of the file. For example, field *CUCOMP* is defined as three digits long, with no decimal places. This field is assumed to be a numeric field because the number of decimal positions is specified in columns 36 and 37. The TEXT keyword beginning in column 45 is used to assign descriptive text to the field. Within the data record, following the data for field *CUCOMP*, will be the data for field *CUCUST*, followed by the data for field *CUNAME*, defined as a 35-character field (because the decimal positions in columns 36 and 37 are blank, field *CUNAME* is assumed to be a character data type). Other data fields follow *CUNAME*.

Finally, the DDS define two key fields (E) — *CUCOMP* and *CUCUST* — the company number and customer number. These fields indicate the order in which the records in the physical file will be accessed on sequential read operations.

To create this physical file, you would enter the DDS into a source member (usually given the same name as the file), then you would type the following command at an AS/400 command line:

```
CRTPF    FILE(CUSTMAS)      +
         SRCFILE(QDDSSRC)   +
         SRCMBR(CUSTMAS)
```

If there were no errors in the DDS source member, the file would be created in your current library. You then could use an HLL program or file editing utility like IBM's DFU (Data File Utility) to add the necessary data records to the file.

DDS for Logical Files

The specifications that define logical files, although similar to those for physical files, are unique in several ways. To create a logical file, you first must create the physical file to which the logical file will refer. Let's assume you wanted to create an alternative view of file CUSTMAS from Figure 15.3, perhaps to access the records within the the customer file by company number and customer name. The DDS in Figure 15.4 would accomplish this goal.

Notice that the DDS source member for this logical file is much shorter than that for the physical file. At (A) we refer to record format *CUSTREC* in physical file

Figure 15.4
DDS for a Logical
File Using
Alternative Keys

```
*...+... 1 ...+... 2 ...+... 3 ...+... 4 ...+... 5 ...+... 6 ...+ ... 7
     A* File name — CUSTMAS1 — Customer master file keyed by name
 (A) A           R CUSTREC                        PFILE(CUSTMAS)
     A           K CUCOMP
 (B) A           K CUNAME
```

CUSTMAS — PFILE(CUSTMAS) — and at (B) we specify different key fields. We don't need to repeat all the field specifications because we want to use the same fields that are in the record format named *CUSTREC*, but we want to access the data records in a different order. To create this file, we would use the following CL command:

```
CRTLF   FILE(CUSTMAS1)    +
        SRCFILE(QDDSSRC)  +
        SRCMBR(CUSTMAS1)
```

Now let's assume that you want to access the records in the customer file in the order specified in logical file CUSTMAS1, but you want to include only those customers whose credit limit is more than $5,000. The DDS in Figure 15.5 would create the necessary logical file.

Figure 15.5
DDS for a
Logical File
Using
Select/Omit
Criteria

```
*...+... 1 ...+... 2 ...+... 3 ...+... 4 ...+... 5 ...+... 6 ...+ ... 7

A* File name – CUSTMAS2 – Customer master file
A*                         Records with high credit limits
A           R CUSTREC                     PFILE(CUSTMAS)
A           K CUCOMP
A           K CUNAME
A           S CULIM$               COMP(GT 5000)
```
(A)

To define this logical file, we add select/omit criteria (A) to select (S in column 17) those records where the field *CULIM$* is greater than 5000. To perform this comparison, we use the COMP keyword: COMP(GT 5000).

Many other DDS options are available when defining logical files. The preceding examples are not intended to provide a comprehensive look at the subject, but rather to give you a basic understanding of how DDS for logical files are defined.

DDS for Display Files

While CL does provide support for database files, you'll find that quite often the files you use in CL are not database files, but display files. The DDS for display files are similar to DDS for database files, but in general, you'll find display files more complex. A display file can contain up to 99 different record formats. Each record format is an individual screen or portion of a screen and can contain:

- Input fields (those fields into which you can enter data)
- Output fields (fields into which you cannot enter data; that is, they are not input-capable)
- Input/output fields (fields that display information you can change)
- Constants (such as titles and descriptive text that you cannot change)
- Conditions (indicators)

As with database files, you create a display file by entering DDS source statements into a source member, which you then compile. To facilitate the process, IBM provides a tool, Screen Design Aid (SDA), that allows you to design the screen interactively without being familiar with all of the DDS conventions. SDA then creates the DDS source statements for you. SDA is part of the Application Development ToolSet/400 (ADTS/400) licensed program product that includes other programming tools, such as PDM and SEU. This tool makes it much easier to design screens than if you had to use SEU to enter individual DDS source statements. If you would like more information about SDA, refer to the IBM publication *Application Development ToolSet/400 — Screen Design Aid,* or the Duke Press publication *Desktop Guide to AS/400 Programmers' Tools.* You can find information about this and other AS/400 technical publications at the end of this book.

Figure 15.6 illustrates a DDS source member that can be used to create a simple display file. The screen generated by this DDS is shown in Figure 15.7.

Figure 15.6
DDS for a
Display File

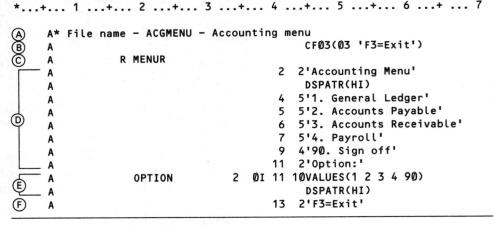

```
*...+... 1 ...+... 2 ...+... 3 ...+... 4 ...+... 5 ...+... 6 ...+ ... 7
   A* File name - ACGMENU - Accounting menu
   A                                           CF03(03 'F3=Exit')
   A          R MENUR
   A                                   2  2'Accounting Menu'
   A                                      DSPATR(HI)
   A                                   4  5'1. General Ledger'
   A                                   5  5'2. Accounts Payable'
   A                                   6  5'3. Accounts Receivable'
   A                                   7  5'4. Payroll'
   A                                   9  4'90. Sign off'
   A                                  11  2'Option:'
   A            OPTION         2  0I 11 10VALUES(1 2 3 4 90)
   A                                      DSPATR(HI)
   A                                  13  2'F3=Exit'
```

Figure 15.7
Screen Created
from DDS in
Figure 15.6

```
Accounting Menu

   1. General Ledger
   2. Accounts Payable
   3. Accounts Receivable
   4. Payroll

  90. Sign off

Option: __

F3=Exit
```

The DDS in Figure 15.6 defines a display file named ACGMENU (A). We include a file-level keyword (B) — file-level keywords are specifications that apply to all record formats within a file. In this case, the file-level keyword enables the F3 function key.

When a user presses F3, your program can identify that condition by testing indicator 03; it will be ON (true). **Indicators** are logical flags used in display files to set conditions; you can define up to 99 indicators (01–99) in a display file. If you use indicators, they are declared within the CL program as logical (*LGL) variables (&in01, &in02, … &in99).

When indicator 03 is defined in a display file, as it is in this example, the CL program accesses the condition of the indicator using the variable named *&in03*. So in the CL program you could test the condition of indicator 03 using the following command:

```
IF    &in03    THEN(GOTO ENDIT)
```

At (C), we name the record format (MENUR). Although this sample display file contains only one record format, a display file can contain multiple record formats (screens), as long as each one has a unique name. Following the record-format specification are entries for several constants (D) that are to be displayed on the screen.

Field OPTION (E) will contain the user's response to the display. The user can enter any one of the values 1, 2, 3, 4, or 90. The input field will be underlined and will also have a display attribute of high intensity, specified by DSPATR(HI), which will cause it to be brighter than other fields on the display. The *I* in column 38 indicates that the field is an input-capable field (i.e., a user can type a value into it).

Finally, the specifications define the constant 'F3=Exit' (F) that will be displayed at the bottom of the screen, as shown in Figure 15.7. This does not enable the F3 Key; it simply shows the workstation user that F3 is a valid function key for this display.

CL File Processing

In addition to the DCLF (Declare File) command, CL primarily uses four *file access commands* to support file input/output (I/O) operations:

- SNDRCVF   Send/Receive File
- SNDF   Send File
- RCVF   Receive File
- WAIT

You can use all the file access commands for display files, but CL allows only input operations for database files, so database operations are limited to the RCVF command.

The DCLF Command

Recall from Chapter 7 that your program must first declare a file if it is to process it (read a record). You can declare only one file per program. When you include the DCLF command in the declarations section of the program, the CL compiler retrieves the file's field descriptions and make them available to the program as CL variables. The DCLF command takes the following form:

```
DCLF    FILE(library-name/file-name)   +
        RCDFMT(record-format-name)
```

The FILE parameter is required. The RCDFMT parameter is optional and defaults to a value of *ALL, indicating that all of the file's record formats will be copied into the CL program at compile time.

Remember that the file must exist on your system when you compile the program. If you do not qualify the FILE parameter with a library name, the file must exist in your library list when you compile the program. The compiler must be able to find the file to use its definitions.

The fields in the file are implicitly declared within the CL program by the DCLF command. You do not need to declare them explicitly. Remember that each of the variables in the CL program will be preceded by an ampersand (&). If you were to declare file *CUSTMAS* from Figure 15.1, CL would define all the fields in the file as CL variables, just as if you had included the following commands:

```
DCL     &CUCOMP    *DEC (3 0)
DCL     &CUCUST    *DEC (7 0)
DCL     &CUNAME    *CHAR 35
DCL     &CUADDR    *CHAR 35
DCL     &CUCITY    *CHAR 21
DCL     &CUSTAT    *CHAR 2
DCL     &CUZIPC    *CHAR 10
DCL     &CUCTRY    *CHAR 35
DCL     &CULIM$    *DEC (11 2)
```

The CL compiler ignores the fact that the file is keyed by company number and customer number. OS/400 data management routines will still present the records in the file in the keyed order; this order is controlled by OS/400, not by the CL program.

The SNDRCVF Command

The SNDRCVF (Send/Receive File) command sends a formatted screen to a workstation, then asks for and optionally reads data from the display. This command effects a two-way communication between a CL program and a workstation user. The CL program sends a screen format to the display, showing the user the current values of those CL variables that correspond to fields defined on the screen. If the screen format includes input-capable fields, the user can enter changes to those fields. The user must then press an action key, such as Enter, or a function key, such as F3. At that point, the CL program continues, and the values entered are passed back to the CL program in the associated program variables.

You can use the SNDRCVF command only with a display file. CL does not support writing records to a database file.

The SNDRCVF command takes the form

```
SNDRCVF    DEV(device-name)                    +
           RCDFMT(record-format-name)          +
           WAIT(wait-parameter)
```

All of the parameters are optional. The default value for the DEV parameter is *FILE, indicating that the workstation device associated with the declared file is the one that

Files Without DDS

In this chapter we cover the use of CL with *externally described* files (i.e., those files created from DDS). Most of the files you will encounter on the AS/400 are externally described files. In CL, all display files must be externally described. Some database files, however, are *program-described*, created with no external data definition. To create a program-described file, you would use the alternative syntax of the CRTPF (Create Physical File) command:

```
CRTPF      FILE(WORKFILE)  +
           RDCLEN(256)
```

In this version of the CRTPF command, you specify a record length for the records in a file, without referring to a DDS source member to define the file format.

You declare a program-described file just like any other file, with the DCLF command. But because there is no defined record format for the file, the CL compiler treats each record in the file as if it contains only one field. CL always declares a variable with the same name as the file and the same length as the file's record length. The following command declares file *WORKFILE* from the previous example and makes available to the program a single 256-character CL variable, *&workfile*.

```
DCLF WORKFILE
```

If your program needs to use individual fields within the file, it must use the built-in %SUBSTRING function to extract fields from variable *&workfile*. You must extract the fields *each* time you read a record from the file. You must also remember that %SUBSTRING supports only character data types; if you need to retrieve numeric data, you first must extract the data as a character field, then use the CHGVAR command to move the data into a numeric variable. The following example illustrates the technique:

```
DCLF      &workfile
DCL       &date      *DEC (6 0)
DCL       &adate     *CHAR 6
CHGVAR    &adate     (%SST(&workfile 1 6))
CHGVAR    &date      &adate
```

In this example, the first CHGVAR command moves the first six characters of the *&workfile* record into the *CHAR variable *&adate*; then the second CHGVAR command assigns the value in *&adate* to variable *&date*. This technique assumes that the value in the substring contains only unpacked numeric data. If the second CHGVAR command encounters any other data type in the substring, the program ends abnormally.

will communicate with the program; you will rarely use any other value for this parameter, so you usually won't need to specify the parameter.

The RCDFMT parameter identifies the screen format that will be processed. Remember that a display file can contain more than one screen format. Use this parameter to specify which format you want to display. The default for RCDFMT is *FILE*, which indicates that the format to be displayed is the one associated with the file declared in the DCLF statement. If the file contains more than one record format, you will usually need to specify a format for this parameter. If the file contains only one record format, the default can be used.

Finally, the WAIT parameter indicates whether you want the program to wait for a response before it continues processing. The default is *YES*. When the user presses Enter or a function key on the display, the program reads the data from the display, placing the values of the fields from the display into the corresponding variables in the CL program. Because you will nearly always need to wait for a response before allowing a program to continue processing, you will usually use the default value. In those very rare instances where you need to do some processing before you read the information from the screen, you would specify *NO*; then later in the program you would include

Figure 15.8
Using the SNDRCVF
Command to
Process a Menu

```
        PGM
        DCLF        ACGMENU

LOOP:
        CHGVAR      &option 0
        SNDRCVF     RCDFMT(MENUR)

        IF          &in03 RETURN

        IF          (&option *EQ 1) DO
                    CALL GLMENU
                    ENDDO

        IF          (&option *EQ 2) DO
                    CALL APMENU
                    ENDDO

        IF          (&option *EQ 3) DO
                    CALL ARMENU
                    ENDDO

        IF          (&option *EQ 4) DO
                    CALL PRMENU
                    ENDDO

        IF          (&option *EQ 90) DO
                    SIGNOFF *NOLIST
                    ENDDO

        GOTO LOOP
        ENDPGM
```

a WAIT command. If you use a SNDRCVF command and specify WAIT(*NO), the CL program continues running until a WAIT command is processed.

The program in Figure 15.8 illustrates the use of the SNDRCVF command to display the menu shown in Figure 15.6 and process a response. Try to follow the logic for every possible response to the menu.

The SNDF Command

Although the two-way SNDRCVF command is by far the most widely used command to communicate between a CL program and a workstation display, it is possible to break down the communications into two one-way commands. The SNDF (Send File) and RCVF (Receive File) commands each perform only half the function of the SNDRCVF command.

The SNDF command sends a record format to a display. This command has the effect of displaying a formatted screen on a workstation. The fields of the screen are filled with the current values of the CL program's variables that correspond to the screen's fields. You cannot use the SNDF command with any type of file other than a display file. CL does not support writing records to a database file. The SNDF command takes the form

```
SNDF    DEV(device-name)              +
        RCDFMT(record-format-name)
```

Both parameters are optional, and both have the same meaning as the DEV and RCDFMT parameters in the SNDRCVF command.

Most programmers prefer to use the SNDRCVF command. If you use SNDF to display a formatted screen, you must subsequently use the RCVF command to read the display.

The RCVF Command

The RCVF (Receive File) command reads a record from a display or a database file. The data fields in the record are loaded into CL program variables.

For display files, the RCVF command reads information from a formatted screen and places the screen's fields into program variables. The command takes the form:

```
RCVF    DEV(device-name)              +
        RCDFMT(record-format-name)    +
        WAIT(wait-parameter)
```

All the parameters are optional and all of them have the same meanings for the RCVF command as they do for the SNDRCVF command. The following code illustrates using the SNDF and RCVF commands to display a menu and then read the information from the menu screen:

```
DCLF    MENUDSPF
 . . .
SNDF    RCDFMT(MAINMENU)
RCVF    RCDFMT(MAINMENU)
```

As you can see, unless there is an overwhelming need to perform some processing in your program between displaying a screen and reading it, the SNDRCVF command will usually serve you better than separate SNDF and RCVF commands.

The RCVF command is the only file access command that you can use with database files. You can read a physical or logical file record into your program, moving the data from the record into CL program variables. When using the RCVF command with database files, you will usually specify the RCVF command without parameters. The following code illustrates the use of the RCVF command to read a record from a database file:

```
DCLF CUSTOMER
. . .
RCVF
MONMSG    CPF0864    EXEC(GOTO EOF)
. . .
EOF:
    RETURN
```

The above example declares a database file named *CUSTOMER*. The fields in CUSTOMER are implicitly defined as CL program variables. Later in the program, the RCVF command reads a record sequentially from the CUSTOMER file, putting the values of the record's fields into the appropriate CL variables. Notice that the example monitors for the message CPF0864 (End of file), branching to the *EOF* label if end-of-file is encountered. Whenever you read a database file in a CL program, you must always monitor for the message CPF0864. This escape message is sent to your CL program whenever end-of-file has been detected for the file being processed.

The WAIT Command
The WAIT command serves the purpose of splitting the WAIT function of the SNDRCVF and RCVF commands into a separate command. If you specify SNDRCVF or RCVF with the WAIT(*NO) parameter value, you must include a WAIT command later in the program. This command is rarely used. The following example shows how you would use the WAIT command in connection with the other data access commands:

```
DCLF    MENUDSPF
. . .
SNDF    RCDFMT(MAINMENU)
RCVF    RCDFMT(MAINMENU)    WAIT(*NO)
. . .
WAIT
```

The WAIT command supports a DEV parameter, just like the other file processing commands, but the default value, *FILE*, will nearly always be sufficient for your program's needs.

CL OUTFILE Support

Many CL commands can create database files as part of their function. Normally, when you enter a CL command, you want the output of the command sent to your workstation screen — by specifying OUTPUT(*) — or to a printer device — by specifying OUTPUT(*PRINT). However, certain CL commands also let you specify OUTPUT(*OUTFILE), enabling you to place the output from the command into a database file. For example, the DSPOBJD (Display Object Description) command displays or prints the descriptions of objects on your system. If you want to put the descriptions into a database file instead, you can specify OUTPUT(*OUTFILE). In this case you must also specify the name of the database file in which to place the data using the OUTFILE parameter of the DSPOBJD command. For example, the following command would place the object description information for all the objects in library ARLIB into a file called OBJECTS in library QTEMP:

```
DSPOBJD    OBJ(ARLIB/*ALL)           +
           OBJTYPE(*ALL)             +
           OUTPUT(*OUTFILE)          +
           OUTFILE(QTEMP/OBJECTS)
```

After this command executes, there will be a file in QTEMP named OBJECTS that will have detailed object description information about each object in ARLIB. The file will contain one record for each object. The format of each record is broken down into data fields describing the different attributes of the individual objects. When the DSPOBJD command is used to create an outfile, the record format of the resulting outfile is predetermined according to the description of an IBM-supplied model file called QADSPOBJ; the record format of the resulting OBJECTS file will contain the same fields as the model file. Each CL command that supports an outfile has its own unique model file. Appendix A lists many commands that support an OUTFILE parameter, along with the name of the corresponding model outfile.

Outfiles are particularly useful for those programs in which you want to perform an action on a number of objects on the system. For example, you could easily write a CL program to move all of the *FILE type objects in one library to another library. The code in Figure 15.9 illustrates such a program.

The program in Figure 15.9 accepts two parameters: the library to move the objects from (*&fromlib*) and the library to move the objects to (*&tolib*). It also declares file QSYS/QADSPOBJ, which is the IBM-supplied model outfile for the DSPOBJD command.

The first command in the procedure section of the program, DSPOBJD, displays all the objects in *&fromlib*, listing them in the outfile QTEMP/QADSPOBJ. (QTEMP is a library used to temporarily store objects, such as work files. Each job on the system has its own unique QTEMP library, which is created automatically when the job starts and is deleted automatically when the job ends.)

The OVRDBF (Override with Database File) command redirects any references to the file QADSPOBJ. From this point in the CL program, references to QADSPOBJ will use the file in library QTEMP, instead of the declared file in QSYS. Although the

Figure 15.9
Using an Outfile
in a CL Program

```
        PGM          PARM(&fromlib &tolib)

        DCL          &fromlib   *CHAR 10
        DCL          &tolib     *CHAR 10
        DCLF         QSYS/QADSPOBJ

        DSPOBJD      OBJ(&fromlib/*ALL)                      +
                     OBJTYPE(*ALL)                           +
                     OUTPUT(*OUTFILE)                        +
                     OUTFILE(QTEMP/QADSPOBJ)
        OVRDBF       QADSPOBJ                                +
                     TOFILE(QTEMP/QADSPOBJ)

READ:
        RCVF         /* Read a record from the outfile */
        MONMSG       CPF0864    EXEC(RETURN)

        IF           (&odobtp = '*FILE')    DO
        MOVOBJ          OBJ(&fromlib/&odobnm)     +
                        OBJTYPE(&odobtp)          +
                        TOLIB(&tolib)
                     ENDDO
        GOTO         READ

        ENDPGM
```

model QSYS/QADSPOBJ was used during the compile process to provide the field definitions, this program will actually place records in, and read records from, the temporary file, QTEMP/QADSPOBJ. (We discuss the OVRDBF command in detail in Chapter 17.)

Once the DSPOBJD command has been executed, the file QTEMP/QADSPOBJ will contain a record for each object in *&fromlib*. Beginning at the READ label, the program reads a record from the file (RCVF command), moving the value of the fields in the record to their corresponding CL variables. Two of those variables created by the compiler are named *&odobnm* (the name of the object) and *&odobtp* (the object type).

Notice the use of the MONMSG command to end the program (RETURN) when it encounters end-of-file (message CPF0864). Otherwise, if the object type is '*FILE', the program performs a MOVOBJ (Move Object) command, using the object name and object type from the record in QADSPOBJ, to move the object from *&fromlib* to *&tolib*. Following the MOVOBJ command, the program loops back to the READ label to process the next record in QADSPOBJ.

Just how did we know the names of the fields in QADSPOBJ? Or for that matter, how did we know that QADSPOBJ is the model outfile for the DSPOBJD command? Good questions. To find the names of the model outfiles, you can refer to Appendix A or to IBM's *AS/400 Programming: Reference Summary*. Alternatively, if you use the command prompter for any command with outfile support, you can press Help or F1; the help text will name the model outfile. Once you know the name of the model outfile, you can use the DSPFFD (Display File Field Descriptions) command to display the individual field names and descriptions for the file.

Data Areas

A **data area** is an AS/400 object (object type *DTAARA) that can be used to hold a small amount of information. You can think of a data area as a "scratch pad" on the AS/400; it is simply an area of memory that you can use to store information of a limited size, for access by any job on the system. You might also think of a data area as a permanent program variable (i.e., a value that will exist on the AS/400 even after a program or job is done using it). Usually, you will use a data area to store a single piece of information, such as the last order number used or last payroll check number used, or to provide an easily changed constant, such as a state sales tax rate. You can also use a data area as a means of passing information from one program or job to another.

In some ways, a data area resembles a file containing a single record, but some of the CL restrictions that apply to data files don't apply to a data area. Most notably, CL can change the information stored in a data area, while it cannot write data to a database file. CL programs can access any number of different data areas in a single program, but when using CL you are restricted to using a single file. You need not declare a data area when you compile a CL program and the data area need not exist when you compile the program.

Data areas are created using the CL command CRTDTAARA(Create Data Area), not DDS. Unlike data files, data areas do not have separately identified fields, but you can extract information from a specific portion of a data area using the RTVDTAARA (Retrieve Data Area) command. CL provides commands to create, retrieve, change, and delete data areas. In addition, the system automatically creates some data areas, which you can use within your programs.

The CL commands provided to specifically manipulate data areas are

- CRTDTAARA   Create Data Area
- DLTDTAARA   Delete Data Area
- DSPDTAARA   Display Data Area
- RTVDTAARA   Retrieve Data Area
- CHGDTAARA   Change Data Area

Creating and Deleting a Data Area

To create a data area, use the CRTDTAARA (Create Data Area) command. The command, with its major parameters, takes the following form:

```
CRTDTAARA    DTAARA(library-name/data-area-name)    +
             TYPE(data-area-type)                   +
             LEN(data-area-length                   +
                 decimal-positions)                 +
             VALUE(initial-value)                   +
             TEXT('description')
```

The DTAARA parameter requires that you specify a name for the data area, following the object naming conventions we discussed earlier. The TEXT parameter allows you to provide some descriptive text for the data area object, to help document its use.

The TYPE parameter specifies the type of data that will be stored in the data area. There are three types from which you can choose. These types should be familiar to you:

- *CHAR Character data
- *DEC   Decimal data
- *LGL   Logical data

The LEN parameter defines the length of the data area, just as it does for a program variable in the DCL command. Data areas of *CHAR type can be up to 2,000 characters long. CL supports *DEC type data areas up to 15 digits long, with up to nine decimal places. (Some other languages may support up to 24 digits, with up to nine decimal places; these data areas cannot be used in a CL program.) Data areas of *LGL type, of course, are only one character long, by definition.

You've probably deduced that the VALUE parameter of the CRTDTAARA command is used to provide an initial value for the data area. You've probably also decided that the same rules for initial values apply when creating a data area as those in effect for the DCL command. Now you're beginning to see how CL's consistency makes it easy to learn. The VALUE parameter does indeed provide a way to initialize a data area with an initial value. If you don't specify a value, the system provides the following defaults:

- Blanks for *CHAR data areas
- 0 for *DEC data areas
- False ('0') for *LGL data areas

Figure 15.10 shows some examples of CL commands used to create data areas. Notice the use of positional notation in some of the examples.

To delete a data area from your system, use the DLTDTAARA (Delete Data Area) command, which identifies the data area to be deleted:

```
DLTDTAARA    DTAARA(library-name/data-area-name)
```

Displaying a Data Area's Contents

You can display or print the description and contents of a data area using the DSPDTAARA (Display Data Area) command, which follows this form:

```
DSPDTAARA    DTAARA(library-name/data-area-name)    +
             OUTPUT(display-or-print)               +
             OUTFMT(output-format)
```

Figure 15.10
Creating Data Areas

```
CRTDTAARA DTAARA(ARLIB/TAXRATE)                              +
          TYPE(*DEC)                                         +
          LEN(6 5)                                           +
          VALUE(0.87500)                                     +
          TEXT('Sales tax rate')

CRTDTAARA CPYNAME    *CHAR 35                                +
          VALUE('Kay Elmnop Enterprises')                    +
          TEXT('Company name')

CRTDTAARA DONEFLAG   *LGL

CRTDTAARA LASTINV    *DEC (9 0)                              +
          TEXT('Last invoice number used')

CRTDTAARA MONTHS     *CHAR 84                                +
          VALUE('January  February March     April-
    May       June      July     August    September-
October   November December ')

CRTDTAARA INPROGRESS *LGL                                    +
          VALUE('1')
```

The DTAARA parameter names the data area you want to display. The OUTPUT parameter can contain either an asterisk (*), if you want to display the data area on the screen (the default), or the special value *PRINT*, if you want to print the output. DSPDTAARA does not support an outfile. The OUTFMT parameter lets you specify the format of the command's output, either the default *CHAR* format, or *HEX* format if you want the data area contents displayed or printed in hexadecimal format.

Retrieving the Contents of a Data Area

Use the RTVDTAARA (Retrieve Data Area) command to retrieve the contents of an entire data area or a portion of a *CHAR data area, copying those contents into a CL program variable. This command retrieves, but does not alter, the contents of the data area. This is the method you use in a CL program to read a data area and make its contents available for processing. The command takes the form:

```
RTVDTAARA    DTAARA(library-name/data-area-name    +
                   (substring-starting-position    +
                     substring-length))            +
             RTNVAR(&CL-variable-name)
```

The DTAARA parameter of the RTVDTAARA command is a list parameter that allows you to name the data area and to define the portion of the data area you want to retrieve. The RTNVAR parameter names the CL variable into which the contents of the data area will be placed. Once you have supplied the name of the data area to be retrieved, the rest of the DTAARA parameter list defaults to retrieving *ALL* of the data area, unless you indicate otherwise.

The following commands, when used in a CL program, would declare a decimal variable &*lastcheck*, then retrieve a decimal data area named LSTCHKUSED (defined as *DEC (5 0)) and copy the value of the data area into the variable (note the use of positional notation for both commands):

```
DCL          &lastcheck    *DEC (5 0)
RTVDTAARA    LSTCHKUSED    &lastcheck
```

If, however, you wanted to retrieve only a portion of a data area, you would define that portion using a construction similar to the %SST built-in function. The following commands declare variable &*month*, then retrieve a portion of the MONTHS data area:

```
DCL          &month           *CHAR 9
RTVDTAARA    (MONTHS (19 9))    &month
```

This RTVDTAARA command would retrieve the nine characters from the MONTHS data area beginning at position 19, placing them into variable &*month*. If the MONTHS data area had been created using the example in Figure 15.10, the value of &*month* would be *March¥¥¥¥*. Note that it wouldn't make sense to substring only a portion of a *DEC type data area; this function is reserved for *CHAR type data areas.

Changing the Contents of a Data Area

The CHGDTAARA (Change Data Area) command changes the contents of an entire data area, or a portion of a *CHAR data area. The new value can be a constant or a CL variable. The command takes the following form:

```
CHGDTAARA    DTAARA(library-name/data-area-name    +
                  (substring-starting-position    +
                  substring-length))               +
             VALUE (new-value)
```

The DTAARA parameter names the data area and defines the portion to be changed, just as it does for the RTVDTAARA command. The VALUE parameter indicates the new value to be placed into the data area, just as it does for the CHGVAR command.

In the following example, CL checks the value of a logical variable, &*leapyear*. If &*leapyear* is on, then the value of the data area *DYSINMONTH* is changed to reflect the correct number of days in February.

```
CRTDTAARA    DYSINMONTH    *CHAR 24                 +
             VALUE('312831303130313130313031')
. . .
IF           &leapyear    DO
             CHGDTAARA    (DYSINMONTH (3 2))        +
                          VALUE('29')
             ENDDO
```

The Local Data Area

For each job in the system, the AS/400 automatically provides a **local data area**. The local data area has several unique characteristics. It is not a permanent AS/400 object; it is created when a job starts, and it disappears when the job ends. Because you don't have to explicitly create or delete a data area, it is quite handy. A data area provides an immediate "scratch pad" that you can use for storing any information you choose. The *LDA is not created in a library, and only the job associated with an *LDA can access the *LDA; a job cannot access another job's *LDA.

Whenever you start an AS/400 job, an *LDA is created automatically just as if you had keyed the following command:

```
CRTDTAARA    *LDA    *CHAR 1024
```

You cannot explicitly create or delete the local data area using the CRTDTAARA or DLTDTAARA commands. You can, however, use the RTVDTAARA, CHGDTAARA, and DSPDTAARA commands by specifying DTAARA(*LDA) for any of these commands. You can also specify the *LDA as an argument in the %SUBSTRING built-in function.

Whenever you use the SBMJOB command to submit a job for batch processing, the submitting job's *LDA is copied to the submitted job's *LDA. After the job is submitted, however, its *LDA exists separately from that of the submitting job; changing the contents of one does not change the contents of the other.

You can use the *LDA to pass values from one program to another within a job, or to pass values when submitting a job, using the SBMJOB command. Using the *LDA allows you to pass values without using parameters. Most HLLs, including RPG and Cobol , can access the *LDA, so you can use it to pass information across language boundaries.

Chapter Summary

CL provides input/output commands for two types of files: database files and display files. You can read information from a database file, or you can send a display to a workstation and subsequently receive user input from that display for use in the program.

There are two major types of database files on the AS/400: physical files and logical files. Physical files contain data defined according to a specific layout, called a record format. Logical files provide sorting and record selection for data in physical files. Logical files contain no data but are indexes to the data records stored in a physical file.

Display files are a special AS/400 *FILE type object called a device file, and as such contain no data. Instead, they contain the descriptions of display screen formats that you can display on a workstation screen.

Database files and display files must exist on your system at the time you compile the program that declares them.

Continued on page 248

Data Queues

A **data queue** is an AS/400 object to which one program can send data and from which another program can receive data. A data queue is the fastest means of communications between two jobs. A data queue differs from a data area. A data area is a static space in memory that can contain information. A data queue, on the other hand, acts as a temporary holding area for information. One program can place a data entry onto a data queue; another program can pick that entry from the data queue and process it. When a data queue entry is read by a program, it is automatically removed from the queue. More than one entry can exist on a data queue at the same time. When you send data to a data queue, the program that receives the data can already be running, waiting for queue entries, or the receiving program can be started at a later time.

Data queues can free a program from doing some work. For example, if an application involves complex transactions (i.e., transactions that update more than one file), you could have several workstations sending transaction entries to a data queue. Then a single batch update program, called a *server program*, could perform the database update, freeing the workstations to perform more immediate work. This scenario could improve overall system performance. Using data queues in this manner can reduce the overhead involved in having workstations directly updating multiple database files.

More than one job can send data to a single data queue. This allows several workstations to dispatch processing to a single data queue to improve performance and simplify database update. You can also have more than one server program receiving data from a single data queue, if your application needs to distribute work among several jobs. For example, you could have several jobs printing orders, taking the information to be printed from a single data queue. One program receives any single entry from a data queue, even if there are several server jobs waiting for entries.

Before you can use a data queue in a program, you must create it. CL provides the CRTDTAQ (Create Data Queue) command for this purpose:

```
CRTDTAQ    DTAQ(library-name/data-queue-name)     +
           MAXLEN(length)                          +
           SEQ(data-retrieval-sequence)            +
           FORCE(force-to-auxiliary-storage)       +
           SENDERID(attach-sender-id)              +
           KEYLEN(key-length)                      +
           TEXT('text')
```

The MAXLEN parameter includes the maximum length of the entries that can be sent to the data queue. This length must be a number between 1 and 64,512.

Continued

Data Queues continued

The SEQ parameter determines in which order entries are retrieved from the data queue. Your choices are the default, *FIFO* (first-in-first-out), *LIFO* (last-in-first-out), or *KEYED* (by key). If you specify SEQ(*KEYED), you must also indicate in the KEYLEN parameter how long the key is to be (1 to 256 bytes).

The FORCE parameter affects performance and recovery. If you specify FORCE(*YES), the data queue is written to disk every time an entry arrives or leaves the queue; the default is FORCE(*NO). Specifying FORCE(*YES) slows the performance of a data queue but ensures that the contents of the queue are retained in case of a system failure.

You can also attach the sender ID to a data queue entry if you specify SENDERID(*YES); otherwise, the default is SENDERID(*NO). The sender ID consists of the qualified job name and the user profile of the job that sent the queue entry.

In addition to the CRTDTAQ command, CL provides a command to remove a data queue from your system: DLTDTAQ (Delete Data Queue). The DLTDTAQ command simply asks for the name of the data queue to delete:

```
DLTDTAQ    DTAQ(library-name/data-queue-name)
```

Beyond the CRTDTAQ and DLTDTAQ commands, CL provides no other commands for use with data queues. To send an entry to a data queue, receive an entry from a data queue, or clear a data queue, you must use IBM-supplied programs called **application program interfaces** (APIs). We discuss APIs in Chapter 19, but for now let's take a brief look at three APIs as they relate to data queues.

Sending an Entry to a Data Queue

To send an entry to a data queue, you must call the QSNDDTAQ API. QSNDDTAQ is *not* a CL command; it is a program. You call an API just like any other program on the system, with the CALL command. For example, you could include the following command in a CL program:

```
CALL PGM(QSNDDTAQ)                            +
     PARM(&qname &qlib &entrylen &entry)
```

The QSNDDTAQ program requires that you provide it with four parameters. These parameters can be constants, or you can use CL program variables, as the example above shows. The first two parameters, *&qname* and *&qlib*, contain the name of the data queue and its library, respectively. The third parameter, *&entrylen*, is a five-digit decimal variable that specifies the number of characters to send to the queue. Finally, the *&entry* parameter contains the actual data to send to the queue.

Continued

Data Queues continued

In addition to the four required parameters, you can call QSNDDTAQ with two optional parameters to support adding key information to the data queue entry. Unless you have created a data queue with SEQ(*KEYED), there is no need for these additional two parameters. For more information about keyed access to a data queue, refer to IBM's *Control Language Programmer's Guide*.

Receiving Entries from a Data Queue

To receive entries from a data queue, use the API named QRCVDTAQ. The following example illustrates the CALL command to receive a data queue entry:

```
CALL PGM(QRCVDTAQ)                                        +
     PARM(&qname &qlib &entrylen &entry &wait)
```

The first two parameters expected by QRCVDTAQ (*&qname* and *&qlib*) are the same ones we discussed when sending a data queue entry. The next two parameters (*&entrylen* and *&entry*) have similar uses, but in this case, the API returns entries to the variables you specify. You need not provide values for these two variables; the API provides the length of the entry in *&entrylen* and the entry itself in *&entry*.

The fifth parameter, *&wait* in this example, is a five-digit decimal variable that specifies how long to wait for an entry to arrive on the data queue. If you indicate a negative value, the program waits for an unlimited time for an entry. A value of zero tells QRCVDTAQ not to wait at all if there are no entries on the queue. Otherwise, a positive number indicates how many seconds to wait for an entry before resuming processing. If zero is specified, and no entry exists when the API is called, the value of the *&entrylen* variable is set to zero. The maximum wait time of 99999 seconds allows the API to wait as long as 28 hours for an entry from the data queue.

The QRCVDTAQ program allows additional parameters to support access by key and sender ID information. If you need support for either of these features, refer to the *Control Language Programmer's Guide*.

Clearing a Data Queue

To clear all the entries from a data queue without reading them, call the QCLRDTAQ program from your program:

```
CALL PGM(QCLRDTAQ)          +
     PARM(&qname &qlib)
```

The two required parameters, *&qname* and *&qlib* in the example, name the data queue to be cleared and its library.

Continued

Data Queues continued

Why Use Data Queues?

It's sometimes difficult to decide whether an application is a good candidate for data queues. They are particularly useful in applications with two parallel processes, where one job could be sending information to another job to be processed *asynchronously* (i.e., at another time). The sending job can send information at a different rate than the server job, and the server simply does its work at its own speed. Neither job cares whether transactions pile up in the data queue; they can both continue processing. Additionally, any number of jobs can be sending to or receiving from a data queue. The data queue acts as a dispatcher for the asynchronous processing to be done.

An application with two or more distinct processes might be a good candidate for a data queue. For example, an order-entry application might process orders and update local inventory interactively, but might use data queues to update inventory records at remote locations, or to print picking lists of ordered items. Using data queues to separate the functions would simplify the interactive order-entry programs, making them more efficient, faster, and easier to maintain. The other parts of the application would also enjoy the same benefits. In addition, each of the functions could execute at a different priority, or at different times, depending upon a company's unique needs.

A job function that requires exclusive use of a system resource might also be a good candidate for a data queue. For example, a hotel reservation system might require the complex update of a room inventory file, updating records covering several days. Using a data queue as a "dispatcher," finding available rooms and assigning them in a single program, instead of requiring individual programs to cooperate with each other in complex multiple-record locking schemes, might make the application easier to code and more reliable.

Why Not to Use Data Queues

Several characteristics of data queues may make them undesirable for certain applications. Once an entry is received from a data queue, it is removed from the data queue, never again to be retrieved; if the program that processes the entry fails before it can process the entry, the entry is lost. As entries are added to a data queue, the size of the data queue increases. As entries are removed from a data queue, however, the size of the data queue does not decrease. The system tries to re-use the space that was occupied by deleted entries, but the data queue always remains the size it was when it had the most entries. The only way to decrease the size of a data queue is to periodically delete it, then re-create it. You should not use data queues for long-term storage of data; database files are a better medium for this purpose.

Continued from page 243

To create a file, you must enter Data Description Specifications (DDS) into a member in a source file (usually named QDDSSRC). The DDS describes the record formats and fields within the records. You then compile the source member to create a file object. The three most common commands used to create file objects are CRTDSPF (Create Display File), CRTPF (Create Physical File), and CRTLF (Create Logical File).

CL primarily uses four file access commands to support file input/output (I/O) processing: SNDF (Send File), RCVF (Receive File), SNDRCVF (Send/Receive File), and WAIT. You can use all the file access commands for display files, but CL allows only input operations for database files, so database operations are limited to the RCVF command.

The DCLF (Declare File) command implicitly declares variables for each field within the declared file. You do not need to declare them explicitly with the DCL command.

The SNDRCVF command sends a formatted screen to a workstation, then asks for and optionally receives data from the display. The SNDF command sends data to a display, then continues processing without waiting for a response. The RCVF command reads information from a display or a database file, making the data fields in the record available as CL program variables. The RCVF command is the only data access command you can use with database files.

Many CL commands can create outfiles as part of their function, placing the output from the commands into database files. Outfiles are particularly useful for those programs in which you want to perform an action on a number of objects on the system.

A data area is a "scratch pad" AS/400 object, identified as object type *DTAARA, that can be used to hold a limited amount of information. CL commands can be used to manipulate the information in a data area. Data areas can be *CHAR, *DEC, or *LGL data types.

The RTVDTAARA (Retrieve Data Area) command retrieves the contents of an entire data area or a portion of a *CHAR data area, copying those contents into a CL program variable. This command retrieves, but does not alter, the contents of the data area.

The CHGDTAARA (Change Data Area) command changes the contents of an entire data area, or a portion of a *CHAR data area. The new value can be a constant or a CL variable.

The local data area is provided automatically by the AS/400 for each job in the system. Whenever you start an AS/400 job, an *LDA is created automatically. You can use the *LDA to pass values from one program to another within a job, or to pass values to a submitted job.

Terms

application programming interfaces	device file	local data area
data area	display file	logical file
data description specifications	indicators	physical file
data queue		

Review Questions

1. Describe each of the following types of files. What is the purpose of each type? Which ones contain data? Which ones can CL read? Which ones can CL write?
   a. Display files
   b. Physical files
   c. Logical files

2. Which of the following commands are used to process file data in a CL program? What is the purpose of each command?
   a. RCVF
   b. SNDRCVF
   c. CRTDTAARA
   d. RTVDTAARA
   e. SNDF
   f. CHGDTAARA
   g. DCLF
   h. WAIT
   i. CRTDSPF

3. Most objects that a CL program uses need not exist at the time you compile the program. Files, however, must exist at compile time. Why?

4. Refer to Appendix A to find five commands that support outfiles. List the commands and the outfiles. What would you expect the contents of each outfile to be?

5. Which of the following types of data would be best stored in a file? Which ones are good candidates for a data area?
   a. Sales tax rate table for a single state
   b. Last-used payroll check number
   c. Employee payroll information
   d. Parameters for a submitted payroll job
   e. Customer names and addresses

6. List three differences between the local data area and a user-created data area.

Exercises

1. In this exercise, you write a program that creates a database file and reads and processes each record in the file. The purpose of the program is to determine the total size of all files in a given library. Typically, this is a function that you would perform in a batch process. In this example, however, the process can be run either interactively or in batch.

   a. Add a member named SA1501*XXX* to source physical file QCLSRC. Substitute your initials for *XXX*.
   b. Add the program information section and the program linkage section to the member.

Exercises continued

Exercises continued

    c. Accept one parameter into the program. This parameter should identify the library for which you want to determine the total of the file sizes. **NOTE:** Select a small library while testing this program, or submit the program for batch processing. If you select a large library and run this program interactively, you can adversely affect the response time of others on the system. If you are unsure of which library to specify, ask your instructor or system administrator.

    d. Using the DSPOBJD command, create an *OUTFILE in library QTEMP that contains one record for each *FILE type object in the library specified on the parameter discussed in c.

    e. Sequentially read each record in the outfile. Add the file size to a variable named &totsize. **Hint:** &odobsz.

    f. When there are no more records in the *OUTFILE, send a message that states, 'Total size of the files in library STUDENT1 is 00000000245000 bytes.' *STUDENT1* is the library that you passed as the parameter and *00000000245000* is the actual size of the files in that library. After sending the message, end the program.

    NOTE: Because this program creates a temporary work file in QTEMP, don't forget to delete the file before ending the program. You always want to clean up after yourself.

    g. Include normal error-handling commands within the program.

    h. Compile and run the program. Again, if you are running the program interactively, select a small library as the parameter — possibly your individual student library.

    i. Using the SBMJOB command, run the program in batch mode. Where does the 'file size' message go? Can you design a better way to send the message back to the message queue of the user who submitted the batch job?

2. In this exercise, you write a program that processes a display file. The display file is a programmer's menu; the DDS source for the display file is shown here:

```
A                                        DSPSIZ(24 80 *DS3)
A                                        CF03(03 'exit')
A           R MENU
A                                     5 33'Programmer Menu'
A                                     8 32'1. Display Job'
A                                    10 32'2. Work with Spooled Files'
A                                    12 32'3. Work with Submitted Jobs'
A           OPTION        1    B    15 46
A                                    15 33'Enter Option'
A                                    20 37'F3=Exit'
```

    a. Add a DSPF member type named SA1503*XXX* to source physical file QCLSRC, or QDDSSRC. Substitute your initials for *XXX*. This member type should be DSPF, instead of CLP.

    b. Add the source statements above into the source member and compile the display file. The name of the display file will be the same as the member name: SA1503*XXX*.

    c. Add a CLP member type named SA1502*XXX* to source physical file QCLSRC. Substitute your initials for *XXX*. This member type should be CLP.

    d. Add the program information section and the program linkage section to the member.

    e. Write a CL program that uses the display file above as a menu. This menu program should perform the following functions:

Exercises continued

Exercises continued

- Show the display file, and accept a response from the user. The allowable responses are

     to press the F3=exit key. (If this key is pressed the program should end.)

  or:

     to place the character '1' in a field called *&option*. (If option '1' is selected, the DSPJOB command should be processed.)

  or:

     to place the character '2' in the *&option* field. (If this option is selected, the WRKSPLF command should be processed.)

  or:

     to place the character '3' in the *&option* field. (If this option is selected, the WRKSBMJOB command should be processed.)

- If the user selects an option other than '1', '2', or '3', the *&option* field is filled with blanks and the screen is redisplayed.
- After each option is selected, the associated command is executed. Then the *&option* field should be filled with blanks and the screen redisplayed, ready to process another option.
- The only way this program will end is if the user presses the F3=exit key.
- Include normal error-handling commands within the program.

   f. Compile the program. Check the compile listing. Did the compiler declare the *&option* variable for use in your program?

   g. Run the program. Test all of the possible options.

3. This exercise is a variation of the program you wrote in Exercise 1. The program performs the same function, but instead of receiving the name of the library from a program parameter, you retrieve it from the job's local data area.

   a. Add a member named SA1504*XXX* to source physical file QCLSRC. Substitute your initials for *XXX*. Here you might want to copy member SA1501*XXX* into the new member.

   b. In the program in Exercise 1 you accepted a parameter to determine which library to use. This program receives no parameters. You should use the RTVDTAARA command to retrieve the name of the library from the first 10 positions of the job's local data area.

   (**Hint:** RTVDTAARA *LDA)

   c. Include normal error-handling commands within the program.

   d. Compile the program.

   e. Before running the program, from a command line, change your local data area so that the first 10 positions of the data area contain the name of the library for which you want to display the total of file sizes. Again, make sure the local data area contains the name of a small library. (**Hint:** CHGDTAARA *LDA)

   f. Run the program interactively.

   g. Run the program in batch mode with the SBMJOB command. Because the library name is in the local data area of your interactive job, that data area is copied to the submitted job's data area. That's how the submitted job can determine the library to use.

Chapter 16

Advanced Message Handling

Chapter Overview

The AS/400 uses messages for a wide variety of purposes. In this chapter we present a general overview of what you can do with messages, and we provide an in-depth look at how you can use messages to communicate between programs.

AS/400 Messages

In Chapter 12 you saw how errors generated within a program are identified by program messages. We discussed the MONMSG command, which allows you to monitor for the occurrence of messages sent to your program, and we discussed briefly how error messages can be received using the RCVMSG (Receive Message) command. In several examples and exercises in this text, you saw how to send messages using the CL commands SNDMSG (Send Message) and SNDPGMMSG (Send Program Message). By now, you probably realize that understanding how messages work is an important part of writing good CL programs. In fact, without at least a basic understanding of messages, your CL programs will be error-prone and, in many cases, unreliable.

The AS/400 is driven by messages. Messages are used for a multitude of different purposes, including initiating jobs, executing commands, communicating between programs, signaling error conditions, allowing users to communicate with each other, and allowing jobs to communicate with users. This chapter helps you understand how to deal correctly with messages in a CL program.

What Is a Message?

In everyday life the concept of a message is quite simple. Webster's dictionary defines a message as "a communication, verbal or written, sent by one person to another." A message, by definition, is sent and is not of any true significance until it is received. Once a message has been received, it can be acted upon. The one who receives the message decides what to do with the information contained in the message.

Messages serve many purposes: to provide information, to ask a question and request a reply, and to request some action on the recipient's part. Regardless of the message type, the recipient determines what will be done after the message has been received. The receiver can ignore the message, act upon the message, or, if requested, choose to send a reply.

AS/400 messages are no different: A message is sent to convey information and the recipient of the message determines what will be done with that information.

AS/400 Message Queues

AS/400 messages may be sent from only two sources: system users and running programs. Messages are not sent directly to other users or programs, but rather to a message queue associated with a user, a program, or a workstation device.

A **message queue** (object type *MSGQ) is a holding area or "in basket" for messages. A message queue usually can store hundreds or even thousands of messages. Once a message has arrived on a message queue, it is up to the recipient to view (or receive) the message, take any action, and remove the message when it is no longer needed.

When a user profile object is created on the AS/400, a **user message queue** is created for that user. This message queue is used whenever a message is sent specifically to that user. Usually, the name of the message queue object is the same as the name of the associated user profile.

Whenever a workstation device is created, a **workstation message queue** is created for that device. Some types of messages are routinely sent to a workstation message queue, rather than to a user message queue. It is the responsibility of the workstation user to view any messages sent to the workstation message queue and to take any action needed. The workstation message queue is usually named the same as the associated workstation device.

In addition, a few special message queues exist on every AS/400: for example, QSYSOPR (the AS/400 system operator message queue) and QHST (the system history log message queue). QSYSOPR lets the system operator receive messages sent by the system, by programs, or by other users, and take appropriate action. The system sends system-related messages to the QHST message queue, which you then can view with the DSPLOG (Display Log) command. You can create other message queues as needed with the CRTMSGQ (Create Message Queue) command.

All the message queues discussed so far are permanent objects on the system. They can be deleted using the DLTMSGQ (Delete Message Queue) command, but they will be permanent until explicitly deleted. The AS/400 also supports two types of *temporary* message queues: a **program message queue** and an **external message queue**.

Immediately before a program begins executing, the system creates a message queue for that program. The program message queue is the program's own "in basket" for messages. Every program that is called on the AS/400 has an associated program message queue. Once a message arrives on the program's message queue, it is up to the program to determine what to do with it. Certain messages can be ignored; others must be dealt with, depending on the message type.

Whenever a job starts on the AS/400, an external message queue is created for that job. The external message queue is used to communicate between the executing job and the job's external requester. Many different message types can be sent to the external message queue as a job runs. Some require attention; others do not.

The structure of all message queues is the same, whether they are permanent or temporary. There is an area for the message and an area for a system-generated message key. The message key is used by the system to uniquely identify each message on the queue. Figure 16.1 illustrates the structure of a message queue.

Figure 16.1
Message Queue Structure

Message Key	Message Storage Area			
	Type	**Severity**	**Message Text**	**etc.**
1AAA	*DIAG	30	0 records copied from file	...
1BBC	*COMP	00	Job completed normally	...
2AFB	*COMP	00	10 records copied	...
3169	*INFO	00	No lunch today for you	...
385B	*INQ	99	What time do we go?	...
39CC	*ESCAPE	99	Job ended abnormally	...

Types of Messages

Several message types can be sent and received. In Figure 16.1 you can see that messages in a message queue have an associated type; for example, *DIAG, *COMP, *INFO, *INQ, and *ESCAPE. Each message type has a unique purpose; the message type sent will depend on the purpose of the message as determined by the sender of the message. Figure 16.2 lists the types of messages, a description of each type, and its purpose.

Figure 16.2
Message Types

Message Type	Description	Purpose
*COMP	Completion	Signals the successful completion of a processing step.
*DIAG	Diagnostic	Indicates that an error condition exists.
*ESCAPE	Escape	Indicates that a severe error has occurred and that the program that sent the message has ended in error. A program that sends an *ESCAPE message ends immediately.
*INFO	Informational	Informs the recipient of any pertinent information. Not generally used to indicate an error.
*INQ	Inquiry	Requests additional information, which is sent back with a *RPY message.
*NOTIFY	Notification	Can be used as an *INQ or *ESCAPE message, depending on the recipient.
*RPY	Reply	Replies to an *INQ or *NOTIFY message.
*RQS	Request	Sends a processing request (i.e., executes a command).
*STATUS	Status	Advises an interactive user of a job's progress. Can also function as an *ESCAPE message.

You must be aware of certain rules about sending and receiving different types of messages. Here is a summary of those rules:

- A CL program can send any of the message types.
- *INFO, *INQ, and *RPY message types can be sent by a workstation user; all other message types cannot.
- Only *INFO, *INQ, *COMP, and *DIAG message types can be sent to a user message queue, a workstation message queue, or the QSYSOPR message queue.
- All message types except *INQ can be sent to a program message queue.
- All message types except *ESCAPE messages can be sent to the job's external message queue.

Commands Used to Send Messages

Four major CL commands are used to send messages:

- SNDMSG   Send Message
- SNDBRKMSG   Send Break Message
- SNDPGMMSG   Send Program Message
- SNDUSRMSG   Send User Message

We discuss each of these commands individually.

The SNDMSG Command

The SNDMSG command sends *impromptu messages* to one or more message queues. The term "impromptu" refers to a message that is not predefined as a message in a message file, as discussed in Chapter 12. This command provides flexibility in specifying the message queue to which the message is sent, and also allows you to specify a message queue that will receive the reply to the message, if one is requested. The SNDMSG command takes the following form:

```
SNDMSG    MSG(message-text)                      +
          TOUSR(to-user-profile)                 +
          TOMSGQ(message-queue-name)             +
          MSGTYPE(message-type)                  +
          RPYMSGQ(message-queue-for-reply)
```

The MSG parameter lets you enter text for an impromptu message. The TOUSR parameter and TOMSGQ parameter are mutually exclusive; you must specify one of the two, but not both. The allowable values for TOUSR are *SYSOPR*, *REQUESTER*, *ALLACT*, or a user profile name. If you specify *SYSOPR*, the message is sent to the QSYSOPR message queue. If you specify *REQUESTER*, the message is sent to the user message queue of the user running an interactive job, or to QSYSOPR if used in a batch job. To send the message to the message queue of all users currently signed on to the system, specify *ALLACT*. If a user profile name is specified, the message is sent to the message queue specified in that user's user profile.

If the TOUSR parameter is not entered, the TOMSGQ parameter must be specified. The allowable values for TOMSGQ are *SYSOPR*, or the qualified names of up to 50 message queues. You can specify TOMSGQ(QHST) to send the message to the QHST message queue for inclusion in the system's history log.

The MSGTYPE parameter specifies the message as either an *INFO* message or an *INQ* message. If it is an *INQ message, you can specify only one message queue in the TOUSR or TOMSGQ parameters. If you do not specify otherwise, the MSGTYPE parameter defaults to a value of *INFO.

If the message is an *INQ message type, you can specify in the RPYMSGQ parameter the name of the message queue to which the reply to the message will be sent. The default value of the parameter is *WRKSTN*; however, you can specify the name of any permanent message queue. When *WRKSTN* is used, the reply is sent to the workstation message queue of the user running the interactive program; if the job is a batch job, the reply is sent to the QSYSOPR message queue.

The following command sends a message to all users currently signed on to the system:

```
SNDMSG    MSG('The system will power down in 5 minutes')   +
          TOUSR(*ALLACT)
```

The next command sends an inquiry message; a reply will be sent to the workstation message queue of the user running the command interactively:

```
SNDMSG    MSG('How about lunch today?')                    +
          TOMSGQ(BOB)                                      +
          MSGTYPE(*INQ)
```

The SNDBRKMSG Command

The SNDBRKMSG command, although similar to the SNDMSG command, has a few notable differences. You can use this command to send messages only to workstation message queues. When you use SNDBRKMSG to send a message, the message is displayed immediately at its destination workstation. If the workstation to which it is sent is currently active, the user will be interrupted. The SNDBRKMSG command has the following form:

```
SNDBRKMSG    MSG(message-text)                    +
             TOMSGQ(to-message-queue)             +
             MSGTYPE(message-type)                +
             RPYMSGQ(reply-message-queue)
```

The MSG parameter lets you enter text for an impromptu message. The TOMSGQ parameter can contain the names of up to 50 workstation message queues, or the value *ALLWS*. If *ALLWS* is specified, the message is sent to all of the workstation message queues defined on the system, whether or not they are currently active.

The MSGTYPE parameter can be specified as *INFO or *INQ. If *INQ is specified, only one message queue can be specified on the TOMSGQ parameter. Also, if *INQ is specified, you can enter the name of the message queue that will receive the reply to the message in the RPYMSGQ parameter. The default for this parameter is to send the reply to the QSYSOPR message queue.

The SNDPGMMSG Command

The SNDPGMMSG command is quite flexible, but it can be used only within a CL program; it cannot be entered on a command line. You can use this command to send an impromptu message or a predefined message from a CL program to any type of message queue on the system, including program message queues and the job's external message queue. The SNDPGMMSG command takes the following form for impromptu messages:

```
SNDPGMMSG    MSG(message-text)                        +
             TOUSR(to-user-message-queue)             +
             TOMSGQ(to-message-queue)                 +
             TOPGMQ(to-program-message-queue)         +
             MSGTYPE(message-type)                     +
             RPYMSGQ(reply-message-queue)              +
             KEYVAR(key-variable-name)
```

For predefined messages, SNDPGMMSG takes this form:

```
SNDPGMMSG    MSGID(message-identifier)                +
             MSGF(qualified-message-file-name)        +
             MSGDTA(message-substitution-data)        +
             TOUSR(to-user-message-queue)             +
             TOMSGQ(to-message-queue)                 +
             TOPGMQ(to-program-message-queue)         +
             MSGTYPE(message-type)                     +
             RPYMSGQ(reply-message-queue)              +
             KEYVAR(key-variable-name)
```

For impromptu messages, you would specify the text in the MSG parameter. For predefined messages, use the MSGID, MSGF, and MSGDTA parameters. The MSG parameter cannot be specified if the MSGID, MSGF, or MSGDTA parameters are specified. Certain message types can be sent only using predefined messages; we talk about this restriction later when we discuss the MSGTYPE parameter.

When you send a predefined message, you specify the identifier of the message to be sent as well as the message file in which the message is defined. For example, to send the message CPF9871 from message file QCPFMSG, you would specify

```
SNDPGMMSG    MSGID(CPF9871)                           +
             MSGF(QCPFMSG)
```

This command would send the message *Error occurred while processing.*

Some messages allow you to specify *message substitution data*, using the MSGDTA parameter. We discussed this topic in Chapter 12, and we have used the MSGDTA parameter with MSGID CPF9898 several times in examples and exercises. CPF9898 is a special blank message provided by IBM; the text consists solely of whatever is in the message data. Consider the following example:

```
SNDPGMMSG    MSGID(CPF9898)                                   +
             MSGF(QCPFMSG)                                     +
             MSGDTA('Cannot find tax rate file')
```

In this example, we send message CPF9898 with the data specified on the MSGDTA parameter.

The TOUSR and TOMSGQ parameters are, again, mutually exclusive (i.e., you must specify one, but not both). The allowable values for the TOUSR parameter are *SYSOPR, *REQUESTER, *ALLACT, or a user profile name. The rules for the TOUSR parameter are the same as those used on the SNDMSG command. The allowable values for the TOMSGQ parameter are *SYSOPR, a qualified message queue name, and the value *TOPGMQ. When *TOPGMQ is specified, the message is sent to the program message queue named on the TOPGMQ parameter.

The TOPGMQ parameter is used to specify the program message queue to which the message will be sent. The parameter has two elements that can be specified. The first element specifies a relationship, and the second element specifies a program used for the relationship. (Because the TOPGMQ parameter can be confusing, "The TOPGMQ Parameter" (pages 260–261) offers additional explanation.)

The MSGTYPE parameter allows you to specify which message type is to be sent to the message queue. The allowable values are *INFO (the default), *INQ, *COMP, *DIAG, *NOTIFY, *ESCAPE, *RQS, and *STATUS.

You need to be aware of certain restrictions, depending on the type of message you are sending. An *INQ (inquiry) message cannot be sent to a program message queue. If an *INQ type message is sent, the reply can only be accessed using the RCVMSG command (discussed later in this chapter). *COMP, *DIAG, *ESCAPE, *NOTIFY, and *STATUS messages can be sent only to a program message queue or to a job's *EXT (external) message queue. *ESCAPE, *NOTIFY, and *STATUS messages can be sent only if the message is predefined in a message file; the MSGID parameter must be specified.

The RPYMSGQ parameter allows you to specify, for *INQ and *NOTIFY message types, which message queue will receive the reply to the message. This message queue may be any type of message queue except the *EXT job message queue. When an *INQ or *NOTIFY message is sent, the default for RPYMSGQ is *PGMQ. This means that the reply will be sent to the program message queue of the program sending the message. You can also specify the qualified name of a message queue.

The last parameter of the SNDPGMMSG command, KEYVAR, is used to retrieve the value of the message key and place that value into a CL program variable. Remember that each message queue uses a message key to keep track of messages within the queue. The message key is not a decimal number like 1, 2, 3, or 4, but

The TOPGMQ Parameter

When you use the TOPGMQ parameter, it is important that you understand how the SNDPGMMSG command works when a program message queue will be the recipient of the message. If a message is to be sent to a program message queue, the program associated with that message queue must currently be within your job's invocation stack. In addition, you cannot send a message to the message queue of a program running within another job. Let's look at an example of the program stack of an interactive job to illustrate how the TOPGMQ parameter can be used (Figure 16A).

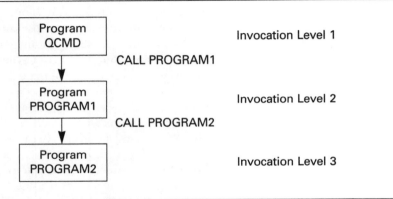

Figure 16A
The Program Stack

Normally, all interactive and batch jobs on the system use the IBM-supplied program QCMD at the first invocation level. This program is automatically placed into the first invocation level by the description of the subsystem in which the job runs. QCMD then calls your initial program, in this case, PROGRAM1. Two programs are in the invocation stack. Suppose that PROGRAM1 calls PROGRAM2; now three programs are in the invocation stack.

Each of the programs in the stack has a distinct program message queue. If PROGRAM2 were to call another program, PROGRAM3, a new program message queue would be created when PROGRAM3 begins execution. When PROGRAM3 ends, its program message queue is deleted and control returns to PROGRAM2.

PROGRAM2 can send a message to the program message queue of any program currently in the stack at the same or at a previous invocation level. So in this example, PROGRAM2 could send a message to its own program message queue, or to the program message queue of PROGRAM1 or QCMD. It

continued

The TOPGMQ Parameter continued

cannot send a message to the program message queue of PROGRAM3 because the message queue of PROGRAM3 does not exist when PROGRAM2 is executing. Using this information, let's see in Figure 16B how the TOMSGQ parameter is used to determine to which program message queue the message is sent.

Figure 16B
The TOPGMQ
Parameter

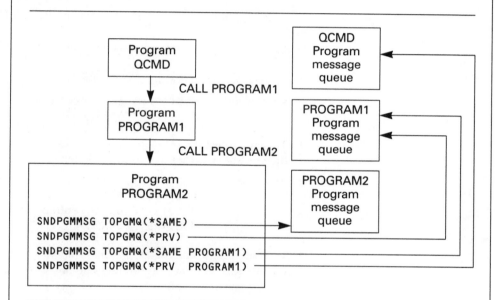

As you can see, when TOPGMQ(*SAME) is used, the message is sent to the program message queue of the same program that sent the message. When TOPGMQ(*PRV) is specified, the message is sent to the program message queue of the previous program in the invocation stack, the current program's caller. To send a message to a particular program's message queue, you can specify the name of the program using the format TOPGMQ(*SAME PROGRAM1), assuming PROGRAM1 is the program you wish to send the message to. To send a message to the caller of a particular program, you specify TOPGMQ(*PRV PROGRAM1), assuming you want to send the message to the caller of PROGRAM1.

You can also specify that you want to send the message to the job's external message queue by specifying TOPGMQ(*EXT).

rather an internal number that the system generates when you send a message to a message queue. You specify the KEYVAR parameter as a CL variable:

```
KEYVAR(&variable)
```

The CL variable must be declared as follows:

```
DCL   &variable   *CHAR 4
```

You might want to retrieve the value of the generated message key so that later in a program you can selectively receive or remove a particular message. This technique is described in more detail when we cover the RCVMSG and RMVMSG commands later in this chapter.

The following examples illustrate use of the SNDPGMMSG command:

- To send a completion message to the previous program's message queue

```
SNDPGMMSG    MSG('Program successfully completed')   +
             MSGTYPE(*COMP)
```

- To send an escape message to the previous program's message queue and cause the current program to end immediately

```
SNDPGMMSG    MSGID(CPF9898)                          +
             MSGF(QCPFMSG)                            +
             MSGDTA('Program ended abnormally')       +
             MSGTYPE(*ESCAPE)
```

- To send a status message to the external message queue. For an interactive job, this message is shown on the message line of the workstation. The message does not appear in the job log.

```
SNDPGMMSG    MSGID(CPF9898)                           +
             MSGF(QCPFMSG)                             +
             MSGDTA('Now processing Step 1.')         +
             TOPGMQ(*EXT)                              +
             MSGTYPE(*STATUS)
```

- To send an informational message to the program message queue used by program PROGRAM1. When the message is placed into the message queue, the message key assigned by the system is returned to the program and placed into the CL variable *&msgkey*, which is defined as *CHAR 4.

```
SNDPGMMSG    MSG('Program3 working ok')               +
             TOPGMQ(*SAME PROGRAM1)                    +
             KEYVAR(&msgkey)
```

The SNDUSRMSG Command

The final command used to send messages is the SNDUSRMSG command. Like SNDPGMMSG, this command can be used only within a CL program; it cannot be entered on a command line. You can use the SNDUSRMSG command to send an impromptu message or a predefined message, but not to send a message to a program message queue. The SNDUSRMSG command includes useful features not available with other message commands. For example, you can both send a message and receive the reply to the message with this one command. You can check for the validity of a reply and optionally translate replies from lowercase to uppercase.

The SNDUSRMSG command uses the following format when sending impromptu messages:

```
SNDUSRMSG    MSG(message-text)                        +
             TOUSR(to-user-message-queue)             +
             TOMSGQ(to-message-queue)                 +
             MSGTYPE(message-type)                    +
             VALUES(list-of-allowable-replies)        +
             DFT(default-reply-value)                 +
             MSGRPY(message-reply)                    +
             TRNTBL(translation-table)
```

The SNDUSRMSG command takes the following form when using predefined messages:

```
SNDUSRMSG    MSGID(message-identifier)                +
             MSGF(qualified-message-file-name)        +
             MSGDTA(message-substitution-data)        +
             TOUSR(to-user-message-queue)             +
             TOMSGQ(to-message-queue)                 +
             MSGTYPE(message-type)                    +
             VALUES(list-of-allowable-replies)        +
             DFT(default-reply-value)                 +
             MSGRPY(message-reply)                    +
             TRNTBL(translation-table)
```

The MSG, MSGID, MSGF, and MSGDTA parameters work the same for this command as they do for the SNDPGMMSG command.

You can specify either the TOUSR parameter or the TOMSGQ parameter, but not both. When you specify the TOUSR parameter, the allowable values are *SYSOPR, *REQUESTER, or the name of a user profile to which you want to send the message.

When you specify the TOMSGQ parameter, the allowable values are *, *SYSOPR, *EXT, or the qualified name of a message queue. If * is specified and the program is running interactively, the message is sent to the job's external message queue; if it is a batch job, the message is sent to the QSYSOPR message queue. If *SYSOPR is specified, the message is sent to the QSYSOPR message queue. If *EXT is specified, the message is sent to the job's external message queue. However, if the job is a batch job and the message is an *INQ message type, the default reply is always returned to the program.

The MSGTYPE parameter identifies the type of message that will be sent. The allowable values are *INFO and *INQ (the default). For *INQ messages, several other parameters are available: VALUES, DFT, MSGRPY, and TRNTBL. These additional parameters are used only with *INQ messages.

The VALUES parameter is used to specify the allowable values that can be used to reply to this message. You can specify up to 20 different valid replies. When an *INQ message is sent to a user, an allowable value must be entered or an error message is issued to the user and the message is re-sent automatically. When this parameter is specified, the MSGRPY parameter must also be specified.

The DFT parameter specifies the default reply that will be used for this message. If, when a recipient is presented with an INQ message, (s)he presses the Enter key, the DFT value is returned to the program. When the DFT parameter is specified, the MSGRPY parameter must also be specified.

The MSGRPY parameter identifies the message's reply. When a user is sent the *INQ message type and a reply is entered, the reply is returned to the program and placed into the CL variable specified on the MSGRPY parameter. If you wanted to store the message reply in a variable named *&reply*, you would specify MSGRPY(*&reply*).

The TRNTBL parameter lets you specify that any reply value a user enters be translated before it is placed into the variable specified on the MSGRPY parameter. The default value of this parameter is *LIBL/QSYSTRNTBL*. QSYSTRNTBL is a translation table used to translate lowercase characters into uppercase. You may specify the name of a different translation table, or *NONE* for no translation.

The following examples illustrate use of the SNDUSRMSG command:

- To send an *INQ message to the QSYSOPR message queue and allow the values *C* and *G* to be entered in reply. *C* is the default value. The reply entered by the system operator will be placed into variable *&reply*, which in this case would be declared as *CHAR 1. After the program issues the SNDUSRMSG command, it waits until a reply is received before processing any further.

```
SNDUSRMSG   MSG('Please load the IRS Tape #5 (C G)')   +
            TOUSR(*SYSOPR)                              +
            VALUES(C G)                                 +
            DFT(C)                                      +
            MSGRPY(&reply)
```

- To send an informational message to an *EXT message queue, if running in an interactive job, or to the QSYSOPR message queue if used in a batch job. The text of the message is in the *&message* variable. The external message queue is displayed on a workstation as the Program Messages display, which we discussed in Chapter 12.

```
SNDUSRMSG   MSGID(CPF9898)      +
            MSGF(QCPFMSG)       +
            MSGDTA(&message)    +
            TOMSGQ(*)           +
            MSGTYPE(*INFO)
```

Receiving Messages

While four CL commands are designed specifically to send messages to message queues, only one command is designed to receive a message: RCVMSG (Receive

Message). The RCVMSG command lets you read messages that are held within a
message queue. Because the RCVMSG command must handle many different types
of message queues, it is remarkably flexible. This flexibility makes the command
complicated to use in some cases, but we'll try to keep things simple. The RCVMSG
command takes the following form (most-used parameters only):

```
RCVMSG    PGMQ(program-message-queue)                      +
          MSGQ(message-queue-name)                         +
          MSGTYPE(message-type)                            +
          MSGKEY(message-key-to-read)                      +
          WAIT(wait-time)                                  +
          RMV(remove-the-message-option)                   +
          KEYVAR(message-key-received)                     +
          MSG(message-text-received)                       +
          MSGLEN(length-of-received-message)               +
          MSGDTA(message-data-received)                    +
          MSGDTALEN(length-of-msgdta-received)             +
          MSGID(id-of-message-received)                    +
          SEV(severity-level-of-message-received)          +
          SENDER(sender-of-the-message-received)           +
          RTNTYPE(return-type-of-message-received)         +
          MSGF(message-file-of-message-received)           +
          MSGFLIB(message-file-used-when-sent)             +
          SNDMSGFLIB(message-file-of-message-received)
```

The first four parameters of the RCVMSG command identify the message you want
to read and the message queue on which the message resides. You can think of the
message queue as being like a database file, with each message being a database
record. When you read a database file, you must identify the file you want to process
and specify which record in the file you want to read. In the case of a message queue,
you identify which message queue (file) you want to process with the PGMQ or MSGQ
parameter; you specify which message (record) you want to read with the MSGTYPE
or MSGKEY parameter.

Reading messages from a message queue, however, differs somewhat from reading
records from a database file. Whenever a message arrives on a message queue, an
attribute is set on the message that indicates it is a new (unread) message. Once a
message is read with the RCVMSG command, the system marks it as an old message.
Certain read (RCVMSG) operations read only new messages; others let you read old
or new messages. Messages are usually read from a message queue in FIFO order —
the first message placed into the queue is the first one read. One exception exists to
this rule: *ESCAPE and *NOTIFY messages are read in LIFO order — the last one
placed on the message queue is the first one read.

Let's look at each of the parameters on the RCVMSG command. As mentioned,
to identify the message queue from which messages are to be read, you can specify
the PGMQ or the MSGQ parameters. The PGMQ parameter follows the same rules as

the TOPGMQ parameter on the SNDPGMMSG command. You can use the PGMQ parameter to specify that you want to receive messages that reside in a particular program message queue or the job's external message queue. If the PGMQ parameter is specified, the MSGQ parameter must be specified as *PGMQ.

If you do not want to read messages from a program message queue or the job's external message queue, you can specify the MSGQ parameter. You may specify a qualified name of a message queue from which you wish to read a message.

Parameter MSGTYPE lets you specify which messages you wish to read, either by message type or by the position of the message within the message queue. You can specify the values *FIRST, *NEXT, *PRV (Previous), or *LAST to position yourself within the message queue to read messages forward or backward. When using these parameter values, you can read both old and new messages on the queue. If you specify *NEXT or *PRV, you must also supply a value for the MSGKEY parameter. To read messages from a message queue according to message type, you can specify *ANY, *COPY, *COMP, *DIAG, *EXCP, *INFO, *INQ, *RPY and *RQS. We discuss only the values you are not familiar with. The value *ANY (the default) is used to read any available new (unread) message from the message queue. *COPY receives a copy of an inquiry message that was previously sent by the program. The value *EXCP is used to receive any exception message; the exception message types are *ESCAPE and *NOTIFY. *RPY receives a reply message type. Note that when reading messages by type rather than by position, you can access only the new (unread) messages from the message queue.

Parameter MSGKEY is used to access a message in the message queue by its internal message key. This provides random access to the old and new messages in the message queue but requires that you first obtain the message key, either with the SNDPGMMSG command or the RCVMSG command. Both commands can place the internal key of a message into a CL variable. While the default for this parameter is *NONE, indicating that you will not read randomly by message key, you can use two other values for those times that you do want to randomly access the messages by key. You can specify the value *TOP, or you can specify the name of a CL program variable; for example, MSGKEY(&msgkey). Variable &msgkey must be declared as *CHAR 4 and contain the value of a valid message key. The message containing that key will then be read. When MSGKEY(*TOP) is specified, the MSGTYPE parameter must contain the value *NEXT or *PRV. When MSGKEY(*TOP) is used, the first message on the message queue is read.

The WAIT parameter is used to specify how many seconds the RCVMSG command should wait for a message to arrive on the queue. This parameter lets you write a CL program that waits for messages to arrive on a message queue and then takes appropriate action based on the message received. This type of program typically runs as a batch job rather than interactively from a workstation. The default value for this parameter is 0 (zero seconds), which means that the program will not wait for a message. If a message is available, it will be read; if a message is not available, the program continues with its next statement. Another value that can be specified for the WAIT parameter is *NOMAX. This value indicates that the program should wait until a message is received before continuing with its next command, regardless of how long it must wait. You can also specify a number of seconds that the RCVMSG command should wait before continuing. For example, specifying the value WAIT(600), indicates that the RCVMSG command should wait for 600 seconds, or 10 minutes, before giving up on the RCVMSG operation.

The RMV parameter determines whether a message is to be removed from the queue after it has been read using the RCVMSG command. The default value is *YES*, indicating that the message would be removed. When you specify RMV(*NO), the message is not removed, but it is marked as an old message.

The remaining parameters, from KEYVAR to SNDMSGFLIB, are used to identify CL variables into which data from the received message will be placed. These are CL return variables like those you used with the retrieve commands (e.g., RTVJOBA and RTVUSRPRF). You can specify the return variables you need and skip those you don't need. When you declare the return variables in your CL program, it is important to declare them with the correct data type and length. Some of the data returned into these variables will have a variable length. If the length of the variable you are using is shorter than the actual data returned, no error occurs, but the data will be truncated. For these types of parameters we provide you with a length that works under almost all conditions. We identify those for you as we discuss the individual parameters.

The KEYVAR parameter stores the message key value of the message received by the RCVMSG command. You can specify this parameter as KEYVAR(&keyvar), where &keyvar is declared as *CHAR 4. If no message is found in the message queue, the variable &keyvar will contain blanks.

The MSG parameter stores the first-level message text of the message received by the RCVMSG command. You can specify this parameter as MSG(&msg), where &msg is declared as *CHAR 132. The first-level message text for a message has a variable length depending upon the message, so your variable could actually be longer or shorter than 132 characters.

The MSGLEN parameter stores the length of the first-level message text placed into the MSG parameter. Because the MSG parameter returns data that is variable in length, this parameter is supplied to tell you how long the MSG actually is. You can specify this parameter as MSGLEN(&msglen), where &msglen is declared as *DEC (5 0).

The MSGDTA parameter stores the message substitution data for the message. You can specify this parameter as MSGDTA(&msgdta), where &msgdta is declared as a *CHAR 200. Message substitution data will be variable in length; you must determine the optimum length for variable &msgdta.

The MSGDTALEN parameter stores the length of the message substitution data placed into the MSGDTA parameter. You can specify this parameter as MSGDTALEN(&msgdtalen), where &msgdtalen is declared as *DEC (5 0).

The MSGID parameter holds the message identifier of the message. You can specify this parameter as MSGID(&msgid), where &msgid is declared as *CHAR 7. If the received message was not sent using a message ID, as in the the case of an impromptu message, or if no message is received, the value of &msgid will be blanks.

The SEV parameter stores the message's severity level. You can specify this parameter as SEV(*&sev*), where *&sev* is declared as *DEC (2 0). If the message was sent as an impromptu message, the value of *&sev* will be invalid.

The SENDER parameter identifies a data structure that contains information about the sender of the message. You can specify this parameter as SENDER(*&sender*), where *&sender* is declared as *CHAR 80. Within variable *&sender* are several pieces of information about the sender of the message. This information can be extracted from variable *&sender* using the %SUBSTRING function. Figure 16.3 shows the information contained in variable *&sender*.

Figure 16.3
SENDER Data
Structure

Character Positions	Data
1–10	Job name of sender
11–20	User name associated with the sender job
21–26	Job number of sender job
27–38	Program name that sent message
39–42	Program statement number that sent message
43–49	Date the message was sent (cyymmdd format)
50–55	Time the message was sent (hhmmss format)

If the message was sent to a program message queue,
the following data is also available:

56–65	The program name of the receiver
66–69	The statement number of the receiver program
70–80	Reserved for IBM's future use

The RTNTYPE parameter stores a code identifying the message type of the message received by the RCVMSG command. You can specify this parameter as RTNTYPE(*&rtntype*), where *&rtntype* is declared as *CHAR 2. You can determine which type of message was received by understanding the code returned. Figure 16.4 lists the RTNTYPE codes and their meanings.

The MSGF parameter identifies the message file that contains the predefined message. You can specify this parameter as MSGF(*&msgf*), where *&msgf* is declared as *CHAR 10.

The MSGFLIB parameter stores the name of the library of the message file in the MSGF parameter. If the command that sent the message used the value *LIBL*, that value is placed into the variable. If the name of a library was explicitly specified on the sending command, that value is placed into the variable. You can specify this parameter as MSGFLIB(*&msgflib*), where *&msgflib* is declared as *CHAR 10. For impromptu messages, both the *&msgf* and *&msgflib* variables will be blank.

The SNDMSGFLIB parameter stores the name of the library containing the message file used in sending the message. If the command that sent the message used the value *LIBL*, that *will not* be the value placed into the variable. Instead, the value of the variable will be the name of the library where the message file actually exists.

Figure 16.4
RTNTYPE Codes
and Values

RTNTYPE Code	Meaning
01	Completion message
02	Diagnostic message
04	Informational message
05	Inquiry message
06	Copy of an inquiry message
08	Request message
10	Request message with prompting message
14	Notify message
15	Escape message
21	Reply message, not checked for validity
22	Reply message, checked for validity
23	Reply message, message default was used
24	Reply message, system default was used
25	Reply message, using system reply list

You can specify this parameter as SNDMSGFLIB(*&sndmsgflib*), where *&sndmsgflib* is declared as *CHAR 10. For impromptu messages, the *&sndmsgflib* variable will be blank. In most cases, this parameter should be used instead of the MSGFLIB parameter to ensure that the message can be located if it is to be sent again to another message queue.

RCVMSG Examples

The program in Figure 16.5 uses the RCVMSG command to read the last message in its program message queue. Under these circumstances, the last message will always be the *ESCAPE message that caused control to be passed to the ERROR label.

Figure 16.5
Reading the
Last Message

```
PGM

DCL       &msg *CHAR 80

MONMSG    MSGID(CPF0000) EXEC(GOTO ERROR)

CHKOBJ    MYLIB/MYFILE                            +
          *FILE                                   +
          AUT(*ALL)

CALL      PROGRAM1

RETURN

ERROR:
    RCVMSG    MSGTYPE(*LAST) MSG(&msg)
    SNDPGMMSG MSG(&msg)
    MONMSG    CPF0000 /* Just in case */

    ENDPGM
```

Because the MSG parameter is specified, the text of the *ESCAPE message is placed into variable *&msg*. That text is then used to send the message to the previous program's message queue using the SNDPGMMSG command.

The program in Figure 16.6 reads all the new messages on the program's message queue and forwards them to the previous program as informational messages.

Figure 16.6
Reading All
New Messages

```
          PGM
          DCL   &msgid   *CHAR 7
          DCL   &msgf    *CHAR 10
          DCL   &msgflib *CHAR 10
          DCL   &msgdta  *CHAR 100
          DCL   &msgkey  *CHAR 4

          CALL PROGRAM2

LOOP:
          RCVMSG     KEYVAR(&msgkey)                          +
                     MSGDTA(&msgdta)                          +
                     MSGID(&msgid)                            +
                     MSGF(&msgf)                              +
                     SNDMSGFLIB(&msgflib)

          IF         (&msgkey = ' ')                          +
          GOTO ENDIT

          SNDPGMMSG MSGID(&msgid)                             +
                     MSGF(&msgflib/&msgf)                     +
                     MSGDTA(&msgdta)                          +
                     MSGTYPE(*INFO)
          MONMSG     CPF0000               /* Just in case */
          GOTO       LOOP

ENDIT:
          RETURN
          ENDPGM
```

Removing Messages

We have seen how messages are sent using the four message-sending commands and how messages are received using the RCVMSG command. Now we address the topic of removing messages from a message queue.

When a program executes, a variety of messages are sent to the program's message queue. IBM-supplied routines send some; your programs can send others. These messages can begin to clutter up the program message queue and, accordingly, the job log. Many times, leftover messages can cause confusion when examining a job log, which is really just a combined look at a job's program message queues. We discuss the job log again in depth in Chapter 21.

When messages are no longer of any use to a program or a job, they should be removed from the message queue. If you use the RCVMSG command, unless you specify RMV(*NO), each message is removed from the message queue as it is received. However, many times there is no need to receive every message in a message queue, so CL also provides a separate command designed specifically to remove messages from a message queue. That command is RMVMSG (Remove Message), which takes the following form:

```
RMVMSG    PGMQ(program-message-queue)    +
          MSGQ(message-queue-name)       +
          MSGKEY(message-key)            +
          CLEAR(clear-option)
```

The parameters PGMQ and MSGQ are used exactly as they were for the RCVMSG command, with one exception: The PGMQ parameter also accepts a value of *ALLINACT. This gives you the ability to remove all messages for programs no longer active in an invocation level.

The MSGKEY parameter lets you specifically remove the message that has the corresponding message key value from a message queue. This parameter may not be specified unless the CLEAR parameter specifies CLEAR(*BYKEY). The CLEAR parameter lets you specify which messages should be removed (cleared). The allowable values are *BYKEY, *ALL, *KEEPUNANS, *OLD, and *NEW. If CLEAR(*BYKEY) is specified, the message specified on the MSGKEY parameter is removed. If you use CLEAR(*ALL), all messages in the specified message queue will be removed. If CLEAR(*KEEPUNANS) is specified, all messages will be removed, except those *INQ messages that have not been answered. If you specify CLEAR(*KEEPUNANS), the message queue cannot be a program message queue. If CLEAR(*OLD) is specified, all old (previously read) messages will be removed; CLEAR(*NEW) removes all new (unread) messages. If you specify PGMQ(*ALLINACT), you must also specify CLEAR(*ALL).

RMVMSG Examples

The following command removes from the job log all messages for all programs no longer in an invocation level:

```
RMVMSG    PGMQ(*ALLINACT)    CLEAR(*ALL)
```

The following command removes all messages from the QSYSOPR message queue, except those that remain unanswered:

```
RMVMSG    MSGQ(QSYSOPR)    CLEAR(*KEEPUNANS)
```

Standard Error-Handling Routines

There are probably as many ways to implement a *standard error-handling routine* as there are programmers to do so. A standard error-handling routine is simply a standard method of implementing an error-handling procedure within your CL programs. When you have an error-handling procedure you know is handling program errors correctly, you simply copy that routine into all your programs that do not require special error-handling procedures.

In this section we examine a few of the standard error-handling routines popular with AS/400 CL programmers and explain how the different routines work. We point out the strengths and weaknesses in the routines and you will see, as we progress, that IBM has not really provided the tools necessary to create a truly bulletproof error-handling routine. In this case, simplicity could be the best solution. But before we begin to analyze different error-handling routines, we need to discuss the concept of handling errors.

When an IBM-supplied program detects a severe error, it sends an *ESCAPE message to the previous program's message queue. Optionally, before the *ESCAPE message is sent, one or more *DIAG messages can also be sent to the previous program's message queue. There is no guarantee that any *DIAG type messages will be sent before the *ESCAPE message; most often, *DIAG type messages are not sent. The wording contained within an *ESCAPE message is sometimes very exact in its explanation of the error that occurred (e.g., *Object FILE1 in library LIBRARY1 not found*); other times the wording is very ambiguous (e.g., *Error occurred while processing*). For the more ambiguous *ESCAPE messages, *DIAG messages are usually sent to provide additional information about the cause of the error.

When an *ESCAPE message is sent to a program's message queue, that program can catch the error using the MONMSG command. However, the MONMSG command cannot catch *DIAG messages that may also be sent before the *ESCAPE message. Both the *DIAG and *ESCAPE messages can be received into the program from the message queue using the RCVMSG command.

Within the CL programs that you write, you want to try to emulate IBM's error-handling techniques. You want to send *ESCAPE messages when your programs encounter severe errors, and at times you want to send *DIAG messages before the *ESCAPE message. This results in a common method for error handling, whether you are calling IBM-supplied programs or the programs that you have written.

In the first error-handling routine shown in Figure 16.7, all the variables needed are declared and the program-level MONMSG command is set to pass control to the label named ERROR if an *ESCAPE message starting with the letters 'CPF' is sent to this program's program message queue.

Three labels are used in the error-handling section of this program: ERROR, ERROR2, and ERROR3. The purpose of the commands at label ERROR is to ensure that the program is not looping within the error routine. The purpose at label ERROR2 is to receive all *DIAG messages in the message queue and forward them to the previous program. At ERROR3, the *ESCAPE message that caused the error routine to be executed is received and re-sent to the previous program's message queue. When the *ESCAPE message is sent, the program immediately ends.

If an *ESCAPE message is sent to the message queue, control immediately passes to the ERROR label, where we first check the value of logical variable *&errorsw*, to see whether it is true. If it is, *ESCAPE message CPF9999 is sent to the previous program's message queue. CPF9999 is the special message used to indicate a **function**

Figure 16.7
Sample Error-Handling
Routine #1

```
            PGM
            DCL         &msgid    *CHAR 7
            DCL         &msgdta   *CHAR 100
            DCL         &msgf     *CHAR 10
            DCL         &msgflib  *CHAR 10
            DCL         &errorsw  *LGL

            MONMSG      CPF0000 EXEC(GOTO ERROR)

            (Include normal program processing here)

            RETURN      /* NORMAL END OF PROGRAM */

ERROR:      IF          &errorsw                              +
                        (SNDPGMMSG MSGID(CPF9999)             +
                                    MSGF(QCPFMSG)             +
                                    MSGTYPE(*ESCAPE))
            CHGVAR      &errorsw '1'

ERROR2:     RCVMSG      MSGTYPE(*DIAG)                        +
                        MSGDTA(&msgdta)                       +
                        MSGID(&msgid)                         +
                        MSGF(&msgf)                           +
                        SNDMSGFLIB(&msgflib)
            IF          (&msgid *EQ ' ')                      +
                        GOTO ERROR3
            SNDPGMMSG   MSGID(&msgid)                         +
                        MSGF(&msgflib/&msgf)                  +
                        MSGDTA(&msgdta)                       +
                        MSGTYPE(*DIAG)
            GOTO        ERROR2

ERROR3:     RCVMSG      MSGTYPE(*EXCP)                        +
                        MSGDTA(&msgdta)                       +
                        MSGID(&msgid)                         +
                        MSGF(&msgf)                           +
                        SNDMSGFLIB(&msgflib)
            SNDPGMMSG   MSGID(&msgid)                         +
                        MSGF(&msgflib/&msgf)                  +
                        MSGDTA(&msgdta)                       +
                        MSGTYPE(*ESCAPE)
            ENDPGM
```

check has occurred in the program. A function check signals that the program can no longer continue because of a severe error. When this *ESCAPE message is sent, the program immediately ends and returns control to the previous program.

If, on the other hand, variable *&errorsw* is false, the program continues to the next command, which sets variable *&errorsw* to true. Recall from Chapter 12 that variable *&errorsw* is used to ensure that the program does not get caught in a never-ending loop within the error-handling procedure.

Next, at label ERROR2, we receive a *DIAG message into our program, placing data from the received message into the return variables listed. Then we check variable *&msgid* to find out whether it contains blanks. This is done in an attempt to determine whether a *DIAG message has been received with the RCVMSG command. When a message cannot be found on the message queue that has the specified type (i.e., *DIAG), the *&msgid* field will contain blanks. The IF (&msgid = ' ') command is used here to determine whether a message has been received. If the *&msgid* field is blanks, the program assumes that no further *DIAG messages exist in the message queue and proceeds to label ERROR3. If variable *&msgid* is not blanks, the *DIAG message is re-sent to the previous program's message queue and the GOTO command causes control to pass to the ERROR2 label, where we again attempt to receive all other *DIAG messages and re-send them. When no more *DIAG messages are left in the program's message queue, control passes to ERROR3. At label ERROR3, the *ESCAPE message is received into the return variables listed, and the *ESCAPE message is re-sent. When the *ESCAPE message is sent, the program immediately ends.

While this error routine is highly effective in some cases, there are problems with it. First, the program re-sends all *DIAG message types found within the message queue to the previous program's message queue. Many times the *DIAG messages within a queue have nothing whatsoever to do with the reason the program failed. They could have been issued by a command under control of a command-level MONMSG command, in which case any *DIAG messages generated by the failed command would still be in the message queue, but the program would continue to process correctly.

The second problem with this routine is that it expects that all *DIAG messages were sent as predefined messages from a message file. In many cases, this is not a valid assumption. *DIAG messages can be sent as impromptu messages where no MSGID is used. When the routine uses the command IF (&msgid = ' ') to determine whether a *DIAG message was received, it can be fooled into thinking there are no more *DIAG messages if the message received does not have a MSGID.

The second example, shown in Figure 16.8, handles the problem of correctly identifying when a *DIAG message is received, but it still does not address the problem of re-sending irrelevant *DIAG messages to the previous program's message queue.

The only difference between this example and the one in Figure 16.7 is that the MSGKEY is placed into variable *&msgkey* when the *DIAG messages are received. If a *DIAG message is received, that variable contains the message key of the message received. This solves the reliability problem; the program now will be able to successfully identify when a *DIAG message is received, even if that message was sent as an impromptu message.

But we still have one problem left to address: how to re-send only those *DIAG messages related to the error that caused our program to fail. The sample routine in Figure 16.9 addresses this problem with a simple solution. It does not re-send any *DIAG messages. Under many situations, this can be an acceptable solution to the problem.

When control is passed to label ERROR, the error-handling routine receives the *ESCAPE message that caused the problem and re-sends it to the previous program's

Figure 16.8
Sample Error-Handling
Routine #2

```
PGM
DCL          &msgid    *CHAR 7
DCL          &msgdta   *CHAR 100
DCL          &msgf     *CHAR 10
DCL          &msgflib  *CHAR 10
DCL          &msgkey   *CHAR 4
DCL          &errorsw  *LGL

MONMSG       CPF0000   EXEC(GOTO STDERR1)

(Include normal processing here)


STDERR1:
          IF           &errorsw                            +
                       SNDPGMMSG MSGID(CPF9999)            +
                                 MSGF(QCPFMSG)             +
                                 MSGTYPE(*ESCAPE)
          CHGVAR       &errorsw '1'
STDERR2:  RCVMSG       MSGTYPE(*DIAG)                      +
                       RMV(*NO)                            +
                       KEYVAR(&msgkey)                     +
                       MSGDTA(&msgdta)                     +
                       MSGID(&msgid)                       +
                       MSGF(&msgf)                         +
                       SNDMSGFLIB(&msgflib)
          IF           (&msgkey *EQ ' ') GOTO STDERR3
          RMVMSG       MSGKEY(&msgkey)
          SNDPGMMSG    MSGID(&msgid)                       +
                       MSGF(&msgflib/&msgf)                +
                       MSGDTA(&msgdta)                     +
                       MSGTYPE(*DIAG)
          GOTO         STDERR2
STDERR3:  RCVMSG       MSGTYPE(*EXCP)                      +
                       MSGDTA(&msgdta)                     +
                       MSGID(&msgid)                       +
                       MSGF(&msgf)                         +
                       SNDMSGFLIB(&msgflib)
          SNDPGMMSG    MSGID(&msgid)                       +
                       MSGF(&msgflib/&msgf)                +
                       MSGDTA(&msgdta)                     +
                       MSGTYPE(*ESCAPE)
          ENDPGM
```

message queue. If the *ESCAPE message is too ambiguous to be useful, the *DIAG messages are still available for viewing in the job's job log.

If you need to resend *DIAG messages, one solution works correctly most of the time. We say "most of the time" because there is really no way to determine whether the *DIAG messages and *ESCAPE message are related. In the routine in Figure 16.10, we make an assumption about the messages on the program message queue. We

Figure 16.9
Sample Error-Handling
Routine #3

```
           PGM

           DCL       &msgid   *CHAR 7
           DCL       &msgf    *CHAR 10
           DCL       &msgflib *CHAR 10
           DCL       &msgdta  *CHAR 100

           MONMSG    CPF0000 EXEC(GOTO ERROR)

(Include normal processing here)

           RETURN      /* Normal  end of program */

 ERROR:    RCVMSG    MSGTYPE(*LAST)          +
                     MSGDTA(&msgdta)         +
                     MSGID(&msgid)           +
                     MSGF(&msgf)             +
                     SNDMSGFLIB(&msgflib)

           SNDPGMMSG MSGID(&msgid)           +
                     MSGF(&msgflib/&msgf)    +
                     MSGDTA(&msgdta)         +
                     MSGTYPE(*ESCAPE)
           MONMSG    CPF0000                 /* Just in case  */
           ENDPGM
```

assume that if the message immediately preceding the *ESCAPE message in the queue is a *DIAG message, that *DIAG message is related to the *ESCAPE message. Most of the time, this assumption is valid. In some cases, where a *DIAG message is not sent immediately before an *ESCAPE message, our assumption will be incorrect. But it will be more correct than assuming that all *DIAG messages in the queue are related to the *ESCAPE message, which is the assumption we made in the first two example routines.

In this routine, the first RCVMSG command receives the *ESCAPE message. That message will always be the last one in the queue, as long as we did not execute any commands before the RCVMSG command that could generate additional messages. When the message is received, we specify RMV(*NO) so that the *ESCAPE message is not removed from the queue when it is received.

When we receive the *ESCAPE message, we also receive its message key. We can then read backward in the queue for the message immediately preceding it. We do this with the second RCVMSG command. We then check the RTNTYPE of the message received to determine whether it is a *DIAG message (&rtntype = '02'). If it is, we send the message to the previous program's message queue. We then receive the *ESCAPE message again, this time removing it from the program's queue, and re-send it.

As stated, this routine gives correct results most of the time; because there is no way to determine whether a *DIAG message is associated with an *ESCAPE message, sometimes it could produce misleading results.

Figure 16.10
Sample Error-Handling
Routine #4

```
            PGM
            DCL         &msgid    *CHAR 7
            DCL         &msgf     *CHAR 10
            DCL         &msgflib  *CHAR 10
            DCL         &msgkey   *CHAR 4
            DCL         &msgdta   *CHAR 100
            DCL         &errorsw  *LGL
            DCL         &rtntype  *CHAR 2

            MONMSG      CPF0000 EXEC(GOTO ERROR)


(Include normal processing here)

            RETURN      /* Normal end of program  */
ERROR:      IF          &errorsw                          +
                        (SNDPGMMSG MSGID(CPF9999)          +
                                   MSGF(QCPFMSG)           +
                                   MSGTYPE(*ESCAPE))
            CHGVAR      &errorsw '1'

            RCVMSG      MSGTYPE(*LAST)                     +
                        RMV(*NO)                           +
                        KEYVAR(&msgkey)

            RCVMSG      MSGTYPE(*PRV)                      +
                        MSGKEY(&msgkey)                    +
                        MSGDTA(&msgdta)                    +
                        MSGID(&msgid)                      +
                        RTNTYPE(&rtntype)                  +
                        MSGF(&msgf)                        +
                        SNDMSGFLIB(&msgflib)
            IF          (&rtntype = '02') DO
                        SNDPGMMSG MSGID(&msgid)            +
                                  MSGF(&msgflib/&msgf)     +
                                  MSGDTA(&msgdta)          +
                                  MSGTYPE(*DIAG)
                        ENDDO
            RCVMSG      MSGKEY(&msgkey)                    +
                        MSGDTA(&msgdta)                    +
                        MSGID(&msgid)                      +
                        MSGF(&msgf)                        +
                        SNDMSGFLIB(&msgflib)
            SNDPGMMSG   MSGID(&msgid)                      +
                        MSGF(&msgflib/&msgf)               +
                        MSGDTA(&msgdta)                    +
                        MSGTYPE(*ESCAPE)
            ENDPGM
```

Chapter Summary

The AS/400 is driven by messages, which are used in many ways, including initiating jobs, executing commands, communicating between programs, signaling error conditions, allowing users to communicate with each other, and allowing jobs to communicate with users. AS/400 messages can be sent from system users and running programs.

Messages are always sent to a message queue, which is a holding area for messages. Some message queues, such as user message queues and workstation message queues, are permanent objects. Others, such as program message queues and external message queues, exist only while a program or job is active.

There are several types of messages, including completion (*COMP), diagnostic (*DIAG), and escape (*ESCAPE) messages. Each message type is used for a specific purpose in a program or job.

Four major CL commands are used to send messages: SNDMSG (Send Message), SNDBRKMSG (Send Break Message), SNDPGMMSG (Send Program Message), and SNDUSRMSG (Send User Message). The SNDMSG command sends impromptu messages to one or more message queues. The SNDBRKMSG command sends impromptu messages to a workstation message queue, interrupting the workstation user. The SNDPGMMSG command sends an impromptu message or a predefined message from a CL program to any type of message queue on the system. The SNDUSRMSG command sends an impromptu message or a predefined message from a CL program to a user, but not to a program message queue. Each of these commands has specific rules regarding which message types it can send and where it can send them.

The RCVMSG command allows you to read the messages that reside within a message queue. You can move information from these messages into CL variables in your program. The command allows you, through the MSGKEY parameter, to access a message in the message queue randomly by its internal message key.

When messages are no longer of any use to a program or a job, they should be removed from the message queue. Unless you specify RMV(*NO) when using the RCVMSG command, each message is removed from the message queue as it is received. CL also provides the RMVMSG (Remove Message) command to remove messages from a message queue.

A standard error-handling routine is simply a standard method of implementing an error-handling procedure within your CL programs. While there are many popular standard error-handling routines, there is no one best routine for all situations; each method has its advantages and weaknesses. Most standard routines pass back both the *ESCAPE message that indicates a program failure and the *DIAG message that may precede it.

Terms

external message queue
function check

message queue
program message queue

user message queue
workstation message queue

Review Questions

1. Identify six different kinds of message queues. What are they used for?

2. Describe the following message types and how each is used:
   a. *COMP
   b. *INQ
   c. *INFO
   d. *ESCAPE
   e. *DIAG

3. Which of the following commands are valid interactively at an AS/400 command line? Which ones can send messages to a user message queue?

   a. SNDMSG
   b. SNDBRKMSG
   c. SNDUSRMSG
   d. SNDPGMMSG

4. Explain the purpose and general flow of a typical error-handling routine.

5. Explain the significance of the message key and message key variables. How are they used in the SNDPGMMSG and RCVMSG commands?

Exercises

1. Write a program (SA1601*XXX*) that will accomplish the following:

   a. Send three *INFO messages to a job's *EXT (external) message queue. The content of these messages should be as follows:

      'This is message number 1'
      'This is message number 2'
      'This is message number 3'

   b. Send an *ESCAPE message to the previous program's message queue stating 'Job ended abnormally'.

   Compile the program. Run the program interactively.

2. Copy the program from Exercise 1 to member SA1602*XXX*. Change the program to send the three messages to the previous program's message queue. This time, at the end, send a *COMP message stating 'Job ended normally'. Compile the program. Run the program interactively.

Exercises continued

Exercises continued

3. This third exercise helps you understand the strengths and weaknesses of the different error-handling routines presented in this chapter.

    a. Enter each of the four standard error routines listed within this chapter into a different source member. Use the member names SA1603*XXX*, SA1604*XXX*, SA1605*XXX*, and SA1606*XXX*.

    b. Within the procedure section of each of the members, enter the following commands after the program level message monitor statement :

        ```
        ADDLIBLE QSYS
        MONMSG CPF0000
        CPYF FROMFILE(AYYY) TOFILE(BYYY)
        ```

    c. Compile and run all four programs. Report on the results.

Chapter 17

Advanced File Techniques

Chapter Overview

In this chapter we introduce you to several tips and techniques for improving performance and getting maximum flexibility when processing database files. You learn how and when to preopen files for an application, how to use OPNQRYF (Open Query File) and CPYFRMQRYF (Copy From Query File) to preselect data in files, and how to position a database file to a specific record.

Using Files in a CL Program

Recall from Chapter 15 that although CL provides input/output commands for two types of files (database files and display files), a single CL program can access only one file. When you declare a file in a CL program (using the DCLF command), the individual fields in the file are implicitly declared as CL program variables, which you can manipulate. Within the program, you use the SNDRCVF (Send/Receive File), SNDF (Send File), and RCVF (Receive File) commands to perform I/O operations on the file.

Before a CL program can use a file, it must *open* the file; the opening process establishes a link between the program and the file and makes records in the file available to the program. A CL program opens a file automatically when it performs its first SNDRCVF, SNDF, or RCVF operation. The file remains open until the program ends, or until the file is explicitly closed.

Using File Overrides

Sometimes you need to make minor changes in the way a program functions without recompiling the program. Maybe it's necessary to change the name of a file, the name of the file member that is processed, or some other attribute of a database or display file. The method that the AS/400 uses to accomplish these minor modifications is called a **function override**. Using overrides, you can make programs more flexible and more general in nature — and, therefore, more useful.

You can use several specific override commands in CL, each of them designed to override a specific type of file. The override commands we introduce in this chapter are

- OVRDBF   Override with Database File
- OVRPRTF   Override with Printer File

Each override command has specific parameters that correspond to specific attributes of the file type the command was designed to work with. For example, the OVRDBF command does not work with printer files because printer files do not have the same characteristics as database files (e.g., file members).

Using the OVRDBF Command

The OVRDBF command has two purposes: to direct a program to use a file other than the one named in the program or to temporarily change the attributes of a file used by a program. All overrides are temporary, and they affect only the job in which the override command is executed. Once a CL program executes an OVRDBF command, the changes made by the command remain in effect until the program ends, until the program encounters a DLTOVR (Delete Override) command, or until the program encounters another override to the same file. The OVRDBF command takes the following form (showing only the parameters used most often):

```
OVRDBF    FILE(overridden-file-name)                           +
          TOFILE(library-name/database-file-name)              +
          MBR(member-name)                                     +
          POSITION(file-positioning-option)                    +
          SECURE(secure-from-previous-overrides-option)        +
          SHARE(open-data-path-sharing-option)                 +
          OVRSCOPE(override-scope)
```

Only the FILE parameter, which specifies the name of a file as it appears in a program, is required. The attributes of the named file will be changed temporarily.

The TOFILE parameter is optional. This parameter, which can be a qualified name, allows you to redirect references to the file named in the FILE parameter with the file you specify in the TOFILE parameter. The default value is *FILE*, indicating that the file named in the FILE parameter will be used, but some of its attributes may be changed temporarily. You can use this command to change the name of the file the program will process, so that a file different from the one specified during program compilation can be processed. The program illustrated in Figure 17.1 uses the OVRDBF command to point to a different file in this manner.

The program in Figure 17.1 may look familiar; it is the same one illustrated in Figure 15.8. The program uses the outfile support of the DSPOBJD command to create a file named QADSPOBJ in library QTEMP; the file will contain the descriptions of all objects in the library specified in variable &fromlib. When the program compiles, it retrieves the variable names it will use for the declared file from file QADSPOBJ in library QSYS. However, when the program executes, the file used will not be file QADSPOBJ in library QSYS, but the outfile QADSPOBJ created in library QTEMP. The OVRDBF command directs the program to use QTEMP/QADSPOBJ instead of QSYS/QADSPOBJ. The remainder of the program reads records from QTEMP/QADSPOBJ and moves each object in the library that is a file to another library, represented by variable &tolib.

Figure 17.1
Using OVRDBF
to Replace a File
in a CL Program

```
         PGM          PARM(&fromlib &tolib)

         DCL          &fromlib  *CHAR 10
         DCL          &tolib    *CHAR 10
         DCLF         QSYS/QADSPOBJ

         DSPOBJD      OBJ(&fromlib/*ALL)                        +
                      OBJTYPE(*ALL)                             +
                      OUTPUT(*OUTFILE)                          +
                      OUTFILE(QTEMP/QADSPOBJ)

         OVRDBF       FILE(QADSPOBJ)                            +
                      TOFILE(QTEMP/QADSPOBJ)

READ:
         RCVF         /* Read a record from the outfile */
         MONMSG       CPF0864    EXEC(RETURN)

         IF           (&odobtp = '*FILE') DO
                      MOVOBJ     OBJ(&fromlib/&odobnm)          +
                                 OBJTYPE(&odobtp)               +
                                 TOLIB(&tolib)
                      ENDDO

         GOTO         READ

         ENDPGM
```

IBM says the OVRDBF command allows you to *replace* a file in a program with another file. But this is not really what happens. The data space occupied by the original file does not change. Instead, the OVRDBF command replaces the *role* of one file with another temporarily. That is, the input/output operations of a program are directed to a different file.

You also can use the OVRDBF command to override certain attributes of a file temporarily without directing the program to process a different file.

Assume you have a mailing list application on your AS/400 that uses names and addresses stored in a file named MAILLIST. Also assume that file MAILLIST contains several distinct mailing lists, each of them stored in a separate member of the file. In our example, an RPG program named UPDMAIL updates the MAILLIST file. Any program, by default, opens the first member of a database file when it opens the file. That means RPG program UPDMAIL always processes the first member of file MAILLIST. To process another member of the file (i.e., a different mailing list), you must use an OVRDBF command.

Program SETMBR in Figure 17.2 accepts the name of a member as an input parameter. It then performs an OVRDBF command to indicate that program UPDMAIL should open a specific member of file MAILLIST, instead of opening the first member. When program UPDMAIL opens file MAILLIST, it opens the member

named in the OVRDBF's MBR parameter. The override specified in CL program
SETMBR remains in effect for any programs it may call; in this example, it calls only
program UPDMAIL. Even though program SETMBR does not process file MAILLIST,
it can issue an override that remains in effect for any programs at a new call level.

Figure 17.2
Using OVRDBF
to Change a
File's Attributes

```
SETMBR:
    PGM         PARM(&member)
    DCL         &member    *CHAR 10
    OVRDBF      MAILLIST   MBR(&member)
    CALL        UPDMAIL
    RETURN
    ENDPGM
```

In addition to specifying a member name for the MBR parameter of the OVRDBF
command, you can specify MBR(*FIRST) to process the first member in a file,
MBR(*LAST) to process the last member, or MBR(*ALL) to process all the members.

The POSITION parameter of the OVRDBF command lets you specify where
processing should start when a file opens. When a database file is opened, a **file
cursor**, much like an "electronic bookmark," is established to indicate which record
in the file should be processed next. Normally, when a file is opened, the file cursor
is set to the first record in the file. Using the POSITION parameter, you can specify
that the cursor be positioned elsewhere. We discuss file positioning in the "Using the
OVRPRTF Command" section.

When a database file is opened within a program, the system provides the program with an **open data path**, a path to the records within the database file. To allow
several programs within a single job to share the same open data path to a file, specify
SHARE(*YES) on the OVRDBF command. You also can specify SHARE(*YES) when
a database file is created; in this case, the file shares its open data path by default and
does not require an override to do so.

For the most part, as long as you keep your program structure simple, you should
have no problems using file overrides. If you must include several call levels or multiple overrides at different levels, however, you need to understand the OVRSCOPE
parameter of the OVRDBF command. OVRSCOPE determines the effective range
(i.e., the scope) of the file override. There are three scoping levels: job level, activation group ("sub-job") level, and call level.

You can specify OVRSCOPE(*JOB) to extend the scope of the override to all
programs that will subsequently run in the current job. This is the highest scoping
level you can specify for an override. When you specify OVRSCOPE(*CALLLVL),
the override is in effect only at the current call stack level and at any newly created
(i.e., lower) call levels; it does not apply to higher call levels. The default,
OVRSCOPE(*ACTGRPDFN), effects different scopes depending upon whether the
program is an Original Program Model (OPM) program or an Integrated Language
Environment (ILE) program. The default scope for OPM programs is at the call
level, just as if you had specified OVRSCOPE(*CALLLVL). For ILE programs, the

default override scope depends upon the activation group in which the program is running. Activation group level scoping is available only for ILE programs. We discuss ILE, activation groups, and more about override scopes in Chapter 22.

The following rules apply generally to file overrides:

- The system applies only one override per database file at any single scoping level. Subsequent overrides to the same database file, at the same scoping level, render previous ones obsolete. For example, two different file overrides cannot be in effect conrurrently at any single call level.

- A program at a lower scoping level can perform an override to a file previously overridden at a higher scoping level. Further, when an override is scoped at the call level, the program at a lower call level can perform an override to a file previously overriden at a higher call level. When this occurs, any attributes in effect at the higher level will also be in effect at the lower level. Any additional attributes specified by the lower level override will also be in effect. Within the lower-level program, you can specify the OVRDBF parameter SECURE(*YES). This causes the lower-level override to ignore previously specified overrides; in this case, only those attributes specified on the current override are in effect at this scoping level.

- When a scoping level ends, any overrides that exist only at that scoping level are removed. Further, when an override is scoped at the call level, the override is removed when that call level ends.

- Issuing an override for a nonexistent file does not generate an error message.

In the example shown in Figure 17.2, if the called program, UPDMAIL, issues an additional override for file MAILLIST, that additional override is in effect only while program UPDMAIL runs. When UPDMAIL returns to calling program SETMBR, the override performed within program UPDMAIL is no longer in effect. Because SETMBR executes at a higher call level than UPDMAIL, any override that UPDMAIL applies is removed when the program ends.

You can apply only one override at a time to a database file in a single scoping level in the program stack. A program always uses the last OVRDBF command it encountered within a scoping level, rendering any previous overrides at that level obsolete. Multiple overrides applied to the *same database file* within the *same scoping level* are not cumulative. In the example code below, only the second override will be in effect after the code executes:

```
OVRDBF    MAILLIST MBR(PROMOLIST)
OVRDBF    MAILLIST SHARE(*YES)
```

After this code executes, the file opens with the first member in the file, not necessarily the PROMOLIST member. The second OVRDBF command removes any existing override, even though the second override set a different parameter than the first one. It's also worth noting that you can apply invalid overrides within a job as long as the override command is syntactically correct. For example, there need not be a file named MAILLIST on your system for you to issue an override command for it; the invalid override is, of course, meaningless, but the system does not generate an error message.

Using the DLTOVR Command

The DLTOVR command lets you remove one or more overrides. The command has a simple format:

```
DLTOVR    FILE(overridden-file-name)  +
          LVL(scoping-level)
```

You identify the overridden file in the FILE parameter and the system removes the appropriate override for the file. You also can specify DTLOVR FILE(*ALL) to remove all overrides at the scoping level you specify. Using the command DLTOVR FILE(*PRTF) removes any printer file overrides, which we discuss next.

The optional LVL parameter allows you to control the scoping level at which you want to delete the override(s). Specifying LVL(*) indicates that you want to delete the override at the current call level; LVL(*JOB) means you want to delete the override at the job level. The default, LVL(*ACTGRPDFN), deletes overrides at different scopes depending upon whether the program is an OPM program or an ILE program. The default scope for OPM programs is at the call level, just as if you had specified LVL(*). For ILE programs, the scope of the deletion depends upon the activation group in which the program is running.

Using the OVRPRTF Command

Even though CL does not directly provide commands to write to a printer file, you can adjust a printer file's attributes. For example, if an RPG program uses a printer file to produce mailing labels, you can adjust the size of the labels and the number of copies to print by issuing an override in the CL program that calls the RPG program. You use the OVRPRTF (Override with Printer File) command to issue overrides to printer files.

The OVRPRTF command, like the OVRDBF command, has two purposes: to direct a program to use a printer file other than the one named in the program or to temporarily change the attributes of a printer file used by a program. These attributes may include which character font to use, the size of the paper used to print a report, or the number of copies of the report to print. Once a CL program executes an OVRPRTF command, the changes made by the command remain in effect until the program ends, until the program encounters a DLTOVR (Delete Override) command, or until the program encounters another override to the same printer file. The command takes the following form (showing only the parameters used most often):

```
OVRPRTF   FILE(file-override-name)                               +
          TOFILE(library-name/printer-device-file-name)  +
          DEV(device-name)                                       +
          PAGESIZE(page-length                                   +
                   page-width                                    +
                   unit-of-measure)                              +
```

```
              LPI(lines-per-inch)                                    +
              CPI(characters-per-inch)                               +
              OVRFLW(overflow-line-number)                           +
              OUTQ(library-name/output-queue-name)                   +
              FORMTYPE(form-type)                                     +
              COPIES(number-of-copies)                               +
              SCHEDULE(print-schedule)                               +
              HOLD(hold-spooled-report)                              +
              SAVE(save-spooled-report)                              +
              SECURE(secure-from-previous-overrides-option)  +
              OVRSCOPE(override-scope)
```

The FILE parameter identifies the name of the printer file to be overridden. The other optional parameters identify the attributes to be overridden. You can refer to Appendix A for a brief description of each of the OVRPRTF command's parameters; we discuss a few of them here.

The use of the OVRPRTF command is similar to that of the OVRDBF command. For example, assume you have a printer file on your system that was created with the following command:

```
CRTPRTF    FILE(QGPL/MLABEL)   +
           PAGESIZE(6 35)      +
           OVRFLW(6)           +
           COPIES(1)
```

The above command would create the printer file definition for a mailing label six lines long by 35 characters wide that has a printer overflow line at line 6 and prints one copy of the labels. If you wanted to temporarily change the size of the label to 18 lines long and you wanted to print three copies, you could issue the following command before running the RPG application program that prints the mailing labels:

```
OVRPRTF    FILE(MLABEL)        +
           PAGESIZE(18 35)     +
           COPIES(3)
```

No changes to your RPG program would be necessary. The system would temporarily override the description stored in the printer file, but only for the duration of the call level in which the override occurred (assuming the override occurs in an OPM program). The CL program shown in Figure 17.3 illustrates the use of OVRPRTF in a CL program that calls an RPG program to print mailing labels.

The program in Figure 17.3 accepts four parameters: the name of the file member containing the mailing list, the length of the label to print (in print lines), the printer device upon which to print the labels, and the number of copies to print. At label A, the program retrieves the name of the currently assigned printer device if the *&prtdev* input parameter has a value of **CURRENT*. At label B, the program overrides references to file MAILLIST to use the member passed in parameter *&mbr*. The program also uses the OVRPRTF command to temporarily adjust the MLABEL printer file to use the printer device named in variable *&prtdev*, the mailing label length specified

Figure 17.3
Using OVRPRTF
in a CL Program

```
MAILLABELS:
      PGM          PARM(&mbr &paglen &prtdev &copies)
      DCL          &mbr       *CHAR 10
      DCL          &paglen    *DEC (15 5)
      DCL          &prtdev    *CHAR 10
      DCL          &copies    *DEC (15 5)

A:    IF           (&prtdev *EQ '*CURRENT    ') DO
                       RTVJOBA     PRTDEV(&prtdev)
                   ENDDO

B:    OVRDBF       FILE(MAILLIST)  MBR(&mbr)
      OVRPRTF      FILE(MLABEL)                  +
                   DEV(&prtdev)                  +
                   OUTQ(*DEV)                    +
                   PAGESIZE(&paglen 35)          +
                   OVRFLW(&paglen)               +
                   COPIES(&copies)
C:    CALL         PRINTLABEL
      RETURN

      ENDPGM
```

in variable *&paglen*, and the number of copies specified in variable *&copies*. At label C, the program calls an HLL program that will print the mailing labels. When program PRINTLABEL opens printer file MLABEL, it overrides the DEV, OUTQ, PAGESIZE, OVRFLW, and COPIES attributes of the printer file to those specified on the OVRPRTF command.

You can apply an OVRPRTF command to all printer files in a call level by specifying OVRPRTF FILE(*PRTF) instead of a specific file name. Consider the following two commands:

```
OVRPRTF      FILE(*PRTF)    +
             DEV(PRT16)     +
             OUTQ(*DEV)     +
             COPIES(2)

OVRPRTF      FILE(MLABEL)   +
             DEV(PRT01)     +
             OUTQ(*DEV)
```

The first command sets all printer files in the call level to print two copies each at device PRT16. The second OVRPRTF command sets printer file MLABEL to print at device PRT01. The program still prints two copies of MLABEL because the generic FILE(*PRTF) specification remains in effect for the attributes not overridden by the second OVRPRTF command. Unlike database file overrides, printer file overrides at the same call level are cumulative.

Positioning Database Files

As we discussed earlier, when a program opens a file, it usually positions the file cursor at the beginning of the file. You can, however, use the POSITION keyword of the OVRDBF command to instruct the system to position the cursor at another record. If you specify OVRDBF MBR(*ALL), however, you must not perform any record positioning; you cannot specify the POSITION parameter in this case.

Specifying POSITION(*START) positions the file cursor at the beginning of the file. Normally, this is where the file cursor would be anyway, so you won't usually use this value.

If you specify POSITION(*END), the file cursor is set at the end of the file; the first time the program tries to read a record from the file sequentially, it will encounter an end-of-file condition. This option is useful for some HLL programs that must read a file backward (called *read previous*); in this case, the first read previous operation would read the last record in the file.

You also can set the file cursor to a specific record in a file, using the *RRN special value. *RRN stands for relative record number and is the order in which records are physically stored within a database file. The following command would specify that when file MAILLIST is opened, the program should start processing at the 501st record in the file:

```
OVRDBF    FILE(MAILLIST) POSITION(*RRN 501)
```

In addition to the positioning values discussed here, a number of positioning values are used primarily for keyed files. These values let you set the file cursor to a specific record, based upon the contents of the record keys. These values are not widely used and are not discussed here.

The CL command POSDBF (Position Database File) also lets you set the position of a database file to either the beginning or the end of a file. While the OVRDBF command is used before you open a file, the POSDBF command is used to position a file that is already open. The following commands would open file MAILLIST and set the file cursor to the end of the file:

```
OPNDBF    FILE(MAILLIST)
POSDBF    OPNID(MAILLIST)    POSITION(*END)
```

The OPNDBF command opens file MAILLIST for processing, then the POSDBF command sets the file cursor to the end of the file. The other allowable value for the POSITION parameter is *START*.

Preopening Database Files

Considerable computer resources are involved in opening a database file. If a particular program opens a large number of files, you may find yourself waiting several seconds for all the file-open operations to complete. This situation would occur each time you call the program. You can improve a program's overall performance by preopening files and letting all your programs access the same preopened files. This would allow you to call a program several times without going through the file-open process each time. Within a CL program, you can open a particular file once and specify that any programs that process the file should share the same open data path. When this is done, other programs that access the file do not cause the full open operation to be performed again. This situation, in which more than one program shares a single open data path to a file, is called a **shared open**. You can accomplish a shared open using either of two methods:

- Use the SHARE(*YES) parameter of the create command used to create the file
- Issue an override to the file, specifying SHARE(*YES)

It is usually useful to preopen files in a "startup" program for an application. Then each program in the application won't have to open the files it needs. The program in Figure 17.4 shows a program that starts a mailing list menu. Before calling the menu program, it preopens all files that will be used.

Figure 17.4
Preopening Files

```
PGM
OVRDBF     FILE(MAILLIST)  SHARE(*YES)
OPNDBF     FILE(MAILLIST)
OVRDBF     FILE(ZIPCODE)   SHARE(*YES)
OPNDBF     FILE(ZIPCODE)
OVRDBF     FILE(ABBREV)    SHARE(*YES)
OPNDBF     FILE(ABBREV)

CALL       MAILMENU

CLOF       OPNID(MAILLIST)
CLOF       OPNID(ZIPCODE)
CLOF       OPNID(ABBREV)

DLTOVR     *ALL
RETURN
ENDPGM
```

The program in Figure 17.4 performs an override to each database file before opening it. The override specifies SHARE(*YES). This value indicates that if the file member is opened more than once, the same open data path to the file's records should be used by each program in the job that opens the member. Each program will not have to perform its own open and overall performance will improve.

Next, the program executes an OPNDBF command to open the file. The file remains open, sharing its data path with any other programs *within this job* that might need the file. After the application ends, the files are closed, using the CLOF (Close File) command. Finally, the overrides are deleted. Even without the DLTOVR command, the overrides would be deleted automatically when the program ends.

Although preopening files is a valuable performance improvement technique, you need to be aware of the implications of open data path sharing. An open data path has only *one* file cursor. Each program that shares the same open data path is responsible for positioning the file cursor to meet its own needs. If a program calls another program and the called program accesses a record in the shared file, the file cursor is repositioned. When the called program returns, the file cursor is still located at the record that was accessed last. The calling program must be able to reposition the file cursor at the record that it now wants to access.

If you are always careful to have each program in an application explicitly set a file's cursor, you should be able to take advantage of preopening files to improve performance. If some of the programs in an application use sequential record processing, however, sharing the open data path may not be a good option; repositioning the file cursor can be much more difficult when using sequential processing.

Using OPNQRYF

You have seen how the override commands can temporarily adjust certain attributes of files you are processing. CL also offers a technique for temporarily adjusting the data records a program processes. For example, in the mailing list application we have discussed, you might want to process only those records from a specific zip code. Or the file might be keyed in alphabetic name order and you might want to print labels in zip code order.

On some other computer platforms, you would use a sort program to order records in a file or to select specific records from a file. The sort program would create a copy of the file with the correct records in the correct order, and the program would process the copy of the file. The AS/400 has such a facility, which it implements with the CL command FMTDTA (Format Data); but it also offers a much more flexible facility, called Open Query File.

The OPNQRYF (Open Query File) command creates a temporary access path with an alternative view of the records in a database file. Only the job that executes the OPNQRYF command can use the access path. This derived file contains a subset of the database records of the original file and can be arranged in the order you specify. An HLL program can process the records in this file, just as if it were processing the file the derived file is based upon — and the file can be processed without any modification to the program. The OPNQRYF command can be used to:

- Select a subset of available records
- Order records by the value of one or more fields in the record
- Join records from different files into one data path
- Group records together
- Calculate new field values for fields that don't exist in a physical file

The OPNQYRF command has many parameters, but the most-often-used ones take the following form:

```
OPNQRYF    FILE(library-name/file-name              +
                member-name                          +
                record-format-name)                  +
           OPTION(open-option)                       +
           FORMAT(library-name/database-file-name    +
                   record-format-name)               +
           QRYSLT('query-selection')                 +
           KEYFLD(file-name/field-name               +
                   collating-order                   +
                   absolute-value)
```

The FILE parameter identifies the database file(s) to be processed by the OPNQRYF command. You can specify a qualified file name. You also can specify a member name within the file. On rare occasions, you specify a record format name (e.g., when you join two files you must specify a record format name).

The OPTION parameter lets you indicate which type of processing you intend to do with the record. Usually, you specify OPTION(*ALL), but you can limit the file operations to input functions, output operations, update operations, delete functions, or a combination of any of these. Specifying OPTION(*INP *OUT *UPD *DLT) is the same as specifying OPTION(*ALL).

The FORMAT parameter indicates the record format the program will use. Usually, you refer to the same record format you used in the FILE parameter, by using the default FORMAT(*FILE). But you can specify a different file and format name; you must do so if you are processing multiple files. If you have specified overrides for a file, they are ignored, unless you also specify FORMAT(*FILE).

The QRYSLT parameter is the one that really demonstrates the power of OPNQRYF. Using this parameter, you can tell the system which records to select from a file. The syntax of the QRYSLT parameter can be as simple as indicating that you want all the records in the database file included:

```
QRYSLT(*ALL)
```

Or you can include a complex expression of up to 2,000 characters describing which records you want to process. The parameter is made up of relational expressions including field names and constant values. Each relational expression includes at least one field name. For example, to select all records that have a zip code (character field name ZIPCOD) equal to 59106, you would use the following syntax:

```
QRYSLT('ZIPCOD = "59106"')
```

Notice that the expression is a quoted string. Also notice that the character value *59106* is enclosed by double quotes. We could also have specified two single quotes, as in the following expression:

```
QRYSLT('ZIPCOD = ''59106''')
```

Double quotes, however, make the expression easier to read. (Note that this convention does not consistently hold true elsewhere in CL. Usually, you are forced to use ' ' instead of " when you want to include a single quote in a quoted CL string.)

The QRYSLT parameter can become very complex, with many string and arithmetic expressions; it can include several built-in functions, such as a substring (%sst) function, a sum (%sum) function, an averaging (%avg) function, a range (%range) function, a character translation (%xlate) function, and even sine (%sin) and cosine (%cos) trigonometric functions, among others. In some ways, the QRYSLT parameter of the OPNQRYF command resembles the record selection techniques used by SQL, a widely used language for performing database operations. The following OPNQRYF command and SQL statement are roughly equivalent:

OPNQRYF command

```
OPNQRYF    FILE(MAILLIST)                              +
           QRYSLT('ZIPCOD = "59106"')
```

SQL statement

```
SELECT    * FROM MAILLIST
          WHERE ZIPCOD = '59106'
```

The KEYFLD parameter of the OPNQRYF command lets you specify an order in which the OPNQRYF command presents records. You can include one or more key fields that determine the order of the records. You can usually specify field names alone; but if you are dealing with more than one file, you can qualify the field names by the file in which they appear (e.g., MAILLIST/ZIPCOD to indicate the ZIPCOD field in file MAILLIST). You also can tell the system to sort the records in ascending or descending order. In rare cases, you might also specify that the order is to be based on the absolute value of the field, without regard to numeric sign. There are three elements in each KEYFLD value: the field name, which is required; the collating order, *ASCEND or *DESCEND, which defaults to *ASCEND; and the optional *ABSVAL entry. Again, there is in SQL a parallel to the KEYFLD parameter; the following examples are roughly equivalent:

OPNQRYF command

```
OPNQRYF    FILE(MAILLIST)                              +
           QRYSLT('COUNTRY = "USA"')                   +
           KEYFLD((ZIPCOD *DESCEND) (CARRTE))
```

SQL statement

```
SELECT    * FROM MAILLIST
          WHERE COUNTRY = 'USA'
          ORDER BY ZIPCOD DESCENDING, CARRTE
```

These statements select the records from MAILLIST that occur in country USA and sort them into order by zip code in descending order, then by carrier route.

To use OPNQRYF in a CL program, you must be aware of some advance setup requirements. First, the file specified on the OPNQRYF command must share its open data path with other programs in the job; this ensures that other programs use the same path to the file that OPNQRYF creates. Next, the path opened by OPNQRYF must be processed by an HLL program. With one exception (the CPYFRMQRYF command, discussed next), CL cannot process the derived file.

How do you use OPNQRYF in a CL program? First, you must execute an override to ensure that the open data path will be shared. Next, execute the OPNQRYF command. Finally, call one or more HLL programs to process the records in the derived file. The program in Figure 17.5 amplifies the mailing list program shown in Figure 17.3. In this case, we added two input parameters to indicate the range of zip codes to process. Then we build a QRYSLT statement using that range of zip codes and process the OPNQRYF command to select and sort records from that range.

Figure 17.5
Using OPNQRYF
in a CL Program

```
MAILLABELS:
        PGM       PARM(&mbr &paglen &prtdev &copies &fromzip &tozip)
        DCL       &mbr      *CHAR 10
        DCL       &paglen   *DEC (15 5)
        DCL       &prtdev   *CHAR 10
        DCL       &copies   *DEC (15 5)
        DCL       &fromzip  *CHAR 5
        DCL       &tozip    *CHAR 5
        DCL       &qryslt   *CHAR 2000

        IF        (&prtdev *EQ '*CURRENT   ') DO
        RTVJOBA PRTDEV(&prtdev)
        ENDDO

/* Build QRYSLT string: 'ZIPCOD = %RANGE("xxxxx" "xxxxx")' */
/*             or: '*ALL'                                   */

A:      IF        (&fromzip *NE '*ALL') DO
        CHGVAR &qryslt                                        +
                  ('ZIPCOD = %RANGE("' *CAT                   +
                  &fromzip *CAT '" "' *CAT                    +
                  &tozip *CAT '")')
        ENDDO
        ELSE      CHGVAR &qryslt ('*ALL')

B:      OVRDBF    MAILMAST MBR(&mbr) SHARE(*YES)

C:      OPNQRYF   FILE(MAILLIST)                              +
                  QRYSLT(&qryslt)                             +
                  KEYFLD((COUNTRY) (ZIPCOD *DESCEND))

        OVRPRTF   MLABEL                                      +
                  DEV(&prtdev)                                +
                  OUTQ(*DEV)                                  +
                  PAGESIZE(&paglen 35)                        +
                  OVRFLW(&paglen)                             +
                  COPIES(&copies)

        CALL      PRINTLABEL

D:      CLOF
        DLTOVR    FILE(*ALL)

        RETURN
        ENDPGM
```

In this program, we have added the necessary support for OPNQRYF and in the process made it capable of handling any zip code range, or all zip codes (when *&fromzip* has a value of **ALL*). At label A in Figure 17.5, we determine whether variable *&qryslt* should be a query-select statement or **ALL*, the special value to include all records. The string expression in the CHGVAR command builds the necessary statement. The override executed at label B specifies the correct file member and also directs the system to use a shared open data path for this file, as required by OPNQRYF. At label C, we perform the OPNQRYF, naming the value of variable *&qryslt* in the QRYSLT parameter and specifying the order in which we want to process the records. After processing the records with the RPG program PRINTLABEL, we close the file (label D) and delete the overrides.

The subject of OPNQRYF can be very broad-ranging and complex. Our discussion here has only scratched the surface. The best way to become proficient with OPNQRYF is to study the subject in IBM's *CL Reference* and do lots of trial-and-error testing.

Using CPYFRMQRYF

Remember that OPNQRYF opens a data path to a file, selecting and sorting records as needed for specific processing. This temporary data path can be accessed only by the current job. That open data path must usually be processed by an HLL program; you cannot directly process an OPNQRYF data path with a CL program. You can, however, make a copy of the records in the data path using the CPYFRMQRYF (Copy From Query File) command. You can copy the records to a physical file or you can print them. Once the records are in a physical file, you can process them directly with CL. Keep in mind, however, that the copy is just that: a copy. If the original file, the one upon which the data path is based, changes, the copy made by CPYFRMQRYF does not change. The CPYFRMQRYF command takes the following form (most-often-used parameters only):

```
CPYFRMQRYF    FROMOPNID(open-id-name)               +
              TOFILE(library-name/file-name)         +
              TOMBR(member-name)                     +
              MBROPT(replace-option)                 +
              CRTFILE(create-file-option)            +
              NBRRCDS(number-of-records)
```

The FROMOPNID parameter is usually the file name from the OPNQRYF command; it identifies the data path to copy. The copy is made to the qualified file name and member specified in the TOFILE and TOMBR parameters. The default TOMBR value is **FIRST*. To print the records instead of copying them to a database file, specify TOFILE(*PRINT). The possible values for the MBROPT parameter are **NONE*, if the TOFILE does not already exist; **ADD*, to add records to an existing TOFILE; or **REPLACE*, to replace existing records in a TOFILE. The CRTFILE parameter allows you to create a TOFILE, if it does not already exist; valid values are **YES* to create the file or **NO* if the file exists. You can copy all records in the data path by specifying NBRRCDS(*END), or you can limit the number of records that will be copied by specifying a number for the NBRRCDS parameter.

Chapter Summary

Function overrides allow you to temporarily change the role of an AS/400 file as it is processed by a program. Overrides allow you to make programs more generic and more flexible, without requiring changes to an application program.

The OVRDBF (Override with Database File) command directs a program to use a database file other than the one named in the program, or temporarily changes the attributes of a database file used by a program. Some common uses for OVRDBF are to open a multiple-member file to a member other than the first one, or to access a temporary file in the job's QTEMP library.

The OVRPRTF (Override with Printer File) command directs a program to use a printer file other than the one named in the program, or temporarily changes the attributes of a printer file used by a program. Some common uses for OVRPRTF are to change the size of a form, to change the number of copies of a report to print, or to change the printer on which a report will be printed.

There are three scoping levels: job level, activation group level, and call level. Overrides are in effect only at the scoping level in which they are applied, and in any lower scoping levels. For overrides scoped at the call level, overrides are in effect only at the call level in which they are applied, and in any lower call levels. You can specify SECURE(*YES) on the override command to secure an override from previously issued overrides. Whenever a program calls another program, if overrides are in effect, the overrides are still in effect for the called program, even if it is an HLL program. The system allows only one override within any scoping level for a single database file; subsequent overrides at the same scoping level render previous ones obsolete. When a scoping level ends, any overrides in effect at that level are deleted. You can also use the DLTOVR (Delete Override) command to explicitly delete overrides.

Usually, when a database file is opened, the file cursor is set to the first record in the file. You can use the POSITION keyword of the OVRDBF command or use the POSDBF (Position Database File) command, to reposition the file cursor to a different record.

Preopening database files and using shared open data paths can improve performance by eliminating the time and resources needed for multiple opens and by decreasing the amount of resources required to maintain multiple open data paths to the same file. Programs that share open data paths must be careful to explicitly set a file's cursor to meet their needs.

The OPNQRYF (Open Query File) command opens a file data path that contains a set of database records to satisfy a specific request. The records can be arranged in the order you specify. This command satisfies the requirements of record sorting and selection. There are several parallels between OPNQRYF and SQL. Using OPNQRYF requires that a file share its open data path with other programs in the job.

The CPYFRMQRYF (Copy from Query File) command copies into a physical file those records selected and sorted by OPNQRYF. Then you can use normal CL file techniques to process the records.

Terms

file cursor   open data path
function override   shared open

Review Questions

1. Specify the override command (including parameters) you would use to prepare a program for the following functions:

    a. Open member COMPANY3 in file CUSTOMERS, which exists in library ARLIB.

    b. Change a sales report, defined in printer file SLSLIB/SLS010P, to print three copies on printer device PRT05.

    c. Process member WAREHOUSE1 in file INVENTORY (in library INVLIB) with OPNQRYF.

    d. Open file SURVEYS in library STATLIB so that the program skips over the first 1,000 records before processing the first one.

    e. Share the open data path for file REZLIB/RESERVMAST among all the programs in the job.

    f. Sequentially update all records in all members of file ARLIB/CASHTRAN.

    g. Specify that all printed reports in a job should print two copies. Payroll checks, defined in file PRLIB/PR160P, however, should only print once, then should be saved on the output queue.

2. In what ways does OPNQRYF differ from conventional sort/selection techniques on other computer platforms? Why would you want to use CPYFRMQRYFs?

3. List two methods for specifying open data path sharing of files.

4. What is the chief advantage of preopening a database file? The chief disadvantage?

Exercises

1. Write a CL program (SA1701*XXX*) that performs the following:

    a. Receive a parameter, *&library*, to contain the name of a library.

    b. Display all the objects in the library to an outfile in library QTEMP. The name of the IBM-supplied model outfile is QSYS/QADSPOBJ.

    c. Perform an OPNQRYF to select all the records in the outfile that are larger than 1,000,000 bytes in size. The size is in variable *&odobsz*. Sort the records by size, in descending order.

    d. Use CPYFRMQRYF to copy the sorted output to database file QTEMP/SELOBJ.

    e. Use the DSPPFM (Display Physical File Member) command to display the records in QTEMP/SELOBJ.

    After you compile the program, call it, passing it the name of a library on your system. Can you identify the five largest objects in the library?

Chapter 18

Advanced Command Prompting

Chapter Overview

You learned in Chapter 4 that the AS/400 command prompting facilities ease the learning curve for interactive entry of CL commands. In this chapter you learn how to use the command prompting facilities within a CL program. We also discuss the selective prompting feature as a means to enhance the usability of your CL programs.

Reviewing the Prompt Facility

Recall that the F4=Prompt key is available from any AS/400 command line and invokes the AS/400 prompter facility. You might also recall that a question mark (?) character can be used within a command prompt to display more information about a selected field contained on the prompt. One thing that you might not be aware of is that the question mark (?) also is the AS/400 prompting character and in many cases works exactly like pressing the F4=Prompt key.

When you are presented with an AS/400 command line, you can press F4=Prompt to invoke the prompting facilities. But, instead of pressing the F4=prompt key, you just as easily could have typed a question mark at the prompt and pressed the Enter key. The result is exactly the same. If the command line is empty when you press F4=Prompt, you are presented with the menu named MAJOR. When you type a question mark on an empty command line and press Enter, you are presented with the same menu. If the command line contains a CL command when the F4=Prompt key is pressed, you are presented with a prompt display for the selected command. Likewise, if you enter a question mark on a command line anywhere before a command, the command will be prompted, just as if you had pressed F4=Prompt.

To help illustrate the use of command prompting, you might try to enter some commands on an AS/400 command line using the prompting character (?). For example, if you type the following command on a command line and press the Enter key, you will be presented with the DSPLIB command prompt, and the OUTPUT(*PRINT) parameter will already be filled in for you.

```
?DSPLIB   OUTPUT(*PRINT)
```

Simple Command Prompting

Within a CL program that is designed to run interactively, you can include **simple command prompting** to enhance the flexibility of the program. With the ability to use the question mark instead of pressing the F4=Prompt key, you can control the display of a prompt screen, as well as control which fields of the prompt the user can modify. In effect, you are allowing the user of the program to change the CL command as the program runs. Consider the following CL program that uses command prompting:

```
PGM
?SNDMSG    TOMSGQ(QSYSOPR)
?SAVLIB    LIB(APLIB1)
RETURN
ENDPGM
```

When this program is called interactively, the user is first presented with the command prompt for the SNDMSG command. Because the TOMSGQ parameter has an assigned value (in this case *QSYSOPR*), the user cannot modify to whom the message is sent. Specifying a value for a command parameter within the program prohibits the user from changing that parameter. The field is displayed on the prompt, but is not input-capable. The user can, however, modify all of the other fields of the SNDMSG command prompt. In this case, the user would probably modify the MSG parameter of the SNDMSG command, thereby using the prompt to simply enter the message text to be sent.

When the user makes any desired changes to the prompted command, then presses Enter, the message is immediately sent. The program then continues to its next command, ?SAVLIB.

Here again, the SAVLIB command is preceded by a question mark, which causes the command prompt for the SAVLIB command to be displayed. Again, because a value is specified for the LIB parameter, this prompt can only be used to save the APLIB1 library; however, the user can modify any of the other fields displayed on the command prompt. In this case, the user would need to specify a device (DEV) to be used for the SAVLIB operation. When the prompt is completed and the user presses the Enter key, the command is immediately processed.

Can you see how you might use the command prompting facilities within a CL program? Here are a few of the possible uses of command prompting within a CL program:

- To provide an end-user tool for sending messages
- To provide a system operator's utility program to perform system backups
- To provide a specialized front-end prompt to restrict programmers from changing compile-time options

Anywhere you want a user to have some control over how a command executes, you can present a prompt for the command and allow the user to modify only those command parameters that you permit.

There are some restrictions when you use command prompting within a CL program. For instance, you cannot include the command prompting character (?) in a program that will run as a batch job. This restriction might already be apparent to you. Because no workstation is attached to a batch job, there is no place to display a command prompt.

Prompting cannot be used on commands contained in an IF, ELSE, or MONMSG command. You can, however, use prompting on commands contained within DO groups associated with an IF, ELSE, or MONMSG command. Also, you cannot prompt for certain CL commands within a CL program. Figure 18.1 contains a list of commands that you cannot prompt for in a CL program.

Figure 18.1
Commands That Cannot
Be Prompted Within a
CL Program

CALL	ENDPGM	RETURN
CHGVAR	ENDRCV	SNDF
DCL	IF	SNDRCVF
DCLF	GOTO	TFRCTL
DO	MONMSG	WAIT
ELSE	PGM	
ENDDO	RCVF	

If a CL program presents a command prompt to the user, it is always the user's prerogative to press the F3 or F12 function key to exit from the prompt. If this occurs, the command is not executed, and an escape message is sent to the program. You should monitor for this escape message whenever you use command prompting in a CL program. Consider the following example:

```
PGM
?CRTLIB
MONMSG MSGID(CPF6801)
RETURN
ENDPGM
```

When this program is executed, the user is presented with a prompt for the CRTLIB (Create Library) command. If the user chooses to use the F3 or F12 key when this prompt is displayed, the escape message CPF6801 is sent to the program. If the program does not monitor for this condition, the program will terminate abnormally. A simple rule to follow is that if you are going to use prompting within a CL program, always follow the prompted command with a MONMSG MSGID(CPF6801).

Selective Prompting

Not only can you provide prompting for CL commands within a CL program, but you may selectively determine which command parameters will be shown to the user on the prompt display and to what extent the user will be able to modify the parameters. This type of prompting is called **selective prompting**, and it can be used in any CL program that will run interactively. Figure 18.2 is an example of a CL program that uses selective prompting.

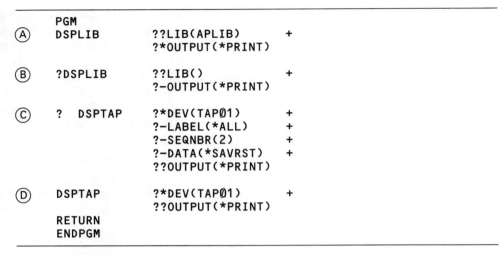

Figure 18.2
Selective Prompting

```
         PGM
(A)      DSPLIB          ??LIB(APLIB)        +
                         ?*OUTPUT(*PRINT)

(B)      ?DSPLIB         ??LIB()             +
                         ?-OUTPUT(*PRINT)

(C)      ?  DSPTAP       ?*DEV(TAP01)        +
                         ?-LABEL(*ALL)       +
                         ?-SEQNBR(2)         +
                         ?-DATA(*SAVRST)     +
                         ??OUTPUT(*PRINT)

(D)      DSPTAP          ?*DEV(TAP01)        +
                         ??OUTPUT(*PRINT)

         RETURN
         ENDPGM
```

Notice that certain special characters are used in conjunction with the question mark in these examples. These are the selective prompting characters ??, ?*, and ?–. Let's examine how they affect the prompts that are displayed to the user.

The example at (A) in Figure 18.2 prompts for the DSPLIB (Display Library) command. Notice that the command itself is not preceded by a question mark. When selective prompting characters are used within a command, the command itself need not be preceded by a question mark. However, if the command is not preceded by a question mark, the only fields displayed on the command prompt are those that are specified on the command. This can be an effective way to reduce the number of parameters that are shown on some commands with many parameters. In this example, only the LIB and OUTPUT parameters will be shown on the prompt. The LIB keyword is preceded by the characters ??. This is the selective prompting designation that causes the command parameter LIB to be displayed on the prompt. The ?? characters also specify that the parameter can be modified by the interactive user (i.e., the field will be input-capable). The value APLIB is specified for the LIB parameter value. When the value is specified, as it is here, and the selective prompting characters used are ??, the value APLIB will appear in the prompt.

The next parameter at (A) is the OUTPUT parameter. It is preceded by the selective prompting characters ?*. These characters specify that the parameter and its value (*PRINT) will be displayed on the prompt, but that the user cannot change the value (i.e., the field is not input-capable).

In the example at (B), the DSPLIB command will be prompted for when the program is executed. Because the DSPLIB command is preceded by a question mark, all of the command parameters will be displayed on the prompt, not just the two specified here. The LIB parameter is preceded by the ?? characters. Again, this specifies that the field will be displayed on the prompt as input-capable. The LIB parameter value itself is specified here as (). This is used to indicate that you do not want to assign any initial value to this parameter, but let it default to the parameter default value. Because LIB is a required parameter for the DSPLIB command, the user is forced to supply a value for it.

The second parameter at (B) is preceded by the characters ?–. These selective prompting characters are used to specify that this particular parameter will not be visible to the user. Because a value of *PRINT is assigned to the OUTPUT parameter here, you are forcing the output of the DSPLIB command to go to a printed report. The user has no control over this. The ?– characters cause the parameter to be hidden from the user even though the question mark preceding the DSPLIB command causes all other command parameters to be displayed.

A rule comes into play when you use the ?– characters: The command itself must be preceded by a question mark whenever ?– is used for CL prompting.

In the example at (C), the DSPTAP command is used. Notice that the ?– characters are used for some parameters. Because of this, the command itself must be preceded by a question mark. Notice also that the question mark and the command itself are separated by some blanks; this is acceptable. The question mark and the command may have any number of intervening blanks.

When the question mark is used before the command, all the parameters will be displayed, unless the parameter is preceded by the characters ?–. In this case, the only parameters that will be displayed are DEV and OUTPUT. The DEV parameter is protected from user changes by the characters ?*. The OUTPUT parameter will be displayed as an input-capable field, changeable by the user, as a result of the characters ??.

In the example at (D), the DSPTAP command will be prompted; DEV and OUTPUT will be the only visible command parameters. The user will not be able to change the DEV parameter value from TAP01, but will be able to change the OUTPUT parameter from *PRINT.

When working with selective prompting, you must understand and adhere to a few rules:

- A command parameter must be presented in keyword notation when selective prompting for that parameter is requested.

- Blanks cannot appear between the selective prompting characters (??, ?*, ?–) and the parameter keyword.

- Any parameter value specified by the prompt or supplied by the user will be used in the execution of the command. If a value is not specified on the prompt and not specified by the user, the parameter default value will be used.

- If a CL program variable is used as a command parameter value that is changeable by the user, a change to the prompt does not change the value of the program variable. But the command will be executed with the changed value supplied by the user and not with the value stored in the variable. If the user does not change the command parameter value, the value of the program variable will be used in the execution of the command.

Figure 18.3 summarizes selective prompting. The figure illustrates each format of selective prompting that we have discussed, tells you what value will be displayed, and indicates whether a user can change the displayed value. The selective prompting characters we have discussed here are not the only ones CL allows. Other character combinations are used only rarely to produce unusual results. Still others are reserved for IBM use. It's unlikely that you'll need these other character combinations; but if you do, you can find them documented in IBM's *CL Programmer's Guide*.

Figure 18.3
Selective Prompting
Summary

Prompt	Value Displayed	Input Allowed
??KEYWORD()	Default	Yes
??KEYWORD(VALUE)	Value	Yes
?*KEYWORD()	Default	No
?*KEYWORD(VALUE)	Value	No
?–KEYWORD()	Parameter not displayed; command will use default	No
?–KEYWORD(VALUE)	Parameter not displayed; command will use value	No

Selective prompting is used mainly to prompt for commands within CL programs. However, if you want to experiment with the selective prompting facility and get a better feel for how it works, you can simply use it on any command line. Try typing a few commands on a command line using the selective prompting characters mentioned above.

In the next chapter, you will see how you can use selective prompting in conjunction with two IBM-supplied programs, QCMDCHK and QCMDEXC, to provide highly versatile and very dynamic programs.

Chapter Summary

The command-prompting facilities available from an AS/400 command line are also available within a CL program. A CL program may prompt a user to enter parameters for most CL commands. The command will then be executed by the CL program.

Command prompting is not valid in a batch environment, and some commands do not allow prompting.

The special command-prompting character is the question mark (?). When it appears, it must precede the command for which prompting is requested. When parameter values are supplied and the question mark is used, these parameters cannot be changed by the user.

In addition to prompting for a command, you may selectively determine which command parameters will be prompted. This selective prompting makes use of special characters ??, ?*, and ?– placed directly before parameters to be prompted.

You must use keyword notation when entering commands that are to use selective prompting. Blanks cannot appear between the prompting characters and the parameter keyword. If you use a program variable as a parameter value in a command that uses selective prompting, changing the value of the parameter does not change the value of the variable.

Terms

selective prompting   simple command prompting

Review Questions

1. Explain the difference between simple command prompting and selective prompting in a CL program. How is each feature implemented?

2. The following examples illustrate prompted CL commands. For each example, explain which parameters will be displayed, which ones the user can change, which ones the user cannot change, and which parameter value will be used by the command if the user doesn't change the displayed value.

   Note: The DSPLIB command supports two command parameters: LIB (with a default value of *LIBL*) and OUTPUT (with a default value of *). Consider both parameters.

```
a. DSPLIB   ??LIB()
b. DSPLIB   ??LIB(*USRLIBL)
c. DSPLIB   ?*LIB(*USRLIBL)
d. ?DSPLIB  ?-LIB(*USRLIBL)
e. ?DSPLIB  ??LIB()   ?-OUTPUT(*PRINT)
f. ?DSPLIB  ??LIB()   ?*OUTPUT(*PRINT)
g. ?DSPLIB  ?*OUTPUT(*PRINT)
h. DSPLIB   ??LIB()   ?*OUTPUT(*PRINT)
i. DSPLIB   ?*OUTPUT(*PRINT)
```

Exercises

1. Write a program (SA1801*XXX*) that does the following:

   Using selective prompting, prompt the user of the program with the command STRSEU. The user should be able to change only the source member name. You should provide appropriate defaults for the other parameters of the STRSEU command. For example, you might supply the defaults that make the user always work with the source file QCLSRC in library STUDENT1. The default source type in this case would be CLP.

2. Write a program (SA1802*XXX*) that does the following:

   Using selective prompting, prompt the user for the RTVUSRPRF command. Allow the user to enter a value for the required USRPRF parameter. The attribute that you retrieve from the user profile will be the TEXT parameter. Once the TEXT parameter is retrieved, send a message (to the bottom of the display using SNDPGMMSG) that includes the text retrieved from the user profile.

   This program allows you to retrieve the text associated with any user profile on the system and to send that text in a message using the SNDPGMMSG command.

Chapter 19

Using IBM-Supplied APIs

Chapter Overview

IBM supplies many application program interfaces (APIs) to provide access to system functions that may be unavailable or inconvenient to access by other methods. In this chapter, you learn the use of the QCMD, QCMDEXC, and QCMDCHK APIs. We also outline other APIs that may be useful in a CL program.

Introduction to APIs

IBM supplies a number of programs called **application program interfaces** (APIs) to make it relatively easy to access low-level machine functions or secured system data from an HLL program. APIs are documented and supported alternatives for gaining access to certain parts of the AS/400's operating system, OS/400, that might be inconvenient or impossible to access using other methods.

One API displays an AS/400 command line. Another API allows an HLL program, such as an RPG program, to execute a CL command. Yet another API scans a character string for a specific pattern. There are APIs to process data queues, user spaces, and other not-so-common AS/400 objects. Chances are, if there is a system function you want to perform, IBM provides an API to perform it. Figure 19.1 lists a few commonly used APIs; there are hundreds of others. In this chapter, we discuss those shown in bold type in the figure. In particular, we discuss those APIs that have a direct relationship to CL. Many of the others have more applicability in other languages. All of the IBM-supplied APIs are documented in several IBM publications, including the *System API Programming* book.

Many of the APIs listed in the figure are directly executable from a CL program. To facilitate performance, an API is generally in the form of a callable program. Not only is it faster to call an API from an HLL than it is to call a CL program to execute a CL command, but it is often easier to code. You might use an API when it would provide better performance than equivalent HLL programming would provide, or when the information or function you need is not available directly from the HLL.

A chief advantage of using APIs is that IBM ensures that the interface to the API remains consistent and compatible from one OS/400 release to the next. So if you use APIs in your programming, you don't need to change your programs if IBM changes the underlying structure of an API when it issues a new release. For example, if you use

Figure 19.1
A Summary of
Commonly Used APIs

API	Function
QCLSCAN	Scans for a string pattern
QCMD	CL command processor
QCMDCHK	Checks the syntax of a CL command string
QCMDEXC	Executes a CL command string
QDCXLATE	Translates a character string
QRCVDTAQ	Receives an entry from a data queue
QSNDDTAQ	Sends an entry to a data queue
QUSCHGUS	Changes the contents of a user space
QUSCMDLN	Pops up a system command line window
QUSCRTUS	Creates a user space
QUSLFLD	Lists a record layout into a user space
QUSLJOB	Lists jobs into a user space
QUSLMBR	Lists database file members into a user space
QUSLOBJ	Lists objects into a user space
QUSLRCD	Lists record formats into a user space
QUSLSPL	Lists spooled files into a user space
QUSRTVUS	Retrieves the contents of a user space

the API named QCMDEXC to execute a CL command from an HLL program, you
would call the API with the following command (or the HLL equivalent code):

```
CALL    QCMDEXC                         +
        PARM(command-string             +
             command-string-length)
```

IBM documents the QCMDEXC command as a callable program that accepts two
parameters: the command string and the length of the command string. This fact does
not change, even if IBM makes major overhauls in the way the system works to execute CL commands; you should not have to change your program or even recompile
it if it uses an IBM-supported and documented API.

Using QCMD

QCMD is the IBM-supplied API that actually executes CL command requests. QCMD
is a multifunction program. When you sign on to the AS/400, QCMD executes the
program specified in your user profile as your initial program, or displays your initial
menu. When you submit a job to batch, QCMD is usually the program at the top level
of the call stack. These functions all happen automatically, but you can explicitly call
the QCMD program to display an AS/400 Command Entry display. You can display a

Command Entry screen such as the one shown in Figure 19.2 by typing the following command at a command line or by including it in a CL program:

```
CALL    QCMD
```

Figure 19.2
AS/400 Command
Entry Display

```
                                    Command Entry                          STUDENT1
                                                                Request level:    8
    All previous commands and messages:
     5> dspcmd dspjob
     5> dspcmd chgjob
     8> dspactjob
        Command DSPACTJOB in library *LIBL not found.
        Error found on DSPACTJOB command.
     8> dspcmd savobj
     9> dspcmd savlib
     5> wrkwtr
     5> dspjob
     5> wrkactjob
      > /* */
     7> call qcmd
                                                                            Bottom
    Type command, press Enter.
    ===> _____
        _____
        _____

    F3=Exit    F4=Prompt    F9=Retrieve    F10=Exclude detailed messages
    F11=Display full         F12=Cancel    F13=Information Assistant    F24=More keys
```

The Command Entry display lets you enter commands that you want to process. Previous commands, along with any messages those commands generated, are shown in a rolling "history" area above the command line. Until now, you have probably dealt only with the AS/400 command line as it is displayed at the bottom of a menu. Many programmers find the Command Entry display more useful, primarily because of its history area and its ability to more precisely display program messages.

For example, you can position the cursor on a CL command in the history area of the display, press F4=Prompt to display the prompter for that command, then press Enter to execute the command. You also can retrieve commands randomly by placing the cursor on a CL command in the history area then pressing F9=Retrieve. If you press F9=Retrieve without placing the cursor on a previous command, QCMD retrieves the last command you entered.

CL commands may be longer than a single line; the QCMD command line is longer than the command line on a menu or in PDM. If the command you want to execute is longer even than the QCMD command line, you can press F11=Display full to lengthen the command line to the entire size of the display.

You can place the cursor on a command or on a message in the history area, then press Help, to display additional information about the command or message.

To the left of the commands in the history area, the Command Entry display shows the call level at which the command was processed. In the example in Figure 19.2, the *dspcmd savlib* command was executed at call level 9, indicated by *9>*.

Using QUSCMDLN

The full-screen Command Entry display may be useful for programmers who need to see the history of the commands they have executed, but typical users usually don't need all the functionality the QCMD display offers. In fact, typical users may never need to see a command line. You can, however, easily include in your CL programs the option to display a *windowed* AS/400 command line, such as the one shown in Figure 19.3.

Figure 19.3
The Command
Line Window

```
ASSIST                    AS/400 Operational Assistant (TM) Menu
                                                        System: STUDENT1
    To select one of the following, type its number below and press Enter.

          1. Work with printer output
          2. Work with jobs
          3. Work with messages
          4. Send messages
          5. Change your password

         10. Manage your system, users, and devices
         11. Customize your system, users, and devices

         75. Information and problem handling

         80. Temporary sign-off
    ..............................................................................
    :                                 Command                                    :
    :                                                                            :
    :  ===> _____        :
    :  F4=Prompt    F9=Retrieve    F12=Cancel                                    :
    :                                                                            :
    :..............................................................................:
```

The menu shown in Figure 19.3 does not normally have a command line on it. (You can display this menu for yourself by typing the command GO ASSIST.) Part of the original menu in the figure is hidden behind the window bordered by the dots at the bottom of the screen. The IBM programmer who wrote the menu assigned a function key (F9=Command line, in this case) to the menu, then instructed the menu program to execute the following command when F9 is pressed:

```
CALL    QUSCMDLN
```

The program QUSCMDLN is an API that always displays a windowed command line over the bottom of an existing display. This command line works the same as any other command line, but it does not take up space on the display unless it is needed; and it is easier to control the security of the command line by calling it explicitly instead of always having it on the display.

Using QCMDCHK

The IBM-supplied API named QCMDCHK performs syntax checking for a single CL command, and optionally prompts for, but does not execute, the command. If you use QCMDCHK to prompt for a command, the API returns to your program the correct command string to execute the command you prompted. You can use QCMDCHK to prompt the user for a command, then store the command for later execution. To use QCMDCHK in your CL programs, use the following form:

```
CALL    QCMDCHK                                 +
        PARM(command-string                     +
             command-string-length)
```

For example, to check the syntax of a simple DSPLIB command, you would use the following command:

```
CALL    QCMDCHK                                 +
        PARM('DSPLIB LIB(1997SALES)' 21)
```

The first parameter is the character string containing the command to be checked. This parameter can be a program variable. If it is a variable and if QCMDCHK performs command prompting, the command the user enters is placed into the variable.

The second parameter is simply the length of the command string in the first parameter. If the first parameter is a quoted string, as in the above example, the second parameter's length must be the exact length of the quoted string. If the first parameter is a program variable, the length of the second parameter is the length of the variable. The second parameter can itself be a variable, which must be defined as *DEC (15 5).

QCMDCHK examines the command string, verifying that all required parameters are included and that all parameters have valid values. If QCMDCHK detects an error, it sends message CPF0006 (Errors occurred in command) to the calling program, along with diagnostic messages that describe the error. You can, of course, monitor for CPF0006 to see whether QCMDCHK determined that the command was invalid.

Prompting with QCMDCHK

You learned in Chapter 18 that you can invoke the CL command prompter by preceding a command name with a question mark (?). You can also request prompting for a command string processed with QCMDCHK by simply preceding the command string with a question mark. You also can place selective prompting characters in front of specific parameters if you wish.

If you use QCMDCHK to invoke the CL prompter, the system checks the syntax of the entire prompted command. If there are no errors, QCMDCHK returns to the calling program a completed command, with the prompting characters removed and with all the parameters filled in. This function occurs only when you pass a program variable as the first parameter to QCMDCHK. For example, the following commands would invoke the CL prompter for the DSPLIB command:

```
DCL       &cmdstr    *CHAR    6000
CHGVAR    &cmdstr                              +
          VALUE('?DSPLIB')
CALL      QCMDCHK                              +
          PARM(&cmdstr 6000)
```

After QCMDCHK has prompted for the DSPLIB command and you have filled in the parameters, the command string is placed in the *&cmdstr* program variable. For example, the string might look like this:

```
DSPLIB    LIB(QGPL QTEMP)    OUTPUT(*PRINT)
```

Whenever you use QCMDCHK to invoke the CL prompter, be sure the command string is passed in a program variable; otherwise, QCMDCHK does not return the completed command to the program and the prompting will not have accomplished anything. In addition, be sure that the program variable is long enough to accommodate the completed command. The maximum command string length is 6,000 characters.

If QCMDCHK detects an error in the command, it sends message CPF0006 (Errors occurred in command) back to the calling program. If you press F3 or F12 while being prompted for the command, QCMDCHK sends message CPF6801 (Command prompting ended) back to the calling program. If you haven't been careful about the length of the return variable for the command string, QCMDCHK may send CPF0005 (Returned command exceeds variable length).

Using QCMDCHK in this way is extremely useful for occasions when you want to interactively prompt for a command and submit the prompted command for batch processing. Because the entire prompted command is returned within the variable, that variable may then be specified on the CMD parameter of the SBMJOB command, as shown here:

```
          DCL       &cmdstr    *CHAR 6000
          MONMSG    MSGID(CPF0000) EXEC(GOTO ERROR)
          CHGVAR    &cmdstr                  +
                    VALUE('?DSPLIB')
PROMPT:   CALL      QCMDCHK                  +
                    PARM(&cmdstr 6000)
          MONMSG    MSGID(CPF6801 CPF0006) EXEC(GOTO PROMPT)
          SBMJOB    JOB(DISPLAY) CMD(&cmdstr)
          ...

ERROR:    ...
```

Using QCMDEXC

Program QCMDEXC executes a single CL command. You can use QCMDEXC to run
a command from an HLL program or from within a CL program. Your program can
call the QCMDEXC program, passing it the command to execute as a program
parameter. But a CL program already executes commands; why would you want to
execute them using QCMDEXC? The answer is that the QCMDEXC API lets you
execute a command within a CL program when you don't know at the time you
compile the CL program which command you will want to execute. The format for
calling the QCMDEXC program is similar to that of QCMDCHK:

```
CALL    QCMDEXC                              +
        PARM(command-string                  +
             command-string-length)
```

The same rules apply to the QCMDEXC parameters that apply to the QCMDCHK
parameters, with some additional restrictions. While the command string itself may
be a program variable, it cannot contain other program variables. Therefore, the
command to be executed cannot be one that returns variables. If a command can be
used only in a program, it cannot be executed by QCMDEXC. The command to be
executed must be valid within the current environment (interactive or batch). You
can determine whether a command is valid to use with QCMDEXC by using the
DSPCMD (Display Command) command, which is discussed in Chapter 20. If a
command is valid with QCMDEXC, the "Where allowed to run" attribute includes
the value *EXEC.

As with QCMDCHK, you can invoke prompting within QCMDEXC by preceding
the command string with a question mark or with special prompting characters. If
QCMDEXC detects an error when it is running the command, it sends an escape
message to the calling program. As with QCMDCHK, if the QCMDEXC API detects
a syntax error, it sends error message CPF0006.

Of course, the real power of both QCMDCHK and QCMDEXC comes into play
when you want to create a variable command string and execute the string while you
are running a program. Using these APIs can add flexibility to your program by letting you change the command to run depending upon other factors in your program.
These two APIs are also the easiest and fastest means to check and execute CL commands from within an HLL program.

The program in Figure 19.4 retrieves the library list of a job, temporarily changes
it, then at the end of the program uses QCMDEXC to restore the library list to the
way it was when the program started. This technique assures that the program has the
libraries it needs to function and, at the same time, takes the security precautions to
ensure that the user's library list outside of this program doesn't change. Note that
the order of processing in this program ensures that the library list is changed back
even if an error occurs during the program. The global message monitor branches to
the ERRTAG label, where the *&errflg* variable is set; then the library list is restored
before escape message CPF9898 is sent back to the caller.

Figure 19.4
Using QCMDEXC
in a CL Program

```
           PGM
           DCL       &usrlibl   *CHAR 275
           DCL       &curlib    *CHAR 10
           DCL       &errflg    *LGL
           DCL       &cmdstr    *CHAR 1000

           MONMSG    CPF0000    EXEC(GOTO ERRTAG)

/* Retrieve library list and current library at start            */
           RTVJOBA USRLIBL(&usrlibl)                      +
                   CURLIB(&curlib)
           IF      (&curlib *EQ '*NONE') DO
                   CHGVAR &curlib '*CRTDFT'
                   ENDDO

/* Change library list for this program                          */
           CHGLIBL LIBL(QPGL PAYROLL GLEDGER QTEMP)       +
                   CURLIB(*CRTDFT)

/* Perform payroll processing                                    */
           CALL    PAYRPROC
           GOTO    ENDTAG

/* If an error occurs, set on the &errflg indicator              */
ERRTAG:
           CHGVAR  &errflg '1'

/* Restore library list using QCMDEXC                            */
/* Build command string: CHGLIBL LIBL(xxxxxxxxxx) CURLIB(xxxxxxxxxx)  */

ENDTAG:
           CHGVAR  &cmdstr ('CHGLIBL LIBL(' *CAT &usrlibl  +
                           *TCAT ') CURLIB(' *CAT &curlib  +
                           *TCAT ')')
           CALL    QCMDEXC PARM(&cmdstr 1000)
           MONMSG  CPF0000 /* Just in case  */
/* Pass back an escape message if an error occurred              */
           IF      &errflg DO
                   SNDPGMMSG       MSGID(CPF9898)          +
                                   MSGF(QCPFMSG)           +
                                   MSGTYPE(*ESCAPE)        +
                                   MSGDTA('Error occurred in payroll processing')
                   MONMSG CPF0000 /* Just in case */
                   ENDDO

           RETURN
           ENDPGM
```

QCMDEXC and Call Levels

Recall that when a CL program calls another program, the called program executes at a new call level. Also recall that when a CL program issues a file override (with call level resource scoping), that override is effective only at the current call level and any lower call levels in the program. Both of these rules are stretched somewhat to accommodate QCMDEXC. Calling QCMDEXC does *not* create a new call level; instead, the command QCMDEXC executes runs at the same level in the call stack as the program that called QCMDEXC.

This exception has implications for file overrides. If QCMDEXC issues a file override command, that override is effective at the same call level as the call to QCMDEXC, and at any lower call levels. Once you understand that QCMDEXC does not cause a new call level to be created, it makes sense that any overrides set by QCMDEXC would be effective at the same level in the call stack. HLL programs, in particular, can take advantage of this exception. You can issue an override from an HLL program by calling QCMDEXC, then have the override be effective for the HLL program that issued the override.

Other APIs

As we mentioned earlier, many APIs are supplied with the OS/400 operating system. As you become more proficient with CL and more familiar with the operating system, you will find that APIs can make your programs more flexible, faster, and easier to code for unique situations.

Program QCLSCAN scans a string of characters to see whether the string contains a pattern you specify. You can begin the search at a specific position in the string, and you can include a "wild-card" character that will match with any character in the string. You can also convert lowercase characters to uppercase before scanning the string. You can use QCLSCAN within an HLL program to perform scan functions that might require a great many lines of code to accomplish using other means.

If you simply want to translate a character string from lowercase to uppercase, you can use the QDCXLATE API. This API also can be used to translate characters from ASCII to EBCDIC format and vice versa.

In Chapter 15, we discussed the APIs that support data queues. These APIs include QSNDDTAQ and QRCVDTAQ. You can make good use of data queues to write *client/server* applications, in which a client program sends processing requests to a server program that actually does the compute-intensive processing. One or more client programs can work with a single server. Data queues also ease implementation of *cooperative processing* applications, a category of client/server programs in which one of the programs actually runs on another computer platform, such as a personal computer. For example, in a cooperative processing environment, a personal computer can request information from the AS/400 through a data queue. The AS/400 can then send the requested information back to the PC, again using a data queue. Then the PC can take advantage of its graphics capabilities to present the information to the user. The use of APIs facilitates this entire process.

There are also APIs that deal specifically with *user spaces*. A user space (object type *USRSPC) is simply an area in memory, similar to a data area, that can be set aside for your use. Many of the APIs use user spaces to store and retrieve information. There are APIs to create and retrieve user spaces. There are also APIs to store system information in user spaces. This information can include lists of objects, file descriptions, record layouts, lists of active jobs, or information about spooled files waiting to print.

Chapter Summary

IBM supplies a number of application program interfaces (APIs) to make it easy to access low-level machine functions or secured system data from an HLL program. Many of these APIs are directly executable from a CL program. To facilitate performance, an API is generally in the form of a callable program. IBM ensures that the interface to the API remains consistent and compatible from one OS/400 release to the next.

QCMD is the IBM-supplied program that actually executes CL command requests. QCMD executes the initial program or menu for an interactive job; it also executes the commands in a batch job. Finally, you can call QCMD when you want to display the Command Entry display. The primary advantages of using the Command Entry display instead of other command lines are the history area of the display, the longer command line, and the ability to more easily interpret job messages.

QUSCMDLN pops up a command line window on the workstation. The command line window is useful when users need a command line only occasionally, or when you want to secure some users from accessing a command line.

QCMDCHK performs syntax checking for a single CL command and optionally prompts for, but does not execute, the command. If you prompt for a command using variables, the QCMDCHK program returns to your program the correct command string to execute. You can use QCMDCHK to prompt for a command, then store the command for later execution, or you can submit the command for batch processing using the CMD parameter of the SBMJOB command.

QCMDEXC executes a single CL command. QCMDEXC is the easiest and fastest means to execute CL commands from within an HLL program. You also can use QCMDEXC from within a CL program when you don't know at the time you compile the CL program which command you will want to execute. QCMDEXC does not cause a new call level to be created in the job's call stack. Any overrides set by QCMDEXC are effective at the same call level as QCMDEXC. HLL programs can use QCMDEXC to issue overrides that will be effective at the same level as the HLL.

QCLSCAN scans a string of characters to see whether the string contains a pattern you specify. You can use QCLSCAN within an HLL program to perform scan functions that might require a great many lines of code to accomplish using other means.

QDCXLATE can be used to translate a character string from lowercase to uppercase, or to translate between ASCII and EBCDIC.

APIs that support data queues allow you to more easily write many client/server and cooperative processing applications. Still other APIs, which make use of user space objects, allow you to easily retrieve system information that might be difficult or impossible to obtain using other methods.

Terms

application program interfaces (APIs)

Review Questions

1. Define an API. Give three reasons for using APIs.

2. Describe the purposes of the following APIs. What are the differences between them?

   a. QCMD
   b. QCMDCHK
   c. QCMDEXC
   d. QUSCMDLN

3. Describe a hypothetical utility program that could make good use of QCMDCHK and QCMDEXC.

Exercises

1. In Exercise 2 in Chapter 15, you built a programmer's menu. Modify the menu so that a command line window will be displayed if the user presses F9.

Chapter 20

Displaying and Changing Command Attributes

Chapter Overview

Certain attributes of a CL command can be modified to suit the specific needs of your organization. In this chapter we discuss those attributes and explain how to customize a command's attributes and parameter default values.

Displaying the Attributes of a CL Command

Every CL command has a set of operational attributes associated with it. These attributes include such things as whether the command can be executed in a batch or interactive environment, whether the command is valid only within a CL program, whether special validity checks will be performed when the command is used, and where the help text for the command resides.

IBM supplies most of your system's CL commands as part of the OS/400 operating system, or as a part of a licensed program product such as RPG/400 or COBOL/400. Others have been supplied by software vendors or may have been created specifically for your organization by a CL programmer. (Chapter 23 instructs you in depth on how to create your own CL commands using the CRTCMD (Create Command) command.) Whether IBM, another software vendor, or you created the command, you can display the command attributes that were assigned to the command when it was created.

The command to display a specific command's attributes is DSPCMD (Display Command). Figure 20.1a shows the workstation display presented when you enter the following command to display the attributes of the CRTCLPGM command:

```
DSPCMD    CMD(CRTCLPGM)
```

As you examine the attributes shown on this display, you should gain an extra level of insight into how a CL command actually performs its processing tasks.

First, the display shows the name of the "Program to process command." You can see that the value for this attribute is *QCLENTR* in library *QSYS*. When a CL command is executed, it always calls a program to actually perform the processing of the command. The data for the command is supplied by the command parameters you

Figure 20.1a
Displaying a
Command's Attributes

```
                            Display Command Information

Command  . . . . . . :    CRTCLPGM      Library  . . . . . . . :    QSYS

Program to process command . . . . . . :    QCLENTR
  Library  . . . . . . . . . . . . . :    QSYS
  State used to call program . . . . . :    *SYSTEM
Source file  . . . . . . . . . . . . :
  Library  . . . . . . . . . . . . . :
Source file member . . . . . . . . . :
Validity checking program  . . . . . :    *NONE
Mode(s) in which valid . . . . . . . :    *PROD
                                           *DEBUG
                                           *SERVICE
Where allowed to run . . . . . . . . :    *IMOD      *BMOD       *IREXX
                                           *BREXX     *BPGM       *IPGM
                                           *EXEC      *INTERACT   *BATCH
Allow limited user . . . . . . . . . :    *NO
Maximum positional parameters  . . . . :    5
                                                                   More...

Press Enter to continue.

F3=Exit    F12=Cancel
```

specify, but it is the called program that actually performs the work. This program is called the **command processing program** or CPP. CPPs are covered in detail in Chapter 24.

Next, the source file and source member are displayed. This attribute is usually blank for IBM-supplied commands (as it is here), but visible for commands that you or others create. This attribute identifies the source member that was used as input to the command compiler.

The "Validity checking program" attribute is shown next. Here the value of the attribute is *NONE*. This indicates that when the command is executed, no program is called to perform additional validity checking of the parameters you have entered. This does not mean that no parameter checking is performed, but rather that a separate program is not used to do the validity checking. We discuss the function of a validity checking program in more detail in Chapter 25.

Next, the "Mode(s) in which valid" attribute is shown. Here is where you can determine the operational mode(s) in which the command can be used. The operational modes here are *PROD*, *DEBUG*, and *SERVICE*. Because these are the only three modes that exist on the AS/400, this means that the CRTCLPGM command can be used in any mode. *PROD* is production mode, the normal operating mode for AS/400 programs. *DEBUG* is debug mode, which programmers use to help find the cause of program problems. *SERVICE* is the AS/400 service mode and is rarely used.

The attribute "Where allowed to run" controls where the command can be executed from. The allowable values you can specify, and their meanings, are shown in Table 20.1.

Table 20.1
Where a Command is Allowed to Run

Attribute Value	Meaning
*BATCH	Can be used as the CMD or RQSDTA parameter on the SBMJOB command, and can be used in an interpreted CL job stream
*BMOD	Can be used within a batch ILE CL module (see Chapter 22)
*BPGM	Can be used within a CL program submitted for batch processing
*BREXX	Can be used within a REXX language procedure submitted for batch processing
*EXEC	Can be processed by the IBM-supplied program QCMDEXC
*IMOD	Can be used within an interactive ILE CL module (see Chapter 22)
*INTERACT	Can be used interactively, but not necessarily as part of an interactive CL program
*IPGM	Can be used within a CL program that is run interactively
*IREXX	Can be used within a REXX language procedure that is run interactively

You can see from Figure 20.1a and Table 20.1 that the CRTCLPGM can run anywhere; all of the allowable values for "Where allowed to run" are specified.

The next attribute on the screen in Figure 20.1a is "Allow limited user." The attribute value is *NO, which means that a **limited user** cannot execute the CRTCLPGM command from an AS/400 command line. When a user profile is created for a new user, (s)he can be designated as having limited capabilities. Limited users can execute only a very few commands (e.g., SIGNOFF) from the command line.

Next is the attribute for "Maximum positional parameters." Here the value is 5, which means that when entering the CRTCLPGM command, you can use positional notation only up to the fifth parameter of the command. After the fifth parameter, you must use keyword notation.

When you press the Page Down (Roll Up) key from the display, you are presented with the next page of command attributes, shown in Figure 20.1b.

The "Message file for prompt text" attribute identifies where the text used for the command prompt display is stored. The "Message file" attribute identifies where the system stores error messages that you can use to indicate command errors.

The "Current library" attribute identifies which library name will be placed in the current library position on the job's library list when the CRTCLPGM command is being processed. Similarly, the "Product library" attribute identifies which library name will be placed in the product library position on the job's library list when the CRTCLPGM command is being processed. In both cases for this example, the value

Figure 20.1b
Displaying a
Command's Attributes
(Second Screen)

```
                         Display Command Information

 Command . . . . . . . :   CRTCLPGM        Library . . . . . . . :    QSYS

 Message file for prompt text . . . . . :   QCPFPMT
   Library . . . . . . . . . . . . . . :     QDEVELOP
 Message file . . . . . . . . . . . . . :   QCPFMSG
   Library . . . . . . . . . . . . . . :     *LIBL
 Current library . . . . . . . . . . . :   *NOCHG
 Product library . . . . . . . . . . . :   *NOCHG
 Help Shelf . . . . . . . . . . . . . . :   *LIST
 Help panel group . . . . . . . . . . . :   QHCLCMD1
   Library . . . . . . . . . . . . . . :     *LIBL
 Help identifier . . . . . . . . . . . :   CRTCLPGM
 Prompt override program . . . . . . . :   *NONE
 Enabled for graphical user interface . :   *YES
 Coded character set ID . . . . . . . . :   37
 Text . . . . . . . . . . . . . . . . . :   Create CL Program

                                                                  Bottom
 Press Enter to continue.

 F3=Exit    F12=Cancel
```

is *NOCHG*, which means that executing this command does not affect the value of the job's current library or product library.

The next three attributes on this display — "Help shelf," "Help panel group," and "Help identifier" — specify where the help text for this command is stored.

The "Prompt override program" attribute is used to identify a program that dynamically changes the command parameter values displayed on the command prompt. We briefly discuss prompt override programs in Chapter 25.

The next two items, "Enabled for graphical user interface" and "Coded character set ID," tell the system whether the command can be used with graphical user interface (GUI) displays or with other language character sets.

Finally, the "Text" attribute determines the descriptive text associated with the command object.

All the command attributes shown in these two figures are assigned appropriate values when a command is created. These attributes allow a high level of customization when you create your own commands. However, for commands IBM has created (e.g., CRTCLPGM), if you do not like one of the command attributes, you cannot re-create it because you do not have the source code IBM used when it created the command. You can, however, change some of a CL command's attributes after the command is created, regardless of who created it.

Changing the Attributes of a CL Command

After a CL command is created, some attributes of the command may be changed to suit your organization's individual needs. For instance, you may want to change the CRTCLPGM command so that it cannot be used interactively. Doing so would ensure that all CL compile operations are performed in a batch process. Or, as another example, you may want to allow "limited users" to execute a command from a command line they normally would not be able to use.

The CL command you use to change a command's attributes is CHGCMD (Change Command). Figure 20.2a shows the display that results when you type the following command and press F4, then F10 (to display additional parameters):

```
CHGCMD    CMD(CRTCLPGM)
```

Figure 20.2a
Changing a Command's
Attributes (First Screen)

```
                            Change Command (CHGCMD)

 Type choices, press Enter

 Command  . . . . . . . . . . . . > CRTCLPGM     Name
   Library  . . . . . . . . . . .     *LIBL      Name, *LIBL, *CURLIB
 Program to process command . . .    QCLENTR     Name, *SAME, *REXX
   Library  . . . . . . . . . .       QSYS       Name, *LIBL, *CURLIB
 Validity checking program  . . .    *NONE       Name, *SAME, *NONE
   Library  . . . . . . . . . . .     _____    Name, *LIBL, *CURLIB
 Mode in which valid  . . . . . .    *PROD       *SAME, *ALL, *PROD, *DEBUG...
                                      *DEBUG
                                      *SERVICE




                                                                 More
 F3=Exit    F4=Prompt    F5=Refresh    F12=Cancel    F13=How to use this display
 F24=More keys
```

Here you can change the name of the program that is used to process the command (the CPP), add a validity-checking program, and change the mode in which the command is valid.

When you press the Page Down (Roll Up) key from the display, you will be shown the display in Figure 20.2b. The screen shows more attributes you can change. For example, if you want the CRTCLPGM command to run only in a batch environment, you can remove the values *IREXX, *IPGM, and *INTERACT.

For IBM-supplied commands, the attribute you would be most likely to change here would be "Allow limited users." Although you may not specifically want to change that attribute for the CRTCLPGM command (because it is a programmer's command), you may find certain other commands that lend themselves to access by limited users.

If you press the Page Down (Roll Up) key again from the display in Figure 20.2b, you will be shown the display in Figure 20.2c. This display shows additional attributes you can change, including the command's current library and product library. Usually, you will not change any of the attributes shown in Figure 20.2c.

Figure 20.2b
Changing a
Command's Attributes
(Second Screen)

```
                              Change Command (CHGCMD)

 Type choices, press Enter.

 Where allowed to run . . . . . .    *IMOD          *SAME, *ALL, *BATCH...
                                     *BMOD
                                     *IREXX
                                     *BREXX
                                     *BPGM
                                     *IPGM
                                     *EXEC
                                     *INTERACT
                                     *BATCH
 Allow limited users  . . . . . .    *NO            *SAME, *NO, *YES
 Help bookshelf . . . . . . . . .    *LIST          Name, *SAME, *LIST, *NONE
 Help panel group . . . . . . . .    QHCLCMD1       Name, *NONE, *SAME
   Library . . . . . . . . . .         *LIBL        Name, *LIBL, *CURLIB
 Help identifier  . . . . . . . .    CRTCLPGM       Character value, *SAME...
 Help search index . . . . . . .     *NONE          Name, *SAME, *NONE
   Library . . . . . . . . . .       _____      Name, *LIBL, *CURLIB
                                                                    More...
 F3=Exit   F4=Prompt   F5=Refresh   F12=Cancel   F13=How to use this display
 F24=More keys
```

Figure 20.2c
Changing a Command's
Attributes (Third Screen)

```
 Change Command (CHGCMD)

 Type choices, press Enter.

 Current library  . . . . . . . .    *NOCHG         Name, *SAME, *NOCHG, *CRTDFT
 Product library  . . . . . . . .    *NOCHG         Name, *SAME, *NOCHG, *NONE
 Prompt override program  . . . .    *NONE          Name, *SAME, *NONE
   Library . . . . . . . . . .       _____      Name, *LIBL, *CURLIB
 Text 'description' . . . . . . .    'Create CL Program
  _____'

                              Additional Parameters

 Enable GUI . . . . . . . . . .      *YES           *YES, *NO, *SAME




                                                                     Bottom
 F3=Exit   F4=Prompt   F5=Refresh   F12=Cancel   F13=How to use this display
 F24=More keys
```

For commands you have created, any of the attributes listed can be changed as needed. Those attributes not listed on the CHGCMD command prompt can be changed only if you re-create the command using the CRTCMD command. And remember that you need the source member for the command to re-create it.

Changing Parameter Default Values

You have seen that customizing certain attributes of a command may enhance your control over the processing of that command. To take this concept of customization one step further, you also can change the default values assigned to command parameters, regardless of whether the command is IBM-supplied or user-created.

For example, the command DSPTAP has several parameters, as shown here:

```
DSPTAP    DEV(tape-device-name)                                 +
          LABEL(*ALL)                                           +
          SEQNBR(1)                                             +
          DATA(*LABELS)                                         +
          OUTPUT(*)
```

The LABEL parameter has a default value of *ALL*, the SEQNBR parameter has a default value of *1*, the DATA parameter has a default value of *LABELS*, and the OUTPUT parameter has a default value of *. Any of these IBM-supplied default values may be changed using the CHGCMDDFT (Change Command Default) CL command. The DEV parameter does not have any default value, and you cannot add a default value for it.

If you wanted to change the default value for the OUTPUT parameter of the DSPTAP command from OUTPUT(*) to OUTPUT(*PRINT) you could simply enter the command

```
CHGCMDDFT    CMD(DSPTAP)                                        +
             NEWDFT('OUTPUT(*PRINT)')
```

If you decided you wanted to change the default for the OUTPUT parameter, as well as the default for the DATA parameter, you could use the CHGCMDDFT command once for each change, or you could use the CHGCMDDFT command once specifying both changes, as in the following example:

```
CHGCMDDFT    CMD(DSPTAP)                                        +
             NEWDFT('DATA(*SAVRST) OUTPUT(*PRINT)')
```

Normally, when you change the parameter defaults for your own custom-created commands, you simply change the command source member and recompile the command using the CRTCMD command. The only commands you typically change using the CHGCMDDFT command are those supplied by IBM or other vendors who do not provide you with the source member used to create the command.

Changing IBM-Supplied Commands

If you decide to change a command that IBM or another software vendor supplied, you must consider at least two issues before you make the change:

- If you change an IBM-supplied command, the change affects all programs that contain or use the command and all system users who use the command.

- Most IBM commands reside in the QSYS library or in licensed program libraries such as QRPG. Whenever a new release of the OS/400 operating system or a licensed program is installed, the library is replaced. Therefore, any changes you have made to the IBM-supplied commands will be gone when the new release is loaded.

To make changes to IBM-supplied commands, you can make the change directly to the command, or you can make the change to a copy of the command. Your requirements and preferences determine which method you choose.

You can make the change directly to the IBM-supplied command using the CHGCMD and/or the CHGCMDDFT commands. This is probably the less desirable of the two methods to effect a change to the IBM-supplied commands, for reasons already mentioned. If you choose to change the IBM commands directly, you want to make sure the changes made are re-applied to the commands when a new release is loaded. You can accomplish this by writing a CL program that applies all the command changes to the new releases of all commands. Once a new release is loaded, you can run the program to apply all the required command changes.

Alternatively, you can make a duplicate copy of the IBM-supplied command, placing the duplicate in a user library. The modifications can then be made to the duplicate copy, instead of the IBM-supplied original. This is really the preferred method of the two. The modified version of the command can then be used selectively by jobs running in the system. To access the new version of the command, a program could place the user library ahead of the QSYS library in the system portion of the job's library list. You can accomplish this by executing the CHGSYSLIBL command within the job. Because the new version is higher in the library list than the IBM-supplied version, the new version would be used by that job.

In addition to providing the capability for an individual job to select which version of the command is used, you also can make all jobs use the new version. You can do this by placing the user library that contains the modified version of the command ahead of the QSYS library in the system library list for all jobs. To accomplish this, change the system value QSYSLIBL to include the user library ahead of the QSYS library; use the CHGSYSVAL command to make the change.

Again, when a new release of the operating system is loaded, all IBM-supplied commands are replaced. Sometimes, the new release of a command is different than the previous release. Sometimes, new parameters are added, parameter defaults are changed, and the allowable values on a parameter may even be changed. Whenever a new operating system release is loaded, your changed commands should be evaluated and, if necessary, re-created to ensure that they are compatible with that new release.

Chapter Summary

When CL commands are created, attributes are specified that affect the way in which the command operates. You can view the attributes for a command using the DSPCMD (Display Command) command.

One of a command's attributes is the name of the command processing program (CPP). This is the program that is called when the command is executed.

Some command attributes can be changed using the CL command CHGCMD (Change Command). You can change the allowable execution environment for a command by changing the "Where allowed to run" attribute. You can enable limited users to execute a specific command from the command line by changing the "Allow limited user" attribute.

The CHGCMDDFT (Change Command Default) command can be used to change command parameter default values. If a command parameter does not already have a default value, you cannot add one with CHGCMDDFT.

You need to be aware of certain considerations when you change IBM-supplied commands. For example, IBM-supplied commands are replaced when a new release of the operating system is installed, so you must have a way, after the new release is installed, to re-create any changes previously made to CL commands.

Terms

command processing program   limited user

Review Questions

1. Which command would you use to make the following changes to IBM commands?

   a. Allow limited users to use the DSPLIB command.

   b. Change the default value for the LIB parameter in the DSPLIB command from *LIBL to *ALLUSR.

   c. Prevent the RPG compiler (command CRTRPGPGM) from running interactively.

   d. Specify that the SIGNOFF command use a user-written program called USRSIGNOFF in library SYSLIB as its command processing program.

   e. Change the default output of the DSPFFD command to be printed instead of displayed.

2. Outline the procedure that should be used when changing IBM command attributes and defaults. Why should you not change the IBM commands directly?

Exercises

1. Display the command attributes for the following commands:

   a. SIGNOFF
   b. IF
   c. RTVSYSVAL
   d. BCHJOB
   e. SNDNETF
   f. WRKMBRPDM
   g. ENDPGM
   h. DSPJOB
   i. CHGJOB
   j. SAVLIB

   For each command:

   - List the qualified name of the command processing program.
   - Indicate whether the command can be run in batch, interactively, or both.
   - Indicate whether the command is valid in a program. Indicate whether the command is valid at an AS/400 command line.
   - Indicate whether the command can be entered at a command line by a limited user.
   - Briefly state the purpose of the command, if you can determine it from the display.

Chapter 21

Understanding the Job Log

Chapter Overview

Every job on the AS/400 generates a job log, which contains information about what processing the job performs. This chapter describes what a job log is, explains how you can control the job log's content, and how you can use the job log to help diagnose problems that may occur during the job's execution.

What Is a Job Log?

Whenever you sign on to the AS/400, an interactive job begins. Likewise, whenever a submitted job begins execution in a batch environment, a batch job starts. Many types of work are being performed on the system at any one time; all this work occurs within the context of a job.

Every job that runs on the AS/400 generates a **job log**.

The job log provides a historical view of what happened during the execution of a job and is a major resource for diagnosing program problems. It can tell you which commands were executed, whether the execution was successful or unsuccessful, and if unsuccessful, why. In the event of an error, it tells you which program instruction caused the error. It also includes runtime information you can use to determine how long it took to execute a particular operation. By understanding the job log and using it to your advantage, you can minimize the amount of time you spend fighting fires.

You learned in Chapter 16 about program message queues and how the system uses messages to communicate between programs. The job log is a user-friendly view of the job's combined external message queue and all its program message queues. The job log is sometimes referred to as the job message queue. In fact, this may be a useful description because all messages generated within a job that have not been removed are contained in the job log. When a job ends, its job log can be written to a spooled output file for printing, or it can be removed from the system. We see in a moment how you control whether the job log is spooled or removed.

Figure 21.1 provides an illustration of the message queues that make up the job log. You can access an active job's job log by using the DSPJOBLOG (Display Job Log) command. After a job ends, its job log is available for viewing only if it was copied to a spooled file. If it was, you can examine the job log in the spooled output file named QPJOBLOG associated with that job.

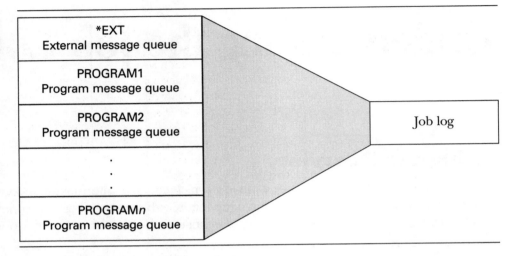

Figure 21.1
The Job Log

The LOG Attribute

Using the LOG attribute of the job description, you can control the level of message detail in the job log and whether the log is spooled or deleted when the job ends. You specify the LOG attribute in the job description. You can permanently change the attribute for a particular job description by using the CHGJOBD (Change Job Description) command; for a batch job, you can also override it by specifying an alternative value on the SBMJOB command. For a job already being executed, you can change the LOG attribute using the CHGJOB (Change Job) command. The shipped default value for job descriptions QBATCH (for batch jobs) and QINTER (for interactive jobs) is LOG(4 0 *NOLIST); the three attribute elements are the message logging level, the message severity level, and the message text level, respectively.

The message logging level controls the kind of messages written to the job log. The allowable values are *0, 1, 2, 3,* and *4;* the higher the number, the more messages the system writes to the job log. Figure 21.2 describes each logging level. The default value of *4* causes the first-level text of all messages to be logged.

Figure 21.2
Message Logging Levels

Level	Message Kept in Job Log
0	No messages
1	Only messages sent to the *EXT message queue
2	Messages sent to the *EXT message queue, messages generated by logged CL commands that issue messages, plus logged commands that issue messages
3	Messages sent to the *EXT message queue, messages generated by logged CL commands that issue messages, plus all logged commands, whether not not they issue messages
4	All messages, plus all logged CL commands

The second element of the LOG attribute controls the message severity level. All messages are assigned a severity level from 0 to 99. Severity level 0 is used for informational messages, while severity level 99 is used for many messages that require immediate attention. The default severity level in the LOG attribute is *0*, which means all messages with a severity level of 0 or higher are included in the job log. If you specify LOG(4 50 *NOLIST), only messages with a severity level of at least 50 are included.

The message text level specifies the level of detail to be logged for each message and whether the log is copied to a spooled file when the job ends. The default value, *NOLIST*, means that if the job ends normally, the job log is not copied to a spooled file. The other available values are *MSG* and *SECLVL*. When you specify *MSG*, only the first-level message text is written to the job log and the log is copied to a spooled output file whether the job ends normally or abnormally. The value *SECLVL indicates that both first- and second-level message text is written to the job log; again, regardless of how the job ends, the log is copied to a spooled output file.

Logging CL Commands

In addition to controlling the message logging, severity, and text levels, you can specify logging for CL commands your job executes. Having a log of executed CL commands is often very helpful when you try to determine what went wrong with a job. When you log commands, the log records the executed commands, the time of execution, and the number of the CL source statement that executed each recorded command. By comparing the CL source with the job log, you can see the program's execution sequence. To log CL commands, the job's message logging level must be 3 or 4.

The job attribute LOGCLPGM controls whether CL commands are logged. The shipped default for job descriptions QBATCH and QINTER is *NO*; you can change the value to *YES* with the CHGJOBD command. For a job already being executed, you can change the LOGCLPGM attribute using the CHGJOB command. You also can override the attribute for a batch job by specifying LOGCLPGM(*YES) on the SBMJOB command.

When you specify LOGCLPGM(*YES), not every CL command is written to the job log. Most commands that are valid only within a CL program (e.g., IF, ELSE, GOTO, DO, MONMSG) are not logged; neither are commands embedded in an IF, ELSE, or MONMSG statement. But commands within a DO group can be logged. Consider the following examples:

Example 1
```
    IF   (&a = &b)   CALL PROGRAM1
```

Example 2
```
    IF   (&a = &b) DO
         CALL PROGRAM1
         MONMSG CPF0000
         ENDDO
```

Because the CALL in the first example is a parameter of the IF command, the CALL is not recorded in the job log. But the CALL command in the second example is embedded in a DO group, so it is recorded in the job log. (This is just one good reason to use DO groups within an IF, ELSE, or command-level MONMSG command.) Because MONMSG isn't a loggable command, it's not logged even though it's within the DO group.

Although you can specify that CL commands cannot be logged by compiling programs with the option LOG(*NO) (something many software vendors do as standard practice to protect their code), you shouldn't use this option on your own programs. If you do and then you have a problem with the program and decide you want to log its commands, you must first recompile it with the option LOG(*YES) or LOG(*JOB). *JOB is the default for the CRTCLPGM (Create CL Program) command; this value means that commands are written to the job log only if the job's LOGCLPGM attribute has the value *YES. If for some reason you always need to log a particular program's commands, compile the program using LOG(*YES); this option logs commands regardless of the job's LOGCLPGM value.

Analyzing the Job Log

It should be clear by now that the job log can be pretty handy to have when you're trying to determine exactly what a job did during execution. Figure 21.3 shows part of a sample log for a batch job. The job that produced this log used the attribute LOG(4 0 *SECLVL) to provide a good level of detail.

The job log heading provides the job and user name and the job number. It also shows the job description used — QGPL/QPGMR in this case. The body of the job log provides several columns of information for each logged message, followed by the message text. The columns are:

- MSGID: If the message is predefined in a message file, this column shows the message's ID.
- TYPE: The message type (e.g., informational, request, escape, diagnostic, command).
- SEV: The message severity level.
- DATE: The date on which the message was sent.
- TIME: The time the message was sent. The format is hhmmss and uses a 24-hour clock (e.g.,130000 is 1:00:00 pm.).
- FROM PGM: The name of the program that sent the message.
- LIBRARY: The name of the library in which the FROM PGM resides.
- INST: The number of the instruction in the FROM PGM that caused the message to be sent. This is not the CL instruction number, but the compiled program's internal instruction number.
- TO PGM: The name of the program to which the message was sent (*EXT indicates the external message queue).

Figure 21.3
Sample Job Log

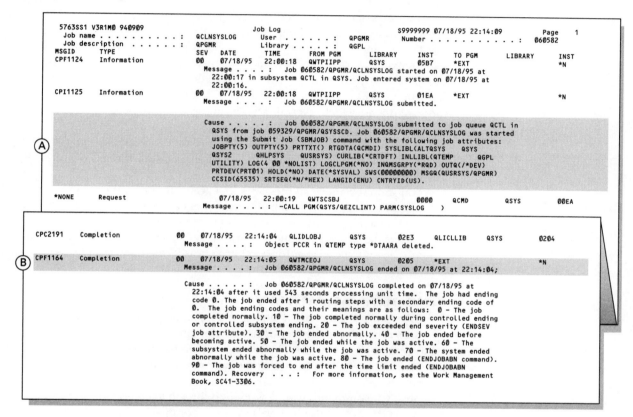

- LIBRARY: The name of the library in which the TO PGM resides.
- INST: Indicates the number of the internal instruction in the TO PGM that received the message.

Below all this information is recorded the first-level message text, with the message data properly inserted. In other words, instead of recording the message as it is stored in the message file (e.g., File &1 not found), the job log shows the value of all variables (e.g., File CUSTOMER not found).

When you specify *SECLVL for the LOG attribute's message text level, the job log shows the second-level message text (A in Figure 21.3). If you don't log the second-level message text, the job log doesn't include the "Cause" paragraph.

At B, you can see that the job ended normally (ending code 0) and that it used 543 CPU seconds. Although active from 22:00 until 22:14 (14 minutes), the job used the CPU for only about 9 minutes of that time. Most of the remaining time was spent waiting for system resources (e.g., disk access, locks).

Keeping a Lean Job Log

The sheer number of messages that can be generated during a job means that the program message queues, and thus the job log, can easily become cluttered with extraneous messages. These in turn can cause confusion when examining the job log. For instance, a program may use a CHKOBJ (Check Object) command to test for the existence of a file. In some cases, perhaps the file is not supposed to exist. In this situation, it's not an error that the file doesn't exist; it's the expected condition. But when CHKOBJ fails to find the file, it sends an escape message to the program message queue, which, even though monitored by the program, can be confusing when the job log is examined.

In such cases, the message should be removed from the program message queue using the techniques for removing messages that were discussed under "Removing Messages" in Chapter 16.

You should remove all messages that aren't useful to the program or job. But it's very difficult to guess which commands may generate messages that should be removed. One way to anticipate them is to do a thorough job of testing your programs. As your testing process produces "noise" error messages, add code to remove them from the log. One criterion for good programs is that they don't leave unnecessary or misleading messages in the job log.

Chapter Summary

Every AS/400 job generates a job log, which contains information about the processing performed by the job. The information contained in the log consists entirely of messages generated by the job. The job log, sometimes called the job message queue, is a combination of all the program message queues used within a job and the job's external message queue.

Most CL commands can be written to the job log, depending on the job attribute LOGCLPGM. The LOG attribute is made up of three separate elements: the message logging level, the message severity level, and the message text level. These determine the amount of detail contained in the job log, and also whether the contents of the job log will be copied to a spooled output file when the job ends.

You can access the job log for an active job by using the DSPJOB (Display Job) command and requesting to see the job log. To access the job log for your own interactive job, you can simply enter the CL command DSPJOBLOG (Display Job Log).

To help diagnose problems in the job, it's important to remove extraneous messages from the job log.

Terms

job log

Review Questions

1. Which message queues make up a job log?

2. Name two job attributes that can affect the contents of a job log. What is the purpose of each one? How do you specify that you want the most detail possible in a job log?

3. Which job attribute setting would ensure that a job log is created if a job ends abnormally but not created if the job ends successfully?

Exercises

1. Display the job log for your current interactive job.

2. Sign on to the AS/400 and perform a programming task assigned by your instructor. The first thing you should do after you sign on is to change your current job attribute LOG to LOG(4 0 *SECLVL) and change LOGCLPGM to LOGCLPGM(*YES). Proceed with your programming assignment as usual. To sign off, use the command SIGNOFF *LIST, and your job log will be copied to a spooled output file QPJOBLOG. Sign back on to the system and examine the job log created by your previous interactive session. If possible, print the job log.

3. Submit a job to the batch environment using the SBMJOB command. Specify that CL commands are to be logged, that you want to see second-level message text in the job log, and that you want to copy the job log to a spooled output file whether the job completes normally or abnormally. After the submitted job ends, view, and if possible print, the job log.

4. Experiment with different message logging levels, message severity levels, and message text levels. Report on the effects.

Chapter 22

Introduction to the Integrated Language Environment

Chapter Overview

With Version 2 Release 3 of OS/400, IBM introduced the Integrated Language Environment (ILE). ILE provides a consistent runtime environment for all the ILE languages on the AS/400. CL is a full participant in the ILE. In this chapter, we provide a basic introduction to the most important ILE concepts and show you how ILE affects CL concepts that we discussed earlier in this text.

What Is ILE?

The **Integrated Language Environment** (ILE) is a new AS/400 program model that provides a consistent environment in which programs execute, regardless of the language in which the program is written. CL is a full participant in ILE, along with ILE RPG/400 (informally referred to as RPG IV), Cobol, and C. ILE provides many benefits to the AS/400, including

- New tools for modular programming
- New ways to call programs
- New ways to subdivide jobs
- Better program performance
- Simpler application maintenance

ILE is the latest evolution of AS/400 program models, available with Version 2 Release 3 of OS/400. In previous versions, most programs (all except those written in C) ran within the **Original Program Model** (OPM). OPM programs can still run under current versions, and you can still create OPM CL programs, but ILE offers an alternative. ILE provides flexible procedure and program calling methods, with resulting improved performance. It encourages programs built from multiple modules, with separate compile and binding steps, reusable components, and service programs. In the case of some languages (most notably RPG), ILE offers new enhanced features not available to OPM programs.

What Is a Procedure?

A **procedure** is an executable segment within a program or a module. It is a set of self-contained HLL statements that perform a function and then return to the procedure that called them. A procedure is not an AS/400 object; it is callable only from within a program, not from a command line.

What Is a Module?

A **module** is a new type of AS/400 object (type *MODULE) that is the result of compiling an ILE language source member. A module is not runnable by itself and cannot be called. To execute the code in a module, you must first **bind** one or more modules into a single ILE program. A module may encompass several procedures.

What Is a Program?

You're already familiar with the concept of a **program**. An ILE program is an AS/400 object (type *PGM) that is the result of binding one or more modules together. You can execute the procedures in a program by calling the program (e.g., by using the CALL CL command). Every program includes a **program entry procedure,** which is the "front door" through which the system begins to execute the program's code.

Creating ILE Modules and Programs

Unlike OPM compilers, which create callable programs from source code, ILE compilers create a *MODULE object, not a *PGM object. Each language has its own specific compiler command. CL compiles ILE CL source code (edited with a source type of CLLE) with the CRTCLMOD (Create CL Module) command:

```
CRTCLMOD    MODULE(library-name/module-name)          +
            SRCFILE(library-name/source-file-name)  +
            MBR(source-member-name)
```

As you can see, the CRTCLMOD command closely resembles the CRTCLPGM command discussed in Chapter 5. But in this case, you create a *MODULE object, not a *PGM object.

After you have compiled an ILE CL source member into a module, you must bind that module (possibly along with other modules) into a callable program. The CRTPGM (Create Program) command accomplishes this binding step:

```
CRTPGM    PGM(library-name/program-name)               +
          MODULE(library-name/module-name)
```

The PGM parameter allows you to name the program that you want to create, while the MODULE parameter names the module that you will bind into the program. The CRTPGM command is not language-specific; you use the same command to create programs from modules compiled by any ILE language. Figure 22.1 illustrates the two-step process of creating an ILE program from CL source.

The *MODULE object is an intermediate object, the result of compiling an ILE source member, and is used to create an ILE program. The system does not need

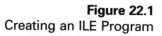

Figure 22.1
Creating an ILE Program

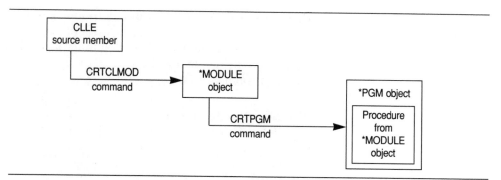

the *MODULE object to actually execute the program. You can use the DLTMOD (Delete Module) command to delete unneeded modules after you have bound them into programs. Deleting unnecessary modules can save disk space on your system.

You should probably save modules, though, if you will need them again (e.g., to bind them into several programs or to rebind a program if one of its modules changes). If a *MODULE object is missing from your system when you want to create a program that needs it, you must recompile the source member to re-create the module.

One-Step Program Creation

You've seen that creating an ILE program is normally a two-step process. First you compile the source member into a module. Then you use the CRTPGM command to bind that module into a program.

The AS/400 offers "shortcut" commands to create a single-module program in a single step. Each ILE language has its own "shortcut" program creation command. To create a single-module ILE CL command, use the CRTBNDCL (Create Bound CL Programs) command:

```
CRTBNDCL    PGM(library-name/program-name)               +
            SRCFILE(library-name/source-file-name)   +
            MBR(source-member-name)
```

This command actually goes through both the compile and binding steps "under the covers," first creating a temporary module, then binding that module into a program, and finally erasing the temporary module. However, restrictions apply to the programs created with this shortcut. We discuss those restrictions later in this chapter, but for now just be aware that the two-step method is the preferred method for creating ILE programs.

Multiple-Module Programs

A single ILE program can comprise several modules. By breaking an application into several modular functions, you can simplify the development of an application, promote reuse of the same modular code in many programs, and improve the reliability of your applications by incorporating well-tested modules into the application's programs.

To create a multiple-module program, you simply compile each source member (they can be written in any ILE language), then bind the modules together with the CRTPGM command:

```
CRTPGM    PGM(library-name/program-name)        +
          MODULE(library-names/module-names)   +
          ENTMOD(library-name/module-name)
```

In the MODULE parameter, list *all* the modules that you want to bind into the program. When you are creating a multiple-module program, you must specify an **entry module** — the "main" module that executes first when the program is called. Name the module in both the MODULE and ENTMOD parameters. Figure 22.2 illustrates the creation of a multiple-module program.

Figure 22.2
Creating an ILE Program

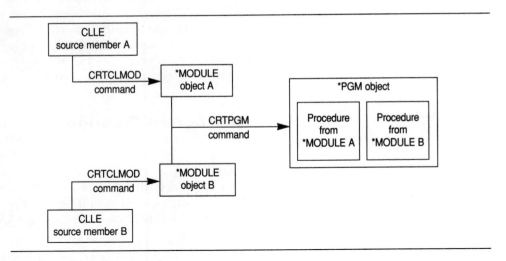

Updating ILE Programs

If you change a source member and then recompile the source member into a module, the change is not automatically reflected in the executable program. To update the program to include the changed module, you must re-bind the program. You can re-bind the program by invoking the CRTPGM command again, naming all the modules that are to be bound into the program. All the modules that you name must exist on the system at the time you re-bind the program. Or you can use the UPDPGM (Update Program) command to simply name the module(s) to be replaced:

```
UPDPGM    PGM(library-name/program-name)        +
          MODULE(library-names/module-names)
```

If you use the UPDPGM command to incorporate changed modules, you need recompile only the changed modules; unchanged modules need not exist at the time you re-bind the program using the UPDPGM command.

Adding Modules

If you decide a program needs additional functionality that an additional module could provide, you must compile the additional module, then use the CRTPGM command to re-bind the program. In this case, all the modules the program uses must exist at the time you re-bind the program.

Calling ILE Programs and Procedures

In Chapter 11, you learned that the CALL command calls, (i.e., runs) a program and passes control to that program. After the called program ends, control returns to the next command in the calling program. This traditional type of call is a **dynamic program call**.

With a dynamic program call, the calling program and the called programs exist as separate *PGM objects on the AS/400. When a CL program encounters the CALL command, the program must find the called program and set up links between the calling program and the called program; this process is called "resolving the call."

Because the system resolves a dynamic program call at runtime rather than when the calling program is compiled, the dynamic program call is very flexible and easy to use. You can make some changes in the called program without recompiling the calling program (as long as the passed parameters don't change). In fact, the called program need not exist when you compile the calling program. The dynamic program call makes good use of AS/400 disk space because the same program can be called by many programs but still exist as a single *PGM object.

There are, however, several potential disadvantages to the dynamic program call. If an application is call-intensive (i.e., if it uses external program calls heavily), the dynamic program call can cause performance problems. In addition, if the calling and called programs are written in two different languages, there may be some obscure compatibility problems between the two languages.

Calling ILE Procedures Using a Static Call

ILE offers an alternative to the dynamic program call: the **static procedure call**. The static procedure call lets you call code originating in separate modules, but within the same ILE program. Recall that you can compile several modules separately, then bind them into an executable program object using the CRTPGM command. The binding step actually copies the code from each module into the *PGM object. This process is called **bind by copy**. Because the call is resolved at binding time, not at runtime, the program can execute the call faster than a dynamic program call.

To execute code across procedures in the program, you use the static procedure call. The CALLPRC (Call Bound Procedure) command implements a static procedure call:

```
CALLPRC    PRC(procedure-name)                    +
           PARM(parameter-values)                 +
           RTNVAL(return-value-variable)
```

You can see that the CALLPRC command is very similar to the CALL command. The PRC parameter, which is required, identifies the procedure you want to call. You must explicitly name the procedure; you cannot code a CL variable for the procedure name.

When you call a bound procedure, you can pass parameters to it. The called procedure can access those parameters and even modify them. The parameter values are listed in the PARM parameter of the CALLPRC command. The same rules that apply to specifying parameters for the CALL command also apply to the CALLPRC command.

The optional RTNVAL parameter allows you to specify a variable to hold a **return value** from the called procedure. Some languages (not CL) allow a procedure to return a value to the calling procedure. If you specify a RTNVAL variable, when control returns from the called procedure, CL places the return value into the variable you specify.

To illustrate the use of the static procedure call in CL, let's look at the following example:

```
CALLPRC    PRC(CALCPMT)                               +
           PARM(&principle &interest &term)           +
           RTNVAL(&payment)
```

This command calls the CALCPMT procedure, which might be an RPG procedure to calculate a monthly installment payment. The calling procedure passes three parameters to CALCPMT: *&principle*, *&interest*, and *&term*. After CALCPMT calculates a payment amount, it returns control to the calling procedure and passes back the value of the payment amount. The calling procedure then places that value into the *&payment* variable.

Using Service Programs

In the previous section, we discussed the bind-by-copy version of the static procedure call. ILE offers a second type of static call that allows you to take advantage of fast procedure calls without actually copying the called modules into an ILE program. This method, called **bind by reference**, uses a new AS/400 object, the **service program** (type *SRVPGM).

You can think of a service program as a procedure "toolbox" that many programs can share. The subject of service program creation and maintenance is beyond the scope of this text. But you can still use the procedures in a service program, even if you don't know how the service program is constructed.

To include a procedure from a service program in an ILE program, you simply name the service program when you bind the program using the CRTPGM command:

```
CRTPGM     PGM(library-name/program-name)            +
           MODULE(library-names/module-names)        +
           ENTMOD(library-name/module-name)          +
           BNDSRVPGM(library-names/service-program-names)
```

The BNDSRVPGM parameter allows you to list service programs that contain procedures you want to bind into the program. The system copies references to the procedures, rather than copying the procedure code itself; hence the term bind by reference. The procedure code remains in the service program object.

At the time the calling program loads, the system immediately resolves any references to service program procedures. When the program actually calls one of those procedures, the call has already been resolved and performs at nearly the same speed as a bind-by-copy static procedure call.

To call a service program procedure, you use the CALLPRC command, just as you do with the bind-by-copy procedure call. Be sure to use the name of the specific procedure that you want to call, *not* the name of the service program. You cannot call a service program itself.

Service programs offer many of the same benefits as dynamic program calls, while still maintaining the performance benefits of the static procedure call. A service program can share a single copy of *MODULE code among many *PGM objects, so it uses memory efficiently. In addition, the calling programs are smaller than with the bind-by-copy concept. For software vendors, service programs are easy to maintain and distribute, and can contain hidden data or procedures.

Understanding Activation Groups

In Chapter 11, you learned that all processing on the AS/400 occurs within the context of a job. ILE provides a finer division within a job, called an **activation group**. Activation groups are ILE's means of partitioning jobs into "sub-jobs." Activation groups are not system objects but are instead a work-management concept that allows you to organize, manage, and process work at a finer level than at the job level.

Activation groups provide finer control of resource **scoping** than jobs provide. Scoping is a term used to describe the extent of influence of a resource; for example, the effect of a file override or a shared open data path. Activation groups allow you to modify the rules for file overrides and shared opens that we discussed in Chapter 17. Activation groups also can improve the performance of ILE program activation (the process of starting up and running a program).

There are four types of activation group options. Each type has its own characteristics and its own uses. The four types are

- Default activation group
- User-named activation group
- System-named (*NEW) activation group
- *CALLER activation group

The activation group (AG) that a program uses is determined at binding time, when the program is created.

Default Activation Group

Every job automatically has a default AG. The default AG exists for the duration of a job. Most system programs and all OPM programs run within the default AG. ILE programs can run within the default AG, but this is usually a bad practice; the default AG is usually limited to dynamic program calls and single module programs.

When you use the CRTCLPGM command to compile an OPM program, there is no option to specify an AG. All OPM programs run within the default AG.

When you use the "shortcut" CRTBNDCL command to create an ILE CL program, the default AG is used by default:

```
CRTBNDCL . . . DFTACTGRP(*YES)
```

If you want to run the program in an ILE AG, you should specify DFTACTGRP(*NO). Then you can use the ACTGRP parameter to specify one of the other AG options.

User-Named Activation Group

You can name an ILE AG that a program will run within. Once created, a named AG usually exists for the duration of a job; that is to say, the AG is "persistent." The first program in a job to use a specifically named AG initializes all the structures and resource control boundaries that the activation needs. Subsequent programs that use this same AG need not perform this activation process because the first program has taken care of this task. Consequently, subsequent programs that use the AG activate faster, saving the overhead of creating the AG. Even if no program is currently using an AG, the structures stay in place unless you specifically destroy the AG by using the RCLACTGRP (Reclaim Activation Group) command.

To specify a named AG, you simply name it in the ACTGRP parameter of the CRTPGM or CRTBNDCL command:

```
CRTPGM . . . ACTGRP(QILE)
CRTBNDCL . . . DFTACTGRP(*NO) ACTGRP(QILE)
```

There's no magic in the name you give an AG. The name merely identifies the group. To simplify your use of AGs, you should standardize on one name that you will use for all ILE AGs, unless you need to separate a specific process in its own AG.

System-Named Activation Group

Unlike a user-named AG, a system-named (*NEW) AG is "nonpersistent"; it exists only during the execution of the program that requires it. The first time a program creates a system-named AG, it builds all the activation structures it needs; then the system destroys all those structures when the program ends. If the same program executes again during a job, it must create an AG again. If this process occurs often during the course of a job, performance can suffer significantly.

To instruct the system to provide a new AG for a program, specify *NEW when you create the program:

```
CRTPGM . . .ACTGRP(*NEW)
CRTBNDCL . . . DFTACTGRP(*NO) ACTGRP(*NEW)
```

Usually, a system-named AG is the least desirable AG option, especially if an application calls many programs. The performance impact of continually building and destroying AGs is noticeable in most applications. Unfortunately, ACTGRP(*NEW) is the default value for the CRTPGM command.

*CALLER Activation Group

The fourth AG option allows a called program to always run in the same AG as the program that called it. This AG can be any of the three types of AGs we've discussed: the default AG, a user-named AG, or a system-named AG. The program does not build any new activation structures and is able to share the same resources as its caller.

As with the other AG options, you specify a *CALLER AG when you create the program:

```
CRTPGM   . . . ACTGRP(*CALLER)
CRTBNDCL . . . DFTACTGRP(*NO) ACTGRP(*CALLER)
```

Activation Groups Made Easy

The subject of AGs can be complex, with many considerations and nuances. But you're usually safe if you remember two easy principles:

- For OPM programs, there's no choice: the program runs in the default AG.
- For ILE programs, use a named AG; for example, ACTGRP(QILE).

Activation Groups and File Overrides

In the previous sections, we said that AGs allow you to control resource scoping at a finer level than the job level. The two areas in which resource scoping becomes most apparent are file overrides and file opens.

With ILE, all the override commands support a new OVRSCOPE parameter that lets you explicitly determine the scope, or the extent of influence, for an override. In Chapter 17, you learned the principles of override scoping for OPM programs. ILE programs offer three scoping options:

- Call stack level
- Activation group level
- Job level

Active file overrides are processed during file open operations and do not affect already opened files. When you specify an override, regardless of the scope that you use, the override only affects subsequent opens.

Call Stack Level Scoping

Call stack level scoping is the narrowest scoping level available. Call stack level scoping is available for either OPM or ILE programs. When an override is scoped at the call stack level in an ILE environment, it is in effect at the current call level and at any subsequent call levels within the same AG. Specify call stack level scoping on the OVRSCOPE parameter of the override command:

```
OVRDBF . . . OVRSCOPE(*CALLLVL)
```

Activation Group Scoping

Activation group scoping is available only for ILE programs. When an override is scoped at the AG, the override affects any subsequent reference to the overridden resource (e.g., a file) in the same AG, regardless of call stack level. Specify activation group scoping on the override command:

```
OVRDBF . . . OVRSCOPE(*ACTGRPDFN)
```

You cannot use activation group scoping within the default AG. Specifying OVRSCOPE(*ACTGRPDFN) within the default AG (or within an OPM program) causes the override to be scoped at the call level.

Job Scoping

Job scoping is available to overrides in both OPM and ILE programs. Specifying a job scoping level extends the influence of the override to all programs that subsequently run in the current job, regardless of the AG or call stack level. The job scoping level is the broadest scoping level available. Specify a job scoping level on the override command:

```
OVRDBF . . . OVRSCOPE(*JOB)
```

ILE Error Handling

In Chapters 12 and 16, we discussed the process that OS/400 uses to report errors. Recall that an error generates an escape message, which you would normally monitor for, using the MONMSG command. The MONMSG command allows you to gracefully handle exceptions.

If you fail to monitor for an escape message in the program that generates the message, the system sends an inquiry message to either the user or the system operator, then waits for a reply. If the reply cancels the program, it creates a special type of escape message known as a function check. This situation is known as an unhandled exception.

ILE changes the way the system treats unhandled exceptions. If there are several call stack levels involved in the execution of a program, ILE uses a process called **percolation** to send the original escape message up the call stack, one step at a time, looking for an exception-handling mechanism such as a MONMSG command. If the system finds a relevant handler *anywhere in the call stack*, it uses the handler to process the escape message. The percolation process repeats until the system finds a handler, or until it reaches an AG boundary. If there is no exception handler, the system finally generates a function check, but only after it has polled all the previous call stack entries looking for a handler.

ILE Error-Handling Tips

Trying to track the route that an escape message takes through the call stack can be a daunting task, and ILE adds yet other potential detours. But you can usually avoid problems with errant messages by following three simple principles:

- Handle the error as soon as it occurs
- Avoid generic handlers
- Avoid handlers that do nothing

Handling the error at its source is the best way to ensure that an exception is processed correctly. If an escape message manages to "escape" the procedure that generated it, another procedure in the call stack could process the message in a way that you hadn't anticipated when you wrote the program. Always include appropriate MONMSG handlers in every procedure.

It's tempting to code MONMSG CPF0000 in every program to monitor for every escape message that might occur. You should resist this temptation, especially if there's a possibility that the message might come from another procedure in the call stack. It's best to monitor for specific messages and take specific appropriate actions.

You should also avoid the temptation to include a message handler that ignores messages entirely. Coding a MONMSG with no EXEC instructions, especially if it is a generic handler, invites the possibility that a program will continue processing, oblivious to the fact that a serious error may have occurred in another procedure within the same program.

Chapter Summary

The Integrated Language Environment (ILE) provides a consistent environment in which programs execute, regardless of the language in which they are written. It also provides tools to encourage modular programming techniques.

A procedure is an executable segment within a program or a module. A *MODULE is an object that is the result of compiling an ILE language source member. You cannot call a module, and the code in a module cannot be executed. To execute a module, you must first bind it into an ILE program, using the CRTPGM (Create Program) command. A program can consist of one or several modules all bound together into a single callable *PGM object.

The CALL command uses a dynamic program call to run a separate program, a separate object distinct from the calling program. The CALLPRC (Call Bound Procedure) command uses a static procedure call to run another procedure within the same program. A static procedure call executes much faster than a dynamic program call.

With a bind-by-copy static procedure call, the called procedure is actually copied into the program at binding time. With a bind-by-reference static procedure call, the called procedure exists in a separate object, called a service program (*SRVPGM).

ILE uses activation groups to subdivide a job into "sub-jobs." Activation groups provide the ability to control resource scoping at a finer level than the job level.

There are four types of activation groups: the default activation group (for Original Program Model programs), user-named ILE activation groups, system-named ILE activation groups, and *CALLER activation groups. At the time you bind a program, you determine which activation group a program will use.

The override commands allow you to control resource scoping — that is, the extent of influence of an override. There are three scoping levels: call stack level, activation group level, and job level.

ILE changes the way the system sends escape messages throughout the procedures in the call stack. Through a method called percolation, an escape message climbs through the entire stack looking for a MONMSG command that can handle the message.

Terms

activation group

bind

bind by copy

bind by reference

dynamic program call

entry module

Integrated Language Environment (ILE)

module

Original Program Model (OPM)

percolation

procedure

program

program entry procedure

return value

scoping level

service program

static procedure call

Review Questions

1. How does the program creation process differ between OPM programs and ILE programs?

2. Explain the differences between a dynamic program call and a static procedure call. Which is faster? Why?

3. Name four different types of activation groups. Which one(s) allow you to run OPM programs, and which one(s) allow you to run ILE programs?

4. What is a generic message handler? Why should you avoid its use with ILE programs?

Exercises

1. In this exercise, you modify the programs from Exercise 2 in Chapter 13 (page 203) to convert the exercise to a single ILE program. The program should accept the date as a parameter, then call a procedure using two parameters: the date in MMDDYY format and a character parameter to contain the translated date. After the procedure ends, the character parameter should be sent as a message to the user who called the program.

   a. Modify program SA1302*XXX* so that it uses CALLPRC to call SA1303*XXX* (substitute your initials for *XXX*).

   b. Use CRTCLMOD to create modules SA1302*XXX* and SA1303*XXX*.

   c. Bind the modules into an ILE program, SA2201*XXX*, using the CRTPGM command.

   d. Call program SA2201*XXX*, supplying different dates. Does the program always work correctly?

2. Using the DSPPGM (Display Program) command, display the attributes of program SA2201*XXX*.

   a. In which activation group does the program run?

   b. How many modules and service programs comprise the program? What are their names?

Chapter 23

User-Defined Commands

Chapter Overview

The AS/400 supports the creation of user-defined commands to allow you to extend and enhance the AS/400 Command Language as needed. This chapter introduces you to the concept of user-defined commands and to the reasons why a command may be the best way to implement a function. We also discuss the components of a command and the procedure for creating one. And we examine the six CL commands used exclusively for command definition. After completing this chapter, you will be able to create your own CL commands.

Why Commands?

You have learned that the more than 1,000 IBM-supplied CL commands simplify the AS/400's operation and provide a consistent user interface to system functions. You also can create your own user-defined commands to simplify your use of the system and to run your own application programs.

What advantages do user-defined commands offer your applications? User-defined commands can simplify the user interface, program design, and system administration functions. By incorporating user-defined commands into your applications, you can take advantage of the same interface IBM uses, and you can let the computer automatically handle many functions that you would otherwise have to explicitly address in a program.

User-defined commands simplify the user interface by providing a single, familiar display for both system and application functions. By providing easily remembered command names, you can allow users to bypass menus. You can easily provide for validation of input and support all the functions of the command prompting facility in your own applications, without designing your own prompting screens. By allowing users to enter parameters in any order (keyword notation) and by providing default values for some parameters, you can provide shortcuts that will make your applications easier to use. You also can easily incorporate the AS/400 help facility into user-defined commands, without additional programming.

User-defined commands simplify system administration by letting you use built-in AS/400 security facilities to authorize user access to specific commands. In many cases, you can automate the addition of libraries to your library list by specifying the library to be used with a command; this will not require additional programming in your application. Command-driven applications simplify user training. Once a person knows how to use one command, (s)he will find it easy to use all the commands in an application.

Finally, user-defined commands can simplify program design by letting you take advantage of the automatic data-conversion capabilities of CL commands. With a command-driven interface you can enter values as character strings, even when your program expects them to be another data type; OS/400 will automatically validate the data and convert it to the necessary type. By exploiting the input validation capabilities of commands, you can reduce or even eliminate from your application the processing steps devoted to checking data input.

Aside from applications, you can also create user-defined commands to help with system functions in your data processing organization. With user-defined commands, you can create abbreviated versions of IBM-supplied commands, create modified versions of IBM-supplied commands, standardize daily routines and functions, and streamline your daily operations.

The Components of a Command

Recall from previous chapters that a command is an object (type *CMD) that resides within an AS/400 library. The name of the command usually consists of a verb and a subject, which make up an imperative statement directing the computer to perform an operation. To simplify the use of user-defined commands, you should use the same naming conventions IBM uses for its commands. The same consistency that makes CL easy to learn can make your application easy to learn and use.

To execute, a command needs at least two components present on the system: a command definition object and a command processing program. You can also have other objects that work in conjunction with a command, but these are the minimum requirements.

The **command definition object**, which is actually the *CMD object you can see on your system, is sometimes abbreviated CDO. The CDO is a description of the command, complete with the parameter keywords, descriptions, and default values. It also contains the validity checking rules, the links to the programs to be called, and information used by the AS/400 command prompter.

The **command processing program** (CPP) is the program that actually performs the work of the command. Every command has a command processing program (or a REXX command processing procedure). The CPP receives the command parameters described in the CDO, then processes them. Many times the command processing program is a CL program, but it can be written in other AS/400 languages, such as RPG/400 or COBOL/400. The CPP can be changed independently of the CDO, as long as the parameters it receives remain consistent with the definition in the CDO.

Instead of a CPP, a command can be associated with a REXX procedure. But because the focus of this text is on CL, not REXX, we do not cover REXX options for user-defined commands.

Command Definition Statements

Just as with a program, a command definition originates from source statements stored in a source physical file member. The source physical file is usually named QCMDSRC.

You can use SEU to enter the statements. The source statements are then compiled into a *CMD object, using the CRTCMD (Create Command) command.

The command definition source specifies the structure of a command. It allows you to define the parameters that will be used by the command and to specify valid values or default values for the parameters. The command definition source is also where you indicate the prompts the user will see when using command prompting.

Unlike a CL program, which can be made up of thousands of different commands, there are only six different command definition statements:

- CMD   Command title specification
- PARM   Parameter definition
- QUAL   Qualified name definition
- ELEM   Elements of a list definition
- DEP   Dependencies between parameters definition
- PMTCTL   Prompt control specification

Most commands you build will need only the first three command definition statements. In fact, if a command has no parameters, you need only one statement, the CMD statement. You can also include comments in a command definition to aid documentation. Comments, following CL convention, are enclosed by /* and */ characters. Like CL program source, command definition source can also include labels.

Figure 23.1 shows the command definition source for a simple user-defined command, EXCCMD (Execute Commands). This command allows you to execute commands stored in a source file member. This command uses most of the principles and techniques we have discussed so far in this text. We discuss the command definition statements in this chapter, then handle the structure of the command processing program in Chapter 24.

When this command is completed, it allows you to execute the CL commands contained in a source member without compiling the member into a CL program. Using this command, you can easily set up procedures to run sequentially and change the commands that are executed as your needs change. The function of this command is similar to that of the IBM-supplied SBMDBJOB (Submit Database Job) command, but it is much more flexible.

The EXCCMD command asks for a member name and a source file name and offers you the option to ignore commands that end in error or abort the procedure if a command within the source member ends in error. This IFERROR parameter defaults to *CANCEL. If the CL commands you want to execute reside in the JOBSTREAM member in file QGPL/QCLSRC, you could execute them by typing the following command:

```
EXCCMD     MBR(JOBSTREAM)      +
           FILE(QGPL/QCLSRC)   +
           IFERROR(*IGNORE)
```

Figure 23.1
Command Definition
for EXCCMD Command

```
/* *********************************************************** */
/* *                                                           */
/* *    Command name - EXCCMD - Execute commands in a source member */
/* *                                                           */
/* *    CRTCMD PGM(EXCCMDC)                                     */
/* *                                                           */
/* *********************************************************** */

EXCCMD:      CMD          PROMPT('Execute Commands from Source')

             PARM         KWD(MBR)                          +
                          TYPE(*NAME)                       +
                          LEN(10)                           +
                          MIN(1)                            +
                          PROMPT('Member')
             PARM         KWD(SRCFILE)                      +
                          TYPE(Q1)                          +
                          PROMPT('Source file name')
             PARM         KWD(IFERROR)                      +
                          TYPE(*CHAR)                       +
                          LEN(7)                            +
                          RSTD(*YES)                        +
                          DFT(*CANCEL)                      +
                          VALUES(*CANCEL *IGNORE)           +
                          PROMPT('Command error action')

Q1:          QUAL         TYPE(*NAME)                       +
                          LEN(10)                           +
                          DFT(QCLSRC)
             QUAL         TYPE(*NAME)                       +
                          LEN(10)                           +
                          DFT(*LIBL)                        +
                          SPCVAL((*LIBL))                   +
                          PROMPT('Library')
```

The CMD Statement

The CMD statement precedes other source statements in the command definition. Only one CMD statement is allowed. It simply provides the prompting text (i.e., the command title) the user sees at the top of a command prompt display. The text can be up to 30 characters long. The CMD statement is required, but the PROMPT parameter is optional. Traditionally, the optional label to the left of the CMD statement identifies the name of the command. In the example in Figure 23.1, the CMD statement identifies the title of the command as *Execute Commands from Source*.

The PARM Statement

Each PARM statement in the command definition defines a parameter for the command. A PARM statement is required for each parameter that will be passed to the command processing program. A command definition can contain up to 75 PARM statements. Specify the PARM statements in the same order in which you want the command processing program to receive the parameters. The PARM statement describes, among other things, the name of the parameter keyword, the type of parameter value, the length of the parameter, the default value (if any), a number of validity checking tests, and the prompt to be displayed on the command prompter. The PARM statement supports many parameters; we discuss the most commonly used ones.

```
PARM KWD(keyword-name)                 +
     TYPE(data-type)                   +
     LEN(length-of-parameter)          +
     RSTD(restricted-values)           +
     DFT(default-value)                +
     VALUES(list-of-valid-values)      +
     SPCVAL(list-of-special-values)    +
     RANGE(range-of-valid-values)      +
     REL(relational-comparison)        +
     MIN(minimum-number-of-values)     +
     MAX(maximum-number-of-values)     +
     PROMPT(prompting-text)
```

To facilitate our discussion of the PARM keyword, consider the following statement from Figure 23.1:

```
PARM KWD(IFERROR)                      +
     TYPE(*CHAR)                       +
     LEN(7)                            +
     RSTD(*YES)                        +
     DFT(*CANCEL)                      +
     VALUES(*CANCEL *IGNORE)           +
     PROMPT('Command error action')
```

The KWD parameter names the command parameter keyword, in this case IFERROR; if you specify the command in keyword notation, this is the keyword you use for this command parameter. The TYPE and LEN parameters allow you to specify the data type and the length of the PARM. You can use any of the valid command parameter data types; Figure 23.2 lists the most common ones. If you don't specify the length of the parameter, the system uses the default length shown in the figure, depending upon the data type.

The RSTD parameter lets you restrict the value of a command parameter to specific values that you set. You set the allowable values in the VALUES or SPCVAL parameter. Many times you will use these parameters in conjunction with the DFT parameter, which lets you set the default value of the parameter. If you specify RSTD(*YES), the command parameter value must be one of the allowable values; if you specify RSTD(*NO), any value will work, as long as its data type matches the TYPE parameter.

The VALUES and SPCVAL keywords describe specific allowable parameter values. When you specify RSTD(*YES) to restrict parameter values, you must use one or more of these keywords to identify the allowable values. For example, in Figure 23.1, the IFERROR parameter is described with two allowable VALUES: *CANCEL* and *IGNORE*. The default value is *CANCEL*.

Figure 23.2
Common Command
Parameter Data Types

Data Type	Description	Default Length	Maximum Allowable Length	Allowable Value
*CHAR	Character	32	3000	Any character string
*CMDSTR	Command String	256	6000	Any CL command
*DATE	Date	7^1	7^1	A character string denoting the date, as in 123197
*DEC	Decimal	(15 5)	(24 9)	A decimal number, as in 5 or 3.14
*GENERIC	Generic Name	10	256	A partial name followed by an (*) asterisk, as in P* or PAY*. Identifies a group of objects
*HEX	Hexadecimal	1	256	A hexadecimal number using digits 0–F
*INT2 or *INT4	Integer	2 or 4^1	2 or 4^1	A numeric integer value as in 1 or 500
*LGL	Logical	1	1	A logical value of 1 or 0
*NAME	Name	10	256	A character string whose first character is alphabetic (A–Z), $, #, or @, and remaining characters are alphanumeric (A–Z, 0–9), $, #, @, _(underscore), or . (period)
*TIME	Time	6^1	6^1	A character string specifying a time of day, as in 123000

[1]You cannot specify a length for this data type.

The SPCVAL keyword has several purposes. First, it allows you to bypass some name-verification logic when entering a parameter. The following example illustrates this function. By specifying special values, we can bypass the normal naming requirements for a *NAME parameter type. In this example, *LIBL* and *ALLUSR* become valid entries, even though both normally are invalid as *NAME type values.

```
PARM KWD(LIB)                         +
     TYPE(*NAME)                      +
     DFT(*LIBL)                       +
     SPCVAL((*LIBL) (*ALLUSR))        +
     PROMPT('Library')
```

The second function of the SPCVAL keyword is to let you assign a translated value to a parameter value the user enters. For example, instead of passing the entire value *CANCEL* or *IGNORE* for the IFERROR parameter, we could pass just a *C* or an *I*. The command processing program would expect to receive a single character parameter with a value of *C* or *I*, indicating whether the procedure should cancel on an error or ignore any errors. But the user could still type either special value *CANCEL* or *IGNORE*; these values would be translated to *C* or *I*, respectively, before the CPP is called. In this case, we would change the PARM statement to

```
PARM KWD(IFERROR)                            +
     TYPE(*CHAR)                             +
     LEN(1)                                  +
     RSTD(*YES)                              +
     DFT(*CANCEL)                            +
     SPCVAL((*CANCEL C) (*IGNORE I))  +
     PROMPT('Command error action')
```

In addition to moving the special values to the SPCVAL keyword, notice that we also changed the length of the IFERROR parameter to *CHAR 1, because that is what would actually be passed.

The RANGE and REL keywords (not used in Figure 23.1) let you validate parameter values based on a range of valid values or on a relational comparison to a value. For example, if you wanted to use a command parameter describing a YEAR, and the command processing program is expecting a year between 1980 and 2000, inclusively, you would use the RANGE keyword as follows:

```
PARM KWD(YEAR)                    +
     TYPE(*DEC)                   +
     LEN(4 0)                     +
     RANGE(1980 2000)             +
     PROMPT('Year to process')
```

If you wanted to ensure that a user could not enter a year before 1960, you could use the REL keyword:

```
PARM KWD(YEAR)                    +
     TYPE(*DEC)                   +
     LEN(4 0)                     +
     REL(*GE 1960)                +
     PROMPT('Year to process')
```

The relational operators valid with the REL keyword are the same mnemonic operators that are valid in other CL commands (e.g., *GT, *EQ, *GE), but not the arithmetic symbols you can use with relational expressions.

The PROMPT keyword lets you specify the prompting text the user sees if (s)he invokes the command prompter. The text is a quoted string, up to 30 characters long. The command prompter automatically fills in the area between the prompt and the parameter input area with filler dots, just as it does for IBM commands. The IFERROR parameter is prompted on the screen as follows:

```
Command error action . . . . . .   *CANCEL      *CANCEL, *IGNORE
```

The specification in Figure 23.1 for the MBR parameter includes one other keyword worthy of mention here. The MIN parameter specifies the minimum number of values that must be entered for a parameter. If the parameter is optional, you can use the default value, *MIN(0)*. If the parameter is required, you must specify the minimum number of values required; usually you will specify *MIN(1)*, as does the specification in Figure 23.1:

```
PARM KWD(MBR)                      +
     TYPE(*NAME)                   +
     LEN(10)                       +
     MIN(1)                        +
     PROMPT('Member')
```

If the parameter is a simple list type parameter, you can indicate that the parameter may have multiple values by using both the MIN and MAX keywords. The MAX keyword specifies the maximum number of entries in the list; the default is *MAX(1)*, indicating that the parameter is a single entry, not a list. If the parameter is a simple list, you must use advanced techniques to determine the contents and length of the value passed to the command processing program. In Chapter 24, we discuss a simple list parameter and describe how the value is passed.

The QUAL Statement

You may have noticed in Figure 23.1 that the SRCFILE parameter is specified with a TYPE (Q1) not listed among the valid data types shown in Figure 23.2:

```
PARM KWD(SRCFILE)                  +
     TYPE(Q1)                      +
     PROMPT('Source file name')
```

This parameter is a **qualified name** (or value), in this case consisting of the file name and the library, usually entered in the format LIBRARY/FILE and shown by the command prompt as

```
Source file . . . . . . . . . .   QCLSRC     Name
      Library . . . . . . . . . .   *LIBL      Name, *LIBL
```

If a parameter is a qualified value (e.g., LIBRARY/OBJECT), you must further define the parameter separately using QUAL statements. Each part of the qualified value must be described with a QUAL statement. The PARM statement that describes the qualified parameter must refer to a label that starts a series of QUAL statements describing the qualified value. In the example in Figure 23.1, specifying TYPE(Q1) simply tells the command compiler that the description for this parameter is defined at label Q1. The label can be any valid label name; it must appear in the command definition source after the PARM statement with which it is associated. A maximum of 300 qualifiers is allowed for a qualified parameter, although in practice you usually use only two or three. The QUAL statements must be specified in the order in which they are passed to the command processing program. Most of the same keywords we discussed earlier for the PARM statement are also valid with the QUAL statement. Here are the QUAL statements from Figure 23.1:

```
Q1:   QUAL  TYPE(*NAME)          +
            LEN(10)              +
            DFT(QCLSRC)
      QUAL  TYPE(*NAME)          +
            LEN(10)              +
            DFT(*LIBL)           +
            SPCVAL((*LIBL))      +
            PROMPT('Library')
```

The first QUAL statement describes the first half of the qualified name (i.e., the source file). Note that the PROMPT for this first portion of the parameter is in the PARM statement, not the QUAL statement. This is normal for the first part of a qualified value. The remaining QUAL statements can have their own prompts.

The length of the qualified parameter is the sum of all the QUAL statements that define the qualified parameter. In this case, the length of the parameter is 20. When the parameter is passed to the command processing program, the file name will be in the first 10 positions of the parameter and the library name will be in the last 10 positions. The command will not pass the qualifier character (/) and will pad each portion of the qualified name to the right with blanks. For example, if the file name is specified as *LIBL/QCLSRC, the command processing program will receive one parameter value:

QCLSRC␣␣␣␣*LIBL␣␣␣␣␣

The command processing program can then break the qualified name into its two parts, using the %SST built-in function.

You may wonder about the curious way that the command sends qualified values; it appears to be backward. For example, you specify *LIBL/QCLSRC when writing the qualified value, but the command processing program receives the value as QCLSRC␣␣␣␣*LIBL␣␣␣␣␣. This notation is a carryover from the System/38, which uses a notation with the period as the qualifier (e.g., QCLSRC.*LIBL) to indicate a qualified value. With the introduction of the AS/400, IBM changed the way to specify qualified values externally, but internally the AS/400 handles them the same way the System/38 does. Even though you specify the library first in a qualified value, the AS/400 reverses the order before sending the parameter to the command processing program.

Other Command Definition Statements

The remaining command definition statements are used in advanced applications of user-defined commands. For the most part, you won't need them for day-to-day programming, but we describe them briefly here. You can find detailed information about these statements in the *CL Programmer's Guide*. Each of these statements must appear after the PARM statement for the parameter it describes, and each is usually found at the end of the source.

The ELEM statement further describes the individual elements that are combined to form a mixed-list type parameter, or a list-within-a-list parameter. A mixed list is a set of separately defined values that usually have different meanings, are of different types, and are in a fixed position in the list. For example, LOG(4 0 *SECLVL) could specify a mixed list. In this case, the specifications that would describe the parameter might follow this format:

```
        PARM KWD(LOG)                               +
             TYPE(E1)                               +
             PROMPT('Logging level')

  E1:   ELEM TYPE(*DEC)                             +
             LEN(1 0)                               +
             RSTD(*YES)                             +
             DFT(4)                                 +
             RANGE(0 4)
        ELEM TYPE(*DEC)                             +
             LEN(2 0)                               +
             RSTD(*YES)                             +
             DFT(0)                                 +
             RANGE(0 99)                            +
             PROMPT('Severity level')
        ELEM TYPE(*CHAR)                            +
             LEN(7)                                 +
             RSTD(*YES)                             +
             DFT(*MSG)                              +
             VALUES(*MSG *SECLVL *NOLIST)           +
             PROMPT('Message text level')
```

Notice that the logic of describing a mixed list is similar to that of describing a qualified value. If the associated PARM statement allows more than one entry (e.g., MAX(2)) and points to an ELEM statement, the parameter being described is a list-within-a-list.

The DEP command definition statement defines the dependencies between parameters. It indicates which parameters are interdependent. For example, you can specify that certain parameters are required if other parameters have specific values. In the following example, if you specified OUTPUT(*PRINT), you would also have to enter a value for the PRTF parameter:

```
        DEP  CTL(OUTPUT *EQ *PRINT)                 +
             PARM(PRTF)
```

The PMTCTL statement is used for prompt control, which defines the conditions under which the parameter will be displayed on the prompt display. When you use the PMTCTL statement to prompt a parameter, the prompting is controlled by another

parameter. For instance, in the following example, the OUTFILE and OUTMBR
parameters will be prompted for only if you specify OUTPUT(*OUTFILE):

```
            PARM        KWD(OUTFILE)                          +
                        TYPE(*NAME)                           +
                        LEN(10)                               +
                        PMTCTL(OUTF)
            PARM        KWD(OUTMBR)                           +
                        TYPE(*NAME)                           +
                        LEN(10)                               +
                        PMTCTL(OUTF)

  OUTF:     PMTCTL      CTL(OUTPUT)                           +
                        COND((*EQ *OUTFILE))                  +
                        NBRTRUE(*EQ 1)
```

The CRTCMD Command

Once you have typed the command definition source into a source file member, you
can create the command object using the CRTCMD (Create Command) command.
This command analyzes the statements in the source, prints a diagnostic listing, and
if no errors are found, creates the *CMD object. You can enter the CRTCMD command on a command line or use option *14* (Compile) on the PDM "Work with
members" display. The CRTCMD command, with its most-often-used parameters,
takes the following form:

```
  CRTCMD      CMD(library-name/command-name)           +
              PGM(library-name/program-name)           +
              SRCFILE(library-name/file-name)          +
              SRCMBR(member-name)                      +
              ALLOW(where-allowed)                     +
              ALWLMTUSR(allow-limited-user)            +
              MAXPOS(maximum-positional-parms)         +
              CURLIB(current-library)                  +
              PRDLIB(product-library)                  +
              TEXT(command-description-text)
```

The CMD parameter identifies the qualified name of the command object as it
will exist on your system. If you don't specify a library name, the command will be
created in your job's current library; the default is *CURLIB*.

You specify the name of the command processing program (CPP) in the PGM
parameter. The CPP is the program that will be run when the command is executed.
We discuss the details of the CPP in the next chapter. The default value for the PGM
parameter is *CMD*, indicating that the CPP is named the same as the command. If
you don't specify a library name, or *CURLIB*, the default value is *LIBL*. The CPP
need *not* exist at the time you compile the command; it must, of course, exist when
you execute the command.

The SRCFILE and SRCMBR parameters identify the location of the command definition source (i.e., the library, source file, and source member). The default value for SRCFILE is *LIBL/QCMDSRC*. The SRCMBR parameter defaults to *CMD*, which tells the compiler that the source is in the member named the same as the command name; otherwise, you must specify the name of the member that contains the command definition source for the command.

The ALLOW parameter indicates in which environment this command can execute. With this parameter, you can prevent a command from being executed within a batch job or used as the command to execute with the QCMDEXC program. This parameter allows you to specify several options, if necessary. Any of the following options are valid (for a complete list, see Table 20.1, page 321):

- *BATCH   The command can be processed in a batch stream, outside of a program.
- *INTERACT   The command can be processed interactively, from a command line.
- *BPGM   The command is valid in a program running in batch.
- *IPGM   The command is valid in an interactive program.
- *EXEC   You can process this command as a parameter on the call command, particularly with the QCMDEXC API. You must also specify *BATCH or *INTERACT if you specify this option.

The default value is *ALL*, to let the command execute in all environments.

To allow users with limited system access to execute the command from a command line, specify ALWLMTUSR(*YES); otherwise, the default value, ALWLMTUSR(*NO), prevents limited-capability users from executing the command.

The MAXPOS parameter lets you specify how many parameters in this command can be specified positionally. Typically, this number should not exceed six, but it can be any number from zero to 75. Usually, you let the system decide how many positional parameters it will allow by using the default, *MAXPOS(*NOMAX)*. There are some restrictions on which kinds of parameters can use positional notation; typically, you do not want to allow positional notation for list type parameters.

The CURLIB and PRDLIB parameters allow you to manipulate some portions of the library list when the EXCCMD command is executed. The CURLIB parameter specifies the name of the current library; the default is CURLIB(*NOCHG), indicating the current library will not change. You can also specify a library name, or CURLIB(*CRTDFT), if you want to specify that no specific current library is active during the processing of the command. Under some circumstances, you may want to use the PRDLIB parameter to specify a product library that will contain the programs needed to execute a command. The default is PRDLIB(*NOCHG); if you accept the default, the product library will not change. If you want no product library during the execution of this command, specify PRDLIB(*NONE); when the command is finished, any previously active product library will be returned to the library list.

Finally, the TEXT parameter lets you document the command by specifying descriptive text within a quoted string. When you display the command description using the DSPCMD (Display Command) or DSPOBJD (Display Object Description) commands, the text will be shown.

To create the sample command in Figure 23.1, you would type the following command (assuming the source is in member EXCCMD in file STUDENT1/ QCMDSRC):

```
CRTCMD      CMD(EXCCMD)                                    +
            PGM(EXCCMDC)                                   +
            SRCFILE(STUDENT1/QCMDSRC)                      +
            ALLOW(*INTERACT *BPGM *IPGM)                   +
            TEXT('Execute commands from source')
```

To prevent execution by QCMDEXC, we have specified

```
            ALLOW(*INTERACT *BPGM *IPGM)
```

For the remainder of the parameters, you could use the default values.

Chapter Summary

You can create your own user-defined commands to simplify your use of the system and to run your own application programs. User-defined commands can simplify the user interface, program design, and system administration functions.

At least two components make up a command: a command definition object (CDO) and a command processing program (CPP). The command definition object (AS/400 object type *CMD) contains the description of the command; the command processing program is the program that runs when the command is executed.

The command definition source specifies the structure of a command. There are six different types of command definition statements:

- CMD   Command title specification
- PARM   Parameter definition
- QUAL   Qualified name definition
- ELEM   Elements of a list definition
- DEP   Dependencies between parameters definition
- PMTCTL   Prompt control specification

Most of the time you need only the CMD, PARM, and QUAL statements.

You create the command object, using the CRTCMD (Create Command) command, after the command definition source has been entered into a source file member.

Terms

command definition object   command processing program
                                                        qualified name

---

Review Questions

1. Give three reasons to implement a user-defined command.

2. Name the two required components of a command. What is the purpose of each?

3. The following command definition statements are the ones most often used in defining a command. What is the purpose of each?

   a. QUAL   b. CMD   c. PARM

4. The command definition statements below describe a command parameter.

```
SORTFILE: CMD    PROMPT('Sort file')
          PARM   KWD(INPUT)                      +
                 TYPE(FILE1)                      +
                 MIN(1)                           +
                 PROMPT('Input file name')


FILE1:    QUAL   TYPE(*NAME)                      +
                 LEN(10)
          QUAL   TYPE(*NAME)                      +
                 LEN(10)                          +
                 DFT(*LIBL)                       +
                 SPCVAL((*LIBL) (*ALLUSR))        +
                 PROMPT('Library')
```

Answer the following questions about the parameter:

a. What is the keyword associated with the parameter?
b. How many entries can you make for the parameter?
c. What type of parameter is it?
d. Is the parameter required or optional?
e. What is the default value for the "Library" portion of the parameter?
f. What special values are allowed for the "Library" portion of the parameter?
g. What type of data is valid in the "Input file name" portion of the parameter?
h. If the user wanted to indicate the file QGPL/SORTIN for this parameter, what would be the contents of the parameter as received by the command processing program?
i. Can you determine the name of the command processing program from this code? Can you determine the name of the command? Why or why not?
j. If the user prompts for this command, what title will be shown on the screen?

Exercises

1. Create the EXCCMD command definition described in this chapter. When you create the command, specify EXCCMDC as the command processing program. Allow the command to execute on a command line, in a batch program, and in an interactive program. Execute the command; what happens?

2. Create a command definition named SA2302*XXX* that accepts two required parameters:

   a. A qualified program name
   b. A "To" library name

3. Create a command definition named SA2303*XXX* that accepts the following parameters:

   a. A qualified object name, required
   b. An object type parameter, default value *PGM
   c. A "To" library name
   d. A yes/no parameter with prompting text "Replace existing objects?" The parameter should pass a *Y* or an *N* to the command processing program.

Chapter 24

Command Processing Programs

Chapter Overview

Programs specified as command processing programs have certain properties and requirements. This chapter examines the characteristics of command processing programs and explains the formats commands use to pass various parameters to a command processing program.

Writing a Command Processing Program

Now that you have written and compiled a command definition object (in Chapter 23), it's time to construct a **command processing program** (i.e., the program that will run when a command is executed). You can write a command processing program (CPP) in CL or any HLL.

Although a command processing program is written specifically for use in conjunction with a command, as long as you supply the correct parameters, you can use the CALL command to execute the program outside the scope of any command. In reality, a CPP is no different from any other program on the system.

The command processing program you would write for the EXCCMD command defined in Chapter 23 is shown in Figure 24.1. Let's examine the characteristics that make it work in connection with the EXCCMD command.

Figure 24.1
Command Processing
Program for the
EXCCMD Command

```
0001.00 /* ***************************************************************** */
0002.00 /*                                                                   */
0003.00 /*      Program name - EXCCMDC - Execute commands on a source file   */
0004.00 /*                                                                   */
0005.00 /*      Command processing program for EXCCMD command                */
0006.00 /*                                                                   */
0007.00 /* ***************************************************************** */
0008.00           PGM          PARM(&mbr &qualfile &iferror)
0009.00
0010.00           DCLF         QGPL/QCLSRC
0011.00
0012.00           DCL          &mbr      *CHAR 10
0013.00           DCL          &qualfile *CHAR 20
0014.00           DCL          &iferror  *CHAR 7
0015.00
0016.00           DCL          &file     *CHAR 10
0017.00           DCL          &lib      *CHAR 10
```

Continued

Figure 24.1
Continued

```
0018.00              DCL      &cmdstr    *CHAR 2000
0019.00              DCL      &cmdidx    *DEC (5 0)
0020.00              DCL      &lftidx    *DEC (5 0)
0021.00              DCL      &rgtidx    *DEC (5 0)
0022.00              DCL      &len       *DEC (5 0)
0023.00              DCL      &symbol    *CHAR 1
0024.00              DCL      &nxtrcd    *CHAR 1
0025.00              DCL      &test      *CHAR 1
0026.00              DCL      &okcnt     *DEC (5 0)
0027.00              DCL      &okcnta    *CHAR 5
0028.00              DCL      &errcnt    *DEC (5 0)
0029.00              DCL      &errcnta   *CHAR 5
0030.00
0031.00              DCL      &errflag   *LGL
0032.00              DCL      &msgid     *CHAR 7
0033.00              DCL      &msgdta    *CHAR 100
0034.00              DCL      &msgf      *CHAR 10
0035.00              DCL      &msgflib   *CHAR 10
0036.00              DCL      &keyvar    *CHAR 4
0037.00
0038.00              MONMSG   CPF0000 EXEC(GOTO ERRTAG1)
0039.00
0040.00              CHGVAR   &file %SST(&qualfile 1 10)
0041.00              CHGVAR   &lib  %SST(&qualfile 11 10)
0042.00
0043.00              CHKOBJ   OBJ(&lib/&file) OBJTYPE(*FILE) MBR(&mbr)
0044.00              OVRDBF   FILE(QCLSRC) TOFILE(&lib/&file) MBR(&mbr)
0045.00
0046.00  NXTCMD:     /* Initialize for next command                            */
0047.00              CHGVAR   &cmdidx 1             /* Index to command area    */
0048.00              CHGVAR   &cmdstr ' '           /* Blank out command area   */
0049.00              CHGVAR   &nxtrcd ' '           /* Set for new command      */
0050.00
0051.00  READ:       /* Read source record                                     */
0052.00              RCVF
0053.00              MONMSG   CPF0864 EXEC(GOTO EOF)
0054.00              CHGVAR   &symbol ' '
0055.00              CHGVAR   &rgtidx 80            /* Right index to &srcdta  */
0056.00              CHGVAR   &lftidx 1             /* Left index to &srcdta   */
0057.00
0058.00              IF       (&srcdta *EQ '    ') GOTO LEN      /* All blank */
0059.00
0060.00  SCANRIGHT:  /* Scan source record from the right                      */
0061.00              CHGVAR   &test %SST(&srcdta &rgtidx 1)
0062.00
0063.00              /* Process blank character                               */
0064.00              IF       (&test *EQ ' ') DO
0065.00                       CHGVAR &rgtidx (&rgtidx - 1)
0066.00                       GOTO   SCANRIGHT
0067.00                       ENDDO
0068.00
0069.00              /* Process + or - continuation character                 */
0070.00              IF       ((&test *EQ '+') *OR (&test *EQ '-')) DO
0071.00                       CHGVAR &symbol &test
0072.00                       CHGVAR %SST(&srcdta &rgtidx 1) ' '
0073.00                       CHGVAR &rgtidx (&rgtidx - 1)
0074.00                       ENDDO
0075.00
```

Continued

Figure 24.1
Continued

```
0076.00                        /* Ignore leading blanks if previous line ended with +  */
0077.00              IF        (&nxtrcd *EQ '+') DO
0078.00
0079.00  SCANLEFT:             /* Scan record from left                     */
0080.00              IF        (%SST(&srcdta &lftidx 1) *EQ ' ') DO
0081.00                        CHGVAR &lftidx (&lftidx + 1)
0082.00                        IF   (&lftidx *LT 81) GOTO SCANLEFT
0083.00                        ENDDO
0084.00              ENDDO
0085.00
0086.00  LEN:                  /* Move &srcdta text to command area         */
0087.00              CHGVAR    &len (&rgtidx - &lftidx + 1) /* Actual len   */
0088.00              IF        (&len *GT 0) DO              /* Positive len */
0089.00                        CHGVAR %SST(&cmdstr &cmdidx &len) +
0090.00                               %SST(&srcdta &lftidx &len)
0091.00                        CHGVAR &cmdidx (&cmdidx + &len)
0092.00              ENDDO
0093.00
0094.00                        /* Read next record if continuation          */
0095.00              IF        (&symbol *NE ' ') DO
0096.00                        CHGVAR &nxtrcd &symbol
0097.00                        GOTO   READ
0098.00              ENDDO
0099.00
0100.00              IF        (&cmdstr *EQ ' ') GOTO NXTCMD
0101.00
0102.00                        /* Execute the command                       */
0103.00              CALL      QCMDEXC PARM(&cmdstr 2000)
0104.00              MONMSG    MSGID(CPF0000) EXEC(DO)
0105.00                        IF   (&iferror *EQ '*CANCEL') GOTO ERRTAG1
0106.00                        CHGVAR &errcnt (&errcnt + 1)
0107.00                        GOTO   NXTCMD
0108.00              ENDDO
0109.00
0110.00              CHGVAR    &okcnt (&okcnt + 1)
0111.00              GOTO      NXTCMD
0112.00
0113.00  EOF:                  /* Remove EOF message, send completion message  */
0114.00              RCVMSG    MSGTYPE(*EXCP)
0115.00              CHGVAR    &okcnta &okcnt
0116.00              CHGVAR    &errcnta &errcnt
0117.00
0118.00              IF        (&errcnt *GT 0) DO
0119.00                        SNDPGMMSG MSG('Errors occurred in'           +
0120.00                                  *BCAT &errcnta *BCAT 'commands.'   +
0121.00                                  *BCAT &okcnta *BCAT                +
0122.00                                  'commands completed successfully.') +
0123.00                                  MSGTYPE(*COMP)
0124.00              ENDDO
0125.00              ELSE      DO
0126.00                        SNDPGMMSG MSG(&okcnta *BCAT                  +
0127.00                                  'commands completed successfully.' +
0128.00                                  *BCAT 'No errors encountered.')    +
0129.00                                  MSGTYPE(*COMP)
0130.00              ENDDO
0131.00
0132.00                        /* Normal end of program                     */
0133.00              RETURN
0134.00
```

Continued

Figure 24.1
Continued

```
0135.00   ERRTAG1:    /* Standard error handling routine                        */
0136.00               IF          &errflag  DO
0137.00                           SNDPGMMSG MSGID(CPF9999)           +
0138.00                                       MSGF(QCPFMSG)          +
0139.00                                       MSGTYPE(*ESCAPE)
0140.00                           ENDDO
0141.00               CHGVAR      &errflag '1' /* Set to fail if error occurs */
0142.00
0143.00   ERRTAG2:    RCVMSG      MSGTYPE(*DIAG)                    +
0144.00                           RMV(*NO)                          +
0145.00                           KEYVAR(&keyvar)                   +
0146.00                           MSGDTA(&msgdta)                   +
0147.00                           MSGID(&msgid)                     +
0148.00                           MSGF(&msgf)                       +
0149.00                           SNDMSGFLIB(&msgflib)
0150.00
0151.00               IF          (&keyvar *NE '    ') DO
0152.00                           RMVMSG     MSGKEY(&keyvar)
0153.00                           SNDPGMMSG MSGID(&msgid)           +
0154.00                                       MSGF(&msgflib/&msgf)  +
0155.00                                       MSGDTA(&msgdta)       +
0156.00                                       MSGTYPE(*DIAG)
0157.00                           GOTO       ERRTAG2
0158.00                           ENDDO
0159.00
0160.00               RCVMSG      MSGTYPE(*EXCP)                    +
0161.00                           MSGDTA(&msgdta)                   +
0162.00                           MSGID(&msgid)                     +
0163.00                           MSGF(&msgf)                       +
0164.00                           SNDMSGFLIB(&msgflib)
0165.00               MONMSG      CPF0000
0166.00               SNDPGMMSG   MSGID(&msgid)                     +
0167.00                           MSGF(&msgflib/&msgf)              +
0168.00                           MSGDTA(&msgdta)                   +
0169.00                           MSGTYPE(*ESCAPE)
0170.00               MONMSG      CPF0000
0171.00
0172.00               ENDPGM
```

Parameters in the CPP

The major requirement for all CPPs is that they must receive all the parameters that commands pass to them. If a parameter is described in a command definition object, it must also be declared and received by the CPP. Furthermore, the parameters must be received in the order they were defined in the command definition (i.e., in PARM statement order). Recall from Chapter 23 that the command definition specified three parameters (MBR, SRCFILE, and IFERROR) in three PARM statements:

```
PARM      KWD(MBR)                          +
          TYPE(*NAME)                       +
          LEN(10)                           +
          MIN(1)                            +
          PROMPT('Member')
PARM      KWD(SRCFILE)                      +
          TYPE(Q1)                          +
          PROMPT('Source file name')
```

```
PARM      KWD(IFERROR)                        +
          TYPE(*CHAR)                         +
          LEN(7)                              +
          RSTD(*YES)                          +
          DFT(*CANCEL)                        +
          VALUES(*CANCEL *IGNORE)             +
          PROMPT('Command error action')
```

Because the command processing program must receive these parameters in the same order they are specified in the command definition, the PGM statement of the CPP must be specified as follows:

```
PGM  PARM(&mbr &qualfile &iferror)
```

Notice that the names of the program variables in the CPP need not match the names of the command parameter keywords. Remember that parameters are passed by position, not by name, so the first receiver variable corresponds to the first command parameter, and so on, regardless of the names of the parameters. Thus, variable *&qualfile* in the above example corresponds to the EXCCMD command's SRCFILE parameter.

You also must declare each of the variables in the CPP to correspond to the data type and length of the command parameter that it will contain. The same rules apply here as those applicable to passing program parameters. Command parameters of *CHAR, *NAME, and *LGL data types are passed to the command processing program as character strings (*CHAR) of the length defined in the PARM command definition statement. Decimal command parameters (*DEC) are passed to the CPP as packed decimal values of the length specified in the PARM command definition. For the example EXCCMD command, the parameters would be defined as follows:

```
DCL  &mbr       *CHAR 10
DCL  &qualfile  *CHAR 20
DCL  &iferror   *CHAR 7
```

Remember from Chapter 23 that the length of the qualified value, returned to variable *&qualfile*, is the sum of the lengths of the parts of the qualified name, in this case 20 characters:

```
QUAL TYPE(*NAME)  +
     LEN(10) ...
QUAL TYPE(*NAME)  +
     LEN(10) ...
```

If the EXCCMD command had decimal parameters, the declarations in the PARM command definition would also have to match the declarations in the CPP, as the following example illustrates:

In the command definition

```
PARM KWD(AMOUNT)    +
       TYPE(*DEC)     +
       LEN(5 0) ...
```

In the command processing program

```
DCL  &amount        +
       *DEC (5 0)
```

Commands offer more data types than CL supports. How do other data types map into CL? The table in Figure 24.2 shows the command parameter types and the requirements for the matching variable declaration in the CPP.

Figure 24.2
Command Parameter
Correspondence
with CL Declarations

PARM Definition	CL Declaration
TYPE(*CHAR) LEN(x)	TYPE(*CHAR) LEN(x)[1]
TYPE(*CMDSTR) LEN(x)	TYPE(*CHAR) LEN(x)[1]
TYPE(*DATE)	TYPE(*CHAR) LEN(7)
TYPE(*DEC) LEN(x y)	TYPE(*DEC) LEN(x y)
TYPE(*GENERIC) LEN(x)	TYPE(*CHAR) LEN(x)[1]
TYPE(*HEX) LEN(x)	TYPE(*CHAR) LEN(x)
TYPE(*INT2)	TYPE(*CHAR) LEN(2)
TYPE(*INT4)	TYPE(*CHAR) LEN(4)
TYPE(*LGL)	TYPE(*LGL) or TYPE(*CHAR) LEN(1)
TYPE(*NAME) LEN(x)	TYPE(*CHAR) LEN(x)[1]
TYPE(*TIME)	TYPE(*CHAR) LEN(6)

[1] If the declared length in the CL program is less than the length passed by the command, the value will be truncated in the CPP.

While a CL program does not directly support binary numbers, a CPP can receive command parameters of type *INT2 and *INT4 as *CHAR variables either two or four characters long, respectively. You can then use the %BINARY built-in function to convert the values to decimal values. Refer to Chapter 8 for more information about the %BINARY function.

Analyzing the CPP

Once you have ensured that the input parameters of the command processing program match the command parameters that will be passed to it, writing the command processing program is just like writing any other CL (or HLL) program. The command processing program in Figure 24.1 uses many of the techniques we discussed earlier. You should now be able to read the program and understand what it does.

So that you'll understand how the EXCCMD command works, we go through the major sections of the program and explain in detail what each section does.

The program must first define (in the PGM command at line 8) the parameters it will receive from the EXCCMD command. Next come the program variable declarations. The program declares file QGPL/QCLSRC, which is a source file that exists on most AS/400s; we use it in this program at compile time as a model file to provide the record layout for a standard source file. All source files contain three fields: *&srcdta*, which holds the actual source data; *&srcseq*, which holds the sequence number; and *&srcdat*, which holds the last change date for the line. This program uses only the *&srcdta* field, which will contain the commands to be executed. We must, of course, declare the variable for the three input parameters: *&mbr*, *&qualfile*, and *&iferror*. The other variables declared in this section are used as work variables within this program.

At line 38, a global message monitor instructs the program to branch to label ERRTAG1 if an unmonitored error occurs.

To use the qualified file name in the *&qualfile* parameter, we must first break it down into its component pieces, *&file* and *&lib*. The CHGVAR commands at lines 40 and 41 accomplish this. Does the file exist, and does the member exist in the file? The CHKOBJ command at line 43 does an existence check, letting the global message monitor handle the situation if the program cannot find the source. If the source does exist, the program issues an override (at line 44) to point to the source member we want to process.

The logic between lines 46 and 100 is a bit complex, but an overview of the technique may help you understand what's happening here. The main purpose of this section of code is to read a record from the source file (line 52) and move the command into variable *&cmdstr*, a 2,000-character string. By itself, that would be a simple task; but don't forget that commands can span several lines, so this program must check for a continuation character at the right end of the command string. If the continuation character (in variable *&symbol*) exists, the program must read the next source record rather than execute an incomplete command. To accomplish this multiple-line support, the program uses a number of indexes (variables *&cmdidx*, *&lftidx*, and *&rgtidx*) and work variables (*&nxtrcd*, *&test*, and *&len*).

Once the program has a complete command in variable *&cmdstr*, it uses the QCMDEXC API to execute the command (line 103), passing variable *&cmdstr* and the constant *2000* as program parameters. If an error occurs during the execution of the command, the command-level message monitor at line 104 is processed. Within the MONMSG, if the value of the *&iferror* variable is *CANCEL*, the program branches to the same ERRTAG1 label that the global message monitor uses. Otherwise, variable *&errcnt* is incremented and the program branches to read the next command in the source member. If the command completes successfully, variable *&okcnt* is incremented (line 110) and the program branches back for more source records.

Notice the MONMSG at line 53. When the program encounters end-of-file when reading the source record, this MONMSG causes a branch to the EOF label at line 113. The end-of-file error message is removed from the program message queue by the RCVMSG command; eliminating this routine message eliminates possible confusion if the job log is examined for errors.

Next (at lines 115 and 116), the program performs a data type conversion for the *DEC variables &errcnt and &okcnt. These variables count the number of successful and unsuccessful command executions. To use these counts in completion messages, the program uses CHGVAR to move the values into character variables. The code from lines 118 to 133 sends one of two completion messages, then ends the program.

The standard error-handling routine (lines 135 through 170) is similar to some of the ones we looked at in Chapter 16. Because a user will want to get detailed diagnostic messages if an error occurs within a command, the error routine receives all the diagnostic messages in the program message queue and returns them to the calling program. After the error routine has processed through all the diagnostic messages, it re-sends the escape message to the caller and ends the program.

Processing List Parameters in the CPP

Remember from Chapter 23 that you can describe a parameter that accepts a list of values instead of a single value. The easiest kind of list to define is the **simple list**, which allows several values of the same type to be specified for a parameter. You specify a simple list by including the MAX keyword on the command definition statement for the parameter. For example, the following code describes a simple list that accepts the names of from one to five user profiles:

```
PARM KWD(TOUSR)                    +
     TYPE(*NAME)                   +
     LEN(10)                       +
     MIN(1)                        +
     MAX(5)                        +
     PROMPT('Send to users')
```

You specify a simple list's maximum number of elements in the MAX parameter. In the above example, a user could specify five elements. For a simple list, you need not include any other command definition statements.

To process a simple list in a command processing program, you must understand the contents of the parameter that the command sends to the CPP. The parameter consists of each of the elements of the list, preceded by a 2-byte binary number that indicates how many elements are in the list. The command passes only the number of elements that the user specifies. In our example, the passed parameter could be from 12 bytes long (if a user enters one element) to 52 bytes long (if a user enters five elements). So if a user entered the TOUSR parameter as follows,

```
TOUSR(BMEYERS DRIEHL)
```

the command would pass a 22-byte parameter to the command processing program. The contents of the parameter would be

```
BMEYERS    DRIEHL
00CDCECDE444CDCCCD4444
022458592000499585000
```

In the above representation, the top line shows the printable characters in the parameter. The two bottom lines depict the hexadecimal representation of the character (e.g., the character *B* is equivalent to a hex *C2*; hex 40 represents a blank). Notice that the first two bytes of the parameter represent a number: *0002*. This number represents the number of elements passed in the simple list.

If a user were to enter three list elements for the TOUSR parameter, the command would pass a 32-byte parameter to the CPP:

```
BMEYERS    DRIEHL     DBERNARD
00CDCECDE444CDCCCD4444CCCDDCDC44
032458592000499585000042595194400
```

If the user were to specify five list elements, the maximum allowed in this example, the passed parameter would be 52 bytes long.

When you specify fewer than the maximum number of elements in a list parameter, the storage immediately following the last element specified is not part of the list. This results in the command sending a variable-length parameter (from 12 to 52 bytes in our example). This variable parameter length presents a challenge to CL. CL does not directly support binary numbers, nor does it directly support variable-length fields. Fortunately, there is a way to handle simple list parameters in a CL command processing program.

For the simple list in the above example, you would declare a receiver variable 52 characters long (i.e., five elements times 10 characters each plus a 2-byte prefix).

```
DCL  &usrlist  *CHAR 52
```

This declaration would ensure that the longest possible parameter would fit in the receiver variable. But in your CL program, you must be careful to process only the number of elements that are actually part of the list. Otherwise, if the command passes a partial list, you might be processing values that are not intended to be part of the list. For example, if there are other parameters following the TOUSR parameter in our example, and the user specifies only three names in the TOUSR parameter, the value in variable *&usrlist* might be something like the following:

```
BMEYERS    DRIEHL     DBERNARD   TUESDAY PARTIAL BACK
00CDCECDE444CDCCCD4444CCCDDCDC44EECECCE4DCDECCD4CCCD
032458592000499585000042595194003452418071839150213 4
```

The last 20 bytes of the variable are not part of the list.

The command processing program must process the binary number in the first 2 bytes of the parameter to know how many elements in variable *&usrlist* are actually part of the list. To do this, the program could use the %BIN function:

```
DCL      &nbrelem  *DEC (5 0)
CHGVAR   &nbrelem  %BIN(&usrlist 1 2)
```

Variable *&nbrelem* would contain the number of elements in the list. Now that you
know how many elements there are in the list, you must loop through each element
and process each one individually. As you know, CL does not directly support a DO
loop, but you can emulate one, using counter and positioning variables:

```
         DCL    &counter    *DEC (5 0)
         DCL    &position   *DEC (5 0)
         DCL    &usr        *CHAR 10

                  ...


         CHGVAR  &counter 0
LOOP:    CHGVAR  &position (&counter * 10 + 3)
         CHGVAR  &usr %sst(&usrlist &position 10)

         ...(Process &usr variable)

         CHGVAR  &counter (counter + 1)
         IF      (&counter *LT &nbrelem) GOTO LOOP
```

As you can see, even a simple list is complicated for CL to process. Mixed element lists and list-within-a-list parameters require careful thought and even more
complexity. The *CL Programmer's Guide* describes how to handle those situations; the
subject is beyond the scope of this text.

Using QCMDEXC as a CPP

We learned earlier that every command on the AS/400 must have a corresponding
command processing program. But you can create a command without writing a
command processing program. The IBM-supplied QCMDEXC program can be used
as a command processing program under some circumstances. Remember that when
you pass this program a command string and the length of the string, QCMDEXC
processes the command. You can use this program in concert with *hidden command
parameters* to create a command without writing a CPP.

One of the less-used keywords on the PARM command definition statement is
CONSTANT. This parameter lets a command pass hidden parameters (constants) to
your CPP. This is useful when you want the command definition object to send a
parameter to the CPP, but you don't want your users to see or change the parameter. IBM uses this technique, for example, to allow multiple commands to use the
same CPP. For example, the CRTUSRPRF (Create User Profile) and CHGUSRPRF
(Change User Profile) commands both use the same CPP; each command passes a
hidden parameter to the CPP to tell it which function to perform.

You can use the CONSTANT feature to specify parameters to pass to QCMDEXC,
thus using QCMDEXC as a command processing program. For example, if you wanted
to create an "alias" command, DP (Display Printed Reports), you could use the following command definition source:

```
CMD
PARM KWD(CMDSTR)              +
     TYPE(*CHAR)              +
     LEN(7)                   +
     CONSTANT('WRKSPLF')
PARM KWD(CMDLEN)              +
     TYPE(*DEC)               +
     LEN(15 5)                +
     CONSTANT(7)
```

When you compile the command, specify QCMDEXC as the command processing program. Now you would have an abbreviated version of the WRKSPLF (Work with Spooled Files) command. You can include prompting characters in the character string in CMDSTR if you want to invoke the command prompter.

Command parameters that use the CONSTANT attribute are completely hidden from the user; if the prompter is invoked, they are not shown. Because this technique merely mimics an existing command, it does have some limitations. First, it can only be used with commands that already exist on your system. Second, except for the flexibility afforded by the command prompter, you can only pass a constant command string to QCMDEXC; variables are not allowed. Finally, CONSTANT parameters are limited to 32 characters, so longer command strings cannot use this technique.

You can use this technique to execute an IBM-supplied command with different default values than those supplied by IBM. Instead of creating a duplicate of an existing command, you can merely specify the command, with the changed defaults, in the CMDSTR parameter of the user-defined command. This method is less release-dependent than the duplicate command technique discussed in Chapter 20. CPPs may change from release to release, thereby invalidating the duplicate command. Using QCMDEXC as the command processing program for an alias command, on the other hand, usually continues to work from one release to the next, because it specifies the CL command to be executed, not the CPP.

Chapter Summary

The command processing program is the program that runs when a command is executed. You can write a CPP in CL or any HLL, and you can directly call a CPP without using its associated command.

If a parameter is described in a command definition object, it must also be declared and received by the command processing program. The parameters must be received in the order they were defined in the command definition. You must declare each of the variables in the CPP to correspond to the data type and length of the command parameter that it will contain. Command parameter data types that CL does not support are mapped directly to *CHAR type CL variables.

Beyond the requirement that a command processing program must properly receive all the variables that the command passes, there is no difference between a command processing program and any other program.

You specify a simple list command parameter by including the MAX keyword on the command definition statement for the parameter. The parameter that is passed to the CPP consists of each of the elements of the list, preceded by a 2-byte binary number that indicates how many elements are in the list. The command passes only the number of elements that the user specifies. When only a portion of the list is specified in a parameter, the storage immediately following the last element is not part of the parameter. Using CL to process simple list parameters, especially partial lists, is not convenient because CL does not directly support binary numbers or variable length fields.

By using the CONSTANT keyword on the PARM command definition statement, a command can pass parameters to a CPP, but the parameter is hidden from the user. You can use this technique to pass a constant value to a CPP (e.g., to use the same CPP for multiple commands, changing the constant parameter to indicate which command is executing the program).

You can also use CONSTANT parameters with QCMDEXC as a CPP to create alias commands (i.e., duplicates of existing commands with changed defaults).

Terms

command processing program   simple list

Review Questions

1. What is a command processing program? What is the main requirement that must be met for a program to be a command processing program?

2. What are the rules that govern the correspondence between a command parameter and a variable in a command processing program?

3. How would you declare a receiver variable in a command processing program to handle each of the following command definitions?

    a. ```
       PARM   KWD(BKPTYPE) TYPE(*CHAR) LEN(7) RSTD(*YES) VALUES(DAILY WEEKLY MONTHLY) +
              MIN(1)
       ```

    b. ```
       PARM   KWD(BKPTYPE) TYPE(*CHAR) RSTD(*YES) VALUES(DAILY WEEKLY MONTHLY)        +
              MIN(1)
       ```

    c. ```
       PARM   KWD(AMOUNT) TYPE(*DEC) LEN(11 2) DFT(0) REL(*GE 0)
       ```

    d. ```
       PARM   KWD(FILES) TYPE(*NAME) MAX(5)
       ```

    e. ```
       PARM   KWD(OUTPUT) TYPE(*CHAR) LEN(1) RSTD(*YES) DFT(*PRINT)   +
              VALUES(* *PRINT *OUTFILE) SPCVAL((*PRINT P) (*OUTFILE F))
       ```

    f. ```
          PARM   KWD(FILE) TYPE(F1) MIN(1) PROMPT('File name')

       F1: QUAL   TYPE(*NAME)
           QUAL   TYPE(*NAME) DFT(*LIBL) SPCVAL(*LIBL) PROMPT('Library')
       ```

Exercises

1. Create the EXCCMDC command processing program described in this chapter.

2. Use PDM and SEU to create source member EXCCMDTST in QCLSRC. Include the following commands:

    ```
    WRKACTJOB
    ?WRKSPLF
    DISPLAYJOB
    DSPLIB QGPL
    ```

    a. Execute the EXCCMD command, using EXCCMDTST as the source member. Use both options for the IFERROR parameter. What is the difference in the way the command executes with each option?

    b. Execute the EXCCMD command, using a non-existent source file or member. What happens?

3. Using QCMDEXC as a command processing program, create a command, DJ, that prompts and executes the DSPJOB command.

Chapter 25

Advanced Command Facilities

Chapter Overview

In this chapter we discuss various features that make user-defined commands more useful. You learn how to build and attach help windows to a command, and how to write programs that will help ensure a command and its parameters are executed properly.

Adding Help to Your Commands

User-defined commands use the same familiar interface and syntax as IBM-supplied commands, including the command prompter, positional and keyword parameters, and validity checking. In addition, you can create help windows. IBM's commands have comprehensive help screens that guide you through the use of the command well enough that you usually don't need any more documentation to use them effectively. IBM allows you to use the same help interface with your user-defined commands, through a function called the **User Interface Manager** (UIM). All the functions IBM designed into its system help interface, including cursor-sensitive help, extended help, search windows, and hypertext linking, are easy to incorporate into your own custom commands.

IBM defines two types of help displays: contextual and extended. **Contextual help** is cursor sensitive, meaning that the information displayed is specific for a section of the display. For example, if you position the cursor on the "Command error action" parameter of the prompted display for the EXCCMD command from Chapter 23, contextual help would provide instructions for completing the IFERROR parameter. **Extended help** describes the entire command, including all parameters and available function keys; the extended help includes all the contextual help for a command.

The AS/400 implements command help through the use of **help panel groups**. A panel group (object type *PNLGRP) is an AS/400 object similar to a display file. Panel groups are the means by which IBM presents most of the operating system displays you see on the AS/400, including menus, list panels, and help displays. The system displays help text in a windowed section of the display, leaving appropriate portions of the underlying display uncovered. The UIM is the operating system function that displays panel groups and automatically handles window sizing and positioning, scrolling, and screen consistency.

To create help panel groups for your own commands, you need to learn some UIM basics. We work with the EXCCMD user-defined command described in Chapter 23 to show you how to implement help for a command. Once you understand the concepts used in building the help panels for the EXCCMD command, you'll be able to apply the same principles to other user-defined commands.

UIM Tag Language

Creating a panel group is simple enough. You enter UIM source statements into a source file member using SEU type PNLGRP (the member type is PNLGRP and the source file member is usually QPNLSRC). Then you compile the member using the CRTPNLGRP (Create Panel Group) command:

```
CRTPNLGRP PNLGRP(library-name/panel-group-name)      +
          SRCFILE(library-name/source-file-name)     +
          SRCMBR(source-member-name)                 +
          TEXT(descriptive-text)
```

As with any language, UIM source has a unique syntax you must follow to ensure that your panel group works properly. The bulk of the source specifications consists of help text information. To format and identify the text, you use UIM tags, special character sequences that tell the UIM compiler how to treat the marked text. UIM tags always begin with a colon (:) and end with a period (.). Most tags work in pairs (e.g., :HP1. marks the beginning of an underlined phrase and :EHP1. marks the end). Some tags, known as *markup tags*, are used to format, highlight, and organize your help text. For example, :HP1. and :EHP1. are the UIM panel markup tags used to demarcate underlined text. So the UIM statement

```
:HP1.This is underlined text.:EHP1.
```

is displayed in a help panel as

<u>This is underlined text.</u>

Other UIM tags define the text's role on the help screen (e.g., whether the text is a comment or module name or the help text itself). IBM's *Guide to Programming Displays* describes the extensive UIM tag language.

Using UIM to Create a Help Panel

Figure 25.1 shows the UIM code required to create EXCCMDH, which will be the help panel group for the EXCCMD command. Every panel group starts with a :PNLGRP. tag and ends with an :EPNLGRP. tag, which are analogous to the PGM and ENDPGM commands in a CL program. Within a panel group, you may have one or more help modules, identified by a :HELP. tag at the start of each module and an :EHELP. tag at the end (A and B in Figure 25.1).

The first help module defined in Figure 25.1, EXCCMD, contains the extended help for the command. The help module should be named the same as the command. (This is not a UIM requirement, but it is a handy convention to adopt.) So the extended help for the EXCCMD command is named by the following statement:

```
:HELP NAME=EXCCMD.
```

Figure 25.1
UIM Help Source for
EXCCMD User-Defined
Command

```
.* ****************************************************
.*
.*      Panel group - EXCCMDH - Help for EXCCMD command
.*
.* ****************************************************
:PNLGRP.
.* ****************************************************
:HELP NAME=EXCCMD.
:P.
The EXCCMD (Execute commands from source) command
allows you to execute commands stored in a source file member, without
compiling the member into a CL program.
Using this command, you can easily set up procedures to
run commands sequentially, and change the commands that are executed as
your needs change.
:EHELP.
.* ****************************************************
.*
.*      Help for parameter MBR
.*
:HELP NAME='EXCCMD/MBR'.
:XH3.MBR (Member)
:P.
Specifies the name of the member that contains
the commands to be executed.
:P.
This is a required parameter.
:EHELP.
.* ****************************************************
.*
.*      Help for parameter SRCFILE
.*
:HELP NAME='EXCCMD/SRCFILE'.
:XH3.SRCFILE (Source file name)
:P.
Specifies the qualified name of the source file that
contains the commands to be executed.
:P.
This is an optional parameter.
:P.
The possible values are:
:PARML.
:PT DEF.QCLSRC
:PD.
The commands are located in a member in file QCLSRC.
:PT.Name
:PD.
Specifies the name of the source file containing
the commands to be executed.
:EPARML.
:XH3.Library
:P.
Specifies the library containing the source file with
the commands to be executed.
:P.
The possible values are:
:PARML.
:PT DEF.*LIBL
```

Ⓐ (next to `:HELP NAME=EXCCMD.`)
Ⓑ (next to `:EHELP.`)

Continued

Figure 25.1
continued

```
:PD.
The library is in the job's library list.
:PT.Name
:PD.
Names the library containing the source file with
the commands to be executed.
:EPARML.
:EHELP.
.* ****************************************************
.*
.*       Help for parameter IFERROR
.*
:HELP NAME='EXCCMD/IFERROR'.
:XH3.IFERROR (Command error action)
:P.
Indicates the action to take if one or more of the commands in the
source file end in error.
:P.
This is an optional parameter.
:P.
The possible values are:
:PARML.
:PT DEF.*CANCEL
:PD.
If any of the commands in the source file end in error,
the procedure will be cancelled; subsequent commands will not be exe-
cuted.
:PT.*IGNORE
:PD.
If any of the commands in the source file end in error,
the error will be ignored; subsequent commands will continue to be exe-
cuted.
:EPARML.
:EHELP.
.* ****************************************************
:EPNLGRP.
```

Figure 25.2 shows the extended help window. This is the overall help that appears when a user working with the command prompter positions the cursor on a word other than one of the parameters, then presses the Help key. It is also the extended help a user gets when (s)he presses F2=Extended help while displaying cursor-sensitive, contextual help.

Each *:P.* markup tag identifies the beginning of a new paragraph, which is separated from the others in the help window by a blank line. UIM automatically formats all lines within a paragraph to fit into the window. For example, the source lines

```
:P.This is
a sample line
of help text.
```

might appear as

```
This is a sample line of help text.
```

depending upon the width of the window. UIM also automatically wraps lines to

Figure 25.2
Extended Help Window

```
                    Execute Commands from Source (EXCCMD)
..............................................................................
:                      Execute Commands from Source                          :
:                                                                            :
:   The EXCCMD (Execute commands from source) command allows you to          :
:   execute commands stored in a source file member, without                 :
:   compiling the member into a CL source program.  Using this command,      :
:   you can easily set up procedures to run commands sequentially, and       :
:   change the commands that are executed as your needs change.              :
:                                                                            :
:  MBR (Member)                                                              :
:                                                                            :
:   Specifies the name of the member which contains the commands to be       :
:   executed.                                                                :
:                                                                            :
:   This is a required parameter.                                            :
:                                                                            :
:  SRCFILE (Source file name)                                                :
:                                                                            :
:                                                                 More ...   :
:  F3=Exit help    F10=Move to top    F12=Vancel   F13=User support          :
:  F14=Print help                                                            :
..............................................................................
```

accommodate narrow windows. Note that comment lines, which do not appear in the compiled panel group, are indicated by .* in columns 1 and 2 of the source.

In addition to extended help, you should create contextual help for each command parameter. Figures 25.3a and 25.3b illustrate a contextual help window for the IFERROR parameter of our EXCCMD command. UIM formats the contextual help within a window, automatically giving it a size and location that usually does not cover the original parameter on the underlying screen. The help module *EXCCMD/IFERROR* in Figure 25.1 contains the specific help text for the IFERROR parameter. You link the help modules to their parameters by using the following syntax in your panel group source code:

```
:HELP NAME='command-name/parameter-name'.
```

The help name is a qualified name consisting of the command name (help identifier) and the parameter name. The help identifier must be identical to the command name (or the name of the extended help module), and the parameter name in the help module must match the parameter name in the command. Note that because we are specifying a qualified name, we must enclose the name in single quotes; in addition, a period is required at the end of the statement.

Now you've learned the basics of creating help screens for user-defined commands. To summarize, the UIM source for command help usually follows this sequence:

```
:PNLGRP.
:HELP NAME='command-name'.
:P.Extended help for command
:EHELP.
:HELP NAME='command-name/parameter-name'.
:P.Contextual help for parameter
:EHELP.
:EPNLGRP.
```

Figure 25.3a
Contextual Help
Window

```
                        Execute Commands from Source (EXCCMD)

 Type choices, press Enter.

 Member . . . . . . . . . . . . .      _____      Name
 Source file name . . . . . . .        QCLSRC        Name
   Library name . . . . . . . .        *LIBL         Name, *LIBL
 Command error action . . . . . .      *CANCEL       *CANCEL, *IGNORE
                     ..............................................................
                     :                              Help                          :
                     :                                                            :
                     :   Indicates the action taken if one or more of the commands :
                     :   in the source file end in error.                          :
                     :                                                            :
                     :   This is an optional parameter.                            :
                     :                                                            :
                     :   The possible values are:                                  :
                     :                                                            :
                     :   *CANCEL                                                   :
                     :                                                More...      :
                     :   F2=Extended help   F10=Move to top    F12=Cancel          :
 F3=Exit   F4=    :   F13=User support   F20=Enlarge       F24=More keys        :
 F24=More keys :                                                               :
                     :..............................................................:
```

Figure 25.3b
Contextual Help
Window After
Pressing Page Down

```
                        Execute Commands from Source (EXCCMD)

 Type choices, press Enter.

 Member . . . . . . . . . . . . .      _____      Name
 Source file name . . . . . . .        QCLSRC        Name
   Library name . . . . . . . .        *LIBL         Name, *LIBL
 Command error action . . . . . .      *CANCEL       *CANCEL, *IGNORE
                 ..............................................................
                 :                              Help                          :
                 :                                                            :
                 :      If any of the commands in the source file end in      :
                 :      error, the procedure will be cancelled; subsequent    :
                 :      commands will not be executed.                        :
                 :                                                            :
                 :   *IGNORE                                                  :
                 :      If any of the commands in the source file end in      :
                 :      error, the error will be ignored; subsequent commands :
                 :      will continue to be executed.                         :
                 :                                                Bottom      :
                 :   F2=Extended help   F10=Move to top    F12=Cancel         :
 F3=Exit   F4= :   F13=User support   F20=Enlarge       F24=More keys       :
 F24=More keys :                                                             :
                 :..............................................................:
```

Formatting UIM Help Text

In addition to sizing and locating windows automatically, UIM helps consistently format and present the help text using special markup tags. We've already touched on the *:HP1.* underlining tag and the *:P.* paragraph tag, but many more tags are available.

There are special tags for various headings and titles. For example, the :XH. tags identify extended headings, which appear as a subheading in the extended help window and as a title within the parameter's contextual help window. The four extended heading tags are

XH1.   indicates centered text, underlining, and boldfaced type

XH2.   indicates left justification, underlining, and boldfaced type

XH3.   indicates left justification and boldfaced type

XH4.   indicates left justification and underlining

The extended heading tags enforce consistency in the way text is formatted on the screen.

The :PARML. and :EPARML. tags identify parameter lists so that the system can automatically format them correctly. For example, the EXCCMD/SRCFILE and EXCCMD/IFERROR help modules in Figure 25.1 each contain a list of parameter values between the :PARML. and :EPARML. tags. This list describes the valid values for the EXCCMD command's SRCFILE and IFERROR parameters. You precede each value on the list with a :PT. (parameter term) tag or :PT DEF. (default parameter term) tag, so that each value will be boldfaced on the screen. You also describe each value with a paragraph, starting with a :PD. (parameter description) tag, and include additional paragraphs, as necessary, using the :P. tag.

Associating a Panel Group with a Command

After you have entered the help panel group source in the source member, you compile it using the CRTPNLGRP (Create Panel Group) command. At that point, you need to associate the panel group with the command for which it will provide the help.

When you create a command that uses help text (in this case, the EXCCMD command), you specify the panel group name in the HLPPNLGRP parameter of the CRTCMD command and indicate the name of the extended help module in the HLPID parameter. So to create the EXCCMD command, you would use the following command:

```
CRTCMD      CMD(EXCCMD)                              +
            PGM(EXCCMDC)                             +
            ALLOW(*INTERACT *BPGM *IPGM)             +
            HLPPNLGRP(EXXCCMDH)                      +
            HLPID(EXCCMDH)                           +
            TEXT('Execute commands from source')
```

You also could use the CHGCMD (Change Command) command to change the help text.

Validity Checking Programs

In the command processing program (CPP) for the EXCCMD command, one of the first things we did was to make sure the source file and member existed in the specified library. If the CPP could not find the objects it needed to run, the default error-handler in the CPP would take over, sending an error message and aborting the program. While it is always desirable to perform such validity checking in the CPP, you can check the validity of command parameters before the command even executes by using a **validity checking program** (VCP). If you use a VCP to check the validity of command parameters, you can give the user feedback earlier, while the command prompter is still displayed; in addition, you can do more detailed validity checking than might be available through the checking facilities built into the command definition.

A VCP is not required. The sole purpose of a VCP is to ensure that the parameters in a command are valid before control passes to the CPP, and to prevent execution if an error occurs when entering the command. You specify the name of the VCP when you create the command

```
CRTCMD     ...     VLDCKR(library-name/program-name)
```

The VCP does not have to exist when you create the command.

A VCP receives the command parameters before the CPP. It has the same basic requirement as the CPP (i.e., it must receive the parameters in the same order and with the same attributes that the command will pass). In addition, the VCP must send messages to the command indicating any errors that it finds. There are several rules regarding these messages:

- The VCP should send *DIAG messages if it detects errors in the command parameters.
- The first four characters of the message data for any *DIAG messages sent by a VCP are reserved for the system.
- The fourth byte of the diagnostic message data should never be blank. Usually, you will specify *0000* as the first 4 bytes of the *DIAG message data.
- After the VCP has sent all its diagnostic messages, it must send *ESCAPE message CPF0002.

Figure 25.4, which is a VCP that might be used for our EXCCMD command, illustrates how these requirements work. This program checks for the existence of the source file and member that are to contain the commands to be executed.

As you can see, some of the code in Figure 25.4 (lines 16 through 19) follows the same logic as the object existence portion (lines 40 through 43) of the CPP for the EXCCMD command. It simply checks for the existence of the source file and member and returns a diagnostic error message if the existence check fails. The program uses message CPD0006, which is a special diagnostic message that IBM provides specifically for validity checking programs.

The routine beginning at line 22 is the global error-handler for the program. It receives the last message (i.e., the escape message that caused the CHKOBJ command to fail) and places the message text in variable *&msg*. Then at line 26 the program

Figure 25.4
Validity Checking
Program

```
0001.00 /* ******************************************************************* */
0002.00 /*                                                                     */
0003.00 /*      Program name - EXCCMDV - Validity checker for EXCCMD command */
0004.00 /*                                                                     */
0005.00 /* ******************************************************************* */
0006.00             PGM          PARM(&mbr &qualfile &iferror)
0007.00
0008.00             DCL          &mbr       *CHAR 10
0009.00             DCL          &qualfile *CHAR 20
0010.00             DCL          &iferror  *CHAR 7
0011.00
0012.00             DCL          &msg       *CHAR 80
0013.00
0014.00             MONMSG       CPF0000 EXEC(GOTO ERRTAG1)
0015.00
0016.00             CHGVAR       &file %SST(&qualfile 1 10)
0017.00             CHGVAR       &lib  %SST(&qualfile 11 10)
0018.00
0019.00             CHKOBJ       OBJ(&lib/&file) OBJTYPE(*FILE) MBR(&mbr)
0020.00             RETURN
0021.00
0022.00 ERRTAG1:    RCVMSG       MSGTYPE(*LAST)              +
0023.00                          MSG(&msg)
0024.00             MONMSG       CPF0000
0025.00
0026.00             CHGVAR       &msg ('0000' *CAT &msg)
0025.00
0026.00             SNDPGMMSG    MSGID(CPD0006)             +
0027.00                          MSGF(QCPFMSG)              +
0028.00                          MSGDTA(&msg)               +
0029.00                          MSGTYPE(*DIAG)
0030.00             MONMSG       CPF0000
0031.00
0032.00             SNDPGMMSG    MSGID(CPF0002)             +
0033.00                          MSGF(QCPFMSG)              +
0034.00                          MSGTYPE(*ESCAPE)
0035.00             MONMSG       CPF0000
0036.00
0037.00             ENDPGM
```

concatenates the character string *0000* with the message text, thus reserving the first 4 bytes for the system, as required. The SNDPGMMSG command at line 26 uses the special message CPD0006 to send the error message back to the command as a diagnostic message. Finally, as required for all VCPs, it sends escape message CPF0002 and ends.

The net result of this VCP is that you can determine immediately whether the source file and member exist. If they do not, you know even before the CPP executes.

Although we have used a VCP to check for the existence of an object, you should be aware that using a VCP to check for object existence may not always be appropriate. A VCP will *always* run whenever you type a command, even if you are not going to execute it immediately. For example, if you use QCMDCHK to check the syntax of a command, then store the command for later execution, you would probably not use a VCP to check for the existence of a needed object. If you do, the object must exist when you type the command, even if you don't really need the object until you execute the command. Even if you were to use SEU to enter the command into a source file, the VCP would run. If the object did not exist, you would not be able to store the command in the source file, even if it were otherwise correct. For most object existence tests, the CPP is probably sufficient; then the object need not exist until you actually execute the command.

Other Advanced Command Topics

In addition to validity checking programs, user-defined commands support a few other types of programs that can make the command facility easier to use. These programs are

- Prompt override programs
- Prompt choice programs
- Prompt control programs

Because these programs are not widely needed when you create user-defined commands, we discuss them only briefly. The IBM *CL Programmer's Guide* explains in detail how to implement each of these features.

A *prompt override program* allows the command prompter to display current values instead of defaults when a command is invoked. For example, the CHGJOB command has a number of parameters that default to the value *SAME*, indicating that the job attribute should not be changed. The prompt override program associated with the CHGJOB command lets you see the current value of the job attribute when you prompt for the CHGJOB command, instead of seeing only *SAME for each attribute. IBM provides prompt override programs for nearly every appropriate command, and you can also write them for your user-defined commands. You specify the name of the prompt override program associated with a command when you create the command:

```
CRTCMD    ...    PMTOVRPGM(library-name/program-name)
```

A *prompt choice program* allows you some flexibility in presenting choices to the user when (s)he prompts for a user-defined command. The choices can be displayed in a 30-character string to the right of the parameter input field on the screen, or if the user presses F4, more choices will be shown on a full-screen display. Usually, the default choice text is sufficient; there may be times, however, when you need to write a prompt choice program to display the choices. This need may occur, for example, if the possible choices are stored in a data file that can be easily and frequently updated. Using a prompt choice program prevents you from having to re-create the command every time the possible choices change. The prompt choice program is usually specified in the PARM or QUAL command definition statement for a parameter; to attach a choice program to a parameter, you specify CHOICE(*PGM), then CHOICPGM(library-name/program-name).

A *prompt control program* lets you perform additional processing to condition parameter prompting for a command when the normal command definition statements won't satisfy your needs. Prompt control programs are used in connection with the PMTCTL command definition statement and the PMTCTLPGM keyword of the PARM statement. The need for prompt control programs is rare.

Chapter Summary

The User Interface Manager (UIM) lets you use the same help interface with your user-defined commands that IBM uses with its commands. UIM supports two types of windowed help displays for commands: contextual and extended. Contextual help is cursor sensitive for a specific parameter, while extended help describes the entire command. UIM uses panel groups to display help screens; a panel group is an object similar to a display file.

The CRTPNLGRP (Create Panel Group) command creates panel groups from UIM source in a source file member. UIM source is mostly the help text itself, but it also contains special character sequences called UIM tags. Markup tags are used to format, highlight, and organize your text. The UIM source for command help usually follows this sequence:

```
:PNLGRP.
:HELP NAME='command-name'.
:P.Extended help for command
:EHELP.
:HELP NAME='command-name/parameter-name'.
:P.Contextual help for parameter
:EHELP.
:EPNLGRP.
```

When you create a command with the CRTCMD (Create Command) command, you specify the help panel group to use with the command.

Validity checking programs (VCPs) allow you to expand on the validity checking capabilities built into user-defined commands. You can use a validity checking program to determine some command errors, such as object existence errors, before the command processing program (CPP) even starts. The VCP, like the CPP, must receive all the parameters from the command. In addition, it must send diagnostic messages to the command if it finds an error; these diagnostic messages must conform to a specific format. Finally, the VCP must send escape message CPF0002 if it finds any errors.

Other programs that help make commands easier to use include prompt override programs, prompt choice programs, and prompt control programs. But these specialty programs are not often needed.

Terms

contextual help   help panel groups
extended help   User Interface Manager

Review Questions

1. Explain the difference between contextual help and extended help.

2. What are panel groups? What is the name of the facility through which the AS/400 supports panel groups?

3. Explain the purpose of a validity checking program. Why would you use one? What are the special requirements of a validity checking program?

Exercises

1. Create the EXCCMDH panel group discussed in this chapter.

2. Create the EXCCMDV validity checking program described in this chapter.

3. Change the EXCCMD command to attach the help panel group and validity checking program.

   a. Execute the command using the EXCCMDTST member from Chapter 24. Use the help facility.

   b. Execute the command using a nonexistent source file or member. Describe the way the validity checking program affects parameter errors.

Appendix A

The Most-Often-Used CL Commands

This appendix serves as a condensed reference to the CL commands used most often in CL programs. While not an exhaustive reference, the appendix includes the CL commands that are most likely to appear within a CL program. The entry for each command includes the following information:

- Brief command description
- Syntax template for most-often-used parameters
- Brief descriptions of most-often-used parameters
- Error messages that can be monitored
- File used, if any

Each command includes a syntax template for the most-often-used parameters and, if necessary, alternative syntax templates. Each template uses the following typographical conventions to indicate attributes of the parameter:

- Positional parameters are *italicized*.
- Required parameters are in **bold type**.
- Default parameter values are <u>underlined</u>.
- Multiple allowable values, including special values, are separated by a vertical bar (I).
- If the syntax template does not include all the parameters for a command, the template ends in ellipses (…).

Error Messages That Can Be Monitored By All Commands

CPF0001	Error found on command.
CPF0010	Command is not supported.
CPF0011	Error detected by prompt override program.
CPF9803	Cannot allocate object.
CPF9805	Object destroyed.
CPF9807	One or more libraries in library list deleted.
CPF9808	Cannot allocate one or more libraries on library list.
CPF9810	Library not found.
CPF9830	Cannot assign library.
CPF9845	Error occurred while opening file.
CPF9846	Error while processing file.
CPF9871	Error occurred while processing.
CPF9901	Request check. Unmonitored message.
CPF9999	Function check. Unmonitored message.

ADDLFM (Add Logical File Member)

Adds a member to an existing logical file.

Syntax

ADDLFM	FILE(*library-name/logical-file-name*)	+
	MBR(*logical-file-member-name*)	+
	DTAMBRS(library-name/physical-file-name	+
	member-name)	+
	SHARE(**NO*|*YES)	+
	TEXT('description')	

Parameters

FILE	Logical file name
	Library: name, **LIBL*, *CURLIB
MBR	Logical file member
DTAMBRS	List of physical file data members
	Physical file: name, **ALL*
	Library: name, *CURRENT
	List of member names: name, *NONE
SHARE	Share open data path: **NO*, *YES
TEXT	Text: description, **BLANK*

Error Messages That Can Be Monitored

| CPF3204 | Cannot find object needed for file. |
| CPF7306 | Member not added. |

Files Used

(None)

ADDLIBLE (Add Library List Entry)

Adds a library name to the user portion of the library list for the process in which the command was entered.

Syntax

| ADDLIBLE | LIB(*library-name*) | + |
| | POSITION(**FIRST*|**LAST*) | |

Alternative Syntax

ADDLIBLE	LIB(*library-name*)	+
	POSITION(*AFTER|*BEFORE|**REPLACE*	+
	reference-library-name)	

Parameters

LIB	Library name
POSITION	Library list position: **FIRST*, *LAST, *AFTER, *BEFORE, *REPLACE
	Reference library name used with *AFTER, *BEFORE, *REPLACE

Error Messages That Can Be Monitored

CPF2103	Library already exists in library list.
CPF2106	Library list not changed.
CPF2110	Library not found.
CPF2113	Cannot allocate library.
CPF2118	Library not added.
CPF2176	Library damaged.
CPF2182	Not authorized to library.

Files Used

(None)

ADDMSGD (Add Message Description)

Describes a message and adds the description to a message file.

Syntax

ADDMSGD	*MSGID(message-identifier)*	+
	MSGF(library-name/message-file-name)	+
	MSG('message-text')	+
	SECLVL('second-level-message-text')	+
	SEV(severity-code)	
	. . .	

Parameters

MSGID	Message identifier
MSGF	Message file name
	Library: name, *LIBL, *CURLIB
MSG	First-level message text
SECLVL	Second-level message: text, *NONE
SEV	Severity code: 00–99

Error Messages That Can Be Monitored

CPF2401	Not authorized to library.
CPF2407	Message file not found.
CPF2411	Not authorized to message file.
CPF2412	Message ID already exists in message file.
CPF2430	Message description not added to message file
CPF2461	Message file could not be extended.
CPF2483	Message file currently in use.
CPF2510	Message file logically damaged.

Files Used

(None)

ADDPFM (Add Physical File Member)

Adds a member to an existing physical file.

Syntax

ADDPFM	*FILE(library-name/physical-file-name)*	+
	MBR(physical-file-member-name)	+
	SHARE(*NO|*YES)	+
	TEXT('description')	
	. . .	

Parameters

FILE	Physical file name
	Library: name, *LIBL, *CURLIB
MBR	Physical file member name
SHARE	Share open data path: *NO, *YES
TEXT	Text: description, *BLANK

Error Messages That Can Be Monitored

CPF3204	Cannot find object needed for file.
CPF7306	Member not added.

Files Used

(None)

ALCOBJ (Allocate Object)

Reserves an object or list of objects for later use by the job.

Syntax

ALCOBJ	*OBJ(library-name/object-name*	+
	object-type	+
	lock-state	+
	member-name)	+
	WAIT(seconds-to-wait)	

Parameters

OBJ   Object name
                Library: name, <u>*LIBL</u>, *CURLIB
                Object type: *DEV, *DTAARA, *DTAQ, *FILE, *LIB, *MENU, *MSGQ,
                    *PGM, *PNLGRP, *SBSD, *USRSPC, ...
                Lock state: *SHRRD, *SHRNUP, *SHRUPD, *EXCLRD, *EXCL
                Member name, if database file: name, <u>*FIRST</u>

WAIT   Time to wait, in seconds: seconds, <u>*CLS</u>

Error Messages That Can Be Monitored

CPF1002	Cannot allocate objects.
CPF1040	Maximum number of objects allocated on system.
CPF1085	Objects not allocated.

Files Used

(None)

CALL (Call Program)

Calls a program, passing control to it. CALL can also pass parameters to the called program.

Syntax

CALL	*PGM(library-name/program-name)*	+
	PARM(parameter-values)	

Parameters

PGM   Name of program to call
                Library: name, <u>*LIBL</u>, *CURLIB
PARM   List of program parameters

Error Messages That Can Be Monitored

CPD0783	Variable must be TYPE(*DEC)
CPF0005	Returned command string exceeds variable provided length
CPF0006	Errors occurred in command
CPF0805	Error found when program started
CPF0806	Error found when procedure started

Files Used

(None)

CALLPRC (Call Bound Procedure)

Calls a bound ILE procedure, passing control to it. CALLPRC can also pass parameters to the called procedure, and receive a return variable back from the called procedure.

Syntax

CALLPRC	*PRC(procedure-name)*	+
	PARM(parameter values)	+
	RTNVAL(return-variable-name)	

Parameters

PRC	Name of bound ILE procedure to call
PARM	List of procedure parameters
RTNVAL	Name of variable to receive return value: variable, <u>*NONE</u>

Error Messages That Can Be Monitored

CPF0806	Error found when procedure started

Files Used

(None)

CHGDTAARA (Change Data Area)

Changes the value of a data area. The data area can be a data area stored in a library, the local data area, the group data area or the program initialization parameter data area.

Syntax

CHGDTAARA	*DTAARA(data-area-name*	+
	(substring-starting-position	+
	substring-length))	+
	VALUE(new-value)	

Parameters

DTAARA	Data area: name, *LDA, *GDA, *PDA
	Library: name, <u>*LIBL</u>, *CURLIB
	Substring starting position: 1–2000, <u>*ALL</u>
	Substring length: 1–2000 (Not used with *ALL)
VALUE	New value for data area

Error Messages That Can Be Monitored

CPF1015	Data area not found.
CPF1018	No authority to change data area.
CPF1019	VALUE parameter not correct.
CPF1020	VALUE parameter too long.
CPF1021	Library not found for data area.
CPF1022	No authority to data area.
CPF1026	VALUE parameter must be '0' or '1'.
CPF1043	Boundary alignment for data area not valid.
CPF1044	AREA parameter not valid for data area.
CPF1045	CPYPTR parameter not valid for data area.
CPF1046	DTAARA(*GDA) not valid because job not group job.
CPF1062	Null string not valid as character value.
CPF1063	Cannot allocate data area.
CPF1067	Cannot allocate library.
CPF1072	DTAARA(*PDA) not valid because job not prestart job.
CPF1087	Substring not allowed for decimal or logical data area.
CPF1088	Starting position outside of data area.
CPF1089	Substring specified for data area not valid.
CPF1138	VALUE parameter not valid type for data area.
CPF1155	VALUE parameter too long for data area.
CPF1162	Boundary alignment for data area not valid.
CPF1163	AREA parameter not valid for data area.
CPF1168	CPYPTR parameter not valid for data area.
CPF1170	Starting position outside of data area.
CPF1192	Substring specified for data area not valid.

Files Used

(None)

CHGJOB (Change Job)

Changes some of the attributes of a job (e.g., its job queue, printer device, output queue, and priority). The job can be on a queue or it can be active.

Syntax

CHGJOB	JOB(*job-number/user-name/job-name*)	+
	JOBQ(library-name/job-queue-name)	+
	JOBPTY(scheduling-priority)	+
	OUTPTY(output-priority)	+
	PRTTXT('print-text')	+
	LOG(message-level	+
	message-severity	+
	logging-level)	+
	LOGCLPGM(*SAME|*YES|*NO)	+
	PRTDEV(printer-device-name)	+
	OUTQ(library-name/output-queue-name)	+
	SCDDATE(date)	+
	SCDTIME(time)	+
	DATE(date)	+
	RUNPTY(machine-running-priority)	
	. . .	

Parameters

JOB	Job: name, *
	User name
	Job number: 000000–999999
JOBQ	Job queue: name, *SAME
	Library: name, *LIBL, *CURLIB
JOBPTY	Job scheduling priority on job queue: 0–9, *SAME
OUTPTY	Output priority on output queue: 1–9, *SAME
PRTTXT	Print text: text, *SAME, *SYSVAL, *BLANK
LOG	Message logging level: 0–4, *SAME
	Message severity: 00–99, *SAME
	Message text level: *SAME, *MSG, *SECLVL, *NOLIST
LOGCLPGM	Log CL program commands: *SAME, *YES, *NO
PRTDEV	Printer device: name, *SAME, *USRPRF, *SYSVAL, *WRKSTN
OUTQ	Output queue: name, *SAME, *USRPRF, *DEV, *WRKSTN
	Library: name, *LIBL, *CURLIB
SCDDATE	Scheduled date: date, *SAME, *CURRENT, *MONTHSTR,
	*MONTHEND, *MON, *TUE, *WED, *THU, *FRI, *SAT
SCDTIME	Scheduled time: time, *SAME, *CURRENT
DATE	Job date: date, *SAME
RUNPTY	Job execution priority: 1 99, *SAME

Error Messages That Can Be Monitored

CPF1317	No response from subsystem.
CPF1321	Job not found.
CPF1332	End of duplicate job names.
CPF1334	BRKMSG(*NOTIFY) only valid for interactive jobs.
CPF1336	Errors on CHGJOB command.
CPF1337	Not authorized to change parameters.
CPF1340	Job control function not performed.
CPF1341	Reader or writer not allowed as job name.
CPF1343	Invalid job type for function.
CPF1344	Not authorized to control job.
CPF1351	Function check occurred in subsystem for job.
CPF1352	Function not done. Job in transition condition.
CPF1634	Specified date or time has passed.

CPF1635	Requested change no longer allowed.
CPF1642	Schedule date not correct.
CPF1644	Scheduled date and time not changed.
CPF1650	Both scheduled date and time must be changed.
CPF1846	CHGJOB did not complete. System value not available.
CPF1854	Value for CCSID parameter not valid.

Files Used

(None)

CHGMSGD (Change Message Description)

Changes an existing message description in a message file.

Syntax

CHGMSGD	*MSGID(message-identifier)*	+
	MSGF(library-name/message-file-name)	+
	MSG('message-text')	+
	SECLVL('second-level-message-text')	+
	SEV(severity-code)	
	. . .	

Parameters

MSGID	Message identifier
MSGF	Message file name
	Library: name, *LIBL, *CURLIB
MSG	First-level message: text, *SAME
SECLVL	Second-level message: text, *SAME, *NONE
SEV	Severity code: 00–99, *SAME

Error Messages That Can Be Monitored

CPF2401	Not authorized to library.
CPF2407	Message file not found.
CPF2411	Not authorized to message file.
CPF2419	Message identifier not found in message file.
CPF2461	Message file could not be extended.
CPF2483	Message file currently in use.
CPF2499	Message identifier not allowed.
CPF2510	Message file logically damaged.
CPF2542	Message description not changed.

Files Used

(None)

CHGMSGQ (Change Message Queue)

Changes the attributes of a message queue, most notably its delivery mode.

Syntax

CHGMSGQ	*MSGQ(library-name/message-queue-name)*	+
	DLVRY(delivery-mode)	+
	PGM(library-name/program-name)	+
	SEV(severity-code)	+
	*RESET(*NO|*YES)*	+
	TEXT('description')	

Parameters

| MSGQ | Message queue: name, *USRPRF, *WRKSTN |
| | Library: name, *LIBL, *CURLIB |

DLVRY	Method of message delivery: *SAME, *HOLD, *BREAK, *NOTIFY, *DFT
PGM	Break handling program: name, *SAME, *DSPMSG
	Library: name, *LIBL, *CURLIB
SEV	Severity code filter: 00–99, *SAME
RESET	Reset old messages: *NO, *YES
TEXT	Text: description, *SAME, *BLANK

Error Messages That Can Be Monitored

CPF2401	Not authorized to library.
CPF2403	Message queue not found.
CPF2406	Not authorized to break program for message queue.
CPF2408	Not authorized to message queue.
CPF2437	MSGQ(*WRKSTN) not allowed unless done interactively.
CPF2446	Delivery mode specified not valid for system log message queue.
CPF2450	Workstation message queue not allocated to job.
CPF2451	Message queue is allocated to another job.
CPF2470	Message queue not found.
CPF2477	Message queue currently in use.
CPF2485	Number of parameters for break program not valid.
CPF2507	MODE(*NOTIFY) not allowed in batch mode.
CPF2534	MSGQ(*USRPRF) specified and no message queue with user profile.
CPF8127	Damage on message queue.
CPF8176	Message queue for device description damaged.
CPF8198	Damaged object found.

Files Used

(None)

CHGSPLFA (Change Spooled File Attributes)

Changes the attributes of a spooled file on an output queue (e.g., the printer device or output queue). The changes affect only the copy of the file currently on an output queue, not the printer file itself.

Syntax

CHGSPLFA	FILE(spooled-file-name)	+
	JOB(job-number/user-name/job-name)	+
	SPLNBR(spooled-file-number)	+
	DEV(device-name)	+
	PRTSEQ(*SAME|*NEXT)	+
	OUTQ(output-queue-name)	+
	FORMTYPE(form-type)	+
	COPIES(number-of-copies)	+
	SCHEDULE(*SAME|*JOBEND|*FILEEND|*IMMED)	+
	SAVE(*SAME|*NO|*YES)	+
	OUTPTY(output-priority)	
	. . .	

Parameters

FILE	Spooled file: name, *SELECT
JOB	Job: name, *
	User name
	Job number: 000000–999999
SPLNBR	Spooled file number: 1–9999, *ONLY, *LAST
DEV	Printer device: name, *SAME, *OUTQ
PRTSEQ	Print sequence: *SAME, *NEXT
OUTQ	Output queue: name, *SAME, *DEV
	Library: name, *LIBL, *CURLIB

FORMTYPE	Form type: name, *SAME, *STD
COPIES	Number of copies: 1–255, *SAME
SCHEDULE	When file becomes available to print: *SAME, *JOBEND, *FILEEND, *IMMED
SAVE	Save file after printing: *SAME, *NO, *YES
OUTPTY	Output priority on output queue: 1–9, *SAME, *JOB

Error Messages That Can Be Monitored

CPF2207	Not authorized to use object.
CPF3303	File not found in job.
CPF3309	No named files are active.
CPF3330	Necessary resource not available.
CPF3335	File attributes not changed.
CPF3340	More than one file with specified name found in job.
CPF3341	File attributes not changed.
CPF3342	Job not found.
CPF3343	Duplicate job names found.
CPF3344	File no longer in the system.
CPF33C6	Priority required to move file exceeds user's limit.
CPF33C7	Cannot move file ahead of other users' files.
CPF33D0	Printer does not exist.
CPF33D1	User does not exist.
CPF33F0	Not authorized to move spooled file.
CPF3401	Cannot change COPIES for files in PRT status.
CPF3464	Not authorized to output queue for device.
CPF3492	Not authorized to spooled file.

Files Used

(None)

CHGSYSVAL (Change System Value)

Changes the current value of a system value (e.g., the system date and time).

Syntax

CHGSYSVAL	*SYSVAL(system-value-name)*	+
	VALUE(new-value)	

Parameters

SYSVAL	System value name: QATNPGM, QDATE, QPRTDEV, QPRTTXT,QSTRUPPGM, QSYSLIBL, QTIME, QUSRLIBL, ...
VALUE	New value

Error Messages That Can Be Monitored

CPF1001	Wait time expired for system response.
CPF1028	Invalid parameter SYSVAL.
CPF1030	System value cannot be changed.
CPF1058	VALUE parameter not correct.
CPF1059	Length of value not correct.
CPF1074	SYSVAL(QMONTH) not valid for Julian date format.
CPF1076	Specified value not allowed.
CPF1078	System value not changed.
CPF1079	Too many or too few values listed.
CPF1127	Device specified for QPRTDEV not printer device.
CPF1132	Specified name not valid.
CPF1203	Keyboard identifier not correct.
CPF1830	Specified values not valid.
CPF1831	User not authorized to change system value.
CPF1832	Cannot change system value during IPL.

CPF1842	Cannot access system value.
CPF1852	System value not changed.
CPF1856	Filter type not correct for system value.
CPF1857	Specified value not a code font.
CPF268D	Unable to access system value.

Files Used

(None)

CHGVAR (Change Variable)

Changes the value of a variable in a CL program.

Syntax

| *CHGVAR* | *VAR(&CL-variable-name)* | + |
| | *VALUE(expression)* | |

Parameters

| VAR | Variable name (preceded by &) |
| VALUE | Expression used to change the value of the variable |

Error Messages That Can Be Monitored

| CPF0816 | %SWITCH mask not valid. |

Files Used

(None)

CHKOBJ (Check Object)

Verifies an object's existence and a user's authority to the object.

Syntax

CHKOBJ	*OBJ(library-name/object-name)*	+
	OBJTYPE(object-type)	+
	MBR(database-file-member-name)	+
	AUT(authority)	

Parameters

OBJ	Object name
	Library: name, *LIBL, *CURLIB
OBJTYPE	Object type: *DEV, *DTAARA, *DTAQ, *FILE, *LIB, *MENU, *MSGQ,
	*PGM, *PNLGRP, *SBSD, *USRSPC, ...
MBR	Member name, if database file: name, *NONE, *FIRST
AUT	List of authorities to check: *NONE, *ALL, *CHANGE, *USE,*EXCLUDE,
	*OBJEXIST, *OBJMGT, *ADD, *DLT, *READ, *UPD, ...

Error Messages That Can Be Monitored

CPF9801	Object not found.
CPF9802	Not authorized to object.
CPF9815	Member not found.
CPF9820	Not authorized to use library.
CPF9899	Error occurred during processing of command.

Files Used

(None)

CLOF (Close File)

Closes a database file that had been previously opened in a CL program using either OPNDBF (Open Database File) or OPNQRYF (Open Query File).

Syntax

CLOF	*OPNID(open-id-name)*

Parameters

OPNID   Open file identifier name

Error Messages That Can be Monitored

CPF4519   Member not closed.
CPF4520   No file open with named identifier.

Files Used

(None)

CLRMSGQ (Clear Message Queue)

Removes all messages from a message queue.

Syntax

CLRMSGQ	*MSGQ(library-name/message-queue-name)*	+
	CLEAR(*ALL|*KEEPUNANS)*	

Parameters

MSGQ   Message queue: name, *WRKSTN
                          Library: name, *LIBL, *CURLIB
CLEAR   Which message to clear: *ALL, *KEEPUNANS

Error Messages That Can Be Monitored

CPF2357   Message queue not cleared.

Files Used

(None)

CLRPFM (Clear Physical File Member)

Removes all data records from a physical file.

Syntax

CLRPFM	*FILE(library-name/physical-file-name)*	+
	MBR(physical-file-member-name)	

Parameters

FILE   Physical file name
                          Library: name, *LIBL, *CURLIB
MBR   Member: name, *FIRST, *LAST

Error Messages That Can Be Monitored

CPF3130   Member already in use.
CPF3133   File contains no members.
CPF3136   File not allowed on command.
CPF3137   No authority to clear, initialize, or copy member.
CPF3141   Member not found.
CPF3142   File not found.
CPF3144   Member not cleared or initialized.
CPF3156   File in use.
CPF3159   Member saved with STG(*FREE).
CPF3160   Operation on member ended. Entry cannot be journaled.
CPF3203   Cannot allocate object for file.
CPF320B   Operation was not valid for database file.

Files Used

(None)

CPYF (Copy File)

Copies a file, or part of a file, to another file. In addition to database (physical and logical) files, CPYF can copy data in external device files, such as tape or diskette files.

Syntax

CPYF	*FROMFILE(library-name/file-name)*	+
	TOFILE(library-name/file-name)	+
	FROMMBR(member-name)	+
	TOMBR(member-name)	+
	*MBROPT(*NONE| *ADD| *REPLACE)*	+
	*CRTFILE(*NO| *YES)*	+
	FROMRCD(starting-record-number)	+
	TORCD(ending-record-number)	+
	NBRRCDS(number-of-records)	+
	INCREL(relational-expression)	+
	FMTOPT(formatting-options)	

Parameters

FROMFILE	File name to copy from
	Library: name, *LIBL, *CURLIB
TOFILE	File to copy to: name, *PRINT
	Library: name, *LIBL, *CURLIB
FROMMBR	Member to copy from: name, generic*, *FIRST, *ALL
TOMBR	Member to copy to: name, *FIRST, *FROMMBR
MBROPT	Replace or add records: *NONE, *ADD, *REPLACE
CRTFILE	Create new output file: *NO, *YES
FROMRCD	Copy starting at record: number, *START
TORCD	Copy ending with record: number, *END
NBRRCDS	Number of records to copy: number, *END
INCREL	List of expressions defining records to copy
	Relationship: *NONE, *IF, *AND, *OR
	Field name
	Relational operator: *EQ, *GT, *LT, *NE, *GE, *LE, *NG
FMTOPT	List of record format field mapping options: *NONE, *NOCHK, *CVTSRC, *MAP, *DROP

Error Messages That Can Be Monitored

CPF2816	File not copied because of error.
CPF2817	Copy command ended because of error.
CPF2818	*FROMMBR value is not allowed on TOMBR parameter.
CPF2835	INCCHAR starting position and length too long.
CPF2857	Multiple member or label copy not allowed with override.
CPF2858	File attributes not valid for printed output.
CPF2859	Shared open data path not allowed.
CPF2864	Not authorized to file.
CPF2875	Wrong file member or label opened.
CPF2883	Error creating file.
CPF2888	Member not added because of error.
CPF2904	Diskette labels not valid for multiple label copy.
CPF2906	Value not valid for INCREL field.
CPF2909	Error clearing member.
CPF2949	Error closing member.
CPF2952	Error opening file.
CPF2968	Position error occurred copying file.
CPF2971	Error reading member.
CPF2972	Error writing to member.
CPF2975	Error while reading from keyed file.
CPF2976	Number of errors greater than ERRLVL value.

CPF3140	Initialize or copy of member canceled.
CPF3143	Increments not allowed.
CPF3148	New records need too much space.
CPF3150	Database copy failed.
CPF9212	Cannot load or unload DDM file.

Files Used

QSYS/QSYSPRT   PRTF Copy file printer file.

CPYFRMQRYF (Copy From Query File)

Copies to a file those database records defined by a previous OPNQRYF (Open Query File) command.

Syntax

CPYFRMQYRF	*FROMOPNID(open-id-name)*	+
	TOFILE(library-name/file-name)	+
	TOMBR(member-name)	+
	MBROPT(*NONE|*ADD|*REPLACE)	+
	CRTFILE(*NO|*YES)	+
	NBRRCDS(number-of-records)	+
	FMTOPT(formatting-options)	
	. . .	

Parameters

FROMOPNID	Open file identifier to copy from
TOFILE	File to copy to: name, *PRINT
	Library: name, *LIBL, *CURLIB
TOMBR	Member to copy to: name, *FIRST
MBROPT	Replace or add records: *NONE, *ADD, *REPLACE
CRTFILE	Create new output file: *NO, *YES
NBRRCDS	Number of records to copy: number, *END
FMTOPT	List of record format field mapping options: *NONE, *NOCHK, *CVTSRC, *MAP, *DROP

Error Messages That Can Be Monitored

CPF2816	File not copied because of error.
CPF2817	Copy command ended because of error.
CPF2858	File attributes not valid for printed output.
CPF2859	Shared open data path not allowed.
CPF2864	Not authorized to file.
CPF2875	Wrong file member or label opened.
CPF2883	Error creating file.
CPF2888	Member not added because of error.
CPF2909	Error clearing member.
CPF2949	Error closing member.
CPF2952	Error opening file.
CPF2971	Error reading member.
CPF2972	Error writing to member.
CPF2975	Error while reading from keyed file.
CPF2976	Number of errors greater than ERRLVL value.
CPF3140	Initialize or copy of member canceled.
CPF3143	Increments not allowed for member.
CPF3148	New records need too much space.
CPF3150	Database copy failed.
CPF9212	Cannot load or unload DDM file.

Files Used

QSYS/QSYSPRT   PRTF   Copy file printer file.

CPYFRMTAP (Copy From Tape)

Copies records from a tape file to an output file or a printer.

Syntax

CPYFRMTAP	FROMFILE(library-name/tape-file-name)	+
	TOFILE(library-name/file-name)	+
	FROMSEQNBR(sequence-number)	+
	FROMLABEL(data-file-identifier)	+
	TOMBR(member-name)	+
	FROMDEV(device-name)	+
	MBROPT(*NONE|*ADD|*REPLACE)	+
	NBRRCDS(number-of-records)	

Parameters

FROMFILE   Tape file name to copy from
                 Library: name, *LIBL, *CURLIB
TOFILE   File to copy to: name, *PRINT
                 Library: name, *LIBL, *CURLIB
FROMSEQNBR Sequence number: 1–9999, *TAPF, *NEXT
FROMLABEL   Tape label to copy from: name, *TAPF, *NONE
TOMBR   Member to copy to: name, *FROMLABEL, *FIRST
FROMDEV   Tape device: name, *TAPF
MBROPT   Replace or add records: *NONE, *ADD, *REPLACE
NBRRCDS   Number of records to copy: number, *END

Error Messages That Can Be Monitored

CPF2816   File not copied because of error.
CPF2817   Copy command ended because of error.
CPF2818   *FROMMBR value is not allowed on TOMBR parameter.
CPF2858   File attributes not valid for printed output.
CPF2859   Shared open data path not allowed.
CPF2875   Wrong file member or label opened.
CPF2888   Member not added because of error.
CPF2909   Error clearing member.
CPF2949   Error closing member.
CPF2952   Error opening file.
CPF2971   Error reading member.
CPF2972   Error writing to member.
CPF9212   Cannot load or unload DDM file.

Files Used

QSYS/QSYSPRT   PRTF   Copy file printer file.

CPYSPLF (Copy Spooled File)

Copies records in a spooled file (usually a printed report) to a database file.

Syntax

CPYSPLF	FILE(spooled-file-name)	+
	TOFILE(library-name/database-file-name)	+
	JOB(job-number/user-name/job-name)	+
	SPLNBR(spooled-file-number)	+
	TOMBR(member-name)	+
	MBROPT(*REPLACE|*ADD)	

Parameters

FILE   Spooled file name
TOFILE   Database file to copy to
              Library: name, *LIBL, *CURLIB

JOB	Job: name, <u>*</u>
	User name
	Job number: 000000–999999
SPLNBR	Spooled file number: 1–9999, <u>*ONLY</u>, *LAST
TOMBR	Member to copy to: name, <u>*FIRST</u>
MBROPT	Replace or add records: <u>*REPLACE</u>, *ADD

Error Messages That Can Be Monitored

CPF2207	Not authorized to use object.
CPF3207	Member not added. Errors occurred.
CPF3303	File not found in job.
CPF3309	No named files are active.
CPF3311	Copy request failed.
CPF3330	Necessary resource not available.
CPF3340	More than one file with specified name found in job.
CPF3342	Job not found.
CPF3343	Duplicate job names found.
CPF3344	File no longer in the system.
CPF3394	Cannot convert spooled file data.
CPF3429	File cannot be displayed, copied, or sent.
CPF3482	Copy request failed. Spool file is open.
CPF3483	Copy request failed.
CPF3486	CHLVAL parameter value not valid.
CPF3492	Not authorized to spooled file.
CPF3493	CTLCHAR parameter not correct for file.
CPF3499	Records in file preceded all assigned channel values.
CPF5812	Member already exists.
CPF9812	File not found.
CPF9837	Attempt made to override file to MBR(*ALL).

Files Used

(None)

CPYTOTAP (Copy To Tape)

Copies records to a tape file.

Syntax

CPYTOTAP	*FROMFILE(library-name/file-name)*	+
	TOFILE(library-name/tape-file-name)	+
	FROMMBR(member-name)	+
	TOSEQNBR(sequence-number)	+
	TOLABEL(data-file-identifier)	+
	TODEV(device-name)	+
	NBRRCDS(number-of-records)	
	. . .	

Parameters

FROMFILE	File name to copy from
	Library: name, <u>*LIBL</u>, *CURLIB
TOFILE	Tape file name to copy to
	Library: name, <u>*LIBL</u>, *CURLIB
FROMMBR	Member to copy from: name, generic*, <u>*FIRST</u>, *ALL
TOSEQNBR	Sequence number: 1–9999, <u>*TAPF</u>, *END
TOLABEL	Tape label to copy to: name, <u>*FROMMBR</u>, *TAPF, *NONE
TODEV	Tape device: name, <u>*TAPF</u>
NBRRCDS	Number of records to copy: number, <u>*END</u>

Error Messages That Can Be Monitored

CPF2816	File not copied because of error.
CPF2817	Copy command ended because of error.
CPF2859	Shared open data path not allowed.
CPF2864	Not authorized to file.
CPF2875	Wrong file member or label opened.
CPF2904	Diskette labels not valid for multiple label copy.
CPF2949	Error closing member.
CPF2952	Error opening file.
CPF2968	Position error occurred copying file.
CPF2971	Error reading member.
CPF2972	Error writing to member.
CPF9212	Cannot load or unload DDM file.

Files Used

(None)

CRTDTAARA (Create Data Area)

Creates a data area, and optionally assigns it an initial value.

Syntax

CRTDTAARA	*DTAARA(library-name/data-area-name)*	+
	TYPE(*DEC| *CHAR|LGL)	+
	LEN(data-area-length	+
	decimal-positions)	+
	VALUE(initial-value)	+
	AUT(authority)	+
	TEXT('description')	

Parameters

DTAARA	Data area name
	Library: name, **CURLIB*
TYPE	Data area type: *DEC, *CHAR, *LGL
LEN	Length of data area: 1–2000
	Decimal positions if TYPE(*DEC): 0–9
VALUE	Initial value
AUT	Authority: authorization list name, **LIBCRTAUT*, *CHANGE, *ALL, USE, *EXCLUDE
TEXT	Text: description, **BLANK*

Error Messages That Can Be Monitored

CPF1008	Data area not created.
CPF1015	Data area not found.
CPF1021	Library not found.
CPF1022	No authority to library.
CPF1023	Data area exists.
CPF1024	TYPE and VALUE parameters not compatible.
CPF1025	LEN and VALUE parameters not compatible.
CPF1026	VALUE parameter must be '0' or '1'.
CPF1047	Length not valid.
CPF1062	Null string not valid as character value.
CPF1092	Cannot create data area.

Files Used

(None)

CRTDTAQ (Create Data Queue)

Creates a data queue in a library.

Syntax

CRTDTAQ	DTAQ(library-name/data-queue-name)	+
	MAXLEN(maximum-entry-length)	+
	FORCE(*NO|*YES)	+
	SEQ(*FIFO|*LIFO|*KEYED)	+
	SENDERID(*NO|*YES)	+
	AUT(authority)	+
	TEXT('description')	
	. . .	

Parameters

DTAQ	Data queue name Library: name, *CURLIB
MAXLEN	Maximum entry length: 1–64512
FORCE	Force to auxiliary storage: *NO, *YES
SEQ	Sequence in which entries are received from the queue: *FIFO, *LIFO, *KEYED
SENDERID	Attach sender-id to message when sending to the queue: *NO, *YES
AUT	Authority: authorization list name, *LIBCRTAUT, *CHANGE, *ALL, USE, *EXCLUDE
TEXT	Text: description, *BLANK

Error Messages That Can Be Monitored

CPF2108	Object not added to library. Function check occurred.
CPF2151	Operation failed.
CPF2283	Authorization list does not exist.
CPF6565	User profile storage limit exceeded.
CPF9820	Not authorized to use library.
CPF9870	Object already exists.

Files Used

(None)

CRTDUPOBJ (Create Duplicate Object)

Copies one or more objects. For physical files, you may copy only the format of the file or you may copy the actual data records as well.

Syntax

CRTDUPOBJ	OBJ(existing-object-name)	+
	FROMLIB(from-library-name)	+
	OBJTYPE(object-type)	+
	TOLIB(to-library-name)	+
	NEWOBJ(new-object-name)	+
	DATA(*NO|*YES)	

Parameters

OBJ	Existing object: name, generic*, *ALL
FROMLIB	From library: name, *CURLIB
OBJTYPE	Object type: *DEV, *DTAARA, *DTAQ, *FILE, *LIB, *MENU, *MSGQ, *PGM, *PNLGRP, *SBSD, *USRSPC, ...
TOLIB	To library: name, *FROMLIB, *SAME, *CURLIB
NEWOBJ	New object: name, *OBJ, *SAME
DATA	Duplicate data in object: *NO, *YES

Error Messages That Can Be Monitored

CPF2105	Object not found.
CPF2109	NEWOBJ must be *SAME when OBJ parameter is *ALL or generic name.
CPF2110	Library not found.
CPF2113	Cannot allocate library.
CPF2116	DATA(*YES) specified and *ALL or *FILE not in OBJTYPE list.
CPF2122	Storage limit exceeded for user profile.
CPF2123	No objects of specified name or type exist in library.
CPF2130	nn objects duplicated. nn objects not duplicated.
CPF2151	Operation failed.
CPF2152	Objects of specified type cannot be created into QTEMP.
CPF2162	Duplication of all objects in library not allowed.
CPF2176	Library damaged.
CPF2182	Not authorized to library.
CPF2185	TOLIB or NEWOBJ parameters not correct.
CPF88C4	Value for NEWOBJ is more than 8 characters.
CPF9827	Object cannot be created in library.

Files Used

(None)

CRTLF (Create Logical File)

Creates a logical database file from the specifications stored in a source file.

Syntax

CRTLF	FILE(library-name/logical-file-name)	+
	SRCFILE(library-name/source-file-name)	+
	SRCMBR(source-file-member-name)	+
	MBR(logical-file-member-name)	+
	DTAMBRS(library-name/physical-file-name	+
	member-name)	+
	MAXMBRS(maximum-members)	+
	MAINT(*IMMED|*REBLD|*DLY)	+
	SHARE(*NO|*YES)	+
	LVLCHK(*YES|*NO)	+
	AUT(authority)	+
	TEXT('description')	

Parameters

FILE	Logical file name
	Library: name, *CURLIB
SRCFILE	Source file containing DDS for logical file: name, QDDSSRC
	Library: name, *LIBL, *CURLIB
SRCMBR	Source file member: name, *FILE
MBR	Logical file member: name, *FILE
DTAMBRS	List of physical file data members
	Physical file: name, *ALL
	Library: name, *CURRENT
	List of member names: name, *NONE
MAXMBRS	Maximum number of file members in logical file: 1–32767, *NOMAX
MAINT	Access path maintenance: *IMMED, *DLY, *REBLD
SHARE	Share open data path: *NO, *YES
LVLCHK	Record format level check: *YES, *NO
AUT	Authority: authorization list name, *LIBCRTAUT, *CHANGE, *ALL, USE,
	*EXCLUDE
TEXT	Text: description, *BLANK

Error Messages That Can Be Monitored

CPF3204	Cannot find object needed for file.
CPF323C	QRECOVERY library could not be allocated.
CPF5702	File either not DDM file or not found.
CPF7302	File not created.

Files Used

QGPL/QDDSSRC	PF	DDS source default input file.
QSYS/QPDDSSRC	PRTF	DDS source listing printer file.

CRTMSGF (Create Message File)

Creates a message file to store message descriptions.

Syntax

CRTMSGF	MSGF(library-name/message-file-name)	+
	SIZE(initial-kilobytes	+
	increment-value	+
	number-of-increments)	+
	AUT(authority)	+
	TEXT('description')	

Parameters

MSGF	Message file name
	Library: name, *CURLIB
SIZE	File size
	Initial storage size in kilobytes: number, 10
	Increment storage size in kilobytes: number, 2
	Maximum number of increments: number, *NOMAX
AUT	Authority: authorization list name, *LIBCRTAUT, *CHANGE, *ALL, USE, *EXCLUDE
TEXT	Text: description, *BLANK

Error Messages That Can Be Monitored

CPF2108	Object not added to library. Function check occurred.
CPF2112	Object already exists.
CPF2113	Cannot allocate library.
CPF2151	Operation failed.
CPF2182	Not authorized to library.
CPF2283	Authorization list does not exist.
CPF2402	Library not found.
CPF2497	Size exceeds machine limit.

Files Used

(None)

CRTPF (Create Physical File)

Creates a physical database file, either from the specifications stored in a source file or from the parameters in the CRTPF command.

Syntax

CRTPF	FILE(library-name/physical-file-name)	+
	SRCFILE(library-name/source-file-name)	+
	SRCMBR(source-member-name)	+
	MBR(physical-file-member-name)	+
	MAXMBRS(maximum-members)	+
	MAINT(*IMMED|*REBLD|*DLY)	+

```
                              SIZE(number-of-records                              +
                                  increment-value                                +
                                  number-of-increments)                          +
                              SHARE(*NO|*YES)                                     +
                              LVLCHK(*YES|*NO)                                    +
                              AUT(authority)                                      +
                              TEXT('description')
```

Alternative Syntax

```
CRTPF                         FILE(library-name/physical-file-name)              +
                              RCDLEN(record-length)                             +
                              MBR(physical-file-member-name)                     +
                              MAXMBRS(maximum-members)                           +
                              MAINT(*IMMED|*REBLD|*DLY)                          +
                              SIZE(number-of-records                             +
                                  increment-value                                +
                                  number-of-increments)                          +
                              SHARE(*NO|*YES)                                     +
                              LVLCHK(*YES|*NO)                                    +
                              AUT(authority)                                      +
                              TEXT('description')
```

Parameters

FILE	Physical file name
	Library: name, *CURLIB
SRCFILE	Source file containing DDS for physical file: name, QDDSSRC
	Library: name, *LIBL, *CURLIB
SRCMBR	Source file member: name, *FILE
RCDLEN	Record length, if no DDS: 1–32766
MBR	Physical file member: name, *FILE, *NONE
MAXMBRS	Maximum number of file members in physical file: 1–32767, *NOMAX
MAINT	Access path maintenance: *IMMED, *DLY, *REBLD
SIZE	Member size
	Initial number of records: 1–2147483646, 10000, *NOMAX
	Increment number of records: 0–32767, 1000
	Maximum number of increments: 0–32767, 3
SHARE	Share open data path: *NO, *YES
LVLCHK	Record format level check: *YES, *NO
AUT	Authority: authorization list name, *LIBCRTAUT, *CHANGE, *ALL, USE,
	*EXCLUDE
TEXT	Text: description, *BLANK

Error Messages That Can Be Monitored

CPF3204	Cannot find object needed for file.
CPF323C	QRECOVERY library could not be allocated.
CPF5702	File either not DDM file or not found.
CPF7302	File not created.

Files Used

QGPL/QDDSSRC	PF	DDS source default input file.
QSYS/QPDDSSRC	PRTF	DDS source listing printer file.

CVTDAT (Convert Date)

Converts a date from one format to another (e.g., from month/day/year format to
year/month/day format).

Syntax

```
CVTDAT                        DATE(date-to-be-converted)                         +
                              TOVAR(&CL-variable-name)                           +
                              FROMFMT(from-date-format)                          +
```

	TOFMT(to-date-format)	+
	TOSEP(separator-character)	

Parameters

DATE	Date to be converted from
TOVAR	CL variable for converted date (preceded by &)
FROMFMT	Format of date in DATE parameter: *<u>*JOB</u>, *SYSVAL, *MDY, *DMY, *YMD, *ISO, *USA, ...
TOFMT	Format to be converted to: *<u>*JOB</u>, *SYSVAL, *MDY, *DMY, *YMD, *ISO, *USA, ...
TOSEP	Date separators to be used in converted date: separator character, *<u>*JOB</u>, *SYSVAL, *NONE, *BLANK

Error Messages That Can Be Monitored

CPF0550	Date too short for specified format.
CPF0551	Separators in date are not valid.
CPF0552	Date contains misplaced or extra separators.
CPF0553	Date contains too many or too few numeric characters.
CPF0554	Variable specified too short for converted date format.
CPF0555	Date not in specified format or date not valid.
CPF0556	Date contains two or more kinds of separators.
CPF0557	Date outside allowed range.

Files Used

(None)

DCL (Declare CL Variable)

Defines a program variable in a CL program.

Syntax

DCL	*VAR(&CL-variable-name)*	+
	*TYPE(*DEC| *CHAR| *LGL)*	+
	LEN(length	+
	decimal-positions)	+
	VALUE(initial-value)	

Parameters

VAR	Variable name (preceded by &)
TYPE	Variable data type: *DEC, *CHAR, *LGL
LEN	Length of data area: number
	Decimal positions if TYPE(*DEC): 0–9
VALUE	Initial value

Error Messages That Can Be Monitored

(None)

Files Used

(None)

DCLF (Declare File)

Declares a file for subsequent processing in a CL program.

Syntax

DCLF	*FILE(library-name/file-name)*	+
	RCDFMT(record-format-name)	
	. . .	

Parameters

FILE   File name
                           Library: name, *LIBL, *CURLIB
RCDFMT   List of record format names: name, *ALL

Error Messages That Can Be Monitored

(None)

Files Used

(None)

DLCOBJ (Deallocate Object)

Releases the allocation of one or more objects so those objects can be used by other jobs.

Syntax

DLCOBJ   *OBJ(library-name/object-name*   +
                    object-type   +
                    lock-state   +
                    member-name)

Parameters

OBJ   Object name
                           Library: name, *LIBL, *CURLIB
                           Object type: *DEV, *DTAARA, *DTAQ, *FILE, *LIB, *MENU, *MSGQ,
                                *PGM, *PNLGRP, *SBSD, *USRSPC, …
                           Lock state: *SHRRD, *SHRNUP, *SHRUPD, *EXCLRD, *EXCL
                           Member name, if database file: name, *FIRST

Error Messages That Can Be Monitored

CPF1005   Objects not deallocated.

Files Used

(None)

DLTDTAARA (Delete Data Area)

Removes one or more data areas from the system.

Syntax

DLTDTAARA   *DTAARA(library-name/data-area-name)*

Parameters

DTAARA   Data area to be deleted: name, generic*
                           Library: name, *LIBL, *CURLIB

Error Messages That Can Be Monitored

CPF2105	Object not found.
CPF2110	Library not found.
CPF2113	Cannot allocate library.
CPF2114	Cannot allocate object.
CPF2117	nn objects. nn objects not deleted.
CPF2176	Library damaged.
CPF2182	Not authorized to library.
CPF2189	Not authorized to object.

Files Used

(None)

DLTDTAQ (Delete Data Queue)

Removes one or more data queues from the system.

Syntax

DLTDTAQ   *DTAQ(library-name/data-queue-name)*

Parameters

DTAQ   Data queue to be deleted: name, generic*
                  Library: name, *LIBL, *CURLIB

Error Messages That Can Be Monitored

CPF2105	Object not found.
CPF2110	Library not found.
CPF2113	Cannot allocate library.
CPF2117	nn objects deleted. nn objects not deleted.
CPF2182	Not authorized to library.
CPF2189	Not authorized to object.

Files Used

(None)

DLTF (Delete File)

Removes one or more files, including any data records in them, from the system.

Syntax

DLTF   *FILE(library-name/file-name)*
                  . . .

Parameters

FILE   File to be deleted: name, generic*
                  Library: name, *LIBL, *CURLIB

Error Messages That Can Be Monitored

CPF0601	Not allowed to do operation to file.
CPF0605	Device file saved with storage freed.
CPF0607	File deleted by another job.
CPF0610	File not available.
CPF0675	Device file is in use.
CPF2105	Object not found.
CPF2110	Library not found.
CPF2114	Cannot allocate object.
CPF2117	nn objects deleted. nn objects not deleted.
CPF2182	Not authorized to library.
CPF2189	Not authorized to object.
CPF2190	Not able to do remote delete or rename request.
CPF3203	Cannot allocate object for file.
CPF320B	Operation was not valid for database file.
CPF3220	Cannot do operation on file.
CPF323C	QRECOVERY library could not be allocated.
CPF324B	Cannot allocate dictionary for file.
CPF3252	Maximum number of machine locks exceeded.
CPF326A	Operation not successful for file.
CPF3273	File or member not created, deleted or changed.

Files Used

(None)

DLTMSGF (Delete Message File)

Removes one or more message files from the system.

Syntax

DLTMSGF   *MSGF(library-name/message-file-name)*

Parameters

MSGF   Message file to be deleted: name, generic*
                        Library: name, *LIBL*, *CURLIB

Error Messages That Can Be Monitored

CPF2105	Object not found.
CPF2110	Library not found.
CPF2113	Cannot allocate library.
CPF2114	Cannot allocate object.
CPF2117	nn objects deleted. nn objects not deleted.
CPF2182	Not authorized to library.
CPF2189	Not authorized to object.

Files Used

(None)

DLTOVR (Delete Override)

Remove one or more file overrides that were previously specified.

Syntax

DLTOVR   *FILE(overridden-file-name)*   +
                       LVL(scoping-level)

Parameters

FILE   List of overridden file names: name, *ALL, *PRTF
LVL   Scoping level of overrides to delete: *ACTGRPDFN*, *, *JOB

Error Messages That Can Be Monitored

CPF9841	Override not found at specified level

Files Used

(None)

DLTSPLF (Delete Spooled File)

Removes a spooled file (usually a printed report) from an output queue.

Syntax

DLTSPLF   *FILE(spooled-file-name)*   +
                     JOB(job-number/user-name/job-name)   +
                     SPLNBR(spooled-file-number)
                     . . .

Parameters

FILE   Spooled file: name, *SELECT*
JOB   Job: name, *
                        User name
                        Job number: 000000–999999
SPLNBR   Spooled file number: 1–9999, *ONLY*, *LAST

Error Messages That Can Be Monitored

CPF3303	File not found in job.
CPF3309	No named files are active.

CPF3330	Necessary resource not available.
CPF3340	More than one file with specified name found in job.
CPF3342	Job not found.
CPF3343	Duplicate job names found.
CPF3344	File no longer in the system.
CPF33D0	Printer does not exist.
CPF33D1	User does not exist.
CPF3478	File not found on output queue.
CPF3492	Not authorized to spooled file.
CPF34A4	File not held or deleted.

Files Used

(None)

DLTUSRSPC (Delete User Space)

Removes one or more user spaces from the system. User spaces are created using an application program interface (API), not a CL command.

Syntax

| *DLTUSRSPC* | *USRSPC(library-name/user-space-name)* |

Parameters

| USRSPC | User space to be deleted: name, generic* |
| | Library: name, *LIBL, *CURLIB |

Error Messages That Can Be Monitored

CPF2105	Object not found.
CPF2110	Library not found.
CPF2113	Cannot allocate library.
CPF2114	Cannot allocate object.
CPF2117	nn objects deleted. nn objects not deleted.
CPF2125	No objects deleted.
CPF2176	Library damaged.
CPF2182	Not authorized to library.
CPF2189	Not authorized to object.

Files Used

(None)

DLYJOB (Delay Job)

Pauses a job for either a specified number of seconds or until a specified time of day.

Syntax

| *DLYJOB* | *DLY(number-of-seconds)* |

Alternative Syntax

| *DLYJOB* | *RSMTIME('time')* |

Parameters

| DLY | Number of seconds to delay job: 0–999999 |
| RSMTIME | Time of day to resume job |

Error Messages That Can Be Monitored

(None)

Files Used

(None)

DMPCLPGM (Dump CL Program)

Prints all variables declared in a CL program and all messages on the program's message queue, then continues processing.

Syntax

DMPCLPGM

Parameters

(None)

Error Messages That Can Be Monitored

CPF0570   Unable to dump CL program.

Files Used

QSYS/QPPGMDMP PRTF CL program dump printer file.

DO (Do)

In conjunction with the ENDDO (End Do) command, the DO groups commands in a CL program.

Syntax

DO

Parameters

(None)

Error Messages That Can Be Monitored

(None)

Files Used

(None)

DSPFD (Display File Description)

Shows file description information (e.g., member list or record format list) for one or more files. You can display or print the description, or direct it to a database file for further processing.

Syntax

DSPFD	*FILE(library-name/file-name)*	+
	TYPE(type-of-information)	+
	OUTPUT(*| *PRINT| *OUTFILE)	+
	FILEATR(file-attributes)	+
	OUTFILE(library-name/database-file-name)	+
	OUTMBR(member-name	+
	*ADD|*REPLACE)	
	. . .	

Parameters

FILE	File to display description: name, generic*, *ALL
	Library: name, *LIBL, *CURLIB, *USRLIBL, *ALLUSR, *ALL
TYPE	Type of information to display: *ALL, *BASATR, *ATR, *ACCPTH,
	*MBRLIST, *SEQ, *RCDFMT, *MBR, ...
OUTPUT	Output destination: *, *PRINT, *OUTFILE
FILEATR	File attributes: *ALL, *DSPF, *PRTF, *DKTF, *TAPF, *PF, *LF, *SAVF, ...
OUTFILE	File to receive output, if OUTPUT(*OUTFILE)
	Library: name, *LIBL, *CURLIB
OUTMBR	Member to receive output, if OUTPUT(*OUTFILE):name, *FIRST
	Add or replace records: *ADD, *REPLACE

Error Messages That Can Be Monitored

CPF3011	TYPE not found for file.
CPF3012	File not found.
CPF3014	No file specified can be displayed.
CPF3020	No files have the specified FILEATR.
CPF3021	File not allowed with SYSTEM(*RMT).
CPF3022	SYSTEM(*RMT) not allowed for files.
CPF3030	nn records added to member.
CPF3061	Record format not found for outfile.
CPF3064	Library not found.
CPF3067	Error while opening file.
CPF3068	Error while writing to file.
CPF3069	Error while closing file.
CPF3070	Error creating member.
CPF3072	File is a system file.
CPF3074	Not authorized to library.
CPF3075	Library not available.
CPF3076	Error occurred when on display.
CPF3077	Error occurred when canceling display.
CPF3084	Error clearing member.
CPF326B	Damage to file.
CPF9851	Overflow value for file too small.
CPF9852	Page size too narrow for file.
CPF9899	Error occurred during processing of command.

Files Used

QSYS/QAFDACCP	PF	Model outfile for access path file information.
QSYS/QAFDBASI	PF	Model outfile for basic file information common to all files.
QSYS/QAFDBSC	PF	Model outfile for BSC file and mixed file device attribute information.
QSYS/QAFDCMN	PF	Model outfile for communications file and mixed file device attribute information.
QSYS/QAFDDDM	PF	Model outfile for distributed data management (DDM) file attribute information.
QSYS/QAFDDKT	PF	Model outfile for diskette file attribute information.
QSYS/QAFDDSP	PF	Model outfile for display file and mixed file display device attribute information.
QSYS/QAFDICF	PF	Model outfile for ICF file attribute information.
QSYS/QAFDJOIN	PF	Model outfile for join logical file information.
QSYS/QAFDLGL	PF	Model outfile for logical file attribute information.
QSYS/QAFDMBR	PF	Model outfile for database member information.
QSYS/QAFDMBRL	PF	Model outfile for database member list information.
QSYS/QAFDPHY	PF	Model outfile for physical file attribute information.
QSYS/QAFDPRT	PF	Model outfile for printer file attribute information.
QSYS/QAFDRFMT	PF	Model outfile for record format information.
QSYS/QAFDSAV	PF	Model outfile for save file information.
QSYS/QAFDSELO	PF	Model outfile for select/omit information.
QSYS/QAFDSPOL	PF	Model outfile for device file spooled information.
QSYS/QAFDTAP	PF	Model outfile for tape file attribute information.
QSYS/QPDSPFD	PRTF	File description printer file.

DSPFFD (Display File Field Description)

Shows field-level information (record layout information) for one or more files. You can display or print the field information, or direct it to a database file for further processing.

Syntax

DSPFFD	*FILE(library-name/file-name)*	+
	OUTPUT(| *PRINT| *OUTFILE)*	+
	OUTFILE(library-name/database-file-name)	+

```
                            OUTMBR(member-name                        +
                              *ADD|*REPLACE)
                            . . .
```

Parameters

FILE   File to display field description: name, generic*, *ALL
                               Library: name, *LIBL, *CURLIB, *USRLIBL, *ALLUSR, *ALL
OUTPUT   Output destination: *, *PRINT, *OUTFILE
OUTFILE   File to receive output, if OUTPUT(*OUTFILE)
                               Library: name, *LIBL, *CURLIB
OUTMBR   Member to receive output, if OUTPUT(*OUTFILE):name, *FIRST
                               Add or replace records: *ADD, *REPLACE

Error Messages That Can Be Monitored

CPF3012	File not found.
CPF3014	No file specified can be displayed.
CPF3024	File not allowed for SYSTEM.
CPF3052	Description for file not available.
CPF3061	Record format not found for outfile.
CPF3063	Output file not physical file.
CPF3064	Library not found.
CPF3066	Error creating output file.
CPF3067	Error while opening file.
CPF3068	Error while writing to file.
CPF3069	Error while closing file.
CPF3070	Error creating member.
CPF3072	File is a system file.
CPF3074	Not authorized to library.
CPF3075	Library not available.
CPF3076	Error occurred when on display.
CPF3077	Error occurred when canceling display.
CPF3084	Error clearing member.
CPF326B	Damage to file in library.
CPF9851	Overflow value for file too small.
CPF9852	Page size too narrow for file.
CPF9899	Error occurred during processing of command.

Files Used

QSYS/QADSPFFD	PF	Model outfile to store file field descriptions.
QSYS/QPDSPFFD	PRTF	File field description printer file.

DSPOBJD (Display Object Description)

Shows names and attributes of one or more objects on the system. You can display or print the object information, or direct it to a database file for further processing.

Syntax

```
DSPOBJD            OBJ(library-name/object-name)                        +
                   OBJTYPE(object-type)                                 +
                   DETAIL(*BASIC| *FULL| *SERVICE)                      +
                   OUTPUT(*|*PRINT|*OUTFILE)                            +
                   OUTFILE(library-name/database-file-name)             +
                   OUTMBR(member-name                                   +
                     *ADD|*REPLACE)
```

Parameters

OBJ   Object to display description: name, generic*, *ALL
                               Library: name, *LIBL, *CURLIB, *USRLIBL, *ALLUSR, *ALL

OBJTYPE	List of object types: *ALL, *DEV, *DTAARA, *DTAQ, *FILE, *LIB, *MSGQ,
	*PGM, *PNLGRP, *SBSD, *USRSPC, ...
DETAIL	Type of information to display: *BASIC, *FULL, *SERVICE
OUTPUT	Output destination: *, *PRINT, *OUTFILE
OUTFILE	File to receive output, if OUTPUT(*OUTFILE)
	Library: name, *LIBL, *CURLIB
OUTMBR	Member to receive output, if OUTPUT(*OUTFILE):name, *FIRST
	Add or replace records: *ADD, *REPLACE

Error Messages That Can Be Monitored

CPF2105	Object not found.
CPF2110	Library not found.
CPF2113	Cannot allocate library.
CPF2114	Cannot allocate object.
CPF2115	Object damaged.
CPF2121	One or more libraries cannot be accessed.
CPF2123	No objects of specified name or type exist in library.
CPF2124	No specified objects can be displayed from library.
CPF2150	Object information function failed.
CPF2176	Library damaged.
CPF2177	OBJTYPE value not compatible with OBJ value.
CPF2182	Not authorized to library.
CPF2189	Not authorized to object.
CPF326B	Damage to file.
CPF9827	Object cannot be created in library.
CPF9847	Error occurred while closing file.
CPF9850	Override of printer file not allowed.
CPF9851	Overflow value for file too small.
CPF9860	Error occurred during output file processing.

Files Used

QSYS/QADSPOBJ	PF	Model outfile for object description entries.
QSYS/QPRTOBJD	PRTF	Object description printer file.

DSPSPLF (Display Spooled File)

Shows the records in a spooled file (usually a printed report).

Syntax

DSPSPLF	*FILE(spooled-file-name)*	+
	JOB(job-number/user-name/job-name)	+
	SPLNBR(spooled-file-number)	
	. . .	

Parameters

FILE	Spooled file name
JOB	Job: name, *
	User name
	Job number: 000000–999999
SPLNBR	Spooled file number: 1–9999, *ONLY, *LAST

Error Messages That Can Be Monitored

CPF2207	Not authorized to use object.
CPF3303	File not found.
CPF3308	Error occurred when trying to display data.
CPF3309	No named files are active.
CPF3330	Necessary resource not available.
CPF3340	More than one file with specified name found in job.
CPF3342	Job not found.

CPF3343	Duplicate job names found.
CPF3344	File no longer in the system.
CPF3359	Not able to display data.
CPF3386	File not a database file.
CPF3387	Cannot display data in file.
CPF3394	Cannot convert spooled file data.
CPF3427	Job not interactive job.
CPF3428	DSPSPLF command ended.
CPF3429	File cannot be displayed, copied, or sent.
CPF3434	Data not in required format.
CPF3435	Requested data not found.
CPF3478	File not found on output queue.
CPF3492	Not authorized to spooled file.
CPF9812	File not found.
CPF9815	Member not found.

Files Used

(None)

ELSE (Else)

Conditionally processes a command if the logical expression on the preceding IF command is false. ELSE must be used in conjunction with an IF command.

Syntax

ELSE   *CMD(CL-command)*

Parameters

CMD   CL command to execute

Error Messages That Can Be Monitored

(None)

Files Used

(None)

ENDDO (End Do)

In conjunction with the DO command, the ENDDO command ends a group of commands in a CL program.

Syntax

ENDDO

Parameters

(None)

Error Messages That Can Be Monitored

(None)

Files Used

(None)

ENDPGM (End Program)

Specifies the end of a CL program.

Syntax

ENDPGM

Parameters

(None)

Error Messages That Can Be Monitored

(None)

Files Used

(None)

GOTO (Go To)

Branches to another part of the program.

Syntax

GOTO   *CMDLBL(command-label)*

Parameters

CMDLBL   Command label to branch to

Error Messages That Can Be Monitored

(None)

Files Used

(None)

IF (If)

Conditionally processes a command if the condition specified in an expression is true.

Syntax

IF   *COND(logical-expression)*   +
                  THEN(CL-command)

Parameters

COND   Logical expression to determine if condition is true
THEN   CL command to execute if condition is true

Error Messages That Can Be Monitored

CPF0816   %SWITCH mask not valid.

Files Used

(None)

MONMSG (Monitor Message)

Establishes a monitor for escape, notify, and status messages. If a monitored message arrives on the program message queue, MONMSG specifies a command to execute.

Syntax

MONMSG   *MSGID(message-identifier)*   +
                      CMPDTA(comparison-data)   +
                      EXEC(CL-command)

Parameters

MSGID   List of message identifiers
CMPDTA   Comparison data: *NONE, data string
EXEC   CL command to execute when message and comparison data are
                      encountered.

Error Messages That Can Be Monitored

(None)

Files Used

(None)

MOVOBJ (Move Object)

Moves an object from one library to another.

Syntax

MOVOBJ	*OBJ(library-name/object-name)*	+
	OBJTYPE(object-type)	+
	TOLIB(to-library-name)	

Parameters

OBJ	Name of object to move Library: name, *LIBL, *CURLIB
OBJTYPE	List of object types: *DEV, *DTAARA, *DTAQ, *FILE, *LIB, *MENU, *MSGQ, *PGM, *PNLGRP, *SBSD, *USRSPC, …
TOLIB	Library to move object to: name, *CURLIB

Error Messages That Can Be Monitored

CPF0601	Not allowed to do operation to file.
CPF0602	File already in library.
CPF0605	Device file saved with storage freed.
CPF0610	File not available.
CPF0678	Operation not performed for file name.
CPF1763	Cannot allocate one or more libraries.
CPF2105	Object not found.
CPF2110	Library not found.
CPF2112	Object already exists.
CPF2113	Cannot allocate library.
CPF2114	Cannot allocate object.
CPF2135	Object already exists in library.
CPF2150	Object information function failed.
CPF2151	Operation failed.
CPF2160	Object type not eligible for requested function.
CPF2182	Not authorized to library.
CPF2189	Not authorized to object.
CPF2193	Object cannot be moved into library.
CPF22BC	Object is not program defined.
CPF2512	Operation not allowed for message queue.
CPF3201	File already exists.
CPF3202	File in use.
CPF3203	Cannot allocate object for file.
CPF320B	Operation was not valid for database file.
CPF320C	File not allowed in SQL collection.
CPF3220	Cannot do operation on file.
CPF322D	Operation not done for database file.
CPF3231	Cannot move file from library.
CPF323C	QRECOVERY library could not be allocated.
CPF323D	User does not have correct authority.
CPF3245	Damage to file prevents operation.
CPF324B	Cannot allocate dictionary for file.
CPF324C	Concurrent authority holder operation prevents move, rename or restore.
CPF325D	Field CCSID values not compatible.
CPF3323	Job queue already exists.
CPF3330	Necessary resource not available.
CPF3353	Output queue already exists.
CPF3373	Job queue not moved. Job queue in use.

CPF3374	Output queue not moved. Output queue in use.
CPF3467	Output queue deleted and then created again.
CPF3469	Operation not allowed for output queue.
CPF7010	Object already exists.
CPF7014	Object cannot be moved to library.
CPF9827	Object cannot be created in library.
OFC1043	Object type not eligible for requested function.

Files Used

(None)

OPNDBF (Open Database File)

Opens a database file member.

Syntax

OPNDBF	*FILE(library-name/file-name)*	+
	OPTION(*INP| *OUT| *ALL)	+
	MBR(member-name)	+
	OPNID(open-identifier-name)	+
	ACCPTH(*FILE|*ARRIVAL	+
	OPNSCOPE(*ACTGRPDFN|*ACTGRP|*JOB)	
	. . .	

Parameters

FILE	File name to be opened
	Library: name, **LIBL*, *CURLIB
OPTION	Open option: *INP, *OUT, *ALL
MBR	File member to be opened: name, **FIRST*, *LAST
OPNID	Open file identifier: name, **FILE*
ACCPTH	Access path to use: **FILE*, *ARRIVAL
OPNSCOPE	Scope of influence of the open operation: **ACTGRPDFN*, *ACTGRP, *JOB

Error Messages That Can Be Monitored

CPF4125	Open of member failed.
CPF4152	Error opening member.
CPF4174	OPNID for file already exists.
CPF4175	Output only and MBR(*ALL) cannot be used together.
CPF4176	File not a database file.

Files Used

(None)

OPNQRYF (Open Query File)

Opens a path to a set of database records that satisfies a database query request.

Syntax

OPNQRYF	*FILE(library-name/file-name*	+
	member-name	+
	record-format-name)	+
	OPTION(open-option)	+
	FORMAT(library-name/database-file-name	+
	record-format-name)	+
	QRYSLT('query-selection')	+
	KEYFLD(file-name/field-name	+
	*ASCEND|*DESCEND	+
	*ABSVAL)	+
	. . .	

Parameters

FILE	List of file names to be processed
	Library: name, *LIBL, *CURLIB
	Member to be processed: name, *FIRST, *LAST
	Record format: name, *ONLY
OPTION	List of open options: *INP, *ALL, *OUT, *UPD, *DLT
FORMAT	Record format specifications for processed records
	File: name, *FILE
	Library: name, *LIBL, *CURLIB
	Record format: name, *ONLY
QRYSLT	Selection values used to determine which records to process: *ALL, expression
KEYFLD	List of key field specifications
	Key field: name, *NONE, *FILE
	File or element: name, *MAPFLD, 1–32
	Key field order: *ASCEND, *DESCEND
	Order by absolute value: *ABSVAL

Error Messages That Can Be Monitored

CPF4174	OPNID for file already exists.
CPF9801	Object not found.
CPF9802	Not authorized to object.
CPF9812	File not found.
CPF9815	Member not found.
CPF9820	Not authorized to use library.
CPF9822	Not authorized to file.
CPF9826	Cannot allocate file.
CPF9899	Error occurred during processing of command.

Files Used

(None)

OVRDBF (Override with Database File)

Temporarily replaces a file in a program, and/or certain attributes of a file.

Syntax

OVRDBF	FILE(overridden-file-name)	+
	TOFILE(library-name/database-file-name)	+
	MBR(member-name)	+
	SECURE(*NO|*YES)	+
	OVRSCOPE(*ACTGRPDFN|*CALLLVL|*JOB)	
	. . .	

Parameters

FILE	Name of file being overridden
TOFILE	Overriding to database file: name, *FILE
	Library: name, *LIBL, *CURLIB
MBR	Overriding to member: name, *FIRST, *LAST, *ALL
SECURE	Secure from other overrides: *NO, *YES
OVRSCOPE	Scope of influence of the override: *ACTGRPDFN, *CALLLVL, *JOB

Error Messages That Can Be Monitored

(None)

Files Used

(None)

OVRPRTF (Override with Printer File)

Temporarily replaces a printer file in a program and/or certain attributes of a printer file.

Syntax

OVRPRTF	FILE*(file-override-name)*	+
	TOFILE*(library-name/printer-device-file-name)*	+
	DEV*(device-name)*	+
	PAGESIZE(page-length	+
	page-width	
	<u>*ROWCOL</u>|*UOM)	
	LPI(lines-per-inch)	+
	CPI(characters-per-inch)	+
	OVRFLW(overflow-line-number)	+
	OUTQ(library-name/output-queue-name)	+
	FORMTYPE(form-type)	+
	COPIES(number-of-copies)	+
	SCHEDULE(*JOBEND|*FILEEND|*IMMED)	+
	HOLD(*NO|*YES)	+
	SAVE(*NO|*YES)	+
	OVRSCOPE(<u>*ACTGRPDFN</u>|*CALLLVL|*JOB)	
	. . .	

Parameters

FILE	Name of file being overridden
TOFILE	Overriding to printer file: name, <u>*FILE</u>
	Library: name, *LIBL, *CURLIB
DEV	Printer device: name, *SYSVAL, *JOB
PAGESIZE	Page length: 1–255.000
	Page width: 1–378.00
	Measurement method: <u>*ROWCOL</u>, *UOM
LPI	Lines per inch: 6, 8, …
CPI	Characters per inch: 10, 15 …
OVRFLW	Overflow line number: 1–255
OUTQ	Output queue: name, *DEV, *JOB
	Library: name, <u>*LIBL</u>, *CURLIB
FORMTYPE	Form type: name, *STD
COPIES	Number of copies: 1–255
SCHEDULE	When file becomes available to print: *JOBEND, *FILEEND, *IMMED
HOLD	Hold the file before printing: *NO, *YES
SAVE	Save file after printing: *NO, *YES
OVRSCOPE	Scope of influence of the override: <u>*ACTGRPDFN</u>, *CALLLVL, *JOB

Error Messages That Can Be Monitored

| CPF7343 | Channel number specified more than once on CHLVAL. |

Files Used

(None)

PGM (Program)

Identifies the start of a CL program and the input parameters that the program will receive when it executes.

Syntax

| PGM | PARM*(&CL-variable-name)* |

Parameters

| PARM | List of parameter CL variable names (each preceded by &) |

Error Messages That Can Be Monitored

(None)

Files Used

(None)

POSDBF (Position Database File)

Sets a database file cursor to the beginning or end of the file.

Syntax

POSDBF	*OPNID(open-identifier-name)* +
	POSITION(*START| *END)

Parameters

OPNID	Open file identifier
POSITION	File position: *START, *END

Error Messages That Can Be Monitored

CPF5213	Positioning of member failed.
CPF5230	No file open with OPNID.

Files Used

(None)

RCVF (Receive File)

Reads data from a display device or a database file.

Syntax

RCVF	*DEV(device-name)* +
	RCDFMT(record-format-name) +
	WAIT(*YES|*NO)

Parameters

DEV	Display device: name, *FILE
RCDFMT	Record format: name, *FILE
WAIT	Wait for data: *YES, *NO

Error Messages That Can Be Monitored

CPF0859	File override caused I/O buffer size to be exceeded.
CPF0860	File not a database file.
CPF0861	File is not a display file.
CPF0863	Value of binary data too large for decimal CL variable.
CPF0864	End of file detected.
CPF0865	File has more than one record format.
CPF0883	*FILE not valid in DEV parameter for file.
CPF0886	Record contains a data field that is not valid.
CPF4101	File not found or inline data file missing.
CPF5029	Data mapping error on member.
CPF502A	Variable length record error on member.
CPF5068	Program device not found.
CPF5070	File has no program devices acquired.

Files Used

(None)

RCVMSG (Receive Message)

Reads a message from a message queue.

Syntax

RCVMSG	PGMQ(*SAME| *EXT| *PRV	+
	program-name)	+
	MSGTYPE(*message-type*)	+
	MSGKEY(*message-key*)	+
	WAIT(*number-of-seconds*)	+
	RMV(*YES|*NO)	+
	KEYVAR(&CL-variable-name)	+
	MSG(&CL-variable-name)	+
	MSGLEN(&CL-variable-name)	+
	MSGDTA(&CL-variable-name)	+
	MSGDTALEN(&CL-variable-name)	+
	MSGID(&CL-variable-name)	+
	SEV(&CL-variable-name)	+
	SENDER(&CL-variable-name)	+
	RTNRYPE(&CL-variable-name)	+
	MSGF(&CL-variable-name)	+
	MSGFLIB(&CL-variable-name)	+
	SNDMSGFLIB(&CL-variable-name)	

Alternative Syntax

RCVMSG	MSGQ(*library-name/message-queue-name*)	+
	MSGTYPE(*message-type*)	+
	MSGKEY(*message-key*)	+
	WAIT(*number-of-seconds*)	+
	RMV(*YES|*NO)	+
	KEYVAR(&CL-variable-name)	+
	MSG(&CL-variable-name)	+
	MSGLEN(&CL-variable-name)	+
	MSGDTA(&CL-variable-name)	+
	MSGDTALEN(&CL-variable-name)	+
	MSGID(&CL-variable-name)	+
	SEV(&CL-variable-name)	+
	SENDER(&CL-variable-name)	+
	RTNRYPE(&CL-variable-name)	+
	MSGF(&CL-variable-name)	+
	MSGFLIB(&CL-variable-name)	+
	SNDMSGFLIB(&CL-variable-name)	

Parameters

PGMQ	Program message queue relationship: *SAME, *EXT, *PRV Program: name, *
MSGQ	Message queue: name, *PGMQ Library: name, *LIBL, *CURLIB
MSGTYPE	Message type: *ANY, *NEXT, *PRV, *INFO, *INQ, *RPY, *FIRST, *COPY, *COMP, *DIAG, *EXCP, *RQS, *LAST
MSGKEY	Message reference key: CL variable (preceded by &), *NONE, *TOP
WAIT	Wait time: number of seconds, 0, *NOMAX
RMVMSG	Remove message: *YES, *NO
KEYVAR	CL variable that is to contain message reference key (*CHAR 4)
MSG	CL variable that is to contain first-level message text (*CHAR up to 132)
MSGLEN	CL variable that is to contain the total length of the message text (*DEC 5 0)
MSGDTA	CL variable that is to contain the message data (*CHAR)
MSGDTALEN	CL variable that is to contain the length of the message data (*DEC 5 0)
MSGID	CL variable that is to contain the message identifier (*CHAR 7)

SEV	CL variable that is to contain the severity code of the received message (*DEC 2 0)
SENDER	CL variable that is to contain the identification of the sender of the message (*CHAR 80)
RTNTYPE	CL variable that is to contain the type code for the message (*CHAR 2)
MSGF	CL variable that is to contain the name of the message file containing the message (*CHAR 10)
MSGFLIB	CL variable that is to contain the name of the MSGF library or *LIBL(*CHAR 10)
SNDMSGFLIB	CL variable that is to contain the name of the MSGF library (*CHAR 10)

Error Messages That Can Be Monitored

CPF2401	Not authorized to library.
CPF2403	Message queue not found.
CPF2408	Not authorized to message queue.
CPF2410	Message key not found in message queue.
CPF2415	End of requests.
CPF2423	Variable specified in SENDER parameter less than 80 bytes.
CPF2433	Function not allowed for system log message queue.
CPF2450	Workstation message queue not allocated to job.
CPF2451	Message queue is allocated to another job.
CPF2470	Message queue not found.
CPF2471	Length of field not valid.
CPF2477	Message queue currently in use.
CPF2479	Program message queue not found.
CPF2482	Message type not valid.
CPF2532	Job message queue logically damaged. Job log ended.
CPF2551	Message key and message type combination not valid.
CPF8127	Damage on message queue.
CPF8176	Message queue for device description damaged.
CPF8198	Damaged object found.

Files Used

(None)

RETURN (Return)

Ends a CL program, returning to the calling program.

Syntax

RETURN

Parameters

(None)

Error Messages That Can Be Monitored

| CPF2415 | End of requests. |

Files Used

(None)

RGZPFM (Reorganize Physical File Member)

Removes deleted records from a physical database file member, optionally reordering the records.

Syntax

```
RGZPFM          FILE(library-name/physical-file-name)          +
                MBR(member-name)
                 . . .
```

Parameters

FILE	Name of file to reorganize
	Library: name, *LIBL, *CURLIB
MBR	Member to reorganize: name, *FIRST, *LAST

Error Messages That Can Be Monitored

CPF2981	Member not reorganized.
CPF2985	Source sequence numbers exceeded maximum value allowed.
CPF3135	Access path already in use.

Files Used

(None)

RMVLIBLE (Remove Library List Entry)

Removes a library name from the library list.

Syntax

RMVLIBLE	*LIB(library-name)*

Parameters

LIB	Name of library to remove from library list

Error Messages That Can Be Monitored

CPF2103	Library already exists in library list.
CPF2104	Library not removed from the library list.
CPF2106	Library list not changed.
CPF2110	Library not found.
CPF2113	Cannot allocate library.
CPF2118	Library not added.
CPF2176	Library damaged.
CPF2182	Not authorized to library.

Files Used

(None)

RMVM (Remove Member)

Deletes one or more members (including the data) from a physical or logical file.

Syntax

RMVM	*FILE(library-name/file-name)*	+
	MBR(member-name)	

Parameters

FILE	Name of database file containing member to remove
	Library: name, *LIBL, *CURLIB
MBR	Member to remove: name, generic*, *ALL

Error Messages That Can Be Monitored

CPF3203	Cannot allocate object.
CPF320A	Member cannot be removed.
CPF320B	Operation was not valid for database file.
CPF3220	Cannot do operation on file.
CPF3273	File or member not created, deleted or changed.
CPF7301	nn members not removed from file.
CPF7310	Member not removed from file.

Files Used

(None)

RMVMSG (Remove Message)

Deletes one or more messages from a message queue.

Syntax

RMVMSG	PGMQ(*SAME|*PRV|*EXT|*ALLINACT	+
	program-name)	+
	MSGKEY(message-key)	+
	CLEAR(clear-instruction)	

Alternative Syntax

RMVMSG	MSGQ(library-name/message-queue-name)	+
	MSGKEY(message-key)	+
	CLEAR(clear-instruction)	

Parameters

PGMQ	Program message queue relationship: *SAME, *ALLINACT, *EXT, *PRV
	Program: name, *
MSGQ	Message queue: name, *PGMQ
	Library: name, *LIBL, *CURLIB
MSGKEY	CL variable that contains message reference key if CLEAR(*BYKEY)
CLEAR	Clear instructions: *BYKEY, *ALL, *KEEPUNANS, *OLD, *NEW

Error Messages That Can Be Monitored

CPF2401	Not authorized to library.
CPF2403	Message queue not found.
CPF2408	Not authorized to message queue.
CPF2410	Message key not found in message queue.
CPF2450	Workstation message queue not allocated to job.
CPF2470	Message queue not found.
CPF2477	Message queue currently in use.
CPF2479	Program message queue not found.
CPF8127	Damage on message queue.
CPF8176	Message queue for device description damaged.

Files Used

(None)

RMVMSGD (Remove Message Description)

Deletes a message description from a message file.

Syntax

RMVMSGD	*MSGID(message-identifier)*	+
	MSGF(library-name/message-file-name)	

Parameters

MSGID	Message identifier to remove
MSGF	Name of message file containing identifier to be removed
	Library: name, *LIBL, *CURLIB

Error Messages That Can Be Monitored

CPF2401	Not authorized to library.
CPF2407	Message file not found.
CPF2411	Not authorized to message file.
CPF2419	Message identifier not found in message file.
CPF2483	Message file currently in use.
CPF2499	Message identifier not allowed.

Files Used

(None)

RNMM (Rename Member)
Changes the name of a member in a physical or logical file.

Syntax

RNMM	*FILE(library-name/database-file-name)*	+
	MBR(member-name)	
	NEWMBR(new-member-name)	

Parameters

FILE	Name of database file containing member to be renamed
	Library: name, *<u>LIBL</u>*, *CURLIB
MBR	Existing name of member
NEWMBR	New name of member

Error Messages That Can Be Monitored

CPF3178	Member not renamed.
CPF3220	Cannot do operation on file.

Files Used

(None)

RNMOBJ (Rename Object)
Changes the name of an object on the system.

Syntax

RNMOBJ	*OBJ(library-name/object-name)*	+
	OBJTYPE(object-type)	+
	NEWOBJ(new-object-name)	
	. . .	

Parameters

OBJ	Name of object to be renamed
	Library: name, *<u>LIBL</u>*, *CURLIB
OBJTYPE	List of object types: *DEV, *DTAARA, *DTAQ, *FILE, *LIB, *MENU,
	*MSGQ, *PGM, *PNLGRP, *SBSD, *USRSPC, ...
NEWOBJ	New name of object

Error Messages That Can Be Monitored

CPF0601	Not allowed to do operation to file.
CPF0602	File already in library.
CPF0605	Device file saved with storage freed.
CPF0610	File not available.
CPF0678	Operation not performed for file name.
CPF1763	Cannot allocate one or more libraries.
CPF2105	Object not found.
CPF2110	Library not found.
CPF2111	Library already exists.
CPF2112	Object already exists.
CPF2113	Cannot allocate library.
CPF2114	Cannot allocate object.
CPF2132	Object already exists in library.
CPF2136	Renaming library failed.
CPF2139	Rename of library failed.
CPF2140	Rename of library previously failed.
CPF2150	Object information function failed.
CPF2151	Operation failed.
CPF2160	Object type not eligible for requested function.

CPF2164	Rename of library not complete.
CPF2176	Library damaged.
CPF2182	Not authorized to library.
CPF2189	Not authorized to object.
CPF2190	Not able to do remote delete or rename request.
CPF22BC	Object is not program defined.
CPF2512	Operation not allowed for message queue.
CPF2691	Rename did not complete.
CPF2692	Object must be varied off.
CPF2693	Object cannot be used for rename.
CPF2694	Object cannot be renamed.
CPF2696	Object not renamed.
CPF3201	File already exists.
CPF3202	File in use.
CPF3203	Cannot allocate object for file.
CPF320B	Operation was not valid for database file.
CPF3220	Cannot do operation on file.
CPF322D	Operation not done for database file.
CPF323C	QRECOVERY library could not be allocated.
CPF323D	User does not have correct authority.
CPF3245	Damage to file prevents operation.
CPF324C	Concurrent authority holder operation prevents move, rename or restore.
CPF3323	Job queue already exists.
CPF3330	Necessary resource not available.
CPF3353	Output queue already exists.
CPF3375	Job queue not renamed. Job queue in use.
CPF3376	Output queue not renamed. Output queue in use.
CPF3467	Output queue deleted and then created again.
CPF3469	Operation not allowed for output queue.
CPF5702	File either not DDM file or not found.
CPF88C4	Value for NEWOBJ is more than 8 characters.
CPF8D05	Library already exists.
CPF9809	Library cannot be accessed.
CPF9827	Object cannot be created.
OFC1043	Object type not eligible for requested function.

Files Used

(None)

RSTLIB (Restore Library)

Restores one or more libraries to the system from a backup medium or from a save file.

Syntax

RSTLIB	*SAVLIB(library-name)*	+
	DEV(device-name)	+
	SAVF(library-name/save-file-name)	+
	RSTLIB(library-name)	+
	OUTPUT(*NONE|*PRINT)	

Parameters

SAVLIB	Saved library: name, *NONSYS, *ALLUSR, *IBM
DEV	List of save devices: name, *SAVF
SAVF	Name of save file if DEV(*SAVF)
	Library: name, *LIBL, *CURLIB
RSTLIB	Restore to library: name, *SAVLIB
OUTPUT	Print a listing: *NONE, *PRINT

Error Messages That Can Be Monitored

CPF3705	Object not journaled.
CPF3706	Object not restored to library.
CPF3707	Save file contains no data.
CPF3709	Tape devices do not support same densities.
CPF370C	Not authorized to ALWOBJDIF parameter.
CPF371B	System/36 environment library not restored.
CPF3727	Duplicate device specified in device name list.
CPF3728	Diskette device specified with other devices.
CPF372C	Library not restored to ASP.
CPF3730	Not authorized to object.
CPF3731	Cannot use object.
CPF3732	Object status changed during restore operation.
CPF3733	Object previously damaged.
CPF3738	Device used for save or restore is damaged.
CPF3739	Database file member damaged.
CPF373E	Library not restored to ASP.
CPF3740	Object not found.
CPF3743	File cannot be restored or displayed.
CPF3748	Object information for library damaged.
CPF3752	No record of save operation exists for library.
CPF3757	Object not restored.
CPF3758	Object not restored.
CPF375F	File not selected. Cannot restore from save type.
CPF3767	Device not found.
CPF3768	Device not valid for command.
CPF3769	File found on media not save/restore file.
CPF376B	File not found.
CPF3770	No objects saved or restored for library.
CPF3773	nn objects restored, nn not restored.
CPF3779	Not all libraries restored.
CPF3780	Specified file not found.
CPF3781	Library not found.
CPF3782	File not a save file.
CPF3783	Cannot determine VOL(*SAVVOL) location. No objects restored.
CPF3784	Restore device specified in the DEV parameter does not match VOL(*SAVVOL) device.
CPF3785	Not all subsystems ended.
CPF378B	Library not created.
CPF3791	End of file.
CPF3793	Machine storage limit reached.
CPF3794	Save or restore operation ended unsuccessfully.
CPF3795	Error while processing.
CPF3796	Storage limit exceeded for user profile.
CPF3805	Objects from save file not restored.
CPF3807	Data decompression error for save file.
CPF3812	Save file in use.
CPF3818	Starting library not found.
CPF3894	Cancel reply received for message.
CPF5729	Not able to allocate object.
CPF9809	Library cannot be accessed.
CPF9812	File not found.
CPF9820	Not authorized to use library.
CPF9822	Not authorized to file.
CPF9825	Not authorized to device.
CPF9829	Auxiliary storage pool not found.

Files Used

QSYS/QPSRLDSP	PRTF	Restored objects status printer file.
QSYS/QSYSDKT	DKTF	Diskette device file used for input.
QSYS/QSYSTAP	TAPF	Tape device file used for input.

RSTOBJ (Restore Object)

Restores one or more objects to the system from a backup medium or from a save file.

Syntax

RSTOBJ	*OBJ(object-name)*	+
	SAVLIB(library-name)	+
	DEV(device-name)	+
	OBJTYPE(object-type)	+
	SAVF(library-name/save-file-name)	+
	FILEMBR(database-file-name	+
	member-name)	+
	RSTLIB(library-name)	+
	OUTPUT(*NONE|*PRINT)	

Parameter

OBJ	List of names of objects to restore
SAVLIB	Name of saved library
DEV	List of save devices: name, *SAVF
OBJTYPE	List of object types: *DEV, *DTAARA, *DTAQ, *FILE, *LIB, *MENU, *MSGQ, *PGM, *PNLGRP, *SBSD, *USRSPC, ...
SAVF	Name of save file if DEV(*SAVF) Library: name, *LIBL, *CURLIB
FILEMBR	List of file members to restore File: name, *ALL List of members: name, generic*, *ALL, *NONE
RSTLIB	Restore to library: name, *SAVLIB
OUTPUT	Print a listing: *NONE, *PRINT

Error Messages That Can Be Monitored

CPF3705	Object not journaled.
CPF3706	Object not restored to library.
CPF3707	Save file contains no data.
CPF3709	Tape devices do not support same densities.
CPF370C	Not authorized to ALWOBJDIF parameter.
CPF3727	Duplicate device specified in device name list.
CPF3728	Diskette device specified with other devices.
CPF3730	Not authorized to object.
CPF3731	Cannot use object.
CPF3733	Object previously damaged.
CPF3738	Device used for save or restore is damaged.
CPF3739	Database file member damaged.
CPF3743	File cannot be restored or displayed.
CPF3748	Object information for library damaged.
CPF374C	No objects restored to ASP.
CPF3767	Device not found.
CPF3768	Device not valid for command.
CPF3769	File found on media not save/restore file.
CPF3770	No objects saved or restored.
CPF3773	nn objects restored, nn not restored.
CPF3780	Specified file not found.
CPF3781	Library not found.
CPF3782	File not a save file.

CPF3783   Cannot determine VOL(*SAVVOL) location. No objects restored.
CPF3784   Restore device specified in the DEV parameter does not match
                 VOL(*SAVVOL) device.
CPF3791   End of file.
CPF3793   Machine storage limit reached.
CPF3794   Save or restore operation ended unsuccessfully.
CPF3795   Error while processing.
CPF3796   Storage limit exceeded for user profile.
CPF3805   Objects from save file not restored.
CPF3807   Data decompression error for save file.
CPF3812   Save file in use.
CPF3867   Contents of FILEMBR parameter not correct.
CPF3868   FILEMBR specified but OBJTYPE must be (*ALL) or (*FILE).
CPF3871   No objects saved or restored; nn objects not included.
CPF3872   Not all objects restored.
CPF5729   Not able to allocate object.
CPF9809   Library cannot be accessed.
CPF9812   File not found.
CPF9820   Not authorized to use library.
CPF9822   Not authorized to file.
CPF9825   Not authorized to device.
CPF9829   Auxiliary storage pool not found.

Files Used

QSYS/QPSRLDSP   PRTF   Restored objects status printer file.
QSYS/QSYSDKT   DKTF   Diskette device file used for input.
QSYS/QSYSTAP   TAPF   Tape device file used for input.

RTVCFGSTS (Retrieve Configuration Status)

Copies the current status of a configuration object, such as a line, controller, or device, into a CL variable.

Syntax

RTVCFGSTS   *CFGD(configuration-description-name)*   +
                 CFGTYPE(configuration-type)   +
                 STSCDE(&CL-variable-name)

Parameters

CFGD   Name of configuration object description to be retrieved
CFGTYPE   Type of configuration object description to be retrieved: *LIN, *CTL, *DEV, ...
STSCDE   Name of CL variable to contain status code

Error Messages That Can Be Monitored

(None)

Files Used

(None)

RTVCLSRC (Retrieve CL Source)

Decompiles a CL program, placing the retrieved source statements into a source file.

Syntax

RTVCLSRC   *PGM(library-name/program-name)*   +
                 SRCFILE(library-name/source-file-name)   +
                 SRCMBR(source-member-name)

Parameters

PGM	Name of program whose source is to be retrieved
	Library: name, *LIBL, *CURLIB
SRCFILE	Name of source file into which CL statements are to be written
	Library: name, *LIBL, *CURLIB
SRCMBR	Source file member into which CL statements are to be written: name, *PGM

Error Messages That Can Be Monitored

CPF0560	Program not a CL program.
CPF0561	Unable to retrieve CL source from CL program.
CPF0562	File not a database source file.
CPF0563	Record length too small for database source file.
CPF0564	Unable to add database member.
CPF0565	Source from CL program not retrieved.
CPF0566	Source not available for CL program.
CPF9801	Object not found.
CPF9806	Cannot perform function for object.
CPF9809	Library cannot be accessed.
CPF9811	Program not found.
CPF9820	Not authorized to use library.
CPF9821	Not authorized to program.
CPF9822	Not authorized to file.
CPF9848	Cannot open file member.
CPF9849	Error while processing file.

Files Used

(None)

RTVDTAARA (Retrieve Data Area)

Copies all or part of a data area into a CL variable.

Syntax

```
RTVDTAARA        DTAARA(library-name/data-area-name              +
                        (substring-starting-position              +
                         substring-length))                       +
                 RTNVAR(&CL-variable-name)
```

Parameters

DTAARA	Data area to be retrieved: name, *LDA, *GDA, *PDA
	Library: name, *LIBL, *CURLIB
	Substring starting position: 1-2000, *ALL
	Substring length: 1–2000
RTNVAR	Name of CL variable to contain value of retrieved data

Error Messages That Can Be Monitored

CPF0811	RTNVAR parameter has incorrect length for data area.
CPF0812	RTNVAR parameter type not valid for data area.
CPF0813	Value in data area not logical value.
CPF1015	Data area not found.
CPF1016	No authority to data area.
CPF1021	Library not found.
CPF1022	No authority to data area.
CPF1043	Boundary alignment for data area not valid.
CPF1044	AREA parameter not valid for data area.
CPF1045	CPYPTR parameter not valid for data area.
CPF1046	DTAARA(*GDA) not valid because job not group job.
CPF1063	Cannot allocate data area.
CPF1067	Cannot allocate library.

CPF1072	DTAARA(*PDA) not valid because job not prestart job.
CPF1087	Substring not allowed for decimal or logical data area.
CPF1088	Starting position outside of data area.
CPF1089	Substring specified for data area not valid.

Files Used

(None)

RTVJOBA (Retrieve Job Attributes)

Copies information about the job in which a program is running into one or more CL variables.

Syntax

RTVJOBA	JOB(&CL-variable-name)	+
	USER(&CL-variable-name)	+
	NBR(&CL-variable-name)	+
	LOGLVL(&CL-variable-name)	+
	LOGSEV(&CL-variable-name)	+
	LOGTYPE(&CL-variable-name)	+
	LOGCLPGM(&CL-variable-name)	+
	OUTQ(&CL-variable-name)	+
	OUTQLIB(&CL-variable-name)	+
	DATE(&CL-variable-name)	+
	TYPE(&CL-variable-name)	+
	RUNPTY(&CL-variable-name)	+
	USRLIBL(&CL-variable-name)	+
	CURLIB(&CL-variable-name)	+
	PRTDEV(&CL-variable-name)	

Parameters

JOB	CL variable to contain name of job (*CHAR 10)
USER	CL variable to contain name of user profile associated which the job (*CHAR 10)
NBR	CL variable to contain unique number of of job (*CHAR 6)
LOGLVL	CL variable to contain message logging level (*CHAR 1)
LOGSEV	CL variable to contain message logging severity level (*DEC 2 0)
LOGTYPE	CL variable to contain level of text that appears for any logged message (*CHAR 10)
LOGCLPGM	CL variable to contain value that determines whether CL commands are logged(*CHAR 10)
OUTQ	CL variable to contain name of output queue (*CHAR 10)
OUTQLIB	CL variable to contain name of OUTQ library (*CHAR 10)
DATE	CL variable to contain job date (*CHAR 6)
TYPE	CL variable to contain job execution environment (0=batch, 1=interactive) (*CHAR 1)
RUNPTY	CL variable to contain job execution priority (*DEC 2 0)
USRLIBL	CL variable to contain list of libraries in user library list (*CHAR 275)
CURLIB	CL variable to contain the name of the current library (*CHAR 10)
PRTDEV	CL variable to contain name of printer device (*CHAR 10)

Error Messages That Can Be Monitored

(None)

Files Used

(None)

RTVMBRD (Retrieve Member Description)

Copies descriptive information about a database file member into one or more CL variables.

Syntax

RTVMBRD	*FILE(library-name/file-name)*	+
	MBR(member-name)	+
	RTNLIB(&CL-variable-name)	+
	RTNMBR(&CL-variable-name)	+
	FILEATR(&CL-variable-name)	+
	FILETYPE(&CL-variable-name)	+
	SRCTYPE(&CL-variable-name)	+
	SRCCHGDATE(&CL-variable-name)	+
	TEXT(&CL-variable-name)	+
	NBRCURRCD(&CL-variable-name)	+
	NBRDLTRCD(&CL-variable-name)	+
	SAVDATE(&CL-variable-name)	+
	USEDATE(&CL-variable-name)	

Parameters

FILE	Name of file containing member to retrieve Library: name, *LIBL, *CURLIB
MBR	Member to retrieve: name, generic*, *FIRST, *LAST, *FIRSTMBR, *LASTMBR Relationship: *SAME, *NEXT, *PRV
RTNLIB	CL variable to contain name of library (*CHAR 10)
RTNMBR	CL variable to contain name of member (*CHAR 10)
FILEATR	CL variable to contain file attribute: *PF or *LF (*CHAR 3)
FILETYPE	CL variable to contain file type: *DATA or *SRC (*CHAR 5)
SRCTYPE	CL variable to contain source file member type (*CHAR 10)
SRCCHGDATE	CL variable to contain date and time source was last changed: CYYMMDDHHMMSS format (*CHAR 13)
TEXT	CL variable to contain member text (*CHAR 50)
NBRCURRCD	CL variable to contain current number of non-deleted records in member (*DEC 10 0)
NBRDLTRCD	CL variable to contain current number of deleted records (*DEC 10 0)
SAVDATE	CL variable to contain date and time member was last saved: CYYMMDDHHMMSS format (*CHAR 13)
USEDATE	CL variable to contain date and time member was last used: CYYMMDD format (*CHAR 7)

Error Messages That Can Be Monitored

CPF3018	Member not available.
CPF3019	File has no members.
CPF3027	File not a database file.
CPF3038	Attributes for return variable not valid.
CPF3039	Return variable too small to hold result.
CPF3049	*NEXT or *PRV member does not exist.
CPF3051	File not available.
CPF325F	Conversion of the text failed.
CPF8109	Damage on physical database file.
CPF8110	Damage on logical database file.
CPF8111	Damage on member.
CPF9806	Cannot perform function for object.
CPF9812	File not found.
CPF9815	Member not found.
CPF9820	Not authorized to use library.
CPF9822	Not authorized to file.

Files Used

(None)

RTVMSG (Retrieve Message)

Copies a message from a message file into one or more CL variables.

Syntax

RTVMSG	*MSGID (message-identifier)*	+
	MSGF (library-name/message-file-name)	+
	MSG (&CL-variable-name)	+
	MSGLEN (&CL-variable-name)	+
	SEV (&CL-variable-name)	

Parameters

MSGID	Message identifier to retrieve
MSGF	Name of message file containing message identifier
	Library: name, <u>*LIBL</u>, *CURLIB
MSG	CL variable to contain text of message (*CHAR 132)
MSGLEN	CL variable to contain length of retrieved message text (*DEC 5 0)
SEV	CL variable to contain severity code of retrieved message (*DEC 2 0)

Error Messages That Can Be Monitored

CPF2401	Not authorized to library.
CPF2407	Message file not found.
CPF2411	Not authorized to message file.
CPF2419	Message identifier not found in message file.
CPF2465	Replacement text of message not valid for format specified.
CPF2471	Length of field not valid.
CPF2499	Message identifier not allowed.
CPF2531	Message file damaged.
CPF2547	Damage to message file QCPFMSG.
CPF2548	Damage to message file.
CPF8126	Message file damaged.

Files Used

(None)

RTVNETA (Retrieve Network Attributes)

Copies network attributes for the system into one or more CL variables.

Syntax

RTVNETA	SYSNAME (&CL-variable-name)	+
	LCLNETID (&CL-variable-name)	+
	LCLCPNAME (&CL-variable-name)	+
	LCLLOCNAME (&CL-variable-name)	+
	DFTMODE (&CL-variable-name)	

Parameters

SYSNAME	CL variable to contain name of system (*CHAR 8)
LCLNETID	CL variable to contain local network identifier (*CHAR 8)
LCLCPNAME	CL variable to contain local control point name (*CHAR 8)
LCLLOCNAME	CL variable to contain default local location name (*CHAR 8)
DFTMODE	CL variable to contain default mode name (*CHAR 8)

Error Messages That Can Be Monitored

| CPF1844 | Cannot access network attribute. |

Files Used

(None)

RTVOBJD (Retrieve Object Description)

Copies descriptive information about an object on the system into one or more CL variables.

Syntax

RTVOBJD	**OBJ**(library-name/object-name)	+
	OBJTYPE(object-type)	+
	RTNLIB(&CL-variable-name)	+
	OBJATR(&CL-variable-name)	+
	TEXT(&CL-variable-name)	+
	OWNER(&CL-variable-name)	+
	SAVDATE(&CL-variable-name)	+
	USEDATE(&CL-variable-name)	+
	SIZE(&CL-variable-name)	+
	SRCF(&CL-variable-name)	+
	SRCFLIB(&CL-variable-name)	+
	SRCMBR(&CL-variable-name)	+
	SRCDATE(&CL-variable-name)	+
	SYSLVL(&CL-variable-name)	

Parameters

OBJ	Name of object description to be retrieved Library: name, *LIBL, *CURLIB
OBJTYPE	List of object types: *DEV, *DTAARA, *DTAQ, *FILE, *LIB, *MENU, *MSGQ, *PGM, *PNLGRP, *SBSD, *USRSPC, …
RTNLIB	CL variable to contain name of library (*CHAR 10)
OBJATR	CL variable to contain expanded object attribute, such as file or program type (*CHAR 10)
OWNER	CL variable to contain name of object owner (*CHAR 10)
TEXT	CL variable to contain member text (*CHAR 50)
SAVDATE	CL variable to contain date and time member was last saved: CYYMMDDHHMMSS format (*CHAR 13)
USEDATE	CL variable to contain date and time member was last used: CYYMMDD format (*CHAR 7)
SIZE	CL variable to contain size of the object in bytes (*DEC 15 0)
SRCF	CL variable to contain name of source file used to create object (*CHAR 10)
SRCFLIB	CL variable to contain name of library for SRCF (*CHAR 10)
SRCMBR	CL variable to contain name of member in SRCF used to create object (*CHAR 10)
SRCDATE	CL variable to contain date and time the source member was updated (*CHAR 13)
SYSLVL	CL variable to contain operating system level under which the object was created: version, release, modification level (*CHAR 9)

Error Messages That Can Be Monitored

CPF2115	Object damaged.
CPF2150	Object information function failed.
CPF2151	Operation failed for object.
CPF2451	Message queue is allocated to another job.
CPF9801	Object not found.
CPF9802	Not authorized to object.
CPF9811	Program not found.
CPF9812	File not found.
CPF9814	Device not found.
CPF9820	Not authorized to use library.
CPF9821	Not authorized to program.
CPF9822	Not authorized to file.
CPF9825	Not authorized to device.
CPF9831	Cannot assign device.

Files Used

(None)

RTVSYSVAL (Retrieve System Value)

Copies a system value (e.g., the system date or time) into a CL variable.

Syntax

RTVSYSVAL	*SYSVAL(system-value-name)*	+
	RTNVAR(&CL-variable-name)	

Parameters

SYSVAL	Name of system value to retrieve: QATNPGM, QDATE, QPRTDEV, QPRTTXT, QSTRUPPGM, QSYSLIBL, QTIME, QUSRLIBL, ...
RTNVAR	CL variable to contain value of system value

Error Messages That Can Be Monitored

CPF1028	Invalid SYSVAL parameter.
CPF1074	SYSVAL(QMONTH) not valid for Julian date format.
CPF1094	CL variable not same type as system value.
CPF1095	CL variable length not valid for system value.
CPF1842	Cannot access system value.
CPF268D	Unable to access system value.

Files Used

(None)

RTVUSRPRF (Retrieve User Profile)

Copies information about a user into one or more CL variables.

Syntax

RTVUSRPRF	*USRPRF(user-name)*	+
	RTNUSRPRF(&CL-variable-name)	+
	SPCAUT(&CL-variable-name)	+
	INLPGM(&CL-variable-name)	+
	INLPGMLIB(&CL-variable-name)	+
	JOBD(&CL-variable-name)	+
	JOBDLIB(&CL-variable-name)	+
	GRPPRF(&CL-variable-name)	+
	OWNER(&CL-variable-name)	+
	GRPAUT(&CL-variable-name)	+
	ACGCDE(&CL-variable-name)	+
	MSGQ(&CL-variable-name)	+
	MSGQLIB(&CL-variable-name)	+
	OUTQ(&CL-variable-name)	+
	OUTQLIB(&CL-variable-name)	+
	TEXT(&CL-variable-name)	+
	PWDCHGDAT(&CL-variable-name)	+
	USRCLS(&CL-variable-name)	+
	CURLIB(&CL-variable-name)	+
	INLMNU(&CL-variable-name)	+
	INLMNULIB(&CL-variable-name)	+
	LMTCPB(&CL-variable-name)	+
	PRTDEV(&CL-variable-name)	+
	PWDEXP(&CL-variable-name)	+
	STATUS(&CL-variable-name)	+
	PRVSIGN(&CL-variable-name)	+
	NOTVLDSIGN(&CL-variable-name)	

Parameters

USRPRF	User profile to retrieve: name, *CURRENT
RTNUSRPRF	CL variable to contain name of retrieved user profile (*CHAR 10)
SPCAUT	CL variable to contain list of special authorities for user profile (*CHAR 100)
INLPGM	CL variable to contain name of initial program that starts when retrieved user profile signs on (*CHAR 10)
INLPGMLIB	CL variable to contain name of library for INLPGM (*CHAR 10)
JOBD	CL variable to contain name of job description associated with retrieved user profile (*CHAR 10)
JOBDLIB	CL variable to contain name of library for JOBD (*CHAR 10)
GRPPRF	CL variable to contain name of group profile (*CHAR 10)
OWNER	CL variable to contain value which specifies user of created objects: *USRPRF or *GRPPRF (*CHAR 10)
GRPAUT	CL variable to contain type of authority granted for created objects: *CHANGE, *ALL, *USE, *EXCLUDE (*CHAR 10)
ACGCDE	CL variable to contain accounting code (*CHAR 15)
MSGQ	CL variable to contain name of message queue associated with user profile (*CHAR 10)
MSGQLIB	CL variable to contain name of library for MSGQ (*CHAR 10)
OUTQ	CL variable to contain name of output queue associated with user profile (*CHAR 10)
OUTQLIB	CL variable to contain name of library for OUTQ (*CHAR 10)
TEXT	CL variable to contain text for user profile (*CHAR 50)
PWDCHGDAT	CL variable to contain date password was last changed: YYMMDD (*CHAR 6)
USRCLS	CL variable to contain user class: *USER, *SYSOPR, *PGMR, *SECADM or *SECOFR (*CHAR 10)
CURLIB	CL variable to contain name of default library for user profile(*CHAR 10)
INLMNU	CL variable to contain name of menu that is displayed when user signs on (*CHAR 10)
INLMNULIB	CL variable to contain name of library for INLMNU (*CHAR 10)
LMTCPB	CL variable to contain value to indicate limitations on AS/400 command line capabilities: *NO, *YES or *PARTIAL (*CHAR 10)
PRTDEV	CL variable to contain name of printer device for user profile (*CHAR 10)
PWDEXP	CL variable to contain password expiration indicator: *YES or *NO (*CHAR 4)
STATUS	CL variable to contain status of user profile: *ENABLED or *DISABLED (*CHAR 10)
PRVSIGN	CL variable to contain previous sign on date and time: CYYMMDDHHMMSS (*CHAR 13)
NOTVLDSIGN	CL variable to contain number of invalid sign on attempts (*DEC 11 0)

Error Messages That Can Be Monitored

CPF2203	User profile not correct.
CPF2204	User profile not found.
CPF2213	Not able to allocate user profile.
CPF2217	Not authorized to user profile.
CPF2225	Not able to allocate internal system object.
CPF2299	Not able to create internal security object.
CPF8134	User profile damaged.

Files Used

(None)

SAVCHGOBJ (Save Changed Objects)

Saves to a backup medium or a save file each specified object or group of objects that has changed since a specific date and time.

Syntax

SAVCHGOBJ	*OBJ(object-name)*	+
	LIB(library-name)	+
	DEV(device-name)	+
	OBJTYPE(object-type)	+
	SAVF(library-name/save-file-name)	+
	OUTPUT(*NONE|*PRINT|*OUTFILE)	+
	OUTFILE(library-name/output-file-name)	

Parameters

OBJ	List of objects to save: name, generic*, *ALL
LIB	List of libraries containing objects to save: name, *ALLUSR
DEV	List of save devices: name, *SAVF
OBJTYPE	List of object types: *DEV, *DTAARA, *DTAQ, *FILE, *LIB, *MENU, *MSGQ, *PGM, *PNLGRP, *SBSD, *USRSPC, ...
SAVF	Name of save file if DEV(*SAVF) Library: name, *LIBL, *CURLIB
OUTPUT	List saved objects: *NONE, *PRINT, *OUTFILE
OUTFILE	Name of file to receive output if OUTPUT(*OUTFILE) Library: name, *LIBL, *CURLIB

Error Messages That Can Be Monitored

CPF3702	nn objects saved; nn not saved; nn not included.
CPF3703	Object not saved.
CPF3708	Save file too small.
CPF3709	Tape devices do not support same densities.
CPF3727	Duplicate device specified in device name list.
CPF3728	Diskette device specified with other devices.
CPF3730	Not authorized to object.
CPF3731	Cannot use object in library.
CPF3733	Object previously damaged.
CPF3735	Storage limit exceeded for user profile.
CPF3738	Device used for save or restore is damaged.
CPF3745	No record of SAVLIB operation exists for library.
CPF3746	System date and time earlier than reference date and time.
CPF3747	Object names cannot be specified with more than one library.
CPF3749	nn objects from library nn not saved.
CPF3767	Device not found.
CPF3768	Device not valid for command.
CPF3770	No objects saved or restored for library.
CPF3774	Not all objects saved from library.
CPF3778	Not all objects saved from all libraries.
CPF377D	Save ended because of read error on internal system resource.
CPF377E	Not enough storage for save-while-active request.
CPF377F	Save-while-active request prevented by pending record changes.
CPF3781	Library not found.
CPF3782	File not a save file.
CPF3789	Only one library allowed with specified parameters.
CPF378A	Message queue not available.
CPF378C	SAVACTMSGQ(*WRKSTN) not valid for batch job.
CPF378E	Library not saved.
CPF3790	No available space on mounted diskette.
CPF3793	Machine storage limit reached.
CPF3794	Save or restore operation ended unsuccessfully.
CPF3795	Error while processing.
CPF3797	No objects saved from library. Save limit exceeded.
CPF3812	Save file in use.
CPF3815	Save file too small for save operation.

CPF3818	Starting library not found.
CPF3867	Contents of FILEMBR parameter not correct.
CPF3868	FILEMBR specified but OBJTYPE must be (*ALL) or (*FILE).
CPF3871	No objects saved or restored; nn objects not included.
CPF3892	Object not saved.
CPF3894	Cancel reply received for message.
CPF5729	Not able to allocate object.
CPF836B	Uncommitted changes prevent save request.
CPF836C	Uncommitted changes prevent save request for library.
CPF836F	Unexpected error during save request.
CPF9809	Library cannot be accessed.
CPF9812	File not found.
CPF9820	Not authorized to use library.
CPF9822	Not authorized to file.
CPF9825	Not authorized to device.

Files Used

QSYS/QASAVOBJ	PF	Model outfile for saved object information.
QSYS/QPSAVOBJ	PRTF	Printer file for saved object information.
QSYS/QSYSDKT	DKTF	Diskette device file used for output.
QSYS/QSYSTAP	TAPF	Tape device file used for output.

SAVLIB (Save Library)

Saves one or more libraries to a backup medium or a save file.

Syntax

SAVLIB	*LIB(library-name)*	+
	DEV(device-name)	+
	SAVF(library-name/save-file-name)	+
	OUTPUT(*NONE|*PRINT|*OUTFILE)	+
	OUTFILE(library-name/output-file-name)	

Parameters

LIB	List of libraries to save: name, *NONSYS, *ALLUSR, *IBM
DEV	List of save devices: name, *SAVF
SAVF	Name of save file if DEV(*SAVF)
	Library: name, *LIBL, *CURLIB
OUTPUT	List saved objects: *NONE, *PRINT, *OUTFILE
OUTFILE	Name of file to receive output if OUTPUT(*OUTFILE)
	Library: name, *LIBL, *CURLIB

Error Messages That Can Be Monitored

CPF3701	nn objects were saved; nn objects were not saved.
CPF3703	Object not saved.
CPF3708	Save file too small.
CPF3709	Tape devices do not support same densities.
CPF3727	Duplicate device specified in device name list.
CPF3728	Diskette device specified with other devices.
CPF3730	Not authorized to object.
CPF3731	Cannot use object.
CPF3733	Object previously damaged.
CPF3735	Storage limit exceeded for user profile.
CPF3738	Device used for save or restore is damaged.
CPF3749	nn objects from library nn not saved.
CPF3751	Some libraries not saved.
CPF3767	Device not found.
CPF3768	Device not valid for command.
CPF3770	No objects saved or restored for library.

CPF3771	nn objects saved. nn not saved.
CPF3777	Not all libraries saved.
CPF377D	Save ended because of read error on internal system resource.
CPF377E	Not enough storage for save-while-active request.
CPF377F	Save-while-active request prevented by pending record changes.
CPF3781	Library not found.
CPF3782	File not a save file.
CPF3785	Not all subsystems ended.
CPF3789	Only one library allowed with specified parameters.
CPF378A	Message queue not available.
CPF378C	SAVACTMSGQ(*WRKSTN) not valid for batch job.
CPF378E	Library not saved.
CPF3790	No available space on mounted diskette.
CPF3793	Machine storage limit reached.
CPF3794	Save or restore operation ended unsuccessfully.
CPF3795	Error while processing.
CPF3797	No objects saved from library. Save limit exceeded.
CPF3812	Save file in use.
CPF3815	Save file too small for save operation.
CPF3818	Starting library not found.
CPF3871	No objects saved or restored; nn objects not included.
CPF3892	Object not saved.
CPF3894	Cancel reply received for message.
CPF5729	Not able to allocate object.
CPF836B	Uncommitted changes prevent save request.
CPF836C	Uncommitted changes prevent save request for library.
CPF836F	Unexpected error during save request.
CPF9809	Library cannot be accessed.
CPF9812	File not found.
CPF9820	Not authorized to use library.
CPF9822	Not authorized to file.
CPF9825	Not authorized to device.

Files Used

QSYS/QASAVOBJ	PF	Model outfile for saved object information.
QSYS/QPSAVOBJ	PRTF	Printer file for saved object information.
QSYS/QSYSDKT	DKTF	Diskette device file used for output.
QSYS/QSYSTAP	TAPF	Tape device file used for output.

SAVOBJ (Save Object)

Saves one or more objects to a backup medium or a save file.

Syntax

SAVOBJ	*OBJ(object-name)*	+
	LIB(library-name)	+
	DEV(device-name)	+
	OBJTYPE(object-type)	+
	SAVF(library-name/save-file-name)	+
	OUTPUT(*NONE*|*PRINT|*OUTFILE)	+
	OUTFILE(library-name/output-file-name)	

Parameters

OBJ	List of objects to save: name, generic*, *ALL
LIB	List of names of libraries containing objects to save
DEV	List of save devices: name, *SAVF
OBJTYPE	List of object types: *DEV, *DTAARA, *DTAQ, *FILE, *LIB, *MENU, *MSGQ, *PGM, *PNLGRP, *SBSD, *USRSPC, ...
SAVF	Name of save file if DEV(*SAVF)
	Library: name, *LIBL, *CURLIB

OUTPUT	List saved objects: *NONE, *PRINT, *OUTFILE
OUTFILE	Name of file to receive output if OUTPUT(*OUTFILE)
	Library: name, *LIBL, *CURLIB

Error Messages That Can Be Monitored

CPF3701	nn objects were saved; nn objects were not saved.
CPF3702	nn objects saved; nn not saved; nn not included.
CPF3703	Object not saved.
CPF3708	Save file too small.
CPF3709	Tape devices do not support same densities.
CPF3727	Duplicate device specified in device name list.
CPF3728	Diskette device specified with other devices.
CPF3730	Not authorized to object.
CPF3731	Cannot use object.
CPF3733	Object previously damaged.
CPF3735	Storage limit exceeded for user profile.
CPF3738	Device used for save or restore is damaged.
CPF3747	Object names cannot be specified with more than one library.
CPF3749	nn objects from library nn not saved.
CPF3767	Device nn not found.
CPF3768	Device nn not valid for command.
CPF3770	No objects saved or restored for library.
CPF3771	nn objects saved. nn not saved.
CPF3774	Not all objects saved from library.
CPF3778	Not all objects saved from all libraries.
CPF377D	Save ended because of read error on internal system resource.
CPF377E	Not enough storage for save-while-active request.
CPF377F	Save-while-active request prevented by pending record changes.
CPF3781	Library not found.
CPF3782	File not a save file.
CPF3789	Only one library allowed with specified parameters.
CPF378A	Message queue not available.
CPF378C	SAVACTMSGQ(*WRKSTN) not valid for batch job.
CPF378E	Library not saved.
CPF3790	No available space on mounted diskette.
CPF3793	Machine storage limit reached.
CPF3794	Save or restore operation ended unsuccessfully.
CPF3795	Error while processing.
CPF3797	No objects saved from library. Save limit exceeded.
CPF3812	Save file in use.
CPF3815	Save file too small for save operation.
CPF3867	Contents of FILEMBR parameter not correct.
CPF3868	FILEMBR specified but OBJTYPE must be (*ALL) or (*FILE).
CPF3871	No objects saved or restored; nn objects not included.
CPF3892	Object not saved.
CPF3894	Cancel reply received for message.
CPF5729	Not able to allocate object.
CPF836B	Uncommitted changes prevent save request.
CPF836C	Uncommitted changes prevent save request for library.
CPF836F	Unexpected error during save request.
CPF9809	Library cannot be accessed.
CPF9812	File not found.
CPF9820	Not authorized to use library.
CPF9822	Not authorized to file.
CPF9825	Not authorized to device.

Files Used

QSYS/QASAVOBJ	PF	Model outfile for saved object information.
QSYS/QPSAVOBJ	PRTF	Printer file for saved object information.

QSYS/QSYSDKT	DKTF	Diskette device file used for output.
QSYS/QSYSTAP	TAPF	Tape device file used for output.

SAVSAVFDTA (Save Save File Data)

Copies the contents of a save file to a backup medium.

Syntax

SAVSAVFDTA	*SAVF(library-name/save-file-name)*	+
	DEV(device-name)	+
	OUTPUT(<u>*NONE</u>|*PRINT|*OUTFILE)	+
	OUTFILE(library-name/output-file-name)	

Parameters

SAVF	Name of save file
	Library: name, <u>*LIBL</u>, *CURLIB
DEV	List of names of save devices
OUTPUT	List saved objects: <u>*NONE</u>, *PRINT, *OUTFILE
OUTFILE	Name of file to receive output if OUTPUT(*OUTFILE)
	Library: name, <u>*LIBL</u>, *CURLIB

Error Messages That Can Be Monitored

CPF3707	Save file contains no data.
CPF3709	Tape devices do not support same densities.
CPF3727	Duplicate device specified in device name list.
CPF3728	Diskette device specified with other devices.
CPF3733	Object previously damaged.
CPF3767	Device not found.
CPF3768	Device not valid for command.
CPF3782	File not a save file.
CPF3793	Machine storage limit reached.
CPF3794	Save or restore operation ended unsuccessfully.
CPF3795	Error while processing.
CPF3812	Save file in use.
CPF5729	Not able to allocate object.
CPF9812	File not found.
CPF9822	Not authorized to file.
CPF9825	Not authorized to device.

Files Used

QSYS/QASAVOBJ	PF	Model outfile for saved object information.
QSYS/QPSAVOBJ	PRTF	Printer file for saved object information.
QSYS/QSYSDKT	DKTF	Diskette device file used for output.
QSYS/QSYSTAP	TAPF	Tape device file used for output.

SBMJOB (Submit Job)

Submits a command or requests data to be run as a batch job.

Syntax

SBMJOB	*JOB(job-name)*	+
	JOBD(library-name/job-description-name)	+
	USER(user-name)	+
	JOBQ(library-name/job-queue-name)	+
	CMD(CL-command)	+
	SYSLIBL(<u>*CURRENT</u>|*SYSVAL)	+
	CURLIB(current-library-name)	+
	INLLIBL(library-name)	+
	PRTDEV(printer-device-name)	+

```
                        OUTQ(library-name/output-queue-name)              +
                        HOLD(*JOBD|*NO|*YES)                              +
                        SCDDATE(date)                                     +
                        SCDTIME(time)                                     +
                        MSGQ(library-name/message-queue-name)
                        . . .
```

Parameters

JOB	Name to be associated with job: name, *JOBD
JOBD	Job description to be used for job: name, *USRPRF
	Library: name, *LIBL, *CURLIB
USER	User profile to be associated with job: name, *CURRENT, *JOBD
JOBQ	Job queue in which job is to be placed: name, *JOBD
	Library: name, *LIBL, *CURLIB
CMD	CL command to run in the batch job
SYSLIBL	System portion of library list for job: *CURRENT, *SYSVAL
CURLIB	Default library for job: name, *CURRENT, *USRPRF, *CRTDFT
INLLIBL	Initial library list for job: names, *CURRENT, *JOB, *SYSVAL, *NONE
PRTDEV	Printer device for job: name, *CURRENT, *USRPRF, *SYSVAL, *JOBD
OUTQ	Output queue for job: name, *CURRENT, *USRPRF, *DEV, *JOBD
HOLD	Hold job on job queue: *JOBD, *NO, *YES
SCDDATE	Scheduled date: date, *CURRENT, *MONTHSTR, *MONTHEND, *MON, *TUE, *WED, *THU, *FRI, *SAT
SCDTIME	Scheduled time: time, *CURRENT
MSGQ	Message queue to receive completion message: name, *USRPRF, *WRKSTN, *NONE

Error Messages That Can Be Monitored

CPF1338	Errors occurred on SBMJOB command.
CPF1634	Specified date or time has passed.
CPF1642	Schedule date not correct.
CPF1854	Value for CCSID parameter not valid.

Files Used

(None)

SIGNOFF (Sign Off)

Ends one or more interactive jobs at a display station.

Syntax

SIGNOFF	LOG(*NOLIST| *LIST) +
	DROP(*DEVD| *YES| *NO)

Parameters

LOG	List job log: *NOLIST, *LIST
DROP	Disconnect switched communications line: *DEVD, *YES, *NO

Error Messages That Can Be Monitored

(None)

Files Used

(None)

SNDBRKMSG (Send Break Message)

Sends a message to one or more workstation message queues in break mode, interrupting the interactive job in progress at the display station.

Syntax

SNDBRKMSG	*MSG ('message-text')*	+
	TOMSGQ(library-name/message-queue-name)	+
	MSGTYPE(*INFO| *INQ)	+
	RPYMSGQ(library-name/message-queue-name)	

Parameters

MSG	Message text
TOMSGQ	List of workstation message queues to receive message: name, *ALLWS
	Library: name, *LIBL
MSGTYPE	Type of message: *INFO, *INQ
RPYMSGQ	Message queue to get reply if MSGTYPE(*INQ): name, QSYSOPR
	Library: name, *LIBL

Error Messages That Can Be Monitored

CPF2428	Only one message queue allowed for *INQ and *NOTIFY type messages.
CPF2469	Error occurred when sending message.

Files Used

(None)

SNDF (Send File)

Sends a display format to a display station.

Syntax

SNDF	*DEV(device-name)*	+
	RCDFMT(record-format-name)	

Parameters

DEV	Display device to which record format is sent: name, *FILE
RCDFMT	Record format to send: name, *FILE

Error Messages That Can Be Monitored

CPF0859	File override caused I/O buffer size to be exceeded.
CPF0861	File is not a display file.
CPF0864	End of file detected.
CPF0883	*FILE not valid in DEV parameter.
CPF0887	Data available from previous input request.
CPF4101	File not found or inline data file missing.
CPF5068	Program device not found.
CPF5070	File has no program devices acquired.

Files Used

(None)

SNDMSG (Send Message)

Sends a message to one or more message queues.

Syntax

SNDMSG	*MSG ('message-text')*	+
	TOMSGQ(library-name/message-queue-name)	+
	MSGTYPE(*INFO| *INQ)	+
	RPYMSGQ(library-name/message-queue-name)	

Alternative Syntax

SNDMSG	*MSG* ('*message-text*')	+
	TOUSR(user-profile-name)	+
	MSGTYPE(*INFO| *INQ)	+
	RPYMSGQ(library-name/message-queue-name)	

Parameters

MSG	Message text
TOUSR	List of users to receive message: name, *SYSOPR, *ALLACT, *REQUESTER
TOMSGQ	List of message queues to receive message: name, *SYSOPR
	Library: name, *LIBL
MSGTYPE	Type of message: *INFO, *INQ
RPYMSGQ	Message queue to get reply if MSGTYPE(*INQ): name, *WRKSTN
	Library: name, *LIBL, *CURLIB

Error Messages That Can Be Monitored

CPF2428	Only one message queue allowed for *INQ and *NOTIFY type messages.
CPF2433	Function not allowed for system log message queue.
CPF2469	Error occurred when sending message.
CPF2488	Reply message queue *WRKSTN not valid for batch job.

Files Used

(None)

SNDPGMMSG (Send Program Message)

Sends a program message to a message queue or to another program within a job.

Syntax

SNDPGMMSG	*MSGID* (*message-identifier*)	+
	MSGF(library-name/message-file-name)	+
	MSGDTA(character-string)	+
	TOMSGQ(library-name/message-queue-name)	+
	TOPGMQ(*PRV|*SAME	+
	program-name)	+
	MSGTYPE(message-type)	+
	RPYMSGQ(library-name/message-queue-name)	

Alternative Syntaxes

SNDPGMMSG	*MSGID* (*message-identifier*)	+
	MSGF(library-name/message-file-name)	+
	MSGDTA(character-string)	+
	TOUSR(user-name)	+
	MSGTYPE(message-type)	+
	RPYMSGQ(library-name/ message-queue-name)	
SNDPGMMSG	*MSG* ('*message-text*')	+
	TOMSGQ(library-name/message-queue-name)	+
	TOPGMQ(*PRV|*SAME	+
	program-name)	+
	MSGTYPE(message-type)	+
	RPYMSGQ(library-name/message-queue-name)	+
SNDPGMMSG	*MSG* ('*message-text*')	+
	TOUSR(user-profile-name)	+
	MSGTYPE(message-type)	+
	RPYMSGQ(library-name/message-queue-name)	

Parameters

MSGID	Message identifier of message to send
MSGF	Name of message file containing message to send
	Library: name, *LIBL
MSGDTA	Message data field: values, *NONE
MSG	Message text
TOMSGQ	List of nonprogram message queues to receive message: name, *TOPGMQ, *SYSOPR
	Library: name, *LIBL, *CURLIB
TOPGMQ	Program message queue relationship: *PRV, *EXT, *SAME
	Program: name, *
TOUSR	User to receive message: name, *SYSOPR, *ALLACT, *REQUESTER
MSGTYPE	Type of message: *INFO, *INQ, *RQS, *COMP, *DIAG, *NOTIFY, *ESCAPE, *STATUS
RPYMSGQ	Message queue to get reply if MSGTYPE(*INQ or *NOTIFY): name, *PGMQ
	Library: name, *LIBL, *CURLIB

Error Messages That Can Be Monitored

CPF2428	Only one message queue allowed for *INQ and *NOTIFY type messages.
CPF2453	Reply queue not sender's program message queue.
CPF2469	Error occurred when sending message.
CPF2499	Message identifier not allowed.
CPF2524	Exception handler not available.
CPF9847	Error occurred while closing file.

Files Used

(None)

SNDRCVF (Send/Receive File)

Sends a display format to a display station, then reads input data from that display station.

Syntax

SNDRCVF	DEV(device-name)	+
	RCDFMT(record-format-name)	+
	WAIT(*YES|*NO)	

Parameters

DEV	Display device to which record format is sent: name, *FILE
RCDFMT	Record format to send: name, *FILE
WAIT	Wait to receive data: *YES, *NO

Error Messages That Can Be Monitored

CPF0859	File override caused I/O buffer size to be exceeded.
CPF0861	File is not a display file.
CPF0863	Value of binary data too large for decimal CL variable.
CPF0864	End of file detected.
CPF0883	*FILE not valid in DEV parameter.
CPF0886	Record contains a data field that is not valid.
CPF0887	Data available from previous input request.
CPF4101	File not found or inline data file missing.
CPF5068	Program device not found.
CPF5070	File has no program devices acquired.

Files Used

(None)

SNDRPY (Send Reply)

Sends a reply to the sender of an inquiry message.

Syntax

SNDRPY	*MSGKEY(&CL-variable-name)*	+
	MSGQ(library-name/message-queue-name)	+
	RPY('reply-text')	+
	RMV(*YES|*NO)	

Parameters

MSGKEY	Name of CL variable that contains message reference key
MSGQ	Name of message queue that received the inquiry message
	Library: name, *LIBL, *CURLIB
RPY	Reply: text, *DFT
RMV	Remove message: *YES, *NO

Error Messages That Can Be Monitored

CPF2401	Not authorized to library.
CPF2403	Message queue not found.
CPF2408	Not authorized to message queue.
CPF2410	Message key not found in message queue.
CPF2411	Not authorized to message file.
CPF2420	Reply already sent for inquiry or notify message.
CPF2422	Reply not valid.
CPF2432	Cannot send reply to message type other than *INQ or *NOTIFY.
CPF2433	Function not allowed for system log message queue.
CPF2460	Message queue could not be extended.
CPF2471	Length of field not valid.
CPF2477	Message queue currently in use.
CPF2547	Damage to message file QCPFMSG.
CPF2548	Damage to message file.

Files Used

(None)

SNDUSRMSG (Send User Message)

Sends a message to a message queue and optionally receives a reply, placing it into a CL variable.

Syntax

SNDUSRMSG	*MSGID(message-identifier)*	+
	MSGF(library-name/message-file-name)	+
	MSGDTA(character-string)	+
	TOMSGQ(library-name/message-queue-name)	+
	MSGTYPE(message-type)	+
	VALUES(allowable-values)	+
	DFT('default-reply-value')	+
	MSGRPY(&CL-variable-name)	+
	. . .	

Alternative Syntaxes

SNDUSRMSG	*MSGID(message-identifier)*	+
	MSGF(library-name/message-file-name)	+
	MSGDTA(character-string)	+
	TOUSR(user-name)	+
	MSGTYPE(message-type)	+
	VALUES(allowable-values)	+
	DFT('default-reply-value')	+
	MSGRPY(&CL-variable-name)	+
	. . .	

SNDUSRMSG	*MSG ('message-text')*	+
	TOMSGQ(library-name/message-queue-name)	+
	MSGTYPE(*message-type)	+
	VALUES(allowable-values)	+
	DFT('default-reply-value')	+
	MSGRPY(&CL-variable-name)	+
	. . .	
SNDUSRMSG	*MSG ('message-text')*	+
	TOUSR(user-profile-name)	+
	MSGTYPE(message-type)	+
	VALUES(allowable-values)	+
	DFT('default-reply-value')	+
	MSGRPY(&CL-variable-name)	+
	. . .	

Parameters

MSGID	Message identifier of message to send
MSGF	Name of message file containing message to send
	Library: name, <u>*LIBL</u>
MSGDTA	Message data field: values, *NONE
MSG	Message text
TOMSGQ	Message queues to receive message: name, <u>*</u>, *EXT, *SYSOPR
	Library: name, <u>*LIBL</u>, *CURLIB
TOUSR	User to receive message: name, *SYSOPR, *REQUESTER
MSGTYPE	Type of message: <u>*INQ</u>, *INFO
VALUES	List of valid replies: value, <u>*NONE</u>
DFT	Default message reply: value, <u>*MSGDFT</u>
MSGRPY	CL variable to contain message reply

Error Messages That Can Be Monitored

| CPF2559 | Error occurred in SNDUSRMSG command. |

Files Used

(None)

TFRCTL (Transfer Control)

Calls a program, transfers control to it, then removes the calling program from the program stack.

Syntax

| *TFRCTL* | *PGM(library-name/program-name)* | + |
| | *PARM(&CL-variable-name)* | |

Parameters

PGM	Name of program to transfer to
	Library: name, <u>*LIBL</u>, *CURLIB
PARM	List of CL variables (preceded by &) to pass as parameters to PGM

Error Messages That Can Be Monitored

| CPF0805 | Error found when program started. |
| CPF0809 | Transfer control (TFRCTL) to C program not allowed. |

Files Used

(None)

WAIT (Wait)

Reads input data from a display device if you have previously specified WAIT(*NO) for a RCVF or SNDRCVF command.

Syntax

WAIT	*DEV(&CL-variable-name)*

Parameters

DEV	CL variable to contain name of responding device: name, *NONE

Error Messages That Can Be Monitored

CPF0859	File override caused I/O buffer size to be exceeded.
CPF0882	No corresponding RCVF or SNDRCVF command for WAIT command.
CPF0886	Record contains a data field that is not valid.
CPF0888	Command not run because job being ended.
CPF0889	No data available for input request within specified time.
CPF4101	File not found or inline data file missing.
CPF5068	Program device not found.
CPF5070	File has no program devices acquired.

Files Used

(None)

Appendix B

Programming Development Manager (PDM)

What Is PDM?

PDM (Programming Development Manager) is a programming environment that provides access to AS/400 functions through a standard list interface. PDM is not a part of the AS/400 base operating system; instead, it is a part of an IBM-licensed program product called Application Development Tools. The Application Development Tools product also includes such things as the AS/400 Source Entry Utility (SEU) and the AS/400 Report Layout Utility (RLU). Almost every AS/400 used for program development and maintenance will contain the Application Development Tools product.

PDM is not an end-user tool. The functions that PDM provides are specifically designed to increase AS/400 programmers' and system administrators' productivity. Functions such as copying files, moving objects from one library to another, compiling programs, and displaying the contents of a library are made easier by using PDM.

The AS/400 Object-Based Structure

To appreciate the usefulness of PDM, it is important to understand a little bit about the AS/400's object-based architecture. Basically speaking, everything that exists on the AS/400 is called an object. An object is simply a unique entity that is identified by its attributes or characteristics. The AS/400 has many types of objects. Figure B.1 lists some of these AS/400 object types and their associated abbreviations.

Figure B.1
Some AS/400
Object Types

Object Type	AS/400 Abbreviation
Command	*CMD
Data area	*DTAARA
Data queue	*DTAQ
File	*FILE
Job Description	*JOBD
Library	*LIB
Message file	*MSGF
Message queue	*MSGQ
Output queue	*OUTQ
Program	*PGM
User Profile	*USRPRF

Object Attributes

One of the object types is the program (object type *PGM). Any program that can be created on the AS/400 will be a *PGM type object. You can have an RPG program, a CL program, a COBOL program, and so on. On the AS/400, each of these different types of programs has different attributes. The program object attributes determine how the AS/400 will run this program type.

As another example of object attributes, consider the object type *FILE. The AS/400 supports many different types of files, such as database files, display files, printer files, and source physical files. Each of these different types of files has different attributes. For instance, a database file can be used to store data, but a display file cannot. Figure B.2 lists some attributes of AS/400 *FILE type objects and *PGM type objects.

Figure B.2
Object Attributes

Object Type	Object Attributes	
*FILE	DSPF	(Display File)
	PRTF	(Printer File)
	PF-SRC	(Source Physical File)
	PF-DTA	(Data Physical File)
*PGM	RPG	(RPG program)
	CLP	(CL program)
	CBL	(COBOL program)

AS/400 Libraries

Any given AS/400 object is stored within a library. You could think of a library as a directory that allows you to find the objects it contains. The concept of an AS/400 library is very similar to that of a directory on your personal computer's hard disk drive. From the DOS prompt on a PC you can type the DOS command DIR, and you will be presented with a listing of all the files and programs stored within that directory. Likewise, on the AS/400 you can use the CL command DSPLIB (Display Library), and you will be presented with a listing of all the objects (files, programs, etc.) stored within a particular AS/400 library.

Just as files and programs are AS/400 objects, an AS/400 library is also an object. A difference, however, is that a library is a special kind of object used to hold other objects.

File Members

As AS/400 libraries can contain objects, certain AS/400 files can contain members. To contain members, an AS/400 *FILE object must have an object attribute of PF-DTA (data file), PF-SRC (source file), or LF (logical file). A member is a construct that the AS/400 uses to contain actual data records.

On the AS/400, a file itself does not contain data records; rather, it is the member within the file that contains the records. A file can have one member, or it can have many members. All of the members within a file will have the same format (i.e., length and data fields), but each member will have its own name. A file actually can be created with no members, in which case the file is incapable of holding data. Figure B.3 shows three PF-DTA files. The first (FILEA) has no members, and therefore can hold no data. The second (FILEB) has one member capable of holding data. The third (FILEC) has four members that can hold data.

Figure B.3
File Members

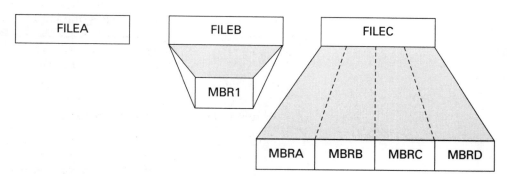

PF-DTA Attribute

AS/400 *FILE type objects with the attribute PF-DTA are database files. PF-DTA is an abbreviation for data physical file. If you needed to create a file on the AS/400 to hold customer names and addresses, you would create a PF-DTA file. After creating the file, you would create a member within that file to hold the actual data. Normally PF-DTA files have only one member, which holds all the data records for the file. Figure B.4 illustrates the structure of a typical data physical file named CUSTMAST, with one member, also named CUSTMAST. The member CUSTMAST contains five data records.

Figure B.4
Data Physical File

CUSTMAST File					
Member CUSTMAST					
John	Jones	125 Bluestop Way	Omaha	NE	33323
Jan	Green	67 Park Lane	Newark	NJ	11323
Phil	Dunn	12365 Bishop S	St. Louis	MO	63128
Trish	Howell	1623 Main St	Olathe	KS	46589
Dave	Bernard	10 Downing St	Billings	MT	54679

PF-SRC Attribute

Files with the attribute PF-SRC are typically used to hold multiple members that contain data records consisting of source statements. PF-SRC is an abbreviation for source physical file. If you need a place to store the source statements for an RPG program or for a CL program, you would create a source physical file, or simply add a member to an existing source physical file. Figure B.5 illustrates a typical source physical file named QCLSRC. In this example, QCLSRC contains three members. The first member (PGM1CL) contains four records, the second member (PGM2CL) contains five records, and the third member (PGM3CL) contains three records.

Figure B.5
Source Physical File

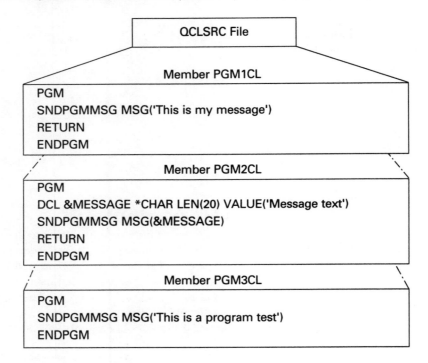

PDM as a Navigational Tool

Figure B.6 illustrates the three levels of the AS/400 object-based architecture: the library level, the object level, and the member level.

PDM is the programmer's environment used to navigate through the various levels of the AS/400 object-based structure. PDM allows you to move easily from one level to the next. For instance, you can start at the library level, then drop down to the object level. From the object level, you can either go back up to the library level or drop down to the member level.

Figure B.6
Object Levels

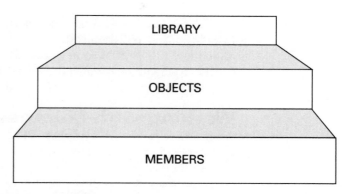

Accessing PDM

You can access a PDM session from your workstation in a number of ways. You can go through an AS/400 menu, such as the PROGRAM menu, and select the PDM menu option. You also can go to any command line and use the IBM-supplied commands that are a part of PDM:

STRPDM	(Start PDM)
WRKLIBPDM	(Work with Libraries Using PDM)
WRKOBJPDM	(Work with Objects Using PDM)
WRKMBRPDM	(Work with Members Using PDM)

The STRPDM Command

When you type the command STRPDM on a command line, you are presented with the PDM main menu shown in Figure B.7. You can choose from any of the four options shown.

Figure B.7
PDM Main Menu

```
                    AS/400 Programming Development Manager (PDM)

     Select one of the following:

          1. Work with libraries
          2. Work with objects
          3. Work with members

          9. Work with user-defined options




     Selection or command
     ===> _____
    _____
     F3=Exit        F4=Prompt       F9=Retrieve         F10=Command entry
     F12=Cancel     F18=Change defaults
```

Selecting option 1 (Work with libraries) in effect executes the same function as the PDM command WRKLIBPDM. Option 2 (Work with objects) has the same effect as using the WRKOBJPDM command. And option 3 (Work with members) has the same effect as typing in the command WRKMBRPDM. The PDM menu option 9 (Work with user-defined options) is discussed in IBM's *PDM Reference*.

Working with Libraries Using PDM

When you select option 1 from the PDM main menu, you are presented with the display shown in Figure B.8. Here you must specify which libraries you wish to work with. In this example, we have chosen to work with all the libraries that start with the letters 'ST', but we could have chosen any of the options listed, such as *LIBL, *ALLUSR, *USRLIBL, and so on. If you are uncertain about what these library options mean, you can position the cursor on the library input-capable field and press the Help key. The help text displayed will explain the different options.

Figure B.8
The Library
Selection Display

```
                          Specify Libraries to Work With

   Type choice, press Enter.

       Library . . . . . . . . . .    ST*          *LIBL, name, *generic*, *ALL,
                                                    *ALLUSR, *USRLIBL, *CURLIB

   F3=Exit      F5=Refresh      F12=Cancel
```

After you press the Enter key from this display, PDM shows you the PDM screen for working with libraries. The libraries listed on the display are determined by your selection on the previous screen. Figure B.9 shows the Work with Libraries Using PDM screen that appears when we select all libraries that start with the letters 'ST'. The same display is presented when we enter the command WRKLIBPDM LIB(ST*) on a command line.

The Work with Libraries using PDM display lists all the libraries you selected. At (A) on this display you are shown the list type. Here the list type is *ALL; the other types of lists are *LIBL and *ALLUSR. In this case, *ALL means that you are being presented with a list of *ALL libraries that match the list criteria (*ALL starting with 'ST').

At (B) is an input-capable field that allows you to position the list starting at a certain library. This is particularly useful for cases in which the list contains more libraries than will fit on one page of the display. If you wanted the listing to start at library STUDENT4, you would enter the characters STUDENT4 into the field.

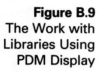

Figure B.9
The Work with
Libraries Using
PDM Display

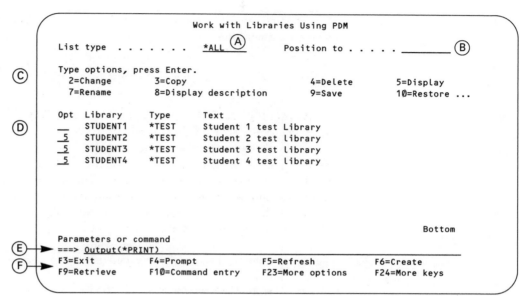

```
                          Work with Libraries Using PDM

      List type . . . . . . .   *ALL (A)        Position to . . . . . _____  (B)

  (C)  Type options, press Enter.
         2=Change          3=Copy                      4=Delete        5=Display
         7=Rename          8=Display description        9=Save         10=Restore ...

       Opt  Library     Type      Text
  (D)   __   STUDENT1    *TEST     Student 1 test Library
         5   STUDENT2    *TEST     Student 2 test library
         5   STUDENT3    *TEST     Student 3 test library
         5   STUDENT4    *TEST     Student 4 test library




                                                                       Bottom
       Parameters or command
  (E) ===> Output(*PRINT) _____
  (F)  F3=Exit           F4=Prompt           F5=Refresh         F6=Create
       F9=Retrieve       F10=Command entry   F23=More options   F24=More keys
```

At (C) you are shown a list of valid options that can be entered next to the list entries to cause some operation to be performed to the corresponding library. For instance, if you wanted to display the contents of a library, you could place the number 5 in the option (Opt) field of an entry on the list and press the Enter key.

Notice in the list of valid options defined at (C) that there are ellipses (...) after the option for 10=Restore. This tells you there are more options than will fit on the screen at one time. You can see the additional options by pressing the F23=More Options key. The valid options from the Work with Libraries Using PDM display are as shown in Figure B.10. Note that all these options cannot fit on the display at one time. But even if these options are not currently shown in area (C) of your display, they are still valid.

Also notice in Figure B.10 that there is a corresponding CL command for most PDM options. The PDM environment provides a user-friendly front-end to allow you to execute CL commands that act upon the system's objects. You do not need to know AS/400 CL commands to use the PDM options; PDM will execute the CL command for you that corresponds to the option you select.

At (D) in Figure B.9 is presented the list of libraries you have selected to work with. From left to right within this list is the Opt field, the Library field, the Type field, and the Text field.

The Opt field is used for entering PDM options. The options we discussed above can be entered into the Opt field. The Library field identifies the library name for this list entry. The Type field identifies whether the library is a *TEST or *PROD type library. This entry is used to specify the type of objects that reside in this library. However, a library's type is taken into account only when you are using the AS/400 debug facility. The Text field shows the descriptive text that is associated with this library.

Figure B.10
Valid Options
with WRKLIBPDM

Option	Operation	CL Command used by PDM
2	Allows you to change the type and text of a library	CHGLIB
3	Copy the contents of a library to another library	CPYLIB
4	Delete a library. Option is valid only when list type is *ALL or *ALLUSR.	DLTLIB
5	Display a list of the objects within a library	DSPLIB
7	Rename a library	RNMOBJ
8	Display a description of the library	DSPOBJD
9	Save the contents of a library to backup media or to a save file	SAVLIB
10	Restore the contents of a library from backup media or from a save file	RSTLIB
12	Go to the Work with Objects using PDM screen. This option allows you to navigate down one level in the object hierarchy. When option 12 is selected, you can work with the objects within the library that option 12 is selected for.	WRKOBJPDM
13	Allows you to change the text associated with a library	CHGOBJD

At (E) in Figure B.9 you can see that the display also includes a command line. This command line can be used like any other AS/400 command line. The F4=Prompt key is available, as is the F9=Retrieve key. The command line also serves another function within PDM. When an option is entered next to an entry in the list, the command entry line can be used to enter command parameters and their values. Figure B.9 shows an example of using option 5 (Display) on three list entries at the same time, and the command line contains the CL command parameter OUTPUT(*PRINT). The reason you can place a command parameter on the command line is that when PDM performs an operation that you specify, it is actually executing one of the CL commands listed in Figure B.10. The command executed when you select option 5 from this display is the CL command DSPLIB. One of the command parameters for the DSPLIB command is OUTPUT. So by placing 5 in the Option field for the library STUDENT2, STUDENT3, and STUDENT4, and placing OUTPUT(*PRINT) on the command line, you are telling PDM to execute three CL commands:

```
DSPLIB LIB(STUDENT2) OUTPUT(*PRINT)
DSPLIB LIB(STUDENT3) OUTPUT(*PRINT)
DSPLIB LIB(STUDENT4) OUTPUT(*PRINT)
```

The function keys that are valid within PDM are shown at (F) in Figure B.9. Because the PDM display does not have enough room to show you all the valid function keys, the F24=More keys key is available to show you the additional function keys allowed. All the function keys listed are always valid, even if they are not currently displayed on the screen. Figure B.11 lists the function keys available within the WRKLIBPDM display.

Figure B.11
WRKLIBPDM
Function Keys

Function Key	Function	Operation
F1	Help	Provides additional information. This function key is cursor sensitive; place the cursor at the location in question before pressing F1.
F3	Exit	To exit from PDM
F4	Prompt	Invokes the AS/400 prompt facility
F5	Refresh	Refresh the display screen
F6	Create or	Prompts you for the CRTLIB command (valid only when list type is *ALL or *ALLUSR)
	Add to List	Allows you to add a library to the library list (valid only when the list type is *LIBL or *USRLIBL)
F9	Retrieve	Retrieves commands previously entered on the command line. Using F9 can help reduce the number of keystrokes when entering CL commands.
F10	Command entry	Calls the IBM-supplied program QCMD. When this program is called, you are presented with an extended AS/400 command line, which allows you to use different functions than are available from the PDM command line.
F11	Display Names and Display Text	This function key is a toggle switch that allows you to flip back and forth between two different methods for displaying the libraries selected.
F12	Cancel	Return to the previous display; do not process any options on the current display.
F13	Repeat	If you type a PDM option next to a list entry and then press F13, that option will be copied into the Opt field for each of the list entries that appear after the one you entered. List entries previous to the one you selected are not affected.
F16	User Options	Allows you to change your user-defined options for PDM.
F17	Subset	Allows you to select a subset of the currently displayed list entries. The subset list will then be displayed, instead of the full list. If you are working with a large number of entries, this allows you to specify a smaller list of entries.
F18	Change Defaults	This option allows you to tailor PDM to meet your special needs.
F21	Print the list	This option will print the entries of the current list.
F23	More options	Allows you to see other options that are valid within this PDM display.
F24	More keys	Allows you to see a listing of other function keys that are available within the PDM display.

Working with Objects Using PDM

When you select option 2 from the PDM main menu, you are presented with the display shown in Figure B.12. Here you must specify which objects you wish to work with and the library in which the objects reside. In this example, we have chosen to work with all of the objects in library STUDENT1. If you are interested in working with only a certain subset of the objects within the STUDENT1 library, the Name, Type, and Attribute fields on the display provide you with the ability to specify your selection criteria. For example, if you want to work with only objects whose names start with the letter 'L', you can type 'L*' into the Name field; or, if you want to work with only objects whose object type is *FILE, you can enter *FILE into the Type field.

Figure B.12
The Object Selection
Display

```
                          Specify Objects to Work With

Type choices, press Enter.

     Library . . . . . . . . . .      STUDENT1      *CURLIB, name

     Object:
       Name . . . . . . . . . .      *ALL          *ALL, name, *generic*
       Type . . . . . . . . . .      *ALL          *ALL, *type
       Attribute . . . . . . .       *ALL          *ALL, attribute, *generic, *BLANK




     F3=Exit      F5=Refresh      F12=Cancel
```

Figure B.13
The Work with Objects
Using PDM Display

```
                         Work with Objects Using PDM
Library . . . . . (A) STUDENT1          Position to . . . . . . . . . _____ (B)
                                        Position to type  . . . . . _____

Type options, press Enter.
   2=Change         3=Copy         4=Delete       5=Display      7=Rename
   8=Display description           9=Save        10=Restore     11=Move ...

Opt   Object      Type      Attribute    Text
___   PGM1        *PGM      RPG          Print a Product Master List
___   STUDENT1    *OUTQ                  STUDENT1 outq for class
___   OPLF001A    *FILE     LF           Order Header by Order Number
___   OPLF001B    *FILE     LF           Order header for RPG class
___   OPLF001CA   *FILE     LF           Invoiced order header records
___   OPLF001D    *FILE     LF           Invoiced order header records
___   OPLF003A    *FILE     LF           Product Mast by Prod number for inq
___   OPLF003B    *FILE     LF           Product Mast by Prod Number for upd
                                                                   More...
Parameters or command
===> _____
F3=Exit           F4=Prompt              F5=Refresh           F6=Create
F9=Retrieve       F10=Command entry      F23=More options     F24=More keys
```

If you do not want to use the PDM main menu to access the Work with Objects Using PDM display, you can use the CL command WRKOBJPDM. When you type the WRKOBJPDM command on a command line and press the F4=Prompt key, you can fill in the prompts to specify which objects in which library you want to work with. The display for the WRKOBJPDM command is shown in Figure B.13.

The Work with Objects Using PDM display shows a list of all the objects you selected. The display works much like the WRKLIBPDM display, except that now you are listing objects within a library, and some of the options are different to correspond to objects instead of libraries. At (A) on this display you are shown the library name. This indicates the current library being displayed. You may overtype the library name with a different library name to work with the objects within a different library. At (B) are two input-capable fields that allow you to position the list starting at a particular object, and/or position the list at a particular object type, within the library.

The rest of the Work with Objects Using PDM screen is similar to the Work with Libraries using PDM screen. All the function keys are the same. Some of the options you can choose are different, but the overall "look and feel" is the same. The options available on the Work with Objects using PDM screen are listed in Figure B.14. Depending on the object type, some options may be invalid. For example, Option 16 (Run an object) is not valid with *FILE objects.

Figure B.14
Valid Options for
WRKOBJPDM Display

Option	Operation	CL Command Used by PDM
2	Change certain attributes of an object	CHGPF CHGPGM etc.
3	Create a duplicate object	CRTDUPOBJ
4	Delete an object	DLTF DLTPGM etc.
5	Display information about an object	DSPFD DSPPGM etc.
7	Rename an object	RNMOBJ
8	Display the object description	DSPOBJD
9	Save an object to backup media or to a Save file	SAVOBJ SAVSAVFDTA
10	Restore an object from backup media or from a Save file	RSTOBJ
11	Move an object from one library to another	MOVOBJ

Continued

	Option	Operation	CL Command Used by PDM
Figure B.14 continued	12	Work with the object If the object type is *FILE and the object attribute is PF-DTA or PF-SRC, the Work with Members Using PDM screen will be displayed. In this way, this option allows you to navigate down one level in the object hierarchy. When option 12 is selected, you can work with the members within thefile that option 12 is selected for.	WRKPGM WRKF WRKMBRPDM etc.
	13	Change the text associated with an object	CHGOBJD
	15	Copy selected records or members from one file to another. (This option is valid only for *FILE type objects with an attribute of DKTF, LF, PF-DTA, and PF-SRC.)	CPYF CPYSRCF
	16	Run an object. If the object type is *CMD, the command will be executed. If the object type is *PGM, the program is called. If the object type is *QRYDFN the query is run.	CALL CHGDTA RUNQRY
	18	Change the data in a file using the Data File Utility. This option is valid only when the object type is *FILE and the attribute is PF-DTA or LF, or when the object type is *PGM and the attribute is DFU.	UPDDTA STRDFU OPTION(3)
	25	Find a selected character string within members of a file. This option is valid only when the object type is *FILE and the attribute is PF-DTA or PF-SRC. (No CL command is executed to perform this function.)	*NONE
	26	Create a program object from *MODULE, *SRVPGM, and/or *BNDDIR objects	CRTPGM
	27	Create a service program from *MODULE, *SRVPGM, and/or *BNDDIR objects	CRTSRVPGM
	34	Invoke interactive source debugger	STRDBG
	54	Compare file members	CMPPFM

Working with Members Using PDM

The lowest level in the object hierarchy that PDM provides access to is file members. Recall that only objects with an object type of *FILE can contain members. Other objects such as programs and data areas do not. PDM provides three ways for you to gain access to the Work with Members Using PDM display: (1) From the PDM main menu, you can select option 3 (Work with members); (2) from the Work with Objects Using PDM display, you can place option 12 (Work with) next to a *FILE object; or (3) you may use the WRKMBRPDM command from any command line.

Figure B.15 shows the display that is presented if you select option 3 from the PDM main menu. Here you specify the name of the file and the name of the library in which the file resides. You can also specify which members of the file you wish to work with, using the Name and Type fields.

Figure B.15
The Member
Selection Display

```
                     Specify Members to Work With

 Type choices, press Enter.

    File  . . . . . . . . .    QCLSRC      Name, F4 for list

      Library . . . . . . .    STUDENT1    *LIBL, *CURLIB, name

    Member:
      Name  . . . . . . . .    *ALL        *ALL, name, *generic*
      Type  . . . . . . . .    *ALL        *ALL, type, *generic*, *BLANK




 F3=Exit      F4=Prompt      F5=Refresh      F12=Cancel
```

The Work with Members Using PDM display in Figure B.16 shows a list of all of the members you selected. Shown at (A) are the names of the file and the library whose members are being displayed. These fields are input-capable, so you can over-type them with a different library name, or a file name, to work with the members of a different file.

Figure B.16
Work with Members
Using PDM Panel

```
                    Work with Members Using PDM

 File . . . . . .    QCLSRC      (A)
   Library . . . .    STUDENT1          Position to . . . . . _____

 Type options, press Enter.
   2=Edit        3=Copy  4=Delete 5=Display     6=Print    7=Rename
   8=Display description 9=Save 13=Change text  14=Compile 15=Create module...

 Opt  Member     Type     Text
  __  BCL810     CLP      DSPLSTSAV CPP
  __  CLRMSGCL   CLP      Clear *PRV Message queue
  __  DSPMSGCL   CLP      Display Messages..remove SFL rec not found
  __  OPCL010    CLP      CUSTOMER REPORT RPG CLASS
  __  RPGINIT    CLP      initial program
  __  SLTC000    CLP      Select Job CL Pgm
  __  SLTC001    CLP      Select Job CL pgm
  __  SLTC002    CLP      Select Job CL Pgm
                                                          More...
 Parameters or command
 ===> _____
 F3=Exit          F4=Prompt           F5=Refresh         F6=Create
 F9=Retrieve      F10=Command entry   F23=More options   F24=More keys
```

At (B) is the listing of members. The type and text fields are both input-capable, so they may be modified from this display. The rest of the Work with Members Using PDM screen is similar to the other PDM screens. As with the other PDM screens, all the function keys are the same, but some of the options are different.

Figure B.17
Valid Options for
WRKMBRPDM
Display

Option	Operation	CL Command used by PDM	
		PF-SRC	PF-DTA
2	Start SEU for this member. Allows editing of a source member.	STRSEU OPTION(2)	N/A
3	Copy a member.	CPYSRCF	CPYF
4	Remove a member.	RMVM	RMVM
5	Display the data in a member.	STRSEU OPTION(5)	DSPPFM
6	Print the member.	STRSEU OPTION(6)	N/A
7	Rename a member.	RNMM	RNMM
8	Display member description (CL command not executed here).	*NONE	*NONE
9	Save the file of which this is a member. (Note: A member can be saved only when the file itself is saved).	SAVOBJ	SAVOBJ
13	Change the text associated with the member.	CHGPFM	CHGPFM
14	Compile an object using this source member as input to the compiler. (This option is valid only for PF-SRC members; the compiler used is dependent upon the source type. For example, if the source type is CL, the CL compiler will be used.)	CRTRPGPGM CRTCLPGM CRTDSPF etc.	N/A
15	Creates a *MODULE from an ILE source member (CLLE, RPGLE, CBLLE, etc.)	CRTCLMOD CRTRPGMOD CRTCBLMOD etc.	N/A
16	Run a procedure specified within the member. (This option is valid only for PF-SRC members; the command used to run the procedure is dependent upon the source type field. For example, for a source type of REXX, the STRREXPRC will be used.)	STRREXPRC STRS36PRC STRBASPRC QSYS38/ EXCBASPRC	N/A

Continued

Figure B.17
continued

Option	Operation	CL Command used by PDM	
		PF-SRC	**PF-DTA**
17	Change using SDA. This option allows you to start the AS/400 Screen Design Aid tool for this member. This option is valid only for PF-SRC members with a source type of DSPF (display file), DSPF36 (Display file System/36), or DSPF38 (Display file System/38).	STRSDA	N/A
18	Change using DFU. Allows you to use the Data File Utility to add/change or delete records from a file. This option is valid only for PF-DTA file members.	N/A	UPDDTA
19	Change using RLU. This option allows you to start the AS/400 Report Layout Utility tool for this member. This option is valid only for PF-SRC members with a source type of PRTF (printer file).	STRRLU	N/A
25	Allows you to find a selected character string within the member. (No CL command is executed.)	*NONE	*NONE
54	Compare file members	CMPPFM	CMPPFM
55	Merge source file members	MRGSRC	N/A

PF-DTA and PF-SRC Differences

When you used the Work with Objects Using PDM screen, you saw that, depending on the object type, certain options are valid and others are invalid. When using the Work with Members Using PDM displays, there are also some differences based upon whether you are working with members of a PF-DTA file or a PF-SRC file. Some options are valid only when working with a PF-SRC file member; others are valid only when working with a PF-DTA file. In fact, the Work with Members Using PDM screen is slightly different depending on the file type. Figure B.17 lists the valid options when you are working with members using PDM. You can see that the options are different based upon the type of file selected (i.e., PF-DTA or PF-SRC). In the figure, N/A is shown when that option is not available for that file type.

Changing Your PDM Defaults

When you start PDM with a command (e.g., STRPDM or WRKOBJPDM), certain defaults are in effect. These defaults affect the way PDM performs certain functions. It is possible for each PDM user on the system to customize the defaults that are in effect. Refer to the *PDM Reference* for information about how to do this, using the F18=Change defaults key.

User-Defined Options

In addition to the standard options shown at the top of each PDM "Work with" display, you may create your own user-defined PDM options. These user-defined options allow you to customize your PDM environment so you can be highly productive while using PDM. With PDM user-defined options, you can easily perform additional operations that are not standard PDM options on libraries, objects, and members. You could also create a shorthand method of calling a commonly used program or of executing a commonly used command. Refer to the *PDM Reference* for information about how to create user-defined PDM options.

Appendix C

Source Entry Utility (SEU)

What Is SEU?

SEU (Source Entry Utility) is a programming tool that facilitates the entry of source statements that can later be used as input to an AS/400 compiler. SEU is what is called a *full-screen editor*, because it allows you to edit (i.e., enter or modify) source member statements appearing anywhere on the workstation screen.

SEU is not a part of the AS/400 base operating system, but instead is a part of an IBM-licensed program product called Application Development Tools. The Application Development Tools product also includes such things as the AS/400 Programming Development Manager (PDM) and the AS/400 Report Layout Utility (RLU). Almost every AS/400 used for program development and maintenance will contain the Application Development Tools product.

Using SEU, you can enter or modify the source statements that will be used to create a CL program, an RPG/400 program, a COBOL/400 program, an externally described file, and many other AS/400 objects. While SEU is by no means a full-function word processor, you can use SEU for typing in notes, or other "text only" documents. Some organizations even use SEU to enter and maintain the documentation for their programs.

SEU Syntax Checking

SEU can check the syntax of source statements to ensure that they meet the requirements of the particular language being used. SEU provides syntax checking capabilities for many AS/400 languages and functions, including the following:

BASIC	COBOL	CL	
FORTRAN	DDS Source	PL/I	RPG

Accessing SEU

There are four major ways to access the SEU facility:

- From the PDM Work with Members display, by selecting options 2 or 5
- By entering the STRSEU command on any command line
- From the Programmer's Menu
- From within the AS/400 Screen Design Aid tool

Figure C.1 shows how you would access SEU using PDM option 2 from the Work with Members Using PDM display.

Figure C.1
Accessing SEU
from PDM

```
                        Work with Members Using PDM

 File . . . . . .   QCLSRC
   Library . . . .    STUDENT1          Position to  . . . . . _____
 Type options, press Enter.
   2=Edit          3=Copy  4=Delete 5=Display     6=Print    7=Rename
   8=Display description 9=Save 13=Change text  14=Compile  15=Create module ...

 Opt  Member      Type     Text
  __   SA0501XXX   CLP      Chapter 5, member 1_____
  __   SA0601XXX   CLP      Chapter 6, member 1_____
  __   SA0701XXX   CLP      Chapter 7, member 1_____
  2    SA0801XXX   CLP      Chapter 8, member 1_____
  __   SA0802XXX   CLP      Chapter 8, member 2_____
  __   SA0803XXX   CLP      Chapter 8, member 3_____
  __   SA0804XXX   CLP      Chapter 8, member 4_____
  __   SA0901XXX   CLP      Chapter 9, member 1_____
                                                                   More...
 Parameters or command
 ===>_____
 F3=Exit        F4=Prompt          F5=Refresh          F6=Create
 F9=Retrieve    F10=Command entry  F23=More options    F24=More keys
```

In this example, the source type of the member that will be edited is CLP (CL program). The source type of the member being edited determines which syntax checker and prompting facilities will be used by SEU for this editing session. Because the source type is CLP, all prompts and syntax checking will be performed according to CL rules. (For ILE CL source, use source type CLLE.)

Figure C.2 shows the SEU edit display that is presented when you place a 2 next to the member SA0801XXX when working with members using PDM.

Four main sections comprise the SEU edit display. At (A) is the section of the edit display used to display the SEU sequence number of the records in the source

Figure C.2
SEU Edit Display

```
 Columns . . . :   1  71              Edit              STUDENT1/QCLSRC
 SEU==> (D)_____    SA0801XXX
 FMT **  ...+... 1 ...+... 2 ...+... 3 ...+... 4 ...+... 5 ...+... 6 ...+... 7
 *************** Beginning of data ***********************************
 0001.00 /*  Program name..... SA0801XXX                              */
 0002.00 /*  Author.......... (Your Name)                            */
 0003.00 /*  Date completed... (enter the current date)              */
 0004.00 /*  Program purpose.. CHGVAR and DMPCLPGM exercise           */
 0005.00 /*  Chapter 8, member 1                                      */
 0006.00
 0007.00              PGM
 0008.00
 0009.00  (B)         DCL       &char10 *CHAR 10
 0010.00              DCL       &char24 *CHAR 24
 0011.00              DCL       &dec50  *DEC (5 0)
 0012.00              DCL       &dec72  *DEC (7 2)
 0013.00              DCL       &lgl1   *LGL
 0014.00
 0015.00
 0016.00              CHGVAR    &char10 'My Library'
 F3=Exit    F4=Prompt   F5=Refresh   F9=Retrieve   F10=Cursor
 F16=Repeat find        F17=Repeat change          F24=More keys
```

member. You can enter special SEU line commands within the sequence number
area by typing over the sequence number. At (B) is the actual typing area for the
source statements. It is here that you enter and edit the statements that will comprise
the source member. At (C) you are shown the function keys that are valid when
using SEU; when you press F24=More keys, you are shown several other valid function keys. At (D) is the SEU command line. This command line is different from the
standard AS/400 command line shown on other screens; it is provided solely as a
means to enter special SEU commands. These commands are different from those
that can be entered over a sequence number.

The SEU Sequence Number Area

The SEU sequence number area shows the SEU line number for each source statement
in the member being edited. The sequence number is displayed in the format of 0001.00.
The sequence number displayed is input-capable, which means you can type data into the
area containing the sequence number.

Although SEU does not allow you to change the sequence number of an existing
line, you can type special *SEU line commands* over the sequence number that is displayed.
The SEU line commands let you manipulate the lines in the source member; they
also let you determine which part of the source member is displayed in the typing
area. You use the SEU line commands to do things such as moving a source line from
one place to another place, deleting a source line, and inserting source lines between
two existing lines. You can also use the line commands to position the display, so that
a specific source line will appear as the first line in the typing area.

Before getting into a full discussion of all the valid SEU line commands, we'll
look at a simple example of moving a source line within the member (Figure C.3).

Figure C.3
Using SEU
Line Commands

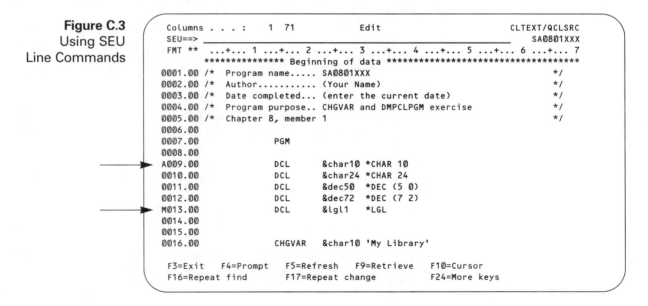

```
 Columns . . . :    1  71              Edit                    CLTEXT/QCLSRC
 SEU==> _____          SA0801XXX
 FMT **  ...+... 1 ...+... 2 ...+... 3 ...+... 4 ...+... 5 ...+... 6 ...+... 7
         *************** Beginning of data ********************************
 0001.00 /*  Program name..... SA0801XXX                                   */
 0002.00 /*  Author.......... (Your Name)                                  */
 0003.00 /*  Date completed... (enter the current date)                    */
 0004.00 /*  Program purpose.. CHGVAR and DMPCLPGM exercise                */
 0005.00 /*  Chapter 8, member 1                                           */
 0006.00
 0007.00            PGM
 0008.00
 A009.00            DCL       &char10 *CHAR 10
 0010.00            DCL       &char24 *CHAR 24
 0011.00            DCL       &dec50  *DEC (5 0)
 0012.00            DCL       &dec72  *DEC (7 2)
 M013.00            DCL       &lgl1   *LGL
 0014.00
 0015.00
 0016.00            CHGVAR    &char10 'My Library'

  F3=Exit   F4=Prompt   F5=Refresh   F9=Retrieve   F10=Cursor
  F16=Repeat find        F17=Repeat change          F24=More keys
```

To move the source line that appears at line 0013.00 in Figure C.3 to the position immediately following line 0009.00, we place the SEU line command **M** (Move) on line 0013.00, and place the SEU line command **A** (After) on line 0009.00, then press the Enter key. The combination of these two SEU line commands tells SEU to **M**ove line 0013.00 **A**fter line 0009.00. The result will be that the statement on line 0013.00 will be moved to the position following line 0009.00, and will be assigned a new sequence number of 0009.01. The sequence number 0013.00 will no longer appear on the display, as shown in Figure C.4. You also can move lines to appear before a line, by specifying **B** instead of **A**.

Figure C.4
Result of the
Move-After Operation

```
Columns . . . :    1  71              Edit                    CLTEXT/QCLSRC
SEU==> _____          SA0801XXX
FMT **  ...+... 1 ...+... 2 ...+... 3 ...+... 4 ...+... 5 ...+... 6 ...+... 7
*************** Beginning of data ****************************************
0001.00 /*  Program name..... SA0801XXX                                  */
0002.00 /*  Author.......... (Your Name)                                 */
0003.00 /*  Date completed... (enter the current date)                   */
0004.00 /*  Program purpose.. CHGVAR and DMPCLPGM exercise               */
0005.00 /*  Chapter 8, member 1                                          */
0006.00
0007.00          PGM
0008.00
0009.00          DCL     &char10 *CHAR 10
0009.01          DCL     &lgl1   *LGL
0010.00          DCL     &char24 *CHAR 24
0011.00          DCL     &dec50  *DEC (5 0)
0012.00          DCL     &dec72  *DEC (7 2)
0014.00
0015.00
0016.00          CHGVAR  &char10 'My Library'

 F3=Exit    F4=Prompt    F5=Refresh    F9=Retrieve    F10=Cursor
 F16=Repeat find          F17=Repeat change            F24=More keys
```

Other commonly used line commands are **C** (Copy) to copy a line to another location while keeping it at the original location, and **D** (Delete) to delete a line from the source member.

In the previous example, we moved one source line to another position. You can also move several lines together in one operation; this is called a *block operation*. Consider the example shown in Figure C.5. Here we want to move the source lines 0009.00 through 0011.00 after line 0014.00.

We place the block move command **MM** on the first and last line to be moved, and place the **A** (After) on line 0014.00. When the Enter key is pressed, the move will be executed.

As an alternative to the block operation using **MM**, you could use the SEU line command **M#**, where # is the number of lines that you want to move. In this example, we could have specified **M3** to move the 3 lines 0009.00, 0010.00, and 0011.00.

Other common block commands are **CC** (Copy) to copy a block of source lines to another location while retaining them at their current location, and **DD** (Delete) to delete a block of lines.

Figure C.5
Using Block Operations

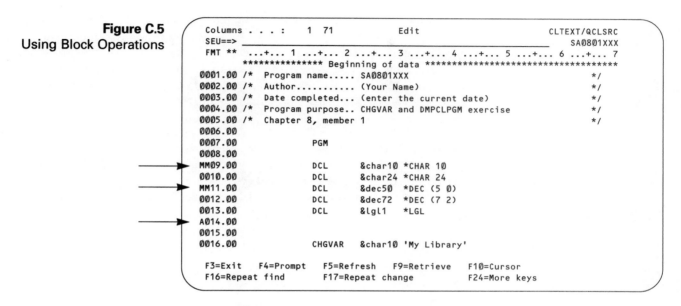

```
Columns . . . :    1  71              Edit                    CLTEXT/QCLSRC
SEU==> _____          SA0801XXX
FMT **  ...+... 1 ...+... 2 ...+... 3 ...+... 4 ...+... 5 ...+... 6 ...+... 7
        *************** Beginning of data ***********************************
0001.00 /*  Program name..... SA0801XXX                                    */
0002.00 /*  Author.......... (Your Name)                                   */
0003.00 /*  Date completed... (enter the current date)                     */
0004.00 /*  Program purpose.. CHGVAR and DMPCLPGM exercise                 */
0005.00 /*  Chapter 8, member 1                                            */
0006.00
0007.00             PGM
0008.00
MM09.00             DCL     &char10 *CHAR 10
0010.00             DCL     &char24 *CHAR 24
MM11.00             DCL     &dec50  *DEC (5 0)
0012.00             DCL     &dec72  *DEC (7 2)
0013.00             DCL     &lgl1   *LGL
A014.00
0015.00
0016.00             CHGVAR  &char10 'My Library'

 F3=Exit    F4=Prompt    F5=Refresh   F9=Retrieve   F10=Cursor
 F16=Repeat find         F17=Repeat change          F24=More keys
```

Line Commands for Positioning Vertically within the Source Member

When a member is originally displayed by SEU, the first record in the source member is displayed at the top of the typing area. When you want to position the member so that a different line is displayed at the top, you can use absolute positioning or relative positioning commands.

To use absolute positioning, type a sequence number over an existing sequence number, and press the Enter key. This will bring the line associated with the sequence number you entered to the top of the typing area. It makes no difference where in the sequence number area this SEU line command is entered.

To move forward or backward in the member, you can use the Page up/down keys; or for more control, you can use relative positioning. To specify relative positioning, overtype a sequence number with a plus sign (+) or a minus sign (−) followed by the number of source lines to be scrolled forward or backward. For example, if you want to move the fifth record on the typing area to the top of the display, you would use the command +5. If you wanted to then move back to the original positioning, you would use the command −5.

Inserting Source Member Lines

When you are editing a source member, the need often arises to add source statements within an existing member. The Insert command is used for that purpose. To insert a line between two existing lines, place the command **I** on the first of the two lines, and press Enter. A new line is inserted for you and you can enter the new source statement into the typing area. After you have entered the new source statement, you can press Enter, and an additional new line will be shown on which you can continue adding another new source member line. SEU will continue to make more empty lines available until you press Enter without previously entering anything into the typing area for the new line.

You can enter the Insert command in such a way that several new lines will be displayed at one time. You can do this by entering the **I** command followed by a number, as in **I5**. This command will insert 5 blank lines into the source member.

SEU Function Keys

When the SEU edit display is presented to you, there are several valid function keys. While not all the function keys are shown on a single display, pressing F24=More keys will display the other available function keys.

The set of function keys that are available from within SEU can be broken down into three categories:

1. Screen Control
2. System Services
3. SEU Services

Screen Control Function Keys

This set of function keys allows you to manipulate the SEU display. The screen control function keys, and a description of the processing each key performs, is presented in Figure C.6.

Figure C.6
Screen Control
Function Keys

Function Key	Processing Performed
F5=Refresh	Refreshes the screen; used for undoing changes and resetting attributes on the screen.
F6=Move the split line	When working in split-screen mode, this function key repositions the split line.
F10=Cursor	Moves the cursor from the typing area to the SEU command line, and vice versa.
F11=Toggle	Moves the source member alternately left or right in the typing area.
F19=Left	Moves the leftmost portion of the source member into the typing area. Many times the source member line cannot be fully contained in the 70-position typing area.
F20=Right	Moves the rightmost portion of the source member into the typing area.

System Services Function Keys

This set of function keys provides access to standard AS/400 system features. The system services function keys, and a description of the processing performed by each key, is presented in Figure C.7.

Function Key	Processing Performed
F1=Help	Invokes the AS/400 Help facility.
F3=Exit	Exits from SEU.
F9=Retrieve	Retrieves the last SEU command entered on the SEU command line.
F21=System command	Displays an AS/400 command line for entry of CL commands.
F24=More keys	Displays the additional function keys that are allowed.

SEU Services Function Keys

This set of function keys provides access to special SEU functions, such as find/change services and browse/copy services, and lets you change your SEU default values. The SEU services function keys, and a description of the processing performed by each key, is presented in Figure C.8.

Function Key	Processing Performed
F4=Prompt	Invokes the SEU prompt facility.
F11=Previous record	When using the SEU prompter, presents a prompt for the previous record in the member.
F13=Change session defaults	Allows you to view and change your SEU session defaults.
F14=Find/Change options	Allows you to find information in the source member, and optionally to change one or all occurrences that are found.
F15=Browse/Copy options	Allows you to browse other source members, or printed reports, and optionally to copy information from them into the source member being edited.
F16=Repeat find	Allows you repeat the last Find operation performed using the Find/Change options.
F17=Repeat change	Allows you to repeat the last Change operation that was performed using the Find/Change options.
F23=Select prompt	Allows you to select an SEU line type prompt. SEU returns to the edit session with the line type and prompt you select.

Find/Change Options

The SEU Find/Change options allow you to locate specific source member lines that match predetermined search criteria, and optionally allow you to change the contents of the source member lines that were found.

When you are dealing with a large source member, it is helpful to be able to find where in the member a particular set of characters is used. For instance, you may want to locate the position in a CL program where the variable name *&error* is used. To find lines containing that variable, you can use the Find portion of the Find/Change options.

You can also use the Find/Change options to locate each occurrence of a set of characters in the member, and change the characters. For example, you may want to find all occurrences of the variable name *&program*, and change each occurrence of the variable to have a new name, *&pgm*. You can also use the Find/Change options to locate the records in the member that were modified on a certain date or since a certain date.

When you press F14=Find/Change options from the SEU work display, you are presented with the screen shown in Figure C.9.

Figure C.9
Find/Change
Options Display

```
                               Find/Change Options

     Type choices, press Enter.

         Find  . . . . . . . . . . . . .     _____
         Change  . . . . . . . . . . . .     _____
         From column number  . . . . . .     1          1-80
         To column number  . . . . . . .     80         1-80 or blank
         Occurrences to process  . . . .     1          1=Next, 2=All, 3=Previous
         Records to search . . . . . . .     1          1=All, 2=Excluded
                                                         3=Non-excluded
         Kind of match . . . . . . . . .     2          1=Same case, 2=Ignore case
         Allow data shift  . . . . . . .     Y          Y=Yes, N=No

         Search for date . . . . . . . .     97/05/19   YY/MM/DD or YYMMDD
           Compare . . . . . . . . . . .     _          1=Less than
                                                         2=Equal to
                                                         3=Greater than

     F3=Exit    F5=Refresh      F12=Cancel    F13=Change session defaults
     F15=Browse/Copy options    F16=Find      F17=Change
```

On this display, you specify the criteria that will be used in finding the record(s) you wish to display; optionally, you can specify the change to be made to the records that match the Find criteria and how the change is to be processed.

First, in the Find prompt, you specify the character string you want to find. This is called the search string. If you want to find syntax errors in the member, you can enter the special value *ERR. In the Change prompt, you optionally specify a string of characters to change the found value to.

The From Column number and To Column number prompts allow you to specify which columns of the source member should be searched for the search string.

The Occurrences to process prompt allows you to specify whether you want to process the next occurrence where the search string is found in the member, the previous occurrence, or all occurrences in the member.

The Records to search prompt allows you to specify whether excluded records are to be included in the find operation. Excluded records are those that have been excluded from the display with the **X** line command.

The Kind of match prompt allows you to specify whether the search is case-sensitive. For instance, if the search string is specified as *&program* and if the value *&PROGRAM* is to be considered an occurrence of the string, you must specify that you want to ignore the case of the search string.

The Allow data shift prompt determines whether the data on a line can be shifted when the search string is not the same length as the Change string. For example, if you are looking for the string *&program*, which is eight characters long, and you are replacing it with the value *&pgm*, which is only four characters long, you will have four additional blanks after the replacement is performed. The value in Allow data shift determines whether you want to shift the remaining characters on the line, thus removing the four new blanks.

The last prompts on the display are Search for date and Compare. These prompts allow you to find the records in a source member that were modified since a certain date. If you specify a value for the Compare prompt, the Search for date operation will be executed. You specify the date to search for in YYMMDD format; you can compare for a value of greater than, less than, or equal to.

When all the prompts are set correctly to perform your Find/Change operation, you press the F16=Find or F17=Change function key to process your request.

While these prompts provide an "ease of use" factor for new SEU users, most experienced AS/400 programmers do not use the Find/Change options display. Instead, they perform the Find/Change operations directly from the SEU work display by typing the Find/Change criteria on the SEU command line. For more information about this approach, see "The SEU Command Line," page 484.

Browse/Copy Options

The SEU Browse/Copy Options allow you to view information from other sources without leaving your current editing session. You can also copy information from other sources into the source member you are currently editing. The Browse/Copy options have two primary purposes: to copy source lines into the member being edited from another member, and to view program compile listings while you are editing the member that was compiled.

To let you view information from another source while you continue editing the current member, a split-screen display is provided. Figure C.10 illustrates the split-screen display used when you are editing member SA0801XXX and viewing (i.e., browsing) member SA0701XXX.

In Figure C.10, you can see that you can copy (the line command C) from the source member you are viewing into the source member being edited (the line command A). This is by far the most heavily used function of the Browse/Copy services: copying source lines from an existing member into a member being edited.

When in split-screen mode, you cannot change the contents of the source member being viewed; you can change only the contents of the member currently being edited. You can, however, copy any lines from the member being viewed into the member being edited.

Figure C.10
Split-Screen Operations

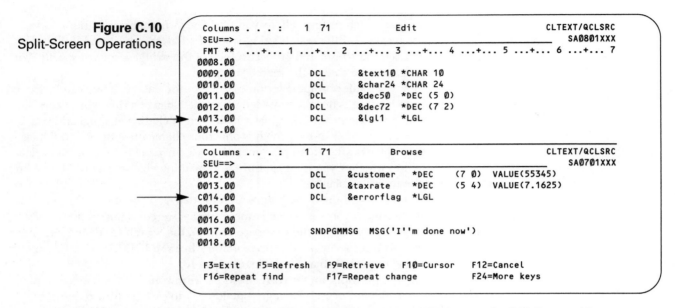

```
Columns . . . :   1  71            Edit              CLTEXT/QCLSRC
 SEU==> _____ SA0801XXX
 FMT **  ...+... 1 ...+... 2 ...+... 3 ...+... 4 ...+... 5 ...+... 6 ...+... 7
0008.00
0009.00            DCL     &text10 *CHAR 10
0010.00            DCL     &char24 *CHAR 24
0011.00            DCL     &dec50  *DEC (5 0)
0012.00            DCL     &dec72  *DEC (7 2)
A013.00            DCL     &lgl1   *LGL
0014.00
          _____
Columns . . . :   1  71            Browse             CLTEXT/QCLSRC
 SEU==> _____ SA0701XXX
0012.00            DCL     &customer  *DEC  (7 0)  VALUE(55345)
0013.00            DCL     &taxrate   *DEC  (5 4)  VALUE(7.1625)
C014.00            DCL     &errorflag *LGL
0015.00
0016.00
0017.00            SNDPGMMSG  MSG('I''m done now')
0018.00

 F3=Exit   F5=Refresh   F9=Retrieve   F10=Cursor   F12=Cancel
 F16=Repeat find        F17=Repeat change          F24=More keys
```

To access the Browse/Copy options of SEU, press the F15=Browse/Copy
Options from the SEU work display. You are then presented with the display shown
in Figure C.11.

Figure C.11
Browse/Copy Options

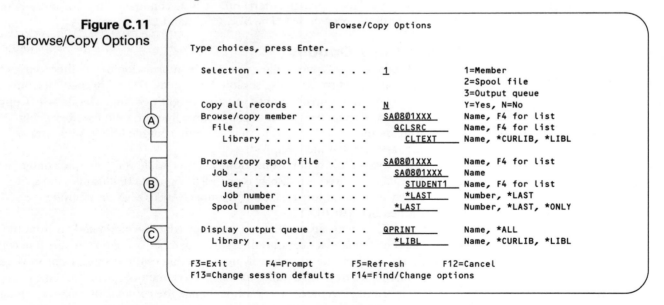

```
                          Browse/Copy Options

  Type choices, press Enter.

      Selection . . . . . . . . . . .   1          1=Member
                                                   2=Spool file
                                                   3=Output queue
      Copy all records . . . . . .      N          Y=Yes, N=No
      Browse/copy member . . . . . .    SA0801XXX  Name, F4 for list
        File . . . . . . . . . . . .      QCLSRC   Name, F4 for list
          Library . . . . . . . . . .      CLTEXT  Name, *CURLIB, *LIBL

      Browse/copy spool file . . . .    SA0801XXX  Name, F4 for list
        Job . . . . . . . . . . . .     SA0801XXX  Name
          User . . . . . . . . . .        STUDENT1 Name, F4 for list
          Job number . . . . . . . .      *LAST    Number, *LAST
        Spool number . . . . . . . .     *LAST     Number, *LAST, *ONLY

      Display output queue . . . . .    QPRINT     Name, *ALL
        Library . . . . . . . . . .      *LIBL     Name, *CURLIB, *LIBL

  F3=Exit     F4=Prompt     F5=Refresh     F12=Cancel
  F13=Change session defaults   F14=Find/Change options
```

The Selection prompt allows you to select whether you want to view a source
member, a spooled output file, or an output queue.

Depending on your answer to this prompt, certain other prompts on the display will be evaluated. For example, if the Selection prompt value is *1*, the prompts shown at (A) are evaluated to determine which member you want to view; the other prompts at (B) and (C) on the display are ignored.

If the Selection prompt contains the value *2*, the prompts at (B) are evaluated to determine which spooled file you want to view. The prompts at (A) and (C) are ignored.

If the Selection prompt contains the value *3*, the prompts at (C) are evaluated to determine which output queue is to be viewed, and the prompts at (A) and (B) are ignored.

Several prompts on the display allow you to press the F4=Prompt key to present a list of possible choices. This is handy when you don't know the exact name of a member or a spooled file that you wish to view.

When you select option 1 or 2 from this display, the result will be a split-screen display, as in Figure C.10. When Option 3 is selected to display an output queue, no split screen is provided; you simply go to the DSPOUTQ (Display Output Queue) display.

At (A) in Figure C.11, you are prompted for Copy all records. Here, if you specify the value *Y*, the copy does not occur immediately, but rather a split-screen display will be presented. When this split screen is presented, a CC (block copy) line command will appear in the first and last line of the member being viewed. You then enter an A (after) or B (before) line command in the member being edited to tell SEU where to copy the records to.

Saving Your Work

When you have completed editing a source member, you can press the F3=Exit command to exit from the current editing session. When you do this, you are presented with the SEU Exit display as shown in Figure C.12. Here you tell SEU what to do with the editing work you have just performed.

Figure C.12
The SEU Exit Display

```
                                   Exit

   Type choices, press Enter.

       Change/create member  . . . . . . .   Y          Y=Yes, N=No
          Member  . . . . . . . . . . . .    SA0801XXX  Name, F4 for list
          File  . . . . . . . . . . . . .    QCLSRC     Name, F4 for list
            Library . . . . . . . . . . .      CLTEXT   Name
       Text  . . . . . . . . . . . . . .    Chapter 8, member 1
       Resequence member . . . . . . . .    Y          Y=Yes, N=No
          Start . . . . . . . . . . . . .    0001.00    0000.01-9999.99
          Increment . . . . . . . . . . .    01.00      00.01-99.99

       Print member  . . . . . . . . . .    N          Y=Yes, N=No

       Return to editing . . . . . . . .    N          Y=Yes, N=No




   F3=Exit    F4=Prompt    F5=Refresh    F12=Cancel
```

The first prompt, Change/create member, tells SEU what to do with the member that you just edited. If you want to save the changes you just made, enter a *Y* in this prompt, then specify where you want the source member to be saved. If you specify the value *N* for the Change/create member prompt, the work performed in your editing session will be lost.

When editing a member with SEU, you are not actually editing the member itself; you are editing a working copy that SEU has temporarily created for you. If you do not save your work by selecting *Y* for the Create/change member prompt, the actual source member will not be changed to reflect your editing changes.

For the Member, File, and Library prompts, you specify where SEU should store the member.

The Text prompt allows you to specify the text that will be associated with the source member you are saving. However, if you are not saving the member, the Text prompt is ignored.

The Resequence member prompts allow you to tell SEU to assign new sequence numbers to the source member lines. This prompt is in effect only if you are saving the member.

The Print member prompt allows you to print the contents of the member to a spooled output file.

The Return to editing prompt allows you to return to the editing session. If syntax errors have been detected by SEU and not resolved in your editing session, SEU will place the value *Y* into this prompt; otherwise, the prompt will default to *N* (Do not return to the editing session).

The SEU Command Line

Most functions that you can perform from the Find/Change Options display, the Change Session defaults display, and the Exit display, you also can perform from the SEU command line. This command line appears at the top of the SEU work display and is used to enter special SEU commands. CL commands cannot be entered into this command line.

The commands allowed from the SEU command line are not the same commands that are entered over a sequence number. For example, in Figure C.13 the SEU command FIND is used. The command FIND CHGVAR will find the first occurrence of the character string CHGVAR in the source member and display that line on the current work display. The FIND command used here invokes the same procedure as that used from the Find/Change Options display.

Figure C.14 shows an example of entering the SEU CHANGE command on the SEU command line; Figure C.15 shows the result of the command.

Several SEU commands can be entered and executed from the SEU command line. The following discussion gives an overview of each of these SEU commands.

Figure C.13
Using the SEU
Command Line

```
Columns . . . :    1  71              Edit                      CLTEXT/QCLSRC
SEU==> FIND CHGVAR_____   SA0801XXX
FMT **  ...+... 1 ...+... 2 ...+... 3 ...+... 4 ...+... 5 ...+... 6 ...+... 7
*************** Beginning of data *************************************
0001.00 /*  Program name..... SA0801XXX                                 */
0002.00 /*  Author........... (Your Name)                               */
0003.00 /*  Date completed... (enter the current date)                  */
0004.00 /*  Program purpose.. CHGVAR and DMPCLPGM exercise              */
0005.00 /*  Chapter 8, member 1                                         */
0006.00
0007.00            PGM
0008.00
0009.00            DCL      &char10 *CHAR 10
0010.00            DCL      &char24 *CHAR 24
0011.00            DCL      &dec50  *DEC (5 0)
0012.00            DCL      &dec72  *DEC (7 2)
0013.00            DCL      &lgl1   *LGL
0014.00
0015.00
0016.00            CHGVAR   &char10 'My Library'

 F13=Change session defaults    F14=Find/Change options
 F15=Browse/Copy options        F24=More keys
```

Figure C.14
Using the CHANGE
Command

```
Columns . . . :    1  71              Edit                      CLTEXT/QCLSRC
SEU==> CHANGE &char10 &text10 ALL_____    SA0801XXX
FMT **  ...+... 1 ...+... 2 ...+... 3 ...+... 4 ...+... 5 ...+... 6 ...+... 7
*************** Beginning of data *************************************
0001.00 /*  Program name..... SA0801XXX                                 */
0002.00 /*  Author........... (Your Name)                               */
0003.00 /*  Date completed... (enter the current date)                  */
0004.00 /*  Program purpose.. CHGVAR and DMPCLPGM exercise              */
0005.00 /*  Chapter 8, member 1                                         */
0006.00
0007.00            PGM
0008.00
0009.00            DCL      &char10 *CHAR 10
0010.00            DCL      &char24 *CHAR 24
0011.00            DCL      &dec50  *DEC (5 0)
0012.00            DCL      &dec72  *DEC (7 2)
0013.00            DCL      &lgl1   *LGL
0014.00
0015.00
0016.00            CHGVAR   &char10 'My Library'

 F13=Change session defaults    F14=Find/Change options
 F15=Browse/Copy options        F24=More keys
```

Figure C.15
Result of the SEU
CHANGE Command

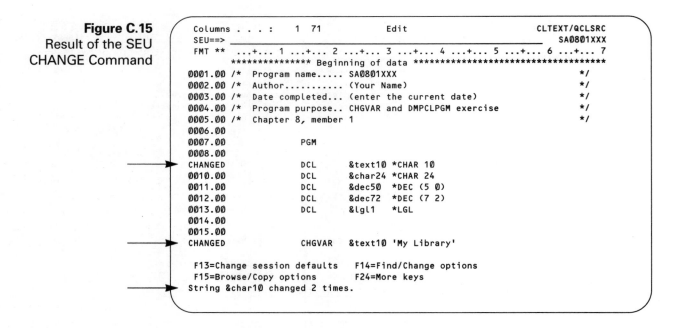

```
 Columns . . . :    1  71              Edit                    CLTEXT/QCLSRC
 SEU==>                                                              SA0801XXX
 FMT **  ...+... 1 ...+... 2 ...+... 3 ...+... 4 ...+... 5 ...+... 6 ..+... 7
 ************** Beginning of data ************************************
0001.00 /*  Program name..... SA0801XXX                                    */
0002.00 /*  Author........... (Your Name)                                  */
0003.00 /*  Date completed... (enter the current date)                     */
0004.00 /*  Program purpose.. CHGVAR and DMPCLPGM exercise                 */
0005.00 /*  Chapter 8, member 1                                            */
0006.00
0007.00              PGM
0008.00
CHANGED              DCL       &text10 *CHAR 10
0010.00              DCL       &char24 *CHAR 24
0011.00              DCL       &dec50  *DEC (5 0)
0012.00              DCL       &dec72  *DEC (7 2)
0013.00              DCL       &lgl1   *LGL
0014.00
0015.00
CHANGED              CHGVAR    &text10 'My Library'

 F13=Change session defaults    F14=Find/Change options
 F15=Browse/Copy options        F24=More keys
 String &char10 changed 2 times.
```

The TOP/BOTTOM Commands

The SEU command TOP is used to position the source member within the work display so that the first page of the member is displayed in the work display. You can alternatively enter the *TOP* command simply as *T*.

The SEU command BOTTOM is used to position the source member within the work display so that the last page of the member is displayed in the work display. You can alternatively enter the *BOTTOM* command simply as *BOT* or *B*.

The SAVE/FILE/CANCEL Commands

The SAVE command is used to save the changes you have made to the current source member. The SAVE command performs the same function as saving your work from the SEU Exit display, but does not end the editing session.

To save the member, simply type the command *SAVE* on the SEU command line. If you want to save the current source member to a different source member, you can specify the command *SAVE libraryname/file-name member-name*. If you are saving the member to a different member of the same source file, you can simply use the command *SAVE member-name*.

The FILE command is similar to the SAVE command except the FILE command ends the current editing session. To end the current editing session and save your work, you would simply enter the command *FILE*; the SEU Exit display would be bypassed. As with the SAVE command, you can use the FILE command to save your work in a different member. Specify the command as *FILE library-name/filename member-name*; or if saving to the same source file, use *FILE member-name*.

You use the CANCEL command to exit from SEU; this command also tells SEU not to save your work. You also can use the CANCEL command on the bottom portion of a split-screen display to remove the split screen. You can alternatively enter the *CANCEL* command as *CAN*.

The FIND/CHANGE Commands

The FIND and CHANGE commands are used to access the SEU Find/Change options without the need to go to the Find/Change Options display.

The FIND command uses the syntax *FIND character-string*, where character-string is a set of characters. *ERR can be the character string to find syntax errors in a compile listing. Also, you can use apostrophes to enclose the character string (e.g., *FIND 'Find this one'*). The *FIND* command can alternatively be specified simply as *F*.

The CHANGE command uses the syntax *CHANGE character-string1 character-string2*, where character-string1 is the string to search for, and character-string2 will replace all occurrences of character-string1. The character strings may be enclosed in apostrophes. The *CHANGE* command may alternatively be entered as *C*.

The SET Command

The SEU command SET is used to set certain attributes of the SEU edit session. The attributes set by the SET command are mainly the options displayed on the Change Session Defaults display. The *SET* command can alternatively be specified as *S*. There are a number of SET commands, but we'll discuss the ones most often used.

The command SET CAPS can be used to set on or off the Uppercase input only attribute of the editing session. Use the command *SET CAPS ON* or *SET CAPS OFF* to allow or disallow mixed case characters.

The command SET ROLL can be used to set the Amount to roll attribute of the editing session. The command can be entered as *SET ROLL HALF*, *SET ROLL FULL*, *SET ROLL CSR*, or *SET ROLL ###*, where ### is the number of lines to roll. *SET ROLL FULL* specifies that the editing screen will roll a full screen when you press Page Up/Down. *SET ROLL HALF* specifies a half-screen roll. *SET ROLL CSR* rolls the screen so that the line where the cursor is currently positioned will be at the top of the screen when you press Page Down (or at the bottom of the screen when you press Page Up).

SEU Session Defaults

When you use SEU, you can customize certain attributes of the SEU edit session for your own personal preferences. To customize SEU for your use, you can press F13=Change session defaults from the SEU work display. The *SEU Reference* manual offers more information about changing your session defaults. These changes will be saved and will be in effect for your current editing session; most will be in effect for subsequent editing sessions as well.

Appendix D

The ILE Debugger

The Integrated Language Environment (ILE) brings with it several features and concepts designed to improve the development process and runtime characteristics of your application programs. The ILE debugger offers many features that facilitate error detection in your programs.

The debug facility lets you

- view the program source, including all modules, while the program is running
- easily set and remove breakpoints
- display or change the values of program variables
- set watch conditions — breakpoints tied to the value of a variable
- step through the program one or more statements at a time

You perform all these functions from the "home base" of the interactive Display Module Source screen.

The Debug Views

Before you can use the ILE debugger with a program, you must provide one or more *debug views* for the modules that make up the program. The debug view specifies the type of debug data you want stored with the module when you compile it. The debug views applicable to CL are

- root source view (*SOURCE)
- compile listing view (*LIST)
- statement view (*STMT)

Each view offers a different level of source detail.

You choose the debug view when you compile the module using the ILE compiler commands. For CL, these commands are CRTCLMOD (Create CL Module) and CRTBNDCL (Create Bound CL Program). (For information about debug views for non-ILE compiler commands, see "Legacy Debugging," page 494.) Specify the debug view in the command's DBGVIEW parameter. For example, you can build a root source view by specifying

```
CRTCLMOD  . . .  DBGVIEW(*SOURCE)
```

DBGVIEW parameter values also include *ALL*, to build all debug views, and *NONE*, to omit debugging information from the compiled module.

The root source view (shown for an RPG program in Figure D.1) includes references to the code from the source member compiled to create the module. The system builds a source view by storing references to the source member code, rather than the code text itself. Consequently, you should make sure that the contents of the source member have not changed between the time you compile the module and the time you debug it and that the source member has not been renamed or moved.

Figure D.1
ILE Debugger
Root Source View

```
                            Display Module Source
Program:   WRKPMT          Library:   BMEYERS         Module:    WRKPMT
        1       FWrkPmtD   CF    E               WORKSTN
        2
        3       /COPY BMEYERS/BSRC,WRKPMTCOPY
        4
        5       D                   DS
        6       D Number                          5S 0
        7       D Char                            5     OVERLAY(Number)
        8
        9       C                   DOU      *IN03 = *ON
       10       C                   EXFMT    WrkPmt1
       11
       12       C                   SELECT
       13
       14       C                   WHEN     *IN03 = *ON
       15       C                   EVAL     *INLR = *ON
                                                                      More...
Debug . . . _____

_____
F3=End program    F6=Add/Clear breakpoint   F10=Step    F11=Display variable
F12=Resume        F17=Watch variable    F18=Work with watch   F24=More keys
```

A compile listing view (Figure D.2) re-creates within the module a representation of the actual compile listing, which includes declarations for externally described files. Unlike the *SOURCE view, the *LIST view is not tied to the original source member, so you can change, move, or rename the source member without affecting this debug view.

The statement (*STMT) view stores debug information by statement number but does not save a representation of the source. Consequently, you can't display the source when debugging a program with the statement view. This view is most useful when you want to distribute debuggable program code but don't want others to be able to see your source.

Which view is best? The answer depends upon your needs. If program object size is your major consideration, you should use the *STMT or *NONE view; both result in smaller program objects than the other options (the *LIST and *ALL options result in the largest program objects). If your program source is reasonably static, the *SOURCE view will probably provide debug capability sufficient for your needs. The *LIST option provides the most stable debug information and the closest correlation between source statement sequence numbers and procedure statement numbers in a program.

Figure D.2
ILE Debugger
Compile Listing View

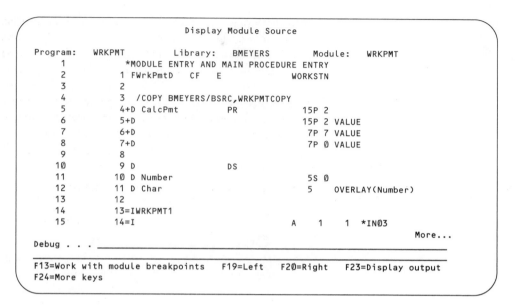

```
                                Display Module Source
Program:   WRKPMT          Library:    BMEYERS          Module:    WRKPMT
     1               *MODULE ENTRY AND MAIN PROCEDURE ENTRY
     2             1 FWrkPmtD   CF    E                WORKSTN
     3             2
     4             3   /COPY BMEYERS/BSRC,WRKPMTCOPY
     5             4+D CalcPmt              PR              15P 2
     6             5+D                                      15P 2 VALUE
     7             6+D                                       7P 7 VALUE
     8             7+D                                       7P 0 VALUE
     9             8
    10             9 D                      DS
    11            10 D Number                                5S 0
    12            11 D Char                                  5     OVERLAY(Number)
    13            12
    14            13=IWRKPMT1
    15            14=I                               A    1    1   *IN03
                                                                      More...
Debug . . . _____

 _____
 F13=Work with module breakpoints    F19=Left   F20=Right   F23=Display output
 F24=More keys
```

If you omit debugging information with the DBGVIEW(*NONE) option, you won't even be able to display variable values using a dump. This option is *not* the same as removing observability from the program object. With ILE, a program's observability information is in two parts: the program template and the debug information. You can omit debug information and still have an observable (and CISC-to-RISC-convertible) program object.

The STRDBG Command

Once you've compiled one or more modules with debug views and bound them into a program, you use the STRDBG (Start Debug) command to start the debug session. The Display Module Source screen appears and shows the corresponding source one module at a time, beginning with the entry module. To view a different module, press F14 and select the module from the Work with Module List display.

When you start the debugger, you usually set at least one breakpoint where you want the program to pause during execution — for example, at statement 1, which is normally the module or main procedure entry point. Once you set a breakpoint, you can press F12 to exit the Display Module Source screen, and then you can execute the program.

When the program pauses at a breakpoint (just before the line of code at which you've set the breakpoint is executed), the Display Module Source screen appears. You can use the screen to set additional breakpoints and watch conditions. To set an unconditional breakpoint at a particular statement, position the cursor at the statement number and press F6. At V3R7, you can also set a *watch* — a special kind of breakpoint that stops the program when the contents of a specific storage location change. For example, you can request a stop in the action whenever the value of

&fromlib changes by placing the cursor on variable *&fromlib* anywhere it appears in the source and then pressing F17.

You can also set breakpoints and watches by entering debug commands on the command line at the bottom of the display. To set a breakpoint for a statement, use the *break* command (*Break 14*, for example); to set a watch, use the *watch* command (e.g., *Watch &fromlib*). You can also use abbreviated versions of the commands: br or w.

Conditional breakpoints and *conditional watches* add flexibility to the debugger. You can condition a breakpoint or watch based on the result of any expression. For example, if you want a breakpoint only when variable *&fromlib* is equal to QUSRSYS, you might type

```
Break 86 when &fromlib = 'QUSRSYS'
```

at the debug command line.

The Debug Commands

Other debug commands and function keys let you display the values and attributes of variables and set variables to specific values. You can display the values of fields, data structures, and arrays; you can also evaluate expressions. Figure D.3 lists all the debug commands and their abbreviated forms.

To display the value of a variable, place the cursor on an instance of the variable in the source display and press F11. Alternatively, you can use the *eval* command to display a variable value. For example, to display the value of *&fromlib*, you could type *Eval &fromlib* on the debug command line.

You can also use the eval command to change the value of a variable. To change *&fromlib*, for example, you might type *Eval &fromlib='QUSRSYS'* on the command line. You can include expressions in an eval command, or you can set the value of a variable to be the same as another variable (for example, *Eval &fromlib=&tolib*).

The *attr* command displays a message showing the attributes of a variable. For example, typing the command *Attr &fromlib* might return the message "TYPE = CHAR(10), LENGTH = 10 BYTES" at the bottom of the display.

Stepping Through a Program

When a program is stopped at a breakpoint, you can resume execution several ways. Simply pressing F12 resumes the program starting with the breakpoint line; when the program encounters another breakpoint, it stops for further debugging. If you want to end the program without further execution, press F3.

You can also step through the program one or more lines at a time. Pressing F10 executes a single line. To advance several lines, use the *step* command; to execute 12 lines, for example, type *Step 12* on the debug command line.

The step command has two modes: *step over* and *step into*. The default mode is step over, which tells the debugger that you want to count OPM program calls and ILE procedure or function calls as a single statement. In step-into mode, the debugger counts each executed statement in the called program, procedure, or function. So, to execute

Command	Abbreviation	Description	Example
Figure D.3			
ILE Debug			
Commands			
Attr	Att	Displays attributes of variable	Attr cpynbr
Bottom	Bo	Shows page with last line of source	Bottom
Break	Br	Sets breakpoint	Break 86 when cpynbr = 2
Clear	C	Removes breakpoint or watch	Clear watch all
Display	Di	Shows Equate definitions or another module	Display ratecalc
Down	Do	Moves source window toward end of source	Down 20
Equate	Eq	Assigns an alias to a variable, expression, or debug command	Equate ratecalc rate*hours
Eval	Ev	Shows or changes the value of a variable, or shows the value of an expression, record, or structure	Eval rate = 5.25
Find	F	Searches for a line number or text string	Find cpynbr
Help	H	Shows online help	Help
Left	L	Moves source window to show source to the left	Left 10
Next	N	Shows next breakpoint	Next
Qual	Q	Defines scope of variables affected by subsequent Eval commands	Qual calcpmt
Previous	P	Shows previous breakpoint	Previous
Right	R	Moves source window to show source to the right	Right 10
Set	Se	Changes debug options	Set updprod yes
Step	S	Runs one or more program statements	Step
Top	T	Shows page with first line of source	Top
Up	U	Shows previous page of source	Up 15
Watch	W	Sets a watch condition	Watch cpynbr

two main procedure statements, including a subprocedure containing 500 statements, you could type any of the following commands:

```
Step 2
Step 2 over
Step 502 into
```

You can also step into a procedure by pressing F22. To step into a program, procedure, or module, the "stepped into" module must have debug data.

You may notice that in single-step mode, the debugger appears to "hang" on certain lines. Because the debugger actually works at the Machine Interface (MI) level, not the source level, the debugger stays on the same source line until all underlying MI instructions have been executed. Some statements generate numerous machine instructions. Single-stepping through a chain operation in an RPG program, for example, causes the debug display to jump to the F-spec for the file and stay there until all the underlying machine instructions have been executed.

Debug Statement Numbers

When you debug an ILE program, the debug statement numbers don't usually match the actual program statement numbers. When a program message indicates an error at a specific statement, you usually won't be able to find the statement in error by going to the indicated statement in the source member or on the source debug display.

Fortunately, the new source debugger ameliorates that situation. When the program modules include debug data and you are in debug mode, the Display Module Source display appears when an error occurs, showing the module in error and highlighting the affected line.

If you're not in debug mode when the error occurs, you must do some detective work to find the actual error line. The error message identifies the procedure in error. The listing view usually provides the closest correlation between procedure statement numbers and module source statement numbers.

Legacy Debugging

At V3R7 of OS/400, you can use the ILE source debugger with Original Program Model (OPM) programs you've compiled to include a debug view. The OPM version of the CL compiler can incorporate a source debug view into a program object. When you compile the program with OPTION(*SRCDBG), the program includes a source view.

To debug an OPM program, start the debugger with the OPMSRC(*YES) option:

```
STRDBG . . . OPMSRC(*YES)
```

If the OPM program doesn't contain a debug view, this command starts the OPM debugger — the traditional pre-ILE debugger.

If you're not on V3R7, you can debug OPM programs using the interactive source debugger that became available with V3R1. The command to start this debugger is STRISDB (Start Interactive Source Debugger). Although this command and the debugger still exist at V3R7, the need for them largely disappears at that release because STRDBG can handle both OPM and ILE programs.

Appendix E

Bibliography

IBM Publications

AS/400 Application Development Tools: Programming Development Manager User's Guide and Reference
Common name: PDM Reference

AS/400 Application Development Tools: Screen Design Aid User's Guide and Reference
Common name: SDA Reference

AS/400 Application Development Tools: Source Entry Utility User's Guide and Reference
Common name: SEU Reference

AS/400 Database Guide
Common name: Database Guide

AS/400 Data Description Specifications Reference
Common name: DDS Reference

AS/400 Data Management Guide
Common name: Data Management Guide

AS/400 Guide to Programming Application and Help Displays
Common name: Guide to Programming Displays

AS/400 Programming: Control Language Programmer's Guide
Common name: CL Programmer's Guide

AS/400 Programming: Control Language Reference
Common name: CL Reference

AS/400 Programming: Reference Summary
Common name: Programming Reference Summary

AS/400 Programming: Work Management Guide
Common name: Work Management Guide

AS/400 System API Programming
Common name: System API Programming

AS/400 System Programmer's Interface Reference
Common name: System Programmer's Interface Reference

Other Useful Publications from 29th Street Press (Formerly Duke Press)

Application Developer's Handbook for the AS/400
　　　Edited by Mike Otey

CL by Example
　　　By Virgil Green

Desktop Guide to AS/400 Programmers' Tools
　　　By Dan Riehl

Desktop Guide to CL Programming
　　　By Bryan Meyers

Desktop Guide to Creating CL Commands
　　　By Lynn Nelson

ILE: A First Look
　　　By George Farr and Shailan Topiwala

Jim Sloan's CL Tips & Techniques
　　　By Jim Sloan

Mastering the AS/400: A Practical Hands-on Guide, Second Edition
　　　By Jerry Fottral

Power Tools for the AS/400
　　　Edited by Dan Riehl

Glossary

Activation group — A "sub-job" in which ILE programs and service programs run. (Chapter 22)

Application programming interfaces (APIs) — IBM-supplied programs that are documented and supported alternatives for gaining access to certain parts of the AS/400 operating system that might be inconvenient or impossible to access using other methods. Examples of API functions are those to display an AS/400 command line, to allow an RPG program to execute a CL command, to scan a character string for a specific pattern, and to process data queues and user spaces. (Chapters 15, 19)

AS/400 name — A character string (up to 10 characters) used to identify objects on the AS/400. The first character in a name is alphabetic (A–Z), $, #, or @; additional characters are alphanumeric (A–Z and 0–9), $, #, @, underscore (_), or period (.). (Chapter 6)

Batch job — A job that requires little or no interaction with the user and usually involves printing reports or processing complex transactions. A batch job usually is submitted from an interactive job, using the SBMJOB (Submit Job) command. *See* Job. (Chapter 11)

Binding — The process of combining one or modules into a callable ILE program. The CRTPGM (Create Program) command performs the binding process. (Chapter 22)

Built-in functions — Predefined capabilities built into CL that you can use with certain CL commands to gain access to additional functions. The three built-in functions are the %SUBSTRING function, the %BINARY function, and the %SWITCH function. (Chapter 8)

Call stack — Term used to refer collectively to an order list of the active programs and procedures within a job. Sometimes called the program stack or program invocation stack. (Chapter 11)

CL compiler — A special IBM-supplied AS/400 program that reads CL source statements in a source member and translates them into machine-readable instructions to create a CL program object. This process is called compiling the program. (Chapter 5)

CL program — An executable AS/400 object (*PGM) consisting of CL commands that define procedures or operations on the AS/400. A CL program is a permanent object on the AS/400. CL programs control an application's workflow. (Chapter 1)

Command — A statement used to request an AS/400 function. CL commands are the primary means of interacting with the AS/400. (Chapter 1)

Command continuation characters — Characters used to continue a CL command on more than one line of a source member. Within a CL source member, acceptable continuation characters are the plus sign (+) and the negative sign (–) or hyphen. Most programmers, however, prefer the + sign. (Chapter 6)

Command definition object (CDO) — One of two components the AS/400 system requires to execute a command. The CDO is the *CMD object that contains a description of the command, complete with parameter keywords, descriptions, and default values. The CDO also contains the validity checking rules, the links to the programs to be called, and information used by the AS/400 command prompter. (Chapter 24)

Command-level message monitor — One of two levels of message monitors available within a CL program, using the MONMSG (Monitor Message) command. The command-level message monitor checks only for messages generated by a single command. (Chapter 12)

Command parameter — A value, specified along with a command, that tells the command explicitly what to do or how to do it. Such values add to a command's flexibility and utility. (Chapters 3, 13)

Command processing program (CPP) — One of two components the AS/400 system requires to execute a command. When a CL command is executed, the CPP is the program that actually processes the command. (Chapters 20, 24)

Command prompt display — A list of commands or command parameter choices that the system provides to help enter CL commands correctly. On the AS/400, the F4=Prompt key invokes the system's prompting facilities. When you press F4 from a screen containing a command line on which you have entered a command, the AS/400 displays a formatted prompt for the command's parameters. (Chapter 4)

Command string parameter (*CMDSTR) — A character string that contains a CL command used as a parameter for another command, such as the SBMJOB (Submit Job) command. A *CMDSTR parameter can contain any valid CL command string not enclosed in single quotes. *CMDSTR parameters offer an additional level of CL prompting. (Chapter 11)

Command token — A compressed representation of a CL command contained in a CL program. This tokenized format is not directly executable. (Chapter 5)

Compiled program object (*PGM) — A set of machine-readable instructions that performs work on the computer. The program object is the result of compiling a source member. The compiler translates source statements into machine-readable instructions, then creates a program object that can be run. Contrast with interpreted job stream. (Chapter 1)

Complex expressions — The result of combining two or more arithmetic, relational, or logical expressions. (Chapter 10)

Complex list — A list within another list that together comprise a parameter value. (Chapter 3)

Concatenate operator — The CL function that joins two character strings and/or values together into one value. CL's concatenation operators are *CAT, *BCAT, and *TCAT. (Chapter 8)

Conditional branching — Refers to program branching that occurs only if certain conditions specified by the IF command are met. (Chapter 9)

Contextual help — One of IBM's two types of help displays for commands. Contextual help is cursor-sensitive; that is, the information displayed is specific for a certain section of the display. (Chapter 25)

Data area — An AS/400 object, identified as object type *DTAARA, that can be used to hold a small amount of information. Think of a data area as a "scratch pad" on the AS/400 — an area of memory that you can use to store information of limited size. (Chapter 15)

Data description specifications (DDS) — The source specifications that describe the attributes and layout of a file. You can enter DDS source for physical, logical, and display files, among others. The system uses the descriptions in the DDS to create files. (Chapter 15)

Data queue (*DTAQ) — An AS/400 object to which one program can send data and from which another program can receive data; a temporary holding area for the data. A data queue is the fastest means of communication between two jobs. (Chapter 15)

Declarations section — That portion of the CL source member that declares (defines) any variables or files that will be used in a CL program. All received parameters, as well as any other variables that will be used in the CL program, must be declared in the declarations section. The declarations section follows the program linkage section. (Chapter 6)

Default values — AS/400-supplied command parameter values for optional parameters that will be used during execution of a command unless you specifically tell the command to use some other value. (Chapter 3)

Device file — A type of AS/400 file that describes the way the AS/400 will interact with a hardware device, such as a printer or workstation. Device files do not contain data. *See* Display file. (Chapter 15)

Display file — An AS/400 *FILE type object that contains the description of display formats that will appear on a workstation screen. A display file is not designed to hold data. On the AS/400, a display file belongs in a special category of files called device files. (Chapter 15)

Dynamic program call — The transfer of control from one program to another at execution time. (Chapter 22)

Entry module — In an ILE program, the "main" module that activates first when the program executes. The entry module is the "driver" for all the other modules in the program. (Chapter 22)

Escape message — A special type of message that reports an error that caused a program to fail. If a program sends an escape message, the program ends immediately. (Chapters 6, 12)

Expression — A group of symbols and values used to represent a single value. The group of symbols in the expression 5 + 1, for example, can be used to represent the value 6. (Chapter 10)

Extended help — One of two types of IBM help displays for commands. Extended help includes all the contextual help for a command plus all other available help information about the command. (Chapter 25)

External message queue — A message queue created by the system whenever a job is started on the AS/400; external message queues are used to communicate between the executing job and the job's external requester (i.e., the user). *See* Message queue. (Chapter 16)

Externally described file — Term that describes an AS/400 database file whose layout is described outside of the program that uses it. Externally described files are usually described using DDS. (Chapter 15)

File cursor — The "electronic bookmark" established by the system when a database file is opened to indicate which record in the file should be processed next. (Chapter 17)

Function check — Notification that a program cannot continue processing because it has encountered an unexpected error. (Chapter 16)

Function keys — Special keys on the keyboard that activate predetermined commands when pressed. Depending on your keyboard, these keys are labeled F1 through F12 or F1 through F24. On the AS/400 command line, for example, F3 is the exit function key; pressing F12 returns you to the previous screen; pressing F9 returns previously entered commands to the command line; and pressing F24 displays any additional function key options. (Chapter 4)

Function override — The method the AS/400 uses to make minor modifications to file attributes or functions at runtime without recompiling the program. Examples of the kinds of changes you would make via a function override are changing a file name, changing a file member name, or changing other attributes of a database or display file. Two frequently used function override commands are OVRDBF (Override with Database File) and OVRPRTF (Override with Printer File). (Chapter 17)

Global message monitor — *See* Program-level message monitor. (Chapter 12)

Global MONMSG command(s) — *See* Program-level message monitor. (Chapter 12)

Help panel groups — An AS/400 object (type *PNLGRP) similar to a display file. A help panel group displays help text. (Chapter 25)

Hexadecimal number — One of a set of numbers in base sixteen that contain the values 0–9 and A–F (where 0 represents 0, 9 represents 9, A represents 10, B represents 11, and so on, with F representing 15, and 10 representing 16) that can be used in CL for such things as manipulating screen attributes, processing lists of values, and assisting in data comparison. To specify hex notation, CL uses an X, followed by a quoted character string consisting of pairs of hexadecimal numbers. (Chapter 7)

Impromptu message — A message on the AS/400 that is not predefined as a message in a message file. (Chapter 16)

Indicator — A logical code used by a program to represent a true/false condition. An indicator can contain the value '1' (true) or '0' (false). (Chapter 15)

Initial program load (IPL) — The AS/400 version of a "boot" process. The IPL loads the system programs, performs hardware diagnostics, and starts the operating system. (Chapter 14)

Integrated Language Environment (ILE) — A common programming model and runtime environment for programs written in any language that conforms to ILE concepts. (Chapter 22)

Interactive job — A job that requires constant interaction between the user and the computer. An interactive job starts when a person signs on to a workstation. *See* Job. (Chapter 11)

Interpreted job stream — A group of commands that are sequentially translated into machine-readable instructions at run time, then executed individually. Contrast with compiled program object. (Chapter 1)

Invocation level — Refers to the nesting levels within a job. Invocation levels identify the relationship between active programs in the program stack. For example, when a program calls another program, the called program executes at a lower invocation level. (Chapter 11)

Job — On the AS/400, the term that refers generally to a unit of work, including all programs, files, instructions, and other objects necessary to perform that work. The two basic types of jobs are interactive and batch. (Chapter 11)

Job description — An AS/400 object (type *JOBD) containing a set of attributes that can be used by one or more jobs. Such attributes include the job's execution priority, the name of the printer upon which reports will be printed, the name of the job queue upon which the job will be placed, and the library list associated with the job. (Chapter 11)

Job log — The AS/400 history of the work a job performs during its execution. Every job that runs on the AS/400 generates a job log. The job log is a combination of all the program message queues used within a job and the job's external message queue. Also referred to as the job message queue. (Chapter 21)

Job message queue — *See* Job log. (Chapter 21)

Job queue — An AS/400 object (type *JOBQ) that acts as a "waiting room" where batch jobs wait in line (queue) for their turn at batch processing. (Chapter 11)

Keyword notation — The presentation of all of a command's parameters preceded by their corresponding keyword. The keyword itself identifies the parameter to the command. (Chapter 3)

Library list — The definition of the path of libraries a job will follow when trying to find programs, files, or other AS/400 objects. (Chapter 11)

Limited user — Any user designated by the system as having limited capabilities to execute commands from a command line. (Chapter 20)

Local data area (LDA) — An area on the system that can be used to pass information between programs in a job. A separate local data area exists for each job. Whenever you start an AS/400 job, an *LDA is created automatically and it disappears when the job ends. Only the job associated with an *LDA can access the *LDA. (Chapter 15)

Localized variable — A variable that exists only in a single program. To localize a variable, you would declare an additional variable with the same data type and length as a program's incoming parameter variable. Then you would use the CHGVAR command to assign the value of the parameter to the localized variable within your called program. (Chapter 13)

Logical file — One of two types of AS/400 database files. Logical files are indexes that provide sorting and record-selection criteria for physical files. Logical files contain no data records, but they can be accessed and manipulated as if they did. (Chapter 15)

Menu — A screen display of a list of items from which a user can make a selection. (Chapter 4)

Message file — An AS/400 file (object type *MSGF) similar to a database file, but used specifically to store message descriptions. Most potential messages that can be generated within a CL program are stored in the IBM-supplied QCPFMSG file in library QSYS. (Chapter 12)

Message identifier — A unique alphanumeric code assigned to each predefined message stored in the system (e.g., for an object not found by the CHKOBJ command, the message identifier is CPF9801). (Chapter 12)

Message queue (*MSGQ) — A holding area, or "in basket," for messages on the AS/400. A message queue can store hundreds, or even thousands, of messages. Some message queues, such as user message queues and workstation message queues, are permanent objects. Others, such as program message queues and external message queues, exist only while a program or job is active. (Chapter 16)

Module — The resulting object (type *MODULE) from compiling an ILE source member. You cannot call or run a module without first binding it into a program. (Chapter 22)

Nested IF control structures — In a CL IF/THEN/ELSE command structure, the situation in which an additional IF command is specified for the THEN parameter to be executed if the first condition is true. The following is an example of a nested IF control structure:

```
IF COND(&user = 'STUDENT1')                              +
    THEN (IF COND(&number = 5)                           +
        THEN(DSPTAP TAP01 OUTPUT(*PRINT)))
```

(Chapter 9)

Nesting level — Term used to describe how many IF statements are nested within a CL IF/THEN/ELSE control structure. (Chapter 9)

Network attributes — Names and attributes that identify your system in a network. Network attributes include such things as the system name and the network name. Network attributes can be retrieved using the RTVNETA (Retrieve Network Attribute) command. (Chapter 14)

Open data path — When a database file is opened within a program, the path that the system provides to the data within the database file. (Chapter 17)

Operand — In an expression, the value or values upon which an action is to be taken or to which an operation is to be done. For example, in the expression 3 + 2, the operands are 3 and 2. (Chapter 10)

Operator — In an expression, the component that represents the action to be taken, or the operation to be performed upon the operand(s) or value(s). For example, in the expression 3 + 2, the operator is the plus (+) sign. (Chapter 10)

Optional parameter — A value that may be specified to further define what a command should do, but that is not required for successful execution of a CL command. (Chapter 3)

Original Program Model (OPM) — The programming model and runtime environment that the AS/400 used before the Integrated Language Environment (ILE) was introduced. (Chapter 22)

Parameter — A value supplied to a program or a command that is used to control the actions of the program or command. (Chapters 3, 11)

Parameter keyword — A significant word that names a command parameter, placed at the beginning of the parameter in keyword notation, that exemplifies the primary meaning of the parameter. In the command `DSPTAP DEV(TAP01)`, the parameter keyword is `DEV`. (Chapter 3)

Parameter value — *See* Parameter. (Chapters 3, 11)

Percolation — The method ILE uses to pass an exception condition through the procedures in a call stack, without handling the exception. (Chapter 22)

Physical file — One of two types of AS/400 database files. Physical files contain data that is defined according to a specific layout or record format. (Chapter 15)

Positional notation — The specification of command parameters in a predetermined order in which the position of each parameter is significant. Keywords are not used. (Chapter 3)

Predefined value — A fixed value defined by IBM that has a special use in CL and is reserved in the AS/400 operating system. A predefined value has an asterisk (*) as the first character in the value. (Chapter 3)

Procedure — A set of computer instructions that performs a particular task, then returns to its caller. A procedure exists only within the context of a program or a service program. (Chapter 22)

Procedure section — The part of a CL program containing CL commands that specify which procedures and processes the program will perform at execution time. This section begins immediately after the declarations section, if present, and ends with the ENDPGM (End Program) command. The procedure section can be divided into two segments: the standard procedure segment, which includes all normal processing performed by the program; and the error procedure segment, which appears in all but the simplest CL programs and includes the major error-handling procedures used by the program. (Chapter 6)

Program — A callable object (type *PGM) that executes computer instructions. (Chapter 22)

Program-described files — AS/400 database files that are processed as if they have no external data definition. The record layout for a program-described file is defined within a program that uses the file. (Chapter 15)

Program information section — The first portion of a CL source member; this section consists entirely of comments whose purpose is to provide information and documentation about the source member and the program created from the source member. (Chapter 6)

Program invocation stack — *See* Call stack. (Chapter 11)

Program-level message monitor — One of two levels of message monitors available within a CL program. A program-level message monitor checks for escape messages issued by all commands within the program. The program-level message monitor is implemented by using the MONMSG as the first command in the procedure section of a CL program. Also referred to as a global message monitor. (Chapter 12)

Program linkage section — The required portion of a CL source member that marks the beginning of the program. The only command in this portion of the source member is the PGM (Program) CL command, plus the optional PARM keyword entry. No other CL command can precede the PGM command within a CL source member. (Chapter 6)

Program message queue — A temporary message queue created by the system immediately before a program begins executing; a program message queue is a program's own "in basket" used to hold messages sent between programs. *See* Message queue. (Chapter 16)

Program parameter — Term referring to a value that a calling program passes to a called program. A program parameter is used either to control the actions of a program or to provide an input value to a program. (Chapter 13)

Program stack — *See* Call stack. (Chapter 11)

Program variables — Fields used within a program to hold values. Unlike a constant, which has a value that never changes, the value stored in a variable can change every time a program is run, or even many times during one execution of a program. Typical uses of CL program variables might be to act as counters within a program to control how many times a loop is processed, or to serve as substitutes for almost all command parameters. (Chapter 7)

Prompt choice program — A program that allows some flexibility in presenting choices to the user when (s)he prompts for a user-defined command. The prompt choice program is specified in the PARM or QUAL command definition statement for a command parameter. (Chapter 25)

Prompt control program — A program that lets you perform additional processing to condition parameter prompting for a command when the normal command definition statements won't satisfy your needs. Prompt control programs are used in connection with the PMTCTL command definition statement and the PMTCTLPGM keyword of the PARM statement. (Chapter 25)

Prompt override program — A program that allows the command prompter to display current values instead of defaults when a command is invoked. (Chapter 25)

Qualified name — An object name, specified together with the name of the library containing the object. A qualified name is specified in the form library/object, with the slash (/) being the qualifier character. (Chapter 23)

Qualified value — Term used for a two- or three-part parameter value; this form of parameter value is usually used when dealing with system objects such as file names or job names. A slash (/) is used to separate, or "qualify," the parts of a qualified value; for example, ARLIB/CUSTOMER or 987654/SHAMM/DSP01. Also referred to as a qualified name. (Chapters 3, 11)

Quoted string — A string of characters enclosed in apostrophes. The character value you specify within apostrophes can consist of any alphabetic, alphanumeric, or special characters. (Chapter 7)

Receiver variable — When used with the CHGVAR command, the term applied to the CL program variable to which you are assigning a value. When used with the PGM command, the term applied to incoming variables received by a called program. (Chapter 8)

Required parameter — A value that must be specified for the AS/400 to execute a CL command. (Chapter 3)

Return value — A value that an ILE procedure returns to its caller. (Chapter 22)

Return variables — Term used to refer to those variables that have significant value only upon their return from another program or command. For example, a program might need to call another program or execute a command to retrieve an external value, such as a date, then place the value into a variable before the program continues processing. (Chapter 14)

Scoping level — The extent of influence of an override or an open data path. There are generally three scoping levels: call level scoping, activation group scoping, and job scoping. (Chapter 22)

Selective prompting — The process of selectively determining which command parameters will be shown to the user on the prompt display and to what extent the user will be able to modify the parameters. Selective prompting can be used in any CL program that runs interactively. The selective prompting characters include ??, ?*, and ?–. (Chapter 18)

Service program — An ILE program object (type *SRVPGM) that performs utility procedures for other ILE programs. (Chapter 22)

Shared open — The situation within a CL program in which more than one program shares a single open data path to a file. You can initiate a shared open with one of the following two methods: by using the SHARE(*YES) parameter of the create command used to create the file; or by issuing an override to the file, specifying SHARE(*YES). (Chapter 17)

Simple command prompting — The insertion of a question mark (?) character at the beginning of a command line in a CL program to control the display of a prompt screen, as well as to control which fields of the prompt the user can modify. (Chapter 18)

Simple list — A list of values of the same type that are defined for a parameter. A simple list is specified by including the MAX keyword on the PARM command definition statement for the parameter. (Chapter 24)

Source physical file — A special kind of AS/400 file intended to hold, among other things, CL source statements. Each source physical file consists of members, and each distinct member contains the actual source statements (e.g., CL commands). (Chapter 5)

Special values — In parameter specification, a special value is the CL equivalent of a reserved word. A special value allows a parameter value to be outside the normal checking rules for parameters. Parameter special values begin with an asterisk (*). (Chapter 3)

Static procedure call — The transfer of control from one ILE procedure to another ILE procedure within the same program. (Chapter 22)

System values — The set of AS/400 characteristics common to the entire system. System values contain systemwide control information you need to control and customize certain day-to-day operating system functions. System values are grouped into the broad categories of date/time, editing, system control, library list, allocation/storage, message/logging, and security. System values are supplied by IBM within the system and can be displayed and often can be changed, but cannot be created or deleted. (Chapter 14)

Unconditional branching — Refers to program branching that occurs when a CL program executes the GOTO command, causing the program to jump to another section. The branch is performed no matter what conditions exist at the time the program encounters the GOTO instruction. (Chapter 9)

User Interface Manager (UIM) — The AS/400 operating system function that displays panels, help text, and other system screens. (Chapter 25)

User message queue — A message queue created when a user profile object is created on the AS/400; the user message queue is used when a message is sent specifically to that user. *See* Message queue. (Chapter 16)

Work management — Term used to identify how the AS/400 organizes, manages, and processes work. Key work management concepts include interactive jobs, batch jobs, job descriptions, job queues, and library lists. (Chapter 11)

Workstation message queue — A message queue that is created on the AS/400 whenever a workstation device is created. *See* Message queue. (Chapter 16)

Index